THE OFFICIAL®
PRICE GUIDE TO
Glassware

**FROM THE EDITORS
OF THE HOUSE OF COLLECTIBLES**

D0802468

THIRD EDITION

THE HOUSE OF COLLECTIBLES
NEW YORK, NEW YORK 10022

Important Notice. The format of *The Official Price Guide Series,* published by *The House of Collectibles,* is based on the following proprietary features: *All facts and prices are compiled through a nationwide sampling of information* obtained from noteworthy experts, auction houses, and specialized dealers. *Detailed "indexed" format* enables quick retrieval of information for positive identification. *Encapsulated histories* precede each category to acquaint the collector with the specific traits that are peculiar to that area of collecting. *Valuable collecting information* is provided for both the novice as well as the seasoned collector: How to begin a collection; how to buy, sell and trade; care and storage techniques; tips on restoration; grading guidelines; lists of periodicals, clubs, museums, auction houses, dealers, etc. *An average price range* takes geographic location and condition into consideration when reporting collector value. *An inventory checklist system* is provided for cataloging a collection.

All of the information, including valuations, in this book has been compiled from the most reliable sources, and every effort has been made to eliminate errors and questionable data. Nevertheless the possibility of error, in a work of such immense scope, always exists. The publisher will not be held responsible for losses which may occur in the purchase, sale, or other transaction of items because of information contained herein. Readers who feel they have discovered errors are invited to *write* and inform us, so they may be corrected in subsequent editions. Those seeking further information on the topics covered in this book are advised to refer to the complete line of Official Price Guides published by The House of Collectibles.

Published by: The House of Collectibles
  201 East 50th Street
  New York, New York 10022

Distributed by Ballantine Books, a division of Random House, Inc., New York and simultaneously in Canada by Random House of Canada Limited, Toronto.

Manufactured in the United States of America

Library of Congress Catalog Card Number: 84-643774

ISBN: 0-87637-311-2

10 9 8 7 6 5 4 3

TABLE OF CONTENTS

ACKNOWLEDGMENTS

The House of Collectibles would like to thank the following individuals for their assistance in publishing this book: Louise Ream, Heisey Collectors of America, Jack Wynne, Palm Harbor, Florida, Frank Hahn, Green Gate Inc., Lima, Ohio, and Sotheby's.

We would also like to thank John and Carol Ney, Orlando, Florida, Lorraine D. Harrington, Ponce Inlet, Florida, and The Glass Hut, Largo, Florida for allowing us to photograph their collections at the Orlando Tupperware Convention Center.

Note to Readers

INTRODUCTION

Nearly everyone collects glass whether they consider themselves to be glass collectors or not. Even in the poorest households in America there is probably at least a piece or two of collectible glassware in the cupboard. Regardless of economic level, there has always been glassware which was affordable to all and which has now become highly collectible.

Pattern glass, art glass, brilliant period cut glass, Carnival glass, and Depression glass are foremost among the types most highly sought by collectors, and the original prices have no bearing on the current values. Indeed, there is much Carnival glass today which far exceeds in price the higher quality, handmade, Brilliant Period cut glass. As a matter of fact, cut glass may be the sleeper of the glass collecting realm. The quality and craftsmanship is so high that comparable glass is rarely produced today. Values in cut glass are sure to escalate in the coming years, making it a very good investment at this time.

Many collections have been started by a single beautiful piece of crystal presented to a newlywed couple. Glassware has long been the most favored choice as a wedding gift. Many of us have been fortunate enough to inherit glass, for among the most treasured of heirlooms are the pieces of old cut glass which are handed down in the family, generation after generation. Perhaps the assorted pieces of Depression glass which were once in your grandmother's cupboard are now displayed prominently in your home. Even if you only have one such piece, can you resist buying another piece in the same pattern when it surfaces at a garage sale for $1.00? With that purchase you begin collecting Depression glass. As you can see, collecting glass is one of the easiest things in the world to get into.

The properties of the glass itself contribute so much to the pleasure in collecting. There is something so aesthetically pleasing in seeing light pass through colored glass or reflect off the countless facets of cut lead crystal. Glass is so pristine and pure in its look, feel, and sound. Whether your passion is the favrile glass of Tiffany, or the diamond splendor of Russian pattern cut glass, this book was written for you. Perhaps you fancy the delicate pastel loveliness of a luncheon table set with Depression glass. The stunning colors and detailed relief of Carnival glass may be your particular favorite. And who does not feel a special sense of history and continuity when holding a fine old piece of pattern glass? So whether your collection consists of one piece or one hundred, we dedicate this book to you in the hope that it will heighten your awareness and enjoyment—welcome to the wonderful world of glass!

MARKET REVIEW

The glassware market is showing great strength and vitality lately. Any accurate market description would have to include the words growth and enthusiasm. Different areas of the market, naturally, are developing at different rates, but glass collectors in general are enjoying dividends on their investments.

Although every area of glassware is exciting, it's Heisey that has drawn the most attention. Always known for its classic elegance and buoyant market value, what is currently attracting the spotlight is the spectacular effort undertaken by the members and friends of the Heisey Collectors of America (HCA) to safeguard the glass they love.

As most people have heard by now, the HCA, by holding a successful fund raising campaign, raised $229,150 to buy all of the existing Heisey molds. They were acquired from Consolidated Colony, the liquidators of the defunct Imperial Glass Corporation of Belleaire, Ohio. This bold venture by the HCA guarantees the integrity of Heisey glass. (To show the far ranging influence of HCA's move, the Cambridge Glass Club is attempting to do the same with the Cambridge molds.) For more information, see the feature on Heisey later in this book.

Depression glass in general is strong. Many manufacturers are popular but Cambridge stands out lately. It's at shows and auctions in increasing amounts and is drawing avid interest and good prices. An all Cambridge auction was held in Old Washington, Ohio recently. Some examples from that show include: an Art Deco cigar humidor that went for $235, an amethyst 12½" Caprice bowl for $300, a Rosepoint 3500/42 12" covered urn for over $600, and a Sea Shell salad bowl in an experimental blue opaque color for $300. But, of course, Cambridge isn't the only glass doing well; Fostoria and Fenton are both enjoying tremendous popularity. The Depression glass market is strong throughout and it is safe to expect continued growth.

Cut glass, especially brilliant period, is gaining momentum. It's still a buyer's market, but it isn't likely to stay that way very much longer. It is still possible to make investments in this market that will pay off in the short term, but the market is tightening. The opportunities for quick gain don't occur as frequently as they used to. An interesting cut glass auction was held in Lenexa, Kansas by the Woody Auction Company recently. Some outstanding sales from the auction included a Royal Flemish vase that went for $1,500 and a 9" × 4" Rex pattern bowl that drew $700. An interesting Harvard pattern ice bucket with an underplate brought in $575 while an Assyrian pattern 10" plate by Sinclaire was taken home for $1,400. A beautiful champagne pitcher in a three-cut octagon pattern with a Hobstar bottom and a sterling silver top by Gorham was snatched up for $1,000. But the sale that really caused a stir at the auction was a Wedgemere ice cream set by Libbey that included an 18" × 10" tray (unsigned) and 12 7" ice cream dishes (signed) that brought in a fantastic $6,000. Keep your eye on cut glass—the market will be changing.

Carnival glass is always popular. Values are so strong these days that it's hard to pick out specific patterns or manufacturers as being expecially popular. Color continues to be the leading factor to the collector. All colors have their fans; blue seems more popular than ever but the iced colors remain the *most* popular.

Art glass is a steady market; values increase slowly but surely. Availability is good in most parts of the country and dealers report brisk sales. Tiffany, of course, is always popular. For example: a Tiffany favrile glass and bronze Crocus lamp was recently purchased for $12,000 at Doyle's. Less high-end Tiffany is available today than before, but it's still out there. A very special Mount Washington Burmese tumbler with a Thomas Hood verse brought a $1,250 value at the Montgomery County Antique Show and Sale held at Silver Spring, Maryland recently. At the same sale a rare French cameo "celery green" vase with pastel pink, white and brown floral cameo decoration, signed, by Burgan and Schverer was $2,350.

So, it was Heisey that made the headlines, but glassware in general is growing at a great rate. There is no end in sight either, but it is always wise to be cautious. The collector who buys hastily might be buying foolishly. Only the collector who does the necessary homework can take a chance on the big decision.

Go to lots of shows, meet lots of people and enjoy lots of glass. But most of all, remember to enjoy the camaraderie of those who share your interest . . . your fellow glassware collectors.

THE HISTORY AND DEVELOPMENT OF GLASS

The development of glass is certainly one of the most important of man's contributions to civilization. Glass has given us very practical solutions to our need for eating utensils and safe storage of foodstuffs, providing very decorative and aesthetic works of art in the process. Through glass we have been able to combine function with beauty, sometimes inexpensively (pattern glass, Carnival glass, and Depression glass), and sometimes at greater expense (cut glass and art glass). Regardless of cost however, we all enjoy the benefits of glass daily.

We do not know the exact date of the discovery of glass but we do know that it predates the time of Christ anywhere from 5,000 to 12,000 years. The first use of glass was probably as a glaze for stone beads which were worn as jewelry in Western Asia. Eventually the beads themselves were made of glass which was thought to have magical properties.

The Egyptians and Syrians developed glass making considerably. Indeed, small blue glass vases from the Egyptian 18th Dynasty have been excavated near Thebes, and they reveal the great glass-making skill which had been attained by the Egyptians. The most significant development in the history of glass was the blowing of glass, which some experts feel was developed by the Syrians around 50 B.C. They originated mold-blown glass and later, free-blown glass.

The expansion of the Roman Empire widely dispersed glass-making skills. Glass was made all over Persia and Europe but it was in Venice, Italy, that glass really achieved its most glorious application to date. Venetian glass was at its height in the 15th and 16th centuries. Despite every attempt to keep Venetian techniques a secret, these methods gradually made their way across Europe. Giacomo Verzelini of Venice managed a glass factory in London in 1575 and glass production flourished all over England. The next great refinement came when George Ravenscroft of England developed lead crystal in 1675. This new heavy glass permitted cutting, engraving, and decoration and was preferred over the paper thin Venetian-style glass. By the 19th century colored glass, especially Bohemian glass was enjoying great popularity.

In the United States, around 1825, molds were developed which pressed patterns into glass imitating the expensive cut glass of Europe. At last decorative glass tableware was within the reach of the middle classes.

By the 1870's American craftsmen were producing ornate cut glass for the wealthy upper classes in America. The years from 1876–1914 are referred to as the brilliant period of cut glass. Heavy lead crystal was deeply cut, faceted, and polished by hand, resulting in pieces which were prismatic and intricate beyond belief.

Art glass came into being during the last half of the 19th century as part of the Victorian preoccupation with the fussy and elaborate. But it was as a result of the worldwide Art Nouveau movement that the beautiful art glass of Tiffany, Galle, Lalique, and others was created. It captured the attention of all with its natural sensual lines and incredible color, shading, and iridescence.

In 1905, taffeta, or Carnival glass as it has come to be known, was born out of the craze for iridescent art glass. Using mass production and new chemical techniques, Carnival glass was widely produced toward the end of the Art Nouveau period. Tastes changed, however, ushering in the streamlined Art Deco period. Even though it continued to be produced until 1930, by 1925 Carnival glass was on the way out. With a dwindling market, this glass was sold by the trainload to fairs and carnivals to be given away as prizes. Hence, it has come to be called "Carnival" glass.

With the Wall Street Crash of 1929, the United States economy collapsed, and the era of Great Depression was ushered in. At this time tank glass production was developed which allowed for the machine molding of huge quantities of glass tableware in just one step. This mass produced tableware has come to be known as Depression glass. It was usually made of colored glass with green, blue, amber, pink, cobalt, red, amethyst, and opaque white being the predominant colors. There was some clear glass produced as well. The patterns were often lacy and elaborate as much to hide the imperfections in the glass itself as for decoration. This glass was often made in complete sets of tableware and given as a premium at gas stations, stores, movie theaters, and in cereal boxes. The prices were incredibly cheap and it was common for a complete service for four to cost a mere $1.99.

A WORD TO THE WISE

Unfortunately, forging of marks and signatures is not uncommon in the glass world. Similarly, reproductions and reissues are passed off on the novice collector as the original item. There are several important steps the collector may take to protect against these possible pitfalls.

1. *Always* deal with a knowledgeable and reputable dealer. Get a written description of the piece along with a certificate of authenticity. Honest dealers will always make good on any piece they sell which turns out to be a fake or reproduction.

2. Study the type of glass you are collecting and learn about its characteristics by seeing as much of it as possible at museums, fine art galleries, and antique shops. Reproductions will always differ from the original even if only slightly.

3. Look for the unmistakable signs of age such as random scratches on the bottom of the base which appear after many years of standing. Glass that is 50–100 years old will not look brand new.

4. Beware of very low prices on an item you know should bring considerably more. Use common sense. Do you really expect to find a genuine signed

Tiffany favrile vase worth several thousand dollars at a flea market for $75.00? As you become more knowledgeable you may indeed spot some real treasures in dusty junk stores. Until then, don't expect to find incredible bargains and when you do, beware.

5. Color is crucial in collectible glassware of all kinds. A number of reissues in pattern, Carnival, and Depression glass have been done in recent years. The colors are different, even if slightly, and are a giveaway that the piece is not original. It is only by seeing a great deal of Depression glass that one learns the true colors of the original. New reissues tend to be in strange tints and hues, and they have a muddy look when compared with the pristine colors of the original.

PERIODICALS

Antiques and Collecting Hobbies, 1006 S. Michigan Avenue, Chicago, IL 60605. General antiques with some glass.

The Antiques Journal, Box 1046, Dubuque, IA 52001. General antiques with some glass.

Antique Monthly, PO Box 37105, Washington, DC 20013. General antiques with some glass.

The Antique Press, 12403 N. Florida Avenue, Tampa, FL 33612. General antiques with some glass.

Antique Review, 12 E. Stafford Avenue, Worthington, OH 43085. General antiques with some glass.

Antique Week, 27 N. Jefferson PO Box 90, Knightstown, IN 46148. General antiques with some glass.

Carnival Glass News and Views, P.O. Box 5421, Kansas City, MO 64131. Reports on auctions, collectors, and carnival glass.

Carnival Glass Tumbler and Mug News, P.O. Box 5421, Kansas City, MO 64131. Provides information about patterns and new discoveries.

Collector's Showcase, PO Box 6929, San Diego, CA 92106. General antiques with some glass.

Encore, Dorothy Taylor, editor, P.O. Box 11734, Kansas City, MO 64138. A bimonthly for Carnival glass collectors.

Depression Glass Daze, P.O. Box 57, Otisville, MI 48463. A monthly newspaper with articles and ads.

The Glass Collector, P.O. Box 27037, Columbus, OH 43227. A quarterly magazine on late 19th century and 20th century American glassware.

Glass Review, P.O. Box 542, Marietta, OH 45750. A monthly magazine on 20th century glassware with articles, pictures, and ads.

Heisey Glass Newscaster, P.O. Box 102, Plymouth, OH 44865. A quarterly pamphlet on identification and research.

Maine Antique Digest, 71 Main Street, Waldoboro, ME 04572. General antiques with some glass.

New England Antiques Journal, 4 Church Street, Ware, MA 01082. General antiques with some glass.

The Paden City Partyline, 13325 Danvers Way, Westminster, CA 92683. A quarterly newsletter about Paden glass on new discoveries and pricing.

CLUBS

American Carnival Glass Association
P.O. Box 273
Gnadenhutten, OH 44629
Publishes *American Carnival Glass News* with club activities, auction results, and information.

American Custard Glass Collectors
P.O. Box 5421
Kansas City, MO 64131
Publishes *Partyline* with sales, and news about rarities and the market.

American Cut Glass Association
P.O. Box 7095
Shreveport, LA 71107
Publishes *Hobstar* monthly, which provides information about cut glass, shows, and sales.

Antique and Historical Glass Foundation
P.O. Box 7413
Toledo, OH 43615

Fenton Art Glass Collectors of America, Inc.
P.O. Box 2441
Appleton, WI 54911
Publishes *Butterfly Net,* a newsletter about club activities and discoveries in Fenton glass.

Fostoria Glass Society of America, Inc.
P.O. Box 826
Moundsville, WV 26041
Publishes *Facets of Fostoria,* a 12-page newsletter.

Glass Art Society
c/o Tom McGlauchlin
Toledo Museum of Art
Toledo, OH 43609
Publishes the *Glass Art Society Newsletter* annually.

Glass Collectors' Club of Toledo
P.O. Box 2695
Toledo, OH 43606

Happy Hunters Carnival Glass Club
Bernice Allen, Secretary
3316 Boston Street
Hopewell, VA 23860

Heart of America Carnival Glass Association
3048 Tamarak Drive
Manhattan, KS 66502
Publishes *The H.O.A.C.G.A. Bulletin* monthly with articles about Carnival glass and information about shows.

Heisey Collectors of America, Inc.
P.O. Box 27
Newark, OH 43055
Publishes *The Heisey News,* a newsletter with information on patterns, history of Heisey, and advertisements.

Imperial Glass Collectors' Society
P.O. Box 4012
Silver Spring, MD 20904
Publishes the *Imperial Collectors Glasszette* quarterly.

International Carnival Glass Association
R.R. #1
Mentone, IN 46539
Publishes the *Carnival Town Pump* newsletter.

Land of Lincoln Carnival Glass Association
5113 North Nordica
Chicago, IL 60656

National Cambridge Collectors, Inc.
P.O. Box 416
Cambridge, OH 43725
Publishes the *Cambridge Crystal Ball* monthly with information about patterns, factory history, and other facts.

National Depression Glass Association, Inc.
8337 Santa Fe Lane
Shawnee Mission, KS 66212
Publishes the *News & Views* monthly, reporting club business and meetings.

The National Duncan Glass Society
P.O. Box 965
Washington, PA 15301
Publishes the *National Duncan Glass Journal* with reprints of early ads for Duncan glass, articles, and club news.

The National Early American Glass Club
c/o Mrs. Shirley Pope
9 Commonwealth Avenue, Apt. 4 A
Boston, MA 02116
Publishes the *Glass Club Bulletin* with articles about old glass and the *National Early American Glass Club Newsletter* which lists events.

National Greentown Glass Association
1807 West Madison
Kokomo, IN 46901
Publishes the *N.G.G.A. Newsletter* quarterly.

New Bedford Glass Society
P.O. Box F 655
65 N. Second Street
New Bedford, MA 02740

Northern California Carnival Glass Club
630 North Lower Sacramento Road
Lodi, CA 95240

Ohio Candlewick Collectors' Club
613 South Patterson Street
Gibsonburg, OH 43431

Pacific Northwest Carnival Glass Club
48900 Middle Fork Road
North Bend, WA 98045

Pairpoint Cup Plate Collectors of America, Inc.
9308 Brandywine Road
Clinton, MD 20735
Publishes *The Thistle* quarterly with news about members, meetings, and information about old glass.

Stained Glass Association of America
1125 Wilmington Avenue
St. Louis, MO 63111
Publishes *Stained Glass Magazine* quarterly.

MUSEUMS

Allen Art Museum
Oberlin College, Oberlin, OH

Art Institute of Chicago
Chicago, IL 60603

Barkley's Museum
Taylor, MO 63471

Bennington Museum
Bennington, VT 05201

John Nelson Bergstrom Art Center and Museum
Neenah, WI 54956

Cambridge Glass Museum, The
Cambridge, OH 43725

Carnegie Institute Museum of Art
Pittsburgh, PA 15213

Chrysler Museum at Norfolk
Norfolk, VA 23510

Corning Museum of Glass and Glass Center
Corning, NY 14830

Currier Gallery of Art
Manchester, NH 03104

Degenhart Paperweight And Glass Museum, Inc.
Cambridge, OH 43725

Edison Museum
Milan, OH

Fenton Art Glass Company
Williamstown, WV 26187

Greentown Glass Museum, Inc.
Greentown, IN 46936

Henry Ford Museum
Dearborn, MI 48121

Historical Society of Western Pennsylvania
Pittsburgh, PA 15213

Jones Gallery of Glass and Ceramics
Sebago, ME 04075

Judy's Museum
Mountain View, MO

Lightner Museum
St. Augustine, FL 32084

Marathon County Historical Society
Wausau, WI 54401

Metropolitan Museum of Art
New York, NY 10028

Morse Gallery
Winter Park, FL

Museum of Modern Art
New York, NY 10019

National Heisey Glass Museum
Newark, OH 43055

New York Historical Society
New York, NY 10024

New Bedford Glass Museum
New Bedford, MA 12742

Old Sturbridge Village
Sturbridge, MA 01566

Oglebay Institute-Mansion Museum
Wheeling, WV 26003

Philadelphia Museum of Art
Philadelphia, PA 19101

Portland Art Museum
Portland, ME

Sandwich Glass Museum
Sandwich, MA 02563

Smithsonian Institution Museum of History and Technology
Washington, D.C. 20560

Study Gallery: A Center for Glass & Ceramics
Douglas Hill, ME 04024

Toledo Museum of Art
Toledo, OH 43697

Wadsworth Atheneum
Hartford, CT 06103

GLOSSARY

ACID ETCHING

A process in decorative glassmaking, in which the glass is first coated with a resistant wax into which a pattern is drawn. When hydrofluoric acid is applied, it cuts a pattern into the areas not protected by the wax. It is most often found on cased glass as it is less expensive than wheel engraving.

AGATA GLASS

Art glassware produced by the New England Glass Company in the late 19th century. It is characterized by brown or purple mottled finish patterns which was achieved by sprinkling alcohol on the color.

AIR TWIST GLASS

A glassmaking process developed and popularized in England during the mid 1700's. Air bubbles were injected into the base of a glass bowl. The base was then pulled down and twisted into a stem, thus the elongated bubbles formed spiralling threads of air.

AKRO AGATE

Founded in 1911 in Akron, Ohio, this company manufactured marbles, moving to Clarksburg, West Virginia several years later. In the early 1930's they added a line of novelty items including ashtrays, planters, vases, flower-pots, and children's toy dishes. These items were made in solid and marble-ized opaque glass.

ALABASTER WARE

Glassware which resembles alabaster in its appearance.

ALBANY GLASS

Albany, New York, was the site of a glass factory that achieved some importance in the late 18th and early 19th century. It was established in the 1780's, temporarily ceased operations about 1790 and resumed in 1792, continuing into the 1820's. Though not noted for remarkable artistry this firm was versatile and its products are eagerly sought by collectors. It manufactured a general line of wares including window glass. It was at one time known as the Hamilton Manufacturing Society.

ALBERTINE

Albertine glass was made by the Mt. Washington Glass Company. It features moderately lavish decor against an opaque ground. Subsequently Albertine became known as Crown Milano. Vases are most abundant. Exceptional specimens can be costly. Albertine was a favorite "parlor glass" of the late Victorian era.

ALEXANDRITE GLASS

A type of English art glass made in the late 19th century by Thomas Webb. This translucent glass was skillfully shaded from blue, through rose, to yellow by reheating it at various temperatures.

AMBER

Yellowish brown color of glass.

AMBERETTE

Amberette is technically pressed glass but by nature of its characteristics and workmanship is generally classified as art glass. Pieces are frosted and stained, the basic color being a velvety yellow. Amberette is still in the modest range of price, perhaps because the attraction common to much art glass—a manufacturer's signature—is not present. It is nevertheless handsome and has attracted increased collecting interest in recent years.

AMBERINA

An American art glass produced in New England during the late 19th century. It was patented by Joseph Locke in 1883. It was a clear, translucent, flint glass with shading from light amber at the base to ruby red at the top. It was usually molded into tableware as well as ornamental objects.

AMELUNG GLASS

A German glassmaker, John Frederick Amelung, established the New Bremen Glassware Factory in Maryland in 1784. The factory operated for only ten years, yet his pieces are considered the finest glass produced in America.

AMERICAN FLINT GLASS WORKS

The American Flint Glass Works, also known by the name of its proprietor, Southwick & Co., was established at Wheeling in what is now West Virginia (but then was Virginia) in the 1840's. The firm was innovative and maintained a quality standard somewhat above the normal for that period. Its products included blown-mold and pressed wares as well as free-blown flint and various colored glass.

AMETHYST

Shades of purple from very light to extremely dark. See BLACK AMETHYST.

ANIMAL DISHES

Covered glass dishes in the shapes of animals came into vogue during the latter part of the 19th century. They were made by a number of firms and specimens representing dozens of animals, both domesticated and wild, can be found. At first, animal dishes were regarded strictly as novelties. Their era of greatest popularity was 1890–1910. Except for scattered exceptions they ceased to be made during the Depression years.

ANNEALING

The tempering of glass immediately following manufacture, whether made by hand or machine, by controlled gradual cooling. This process strengthens the glass, thus making it more practical. See also ANNEALING CRACK; LEER.

ANNEALING CRACK

A crack or fissure in the glass due to its improper cooling.

APPLICATION

Applying hot rods of glass to blown or pressed blanks to form pedestals, handles, etc.

APPLIED STEM

The stem is applied to a piece rather than blown when making the object.

APRICOT

Deep yellow color.

A O P

Abbreviation for "all-over pattern."

ART GLASS

Various kinds of late 19th century American decorative glassware in the Victorian style. It was ornamental glass that was fabricated into free-blown, pressed tableware, and decorative glassware. Ornate designs and various color effects were employed to achieve many successful varieties.

ART NOUVEAU (1885–1925)

An artistic movement which literally translated means "new art." Breaking away from past historic academic styles, it was a style of architecture and decoration which used bolder colors, free flowing designs, asymmetrical shapes, celestial figures, tall swirling plant forms, and whiplash curves. It was strongly influenced by Gothic and Japanese art forms. Realism was rejected as it was an inspired return to nature. Its rich linear rhythm was found not only in architecture and art, but it also decorated every kind of furnishing, jewelry, and glass. Ornament became so profuse as the movement advanced that construction of a piece was sometimes concealed.

AURENE GLASS

A brightly colored iridescent ornamental glass created by Frederick Carder, manager of the Steuben Glass Works, New York, in 1905. Although inspired by Tiffany, it has a far greater variety. See ART GLASS.

AVENTURINE

A type of lustrous Venetian glass that combined small flakes of gold and copper, in suspended state, with colored glass. Although an ancient technique, this decorative process was revived during the 19th century.

BACCARAT GLASS

Fine quality glassware for tableware and decorative glass, especially paperweights. Glassworks in France and Belgium manufactured this quality glass from the late 18th century and throughout the 19th century.

BALTIMORE GLASS

Products of any one of several glassworks in Baltimore, Maryland, including Amelung glass and Baltimore flint glass.

BANANA DISH

A glass dish with two highly curved sides and two ends left open on a pedestal base.

BASKET

Basket shaped glass piece used for decoration, food service, or vase.

BELL

Novelty item made in every type of glass, often ringable. Used at the dinner table as a signal to the servants that it was time to serve.

BERRY BOWL

Small round bowl.

BITTERS BOTTLE

Small decanter used for holding Angostura bitters which is used in making mixed alcoholic drinks.

BLACK AMETHYST

Purple glass so dark it appears almost black.

BLANK

Uncut glass objects which were cut or decorated into the finished product.

BLOWN-MOLDED GLASS

A method of glassmaking in which hot glass was blown through a blowpipe into a pre-formed metal mold. The mold was used for giving shape to a glass vessel and for impressing a design on its surface. It was used as a means of quick and inexpensive glass production. It is easily discernible from pressed glass since the pattern undulations are also on the inside of the vessel. See FREE-BLOWN GLASS.

BLOWN MOLDED

Glass is blown into a mold to reproduce the design of the inner mold.

BLOWPIPE

A long metal tube used in blowing glass.

BLUE, ELECTRIC

Royal blue.

BLUERINA

Bluerina was named for Amberina and shares its characteristic of embodying tones which meld from one distinct color into another, in this case blue to amber. Guidelines on classification are not firm, as the name may be applied to the glassware of any manufacturer that exhibits such coloring, even if known better by a product designation; for example some Alexandrite glass falls into the realm of Bluerina.

BOHEMIAN GLASS

An ornamental glass manufactured during the latter part of the 17th century in an attempt to imitate Venetian glass. Coming from one of the chief European glassmaking regions, Bohemian glass was especially suitable for ornate engraved and cut decorations. It was renowned for its rich colors, such as bright yellow, ruby red, etc.

BON BON

Small, uncovered candy dish.

BREAD AND BUTTER PLATE

Six inch plate.

BRIDES' BASKET

Glass bowl held in a silverplated frame. Very often the bowl has a delicately ruffled, fluted, or crimped edge. Although made in all sizes, most ranged from 9–14 inches in diameter and 9–16 inches in height. Brides' baskets were made of every type of glass and first captured the imagination of the public at the World's Columbian Exposition in Chicago in 1893. These bowls were a favorite wedding gift from the 1890's–1920, hence the term "brides' basket." This term surfaced in the 1960's.

BRILLIANT PERIOD

The term given to cut glass of the golden age of its manufacture, the second half of the 19th century, when great energy was spent in creating intricate, luxurious patterns. This ware was deeply cut and highly polished. The best American examples date from about 1870 to 1895. Brilliant period cut glass is considered the most desirable variety of its species by collectors and has gained considerably in value over the years, enhanced by the fact that production ceased more than half a century ago.

BRISTOL GLASS

An English decorated clear and colored glassware produced in Bristol factories during the 17th and 18th centuries. Dark blue, red, and green were used to create snuffboxes, candlesticks, vases, decanters, jars, mugs, etc. They were noted for their fine production of small articles in white opaque milk glass, which was an imitation of porcelain and painted with enamel colors.

BRISTOL-TYPE GLASS

A plentiful Victorian art glass sold by a number of manufacturers in the 19th century. Its name is taken from the city of Bristol in Great Britain, which at one time served as headquarters for numerous glassmakers. After being imported to (and becoming popular in) the U.S. domestic factories began producing it and it was commonly sold in variety shops and other outlets for many years. The pieces were generally opaque, with enameled hand painting. Originally it was regarded as a better-than-nothing substitute for those who could not afford the more expensive varieties of fine glass. Passage of time and heightened collector interest has resulted in increased prices.

BURMESE GLASS

Burmese glass was introduced late in the 19th century by the Mt. Washington Co., then subsequently produced by Webb of England. An addition of uranium was made to the fabric, producing pleasing tonal effects shading from pink to pastel yellow. So-called Gunderson Burmese is of much later manufacture than the Mt. Washington and Webb varieties but is nevertheless collectible and can be a worthy alternative for those unable to afford the high prices often obtained for "old Burmese."

BUTTERBALL OR CONFECTION DISH

Shallow glass dish which has long center pole with closed handle at top. Butterballs or tidbits are arranged on the dish around the center pole.

BUTTER PLATE, INDIVIDUAL

Tiny glass plate used for serving individual portions of butter.

BUTTER TUB

Small pail shaped glass holder used to hold butter balls or pats.

CAKE PLATE

Large flat plate with three short legs.

CALCITE GLASS

A glass resembling, but not manufactured from, the mineral calcite, having a rich cream-white color. The most notable examples were the work of Frederick Carder at the Steuben company, who pioneered their manufacture. The method of decoration varied. Calcite glass is frequently termed "Aurene."

CAMBRIDGE GLASS CO.

The Cambridge Glass Co., located in the Ohio town of that name, was chiefly a producer of cut glass, though it sold other types as well. Its operations were very extensive and for many years, especially during the 1920's and 1930's, it maintained a near monopoly on the manufacture of cut glass tableware. Some of its designs were most creative.

CAMEO GLASS

Ornamental glassware made from layers of different colors, often white on blue, in which the outer opaque layer was cut away so that the background color showed. It could also be made in three or more layers. Although a rare and difficult technique developed by the Romans in the first century, it was almost unknown until the 19th century.

CAMPHOR GLASS

A white American pressed glass, that was semiopaque blown molded glass.

CANARY

Yellow glass or crystal.

CANDELABRUM

A candlestick lampstand or chandelier with two or more branches.

CANDLESTICK

A moveable candle holder from the mid 16th century. It is a simple tube with a socketed glass holder at one end and a flattened base at the other.

CARAFE

A bottle used for serving wine or water. Their era of most extensive use was from about 1760 to 1820, when the water carafe (or, more likely, a series of them) could not be omitted from a well-appointed dining table without causing comment. Crushed or cubed ice could be included in the carafe to keep water at lower than room temperature; this was looked upon as a novelty, and the beverage as a welcome refreshment, in the days before electrical refrigerators. Carafes again came into vogue in the late Victorian age, when a number of American manufacturers produced them.

CARDER, FREDERICK

Founder of the Steuben Glass Co. (1903). Products of Steuben from that year until 1932 are sometimes, though confusingly, referred to as "Carder glass." Frederick Carder lived to the age of 100; he died in 1963.

CARNIVAL GLASS

An inexpensive glass produced after World War I and later used as prizes awarded at a carnival or fair. It consisted of fruit bowls, sugar bowls, pitchers, creamers, etc. with molded decorations in iridescent colored glass. It was manufactured in both Europe and America in red, blue, green, mauve, silver, gold, and more.

CASED GLASS

A blown glass in two to five layers of different colors, including clear glass and opaque white. The layers were fused one inside the other while the glass was hot. It was blown into decanters, glasses, etc. and decorated by cutting away parts of each layer, which offered many diverse decorative effects. It was produced mainly in the 19th century.

CASTOR SET

Glass condiments held in a silver plated metal frame with handle. There were breakfast, lunch, and dinner castor sets which held the different condiments required for each specific meal. For example, the breakfast castor set would contain salt and pepper shakers, syrup pitcher, and jelly or marmalade jar. Dinner castor sets would contain salt and pepper shakers and oil and vinegar cruets, etc. They were used during the Victorian period.

CELERY

Either a tall cylindrical vessel or a long flat narrow dish for serving celery.

CHAIN

Guilloche, trailed circuit. Heavy glass threads are applied in a chain design.

CHAMPAGNE GLASS

The classic or traditional shape of champagne glass—a wide shallow bowl surmounting a stem, with circular base—evolved in the second quarter of the 19th century.

CHARTREUSE

Opaque glass of yellow-green.

CHECKERED DIAMOND

Motif featuring a large diamond with four small diamonds cut in each.

CHEESE AND CRACKER DISH

Two tiered glass serving dish for cheese and crackers.

CHEESE DISH

Round dome shaped cover with flat bottom dish.

CHERRY JAR

Glass jar with large mouth and lid for holding maraschino cherries.

CHIGGER BITE

Term used by the glass trade and auctioneers to describe small chips on a piece of glass.

CHOP PLATE

Salver; large serving plate.

CHUNKED

Damaged glass in very poor condition.

CIGAR JAR

Large mouthed glass humidor or canister with lid for storing cigars or tobacco.

CLAM BROTH

Semi-opaque grayish glass.

CLARET

Stemmed glass for serving claret wine.

CLOSED HANDLED

Solid tab handles.

COASTER

Small round object with shallow rim, used under glassware to protect the furniture.

COBALT BLUE

Dark, rich, deep shade of blue glass, highly prized. It was produced by mixing cobalt and aluminum oxides.

COCKTAIL GLASS

Small drinking glass for cocktails with a stemmed foot and a bowl.

COIN GLASS

A drinking vessel, usually a glass or a tankard, with a coin visibly placed in the foot.

COLOGNE BOTTLE

A bottle used for holding cologne or toilet water. Uses a glass stopper.

COMPANION PIECE

One of two or more pieces that together make up a pair or set.

COMPORT

Compote. Usually stemmed, open shallow dish or bowl.

CONCENTRIC RINGS

Design motif of circles within circles.

CONSOLE BOWL

Centerpiece bowl, often accompanied by matching candlesticks as a set.

CORAL

Opaque glass covered with heat sensitive glass resulting in yellow-to-red shading. See Wheeling Peach Blow.

CORALENE GLASS

A type of art glass that was introduced in America, but popular in Europe. It was ornamented with raised branches that looked like coral. They were formed from enamel to which drops of clear or opalescent glass were applied.

CORDIAL GLASS

Very much like a wine glass, only smaller; 1 to 2 oz. capacity. Has a tall stem and a wide circular foot.

CORNING GLASS WORKS

An important American glass factory, established in the 19th century and still flourishing at the present. For more than 100 years it has been in the control of successive generations of the Houghton family. Today the firm, which has long operated Steuben Glass, maintains a museum of glass at its headquarters in Corning, New York, in which are displayed various examples of important ancient and modern glass. Its first year of operation at the present location was 1868, at which time it was known as the Corning Flint Glass Co. In 1875 the name was changed to Corning Glass Works.

COSMOS

Milk glass (pressed) decorated by staining. Sold extensively in the early years of this century, Cosmos glass was traditionally of little regard in the collecting fraternity. It has now gained a moderate following, with prices in triple digits being not uncommon.

COVERED BON BON

Covered candy dish.

COVERED BUTTER DISH

Round dome shaped glass cover over flat bottom glass dish. Smaller than covered cheese dish.

CRANBERRY GLASS

A type of Victorian blown molded glass with a light bright red tint. It was made into vases or bowls with fluted rims. The color was light so as to mask the imperfections in the glass itself. An inexpensive glass it was easily discernible from the better quality ruby glass.

CRAQUELLE GLASS

Very rough texture which is produced by rolling in crushed glass and reheating and reblowing or by dipping hot glass into cold water.

CREAM SOUP

Small two handled dish.

CROWN MILANO

See ALBERTINE.

CRUET

Small decanter, often handled, used in tandem to serve oil and vinegar.

CRYSTAL GLASS

A brilliant colorless glass which contains a high amount of lead oxide. Originally it was the *cristallo* glass developed in Venice in the mid 15th century. It derived its name from its resemblance to rock crystal. See FLINT GLASS: LEAD GLASS.

CULLETS

Scraps of broken glass which were remelted and added during glassmaking to encourage fusion.

CUSTARD GLASS

A creamy or yellowish milk glass popular in the early 20th century.

CUT GLASS

Glass decorated with faceted designs. The glass was carved or ground into deep sparkling facets by revolving wheels layered with an abrasive. It developed during the 16th century in Bohemia and was very popular until the invention of molded pressed glass in America about 1825 which was an inexpensive imitation of cut glass. It enjoyed a revival during the brilliant period of cut glass in America which dated from 1876–1916.

DAISY-IN-HEXAGON

Motif which features a flower enclosed in a hexagon.

DAUM

A French glassworks, noted for its production of art glass. As a result of its location in the town of Nancy, the ware is often referred to as Nancy Daum —suggesting the existence of a glassmaker named Nancy Daum. The firm has had a distinguished history, for more than 100 years, and continues in operation today, though the word "Daum" has now been deleted from its title: the new name is Cristalleries de Nancy. Its beginnings date to 1875 when an already existing factory was acquired by Jean Daum. The era of its most noteworthy achievements was from about 1895 to the outbreak of World War I, when it was a leader in the production of Art Nouveau glass and was influential in setting styles followed or imitated by other manufacturers, notably in America.

DECANTER

A glass vessel used originally to pour wine at the table. Use has been expanded to now include spirits of all types. Usually has a glass stopper. Types include: bell, claret, ship's, and whiskey.

DELPHITE

Blue milk glass. It is opaque and a pale blue in color.

DENNIS GLASSWORKS

English factory, near Stourbridge, run by the Webb family. It was founded in 1855 and is still in operation; the era of greatest achievement was in the later 1800's, when it produced much fashionable art glass.

DEPRESSION GLASS

Colored glassware which was produced in America primarily from the late 1920's through the 1930's. Inexpensively made, this glassware was turned out in quantity and sold at dime stores or given away as promotions or inducements to buy other products.

DIAMOND-DAISY

Diamond shaped squares containing a daisy pattern.

DIAMOND POINT

Design which features faceted diamond projections which come to a point.

DIATRETA GLASS

A form of art glass where small, ornamental pieces of glass are fastened to a glassware object. This process was developed by F. Carder at Steuben Glass Works.

DIP MOLD

One piece mold used for imprinting a decoration; has open top.

DISPENSERS

Glass container with a spigot for dispensing cold water from the refrigerator. Also includes the juice dispensers found in drugstore soda fountains.

DOMINO TRAY

Tray for holding creamer and sugar cubes. Has built in container for creamer.

DORFLINGER GLASS WORKS

The Dorflinger Glass Works was established at White Mills, Pennsylvania, by Christian Dorflinger, a German immigrant. He came to the U.S. in 1846 and six years later was operating the Long Island Flint Glass Works of Brooklyn, New York. The Pennsylvania factory was shut down in 1921. It specialized in high grade tableware.

DOUBLE CRUET

A glassware object where two bottles are made separately and then joined together to make one bottle with an interior separation. Usually made for serving oil and vinegar.

DRESSER SET

Glass accessories with glass tray for dressing table. Includes items such as hair receiver, puff box, glove box, hat pin holder, hair pin tray or box, perfume and cologne bottles, etc.

DRESSER TRAY

Large glass tray which holds dressing table accoutrements such as hair receiver, cologne bottles, glove box, puff box, ointment jars, etc.

EDINBURGH CRYSTAL GLASS CO.

Important producer of cut glass, from the later 19th century to the present. The factory is now located outside Edinburgh in the Scottish village of Penicuik.

EBONY

Black colored glass.

EMBOSSING

Patterns are in bas relief, that is they project slightly from the ground of the piece.

ENAMEL

A glass coating colored with pigments derived from metallic oxides. It was applied to glassware by firing to fuse the enamel to the original glaze.

ENGRAVED GLASS

A design is cut in the glass surface by small wheels coated with an abrasive, such as emery, or diamond-point.

EPERGNE

An ornamental centerpiece for a dining table, it incorporated a number of small dishes around a central bowl.

ETCHED GLASS

An inexpensive substitute for hand-cutting on Victorian cased glass. Patterns are scratched in acid-resistant wax and acid is then applied.

EWER

A jug-like object with a globe body and a long handle resting on a wide footed base. Has a pouring spout which comes upward out of the body.

FAKE

A glassware object that is genuinely antique but has been purposefully altered in its body or adornments so as to artificially raise its value.

FAVRILE

The trade name for the American art glass marketed by Louis Tiffany, in the Art Nouveau style.

FENTON ART GLASS COMPANY

Founded in Martin Ferry, Ohio, this company has been producing fine glassware since 1907. In the early years they made carnival, custard, opalescent, and a variety of other pressed and molded wares. Over the years they added hobnail, stretch, slag, and overlay pieces to their line. Famous for the hand decoration work, Fenton is still producing quality glassware in Williamsburg, West Virginia today.

FERN BOWL

Glass container for holding potted ferns. It has a liner and is tri-footed.

FERN GLASSWARE

Glassware decorated with engraved representations of ferns.

FIGURINE

A small individual figure.

FINDLAY GLASS

A type of art glass molded in several different patterns and in many colors, usually brown.

FINGERBOWL

This table convenience is of earlier origin than might be imagined and has a long history, encompassing many styles, shapes, sizes, and motifs. Silver or pewter fingerbowls were at times favored over glass. Nevertheless, a great number were made of glass, in both Europe and America. They were most popular during the Victorian era and the early 20th century.

FIRED-ON

Baked on color.

FIRE POLISHING

A detail work on glass of a final firing to give added glaze and smooth finish to pressed glass.

FLASK

A small container for carrying spirits. They are usually made from metal to better withstand rough usuage, but they have been made from glass.

FLASHED GLASS

A glass, popular in Victorian America, with a thin coat of colored glass over a clear base.

FLINT GLASS

The name by which English lead glass was known in the 17th and 18th century and occasionally afterward. So entrenched did this terminology become that, even to this day, English glass of that era is called "flint glass." A small quantity of pulverized flint was used as an ingredient, later replaced by sand.

FLOWER BOWL

Large shallow bowl used for floating flowers with short stems.

FLUX

Chemicals or metals such as oxide of lead, carbonate of soda, and potash which, when added to silica, cause it to fuse into glass.

FLUTED

Scalloped edge.

FLUTING

Glassware ornamentation in the form of parallel grooves.

FOOT

The part of a glassware object that it rests upon. However, to be a *foot* and not a *base,* it must be separated from the rest of the object by a stem, which can be either short or long.

FOSTORIA GLASS COMPANY

Founded in Fostoria, Ohio in 1887, Fostoria continues in production at their Moundsville, West Virginia factory today. Many of their lovely glassware lines are considered to be "elegant" depression era glass and these patterns are avidly sought by collectors today.

FREE-BLOWN GLASS

Hand-maneuvered glass blowing without a mold, an ancient technique of high-quality craftsmen.

FROG

Round, domed, heavy glass object with holes drilled for placing in vases to hold flowers in place.

FROSTED GLASS

Glass with an opaque outer surface made by exposing the surface to the vapor of hydrofluoric acid. Can also refer to glassware with small cracks on the surface.

FRY, H.C.

American manufacturer, born 1840, founded the Rochester Tumbler Co. in 1872 and the H.C. Fry Glass Co. in 1901, both located at Rochester, Pennsylvania. "Fry glass" includes art glass and other varieties. Fry died at the age of 89 in 1929 and the business succumbed to the Depression several years later.

FUSION

The melting point of glass which occurs at 2500° Fahrenheit. At this point glass is blown or pressed into the desired shape.

GADROON

A border trim of reeds and flutes, sometimes referred to as knurling.

GAFFER

Master glass blower and shop foreman.

GALLÉ, ÈMILE

Pioneer in the French Art Nouveau movement who gained fame for his Cameo glass in the late 1880's. His art glass featured floral designs in natural colors and an oriental style was often followed.

GILDING

Application of gold or gold paint to an object for decoration.

GLASSBORO

The Glassboro Glassworks was established at Glassboro, New Jersey, early in 1781 by Jacob Stanger. It was New Jersey's second glass manufacturing establishment. Successful in enduring many hardships and periods of economic uncertainty, the factory continued into the 20th century—one of very few American business enterprises, glass or otherwise, to span three centuries. Positive identification of its early products is difficult.

GLASS PICTURE

A picture or depiction on a flat sheet of glass.

GLOVE BOX

Glass rectangular box used on dressing table or vanity to hold gloves.

GOBLET

A glass vessel with a large bowl and a wide stemmed foot.

GONE WITH THE WIND LAMP

Parlor lamp, either kerosene or electric, consisting of a glass base and round globe glass shade.

GRAPEFRUIT GLASS

A glassware object with a bowl resting on a wide foot used to serve a ½ grapefruit.

GRAVY BOAT

Oval shaped spouted bowl often with pedestal.

GREEN, APPLE

Light green glass.

GREEN, EMERALD

Deep green, the shade of an emerald.

GREEN GLASS

The natural color of alkaline or lime based glass.

GREGORY, MARY

Designation for a particular variety of 19th century glassware, painted with white or pastel pink enamel, featuring a likeness of a boy, a girl, or boy and girl. Traditional legend holds that "Mary Gregory" was an enameler for the Boston & Sandwich Glass Co. in the 1870's, where this type of ware was once believed to have originated.

GRILL PLATE

Plate divided into three sections by means of raised ridges.

GROUND

The name given to the background on which decoration is imposed.

HAIR PIN BOX

Small box, part of dresser set, used to hold hair pins on a dressing table.

HAIR RECEIVER

Small round box with lid which has a large hole in the middle. Used on Victorian dressing tables to hold hair which accumulated in hair brush.

HAMMONTON

The Hammonton Glassworks was established at the New Jersey town of that name by William Coffin and Jonathan Haines in 1817. It remained in operation for a number of years under the name Coffin & Haines. Its products are classified as South Jersey type glassware.

HAND BLOWN

See FREE BLOWN.

HANDEL, PHILIP J.

An American glassmaker who established the Handel Company in 1885 in Meriden, Connecticut; a branch factory was later started in New York City. Popular products included acid-cut-back cameo vases in the Art Nouveau style and lamps similar to Tiffany lamps but less expensive.

HAT PIN HOLDER

Tall cylindrically shaped glass Victorian dressing table accessory, used to hold hat pins.

HAWKES, T.G. & CO.

A glassware manufacturing company established at Corning, N.Y. in the late 19th century, it manufactured mostly cut glass. Later joined with F. Carder to form Steuben Glass Works.

HAZEL ATLAS GLASS COMPANY

This large company produced pressed wares from 1902 to 1956. Factories were located in Pennsylvania, Ohio, and West Virginia.

HEISEY

The A.H. Heisey Glass Co. was established in the 1860's at Newark, Ohio, by a partnership which included George Duncan and Daniel C. Ripley. It manufactured cut and pressed wares.

HIGHBALL OR BEER GLASS

Tall tumbler used for serving highballs or beer.

HOBNAIL

A manner of decorating glassware, either by pressing or cutting, with an overall pattern of small raised knobs known technically as prunts. The pattern became popular in Britain as early as 1800 but not in the U.S. until after the Civil War.

HOCKING GLASS COMPANY—ANCHOR HOCKING CORPORATION

The history of Anchor Hocking Corporation is the story of a company that started small, but grew through initiative and desire on the part of its founders and employees. In the years that have passed since the Hocking Glass Company was founded in 1905 in Lancaster, Ohio by I. J. Collins, it has grown into the Anchor Hocking Corporation worldwide. The company is a leading manufacturer of glass and ceramic tableware, glass and plastic containers, plastic and metal closures, plastic dinnerware, decorative hardware and plastic and glass forming equipment. Manufacturing facilities and sales offices are located in the United States, Canada, the Netherlands, and the company has licensing agreements with a number of foreign companies.

HONESDALE

The Honesdale Decorating Co. was founded at Honesdale, Pennsylvania, in 1901 by the Dorflingers. It was active until 1932. Some of its ware was gold decorated and is highly regarded by collectors.

HORSERADISH JAR

Glass jar with lid used to serve horseradish.

HOT PLATE

Glass plate used to sit under hot items in order to protect surface beneath.

HYDROFLUORIC ACID

A highly corrosive substance used in creating frosted glass. When combined with ammonium sulfide, it can be used to test the authenticity of lead glass.

ICE BLUE

Light crystal blue.

ICE BUCKET OR TUB

Deep pail shaped container usually with closed handles for holding ice.

ICE CREAM PLATE

Small glass plate.

ICE CREAM TRAY

Large glass tray with shallow rim, usually made of cut glass, for serving ice cream.

ICE GLASS

A form of art glass with a rough surface resembling cracked ice.

ICE LIP

A rim which prevents ice from spilling out of the spout of a pitcher.

IMPERIAL

The Imperial Glass Co., a major producer of Carnival ware, was established at Bellaire, Ohio, in 1901. After enjoying great success, the company went bankrupt during the Depression but was reorganized and saved.

INCISING

The decorative technique of engraving or cutting into a surface of glass, as opposed to relief decoration.

INDIANA TUMBLER & GOBLET CO.

Firm noted for its manufacture of pressed glass in the late 19th/early 20th centuries. It was also the producer of Carmel Slag glass, a bizarre ware featuring striations of color that suggest medieval German glass. Holly Amber was another of its lines. In general its articles are not expensive, and have been receiving increased attention.

INKWELL

Small heavy glass bottle for holding ink.

INTAGLIO

A design cut underneath a surface leaving a reverse relief.

INTARSIA

A variety of glass produced during the 1920's by Steuben when under directorship of Frederick Carder. It consisted of a core of colored glass sandwiched between layers of clear, decorated by etching. Painstaking and costly to manufacture, Intarsia Ware was never circulated in large numbers and is quite scarce today. The designs are sometimes said to be suggestive of patterns in ancient glassware; this was probably more accidental than intentional.

IRIDESCENT GLASS

An American art glass with a shimmering quality, used by Tiffany in the early 20th century.

IVORY

Term used to describe custard glass in the "Vermont" and "Delaware" pattern.

IVRENE

Opaque white glass by Steuben with an iridescent pearlized quality.

JADEITE

Pale green opaque glass color.

JAM JAR

Small jar with lid which usually has opening for spoon handle. Used to hold jams, jellies, and preserves.

JARVES, DEMING

Founder of the New England Glass Co. (1818), and the Boston & Sandwich Glass Co. (1825). In 1837 he set up the Mt. Washington Glass Works, though he played no role in its operations; its directorship was assigned to George Jarves, his son. The last company he established was the Cape Cod Glass Co. in 1858. Jarves died at age 79 in 1869, by all odds the most influential and financially successful American glass executive of the middle 19th century.

JELLY TRAY

Small shallow tray with rim for serving sliced cranberry jelly or jellied consomme.

JEANNETTE GLASS COMPANY

This company has been producing glassware in Jeannette, Pennsylvania since around the turn of the century.

JENNYWARE

Kitchenware items made by Jeannette are called Jennyware by collectors. The aquamarine pieces are the most sought after and the most common.

JERSEY GLASS CO.

The Jersey Glass Co. was founded at Jersey City, New Jersey, in 1824 by George Drummer. It manufactured chiefly tableware, both cut and pressed.

JUG

A vessel for storing liquid, it usually has a wide mouth, pouring spout, and handle. Often referred to as a pitcher.

JUICE GLASS

A tall narrow glass used for drinking fruit and vegetable juices.

KEW BLAS

An iridescent variety of art glass, introduced by the Union Glass Co. in the 1890's. The chief color is brown, shading into various hues and intermixed with green.

KICK

A small indentation in the bottom of any glass object.

KNIFE REST

Small, glass, barbell-shaped table accessory used to hold knife blade off table while eating.

KNOP

A ball-shaped swelling on the stem of a wine glass.

LACE GLASS

See-through Venetian glass with a glassy, thread-like motif. Layered on either side in clear glass. Popular in the mid-16th century.

LACY PRESSED GLASS

An American variety of pressed glass distinguished by motifs of angular and round compositions, encompassing a complete surface. Popular in the mid-19th century.

LALIQUE

A leader of the Art Nouveau movement in glassware, Rene Lalique was, for many years, one of the more influential designers and manufacturers. His factory was located at Combs, France, and supplied the Parisian market as well as exporting heavily to the U.S. Unlike many of his contemporaries he continued to enjoy success after Art Nouveau had waned, following World War I, and in fact some of his greatest successes came in the 1920's and 1930's. He died in 1945 at the age of 85, having spent more than 60 years in the glass industry.

LATTICINO

Refers to solid, Venetian glass from the 16th century, with white opaque threadwork contrasting with the clear glass.

LAVA GLASS

Tiffany glass of dark blue hue with tendrils or coated decorations in gold or silver.

LAYERED GLASS

Glassware made with two or more layers of glass.

LEAD GLASS

In the 17th century, George Ravenscroft, an English glassmaker, invented a type of glass of extreme brilliance, fused with an oxide of lead.

LEER

Lehr glassmaker's oven for gradually toughening ware. Improved designs led to more ornate glass from the mid to late 18th century.

LIBBEY GLASS

Late 19th century glassworks from Toledo, Ohio, known for cut and pressed glass wares of high quality. Also known for Peachblow and Amberina.

LIBERTY WORKS

This glass company was located in Egg Harbor, New Jersey and produced glassware from 1903 to 1932.

LILY-PAD

The name given to an applied decoration in American glass. The lily-pad motif was shaped from a superimposed layer of glass, and varied in design. One typical motif had a curving stem which supported a flat leaflike ovoid pad.

LIME GLASS

Discovered in 1864 as a substitute for lead glass by William Leighton, a chemist employed by a glass works at Wheeling, West Virginia. It was cheaper than lead glass, cooled quicker, and was lighter in weight, even though its appearance was inferior. Employed for glass or domestic utility, later became more widely used.

LOCKE, JOSEPH

English glassmaker and designer, active in the United States in the late 19th and 20th centuries. Pioneer of a number of varieties of art glass, including Agata. Locke died in 1936 at age 90.

LÖTZ GLASS OR LOETZ GLASS

Austrian Art Nouveau glass from the factory of Johann Lötz. Influenced by Tiffany glass.

LOVING CUP

Large footed tri-handled glass cup.

LOW RELIEF

Relief adornment where the relief or projected portion is only raised a small degree.

LUNCHEON PLATE

Eight to nine inch plate, smaller than a dinner plate, larger than a salad plate.

LUTZ GLASS

A thin clear glass striped with colored twists in the Venetian style. Introduced at the Boston and Sandwich Glass Works by Nicholas Lutz. Sometimes referred to as "candy stripe glass."

MACBETH EVANS GLASS COMPANY

With several locations in Indiana, Macbeth Evans has produced glassware since 1899.

MARBLED GLASS

Decorative glassware with random coloration to resemble marble.

MARVER

A marble plate on which blown glass is shaped.

MAYONNAISE

Open compote often with underplate. Used for serving mayonnaise.

McKEE

Involved in United States glassmaking since the 1840's, the McKee Glass Company was organized in the late 1800's in Jeannette, Virginia. In 1961, it was bought by the Jeannette Corporation.

MERCURY GLASS

Two layers of glass sandwiching a coating of mercury or silver nitrate between.

MERESE

Pediment of glass bridging the bowl and stem.

METAL

When referring to glassmaking, the molten material from which it is made.

MILK GLASS

An opaque glass, handblown and decorated like porcelain, in the 17th and 18th century, popular for pressed glass.

MORGANTOWN GLASS WORKS

Located in Morgantown, West Virginia, Morgantown Glass Works produced glassware from the 1800's to 1972.

MILLEFIORI

A paperweight with a stylized floral motif achieved by using several different colored glass rods together in a pattern and covering them with a thick glass metal, popular in the 18th century.

MILLERSBURG

An important producer of Carnival glass, though short-lived. The Millersburg Glass Co. was founded by John Fenton of the Fenton Art Glass Co. in 1909. It pioneered a variety of ware featuring so-called radium finish (which did, indeed, carry measurable traces of radiation; this was overlooked at the time, but after World War II, when the public became radiation-conscious, some persons disposed of their Millersburg wares out of fear of radium poisoning. It has since been demonstrated that the quantities are far too minute to cause harm.)

MOLD PRESSED

Another name for pressed glass: ware manufactured by pressing into a mold, rather than by blowing. It was made extensively in the U.S. from the second quarter of the 19th century onward.

MONART GLASS

A Spanish glass oxidized with marbling effects.

MONAX

Thin white glass produced by Macbeth Evans.

MOSS AGATE

A variety of art glass manufactured by Steuben, featuring a marbleized overall effect worked up from the use of powdered glass and injection of cold water. The normal colors are red or brown.

MOTHER-OF-PEARL

Layered glass with air trapped in between.

MOTIF

Design or pattern of glass.

MOUNT VERNON GLASS

American art glass from the 19th century, blown-molded vases and novelties.

MOUNT WASHINGTON GLASS WORKS

An American art glass manufacturer established in South Boston in 1837 by Deming Jarves. Was best known for cameo glass and other fine glass such as Burmese and Crown Milano. The firm was acquired by Pairpoint Manufacturing Co. in 1894.

MUFFINEER

See SUGAR SHAKER.

MUG

A drinking vessel on a flat base with no stem or floor. It may also have a lid and is usually made of metal; in glass it is often referred to as a stein.

MURANO GLASS

The finest of Venetian glasses produced on a small island in southern Italy.

MUSTARD JAR

Small glass jar with lid which has indention for spoon. Used to serve mustard.

NAILSEA GLASS

Produced by Nailsea Glass House which was founded in the late 18th century at Nailsea in Somerset, Great Britain. Manufactured many unusual pieces such as canes and rolling pins. The term "Nailsea" has become vague over the years, now referring to a wide range of articles; many are attributable to Nailsea, but many are not.

NAPOLI

Object is covered with enamel and gilt all over—outside and inside.

NAPPY

Refers to a bowl. Old English term. Often found with one or two handles.

NASH

Prominent family of Anglo-American glass designers and manufacturers, founders of the A. Douglas Nash Corporation, noted for its art glass in the Tiffany manner. Unlike cheap imitators of Tiffany, who were plentiful in the World War I era, Nash worked in the Tiffany manner because of the family's close association with that firm, and produced wares of high quality.

NECK

The part of any glass vessel between the body and the mouth.

NEW BREMEN

One of the most influential factories in America in the Federal period. The New Bremen Glass Manufactory was located at New Bremen (from Bremen, a town in Germany), Maryland, founded by Johann F. Amelung in 1784. Unlike most makers of that era it signed and even dated some of its work. New Bremen or "Amelung" glass is scarce and eagerly sought; most recorded examples are found in museums.

NEW ENGLAND GLASS COMPANY

A leading glassmaking company established at Cambridge, Massachusetts, by Deming Jarves and associates in 1818 and which remained active until c. 1880; known for all kinds of glassware, including pressed and cut glass and a variety of art glasses, such as Agata, Amberina, Pomona, and Wild Rose Peachblow. Was incorporated into the Libbey Glass Co. in 1890.

NEW GENEVA

Glass works established 1797 in Fayette County, Pennsylvania, by Albert Gallatin. This was the farthest west that a glassworks was set up prior to the 19th century. Gallatin later gained notoriety by serving twelve years as U.S. Secretary of the Treasury, under John Adams and Jefferson. Its chief output was household ware of modest design, and it made some sheet glass for windows. The name "New Geneva" was chosen because of the preponderance of Swiss immigrants in the area.

NEW MARTINSVILLE GLASS COMPANY

Starting in 1901, New Martinsville Glass Company produced art glass for many years. The company later produced pressed pattern glass, novelty items, and Depression glass. In 1944, New Martinsville was bought by another company and became The Viking Glass Company.

NIPT DIAMOND WAVES

A diamond pattern on glassware produced by pinching together thick vertical threads of applied glass.

OBSIDIAN

A mineral that looks very much like glass. Modern glass, when colored black, is often referred to as "obsidian glass."

'OFF-HAND' GLASS

The curiosity glassware that craftsmen made from the leftover glass at factories; some were works of art, some utilitarian, some vulgar.

OGIVAL-VENETIAN DIAMOND

Diamond formation pattern in pattern glass. Also called reticulated or expanded diamond.

"OLD GOLD"

Deep amber stain.

OLIVE DISH

Small shallow relish dish.

OLIVE JAR

Glass container with wide mouth and lid used to serve olives.

OPAL GLASS

Milk glass.

OPALESCENT GLASS

Same as iridescent.
1. An art glass made by covering a bubble of colored glass with a layer of clear glass. The bubble was then placed into a pattern mold and blown so that the relief design was on the outer layer. It was then reheated causing the

raised portion to become opalescent against the colored background. This technique was most popular in the United States during the 19th century.

2. An art glass developed by F. Carder of Steuben Glass. While the glass was still hot, a strong jet of compressed air was blown over certain areas of the object. This jet of air resulted in an iridescence. It was manufactured in four colors: blue, pink, yellow, and green.

OPALINE GLASS

A luxurious variety of glass, employed in the manufacture of pressed and art wares. It seems to have been introduced, or at any rate popularized, by Baccarat in the 1820's, but they in no way held any monopoly on its manufacture.

OPAQUE GLASS

A glass with little or no translucency and highly colored.

OPAQUE-WHITE GLASS

A porcelain-like glass with a milky quality.

OVERLAY GLASS

A glass molding technique of placing one colored glass over another, with designs cut through one layer only.

OVERSHOT GLASS

Novelty glass of Sandwich and Reading which has rough icy finish which is acquired by rolling molten wares in crushed glass.

OWENS, MICHAEL J.

Co-founder of the Owens-Illinois Company. Inventor of the automatic bottle blowing machine.

OWENS-ILLINOIS INC.

A glass manufacturing company established at Toledo, Ohio in 1929. The company was formed by a merger of the Owens Bottle Machine Company and the Illinois Glass Company. In 1936 it acquired the Libbey Glass Company. Owens-Illinois made many items ranging from bottles to tableware.

PADEN CITY GLASS COMPANY

Known primarily for the glass it produced, Paden City also produced pottery. The company started in 1916 in Paden City, West Virginia, and closed in 1951. Many of the elegant Depression glass patterns were made by Paden City.

PAIRPOINT

The Pairpoint Manufacturing Co. was established in 1865 at New Bedford, Massachusetts. Eventually it acquired the prestigious Mt. Washington Glass Co. The firm, with various changes of name, operated until 1958.

PARISON

Mass of molten glass which is gathered on the end of the blowpipe.

PARFAIT

Tall, footed ice cream dish in which sundaes are served.

PATE DE VERRE

"Paste of glass" or "glass paste." Made from powdered glass, melted and colored, pate de verre is of ancient origin and has been used in the manufacture of various articles. It is sometimes carved.

PATTERN GLASS

A kind of pressed glass, popular in the 1830's when it was imitative of the design and appearance of cut glass. In time the patterns became more complex, including circular, oval, and elliptical patterns. In the 1860's the New England Glasshouse developed a way to press soda-lime glass, which was of inferior quality and did not make a bell-like ring when struck, as did the formerly used flint glass. To compensate for such imperfections, the entire surface was covered with more ornate designs. This type of glass was extensively produced in the second half of the 19th century.

PATTERN-MOLDED GLASS

A blown-molded glass in which the pattern is first impressed in a small mold before the glass is blown to full size.

PEACH BLOW GLASS

An American art glass of the late 19th century, characterized as a partially opaque glass shaded from cream or bluish-white to pink or violet-red. It was manufactured by several companies, including: New England Glass, Mt. Washington Glass, and Thomas Webb & Sons.

PEARL ORNAMENTS

Molded all-over patterns of ogivals or diamonds.

PEARLINE GLASS

Late 19th century art glass, varying from deep to pale opaline blue in the same piece.

PEGGING

A process whereby a metal tool was used to prick a glass object while still molten. The resulting rip was covered with more molten glass resulting in a bubble of trapped air. The air would then expand due to the heat resulting in a tear-shaped bubble inside the glass.

PHILADELPHIA GLASS

A term usually applied to glassware from an 18th century glassworks in Kensington, Philadelphia, of which no examples can be certifiably identified.

PHOENIX GLASS

A term especially applied to a cased milk glass known as mother-of-pearl glass, produced by the Phoenix Glassworks Company in Pittsburgh, late 19th century.

PHOTOCHROMIC GLASS

A glass developed in 1964 by Corning Glass Works. When exposed to ultra-violet radiation (e.g. sunlight), the glass darkens. When the radiation is removed, the glass clears.

PICKLE CASTOR

Glass jar held in a silver plated metal frame with handle and spoon. Used during the Victorian period for serving pickles.

PICKLE DISH

Oblong tray smaller than a celery dish.

PIGEON BLOOD

Brown highlighted ruby glass.

PITCHER

See JUG.

PITTSBURGH FLINT GLASS WORKS

In American glass, the formal name for Bakewell's glass works, established in 1808.

PITTSBURGH GLASS

Late 18th century and 19th century American glass, especially known for high-quality pressed glass.

PLATED GLASS

Layered glass made by dipping blown glass into different colored glass.

PLATINUM BAND

Ornamental silver colored rim.

PLATONITE

Heat resistant white glass by Hazel Atlas.

POKAL

A large standing cup with a cover, especially one featuring fine decoration and artistic merit.

POLYCHROMIC

Two or more colors.

POMONA GLASS

An art glass developed at the New England Glass Company by Joseph Locke. There were two manufacturing methods, but the basis of both was that some portion of a glass object was covered with an acid-resistant substance and some was not. The object was then dipped in acid, resulting in a mottled appearance. Some of the object would be frosted and etched by the acid, and the rest would remain smooth. The smooth areas were usually amber tinted.

PONTIL, PUNTEE, OR PUNTY ROD

Long iron bar which holds vessel after it has been detached from the blowpipe and while the final touches are being done.

PRESERVE DISH

Footed candy dish.

PRESSED GLASS

An inexpensive substitute for free-blown cut glass, thicker and heavier, and formed in a mold by mechanical pressure rather than by blowing. It was developed in the early 19th century and soon was in general use in American glasshouses.

PRISM CUTTING

A style in cut glass with long horizontal grooves cut into the glass. The lines are parallel and usually meet somewhere on the object.

PRUNTS

A glass-drop ornament attached to some early drinking vessels, notably used by the Germans on such glasses as the Krautstrunk and Roemer.

PUFF BOX

Small lidded box used for powder and powder puff, found on Victorian dressing tables.

PUMICE

Volcanic rock which has been ground into a powder and is used for polishing.

PURLED GLASS

Ribbing added around the base of a vessel.

PYREX

Trade name for "borosilicate glass" developed by Corning Glass in 1912. It is extremely heat resistant and inexpensive as well, making it one of the most popular kitchen wares today.

QUARTZ GLASS

An art glass introduced by Steuben, designed to imitate the appearance of quartz. It was produced in a variety of colors and shades.

QUATREFOIL

A form based on four leaves or a four-petalled flower, a gothic motif in architecture and window tracery.

QUEZAL ART GLASS & DECORATION COMPANY

A glassware manufacturing company founded in Brooklyn, N.Y. in 1901. It was best known for "Quezal" glass but it also manufactured several other types of art glass including opalescent pieces.

QUEZAL GLASS

An iridescent semi-opaque imitation of Tiffany's 'Favrille' glass which is sometimes molded. It was made in Brooklyn about 1917.

QUILLING

On glass, a wavy ornament worked into a pattern by nips with the pincers at regular intervals.

RANGE SETS

Also called grease sets or drip sets for range tops that include a large salt and pepper and a drippings jar. Other items in a range set could include a flour jar, sugar jar, or spice shaker. Found in depression era glass.

RATAFIA GLASS

See CORDIAL GLASS

RAVENSCROFT

George Ravenscroft (1632–1683) is commonly regarded as the first commercially successful glassmaker in England and responsible for popularizing lead glass. He in fact may be credited with a larger accomplishment; as the result of his efforts, glass for use in tableware gradually began to replace pewter and other materials. Pieces proven beyond doubt to be his work are rare (not for lack of output, but breakage over the years) and sell for high prices. Much research has been done on his life and work.

RAYED

Design of sunburst cuts on bottom of glassware.

REAMER

Juice extractors, reamers consist of a handled, highsided saucer with a pouring lip. In the center of the saucer is a pointed cone reaming section. The citrus half is seated on the reaming section and turned to produce juice.

REFRIGERATOR CONTAINERS

Refrigerator containers are glass kitchenware items made for use in the refrigerator. Some are made to hold butter, vegetables or leftovers, and some are made for easy stacking in the refrigerator.

RELIQUARY

A glass vessel used for storing a religious relic.

RELISH

Pickle dish; oblong tray, sometimes with one or two handles.

RESONANCE

The sound that results from a glass object being struck. Is thought by many to be a test for crystal, but this is not necessarily true as there are certain kinds of glass that have a resonance similar to crystal.

RETICULATION

See OGIVAL.

REVERSE PAINTING

Designs are painted on the back of glass, appearing in proper perspective when viewed from the front.

RIGAREE

Applied decoration of glass with close-set, narrow, vertical bands, sometimes in different colors.

ROLLED EDGE

Curved lip or edge which may roll either toward the center or away.

ROMAN GLASS

A term referring to glass made during the Roman period.

ROPE EDGE

Rope-like design around the edge of a piece of glassware.

ROSE

Deep red cranberry stain flashing.

ROSE BOWL

Small, round, often tri-footed bowl having small opening in center.

ROYAL FLEMISH GLASS

Type of art glass made by the Mount Washington Glass Works decorated with thin surface staining and raised gilding.

RUBINA

Crystal which gradually goes from rich cranberry at top to clear at the bottom.

RUBINA VERDE

Crystal which gradually goes from rich cranberry at top to yellow-green at the bottom.

RUBY GLASS

Popularized by Carder of Steuben, ruby glass was a kind of handsome art glass with delicate impressive coloring, either of pastel pink or strong red.

SALAD PLATE

Seven to seven-and-a-half inch plate.

SALT CELLAR

A bowl for holding salt at the table, common prior to the use of shakers and even for a while thereafter. It was open at the top so that users could take pinches of salt between the fingers and sprinkle on food. Salt cellars vary considerably in size. There are individual salt cellars used with tiny spoons, also. Salt cellars were sometimes footed.

SALTS BOTTLE

Small glass bottles with silver tops carried by Victorian ladies and containing smelling salts should they feel faint.

SALVE BOX

Small lidded jar used to hold salves, ointments, creams, etc., found on Victorian dressing tables.

SALVER

Large platter, 11–12 inches.

SANDWICH GLASS

An American pressed glass, popular in America and Europe as a substitute for cut glass, produced in Massachusetts during the 19th century.

SANDWICH SERVER

Center handled salver.

SASE

Abbreviation for self addressed stamped envelope. Used in mail order advertisements in glass and antique publications.

SATIN-GLASS

An American art glass consisting of layers of colored glass covered with square indentations, then given an acid-vapor bath to produce a satin finish.

SAUCE BOAT

A glass vessel used for serving sauce or gravy. These items are shaped like boats with handles on both ends.

SHERBET

Small, footed dessert dish.

SICK GLASS

Poor quality glass which has either been damaged by external factors or was simply made from inferior materials and with inferior processes.

SIGNATURE

Mark of the maker and/or manufacturer.

SILVER DEPOSIT

Silver decoration on glassware often in floral motif.

SILVERIA GLASS

A technique of rolling a thin layer of silver over glass, sealing it and then blowing, which shatters the foil into glittering flecks.

SILVERINA

A variety of art glass pioneered by Steuben in the 1920's, using flakes of mica.

SILVER ONYX GLASS

Pressed opaline glass decorated by staining parts of the pattern with platinum lustre.

SLAG GLASS

A leaded glass first produced in England in the middle 19th century. It employs slag, which is the refuse from steel works. The glass could be molded in many forms.

SODA GLASS

A light, easily worked glass from the Renaissance on in Venice.

SOUTH BOSTON GLASS

Associated with the Boston Glass Co., the originators of the three mold glass.

SOUTH JERSEY GLASS

Eighteenth century tableware produced by the glassworks of Caspar Wistar and other factories in the New Jersey area. First made for the workers' private use and local markets, the pieces are characterized by bold, almost crude, form. The style gradually spread throughout New England and New York.

SOWERBY'S ELLISON GLASS WORKS

Founded by George Sowerby, this glasshouse has specialized in pressed glass, which it began to produce in the 1880's. Its output has included slag glass, opalescent glass, and an opaque glass called vitro-porcelain used for imitating porcelain services.

SPANGLED GLASS

A late 19th century American art glass principally made into glass baskets with fancy decorated handles and rims. Flakes of mica were incorporated in the clear glass inner layer, and an overlay of clear tinted glass of various colors was applied.

SPATTER GLASS

Type of opaque white or colored glass in both England and America. The English color version usually has a white lining. The exterior is mottled with large spots of differently colored glass.

SPOON DISH

Rectangular or oval shaped shallow glass dish used for holding dessert spoons.

SPOON HOLDER OR SPOONER

Tall cylindrically shaped holder with or without handles, used to hold dessert spoons.

STAINED GLASS

Imitation colored glass achieved by painting clear glass with metallic stain.

STEUBEN

Manufacturer of art glass, noted today for figurines and elaborate decorative pieces created as objets d'art rather than for utilitarian purpose. The firm was begun by Frederick Carder at Corning, New York, in 1903, and soon became an influential style-setter whose products were copied by others. It was absorbed (though still under Carder) by the Corning Glass Works in 1918.

STRIPED GLASS

An American art glass from the late 19th century, characterized by wavy bands of contrasting color on a background.

SUGAR AND LEMON TRAY OR DISH

Two-tiered serving dish. Cut lemons were placed on the bottom tier and sugar was held by bowl which made up the top tier.

SUGAR SHAKER

Resembles salt shaker except that it is larger in size with bigger holes in the lid, used for sprinkling sugar. It is also called a muffineer.

SUNSET-GLOW GLASS

A glass evolving in the late 18th century which was milky white and opalescent.

SUPERIMPOSED DECORATION

Decorations and designs are tooled in glass and applied on the original surface.

SYRUP PITCHER

Small pitcher with hinged metal lid for serving syrup.

TAZZA

A decorative drinking vessel, usually mounted on a stem and made of glass. The beautifully wrought pieces of the 16th century are especially valued.

TEA CADDY

Large wide-mouth glass canister with lid used for storing loose tea.

TEAL

Blue-green glass.

TEAR

Bubble of air trapped in glass. Sometimes purposefully blown in stem for decoration.

THREAD CIRCUIT

A decorative motif on glass of applying threads of twisted glass on the bowl or neck of a vessel. Sometimes the appliques are of different colored glass, in concentric circles or symmetrical patterns. It had its beginnings in Venetian glass during the Renaissance.

TID-BIT TRAY

Tiered dish for serving hors d'oeuvres. Generally a metal pole runs through the center of each tier which is largest on the bottom, becoming smaller as they go up.

TIFFANY

Louis Comfort Tiffany, the most celebrated of American glassmakers, was born in 1848. He traveled abroad as a youth, studied painting, and became introduced to the beginnings of the Art Nouveau movement, at that time unknown in the U.S. By 1885 he had set up a glass factory on Long Island, New York. As the result of vast publicity achieved through the exhibition of his products at world's fairs and their popularity among the social elite, he soon gained an unrivaled reputation. The business was expanded to include not only glassware but decorative household objects, furniture, jewelry and miscellaneous lines, as well as interior decoration service. Tiffany pioneered a number of varieties of art glass, sold in the studios he established and in fashionable shops. Of these, favrile was undoubtedly the foremost, and the style with which he came to be best identified. Every piece of Tiffany glass is now in the rank of prime collectors' item, with prices for certain of them, such as lamps, going into five figures. Tiffany died in 1933 at age 85.

TIFFIN GLASS COMPANY

Based in Tiffin, Ohio, the Tiffin Glass Company was a subsidiary of U.S. Glass Company. It closed in 1980.

TOILET WATER BOTTLE

Bottle which is larger than cologne bottle used for holding toilet water on dressing table.

TOOLS

In glassmaking these include: block, blowpipe, caliper, compass, crimper, punty rod, and pucellas.

TOOTHBRUSH BOTTLE

Tall cylindrical glass bottle with cap, used to store toothbrush.

TOOTHPICK HOLDER

Small glass container found in novelty shapes and sizes used to hold toothpicks.

TOOTHPOWDER JAR

Small lidded jar for holding toothpowder.

TOPAZ

Bright yellow glassware.

TRANSLUCENT

Glass which diffuses light in such a way that objects cannot be clearly seen through it.

TRANSPARENT

Glass which permits light to pass through which makes it easy to see through.

TRIVET

Footed hot plate.

TUMBLER

A glass vessel, not having a stem or handle, resting upon a base rather than a foot or other support. The normal shape is cylindrical and capacity varies.

TUMBLE UP

Water bottle and inverted glass set which is intended for a night stand.

ULTRA-MARINE

Blue-green by Jeannette.

VASA MURRHINA

An art glass with an inner layer of colored glass that has various colored metals in flake or dust form used in it. Produced in Boston during the late 19th century.

VASELINE BOX

Small lidded ointment box; part of Victorian dressing table accoutrements.

VASELINE GLASS

A decorative glass originally from France. Produced during the second half of the 19th century in England and America, it is characterized by its greenish-yellow tone resembling the ointment. Often referred to as yellow opaline.

VERRE-DE-SOIE

Art glass produced by Steuben, among others, which is distinguished by its translucent silky irridescence.

WAFER DISH

Small square or rectangular glass dish used for serving wafers and crackers.

WATERFORD

Irish glass produced in Ireland from the 18th century onwards, associated with deep-cut glass of a bluish tint, avidly collected.

WESTMORELAND GLASS

An American glass in the 19th century imitating earlier styles.

WHEELING GLASS

Table glass from Virginia in the 19th century.

WHISKEY JUG

Whiskey decanter shaped like a jug, with or without handle.

WHISKEY TUMBLER

Small flat bottom glass for serving whiskey.

WHITNEY GLASS

An American glass from the 18th century producing bottles and flasks.

WINE GLASS

Stemmed glass for serving wine.

WINE SET

Decanter and wine glasses usually on a matching tray.

WRYTHING ORNAMENTATION

Fluting and/or swirled ribbing.

ZANESVILLE GLASS

An American art glass, produced in Ohio in the early 19th century.

ZWISCHENGOLDGLAS

A form of glass, popular in 18th century Bohemia, which was gilded and inlaid in another straight-sided glass.

GLASS ARTICLES

Goblet

Champagne

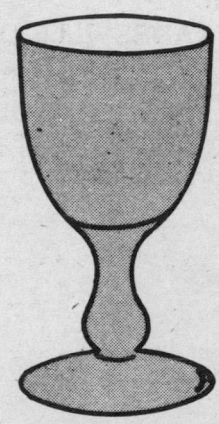

Claret

Sherry

Wine

Cordial

Comport

Basket

Decanter

Cruet

**Creamer
and
Sugar**

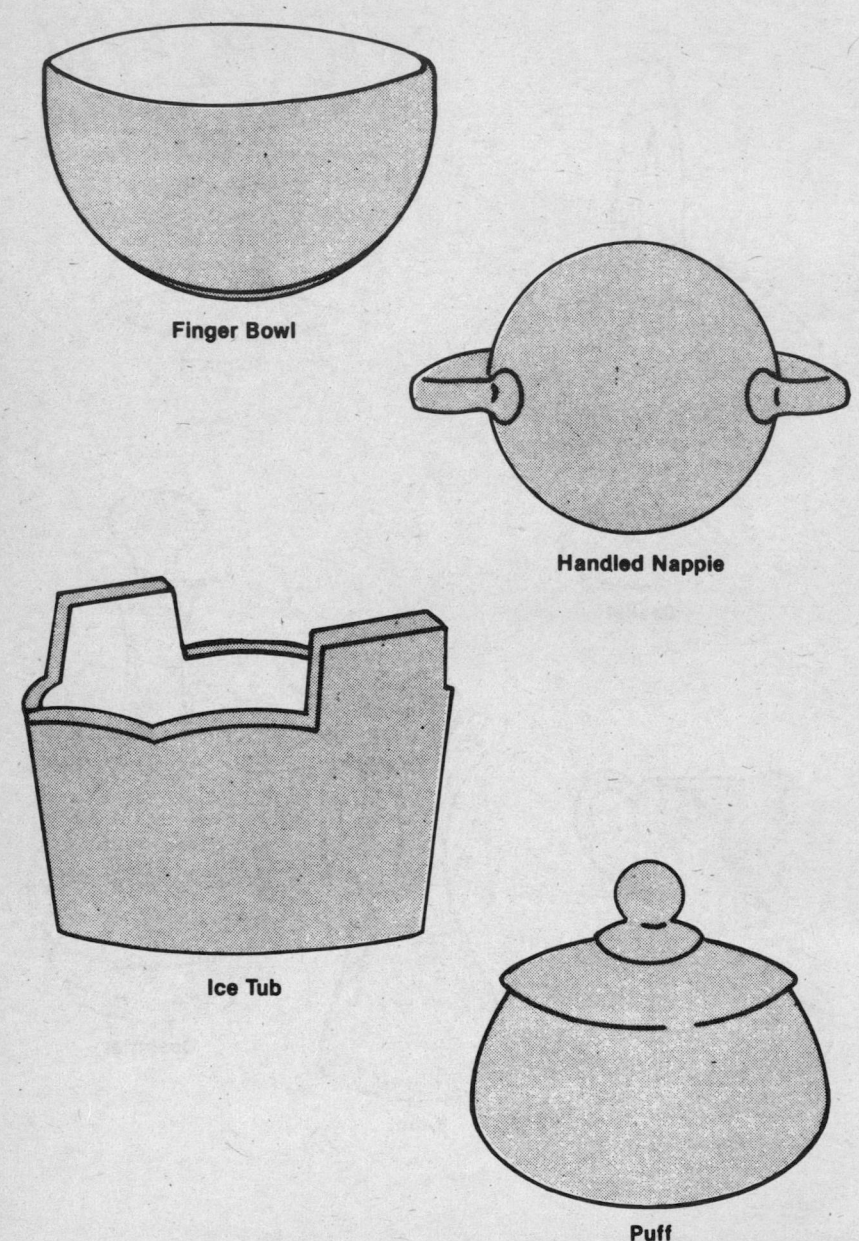

Finger Bowl

Handled Nappie

Ice Tub

Puff

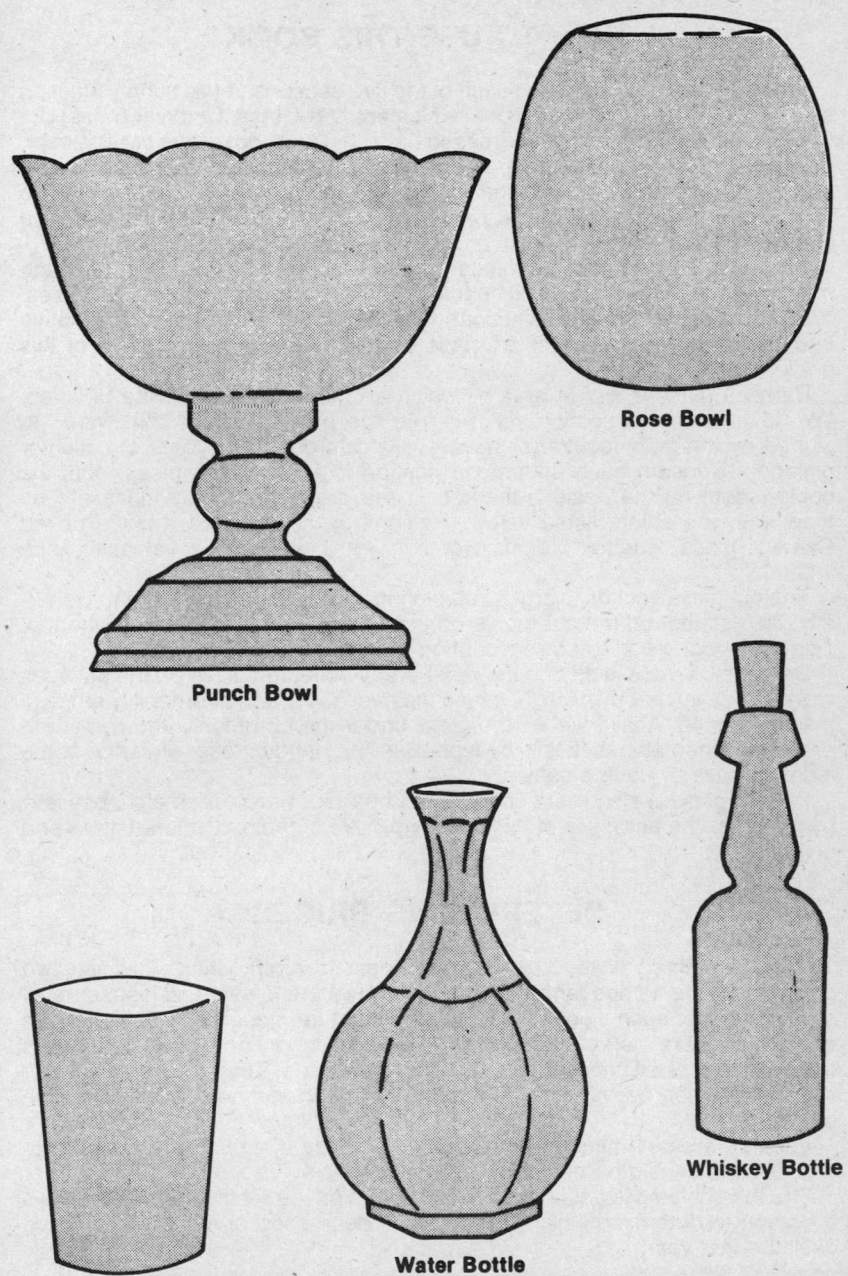

Rose Bowl

Punch Bowl

Tumbler

Water Bottle

Whiskey Bottle

HOW TO USE THIS BOOK

We have attempted to make each of the five sections of this survey function as a complete book. The sections, which are: Art Glass, Carnival Glass, Cut Glass, Depression Glass, and Pressed Pattern Glass, cover the history, care, display, and collecting tips that are indigenous to each type of glass, as well as the representative listings that can guide you to relative value. How the listings are organized depends on the collecting trends and the available information.

Art glass is often collected according to manufacturer or artist, although many collectors have gathered beautiful displays of certain pieces, i.e. vases. We have grouped the listings according to maker or type of glass. Descriptive information on each type of art glass can be found in the glossary of this book.

Carnival glass is a vast area to which an entire book could be devoted. We have listed the section according to the pattern names that were assigned by the manufacturer or have evolved through fifty years of collector dialogue. Beneath each pattern description is a list of the pieces that we could locate on the dealer's market. These are arranged alphabetically by type, with the colors listed below. Remember, if you have a piece of red Carnival glass, whether we list it or not, you have quite a valuable piece indeed.

The cut glass section is organized alphabetically according to item. Generally, the listings run the cut motifs on the article from the bottom to the top. Compare your piece to our description to find its relative value.

Depression glass is among the most avidly collected glass on the antiques market today. A happy thing, because the availability and affordability of these pieces is good. Again, we list the glass under the commonly known pattern name and then alphabetically by type. Use the handy cross reference in the index in case of double names.

Pattern glass is also listed under the old pattern name, then alphabetically by type. For the purposes of this book, we have combined colored glass and crystal.

DETERMINING PRICES

There are three price columns found next to each listing. The first two columns create a price range. The range shows the lowest and highest retail selling price for each piece. These prices reflect the geographical differences of the glassware market, as well as the laws of supply and demand. Dealers usually sell at retail price, but buy at wholesale value. Therefore, if a collector sells to a dealer, he should expect a lower price than if he sold at an auction or flea market.

Values were determined by averaging the prices of actual sales across the country and should be used only as a guideline.

The third column is an average of last year's prices for the item. This allows a person to determine which objects have decreased or increased in value over the last year.

ART GLASS

INTRODUCTION

Collectible art glass refers to various types of decorative glass which was developed all over the world and hand worked in one or all stages of development from the last half of 19th century until the 1930's and 1940's. It includes glass from the Victorian, Art Nouveau, and Art Deco periods. Victorian art glass consists of the Amberina, Burmese, Peach-Blow, Opal, Silverina, Agate, Crown Milano, Napoli, Satin, and Royal Flemish, to name a few. With the decline of the Victorian period and the emergence of Art Nouveau, iridized glass appeared, made in America by Louis Comfort Tiffany and Steuben, in Austria by Lötz, in France by Gallé, and in England by Thomas Webb and Sons.

Art Deco replaced Art Nouveau in the 1920's and the glass of Lalique of France epitomized the sleek styles of the day.

BUYING AND SELLING

In buying art glass there is no substitute for education. Read, research, and study this field; then go out and look at as much art glass as you can find in local museums and galleries. Dealing with reputable established dealers is a must, for forgeries of marks and fake art glass are not at all uncommon. Often times even experts are fooled. Making a mistake in this field can be costly. Art glass values are typically the highest in glass collecting.

When considering a purchase ask yourself the following questions. Is the piece signed? Does the base show tell-tale signs of wear? Is the piece the same shape and color as other documented examples of the same type? Even slight variations in shade, hue, and shape can indicate a reproduction. Is the price in keeping with the known value of similar pieces or is it too good a bargain to be true?

Is the dealer willing to stand behind the sale in writing? Educating yourself and dealing with reputable professionals are the keys to successful buying in the art glass world.

CARE AND REPAIR

The utmost care must be exercised in cleaning art glass. Enameled or flashed pieces can be damaged by washing. It is always wise to first wipe the object with a dry, flannel cloth, buffing gently to remove accumulated dirt and dust. Then, if need be, use a damp cloth and wipe carefully. Dry the piece thoroughly. If a piece needs washing use only mild soap in lukewarm water. Do not soak. Wash and dry quickly.

Repairs must be made by an expert. To find one in your area, call local galleries or museums. But remember, generally speaking, any serious damage renders art glass virtually worthless. And most damaged glass is impossible to repair.

AMERICAN ART GLASS

Art glass in America began to be produced as a result of the Victorian preference for ornate and colorful decorative objects. The last half of the 19th century saw the development of this glass in America. One of the first types of art glass was silvered or mercury glass which consisted of sandwiching a layer of silver foil between two outer layers of glass. It was produced by the New England Glass Company. Next, opal or milk glass was offered by first the Boston and Sandwich Glass Company and then the Mount Washington Glass Works.

In 1883, Joseph Locke, an Englishman, employed by the New England Glass Company near Boston, Massachusetts, obtained a patent for the first shaded art glass which he called Amberina. This glass was amber at the base gradually becoming deep ruby at the top.

In 1885, Frederick Shirley, another Englishman, employed by the Mount Washington Glass Company, patented Burmese glass which was an opaque glass; pale yellow at the base gradually shading to a salmon color. He made a tea set in Burmese and sent it to Queen Victoria, who immediately ordered more pieces. In 1886, the Mount Washington Glass Company permitted Thomas Webb and Sons of England to make Burmese glass in Great Britain. It was signed "Queen's Burmese."

The next glass produced by the Mount Washington Glass Company was called Peach Blow. It was blue tinted white glass at the base gradually shading to deep rose pink at the top. Peach Blow was immediately copied by the New England Glass Company and Hobbs-Brockunier of Wheeling, West Virginia. It was called Wild Rose, Coral, Wheeling Peach Blow and Plated Amberina by the various companies who made it. It was usually white with blue or yellow tints at the base shading to deep pink or deep red at the top.

One of the more popular types of art glass was developed by Frederick Shirley in 1886 for the Mount Washington Glass Company called Pearl Satin Ware. This was white mold blown glass which was dipped into colored glass and then exposed to acid fumes, producing a satin matte sheen.

Joseph Locke of the New England Glass Company patented Agata glass in 1887 which had mottled areas of brown and purple over Wild Rose glass. These effects were obtained by splashing the glass with various chemicals and refiring, creating a permanent glaze.

The Mount Washington Glass Company must be regarded as the most important producer of early commercial art glass in America. They produced a wide variety of glass such as: Opal, Burmese, Peach Blow, Pearl Satin Ware, Cameo, Albertine, Crown Milano, Royal Flemish, and Napoli. This early art glass flourished until the turn of the century when the era of the Art Nouveau ushered in the art glass of Louis Comfort Tiffany.

Louis Comfort Tiffany was a well-known decorator by the 1880's and a devotée of the infant Art Nouveau movement in America. The Art Nouveau style was a rebellion against the imitativeness of the Victorian period and the mass production of the Industrial Revolution. It came out of the Arts and Crafts movement in England and the belief of its founder, William Morris, that all decorative arts should be handmade. The Art Nouveau style is characterized by a return to nature in motifs executed by sensual, flowing lines with a heavy oriental influence.

Tiffany, the son of the famous jeweler, Charles Louis Tiffany, studied painting as a young man and spent ten years pursuing a career as a fine artist. Realizing he would never achieve worldwide recognition as a painter, he decided to go into the new field of interior decoration and it was here that he quickly gained fame. He had been experimenting with glass making in order to produce decorative objects for his design work and he devoted more and more of his time to glass. Tiffany had been collecting ancient glass for years and was particularly captivated by the iridescence found on ancient glass as a result of chemical changes. In 1880 he obtained a patent for his "favrile" glass, favrile meaning handmade. Gold chloride was used either in the glass or as a spray to achieve the iridized gold sheen which characterizes favrile. Indeed, Tiffany's colored glass was incredibly deep and true in its color due to the use of expensive metal oxides which produced the most intense colors. His blown glass was reheated as many as twenty times to achieve the desired effect. He absolutely believed that the decoration in glass must be a part of the glass itself, not applied externally.

Tiffany did not strictly adhere to the Art Nouveau movement. He was far too ornate and exotic to qualify as true Art Nouveau. His unique design sense and great love of beauty produced a style uniquely his own. In his older years his popularity declined as America moved into the streamlined world of the Art Deco period. There was a tremendous resurgence of interest in his work in the 1960's and now his decorative pieces are highly sought by collectors. The high quality of Tiffany's work has stood the test of time and while he did not personally make the art glass, it was nonetheless his alone. Tiffany was a man of unwavering standards of quality. He was also a stern taskmaster presiding over his workshop with a firm hand. He permitted nothing to leave without his approval. Tiffany was subsidized by his father's jewelry company; therefore, he never really had to consider cutting corners in order to stay in business. Because of this, the quality of his output was extremely high; indeed, cost alone would prohibit his glass from being reproduced today.

The Steuben Glass Company produced some of the finest art glass in America. Founded in 1903 in Corning, New York by Thomas Hawkes and Frederick Carder, the Steuben Glass Company became the Steuben Division of Corning Glass Company in 1918. Steuben continues to produce exquisite crystal art glass to the present day.

It was in the early years from 1903–1933 under the direction of Frederick Carder that Steuben produced its most famous art glass. Carder developed the beautiful iridescent aurene glass and also produced pieces in colored and clear crystal. No colored glass has been produced by Steuben since 1933 except for a few limited editions and some gold and silver decorative pieces. Therefore, if the glass is Steuben Aurene, Centra,

Cluthra, Dietreta, Florentia, Intarsia, Ivory, Iverene, Jade, Moss Agate, Oriental Poppy, Rosaline, Rouge Flambee, Verre de Soie, or Tyrian, it must be early Steuben. Their crystal sculptures of the finest lead crystal date from 1933 to the present day and are an art form in themselves. Steuben glass is signed "Steuben" in very fine script with a diamond point.

AUSTRIAN ART GLASS

Austria joined the worldwide fascination with the Art Nouveau movement rather late in the game. The primary art glass factories were those of Lötz, Lobmeyer, E. Bakalowits, Adolph Zasche, Graf von Harrach, and Moser and Sons.

Austrian art glass is characterized by beautiful, flowing iridescence and the graceful, sensual shapes of the Art Nouveau. The earliest maker of iridescent glass was Lobmeyer who was copied by Thomas Webb and Son in England, who were in turn copied by Louis Comfort Tiffany of America. Tiffany eventually inadvertently returned the favor to Austria, for one of his master glass blowers defected to the Lötz glasshouse.

Johann Lötz died in 1848 and his widow ran the firm until 1879 when a grandson, Max von Spaun of Vienna, took over. Under his direction, the firm achieved international fame, winning prizes and awards in many turn of the century fairs and expositions. Most Lötz glass is unsigned but there are signed pieces: "Löetz Austria" and "Lötz, Klostermuhle" with a mark depicting a circle which encloses crossed arrows. Signed pieces are not necessarily more valuable than unsigned pieces attributed to Lötz because of the beauty and quality of all pieces. Lötz glass was copied widely by other Austrian firms. Therefore, research and careful study are invaluable to the collector in the area of Austrian art glass. Perhaps one day the original catalogs of the primary Austrian glassmakers will be republished. This would be of tremendous help to collectors.

ENGLISH ART GLASS

English cameo glass was introduced in the 1850's and produced by the craftsmen in Stourbridge. Cameo glass was achieved by cutting layered or cased glass in such a way that a design of a different color from that of the ground appears in relief. This style of art glass was a result of the 19th century revival of classicism in the Victorian decorative arts. The outstanding ancient impetus for cameo glass was the famous Portland vase. This ancient glass vase, dating from first century A.D. and excavated from the sarcophagus of Alexander Severus who died in 235 A.D., depicts the Greek sea goddess Thetis, mother of Achilles. The relief is in white opaque glass carved against a dark blue ground. It was purchased by the Duchess of Portland, hence the name. (In 1845, while on loan to the British Museum, the vase was smashed by an Irish madman. It was repaired and became a part of the permanent collection of the British Museum in 1945). John Northwood, an English glassmaker, completed an exact replica of the Portland vase in 1876. Acid was used to obtain an outline of the pattern, then the outer layer of glass was painstakingly carved away. The project took years to complete and the copy by Northwood was exhibited in the Paris exhibition of 1878.

Thomas Webb and Son, along with the master craftsmen of their firm, Thomas and George Wood, produced exquisite commercial cameo glass from the 1880's until 1910. This glass is available to collectors today.

FRENCH ART GLASS

The handmade art glass of France, which first appeared in 1878, was an immediate success with the public. It was a complete departure from the factory made glassware which preceded it and it helped to introduce the Art Nouveau style to France. The earliest pieces were made by Eugene Rousseau. His glass was usually smoke-colored and had a crackled finish. His inspiration was Japanese art and many traditional oriental motifs and shapes were incorporated into his vase designs. Leveille was his protege and when he eventually took over the firm he continued to produce this tyle of art glass.

The greatest of all the French art glass makers was Emile Gallé who directed the acclaimed Nancy School of Art in Nancy, France. This academy was formed to espouse the great Art Nouveau movement in France. Nancy developed into a colony for the artisans of this movement.

Early in his career, Gallé, produced enameled and gilded transparent amber, green, or white pieces using historical themes. In the mid 1880's, he began to make pieces decorated with realistic motifs drawn from the world of nature. Flora, fauna, and even insects appeared on transparent glass objects. Gallé is probably most famous for his exquisite cameo glass which he introduced in the 1890's. With improved mass production techniques, Gallé used acid to etch designs on cased glass and remove layers of glass, leaving bas-relief designs which were then further carved by hand.

Emile Gallé died in 1904 and the quality of the work produced by his factory declined dramatically. He signed his glass "Gallé"; after his death the mark "Gallé*" appeared.

August and Jean Daum of Nancy also produced exquisite cameo glass although they had never received their just due until recent years. Their work is similar to that of Gallé but the background colors differ; Daum-Nancy cameo glass often has orange and yellow grounds as contrasted to the cream ground so often used by Gallé.

Rene Lalique first achieved fame as a maker of Art Nouveau jewelry in the 1890's. He experimented with glass then, incorporating it into his jewelry designs. His fame as a glassmaker, however, came as a result of his commission by Coty Parfums to produce decorative bottles for their fragrances. His most famous work was produced during the Art Deco period and included illuminated, frosted glass sculpture, vases, and even car hood ornaments.

	Current Price Range		Prior Year Average

AGATA

☐ **Spooner,** green opaque, very good mottling and gold band, 4½″ high ... **625.00** **725.00** **635.00**

☐ **Tumbler,** green opaque, excellent mottling and gold band, bottom has optic rib, 3¾″ high **575.00** **675.00** **585.00**

☐ **Tumbler,** green opaque, good mottling and gold band, glass is somewhat thick, 3¾″ high **475.00** **575.00** **485.00**

☐ **Tumbler,** green opaque, good mottling and gold band, bottom has optic rib, 3¾″ high......................... **550.00** **650.00** **595.00**

AMBER

☐ **Beer Stein,** amber applied handle, green applied berry prunts, pewter base and hinged lid with thumbpiece, hold ¼ liter, 6⅞″ high, 3″ diameter **180.00** **230.00** **190.00**

☐ **Cologne Bottle,** cut glass with matching stopper, 7″ high, 3¾″ diameter .. **150.00** **200.00** **155.00**

☐ **Liqueur Cruet,** pewter stopper, pewter mounted, 8″ high, 3″ diameter **100.00** **130.00** **105.00**

☐ **Liqueur Cruet,** swirl, amber rigaree, applied foot, pewter stopper, 8½″ high, 3⅛″ diameter **125.00** **160.00** **135.00**

☐ **Vinegar Cruet,** applied handle and ball stopper with enameled decorations, enameled, white dabs and blue fans on cruet, bulbous shaped mouth, 6¾″ high, 3½″ diameter **130.00** **180.00** **135.00**

☐ **Vinegar Cruet,** inverted thumbprint style, applied handle and bubble stopper, bulbous shape, 5¼″ high, 3″ diameter **105.00** **160.00** **120.00**

AMBERINA

☐ **Bowl,** swirl, deep fluted, rich cranberry shades evenly to amber, amber wafer foot, decorated with gold branches, berries and leaves, 7½″ x 10¾″ **350.00** **450.00** **365.00**

☐ **Bowl,** swirl, fluted, rich red shades to amber, iridized finish, 4″ high, 7⅝″ diameter **140.00** **190.00** **150.00**

☐ **Champagne Glass,** hollow stem, 6″ high **175.00** **250.00** **185.00**

	Current Price Range		Prior Year Average

☐ **Cruet,** Mt. Washington, Venetian Diamond, deep fuschia shading to honey amber, original stopper **250.00 350.00 275.00**

☐ **Cruet,** ruby shaded to amber, applied handle, 5″ high **45.00 75.00 50.00**

☐ **Fingerbowl and Underplate,** Libbey, bowl is more red than underplate which is fuschia, 2½″ high, signed LIBBEY, 1917 . . . . **525.00 625.00 535.00**

☐ **Pitcher,** diamond quilted, applied amber handle, red shaded to amber, round mouth, shape of tankard, belltone, 7″ high, 4⅛″ diameter **350.00 400.00 375.00**

☐ **Ramekin,** rich color, glass has minute ribbing, belltone, 2¼″ high, 2¾″ diameter **230.00 280.00 250.00**

☐ **Salt and Pepper Shakers,** set, inverted thumbprint, deepest fuschia color, original tops, 1880s **250.00 350.00 265.00**

☐ **Spooner,** Mt. Washington, diamond quilted, deep fuschia, square top **275.00 350.00 290.00**

☐ **Tumbler,** cranberry shaded to amberina, quilted design, 3″ high **30.00 60.00 42.00**

☐ **Vase,** flower petal shaped top, fancy amber applied spiral trim, cranberry shades evenly to amber, 10″ high, 5⅝″ diameter **150.00 205.00 165.00**

☐ **Vase,** swirl, fan shaped top, rich cranberry shaded to golden amber, amber edging around top, amber applied wishbone feet, 8⅛″ high, 6⅜″ diameter **120.00 175.00 130.00**

☐ **Vase,** Jack-In-Pulpit, decorated in gold with amber edging around top, cranberry shaded to amber, decoration of flowers and leaves in heavy gold, pair, 14¾″ high, 5⅜″ diameter **475.00 520.00 480.00**

☐ **Water Tumbler,** diamond quilted, belltone, 3⅝″ high, 2½″ diameter **110.00 130.00 120.00**

☐ **Whiskey Tumbler,** diamond quilted, deep red shaded to amber, belltone, 2⅝″ high, 2⅛″ diameter **170.00 200.00 185.00**

AMBERINA, REVERSE

☐ **Pitcher,** bulbous, olive amber shades evenly to cranberry, round mouth, clear reeded applied handle, colored enam-

	Current Price Range		Prior Year Average

eled leaves and flowers, red and green jewel decorations, 7⅞" high, 5¼" diameter **225.00** **325.00** **240.00**

☐ **Salt Shaker,** inverted baby thumbprint, pewter top **150.00** **220.00** **160.00**

☐ **Tumbler,** amber shaded to cranberry at base, pink, yellow, and blue enameled flowers with applied red jewels to centers, 5⅛" high, 2⅝" diameter ... **90.00** **130.00** **95.00**

ARGY-ROUSSEAU

☐ **Bowl,** pâte-de-verre, cylinder shape tapering towards the base, red background, molded with pineapples and leaves inside medallion-like designs which encircle the shoulder in a band, in black and red, signed, 4½" diameter, c. 1925 .... **1100.00** **1400.00** **1150.00**

☐ **Bowl,** pâte-de-verre, expanding cylinder, mottled lavender and green background, molds with roses, signed, 2¾" high, c. 1925 .... **800.00** **1200.00** **850.00**

☐ **Box,** covered, circular, light amber, orange, and gray, molded with leaves, strapwork, and stars with a red mask on the lid, signed, 6" diameter, c. 1925 **2200.00** **2800.00** **2250.00**

☐ **Pendant,** pâte-de-verre, flattened oval, double-pierced for stringing, molded with a moth, lavender and brown, 2½" long, c. 1920 .... **1200.00** **1400.00** **1250.00**

☐ **Shade,** pâte-de-verre, flaring bell shape, molded vertical ribs, mottled lavender and black background, molded in relief with black diamond shapes with black and magenta berries, signed, 6" high, c. 1925 .... **800.00** **1200.00** **850.00**

☐ **Vase,** elongated ovoid body tapering towards the base, light green background with streaking, overlaid with three bunches of poppies with long stems in orange and dark green, signed, 7⅛" high, c. 1920 .... **700.00** **900.00** **750.00**

☐ **Vase,** inverted bell shape, flaring panels on two sides, everted rim, spreading panelled foot, gray streaked with ochre shading to brown, lug handles with stars molded on sides, signed, 9½" high, c. 1925 .... **2000.00** **3000.00** **1900.00**

	Current Price Range		Prior Year Average

☐ **Vase,** ovoid shape, mottled ochre streaked with orange, lower portion molded with Greek Key pattern in yellow, orange, and gray, upper portion molded with three women picking apples in orange, yellow, gray, and brown, signed, 10″ high, c. 1925 .... **3000.00 5000.00   3100.00**

AUSTRIAN

☐ **Bowl,** circular, deep, pinched rim which curves inward, green background, acid-etched swirls and scrolls in strapwork pattern, silvery-blue oil spots, 5″ high, c. 1900 .... **200.00   300.00   225.00**

☐ **Comport,** trumpet shape, flaring rim with ruffling, amber iridescent, with short stem and circular foot, 4¾″, c. 1900 .... **250.00   350.00   275.00**

☐ **Cruet stand,** in form of an Asian elephant, textured skin, amber iridescent, metal rack strapped on its back, 11″ high, c. 1905 .... **350.00   540.00   365.00**

☐ **Vase,** bulbous base tapering to cylinder neck, slightly flared rim, short circular foot, blue iridescent background, applied lily pads, overlaid in flowers of silver mounts, 4¼″ high, c. 1900 .... **800.00   900.00   850.00**

☐ **Vase,** cylinder shape which tapers in towards the bottom then flares out to a circular flattened base, blue, purple, and green iridescent background, overlaid with silver foliage, 4¼″ high, c. 1900 .... **520.00   720.00   525.00**

☐ **Vase,** cylinder shape expanding towards the neck, slightly flaring rim, yellow background, overlaid in gray, cut with bellflowers and geometric designs, 10¼″ high, c. 1913 .... **900.00 1000.00   950.00**

☐ **Vase,** cylinder shape with slightly swollen base and shoulder, short circular foot, opalescent gray shading to pale orange, silvery-blue designs of striated feathering and oil spotting, 9⅛″ high, c. 1900 .... **800.00 900.00   850.00**

	Current Price Range		Prior Year Average

☐ **Vase,** double-bulbous shape, streaked ochre, rust and green background, silver mounts of poppy blossoms around bulbous neck with tendrils twining to the base, 6¼″ high, c. 1900 . . . . **300.00** **500.00** **325.00**

☐ **Vase,** inverted trumpet shape, cylinder neck, trefoil rim, green background, rectangular weave stringing, 6¼″ high, c. 1900 . . . . **85.00** **100.00** **85.00**

☐ **Vase,** long cylinder neck ending in flattened bulbous base, flattened flaring rim, amber iridescent background, overlaid with intricate silver foliage, 4″ high, c. 1900 . . . . **200.00** **300.00** **215.00**

☐ **Vase,** ovoid shape, waisted neck, flaring rim, yellow iridescent background, silver leaves, 3¾″ high, c. 1900 . . . . **300.00** **500.00** **325.00**

☐ **Vase,** ovoid shape, waisted neck, ruffled rim, salmon iridescent background, band around base of blue, white and red folds, fits into a cast stand of blossoms and leaves, 15″ high, c. 1900 . . . . **150.00** **200.00** **175.00**

☐ **Vase,** pear shape, amber iridescent background, overlaid with silver foliage, 4″ high, c. 1900 . . . . **200.00** **300.00** **215.00**

☐ **Vase,** pear shape, amber iridescent oil streaked background, intricate silver foliage, 4″ high, c. 1900 . . . . **200.00** **300.00** **215.00**

☐ **Vase,** spherical shape, flattened, cylinder neck, bulbous mouth, light green background, stringing, bronze handles in flower shapes, 6½″ high, c. 1900 **85.00** **100.00** **90.00**

☐ **Vase,** spherical shape, flattened, thin cylinder neck, clear background, green stringing, 6¼″ high, c. 1900 . . . . **85.00** **100.00** **90.00**

☐ **Vase,** spherical shape, tapering towards neck, lightly ribbed sides, emerald green lower body with flowers and leaves in silver, 5″ high, c. 1900 . . . . **110.00** **162.00** **125.00**

☐ **Vase,** spherical shape, waisted neck, green background, overlaid in silver blossoms and leaves, 13¾″ high, c. 1900 . . . . **300.00** **500.00** **325.00**

BACCARAT

	Current Price Range		Prior Year Average
☐ **Centerpiece Bowl,** Rose Teinte, embossed sunburst swirl, amberina-like coloring, scalloped edging, ormolu feet, 5½" high, 10¾" diameter	260.00	300.00	270.00
☐ **Cologne Bottle,** Rose Teinte, embossed swirl, 6¾" high, 2½" diameter	80.00	130.00	85.00
☐ **Cologne Bottle,** Rose Teinte, embossed swirl, amberina-like coloring, matching stopper, 8" high, 3" diameter	100.00	150.00	110.00
☐ **Epergne,** Rose Teinte swirl glass, scalloped edges, amberina-like coloring, three pieces unscrew, marked, rare, 15" high, 10" diameter	475.00	520.00	480.00
☐ **Fairy Lamp,** Rose Teinte, embossed sunburst glass, amberina-like coloring with matching saucer, 3¾" high, 5¾" diameter	215.00	240.00	220.00
☐ **Goblet,** Rose Teinte, amberina-line embossed swirl, marked, 4½" high, 2⅞" diameter....................	70.00	100.00	75.00
☐ **Lamp Base,** Rose Teinte, embossed sunburst with amberina-like coloring, square shape, 7½" high, 2¾" diameter................................	130.00	180.00	140.00
☐ **Perfume Bottle,** Rose Teinte, embossed swirl, 5¾" high, 2¼" diameter	85.00	100.00	90.00
☐ **Sugar Bowl,** Rose Teinte, amberina-like embossed swirl, marked, rare, 4¾" high, 4½" diameter	110.00	140.00	115.00
☐ **Tray,** Rose Teinte, embossed swirl, amberina-like coloring, round, scalloped edge, marked, 11⅛" diameter	100.00	150.00	110.00
☐ **Wine Decanter,** Rose Teinte, embossed swirl, amberina-like coloring, matching stopper, 9¾" high, 4⅞" diameter	130.00	170.00	135.00
☐ **Trumpet Vase,** . Rose Teinte, amberina-like coloring, ormolu base, 14⅝" high, 6½" diameter	240.00	300.00	250.00
☐ **Vase,** Rose Teinte, swirl glass, trumpet shape with scalloped top, amberina-like coloring, ormolu base, 14⅜" high, 6½" diameter	240.00	300.00	245.00
☐ **Vase,** tapered sides with panels, hexagon shape base, signed, 7" high	80.00	140.00	110.00

BOHEMIAN

	Current Price Range		Prior Year Average
☐ **Bowl,** overlay of cobalt, cut hobstars and fans, starcut design on base, tapered sides, round shape, 3½″ high, 12″ diameter	65.00	87.50	75.00
☐ **Bowl,** overlay of cobalt, cut hobstars and fans, tapered sides, starcut design on base, tapered sides, round shape, 3½″ high, 12″ diameter	60.00	80.00	70.00
☐ **Cake Plate,** overlay of amethyst, cut wave design surrounding hobstars and diamonds, notched and scalloped rim, 11¼″ diameter	40.00	60.00	50.00
☐ **Cologne Bottle,** ruby red with frosting around center, ruby circles and medallion have etched scene of deer, ruby cut stopper, 7⅜″ high, 2½″ diameter	150.00	200.00	160.00
☐ **Compote,** overlay of green, triangles with caning, thumbprints and sunburst design, notched and paneled shafts, starcut design on base, 6″ high, 7½″ diameter	35.00	70.00	45.00
☐ **Decanter,** cobalt with bullseye and fan cuts, paneled neck, clear stopper, 12½″ high	55.00	75.00	65.00
☐ **Dish,** overlay of green with three large cut fans, thumbprint, and marquise on border, footed, round shape, 3¼″ high, 8″ diameter	45.00	65.00	50.00
☐ **Vase,** overlay of amethyst, graduated sizes of cut panels, 10″ high	27.50	52.50	37.50
☐ **Vase,** overlay of cobalt, trumpet shape, cut pinwheels, diamonds and fans, 12″ high	60.00	100.00	80.00
☐ **Vase,** overlay of cobalt, trumpet shape, graduated sizes of cut panels, 7″ high	30.00	50.00	40.00
☐ **Vase,** overlay of cranberry, cut spiked diamond, and notched leaves, tapered base, cylindrical shape	60.00	80.00	70.00
☐ **Vase,** overlay with diamond cuts	80.00	110.00	90.00

BRISTOL

	Current Price Range		Prior Year Average
☐ **Cologne Bottle,** finish of apple green satin, green reeded handles trimmed in gold, matching scalloped stopper, 9⅜″ high, 3⅜″ diameter	130.00	190.00	140.00

Bohemian Decanter, *cranberry forest design, etched, 15" high,* **$185.00-$200.00**

	Current Price Range		Prior Year Average
☐ **Lustres,** gold decorated blue combination of glossy and satin finish, each lustre has eight crystal cut, spear point prisms, 10¾" high, 5" diameter	320.00	370.00	325.00
☐ **Sweetmeat Jar,** of pink overlay, silver plated lid, handle and rim around base, white interior, floral decoration of blue and white and enameled duck in flight, 5" high 3" diameter	120.00	160.00	135.00
☐ **Vase,** decorated turquoise blue, gray, purple and yellow bird of enamel on front, flowers of pink and white with green leaves, bug decoration on back, dots of white and bands of gold adorn pedestal base, flattened oval shape, 2½" high, 4¼" diameter	200.00	240.00	210.00

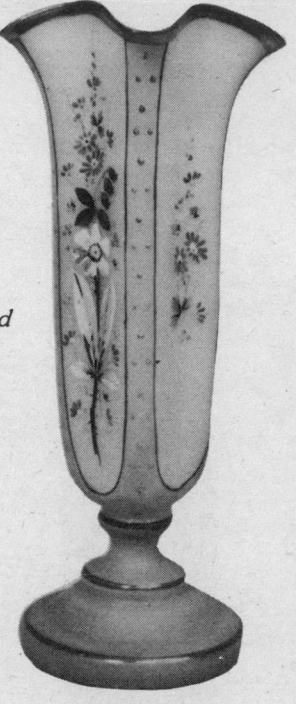

Bristol Vase, *frosted mauve and white, enamel floral decoration, 10½" high,* $85.00-$100.00

	Current Price Range		Prior Year Average
☐ **Vase,** of pink overlay, scalloped cut top with gold trim, decorated in blue, white, and orange enameled flowers, white heron outlined in blue dot pattern, 15" high, 5" diameter	210.00	270.00	230.00
☐ **Vases,** narrow necks, globular shape, 6½" high	28.00	44.00	34.00

BURGUN & SCHVERER

☐ **Bowl,** half-spherical, wide mouth with sawtooth, light green streaked with red, enameled with cherry blossoms and leaves in light pink, white, green, and brown, overlaid and carved in clear, gilding, 7" diameter, c. 1895 . .	4000.00	6000.00	4100.00
☐ **Bowl,** waisted dome body, flaring rolled lip, lobed circular foot, brownish-yellow streaked with green background, cut with wild animals and flow-			

	Current Price Range		Prior Year Average

ers within black enamel bands, background cut with spiraling garlands, enameled orange leaves around mouth, 5⅛" diameter, c. 1895 . . . . . .   **3000.00   4000.00   3250.00**

☐ **Bowl,** wide circular body, waisted standard, slightly flaring foot, sawtooth rim, light green with red-streaked background, enameled with poppies, grass, and leaves in light pink, white, green, and brown, overlaid clear with carving, gilding, 6" diameter, c. 1895 . . . .   **4000.00   5000.00   4100.00**

☐ **Vase,** bulbous body, cylinder neck slightly expanding towards sawtooth lip, pale yellow with brown streaks, enameled with flowers and leaves in blue and green, overlaid in clear, an applied scroll of foliage twining around neck, gilding, 5½" high, c. 1895 . . . .   **2000.00   3000.00   2100.00**

☐ **Vase,** bulbous body with long cylinder neck, gray shading towards base to lavender, overlaid in clear, carved with flowers and leaves of white, light yellow, and green, sawtooth neck, gilding, 5¾" high, c. 1895 . . . .   **2000.00   3000.00   2100.00**

☐ **Vase,** cabinet, baluster shape, sawtooth neck, yellow and beige background, overlaid in clear, carved with flowers and leaves of lavender, white, green, and brown, gilding, 5¼" high, c. 1895 . . . .   **3000.00   4000.00   3100.00**

☐ **Vase,** cabinet, spherical body, short cylinder neck with flaring lip, three clear feet, frosted gray with lavender streaked background, overlaid in lavender, cut with bleeding hearts and leaves, gilding highlights, 3⅛" high, c. 1895 . . . .   **600.00   800.00   615.00**

☐ **Vase,** compressed ovoid body, cylinder neck with lobing, light pink shading to magenta towards base background, etched and enameled with flowers, and leaves, in mottled yellow, green and brown, 4¾" high, c. 1895 . . . . . .   **4000.00   6000.00   4200.00**

☐ **Vase,** cylinder body expanding towards the shoulder, waisted neck with knob topped by inverted bell shape portion, short circular foot, gray with

	Current Price Range		Prior Year Average

splashes of lavender background, overlaid in lavender, cut with irises and leaves, 9⅜" high, c. 1895 .... **1600.00 2000.00 1700.00**

☐ **Vase,** cylinder shape tapering towards neck, milky opalescent, and lavender, enameled white flowers and green leaves enclosed, flower designs carved and in gilt, 5½" high, c. 1895 **1000.00 1400.00 1100.00**

☐ **Vase,** cylinder shape with expanded base, waisted neck, sawtooth neck, light green with red spiraling streaks, overlaid in clear, carved flowers and leaves of mottled pink, yellow, brown, green, and white enamel, gilding, 9" high, c. 1895 .... **6000.00 8000.00 6100.00**

☐ **Vase,** double cone shape, flaring lip curves outward, short circular foot, green streaked with dark red background, enameled with flowers and leaves of rose, dark red, green, brown, and white, gilding, 6¾" high, c. 1895 **4000.00 6000.00 4100.00**

☐ **Vase,** elongated ovoid body, waisted neck, sawtooth neck, etched green with red-streaked background, enameled rhododendrons and leaves of mottled pink, yellow, green, and brown, gilding, 9½" high, c. 1895 .... **6000.00 8000.00 6100.00**

☐ **Vase,** elongated ovoid shape, waisted neck, sawtooth lip, light yellow shading to green background, overlaid in clear, carved peonies and leaves of light pink, white and green enameling, gilding, 9½" high, c. 1895 .... **6000.00 8000.00 6100.00**

☐ **Vase,** elongated ovoid, swollen, waisted neck, slight flaring lip, green etched background, overlaid in clear, carved with poppies and leaves of mottled pink, green, and brown enamel, gilding, 9" high, c. 1895 .... **6000.00 8000.00 6100.00**

☐ **Vase,** elongated ovoid tapering towards base, short cylinder neck, lavender shading to pale lavender towards base, enameled in flowers and leaves of green, white, light yellow, overlaid in clear, sawtooth neck, gilding, 4½" high, c. 1895 .... **2000.00 3000.00 2100.00**

☐ **Vase,** inverted bell shape, pedestal foot slightly domed, wide flaring flip, clear amber background, green streak-

	Current Price Range		Prior Year Average

ing inside decorated with band of mythological animals and leaves, enameled band of roses at lip, black scroll against white band around foot, gilding, 5¼″ diameter, c. 1895 . . . . . . **4000.00** **6000.00** **4100.00**

BURMESE

☐ **Cruet,** Mt. Washington, acid finish, melon ribbed, undecorated, second fired yellow edge on spout, very fine color, 6½″ high **900.00** **1400.00** **950.00**

☐ **Cruet,** Mt. Washington, acid finish, ribbed, matching ribbed stopper, yellow handle, 7″ high, 3¾″ diameter . . **775.00** **900.00** **785.00**

☐ **Fairy Lamp,** acid finish, superb color, deep salmon pink shades evenly to creamy yellow, rare pressed Burmese base, clear inside cup, base marked Clarke, 5″ high, 3⅞″ diameter **375.00** **475.00** **385.00**

☐ **Fairy Lamp,** acid finish, superb color, rich salmon pink shades evenly to yellow, on matching ruffed reversible base, clear marked Clarke cup, 5¾″ high, 7″ diameter **500.00** **700.00** **525.00**

☐ **Fairy Lamp,** Webb, acid finish, dome on signed Clarke candle cup **225.00** **250.00** **230.00**

☐ **Fairy Lamp,** Webb, acid finish, gold decorated Aladdin shape muted green Tunnecliffe pottery base, shade is decorated with red flowers and green leaves, base marked Clarke inside, 6½″ high **675.00** **750.00** **685.00**

☐ **Fairy Lamp,** Webb, acid finish, superb color, matching unsigned fluted Burmese bowl base with three yellow feet, pressed Burmese insert signed Clarke, clear candle cup, large Burmese dome shade, 6½″ high, 4¼″ diameter **685.00** **800.00** **700.00**

☐ **Muffineer,** Mt. Washington, acid finish, white and colored dots form delicate blossoms, attributed to Timothy Canty, 4½″ high **575.00** **650.00** **580.00**

☐ **Rosebowl,** miniature, Webb, acid finish, crimped top, decorated with red berries, green and brown leaves, unsigned, 2½″ high, 2¾″ diameter **275.00** **350.00** **285.00**

	Current Price Range		Prior Year Average
☐ **Sugar and Creamer Set,** Mt. Washington, acid finish, no decoration, 3¾" creamer has applied handle, open sugar is 2⅛" high	550.00	650.00	575.00
☐ **Table Lamp,** probably Mt. Washington, shade has satin exterior, shiny interior, fine color, base is originally Kerosene, converted to electricity, made of Brittania metal in England, has embossed florals, shade is 10" diameter, total height is 15"	1000.00	2000.00	1200.00
☐ **Toothpick Holder,** acid finish, bulbous with square top, decorated with dainty brown leaves, white and blue enameled flowers, 3" high, 2½" diameter	230.00	330.00	245.00
☐ **Toothpick Holder,** acid finish, square top, 2⅝" high, 2½" diameter	130.00	190.00	142.00
☐ **Vase,** acid finish, ribbed, scalloped top, 3¾" high, 2½" diameter	150.00	225.00	165.00
☐ **Vase,** shiny finish, ruffled top, 3¾" high, 3" diameter	150.00	200.00	160.00
☐ **Vase,** acid finish, salmon pink shades evenly to yellow, enameled decoration features red buds and green leaves unsigned but attributed to Webb, 8" high, 4" diameter	700.00	900.00	725.00
☐ **Vase,** acid finish, undecorated, 3¾" high, 5¼" diameter at widest point . .	175.00	275.00	180.00
☐ **Vase,** Mt. Washington, beautiful coloration, enameled multicolor stylized blossoms and foliage, two applied handles, 10½" high	1150.00	1350.00	1200.00
☐ **Vase,** Mt. Washington, bottle, acid finish, salmon pink evenly shaded to yellow, white enameled mums and dainty green foliage, 6⅜" high, 3¼" diameter	225.00	325.00	250.00
☐ **Vase,** Mt. Washington, bulbous base, long slender neck, decorated with sacred ibis, oasis scene in raised gold, 12" high, 7" diameter at widest point	2500.00	3500.00	2750.00
☐ **Vase,** Mt. Washington, egg shaped, acid finish, decorated with daisies and foliage in three shades of gold enamel, designs outlined in raised gold, 9" high, 4¾" diameter at widest point	650.00	750.00	675.00
☐ **Vase,** Mt. Washington, jack-in-pulpit, acid finish, very good color, flared crimped top, 12½," high, 5" diameter at top	600.00	700.00	625.00

	Current Price Range		Prior Year Average
☐ **Vase,** Mt. Washington, teardrop shape, elaborate blossom and foliage multicolored and gold decoration, raised gold dots, fancy scrolls, 10½" high, 5½" diameter at widest point	1500.00	2500.00	1750.00
☐ **Vase,** Webb, acid finish, flower petal top, salmon pink shades evenly to yellow, decorated with green leaves and red berries, 3⅜" high, 3⅛" diameter	300.00	385.00	315.00
☐ **Vase,** Webb, acid finish, fluted top, slightly embossed striped effect, 3½" high, 3" diameter	175.00	270.00	185.00
☐ **Vase,** Webb, acid finish, ruffled top and base, 4½" high, 2¾" diameter	175.00	270.00	185.00
☐ **Vase,** Webb, acid finish, ruffled top, salmon pink shades evenly to yellow, decorated with lavender five petal flower, green and brown leaves, unsigned, 4⅛" high, 2¾" diameter	295.00	395.00	300.00
☐ **Vase,** Webb, acid finish, ruffled top, widely flared, ball shape body, unsigned, 3⅛" high	175.00	275.00	180.00
☐ **Vase,** Webb, acid finish, salmon pink shades evenly to yellow, decorated with green foliage and red buds, unusual shape, 4⅜" high, 2½" diameter	300.00	400.00	325.00
☐ **Vase,** Webb, Queen's, acid finish, bottle, salmon pink shades evenly to yellow green ivy leaf enameled decoration, signed Thos. Webb Queens Burmese Ware, 7¾" high, 4½" diameter	800.00	1000.00	825.00
☐ **Vase,** Webb, Queen's, acid finish, flower petal top, salmon pink shades evenly to yellow, decorated with green and brown leaves, red berries, signed Thos. Webb Queens Burmese Ware, 2¾" high, 3¼" diameter	375.00	475.00	400.00
☐ **Vase,** Webb, Queen's, acid finish, flower shaped top, unusual frosted edging, salmon pink shades evenly to yellow, tan pine cone enameled decoration, signed Thos. Webb Queens Burmese Ware, 5⅝" high, 3⅛" diameter	500.00	700.00	550.00
☐ **Whiskey Tumbler,** Mt. Washington, acid finish, diamond quilted, reheated yellow top edge, 2¾" high, 2¼" diameter	150.00	220.00	165.00

CAMEO

	Current Price Range		Prior Year Average

☐ **Bowl,** English, ribbed, thin outer layer of various pink shades, white inner layer, acid cut back in fish scale motif, decorated with morning glory vine and butterfly in gold enamel, 3″ base, 7½″ at widest point, 6¼″ top diameter, signed in enamel G.L.F., paper label Whitlow collection **900.00   1100.00   950.00**

☐ **Perfume Bottle,** English, round, dark blue ground, profusely decorated with deeply carved and finely detailed white blossoms, foliage and butterfly, sterling, screw-type stopper, 7¼″ high, 5″ diameter **1800.00   2500.00   1900.00**

☐ **Vase,** English, four layers, white to red to clear to green, depicts raspberries and foliage, very elaborate top border, 7″ high, 4½″ diameter at widest point, unsigned **2000.00   3000.00   2250.00**

☐ **Vase,** signed by Michel Paris, translucent, frosted background with brown cut to yellow, sailboat scene, three detailed acid cuttings, 8½″ high, 3½″ diameter **800.00   850.00   820.00**

CASED

Cased Glass—Czechoslovakian

☐ **Lustres,** white with cranberry banding, circular medallions, hand painted flowers, ruffled rims, pedestal bases, spearpoint prisms, 12⅝″ high **74.00   150.00   100.00**

☐ **Perfume Bottle,** decorated yellow, clear ball stopper has covering of gold, sanded gold leaves and ribbon studded with applied jewels of green and red, 5½″ high, 2⅛″ diameter **100.00   140.00   110.00**

☐ **Rose Bowl,** amethyst, applied flower in white with transparent, applied branch and leaf, 3¾″ high, 4″ diameter, rare **150.00   200.00   175.00**

☐ **Rose Bowl,** pink hobnail design, eight crimp top, 3⅛″ high, 3⅝″ diameter **95.00   125.00   115.00**

CORALENE	Current Price Range		Prior Year Average
☐ **Pitcher,** orange glass, amber applied handle and rigaree of amber surrounds neck, water lilies of white and green leaves in Coralene beading decoration, 6¼" high, 4" diameter	210.00	250.00	215.00
☐ **Lamp Base,** satin glass of decorated yellow, fern leaf sprays of pale yellow in beaded Coralene of yellow, original brass burner, 7⅝" high, 3" diameter	160.00	192.00	160.00
☐ **Vase,** seaweed decoration on pale blue diamond quilted mother of pearl, coralene blossoms have applied jewel center, 7" high	450.00	550.00	475.00
☐ **Vase,** seaweed, pink decoration on gold diamond quilted mother of pearl, 6¾" high	450.00	550.00	475.00

CRANBERRY

	Current Price Range		Prior Year Average
☐ **Bowl,** applied crystal berries on top edge, berry pontil plus three crystal fans applied around top, three reeded scroll feet, 5½" high, 5½" diameter	280.00	330.00	290.00
☐ **Bowl,** clear reeded scroll feet, six clear berry prunts around top, three crystal fan shaped applied designs on bowl, berry on base, 5⅜" high, 6⅛" diameter	225.00	300.00	250.00
☐ **Bowl,** two rows of crystal applied shell trim, applied rigaree around center, three crystal reeded scroll feet, base has berry prunt, 4¾" high, 8" diameter	420.00	480.00	430.00
☐ **Cologne Bottle,** frosted with gold decorations, clear ball stopper adorned in gold, 5¾" high, 3⅛" diameter	185.00	215.00	185.00
☐ **Fairy Lamp,** frosted, shade has crimped top, signed Clarke base, 3¾" high, 2⅞" diameter	110.00	150.00	115.00
☐ **Liqueur Set on Tray,** decorated in heavy gold, tray has square, scalloped edge, 8" diameter, bottle has applique on sides with flower basket and butterfly decoration, 9¼" high, set of six glasses, matching, 2" high	250.00	300.00	255.00
☐ **Lustres,** clear crystal prisms, pair, 11" high	110.00	160.00	130.00
☐ **Pitcher,** inverted thumbprint, bulbous with square top, clear applied handles, 5⅞" high, 3½" diameter	87.00	110.00	94.00

	Current Price Range		Prior Year Average

☐ **Vase,** clear reeded applied handles, enameled flowers of blue and white with gold foliage, 11½" high, 6¾" diameter 320.00 360.00 325.00

☐ **Vase,** decorated with gold enamel and blue and white forget-me-nots, 11" high, 4" diameter 120.00 160.00 130.00

Left to Right: **Cranberry Pickle Castor,** *sterling holder with fork, 11¾" high,* **$225.00-$250.00; Cranberry Thumbprint Basket,** *applied crystal handle, 10" high,* **$70.00-$85.00**

	Current Price Range		Prior Year Average

☐ **Vase,** ewer, Moser-type, enameled, clear twig handle, 11½" high 30.00 70.00 45.00

☐ **Vase,** fan shaped, deep cranberry color, clear applied ruffle around top edge, clear applied wishbone feet, decorated with small enameled multi-colored leaves, blue and white flowers on gold panel, 10¾" high 185.00 225.00 190.00

☐ **Vase,** hand painted circular plaque of young child in porcelain, some fired gold foliage and bird design, pedestal base, inverted heart shape, 5" high 30.00 60.00 45.00

☐ **Vases,** pair, decorated with gold sanded flowers and leaves outlined in white with blue centers, small white enameled flowers and branches, gold sanded top and bottom bands, 10" high, 3¾" diameter 275.00 330.00 285.00

☐ **Vases,** pair, deep cranberry color, lavishly decorated with gold, blue, and white flowers and leaves, 11" high, 4" diameter 300.00 400.00 325.00

☐ **Water Pitcher,** optic effect, clear applied handle, very large, 12¾" high, 6¼" diameter..................... 250.00 320.00 275.00

☐ **Wine Glasses,** cranberry bowls with clear stems and feet, belltone, set of six, 5⅛, 2¼" diameter 165.00 195.00 170.00

CROWN MILANO

☐ **Ewer,** Mt. Washington, applied handle, profuse eight-color geometric decoration, 13" high, unsigned 1600.00 2000.00 1700.00

☐ **Ewer,** Mt. Washington, unusual pastel lilac decoration depicts reclining shepherdess with her sheep, back decorated with birds and roses, raised gold wreaths surround both panels, small pastel lilac wreaths elsewhere, 10½" high, 8½" diameter across front 2500.00 3500.00 2650.00

☐ **Cracker Jar,** Mt. Washington, melon ribbed, cream ground, colorful nasturtium enameled decoration, silver plated bail and lid, lid is signed J.P.C.E.P.N.S., 8" high to top of fully extended bail, 7" diameter 500.00 600.00 530.00

	Current Price Range		Prior Year Average

☐ **Decanter,** with hollow stopper, shiny finish, decorated with exquisite enamel roses and profuse gold scrolls on neck and stopper, 10″ high and 6″ wide at bulbous base, rare early Albertine/Crown Milano signature **1000.00 1400.00   1150.00**

☐ **Jam Jar,** white body, slightest hint of pink at shoulders and base, decorated with very delicate blue and white forget-me-nots, silver plated lid and bail is signed Sant & Co., signed jar, body is 4″ high, overall height to top of extended bail is 7″ **350.00   450.00   375.00**

☐ **Pickle Castor,** Mt. Washington-Pairpoint, pansy decoration, silver plated lid signed M.W., holder has Pairpoint mark, both resilvered, bowl is 4″ high, 4½″ diameter, holder is 10″ tall **1000.00 1200.00   1025.00**

☐ **Plate,** rose and fired gold scrolling, enameled dots on three reserves, 11″ diameter **120.00   180.00   150.00**

☐ **Rose Bowl,** Mt. Washington, all over decoration of roses, buds, leaves, gold trim, purple numbered pontil **350.00   425.00   365.00**

☐ **Salt Shaker,** cockle shell, Mt. Washington, white satin body, dainty enamel blossoms, silver plated top shaped like seashell **385.00   485.00   390.00**

☐ **Tray,** Mt. Washington, shiny finish, rolled and serrated edges, enamel thistle and foliage decoration, outlined with raised gold, 9½″ long, 7″ wide, signed **840.00   980.00   860.00**

☐ **Urn,** with rare crown shaped lid, raised gold blossom and foliage decoration, 16½″ high, 8″ wide, 5½″ deep, signed **2800.00 3300.00   2900.00**

☐ **Vase,** early Guba, tall and slender, shiny finish, decorated with four flying ducks over raised gold wheat field, 17″ high, 4½″ diameter, signed with Crown Milano/Albertine mark which features a crown within a crown **3500.00 4200.00   3650.00**

☐ **Vase,** Guba, decorated with five ducks on front, three in back, two applied handles, excellent professional repair to base **2000.00 2250.00   2100.00**

☐ **Vase,** Mt. Washington, bulbous, cream colored body with slender neck, gold blossoms and jewels covered with gold enamel, 12½″ high, signed **825.00 1000.00   840.00**

	Current Price Range		Prior Year Average

☐ **Vase,** Mt. Washington, cone shaped, enamel floral bouquet decoration, 8¾" high, signed **850.00** **975.00** **865.00**

☐ **Vase,** square shaped, rounded corners, two delicate applied handles, decorated with pastel enamels in tiny free form geometric patterns, 8" high, unsigned **720.00** **820.00** **730.00**

☐ **Vase,** Mt. Washington, square with rounded corners, two applied scroll handles, cream ground, decoration of gold and colorful enamel oak leaves and gold acorns, original paper label, 8¼" high **950.00** **1100.00** **975.00**

D'ARGENTHAL

☐ **Bowl,** double-conical shape, wide with waisted neck and foot, slightly flaring rim, yellow background, overlaid in red, carved with roses, leaves, and branches, signed, 12" diameter, c. 1900 .... **1000.00** **1400.00** **1100.00**

☐ **Bowl,** swollen spherical, indulated rim scalloped, yellow background, overlaid in maroon, cut with roses, signed, 6" diameter, c. 1900 .... **600.00** **700.00** **650.00**

☐ **Box,** covered, shallow circular shape, dark yellow background, overlaid in brown and umber, cut with wildflowers and leaves, signed, 3¾" diameter, c. 1915 .... **400.00** **600.00** **425.00**

☐ **Vase,** baluster shape, light yellow background splashed with red, overlaid in red, cut with landscape of lake, arched bridge, and trees, signed, 13¾" high, c. 1910 .... **2000.00** **3000.00** **2100.00**

☐ **Vase,** baluster shape, turquoise background, overlaid in dark blue, cut with flowers and leaves, signed 7" high, c. 1900 .... **400.00** **500.00** **425.00**

☐ **Vase,** cylinder shape tapering towards lip, short circular foot, orange-yellow background, overlaid in red, cut with leafy branches, trumpet blossoms, signed, 11¾" high, c. 1900 .... **700.00** **1000.00** **750.00**

	Current Price Range		Prior Year Average
☐ **Vase,** cylinder, slight tapering towards base, waisted neck, flaring lip, frosted yellow background, overlaid in brown, cut with scrolling vines in bloom, signed, 13¾″ high, c. 1900	1000.00	1500.00	1100.00
☐ **Vase,** ovoid body, pink shading to lavender, cut with orchids and leaves, signed, 6″ high, c. 1900	400.00	600.00	425.00

DAUM NANCY

☐ **Beaker,** flaring cylinder, gray shading to light pink and green, enameled black winter landscape, signed, 6″ high, c. 1910	600.00	800.00	610.00
☐ **Bottle,** compressed spherical body, inverted bell shaped lid, mottled gray shading to lavender, overlaid and enameled in lavender and green, gilding, cut with violets and leaves, strap work on base, signed, 4″ high, c. 1910	700.00	800.00	710.00

Daum Nancy Vase, *French Cameo glass, sterling base and feet, thistle design, 5″,* **$550.00-$650.00**

	Current Price Range		Prior Year Average

☐ **Bottle,** perfume, stopper, ovoid shape flattened on two sides, tapering to cylinder neck, concave disc-shaped stopper, mottled blue background, overlaid, cut and enameled with yellow iris and green leaves, signed, 5½" high, c. 1910 . . . . — 600.00 — 700.00 — 620.00

☐ **Bottle,** perfume, stopper, ovoid shape, short cylinder neck, fan-shaped stopper, gray background shading to darkish-yellow and pink, cut and enameled with wildflowers in blue, red, and gray, gilding, 3½" high, c. 1910 . . . . . — 550.00 — 650.00 — 565.00

☐ **Bowl,** circular, expanding, short sloping shoulder, mottled yellow shading to orange at base, overlaid in green, cut with trumpet blossoms and leaves, signed, 8¾" diameter, c. 1915 . . . . . . — 600.00 — 900.00 — 625.00

☐ **Bowl,** cameo, gray glass shades to pale blue, overlaid in white, cut with edelweiss, heightened in enamel, cameo mark, 6¾" high, c. 1900 . . . . — 750.00 — 850.00 — 800.00

☐ **Bowl,** acid etched, geometrical pattern, c. 1930 . . . . — 2800.00 — 3000.00 — 2900.00

☐ **Bowl,** cone shape, flattened flaring rim, cylinder foot, blue, cut with lattice pattern, signed, 15¾" diameter, c. 1922 — 2000.00 — 3000.00 — 2100.00

☐ **Bowl,** cylinder shape, slightly flaring, waisted above circular foot, applied angular handles, mottled green and blue deepening to deep blue at base, intaglio cut with cherry blossoms and leaves, signed, 5⅜" high, c. 1910 . . . — 400.00 — 600.00 — 420.00

☐ **Bowl,** deep canoe shape, bright green shading to pale green at the base, cut and enameled on front side with river scene, signed, 5½" long, c. 1900 . . . — 350.00 — 450.00 — 370.00

☐ **Bowl,** deep canoe shape, undulating rim, pale orange and citron background, cut and enameled with winter scene in white, gray, and brown, purple tinge, signed, 6" high, c. 1900 . . . . . . — 450.00 — 550.00 — 460.00

☐ **Bowl,** deep ovoid shape, short circular foot, two applied handles, opalescent background, overlaid in magenta shading to deep red, cut with flowers and leaves, signed, 6¾" high, c. 1900 . . . — 2400.00 — 2600.00 — 2450.00

	Current Price Range		Prior Year Average

☐ **Bowl,** double cone shape, mottled yellow background, drippings of dark yellow and brown, signed, 3¼" high, c. 1915 . . . . **150.00   250.00   165.00**

☐ **Bowl,** elongated diamond shape, waisted shoulder, dipped rim, mottled pink and blue background, overlaid and enameled with flowers and leaves in blue, green, dark brown, signed, 12" high, c. 1910 . . . . **800.00   1000.00   850.00**

☐ **Bowl,** enameled, short ovoid body, background of yellow sea and orange and gray sunset, overlaid with grayish-brown sailboats, signed, 5¼" high, c. 1900 . . . . **400.00   600.00   420.00**

☐ **Bowl,** enameled, frosted and yellow background, cut with trailing violets and leaves enameled in light green and lavender, 4⅜" high, c. 1900 . . . . **300.00   350.00   320.00**

☐ **Bowl,** fish bowl shape, shading from green at neck to pale green at base, cut and enameled into bowl is river scene, signed, 5½" high, c. 1900 . . . **350.00   450.00   375.00**

☐ **Bowl,** frosted, mottled gold background, winter scene of barren forest and snow, one acid cutting and enameled, signed, 2½" high, 5¾" diameter **720.00   800.00   740.00**

☐ **Box,** covered, bulging circular, domed lid with knop finial, mottled brown and green with gilt foil inclusions, signed, 6" diameter, c. 1925 . . . . **400.00   500.00   420.00**

☐ **Box,** covered, circular, domed lid, mottled gray background, overlaid in pink, green, red, cut with blossoms and leaves, signed, 3½" diameter, c. 1915 **300.00   500.00   325.00**

☐ **Box,** covered, flattened circular lid, enameled gray winter scene, bowl enameled with river scene, opalescent background, signed, 6" diameter, c. 1910 . . . . **800.00   1000.00   825.00**

☐ **Box,** covered, waisted spherical shape, domed lid, mottled aquamarine and gray shading to dark blue, overlaid in green and blue, cut with peacock feathers, signed, 6" diameter, c. 1910 **900.00   1100.00   935.00**

☐ **Creamer,** ovoid shape, applied silver handle with foliage, silver flattened lid chased with lilies of the valley and

	Current Price Range		Prior Year Average

leaves, opalescent, enameled scene with windmills and sailboats in charcoal, signed, 4¼" high, c. 1910 . . . . .   **600.00   800.00   625.00**

☐ **Dish,** clover shape, mottled ochre, etched and enameled with columbines and leaves in rust and green, signed, 5¾" diameter, c. 1915 . . . .   **400.00   600.00   450.00**

☐ **Ewer,** elongated teardrop, applied loop handle, short circular foot, mottled yellow and orange, overlaid and enameled in red and green poppies and leaves, band of flowers around base, 9½" high, c. 1910 . . . .   **800.00 1200.00   850.00**

☐ **Figure,** woman in classical dress, standing on rectangular base, hand raised over head, glass shading progressively downward from light purple to green and dark purple, signed, 10" high, c. 1915 . . . .   **3500.00 4500.00 3600.00**

☐ **Goblet,** miniature, gilded and enameled, flowers, signed, 2" high, c. 1900   **375.00   430.00   400.00**

☐ **Lamp,** domed shade with upper section lobed, on three-arm support of wrought-iron, baluster shape stand with knopped neck and circular spreading foot, deep blue shading to light blue with gold foil inclusions, signed, 18½" high, c. 1920 . . . .   **1500.00 2000.00 1600.00**

☐ **Lamp,** helmet shape shade with large domed finial, supported by angular wrought-iron arms, baluster standard, knopping above the spreading circular foot, signed, 15" high, c. 1910 . . . . . .   **3500.00 4500.00 3600.00**

☐ **Lamp,** cameo, mottled yellow and orange glass overlaid in claret, shade is cut with bay scene, signed, 15" high, c. 1900 . . . .   **2200.00 2800.00 2400.00**

☐ **Lamp,** table, acid etched, marked "Daum Nancy France," 16" high x 13" wide c. 1925 . . . .   **5000.00 6000.00 5400.00**

☐ **Lamp,** etched glass and bronze, Daum and Edgar Brandt, two-armed, footed, 19⅜" high, c. 1925 . . . .   **3400.00 3800.00 3550.00**

☐ **Lamp,** table, marked "Daum Nancy France," frosted gray glass mottled with pale yellow, 16" high, c. 1920 . .   **6300.00 7000.00 6600.00**

☐ **Lamp,** lobed domed shade supported by wrought-iron angular arms, baluster standard, knopped above the slightly

	Current Price Range		Prior Year Average

domed foot, mottled yellow-brown background overlaid in lavender, cut with lake scene, signed, 14¾" high, c. 1910 .... **6000.00 7000.00 6100.00**

☐ **Lamp,** lobed domed shade with uneven edge, supported by angular wrought-iron arms, baluster standard with spiraling grooves and knopped above slightly domed foot, mottled blue shading to green, standard mottled in green shading to blue-green and lavender, signed, 21½" high, c. 1915 **700.00 800.00 720.00**

☐ **Pitcher,** ovoid shape, slightly flaring rim with small spout, scrolling handle, mottled blue shading to green, cut and enameled with wildflowers and leaves, signed, 3½" high, c. 1910 .... **700.00 800.00 720.00**

☐ **Pitcher,** slender cylindrical body, flat shoulder, straight cylindrical neck, elongated spout, streaked burgundy sides overlaid in purple shading to blue, cut around neck and shoulder with scrolling strap work against a tooled ground, sides tooled with lily blossoms and leaves, signed, 16½" high, c. 1900 .... **800.00 900.00 850.00**

☐ **Rose Bowl,** French cameo glass, satin finish background with mottled gold and tan, trees in brown along lake in an acid cutting and enameled, three petal top, 3" high, 3¼" diameter **650.00 750.00 690.00**

☐ **Rose Jar,** overlay of yellow and pink flowers over mottled background, etched leaves, green branches, bulbous shape, signed, 5¾" high **350.00 500.00 400.00**

☐ **Salt,** circular bowl shape with two notched portions of the rim extending as handles, gray background, enameled Dutch scene of the seashore in gray, signed, 1¾" high, c. 1910 ..... **300.00 400.00 320.00**

☐ **Tumbler,** cylinder shape, expanding towards the rim, gray streaked with ochre, burgundy, and yellow, overlaid in ochre, green, yellow, blue, burgundy, and rust, cut with leafy branches with raspberries, signed, 5" high, c. 1915 **600.00 800.00 610.00**

☐ **Vase,** baluster shape tapering towards the neck, waisted neck and base, knopped base with spreading foot,

	Current Price Range		Prior Year Average

mottled gray streaked with green and mustard background, etched and enameled with wildflowers, leaves, and grass in pink, green, and brown, signed, 16¾″ high, c. 1915 . . . .

| | 600.00 | 700.00 | 615.00 |

☐ **Vase,** baluster shape, waisted neck and foot, slightly flaring rim, short circular foot, mottled orange, bright green, and yellow, overlaid in black, cut with junks sailing, signed, 14¼″ high, c. 1900 . . . .

| | 1400.00 | 1600.00 | 1450.00 |

☐ **Vase,** opalescent, bulbous body, long cylinder neck, pattern of leaves and flowers, signed, 19½″ high, c. 1900

| | 2400.00 | 2800.00 | 2600.00 |

☐ **Vase,** peacock feather design, purple at base shades to blue on top, overlaid in green, cameo mark, 11½″ high, c. 1900 . . . .

| | 650.00 | 750.00 | 700.00 |

☐ **Vase,** cameo, landscape scene, gray sides mottled with rose and apricot, overlaid in emerald green and reddish-brown, cameo signature, 21″ high, c. 1910 . . . .

| | 2500.00 | 2900.00 | 2650.00 |

☐ **Vase,** landscape scene, signed in enamel, bulbous body, long cylinder neck, 16½″ high, c. 1910 . . . .

| | 1000.00 | 1225.00 | 1100.00 |

☐ **Vase,** cameo, round foot, mottled gray-amber glass, cameo mark, wide mouth, 17″ high, c. 1900 . . . .

| | 1150.00 | 1225.00 | 1225.00 |

☐ **Vase,** cameo, etched, gilded and enameled, frosted glass overlaid in clear green, gilt mark, 8⅛″ high, c. 1900 . . . .

| | 900.00 | 950.00 | 920.00 |

☐ **Vase,** cameo, gray-yellow tinted glass streaked with patches of deeper yellow, overlaid in pink and gray-green, engraved mark, flowers, footed, 8¼″ high, c. 1900 . . . .

| | 1000.00 | 1200.00 | 1100.00 |

☐ **Vase,** etched and gilded, gray glass tinted with deep pink-purple at the top, gilt mark, 13⅝″ high, c. 1900 . . . .

| | 750.00 | 830.00 | 775.00 |

☐ **Vase,** etched, signed, 6″ high, c. 1920

| | 3300.00 | 4000.00 | 3700.00 |

☐ **Vase,** etched glass, bulbous, small mouth, 14¾″ high, c. 1930 . . . .

| | 830.00 | 920.00 | 875.00 |

☐ **Vase,** orange and rose sides overlaid in brown, mottled enameled, 23¼″ high, c. 1900 . . . .

| | 1100.00 | 1400.00 | 1250.00 |

	Current Price Range		Prior Year Average

☐ **Vase,** bulbous base, long cylinder neck expanding to a flaring neck, mottled orange-yellowish background shading to dark maroon towards the base, cut and enameled with orchids and leaves in deep pink, green, and ochre, cut with two spider webs in the background of the flowers, signed, 6¾" high, c. 1910 — **1100.00 1400.00 1200.00**

☐ **Vase,** bulbous base, slight lobing as it tapers to slender cylinder neck, gray background, overlaid in mottled yellow and red, cut with handing branches with berries, band of grass around the lower portion of the base, signed, 13¼" high, c. 1910 . . . . **900.00 1100.00 980.00**

☐ **Vase,** bulbous base, sloping shoulders, long cylinder neck which expands towards the rim, hammered background in lavender shading to beige then charcoal, overlaid in orange and dark green, carved with tulips, cut with grass around the base, signed, 12¼" high, c. 1900 . . . . **7000.00 8000.00 7200.00**

☐ **Vase,** compressed baluster, flaring circular foot, dark amethyst background, etched with thistles, leaves and croix de Lorraine, gilding, signed, 12½" high, c. 1900 . . . . **400.00 600.00 430.00**

☐ **Vase,** compressed ovoid, rectangular rim, mottled beige shading towards the base to green and pink, etched and enameled with wildflowers and leaves in light blue, green, and brown, signed, 7" long, c. 1910 . . . . **400.00 500.00 425.00**

☐ **Vase,** cameo, cylinder body, narrows towards top, free-form rim, yellow-brown sides overlaid in red and yellow, molded in medium relief of leaves and branches, marked, 16½" high, c. 1910 **2900.00 3200.00 3000.00**

☐ **Vase,** compressed spherical body, cone-shaped neck, short circular foot, green shading to lavender and gray, overlaid in lavender and green, cut with lily-of-the-valley flowers, signed, 3¾" high, c. 1910 . . . . **1000.00 1400.00 1100.00**

	Current Price Range		Prior Year Average

☐ **Vase,** small globular body, long cylinder neck, flaring lip, purple sides, overlaid in lavender, carved with flowers, leaves, a bee and a dragonfly, marked, 19½" high, c. 1900 . . . . **1200.00   1600.00   1500.00**

☐ **Vase,** cylinder body, bulbous base, slightly expanding neck, mottled dark purple background, overlaid in lightly iridescent green and lavender, cut with raspberry branches and insects, foil inclusions, signed, 17⅝" high, c. 1900   **6000.00   8000.00   6200.00**

☐ **Vase,** eggshaped body, cylindrical neck, short circular base, amber streaked opal sides overlaid with bellflowers and bees in brown and green, base has band of petals, neck has elongated brown streaks, signed, 12" high, c. 1900 . . . .   **500.00   700.00   550.00**

☐ **Vase,** cameo, short bulbous body, cylinder neck flares towards top, body is deep green overlaid in light green, neck is gray overlaid in deep and light green, cut with flowers and leaves, marked, 5" high, c. 1900 . . . .   **1400.00   1700.00   1600.00**

☐ **Vase,** egg shaped body, short circular base, yellow overlaid in deep green and brown, lilies-of-the-valley design cut into glass, signed, 6¾" high, c. 1900 . . . .   **900.00   1000.00   920.00**

☐ **Water Tumbler,** barrel shape, frosted background of mottled chartreuse and blue, trees beside a lake in one acid cutting and enameled, signed, 4¾" high, 2⅜" diameter **670.00   750.00   680.00**

☐ **Water Tumbler,** barrel shape, frosted background of mottled gold shaded to yellow, sailboats in black silhouette in one acid cutting and enameled, signed, 4¾" high, 2⅜" diameter **670.00   750.00   680.00**

☐ **Water Tumbler,** barrel shape, frosted background of mottled white with leafy trees of green and yellow, one acid cutting and enameled, 4⅞" high, 2⅜" diameter **670.00   750.00   680.00**

DESIRÉ CHRISTIAN

	Current Price Range		Prior Year Average

☐ **Bowl,** bulbous shape, wide mouth, short circular foot, pale green shading to lime green and turquoise, overlaid in lime green, carved lily pads, blossoms, and flying dragonfly, signed, 6" diameter, c. 1895 . . . .   1200.00   1400.00   1250.00

☐ **Vase,** bud, compressed spherical body with long cylinder neck tapering towards flared rim, dark burnt brown with lavender tinge shading to olive green and beige, overlaid in lavender, carved with milkweeds, leaves, and grass, signed, 12⅝" high, c. 1895 . . . .   3000.00   4000.00   3100.00

☐ **Vase,** elongated cylinder expanding to swollen neck, knopped base, spreading foot, gray splashed with red background, carved with two orchids on two long stems and leaves and grass around base, signed, 14⅜" high, c. 1895 . . . .   2000.00   3000.00   2100.00

DE VEZ

☐ **Vase,** acid finish background, dark green shaded to rose landscape scene in three acid cuttings, signed, 9⅜" high, 2⅝" diameter 620.00   680.00   630.00

☐ **Vase,** acid finish background of blue with mountain landscape scenes on three, detailed acid cuttings, signed, 11½" high, 3¾" diameter 720.00   770.00   730.00

☐ **Vase,** acid finish background of shell pink with navy blue shaded to yellow shaded to pink in three acid cuttings, mountain scene, signed, 6½" high, 2⅞" diameter 630.00   690.00   640.00

☐ **Vase,** bulbous body sloping towards long cylinder neck, light pink background, overlaid in yellow and blue, cut with scene with squirrels in trees in the foreground and mountains in the distance, signed, 13" high, c. 1900 . . . .   1100.00   1400.00   1150.00

☐ **Vase,** cylinder shape expanding toward a flaring rim, flaring circular foot, yellow background splashed with orange and green, cut with river scene, signed, 5¼" high, c. 1910 . . . .   700.00   800.00   725.00

	Current Price Range		Prior Year Average

☐ **Vase,** cylinder shape tapering toward the neck, milky, overlaid in lavender shading to pink, cut with cartouches enclosing river landscape, signed, 9¾″ high, c. 1900 .... **800.00 1000.00 810.00**

☐ **Vase,** elongated pear shape, short cylinder neck, yellow background streaked with orange, overlaid in dark blue, cut with river scene, signed, 5½″ high, c. 1910 .... **700.00 800.00 725.00**

☐ **Vase,** pear shape body, long cylinder neck, flared rim, yellow background, overlaid in orange and blue, cut with a river scene, signed, 6″ high, c. 1910 **700.00 800.00 725.00**

☐ **Vase,** trumpet, acid finish background, navy blue shaded to rose in three acid cuttings, bird on branch, foliage frames scene, gold plated brass base with leaves, 18¾″ high, 6⅜″ diameter ... **2000.00 2200.00 2100.00**

DURAND

☐ **Plate,** flashed ruby with white pulled feathers, hatched pontil, underside features Bridgeton Rose engraving by Charles Link, 8″ diameter **275.00 375.00 285.00**

☐ **Vase,** baluster shape, waisted and flaring neck, flattened circular foot, amber iridescence with opalescent trails, 8⅛″ high, c. 1900–1930 .... **300.00 400.00 350.00**

☐ **Vase,** bulbous shape, iridescent blue, wide flared neck, 8½″ high **175.00 230.00 210.00**

☐ **Vase,** compressed bulbous, flattened shoulders, waisted and lobed neck, flaring rim, blue iridescence, signed, 8½″ diameter, c. 1905–1930 .... **350.00 450.00 375.00**

☐ **Vase,** compressed spherical base, cylinder neck expanding into trumpet-shape, green background, undulating bands in amber iridescence, signed, 12″ high, c. 1905–1930 .... **1200.00 1600.00 1250.00**

☐ **Vase,** compressed spherical body, lobed neck, blue, 8½″ high **350.00 450.00 375.00**

☐ **Vase,** compressed spherical, trumpet-like neck, short circular foot, blue iridescence, signed, 9¼″ high, c. 1905–1930 .... **300.00 400.00 350.00**

☐ **Vase,** conical, iridescent gold leaf and vine design, flared rim, 7″ high **250.00 400.00 310.00**

	Current Price Range		Prior Year Average
☐ **Vase,** cylindrical, flaring rim, circular base, amber decorated with opalescent interlacing designs, 8⅛" high ..	700.00	800.00	725.00
☐ **Vase,** cylindrical, iridescent platinum "King Tut" pattern, wide, narrow mouth, 8" high	250.00	400.00	310.00
☐ **Vase,** cylindrical, scalloped rim, short circular base, opalescent glass decorated with green hearts and vines, 11" high	700.00	800.00	725.00
☐ **Vase,** cylindrical, expanding towards the shoulders, waisted neck, flaring rim, flattened circular foot, blue iridescent, amber iridescent foot, signed, 14¼" high	300.00	400.00	375.00
☐ **Vase,** cylindrical, swollen shoulders, everted lip, silvery-blue, signed, 6⅛" high, c. 1905–1920	300.00	500.00	375.00
☐ **Vase,** elongated ovoid, waisted neck, flattened flaring rim, short circular foot, blue iridescent background, opalescent clinging heart vine, 10½" high, c. 1905–1930	300.00	500.00	375.00
☐ **Vase,** ovoid shape, flaring neck, iridescent blue, signed, 10¼" high, c. 1905–1925	400.00	500.00	425.00
☐ **Vase,** urn shape, blue iridescent background, with white heart and trailing vine overlay, 7⅛" high, 1905–1925 ..	400.00	600.00	425.00

GALLÉ

☐ **Beaker,** cylinder shape, protruding horizontal rib around lower portion, sits on a gilt-bronze foot with scalloped design, pale blue background, overlaid in red, orange, and maroon, cut with an orchid and leaves, signed, 5¼" high, c. 1900	3500.00	4500.00	3550.00
☐ **Beaker,** cylinder shape tapering towards base and rim, Islamic-like designs enameled in red, white, blue, mauve, and gray, on front side cut with cartouche enclosing a woman and birds, reverse side with oval panel enclosing a king, figures yellow, signed, 4¼" high, c. 1890	800.00	900.00	815.00

	Current Price Range		Prior Year Average

☐ **Bon Bon,** with cover and underplate, pastel enamel decoration featuring ribbons, bows, flying insects, dots, 5½" high, underplate diameter is 7¼", signed in enamel, Galle a Nancy, c. 1880 .... **925.00 1100.00 940.00**

☐ **Bottle,** glass stoppered, gray body streaked with pale lavender, fire-polished, cameo signature, 5¼" high, c. 1900 .... **850.00 950.00 900.00**

☐ **Bowl,** circular with cylinder ridged foot, yellow background, overlaid in maroon, and beige, carved with a lakeside scene with sailboats in the background and trees, in the foreground, 9¼" diameter, c. 1900 .... **3500.00 4500.00 3600.00**

☐ **Bowl,** cylinder shape, beige background, overlaid in amber and brown, cut with fruit-laden and leafy branches in the foreground and trees and clouds in the background, signed, 9¼" diameter, c. 1900 .... **1800.00 2500.00 1900.00**

☐ **Bowl,** deep bulbous shape with ruffled flaring rim, deep yellow, enameled with a cross of Lorraine encircled by a garland of thistles in pale orange, ivory and gilt, signed, 9" high, c. 1885. ... **800.00 900.00 815.00**

☐ **Bowl,** half-spherical shape with spreading cylinder foot, yellow background, cartouche in center, flowers and leaves in ivory, rose, green, and brown, gilt, decorative band around the rim, floral repousse around the bottom edge of the foot, signed, 9½" diameter, c. 1895 .... **3000.00 3500.00 3100.00**

☐ **Bowl,** mold-blown, opalescent olive-green walls, overlaid in rust, cameo signature, 12½" high, c. 1920 ...... **5500.00 6500.00 6000.00**

☐ **Bowl,** half-spherical with lobed lip, light gray background, frosted inside, overlaid in orange, cut with hanging grapes, signed, 4¾" long, c. 1900 .... **450.00 550.00 475.00**

☐ **Bowl,** shallow with wide mouth, mottled amber shading pale to dark, green lower body, fire polished, signed, 5¼" diameter, c. 1890 .... **600.00 800.00 625.00**

	Current Price Range		Prior Year Average

Bowl, triangular shape, straight-sided, red background, overlaid in burgundy, cut with orange blossoms and leaves, signed, 4" high, c. 1900 . . . . **300.00 500.00 310.00**

Box, covered, circular shallow shape, flattened lid, light orange background, overlaid in blue, cut with morning glories, leaves and trailings, signed, 3" diameter, c. 1900 . . . . **700.00 800.00 720.00**

Box, cameo, gray overlaid in shades of green and white, decorated with leaves and flowers, signed, 6½" high, c. 1900 **500.00 600.00 560.00**

Box, covered, hexagonal, mottled gray, yellow, and pink background, overlaid in various shades of brown, cut with butterflies on lid, river scene with blossoming trees on box, signed, 6¾" diameter, c. 1900 . . . . **550.00 800.00 550.00**

Box, covered, cylinder body which tapers, yellow background with reddish brown overlay, carved branches with flowers and leaves, matching cover with three butterflies, box and cover signed, 2⅞" diameter, c. 1900 . . . . . . **300.00 500.00 315.00**

Cordial Set, decanter and six cups, decanter swollen ovoid body, short cylinder neck with spout, large applied handle, cups cylinder shape expanding towards the rims, mottled gray and yellow background, overlaid in bright red, cut with hanging grape vines with berries and leaves, signed, decanter 8½" high, cups 2½" high, c. 1900 . . . . **1700.00 1800.00 1750.00**

Cup, gilded and enamelled with lilies in shades of white, purple, and green, light surface **2200.00 3000.00 2600.00**

Cup, with cover, gilded and enameled with lilies in shades of white, purple and green, light surface opalescence, etched, footed, 10½" high, c. 1900 . . **3800.00 4200.00 4000.00**

Decanter, bell shape body with waisted shoulder, baluster neck, trumpet-shaped stopper with flaring, scalloped rim, short circular foot, spiral ribbing, upper knop above shoulder and lower portion of body carved with wildflowers, green background, signed, c. 1895 . . . . **1800.00 2200.00 1850.00**

	Current Price Range		Prior Year Average

☐ **Ewer,** cameo, silver mounts, opal glass with green inclusions, overlaid with pink, decorated with flowers and foliage, cameo signature, 13⅛", c. 1900 **4200.00 5000.00 4600.00**

☐ **Lamp,** domed shade, baluster standard with spreading foot, yellow background, overlaid in blue and brown, cut with mountain and lake scene, signed 14⅜" diameter, c. 1900 . . . .**18000.00 20000.00 18100.00**

☐ **Lamp,** flaring cone shape shade, supported by three gilt-bronze arms, trumpet shape standard, pale orange, overlaid in blue and green, cut with pansies and leaves, standard overlaid with brown, cut with oak leaves and acorns, signed, 25" high, c. 1900 . . . . **4500.00 5500.00 4650.00**

☐ **Lamp,** gray glass overlaid in blue and mauve and cut with stylized flowers shaped like stars, signed, 10½" high, c. 1900 . . . . **5000.00 5500.00 5200.00**

☐ **Lamp,** cameo, yellow glass overlaid in red and cut with magnolias, signed, footed, 22" high, c. 1900 . . . .**10000.00 11000.00 10500.00**

☐ **Lamp,** cameo, base and shade are both glass, baluster-shaped base, footed, gray frosted glass overlaid in orange, etched with flowers; shade is domed, blue frosted glass overlaid in orange, rondels with etched dragonflies, marked, 18¾" high, c. 1900 . . . **3100.00 3000.00 3500.00**

☐ **Lamp,** pear shape, expanding, yellow background, overlaid in blue and purple, cut with landscape of lake and mountains, bronze collar at neck, signed, 10¼" high, c. 1900 . . . . **1400.00 1600.00 1450.00**

☐ **Lamp,** swollen conical shade, lower border lobed, standard in baluster shape, spreading foot, shade supported by three arms of bronze, pink and gray background, overlaid in violet shading to green, cut with primroses and leaves, signed, 22¼" high, c. 1904–1914 . . . . **4500.00 5500.00 4600.00**

☐ **Lamp,** cameo, base and shade are both glass, base is baluster shaped, footed, gray glass with yellow mottling, overlaid in purple-blue, cut with flowers; shade is domed with cut design of

	Current Price Range		Prior Year Average
leaves, same colors as base, marked, 21¼" high, shade is 8⅝" wide, c. 1904–1910	4700.00	5200.00	5000.00
☐ **Lamp,** base and shade are both glass, shade support is bronze, base is globular, yellow glass overlaid in blue and etched with foliage, shade is conical with same decoration, marked, 7¼" high, shade is 8" wide, c. 1900	3400.00	3900.00	3700.00
☐ **Lamp Base,** baluster shape, waisted neck, flaring foot, yellow background, overlaid in red, carved roses and leaves, signed, 16½" high, c. 1900 ..	600.00	800.00	610.00
☐ **Sconces,** ovoid shape with flat top and lower section coming to a point, gilt-bronze lines the sides ending in a scrolling design at the rim and a small paneled design at the bottom, pale pink background, overlaid in purple, cut with scrolling morning glories, signed, 11" high, c. 1900	1200.00	1300.00	1250.00
☐ **Shade,** ceiling, half-spherical, flared rim, pale yellow background, overlaid in bright red, cut with cactus blossoms and leaves, signed, 21¼" high, c. 1900	1000.00	2000.00	1075.00
☐ **Shade,** ceiling, half-spherical, flaring rim, pale yellow background, overlaid in orange, red, yellow, and maroon, cut with branches with acorns, leaves and a squirrel, signed, 20" diameter, c. 1910	19000.00	21000.00	19100.00
☐ **Tumbler,** cylinder shape, tapering towards neck and base, light amber background, enameled with two dragonflies in red, pink, blue, green and white, carved pinwheels, signed, 4½" high, c. 1900	600.00	900.00	630.00
☐ **Vase,** baluster shape, swollen shoulders, slightly flaring foot, gray with orange streaked background, overlaid in orange, cut with chrysanthemums and leaves, signed, 7⅞" high, c. 1900 ...	800.00	1200.00	840.00
☐ **Vase,** gray and yellow overlaid in deep blue, landscape scene, cameo signature 11" high, c. 1900	5600.00	6200.00	5900.00
☐ **Vase,** cameo, mold blown, yellow glass overlaid in purple, decorated in high relief with branches with plums, cameo mark, 12⅝", c. 1900	5800.00	6200.00	5900.00

	Current Price Range		Prior Year Average

☐ **Vase,** gray and pink overlaid in brown, cameo mark, footed, landscape, 20½" high, c. 1900 .... **3400.00 3900.00 3600.00**

☐ **Vase,** half-moon shape, gray and yellow overlaid in mauve, decorated in cameo waterlilies, signed, c. 1900 ... **700.00 1000.00 800.00**

☐ **Vase,** cameo, yellow glass overlaid with amber, decorated with lilies, wide base, 18¾" high, c. 1900 .... **1100.00 1500.00 1200.00**

☐ **Vase,** decorated with lilies, yellow glass overlaid in amber, footed, 18¾" high, c. 1900 .... **1200.00 1600.00 1300.00**

☐ **Vase,** bottle-shaped, cameo signature, decorated with flora, footed, neck narrows towards top, 9½", c. 1900 ..... **500.00 600.00 550.00**

☐ **Vase,** green glass with inserted pockets of bright blue, deep blue, red and yellow, cameo signature in light relief, decorated with leaves, 26⅞" high, c. 1900.......................... **8700.00 9400.00 9000.00**

☐ **Vase,** baluster shape, trumpet base, mottled amber background, overlaid in purple, carved with delphiniums, signed 17⅛" high, c. 1900 .... **700.00 1000.00 715.00**

☐ **Vase,** baluster shape, waisted neck and foot, rolled foot, gray shading to turquoise background, overlaid in rose and avocado, cut with poppy blossoms, buds and leaves, signed, 11½" high, c. 1904 .... **700.00 1000.00 725.00**

☐ **Vase,** mold blown, cameo, yellow glass overlaid in green and brown, bulbous, cameo signature, 9¾" high, c. 1920 **3000.00 3500.00 3200.00**

☐ **Vase,** cameo, plum decoration, small foot, bulbous, wide mouth, yellow glass overlaid in red, cameo signature, 13", c. 1925 .... **6600.00 7000.00 6800.00**

☐ **Vase,** cameo, decorated with rosehips, mold blown, small foot, bulbous body, yellow glass overlaid in violet shadings, cameo signature, 9¾" high, c. 1925 .... **1800.00 2100.00 1900.00**

☐ **Vase,** baluster shape, waisted neck, flaring rim, domed foot, off-white background, overlaid in red, cut with leafy branches and fuchias hanging, signed, 8" high, c. 1900 .... **1500.00 2000.00 1575.00**

☐ **Vase,** etched, footed, gray overlaid in pink-brown, 7¼" high, c. 1900 ...... **1200.00 1400.00 1300.00**

	Current Price Range		Prior Year Average
☐ **Vase,** cameo, pale gray shaded with amber, lavender foil inclusions, footed, bulbous body, 13" high, c. 1900	4000.00	4600.00	4300.00
☐ **Vase,** gray sides shaded with pink, overlaid in salmon, 7½" high, c. 1900	600.00	700.00	650.00
☐ **Vase,** gray sides, overlaid in pink and brown, signature in low relief, footed, 10" high, c. 1900	700.00	900.00	750.00
☐ **Vase,** baluster shape, waisted neck with slightly flaring rim, spreading foot with knob, mottled amber shading to lavender, overlaid in dark amber shading to lavender, carved with iris blossoms and leaves, signed, 13¾" high, c. 1900	1500.00	2000.00	1600.00
☐ **Vase,** fire polished, light surface opalescence, gilded and enameled with roses, 6½" high, c. 1900	900.00	1100.00	1000.00
☐ **Vase,** wheel-carved, internally decorated, carved signature, 5⅜" high, c. 1900	8000.00	9000.00	8600.00
☐ **Vase,** "Rose de France," pale green glass etched with branches; stems, leaves, and rose in several tones of pink, rose in relief, 7½" high, c. 1900	18000.00	22000.00	20000.00
☐ **Vase,** gray sides overlaid with pink, gilded, enameled flowers, footed, 11¼" high, c. 1900	2100.00	2600.00	2300.00
☐ **Vase,** cameo, gray-yellow glass overlaid with pink-brown, etched with oriental-style floral design, signed, 7¼" high, c. 1900	1000.00	1200.00	1100.00
☐ **Vase,** cameo, gray sides shaded to blue-green at the base, fire polished, landscape scene, 18" high, c. 1900	3000.00	3600.00	3300.00
☐ **Vase,** baluster shape with slightly everted rim, short rolled foot, gray opalescent background, overlaid in pink, rose, deep red, cut with wild roses and leaves, signed, 11¾" high, c. 1900	2000.00	2200.00	2050.00
☐ **Vase,** cameo, pale blue overlaid in brown and pink, enamelled flowers, 6½" high, c. 1900	800.00	1000.00	900.00
☐ **Vase,** cameo, peach overlaid in red-brown, cut with flora, cameo mark, bulbous body, long cylinder neck, 6¾" high, c. 1900	400.00	500.00	470.00

	Current Price Range		Prior Year Average

☐ **Vase,** cameo, yellow sides overlaid in orange, enameled, cameo signature, 16¾" high, c. 1920 . . . . **4000.00 4700.00 4400.00**

☐ **Vase,** baluster shape, yellow and gray background, overlaid in red and burgundy, cut with primroses and leaves, signed, 14¼" high, c. 1900 . . . . **800.00 1200.00 850.00**

☐ **Vase,** cameo, ovoid body, gold-colored frosted sides overlaid with golden-yellow and purple, cut with vines, berries, and leaves, marked, 11½" high, c. 1900 . . . . **4200.00 4600.00 4400.00**

☐ **Vase,** cameo, mold-blown, ovoid body, waists near top, flared lip, yellow sides overlaid with blue and purple, cut with designs of plums, branches and leaves, marked, 13¼" high, c. 1925 **4700.00 5200.00 5000.00**

☐ **Vase,** cameo, landscape scene, cylinder body narrows towards top, flaring lip, gray frosted glass overlaid with yellow, blue and violet, etched, marked, 9½" high, c. 1900 . . . . **2700.00 3400.00 3200.00**

☐ **Vase,** blue gray with landscape scene, signed in cameo, 7" high **335.00 390.00 350.00**

☐ **Vase,** smoked glass, flowers enameled in red and green, broad base, long cylinder body, stems and leaves in high relief, gilded, 23¼" high, c. 1900 . . . . **1200.00 1500.00 1300.00**

☐ **Vase,** gilded, green glass with acid etching, enameled with daisies and poppies in white, green, and red enamel, 7½" high, c. 1900 . . . . **1000.00 1400.00 1200.00**

☐ **Vase,** bud, compressed spherical body, thin cylinder neck, gray and lavender background, overlaid in lavender, cut with blossoms and leaves, polished, signed, 8½" high, c. 1900 . . . . **250.00 350.00 275.00**

☐ **Vase,** cameo, tall cylinder body, narrows sharply at top, broad foot, yellow glass overlaid in red, etched with flowers, branches and leaves, marked 28½" high, c. 1900 . . . . **7600.00 8500.00 7900.00**

☐ **Vase,** cameo, mold blown, elephant decoration, small foot, bulbous body, green overlaid in brown and blue, 15¼" high, c. 1925 . . . .**10000.00 12000.00 11000.00**

	Current Price Range		Prior Year Average

□ **Vase,** bud, cylinder shape, compressed spherical foot, frosted, overlaid in lavender, cut with vine and leaves, signed, 11½" high, c. 1900 .. **700.00 800.00 710.00**

LALIQUE

□ **Ashtray,** circular form, wide flat rim, amber, molded in high relief with scarabs with leaves, signed, 5¼" high, c. 1925 .... **300.00 500.00 350.00**

□ **Ashtray,** square, stepped corners, frosted, molded with interweaving bands—one plain, the other of daisies, signed, 10" long, c. 1925 .... **400.00 600.00 425.00**

□ **Bottle,** with stopper, ovoid body, frosted, molded with pairs of dancing figures, twelve figures in all, stopper is of a kneeling nude female figure, 11½" high, c. 1925 .... **2000.00 2300.00 2100.00**

□ **Bottle,** flattened square shape, rectangular slightly domed stopper, clear and frosted, molded with thorny branches, signed, 3⅜" high, c. 1925 .... **1200.00 1600.00 1200.00**

□ **Bottle,** perfume, compressed spherical, short cylinder neck, slightly domed lid molded with three moths, frosted, molded with fluting, pinkish-brown wash, 2½" high, c. 1925 .... **400.00 600.00 425.00**

□ **Bottle,** perfume, flattened circular body, cylinder neck with scalloping, flaring circular foot, cylinder stopper expanding, trimmed in blue enamel, signed, 6½" high, c. 1925 .... **300.00 400.00 350.00**

□ **Bottle,** gray staining, molded with sylvan scene, stopper molded with flower, 5" high, c. 1925 .... **410.00 460.00 435.00**

□ **Bottle,** perfume, flattened circular, clear, molded with protruding bosses and beaded spirals, domed circular cover, signed, 5¾" high, c. 1925 .... **600.00 800.00 650.00**

□ **Bottle,** perfume, flattened circular shape, short circular neck, flattened circular stopper, flattened sides molded with chevron designs in graduated bands, dark ochre shading to yellow, signed, 4¼" high, c. 1925 ..... **400.00 600.00 425.00**

	Current Price Range		Prior Year Average

☐ **Bottle,** perfume, with glass stopper, swollen tear-drop shape, brown staining, small mouth, molded with flowers, marked, 5¼" high, c. 1925 .... **230.00 275.00 245.00**

☐ **Bottle,** cylinder body, waisted neck, ribbed, blue, turquoise glass stopper, marked "R Lalique France," 11" high, c. 1930 .... **370.00 420.00 400.00**

☐ **Bottle,** perfume, square shape, flattened rectangular stopper, clear, molded on two sides with flying sparrows, blue wash, signed, 3½" high, c. 1930 .... **150.00 250.00 175.00**

☐ **Bottle,** perfume, spherical body, short cylinder neck, bud-shaped stopper, clear, molded with graduated bands of upright leaves, signed, 3" high, c. 1925 **750.00 850.00 775.00**

☐ **Bowl,** circular, flaring, opalescent, molded in high relief with lovebirds on flowering branches, gray-blue wash, signed, 9½" diameter, c. 1925 ...... **600.00 900.00 650.00**

☐ **Bowl,** bulbous body, small foot, wide mouth, decorated with flowers with black enamel centers, marked, 5" high, c. 1920 .... **375.00 425.00 400.00**

☐ **Bowl,** circular shape, enameled, deep, molded with graduated bands of daisy blossoms with black enameled centers, signed, 10" high **150.00 300.00 160.00**

☐ **Bowl,** circular, flaring sides, opalescent, molded with design of swimming fish and the center with bubbles, 11¾" diameter, c. 1925 .... **300.00 400.00 350.00**

☐ **Bowl,** circular shape, deep, opalescent, molded with lovebirds, background of molded blossoms, signed, 9⅝" diameter, c. 1925 .... **300.00 500.00 310.00**

☐ **Bowl,** flaring sides, flat everted rim, molded in concentric sawtooth in wavy lines, signed, 8¼" diameter, c. 1925 **300.00 500.00 325.00**

☐ **Bowl,** helmet shape, molded with branches of berries and leaves, signed, c. 1925 .... **350.00 500.00 375.00**

☐ **Bowl,** molded, opalescent, wave and bubble pattern over entire surface, 9¾" diameter, c. 1925 .... **300.00 400.00 325.00**

☐ **Bowl,** opalescent, deep with sloping sides, molded with scrolling fish and bubbles, signed, 9¼" high, c. 1925 .. **250.00 350.00 275.00**

	Current Price Range		Prior Year Average
☐ **Bowl,** shallow domed-shaped, yellow and ochre, molded with twining blossoms, 8½" diameter, c. 1925	200.00	300.00	250.00
☐ **Bowl,** shallow, frosted, flattened lip with molded design of foliage, signed, 7⅛" diameter, c. 1925	350.00	500.00	375.00
☐ **Box,** covered, circular-shaped, shallow, frosted, molded with three bands of foliage, flattened lid molded with the three Graces, 3¾" diameter, c. 1925	100.00	125.00	110.00
☐ **Box,** covered, straight sides, circular domed lid, opalescent, molded with flying dragonflies, sits on circular opalescent glass box, 6¾" diameter, c. 1925	600.00	800.00	615.00
☐ **Box,** covered, straight sides, domed lid, opalescent, molded with dahlias, sits on board box covered in blue, 8¼" diameter, c. 1925	400.00	600.00	425.00
☐ **Buckle,** rectangular shape with rounded corners, amber, molded and pierced with two twining cobras with open mouths, signed, 1¾" long, c. 1925	800.00	1000.00	810.00
☐ **Brooch,** circular, depicts a fantastic, grotesque face, metal molded, backed with orange foil, low relief, 1⅝" diameter, c. 1920	450.00	525.00	470.00
☐ **Centerpiece,** round bowl with large looped-shaped handles with pierced scrolls, frosted handles molded with leaping gazelles, signed, 18½" long, c. 1925	800.00	1200.00	825.00
☐ **Chandelier,** domed shape, clear, molded with three bands of grape clusters and vines, pierced, signed, 13¾" diameter, c. 1925	800.00	1000.00	850.00
☐ **Chandelier,** domed shade, pierced and supporting four hooks, molded in high relief with peaches and leaves, 15" diameter, c. 1930	1000.00	1400.00	1000.00
☐ **Chandelier,** domed shape shade, frosted, molding on exterior of bouquets of primroses, brown wash, signed, 12" diameter, c. 1925	600.00	800.00	615.00
☐ **Clock,** flat panel with arched crest, molded with two females in classical dress holding garland circling etched			

	Current Price Range		Prior Year Average

circular clock face, on rectangular base silver painted, on four ball feet, 15¼" high, c. 1925 . . . . 8000.00 10000.00 8500.00

☐ **Clock,** flattened rectangular frame, expands into rectangular base, clear, molded in low relief with birds perched in cherry branches, signed, 6" high, c. 1930 . . . . 800.00 1000.00 815.00

☐ **Clock,** flattened rectangular, stepped rectangular base, clear, background of molded flowers, molded swallows flying in black enamel, signed, 6" high, c. 1925 . . . . 600.00 800.00 610.00

☐ **Clock,** flattened square, clear and frosted, molded with nude females swimming, signed, 4½" high, c. 1925 400.00 600.00 425.00

☐ **Clock,** rectangular shape, frosted, pierced, molded with sparrows perched on leafy branches, signed, 6" high, c. 1925 . . . . 800.00 1000.00 800.00

☐ **Cordial Set,** decanter with stopper, eight glasses, tinted pink, stencil marked "R Lalique France," 7⅜" high, c. 1930 . . . . 475.00 525.00 500.00

☐ **Decanter,** bell shape, short neck, clear, slightly domed stopper with molded branches of berries and leaves, signed, 8½" high, c. 1930 . . . 600.00 800.00 650.00

☐ **Decanter,** with stopper, gray body, clear neck, body is octagonal, four sides depict frogs' heads, alternate with four panels of sirens, stopper is clear and comes to a sharp point, marked, 15½" high, c. 1920 . . . . 3300.00 3650.00 3500.00

☐ **Decanter,** ovoid shape, molded in pattern of blossoms on one side, the other flattened side has a large molded blossom, stopper in shape of disc with blossom design, signed, 8" high, c. 1925 . . . . 300.00 500.00 325.00

☐ **Dish,** molded, opalescent, circular-shaped, molded with sirens, signed, 11" diameter, c. 1925 . . . . 300.00 400.00 325.00

☐ **Flacon,** elongated ovoid, short cylinder neck, opalescent, molded with thistle branches, blue wash, 9½" high, c. 1925 . . . . 800.00 1000.00 850.00

	Current Price Range		Prior Year Average
☐ **Flacon,** ovoid body, tapering to short cylinder neck, figural stopper of a female, frosted, molded in relief of nude males and females, signed, 11½" high, c. 1925	800.00	1000.00	850.00
☐ **Figure,** mold of a mermaid holding a conch shell to her ear, on circular base, blue-gray wash, signed, 5¼" high, c. 1920	1400.00	1600.00	1450.00
☐ **Figure,** nude female with arms extended holding draping material, rectangular stand, milky opalescent with light amber, signed, 8¾" high, c. 1925	2000.00	3000.00	2050.00
☐ **Figurine,** mermaid figure, opalescent, wide foot, figure is leaning to its own right, engraved "R. Lalique France," 4" high, c. 1920	600.00	675.00	640.00
☐ **Glass,** wine, clear, double-cone shape, black knop, c. 1925	25.00	30.00	24.50
☐ **Hood Ornaments,** pair, entitled "Epsom," chrome mounts, onyx base, head of a horse with molded mane, 6" high, c. 1932	2300.00	2700.00	2500.00
☐ **Hood Ornament,** in the shape of a rooster's head, clear, signed, 7⅛" high, c. 1930	1800.00	2500.00	1850.00
☐ **Hood Ornament,** rooster figure, head down, plumage held high, light amethyst, mounted in chrome radiator cap, 8½" high, c. 1925	750.00	1100.00	950.00
☐ **Hood Ornament,** stylized head of woman with open mouth and windswept hair in stylized horizontal pattern, frosted gray, "The Spirit of the Wind," 10¼" long, c. 1930	1800.00	2200.00	2000.00
☐ **Incense Burner,** cylinder body tapering towards the neck, ovoid domed cover, mold of fantastic sirens, 6¾" high, c. 1920	1200.00	1400.00	1250.00
☐ **Incense Burner,** spherical shape, cylinder neck, dark gray, body molded with graduating bands of stylized leaves which overlap, 5½" high, c. 1925	800.00	1200.00	815.00
☐ **Jar,** cylinder shape tapering slightly towards the neck, two thick angular handles molded with sparrows and berries, 7½" high, c. 1925	300.00	500.00	315.00

	Current Price Range		Prior Year Average

☐ **Lamp,** figurine of fish with open mouth, clear, fits onto circular light base of bronze, base with underwater plants, signed, 15¼″ high, c. 1925 .... **1000.00 1100.00 1050.00**

☐ **Lamp,** body and shade are both glass, footed, shade is conical with molded figures of females dancing with flowers, base is cylindrical narrowing sharply approaching the foot, base is molded with garlands of flowers, marked, 12¾″ high, shade is 9¼″ wide, c. 1932 .... **4400.00 4800.00 4700.00**

☐ **Ornament,** St. Christopher, intaglio marking "Lalique France," 4½″ high, c. 1930 .... **225.00 280.00 260.00**

☐ **Pendant,** flattened triangular shape with rounded corners, mold on one side with scrolling branches with berries, pierced for stringing, signed, 2″ long, c. 1925 .... **800.00 1200.00 810.00**

☐ **Set,** seven champagne glasses, six wine glasses, six small bowls, wine glasses and bowls are molded with naked figures, 4⅜″, 6⅛″, 2¼″ high, c. 1930 .... **800.00 900.00 850.00**

☐ **Tray,** perfume, rectangular shape with five apertures, blossom-shaped stoppers, clear, molded with pattern of thistle branches, 8¾″ long, c. 1930 .... **600.00 800.00 600.00**

☐ **Tray,** perfume, shallow rectangular shape, pierced with five openings for bottles, molded with branches with thistles, 8¾″ long, c. 1925 .... **300.00 500.00 350.00**

☐ **Vase,** bulbous body, conical neck, pearly opalescent, molded around body in pattern of flowers, signed, 6″ high, c. 1925 .... **300.00 500.00 325.00**

☐ **Vase,** leaves in low relief, overlaid in blue-gray, ovoid body, marked, 9¼″ high, c. 1920 .... **630.00 680.00 650.00**

☐ **Vase,** pear shape, opalescent, pattern of stylized flowers, green shading to blue near the top, 7″ high, c. 1920 .. **1100.00 1400.00 1250.00**

☐ **Vase,** yellow walls, molded in relief with branches, cylinder body with slight flaring, small foot, 9½″ high, c. 1930 ... **820.00 900.00 870.00**

☐ **Vase,** circular neck, small base, red glass, sides molded with spirals, marked, 8¼″ high, c. 1925 .... **3600.00 4000.00 3800.00**

	Current Price Range		Prior Year Average

☐ **Vase,** opalescent, molded in high relief of nude female dancing figures, body flares towards top, plain rim, marked, 9¾" high, c. 1925 . . . . **2600.00 3000.00 2700.00**

☐ **Vase,** bulbous body, cylinder neck flaring, clear and frosted, molded with leafy branches and a band of running rabbits, 6½" high, c. 1925 . . . . **400.00 600.00 450.00**

☐ **Vase,** bulbous body, short cylinder neck, blue, molded in relief with gourds and vines, 7" high, c. 1925 . . . . **3000.00 5000.00 3100.00**

☐ **Vase,** bulbous body, thick flattened lip, opalescent, molded in high relief of swimming fish, 10" high, c. 1930 . . . . **1000.00 1400.00 1100.00**

☐ **Vase,** frosted, hobnail design, ovoid body, wide mouth, marked, 7¼" high, c. 1920 . . . . **325.00 375.00 350.00**

☐ **Vase,** bulbous body with tapering neck, amber, molded with upright leaves, signed, 9" high, c. 1925 . . . . **700.00 900.00 725.00**

☐ **Vase,** bulbous shape, clear and frosted, molded in relief with tulips and leaves, 8¼" high, c. 1920 . . . . **600.00 800.00 615.00**

☐ **Vase,** compressed spherical body, short cylinder neck, molded flowers with black enameled centers, gray wash, signed, 7" diameter, c. 1925 . . **600.00 800.00 625.00**

☐ **Vase,** white, molded with leaves, ovoid body, waisted neck, flaring rim, 6¾" high, c. 1920 . . . . **450.00 535.00 480.00**

☐ **Vase,** cone shape, waisted neck, flaring lip, frosted, clear, molded with bands of flowers, bands give tiered appearance, signed, 6¾" high, c. 1925 **600.00 700.00 625.00**

☐ **Vase,** cylinder body and neck, frosted background with light gray wash, molded with berries and leaves, signed, 7" high, c. 1925 . . . . **150.00 300.00 160.00**

☐ **Vase,** bulbous body, wide mouth, slightly waisted neck, amber glass, with low relief of foliage, marked, 7" high, c. 1925 . . . . **2100.00 2400.00 2250.00**

☐ **Vase,** cylinder body flaring, wide-mouth concave rim, opalescent, molded in high relief with bosses, strapwork crisscrossing in background, brown wash, signed, 5¾" high, c. 1925 **600.00 800.00 625.00**

	Current Price Range		Prior Year Average

☐ **Vase,** frosted, bulbous body, shades to red near top, medium relief of wheat and parrots heads, marked, 10″ high, c. 1930 .... **2000.00 2400.00 2200.00**

☐ **Vase,** cylinder flaring body, opalescent, molded with pairs of lovebirds on branches, background of leaves, tails extend to base to form four arches, blue wash, signed, 9½″ high, c. 1925 **800.00 1200.00 815.00**

☐ **Vase,** cylinder body, slightly waisted, flaring rim, gray sides with low relief of a pastoral scene including horses and trees, marked, 7¼″ high, c. 1925 ... **1800.00 2200.00 2000.00**

☐ **Vase,** ovoid body, small base, amber body, low relief of birds perched on a branch, marked, 10″ high, c. 1932 ... **3000.00 3500.00 3300.00**

☐ **Vase,** cylinder shape with slight flaring, flattened flaring rim, cut with design of thistles and twining stems, signed, 8½″ high, c. 1925 .... **400.00 600.00 425.00**

☐ **Vase,** cylinder shape with tapering, frosted clear background, molded with scrolling grapevines around the top portion and roosters with their tails extended around the main body, signed, 6¼″ high, c. 1925 .... **250.00 400.00 275.00**

☐ **Vase,** diamond shape body, two side handles of three gadrooned scrolls with satin-finish, light brown wash, signed, 7¼″ high, c. 1925 .... **600.00 900.00 625.00**

☐ **Vase,** elongated ovoid body, short cylinder neck, molded with thorny thistle branches, signed, 10¼″ high, c. 1925 **3000.00 5000.00 3200.00**

☐ **Vase,** elongated ovoid, slightly waisted neck, bright blue, molded peacock heads around upper body, signed, 9¼″ high, c. 1925 .... **2000.00 3000.00 2100.00**

☐ **Vase,** flattened circular, short cylinder neck, molded on front with two sparrows encircled by a thistle branch, 8″ high, c. 1925 .... **400.00 600.00 415.00**

☐ **Vase,** inverted bell shape, clear, lower portion of body molded in berries which become smaller with each descending band, signed, 8″ high, c. 1925 ...... **300.00 500.00 325.00**

☐ **Vase,** inverted bell shape, frosted, molded with vertical bands of chevrons, signed, 8½″ high, c. 1925 ..... **300.00 400.00 325.00**

	Current Price Range		Prior Year Average
☐ **Vase,** inverted helmet shape, clear, molded with birds and cherries in light opalescence, signed, 5¾" high, c. 1925	600.00	700.00	625.00
☐ **Vase,** inverted helmet shape, flattened circular foot, bird-shaped handles, frosted, clear, signed, 7½" high, c. 1925	700.00	800.00	715.00
☐ **Vase,** inverted helmet shape, flattened spreading foot, two handles molded as antelopes, signed, 7½" high, c. 1925	700.00	800.00	750.00
☐ **Vase,** molded, frosted, ovoid shape, molded with lovebirds on flowering branches, signed, 10" high, c. 1930	500.00	700.00	550.00
☐ **Vase,** molded opalescent, spherical shape, pattern of stylized fish, signed, 6¾" high, c. 1925	300.00	400.00	325.00
☐ **Vase,** molded, opalescent, urn shape, molded with pattern of thistles and leaves, 8½" high, c. 1925	500.00	600.00	550.00
☐ **Vase,** opalescent, cylinder shape, flaring rim, molded with eucalyptus leaves and berries, 6½" high, c. 1925	300.00	500.00	325.00
☐ **Vase,** opalescent, trumpet shape, frosted background, molded with bands of overlapping leaves, signed, 5⅛" high, c. 1925	300.00	500.00	325.00
☐ **Vase,** ovoid body, rimmed neck, frosted, molded in high relief with grasshoppers and blades of grass, green and blue wash, signed, c. 1925	1000.00	1400.00	1100.00
☐ **Vase,** ovoid body, short cylinder neck, amber, molded in relief with archers hunting flying birds, signed, 10¾" high, c. 1930	2000.00	3000.00	2200.00
☐ **Vase,** ovoid body, short cylinder neck, dark amber, molded frieze of nude men with bows and arrows hunting birds in flight, signed, 10½" high, c. 1925 . . .	2000.00	3000.00	2200.00
☐ **Vase,** ovoid body, short cylinder neck, flaring rim, molded with thistles and leaves, signed, 9" high, c. 1925	600.00	800.00	625.00
☐ **Vase,** ovoid body, short flaring cylinder neck, opalescent, molded in relief with three graduated bands of running gazelles and leafy branches with berries, signed, 7" high, c. 1930	600.00	900.00	625.00

	Current Price Range		Prior Year Average

☐ **Vase,** ovoid shape, gray, molded in relief with thistles, blossoms, and leaves, light orange wash, signed, c. 1925 .. | 600.00 | 800.00 | 650.00

☐ **Vase,** ovoid shape, short cylinder neck, clear, molded with pattern of wheat sheaves, signed, 7″ high, c. 1925 ... | 300.00 | 500.00 | 325.00

☐ **Vase,** ovoid shape, short cylinder neck, flaring rim, opalescent, molded in high relief with tulips and stalks, blue-gray wash, signed, 8½″ high, c. 1925 .... | 1000.00 | 1400.00 | 1050.00

☐ **Vase,** ovoid shape, short cylinder neck, flattened flared rim, amber, molded with four protruding panels of stylized thistles which run vertically, signed, 7½″ high, c. 1925 .... | 800.00 | 1000.00 | 850.00

☐ **Vase,** pear shape tapering to cylinder neck, flaring rim, bright green, molded with graduated bands of stylized leaves, signed, 9″ high, c. 1925 ..... | 1800.00 | 2400.00 | 1900.00

☐ **Vase,** pear shape, tapering to a thin neck, frosted with blue-gray background, fern leaves molded, signed, 8¼″ high, c. 1925 .... | 300.00 | 400.00 | 325.00

☐ **Vase,** spherical body, flaring rim, opalescent frosted, molded with snail shells, blue-gray wash, signed, 6¾″ high, c. 1925 .... | 800.00 | 1000.00 | 815.00

☐ **Vase,** spherical body, short cylinder neck, molded with swimming fish, signed, 7″ high, c. 1925 .... | 600.00 | 800.00 | 625.00

☐ **Vase,** spherical body, short flaring neck, frosted, molded with graduated panels of raised bosses running vertically, background stippled, brown wash, signed, 7″ high, c. 1925 ...... | 400.00 | 600.00 | 415.00

☐ **Vase,** spherical body, waisted neck, flaring rim, frosted, molded with sunflowers, blue wash, signed, 4¾″ high, c. 1925 .... | 400.00 | 400.00 | 310.00

☐ **Vase,** spherical, short cylinder neck, bright green, molded with pattern of large beetles, signed, 11½″ high, c. 1925 .... | 8000.00 | 12000.00 | 8100.00

☐ **Vase,** spherical, short cylinder neck, flaring rim, frosted dark amber, molded with pattern of stylized leaves, signed, 6½″ high, c. 1925 .... | 700.00 | 800.00 | 750.00

	Current Price Range		Prior Year Average

☐ **Vase,** swollen ovoid body, short cylinder rim, golden yellow, molded with pairs of lovebirds perched on blossoming branches, signed, 10¼″ high, c. 1925 .... **3000.00 5000.00 3100.00**

☐ **Vase,** swollen spherical body, short cylinder neck, opalescent, molded in relief with swimming fish, 10″ high, c. 1930 .... **1000.00 1500.00 1050.00**

☐ **Vase,** swollen teardrop shape, everted rim, frosted, molded in relief with vertical leaves, gray wash, signed, 9¼″ high, c. 1925 .... **600.00 800.00 615.00**

☐ **Vase,** teardrop shape, swollen, flattened flaring rim, frosted, molded with vertical leaves, brown wash, signed, 9¼″ high, c. 1925 .... **800.00 1000.00 850.00**

☐ **Vase,** trumpet shape, clear, molded with pattern of sparrows perched on branches, signed, 7¼″ high, c. 1925 **300.00 500.00 325.00**

☐ **Vase,** trumpet shape, clear, molded with protruding diamond-shaped bands, molded blossom and leaves in background, blue wash, signed, 5″ high, c. 1925 .... **400.00 600.00 425.00**

☐ **Vase,** trumpet shape, clear, molded with protruding diamond shapes, opalescent, background molded with blossoms and leaves, brown wash, signed, 5″ high, c. 1925 .... **600.00 800.00 615.00**

☐ **Vase,** trumpet shape, frosted background, molded with vertical panels of overlapping leaves, blue-gray wash, 5⅛″ high, c. 1925 .... **300.00 500.00 325.00**

☐ **Vase,** wide cylinder shape expanding towards the rim, thick-walled, opalescent, molded in high relief with dahlias and leaves, signed, 10¼″ high, c. 1925 **2000.00 3000.00 2100.00**

LEGRAS

☐ **Vase,** bulbous shape, waisted neck, with three pinches, light brown background, cut and enameled sea plants in red and green, signed, 7¾″ high, c. 1900 .... **200.00 300.00 250.00**

☐ **Vase,** cylinder shape tapering towards the base, waisted cylinder neck, high domed foot, mottled green shading to

	Current Price Range		Prior Year Average

yellowish-green to mottled blue, enameled with spring scene in green, rust, and black, signed, 12¼" high, c. 1910 — **800.00** — **900.00** — **825.00**

☐ **Vase,** cylinder shape tapering towards the top, slightly lobed then tapering neck, bright green background shading to mottled blue and green, overlaid with blue, cut with a branch green, ochre, and brown, gilt neck, signed, 16¼" high, c. 1900 . . . . — **1400.00** — **1600.00** — **1450.00**

☐ **Vase,** cylinder shape, square mouth, etched and enameled in green, peach, and brown, landscape of lake, mountains, and evergreens, signed, 7" high — **400.00** — **600.00** — **415.00**

☐ **Vase,** four-sided, waisted, cut and enameled in pale orange, green and brown, landscape of shepherdess and her flock on a mountainside, signed, 11¾" high . . . . — **300.00** — **500.00** — **325.00**

☐ **Vase,** miniature, flattened ovoid shape, gray streaked with orange, and yellow, enameled in white, gray, and brown, landscape of a pond, signed, 4" high, c. 1910 . . . . — **700.00** — **900.00** — **725.00**

☐ **Vase,** ovoid base, long cylinder neck expanding at neck, flattened triangular foot, blue background, overlaid in lavender and brown, cut with hanging wisteria, signed, 23¾", c. 1900 . . . . — **700.00** — **800.00** — **725.00**

☐ **Vase,** spherical base, long cylinder neck, sloping shoulders, beige background, overlaid in mottled brown, maroon, and green, cut with chestnut leaves and fruit, 20" high, c. 1915 . . . — **700.00** — **900.00** — **750.00**

☐ **Vase,** tapering cylinder shape, black background, white particles in chevrons, signed, 5½" high, c. 1927 . . . . . — **600.00** — **700.00** — **625.00**

LE VERRE FRANCAIS

☐ **Vase,** cameo, ovoid-shaped, waisted neck, flaring rim, mottled pink background, cut in daisies around the shoulder, overlaid in lavender deepening to amethyst around the base, 4½" high, c. 1925 . . . . — **200.00** — **300.00** — **250.00**

☐ **Vase,** cameo, trumpet-shaped, mottled orange and yellow background, cut with bouquets of flowers and

	Current Price Range		Prior Year Average

leaves in bright orange darkening to a deep purple, signed, 18⅛″ high, c. 1925 . . . . 200.00   300.00   250.00

☐ **Vase,** compressed spherical tapering to trumpet-shaped neck, green background, overlaid in mottled orange, brown, and green, carved with flowers with honeycomb pattern around the base, 16¾″ high, c. 1920 . . . . 400.00   600.00   425.00

☐ **Vase,** cylinder body tapering towards neck, waisted neck and foot slightly flaring rim, mottled pink background, overlaid in orange shading to green and turquoise, cut with blossoms and leaves, honeycomb design on neck, 26″ high, c. 1930 . . . . 600.00   800.00   650.00

☐ **Vase,** spherical-shaped with thin cylinder neck, flaring rim, yellow background, cut in flowers and tendrils in blue and orange, signed, 12″ high, c. 1925 . . . . 250.00   400.00   275.00

Le Verre Francais Vase, *French Cameo glass, orange and blue, signed, 5″ high,* **$600.00-$700.00**

LÖETZ

	Current Price Range		Prior Year Average

☐ **Biscuit Jar,** iridescent purple shaded to black, swing handle, silverplate lid, 9" high 60.00 120.00 90.00

☐ **Bowl,** bulbous body with waisted base and neck, flaring rim, magenta background, silvery-blue designs of ripples, 10" diameter, c. 1900 .... 900.00 1100.00 950.00

☐ **Bowl,** bulbous shape, green iridescent, swirl decoration, pinched form, 5½" high 80.00 130.00 100.00

☐ **Bowl,** circular, green iridescent, fluted, 7½" diameter 70.00 100.00 85.00

☐ **Bowl,** deeply curved, pinched rim which curves in, clear, silvery-blue oil spots, 7" high, c. 1900 .... 100.00 150.00 115.00

☐ **Bowl,** ovoid shape, crimped lip and sides, slightly flaring rim, short circular foot, oil-spotted yellow background with blue striations, 10¼" long, c. 1900 900.00 1000.00 920.00

☐ **Bowl,** ovoid-shaped, silvery amber iridescent background, amber iridescent wave pattern, ruffled neck, unsigned, c. 1900 .... 300.00 400.00 310.00

☐ **Lamp,** iridescent cylinder body with spherical shade, sits in bronze stand which encircles the cylinder body and ends in a triangular base, body in salmon with amber and silvery-blue oil spots, 19½" high, c. 1900 .... 600.00 1000.00 700.00

☐ **Lamp,** melon-shaped based, silvery-blue oil spots, helmet-shaped shade in avocado green, both with four vertical hobnail bands, 11" high, c. 1900 .... 1000.00 1500.00 1100.00

☐ **Vase,** baluster body, expanding to swollen ovoid at upper portion, waisted neck, flaring lip, flaring circular foot, amber iridescent background, loops and trails in orange, silvery-blue, and amber iridescent, 6¼" high, c. 1900 600.00 800.00 650.00

☐ **Vase,** baluster shape, flaring lip, spreading circular base, pale iridescent orange, orange striated lappets around lip, rose spotting around the foot, 8¼" high, c. 1900 .... 200.00 300.00 220.00

☐ **Vase,** inverted pear-shape, wide mouth, green-purple, peacock feather decoration, marked, 9¼" high, c. 1900 .... 11000.00 14000.00 13000.00

	Current Price Range		Prior Year Average
☐ **Vase,** salmon glass with blue waves, iridescent, iris blossom overlay, unsigned, 6″ high, c. 1900	750.00	850.00	800.00
☐ **Vase,** baluster shape, triangular mouth, orange oil spots, loops and swirls in silvery-blue and iridescent amber, 8¼″ high, c. 1900	200.00	300.00	215.00
☐ **Vase,** bulbous base tapering to long cylinder neck, everted rim, light orange background, lavender feathering, silvery-blue iridescent oil spots, overlaid in silver, 10½″ high, c. 1900	600.00	1000.00	650.00
☐ **Vase,** blue and green, iridescent pinched shoulder and ruffled collar, Loetz Austria etched on bottom, 7″ high	320.00	420.00	375.00
☐ **Vase,** yellow glass with a medial stripe of green flowing into pink-red and blue, bulbous body, wide mouth, wide base, vase narrows towards top, marked, 6″ high, c. 1900	4400.00	4800.00	4500.00
☐ **Vase,** bulbous shape, cylinder neck, flaring rim, blue background, silvery-blue oil spots, 12″ high, c. 1910	250.00	350.00	260.00

Loetz Vase, *art nouveau design, metallic overlay, 6″ high,* **$345.00–$370.00**

	Current Price Range		Prior Year Average
☐ **Vase,** bulbous shape, green iridescent bark design, fluted rim, 9¾" high	60.00	90.00	75.00
☐ **Vase,** bulbous shape, gold iridescent with purple wave motif, narrow, flared rim, 5¾" high	100.00	200.00	150.00
☐ **Vase,** bulbous shape, iridescent herringbone design, flared rim, slender neck, 8" high	30.00	50.00	40.00
☐ **Vase,** pair, baluster shape, small foot, iridescent, unmarked 7" high, c. 1900	780.00	825.00	800.00
☐ **Vase,** bulbous trumpet shape, amber iridescent, petal shape rim, signed Loetz Austria, 10" high	100.00	200.00	135.00
☐ **Vase,** cone shape, tapering neck, iridescent amber background, silvery-blue folds, applied scrolling tendrils in orange and silvery-blue iridescence, signed, 9" high, c. 1900	1400.00	2000.00	1500.00
☐ **Vase,** cylinder shape expanding to shoulders, waisted cylinder neck, flaring rim, silvery-blue designs in background, overlaid in silver scrolls, signed, 5" high, c. 1900	300.00	400.00	320.00
☐ **Vase,** amber walls shade to green, iridescent, bulbous body, wide mouth, silver mounts, unmarked, 8¾" high, c. 1900	1150.00	1350.00	1200.00
☐ **Vase,** cylinder shape flaring towards the rim, short circular foot, applied rectangular handles in yellow, blue background with silvery-blue oil-spotting, 7½" high, c. 1900	600.00	700.00	650.00
☐ **Vase,** cylinder shape wide everted rim, fits into openwork pewter mount with stems, leaves, berries, and female masks, amber and silvery-blue iridescent oil spotting, 7½" high, c. 1900	400.00	600.00	450.00
☐ **Vase,** elongated bulbous-shape, flaring rim with ruffling, amber iridescent background, molded leaves, signed, 9¾" high, c. 1900	400.00	600.00	415.00
☐ **Vase,** floriform, waisted onion formed bowl, cylindrical stem, wide circular base, light brown sides decorated with ruby and opal striated feather designs, signed, 12¼" high, c. 1900	1400.00	1600.00	1450.00
☐ **Vase,** green, decorated with eye of peacock, reticulated holder, rare, 5" diameter	125.00	200.00	150.00

	Current Price Range		Prior Year Average

☐ **Vase,** green iridescent, crimped rim, handles on side, 7″ high .... | 80.00 | 130.00 | 100.00

☐ **Vase,** hour glass shape, orange and green iridescent, 11¾″ high .... | 60.00 | 90.00 | 75.00

☐ **Vase,** inverted trumpet shape, wide flaring mouth, wide bulbous body, coiling serpent around neck in blue and green iridescent, amber and blue iridescent oil spotting, 8″ high, c. 1900 | 400.00 | 600.00 | 425.00

☐ **Vase,** Jack-in-the-Pulpit, spherical shape, flattened, tapering into cylinder neck with highly ruffled rim, silvery-blue iridescence, 12½″ high, c. 1900 .... | 400.00 | 600.00 | 415.00

☐ **Vase,** ovoid body, lobed rim, blue iridescent folds against dark amber iridescent background, 12¼″ high, c. 1900............................. | 400.00 | 500.00 | 420.00

☐ **Vase,** ovoid shape, cylinder neck flaring slightly, silvery background, striated ribbonwork in amber, signed, 4¼″ high, c. 1900 .... | 300.00 | 400.00 | 320.00

☐ **Vase,** ovoid shape, short tapering rim, clear, amber oil spots, signed, 7½″ high, c. 1900 .... | 100.00 | 175.00 | 120.00

☐ **Vase,** ovoid shape, waisted neck, flaring rim with ruffling, turquoise background, impressed circles and designs of silvery-blue oil spots, 6½″ high, c. 1900............................. | 100.00 | 200.00 | 110.00

☐ **Vase,** ovoid shape, waisted neck, short cylinder neck, slightly flaring rim, short circular foot, red background, silvery-blue iridescent patterns of undulating bands, 8″ high, c. 1900 .... | 900.00 | 1000.00 | 920.00

☐ **Vase,** ovoid shape, waisted neck, slightly flaring lip, iridescent blue pattern of undulating ripples, 10½″ high, c. 1900 .... | 700.00 | 800.00 | 720.00

☐ **Vase,** ovoid shape, waisted neck, spreading foot, clear, amber oil spots, overlaid with silver blossom and leaves, rim with band of silver, 4¾″ high, c. 1900 .... | 50.00 | 75.00 | 55.00

☐ **Vase,** ovoid shape with pinching, short neck with flares, iridescent amber oil spot glaze surface, 6⅛″ high, c. 1900 | 150.00 | 200.00 | 165.00

☐ **Vase,** ovoid shape with pinched sides, waisted neck, ruffled, rim, clear, amber oil spots, 10″ high, c. 1900 .... | 100.00 | 175.00 | 115.00

	Current Price Range		Prior Year Average

☐ **Vase,** pear shape, clear background, amber iridescence and orange oil spots, thumbprints pressed in two rows on sides, 6⅜" high, c. 1900 . . . . **300.00 500.00 310.00**

☐ **Vase,** pear shape, pinched triangular sides, cloverleaf lip, green shading to pink, silvery-blue lappets with vertical bands, signed, 5" high, c. 1900 . . . . . **800.00 1200.00 900.00**

☐ **Vase,** pear shape, short neck with flaring iridescent amber, unsigned, 10¼" high, c. 1900 . . . . **200.00 300.00 210.00**

☐ **Vase,** pear shape, waisted neck, ruffled rim, rectangular panels on sides and shoulders, pink opaque with silvery-blue oil spots, 8" high, c. 1900 **100.00 175.00 115.00**

☐ **Vase,** pear shape, waisted neck spreading foot, clear background, amber and purple iridescence, 6½" high, c. 1900 . . . . **100.00 200.00 110.00**

☐ **Vase,** short urn shape, short cylinder neck, flaring rim, short circular base, red background, amber and blue iridescent waves, 5½" high, c. 1900 . . . . . **200.00 300.00 215.00**

☐ **Vase,** slender bulbous shape tapering into cylinder neck, ruffled flaring rim, short circular foot, amber background, silvery-blue designs, signed, 9¼" high, c. 1900 . . . . **1100.00 1400.00 1200.00**

☐ **Vase,** spherical shape, flattened, short waisted neck, pale yellow background, overlaid with silver poppy blossoms and leaves and amber iridescence, 2½" high, c. 1900 . . . . **50.00 75.00 55.00**

☐ **Vase,** spherical shape, flattened, thin cylinder neck, opaque white background, overlaid in medium brown, cut with blossoms and leaves around the shoulder and neck, signed, 4½" high, c. 1900 . . . . **100.00 150.00 120.00**

☐ **Vase,** square shape, waisted neck, ruffled rim, amethyst background with applied lavender stringing, 11¼" high, c. 1900 . . . . **600.00 700.00 650.00**

☐ **Vase,** thin, elongated pear shape, flaring rim, flattened circular foot, dark amber background, undulating designs in silvery-blue, 10" high, c. 1900 . . . . **200.00 400.00 250.00**

	Current Price Range		Prior Year Average
☐ **Vase,** triangular shape, twisting, waisted neck, trefoil rim, blue background, silvery-blue oil spots, 6½" high, c. 1900	100.00	200.00	120.00
☐ **Vase,** urn shape, flaring rim, short circular base, red background, amber and blue iridescent waves, interior of rim gold iridescence, 7¼" high, c. 1900	500.00	750.00	550.00
☐ **Vase,** waisted cylinder with bulging shoulders, waisted neck, flaring rim, amber iridescent background, silvery-blue feathering, 5½" high, c. 1900 ..	350.00	450.00	370.00

MARINOT

☐ **Bottle,** with stopper, ovoid body, decorated the same externally and internally, orange-red ground covered with moss-like green tufts of color, stopper is clear glass, marked, 5¼" high, c. 1925	5600.00	6200.00	5900.00
☐ **Bottle,** with stopper, rectangular body, body is decorated with free-form design over a deep red ground, deep wavering cuts are made at each corner, decorated the same externally and internally, stopper is clear glass, marked, 5" high, c. 1925	4400.00	4900.00	4600.00
☐ **Jar,** body flares towards the top, indented on the sides, walls are dappled with red, gray, and ochre against a black ground, cover is similarly decorated and is domed, marked, 5¼" high, c. 1925	4600.00	5400.00	5200.00

MARY GREGORY

☐ **Box,** cobalt blue, round, hinged lid, ormolu feet, white enameled decoration depicts young girl holding bird, white floral sprays, 5" high, 5⅜" diameter	350.00	450.00	365.00
☐ **Box,** emerald green, puffy shape, lift off lid, white enameled decoration depicts young girl, 3" high, 3⅝" diameter ...	90.00	130.00	95.00
☐ **Box,** lime green, hinged lid, white enameled decoration depicts young boy, hinged, 1¾" high, 2⅜" diameter	120.00	150.00	125.00

	Current Price Range		Prior Year Average

☐ **Box,** lime green, round, hinged lid, white enameled decoration depicts young girl, floral sprays on sides, 3″ high, 3¼″ diameter **130.00   175.00   135.00**

☐ **Box,** patch, cobalt, round, hinged lid, white enameled decoration depicts little boy, white enamel dots around sides, 1⅛″ high, 2″ diameter **150.00   180.00   155.00**

☐ **Box,** patch, round, lime green, white enameled decoration depicts young girl, hinged, 1⅜″ high, 2⅛″ diameter   **120.00   150.00   125.00**

☐ **Box,** sapphire blue, round, hinged lid, white enameled decoration depicts young girl, white dot trim around sides, 2⅝″ high, 3¼″ diameter **130.00   175.00   135.00**

☐ **Plate,** cobalt, white enameled decoration depicts girl with butterfly net, original ormolu compote stand, three round rings hang from holder, 6¼″ diameter   **140.00   170.00   145.00**

☐ **Spa Glass,** amber, flattened oval shape, white enameled decoration depicts little girl carrying basket, 4⅛″ high, 2⅜″ diameter **90.00   120.00   95.00**

☐ **Tumbler,** cranberry, white enameled decoration depicts young girl, 4¼″ high, 2½″ diameter **50.00   85.00   60.00**

☐ **Vase,** covered, cobalt blue, white enameled decoration depicts young girl carrying flower basket, enameled dot bands around top and lid, 14″ high, 5½″ diameter **275.00   375.00   285.00**

☐ **Vase,** cranberry, white enameled decoration depicts young boy wearing hat, 7¾″ high **100.00   150.00   110.00**

☐ **Vase,** green, with applied handles in clear, boy picking flowers decoration in white enamel, 10½″ high **130.00   180.00   145.00**

☐ **Vase,** sapphire blue, cut scalloped top, white enameled decoration depicts young boy holding goblet, fancy metal base mount of plated brass with woman's head handles on each side, 14¼″ high, 3¾″ diameter **200.00   275.00   220.00**

☐ **Wine Bottle,** cranberry, white enameled decoration depicts girl holding bouquet, original clear bubble stopper, 9″ high, 3⅛″ diameter **140.00   170.00   145.00**

MOSER

	Current Price Range		Prior Year Average
Box, decorated amethyst, three applied salamanders in amber for feet that are trimmed in gold, amber salamander trimmed in gold on lid, enameled flowers of pink and green foliage, hinged, 4⅜" high	600.00	650.00	610.00
Juice Glass, cranberry, gold enamel branches, yellow, pink, turquoise and blue enamel leaves, leaves and veins outlined in raised gold, acorns, gold band at rim and base, 4" high	150.00	225.00	175.00
Libation Jug, enameled decorations, strap, twig handle, signed, 9½" high	30.00	70.00	45.00
Tumbler, crystal top shades to blue at base, engraved with ruffed grouse and landscape scene, acid cut decorative band at rim with gold enamel, cutting at base, 5" high, 3" diameter, signed	350.00	400.00	360.00
Vase, decorated opaque pink shaded to clear, four amber reeded applied scroll feet covered in gold, gold rigaree on sides of vase, enameled eagle in relief on front, multicolored oak leaves, enameled insect decoration, applied glass acorns, 7⅞" high, 7" diameter	1500.00	2000.00	1600.00
Vase Ewer, gold over crystal, enameled, multicolored flowers and green leaves, pedestal base, 5¾" high, 2¾" diameter	150.00	200.00	160.00
Vase, opalescent deep pink at top shading to almost clear at base, applied crimped glass handles burnished with gold on each end of the flattened oval shape body, parrot, acorns, leaves, and branches in relief and gold and multicolor enamel decoration, elaborate decoration around neck, 7½" high, 7¾" at widest point, 2½" deep, Moser signature	850.00	950.00	875.00
Vase, multicolored enameled grape leaves and bee with applied yellow and red grape bunches, four applied feet of amber rosette, 5½" high, 2¼" diameter	350.00	400.00	360.00

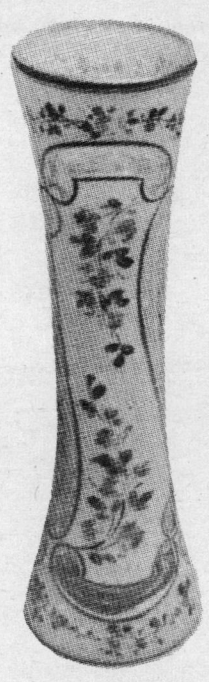

Left to Right: **Moser Karlsbad Bud Vase,** *cut scroll design frames enamel floral decor, 6" high,* **$125.00–150.00; Moser Cup and Saucer,** *lavender with gold gild decor,* **$150.00–$170.00**

MOTHER-OF-PEARL

	Current Price Range		Prior Year Average
☐ **Bowl,** blue diamond quilted, oblong, four applied feet, 8" long, 7" wide, 3" high	250.00	350.00	275.00
☐ **Creamer,** satin, blue raindrop, bulbous, round top, white lining, blue frosted reeded applied handle, 4½" high, 3⅛" diameter	200.00	250.00	215.00
☐ **Fairy Lamp,** satin glass, swirl shaded pink, white interior, clear insert cup for bulb, ruffled lampshade and base, 5" high, 5½" diameter	420.00	480.00	435.00

	Current Price Range		Prior Year Average

☐ **Fruit Bowl,** thin pink interior layer, air trap of interlocking diamond mother of pearl, thick exterior layer of white glass, thorn handle at one end, 10½" long, 5¾" high **530.00 630.00 540.00**

☐ **Peg Lamp,** swirl satin glass ruffled shade and font, clear chimney, classical lady candlestick of heavy brass, 19½" high, 3½" diameter **620.00 700.00 640.00**

☐ **Perfume Bottle,** satin glass, diamond quilted blue, white interior, silver top, 4½" high, 2⅝" diameter **250.00 300.00 270.00**

☐ **Rose Bowl,** swirl, air trap swirls are pale brown at crimped rim, area between swirls is teal blue at the base shading to olive in center to golden brown at top, robins egg blue interior, 3" high, 6½" diameter at widest point **750.00 850.00 775.00**

☐ **Sweetmeat,** rainbow with silverplate bail and lid, horizontal bands on airtrap, six yellow, six blue, and six pink alternating vertical bands, lid is embossed with florals and has ivory finial, 6" high when bail is fully extended upright, 5½" base diameter, 4½" lid diameter **930.00 1000.00 935.00**

☐ **Sweetmeat Jar,** satin glass, diamond quilted pink, silverplated top, lip and handle, white interior, 5¼" high, 3⅜" diameter **320.00 370.00 340.00**

☐ **Sweetmeat Jar,** satin glass, diamond quilted rose, embossed, ribbed, silverplated top, lip and handle, white interior, 3⅛" high, 4¾" diameter **400.00 460.00 435.00**

☐ **Vase,** blue diamond quilted, frosted thorn handles and rim **185.00 300.00 190.00**

☐ **Vase,** diamond, quilted butterscotch, silverplated Victorian motif holder, 6½" high **430.00 520.00 440.00**

☐ **Vase Ewer,** satin glass, shaded blue herringbone, frosted applied handle, three way top, white interior, 8¼" high, 3⅞" diameter **220.00 270.00 225.00**

☐ **Vase Ewer,** satin glass, shaded blue herringbone, white interior, applied frosted handle, top is three petal, 8½" high, 4" diameter **220.00 270.00 240.00**

	Current Price Range		Prior Year Average

☐ **Vase,** Feredzeichnung, butterscotch, gold tracery decoration, gold around rim, 10¾" high, 8" diameter at widest point, signed Patent 9159 .... 1600.00 2000.00 1700.00

☐ **Vase,** frosted clear hobnail, gradually shading to gold at the square fold-in top, each raised rounded hobnail looks like a pearl, rare 575.00 700.00 585.00

☐ **Vase,** satin glass, blue ribbon, ball shape, with fluted top, white interior, 4⅛" high, 3⅛" diameter 240.00 300.00 245.00

☐ **Vase,** satin glass, decorated blue herringbone with frosted handles, oval shape ruffled top, white interior, 7⅜" high, 4⅛" diameter 235.00 275.00 240.00

☐ **Vase,** satin glass, diamond quilted bright yellow shaded to white, white interior, top is three petal, 6⅛" high, 3⅝" diameter 210.00 260.00 230.00

☐ **Vase,** satin glass, diamond quilted chartreuse green, white interior, ormolu foot and flower decorations, frilled top, 10" high, 4" diameter 500.00 590.00 540.00

☐ **Vase,** satin glass, rose shaded to pink swirl, white interior, 11¼" high, 5" diameter 280.00 330.00 285.00

☐ **Vase,** satin glass, shaded blue, white interior, folded over square top, 5⅛" high, 3⅞" diameter 250.00 300.00 265.00

☐ **Vase,** satin glass, shaded peach herringbone, ruffled top, 9¼" high, 4" diameter 200.00 250.00 225.00

☐ **Vase,** satin glass, shaded yellow herringbone, fan shape ruffled top, white interior, 7⅜" high, 2½" diameter 160.00 200.00 165.00

☐ **Vase,** satin glass, swirl, reverse amberina coloring, golden yellow top shades to rose red, at base white lining, lacy gold enameled flowers, 9¼" high, 4½" diameter 900.00 1300.00 1000.00

☐ **Water Tumbler,** satin glass, diamond quilted pink, decorated with blue daisies and yellow and green leaves, 3⅞" high, 2⅞" diameter 210.00 260.00 225.00

☐ **Vase,** satin glass, coinspot, cream with white interior, ruffled, 8⅜" high, 4" diameter 180.00 220.00 185.00

MT. WASHINGTON

	Current Price Range		Prior Year Average
☐ **Biscuit Barrel,** painted flower decoration, swing handle, covered	80.00	130.00	100.00
☐ **Bowl,** cameo, with original gold wash holder, pink cut to white, winged birds and flowers, bowl is 8″ square, 4½″ high, holder is signed Reed and Barton	825.00	925.00	835.00
☐ **Flower Frog,** mushroom shaped, satin finish in beige with leaves decoration in gold, brown and green, 2¾″ high, 5″ diameter	140.00	192.00	150.00
☐ **Muffineer,** egg shaped, clear with satin finish, decorated with colorful enameled daisies, one hole in top	275.00	350.00	280.00
☐ **Muffineer,** egg shaped, decorated with autumn leaves and blue berries, pewter top, 4½″ high	300.00	375.00	325.00
☐ **Muffineer,** egg shaped, raised enamel dots form pink and white blossoms, attributed to Timothy Canty	300.00	375.00	325.00
☐ **Pitcher,** tankard style, clear, applied handle, decorated with shrimp, crabs, seaweed, brushed gold highlighting on handle and rim, 8¾″ high	900.00	1025.00	925.00
☐ **Salt and Pepper Shakers,** each has six panels with hand painted delicate enamel floral decoration, silverplated tops	185.00	240.00	200.00
☐ **Salt and Pepper Shakers,** set, fig shaped, salt is decorated with yellow flowers and ferns in two shades of green, pepper has white flowers and green foliage with multicolor accents	325.00	375.00	330.00
☐ **Salt Shaker,** sitting hen, floral enamel on red body, silverplated top forms chicken's head, original paper label . .	350.00	400.00	355.00

MÜLLER FRÈRES

☐ **Bowl,** inverted cone shape, waisted neck and foot, flaring rim, short circular foot, overlaid, carved, and enameled in flurogravure, harvest scene of workers in rust, orange and ochre, signed, 6¼″ high, c. 1900	2000.00	3000.00	2250.00
☐ **Ewer,** inverted cone shape, cylinder neck, upright spout, applied, c-scroll handle, waisted short circular foot, frosted and green background, over-			

	Current Price Range		Prior Year Average

laid, carved, and enameled in flurogravure with blossoms and leaves, signed, 19″ high, c. 1900 . . . . **2000.00 3000.00 2200.00**

☐ **Lamp,** base is wrought-iron, shade is cameo, yellow, and gray overlaid in blue, cut with flowers, marked, 26″ high, c. 1925 . . . . **4200.00 4700.00 4400.00**

☐ **Lamp,** base is bronze, shade is orange glass, stenciled mark on shade, shade is connected to base by a single, thick, curved strand of bronze, 17½″ high, c. 1905 . . . . **275.00 325.00 300.00**

☐ **Lamp,** cameo, landscape scene, base and shade in lightly tinted glass overlaid in orange-pink and blue-brown, 26¾″ high, c. 1900 . . . . **8200.00 9000.00 8700.00**

☐ **Luminiere,** rectangular glass panel, etched with an arctic scene depicting four polar bears standing on icebergs, top of panel is domed, stands on rectangular metal platform, marked, 33½″ long, c. 1930 . . . . **5300.00 6000.00 5600.00**

☐ **Vase,** baluster shape, waisted neck, spreading circular foot, frosted blue background, overlaid, carved, and enameled in flurogravure in yellow and off-white, winter scene with two dogs and hanging pheasant, signed, 9″ high, c. 1900 . . . . **1800.00 2200.00 1900.00**

☐ **Vase,** cylinder body expanding towards shoulder, cylinder neck, applied serpentine handle, green background, enameled in flurogravure of branches of berries and leaves, in orange, brown, mustard, and gray, signed, 10¼″ high, c. 1910 . . . . **1000.00 1400.00 1100.00**

☐ **Vase,** cylinder shape expanding towards the sloping shoulders, short cylinder neck, mottled orange-pink background shading to ivory, overlaid in blue, cut with iris, signed, 9″ high, c. 1910 . . . . **700.00 800.00 750.00**

☐ **Vase,** cameo, cylinder body, waisted neck, yellow glass overlaid in blue-gray and red, etched with flowers, area around base is completely blue, marked, 9⅛″ high, c. 1920 . . . . **2500.00 3300.00 2800.00**

	Current Price Range		Prior Year Average

☐ **Vase,** cameo, baluster-shaped, gray walls with green, white, ochre, and red, overlaid in ochre, red, and white, cut with foliage design, marked, 11¾" high, c. 1920 .... **1200.00 1500.00** 1350.00

☐ **Vase,** cameo, cylinder body, narrows severely towards the top, widens slightly at the very top, yellow glass sides molded with mushrooms and foliage, marked, 15½" high, c. 1915 .. **2800.00 3400.00** 3100.00

☐ **Vase,** cameo, landscape scene, ovoid body, gray glass shades to salmon at neck and base, overlaid in blue and black, cut with oasis scene, marked, 15¾" high, c. 1925 .... **3200.00 3800.00** 3400.00

☐ **Vase,** elongated ovoid body, bulbous neck, mottled green and gray background, overlaid, carved, and enameled in flurogravure of scene with house and trees in salmon, gray, brown, and ochre, signed, 17¼" high, c. 1900 .... **3000.00 5000.00** 3200.00

☐ **Vase,** elongated ovoid, waisted neck, mottled orange, and yellow shading to aquamarine and green background, cut and enameled with flowering trees in red, green, yellow, and brown, signed, 8¾", c. 1915 .... **800.00 1200.00** 850.00

☐ **Vase,** frosted background of mottled off-white, landscape scene of maroon shaded to rose in three acid cuttings, signed, 8¼" high, 4⅝" diameter **720.00 770.00** 730.00

☐ **Vase,** frosted off-white background, three layer acid cut back, maroon to rose, depicts river and tree landscape, signed, 8⅝" high, 4⅝" diameter **500.00 900.00** 600.00

☐ **Vase,** cameo, landscape scene, lemon-yellow glass, overlaid in brown, cut with a view of two nomads sitting, a women standing near them and a mosque-like structure in the background, palm trees are also visible, marked, 17" high, c. 1925 .... **5000.00 6000.00** 5200.00

☐ **Vase,** rectangular body, tapers towards top, gray glass sides with purple, overlaid in violet, cut with foliage decoration, against a river background, two c-shaped handles, marked, 10¾" high, c. 1900 .... **2900.00 3200.00** 3100.00

	Current Price Range		Prior Year Average

☐ **Vase,** cameo, landscape scene, yellow walls, overlaid in pink-red, cut with an oasis scene with two musicians sitting while two dark figures stand nearby, a running band of arches surrounds the base, cylinder body bulges slightly near the top, 16½″ high, c. 1925 .... **5000.00 6000.00 5500.00**

☐ **Vase,** yellow glass, overlaid with red and rose, cut with flowers and branches, bulbous body, flaring lip, marked, 11″ high, c. 1925 .... **3200.00 3800.00 3600.00**

☐ **Vase,** frosted pink background, five layer acid cut back, maroon to red to rose to yellow to pink, depicts three roses and foliage, signed, 7½″ high, 5⅜″ diameter **950.00 1400.00 1050.00**

☐ **Vase,** ovoid body, flattened at the shoulders, short cylinder neck, mottled orange and off-white background, overlaid and carved in flurogravure of oak leaves, acorn cabochons, 4½″ high, c. 1900 .... **600.00 900.00 615.00**

☐ **Vase,** ovoid shape, short cylinder neck, flattened flaring rim, short circular foot, bright yellowish-green background, overlaid in dark green, carved with water lilies and leaves, signed, 10¼″ high, c. 1900 .... **2000.00 2200.00 2100.00**

☐ **Vase,** ovoid shape, small bulbous neck, two lug handles, mottled green and gray background, overlaid with salmon and white, cut fuchsias, flurogravure pistols, snail, and leaves, in dark peach, light peach, and beige, 8¾″ high, c. 1900 .... **2000.00 3000.00 2100.00**

☐ **Vase,** ovoid shape, waisted and lobed neck, flaring rim, yellow background, overlaid in brown, cut with landscape of workmen in the fields at sunset, signed, 6″ high, c. 1910 .... **350.00 450.00 375.00**

☐ **Vase,** ovoid shape, waisted neck, slightly flaring rim, mottled yellow and orange background, overlaid in brown and yellow, scene of autumn forest, signed, 5¾″ high, c. 1910 .... **500.00 700.00 550.00**

	Current Price Range		Prior Year Average
☐ **Vase,** spherical shape, waisted neck, flaring lip, mottled yellow background, overlaid in turquoise, and black, cut with river scene, signed, 7½" high, c. 1910	800.00	1200.00	850.00
☐ **Vase,** translucent frosted gold background, four layer acid cut back, depicts two black storks, chateau, mountain scene, signed, 7¾" high, 4⅜" diameter	1300.00	1700.00	1400.00
☐ **Vase,** urn-shaped with ovoid shoulders, beige with gold and silver foil inclusions on background, overlaid with blossoms and leaves in deep blue, signed, 6½" high, c. 1920	700.00	1000.00	710.00
☐ **Vase,** wide cylinder body, tapering to a narrow cylinder neck, frosted with splashes of red, pink, and orange, overlaid, carved, and enameled in yellow, brown, ochre, and white with strawberries, peach blossoms and leaves, signed, 9½" high, c. 1900 ...	1600.00	2000.00	1700.00

OPALESCENT

	Current Price Range		Prior Year Average
☐ **Bowl,** diamond quilted light green shaded to pink, ruffled, polished pewter frame, 17¾" high, 11¾" diameter	210.00	250.00	215.00
☐ **Bowl,** flashed rainbow, fluted edge, decorated with enamel florals, 5" high	270.00	330.00	275.00
☐ **Ewer,** striped white shaded to green, vaseline applied leaf and handle, appliqued flowers in pink, 8½" high, 3" diameter	130.00	180.00	140.00
☐ **Fairy Lamp,** amber swirl, signed Clarke base, shaped like a pyramid, 3¾" high, 3⅛" diameter	100.00	120.00	110.00
☐ **Fairy Lamp,** blue swirl satin finish, light blue glass cup and candle cup, matching square ruffled base, rare, 6½" high, 5¾" diameter	530.00	590.00	540.00
☐ **Fairy Lamp,** pink and white frosted swirl decoration, dome shape, signed Clarke candle cup, matching square ruffled vase, 5½" high, 6" diameter	520.00	600.00	535.00
☐ **Fairy Lamp,** pressed glass, blue embossed rib design, signed Clarke base, 3¾" high, 2⅞" diameter	100.00	150.00	110.00

	Current Price Range		Prior Year Average

☐ **Vase,** Jack-In-Pulpit, fluted with purple edge, 7" high, 3⅞" diameter 70.00 100.00 80.00

☐ **Vase,** white opalescent Monot Stumpf, pink shaded to off-white, pantin fan shape, belltone, interior is of lustered glass, 7" high, 6⅛" diameter 220.00 270.00 230.00

☐ **Vase,** white opalescent Monot Stumpf, pink shaded to striped white, pantin ruffled fan shape, belltone, 7¾" high, 7½" diameter 280.00 330.00 290.00

☐ **Water Tumbler,** cranberry, ten row hobnail, 3¾" high, 2¾" diameter ... 125.00 160.00 140.00

☐ **Water Tumbler,** decorated peach, white flowers have gold leaves and centers, 4" high, 2¾" diameter 50.00 100.00 60.00

☐ **Water Tumbler,** lavender, light row hobnail, 3¾" high, 2¾" diameter ... 125.00 160.00 140.00

ORREFORS

☐ **Beaker,** cylinder body, flaring neck, four ball feet set on flattened dome base, clear, etched jungle scene with men, women, children, palm trees, exotic birds, squirrels, and monkeys, signed, 10½" high, c. 1930 .... 1000.00 1400.00 1100.00

☐ **Bottle,** cylinder body, short cylinder neck, elongated dome stopper, light green, clear, decorated internally with sea grass and star-fish in maroon, signed, 6¼" high, c. 1938 .... 1200.00 1400.00 1275.00

☐ **Bottle,** cylinder, thick-walled, clear, cartouche with dove and strapework, signed, 6¼" diameter, c. 1940 ...... 2500.00 3000.00 2600.00

☐ **Bottle,** circular, thick-walled, stepped interior, green garlands and air bubbles embedded in walls, signed, 6½" diameter, c. 1940 .... 600.00 700.00 620.00

☐ **Bottle,** cylinder with expanding neck, clear, cut with hunting scenes, signed, 8¾" long, c. 1927 .... 700.00 800.00 780.00

☐ **Bottle,** flaring, blue-tinted background, engraved scene of two maidens catching a dolphin in a net on one side, engraved dolphin on the other, stylized sunset and clouds above, scalloped border engraved around the rim, with stand, 8½" long, c. 1925 .... 500.00 700.00 550.00

	Current Price Range		Prior Year Average
☐ **Bottle,** octagon shape, light gray, cut with nude females and foilage, signed, 11½" long, c. 1928	550.00	650.00	575.00
☐ **Decanter,** clear, intaglio-carved figurines of Pan and nude female, signed, 10½" high, c. 1925	700.00	900.00	750.00
☐ **Decanter,** elongated helmet shape, elongated dome stopper, fluted sides, clear, cut with nude female, signed, 7" high, c. 1940	350.00	450.00	380.00
☐ **Vase,** beaker shape, slight flaring at lip, clear, etched with five nude females with long hair, standing on Herm pedestals, signed, 6¾" high, c. 1929 . . .	1000.00	1400.00	1150.00
☐ **Vase,** cylinder shaped, hexagonal with panels, clear, engraved with nude female dancing, signed, 9¾" high, c. 1951	350.00	450.00	375.00
☐ **Vase,** exaggerated urn-shape, waisted neck, cylinder neck, blue, vertical striations in dark blue, signed, 4" high, c. 1935	700.00	800.00	715.00
☐ **Vase,** inverted cone with undulating sides, flattened circular foot, clear, cut with male nude diving, 8½" high	350.00	450.00	375.00
☐ **Vase,** pear shape, waisted neck, applied double-c scrolling handles at neck, gray, cut with design of nude females in revelry, bands of geometric patterns above and below, signed, c. 1928	900.00	1100.00	980.00
☐ **Vase,** triangular sides rounded, thick-walled, clear, undulating striations, signed, 4½" diameter, c. 1940	350.00	550.00	375.00

OVERLAY

	Current Price Range		Prior Year Average
☐ **Bowl,** shaded pink, fan shape with amber applied edging, hobnail effect around top, ormolu holder with tassels, 7¼" high, 9¾" diameter	260.00	300.00	265.00
☐ **Fairy Lamp,** candy striped in pink, matching candle cup, embossed, pink rib dome shade, clear applied feet, ruffled base, white interior, three parts, 5¼" high, 4⅜" diameter	375.00	420.00	380.00
☐ **Fairy Lamp,** dark green, shade has white interior, signed Clarke base, 4⅜" high, 3⅞" diameter	130.00	180.00	140.00

	Current Price Range		Prior Year Average

☐ **Fairy Lamp Shade,** dark green with white interior, signed Clarke base, 4½" high, 4" diameter **120.00   170.00   125.00**

☐ **Finger Lamp and Chimney,** blue, shaded, clear reeded applied handle, pink and white enameled flowers and gold color foliage, 5½" high, 4¼" diameter **125.00   165.00   130.00**

☐ **Finger Lamp and Chimney,** pink shaded, clear handle, red roses trimmed in green and dots of white, 6" high, 5" diameter **175.00   225.00   200.00**

☐ **Finger Lamp and Chimney,** satin, lemon yellow, embossed shell and leaf, frosted reeded applied handle, 5" high, 3⅞" diameter **150.00   180.00   160.00**

☐ **Finger Lamp,** blue, shaded, clear reeded, applied handle, embossed designs, 6" high, 4¼" diameter **135.00   175.00   140.00**

☐ **Goblet,** white on crystal, dainty multi-color floral decoration, white cut to clear and outlined in gold in places, continental **140.00   160.00   145.00**

☐ **Hand Lamp and Chimney,** shaded chartreuse green, clear reeded applied handle, scroll decoration in beige, base has panelled pattern, 5" high, 3⅝" diameter **130.00   180.00   140.00**

☐ **Rose Bowl,** diamond quilted rose satin cut velvet, eight crimp top, white interior, 3½" high, 3¼" diameter **220.00   270.00   230.00**

☐ **Rose Bowl,** shaded blue with embossed swirl rib design, eight crimp top, white interior, 5" high, 6" diameter **180.00   210.00   185.00**

☐ **Table Lamp,** mushroom shape shade has pink embossed flowers and a ruffled top and clear chimney, white interior, silverplated base, 17¼" high, 6" diameter **330.00   380.00   340.00**

☐ **Vase,** Jack-In-Pulpit, amber edged ruffled top, pink and white applied flowers with amber leaves on cream, white interior, 6⅞" high, 6⅛" diameter **150.00   200.00   160.00**

☐ **Vase,** Jack-In-Pulpit, cranberry edged, white background, 7½" high, 6" diameter **130.00   180.00   140.00**

	Current Price Range		Prior Year Average

☐ **Vase,** Jack-In-Pulpit, decorated blue with multicolored, enameled flowers, branches and butterfly, decorated blue interior, 5⅝" high, 4⅝" diameter **130.00   170.00   135.00**

☐ **Vase,** Jack-In-Pulpit, green, white background, clear applied feet, 7" high, 5" diameter **120.00   150.00   130.00**

☐ **Vase,** Jack-In-Pulpit, purple, ruffled top, white background, 7½" high, 6" diameter **130.00   180.00   140.00**

☐ **Vase,** Jack-In-Pulpit, purple shaded to lavender, ruffled, 7¼" high, 6" diameter **120.00   170.00   125.00**

☐ **Vase,** Jack-In-Pulpit, shaded green, clear applied feet, scalloped edges, 6⅝" high, 5½" diameter **120.00   170.00   125.00**

☐ **Vase,** Jack-In-Pulpit, shaded maroon, white background, ruffled edging, 7" high, 6½" diameter **140.00   175.00   150.00**

☐ **Vase,** pink, large applied crystal flower and branch, crystal around base, white interior, 8¾" high, 4⅜" diameter **130.00   180.00   140.00**

☐ **Vase,** silver floral leaves and swag etched over green, narrow, flaring neck, pear shape, 5" high **40.00   80.00   50.00**

☐ **Vases,** white with enameled blue flowers, clear applied edge around ruffled top, ormolu handled holder, pink interior, 12¾" high, 7" diameter **260.00   310.00   265.00**

☐ **Water Tumbler,** overlay of decorated shaded pink, with satin blue and white flower with green leaves, gold trim, white interior, 4⅛" high, 3" diameter **150.00   200.00   160.00**

OVERSHOT

☐ **Fairy Lamp,** amber embossed swirl, signed Clarke base, 3½" high, 2⅞" diameter **120.00   170.00   125.00**

☐ **Fairy Lamp,** cranberry, embossed hob design, signed Clarke base, 4" high, 3" diameter **140.00   200.00   160.00**

☐ **Fairy Lamp,** cranberry, embossed ribs, signed Clarke base, 3¾" high, 2⅞" diameter **135.00   195.00   155.00**

☐ **Fairy Lamp,** opaque yellow, with embossed swirl pattern, signed Clarke base, 3½" high, 2⅞" diameter **150.00   200.00   170.00**

	Current Price Range		Prior Year Average

☐ **Pitcher,** ruffled, pink and white spatter glass, bulbous three way top, clear reeded applied handle, 7⅞" high, 5¼" diameter **150.00 200.00 160.00**

PEACHBLOW

☐ **Bowl,** New England, flared scalloped rim, 2¾" high, 5½" at widest point .. **700.00 800.00 725.00**

☐ **Bowl,** porridge, New England, shiny finish, deep rich color dominates, 2¾" high, 4½" diameter **400.00 475.00 425.00**

☐ **Cruet,** Wheeling, deepest mahogany color at top gradually shading to cream at base, clear amber faceted handle, reeded handle, 6¾" high **1100.00 1400.00 1200.00**

☐ **Pitcher,** Wheeling, shiny finish, exquisite color, applied amber handle, 9½" high **1000.00 1500.00 1100.00**

☐ **Shade,** gas light, New England, shiny finish, very good color, 4½" high, 6¼" diameter at top, 2¼" fitting, rare **350.00 450.00 375.00**

☐ **Sugar and Creamer Set,** Mt. Washington, pink to gray shading, eggshell-thin glass, squatty creamer is 1¾" high and 5½" across including extension of two applied handles, corset shaped pitcher is 3¾" high and 2" wide at base **4000.00 5000.00 4300.00**

☐ **Toothpick Holder,** ruffled rim, cylindrical shape, 2¼" high **110.00 130.00 120.00**

☐ **Tumbler,** New England, shiny finish, wild rose upper half, 3¾" high **350.00 425.00 375.00**

☐ **Vase,** lily, New England, satin finish, beautiful wild rose color, original paper label, 8¼" high **820.00 920.00 830.00**

☐ **Vase,** lily, New England, shiny finish, deep wild rose color covers 3" of this 9¾" high piece **750.00 850.00 775.00**

☐ **Vase,** Morgan, Wheeling, shiny finish, exquisite candy apple red, 7¾" high **900.00 1100.00 935.00**

☐ **Vase,** Mt. Washington, acid finish, cast in Webb Burmese shape, pink shaded to blue, flower top, very rare, 3¼" high, 3" diameter **800.00 1200.00 850.00**

☐ **Vase,** Mt. Washington, trumpet (lily), acid finish, pink shaded to blue, rare, 6¼" high, 2½" diameter **900.00 1400.00 1000.00**

	Current Price Range		Prior Year Average

☐ **Vase,** New England, Wild Rose, satin finish, double gourd, deepest raspberry shading to white, 7″ high, 1880s .... | 500.00 | 700.00 | 550.00

☐ **Vase,** satin finish, ribbed pear design, narrow neck, 9″ high .... | 65.00 | 100.00 | 75.00

☐ **Vase,** Webb, glossy, dark red and pink with raised gold prunus, cream lining, 3¼″ high, 2⅜″ diameter .... | 250.00 | 450.00 | 275.00

☐ **Vase,** Webb, glossy, rose red and pink with raised gold prunus and bird decoration, cream lining, 9″ high, 4″ diameter .... | 400.00 | 700.00 | 450.00

☐ **Vase,** Webb, satin, rose and pink with floral and butterfly decoration in heavy gold, cream lining, 8″ high, 3″ diameter | 375.00 | 600.00 | 425.00

☐ **Vase,** Webb, two applied handles, raised gold, green and silver decoration features squirrels, grapes and grape vines, 10″ high .... | 450.00 | 550.00 | 475.00

☐ **Vases,** rose shaded to cream, Japanese style blossoming branches, slender necks, pair, 7″ high .... | 210.00 | 310.00 | 250.00

☐ **Water Pitcher,** Wheeling, finest color, square top, applied amber handle, 10″ high .... | 1000.00 | 1500.00 | 1200.00

POMONA

☐ **Juice Glass,** first grind, delicate hobnail interior, tapered, 3¾″ high, base 1½″ in diameter, 2¼″ in diameter at top .... | 60.00 | 80.00 | 65.00

☐ **Lemonade Pitcher,** first grind, cylindrical shape, two rows of blue tinted cornflowers, 12″ high, 4″ diameter at base, 3″ diameter at top .... | 950.00 | 1075.00 | 975.00

☐ **Pitcher,** New England, first grind, miniature, square top .... | 90.00 | 130.00 | 100.00

☐ **Tumbler,** New England, second grind, cornflower staining .... | 60.00 | 100.00 | 70.00

☐ **Water Carafe,** New England, second grind, cornflower staining .... | 175.00 | 225.00 | 185.00

☐ **Water Set,** pitcher and six tumblers, first grind, pitcher is 6¾″ high ...... | 700.00 | 900.00 | 725.00

☐ **Water Tumbler,** New England, blue cornflower pattern, second grind, 3¾″ high, 2½″ diameter .... | 160.00 | 200.00 | 165.00

QUEZAL	Current Price Range		Prior Year Average
☐ **Bowl,** circular, shallow, flaring lip, mounted on circular base, iridescent, signed, 11¾" diameter, c. 1901-1925	300.00	400.00	320.00
☐ **Dish,** circular shape, two ribbed handles, amber iridescence, 5½" diameter, c. 1901-1925	125.00	175.00	135.00
☐ **Light Shade,** flower form, with scalloping, flared rim, iridescent yellow, signed, 5¼" high, c. 1900	150.00	200.00	160.00
☐ **Vase,** elongated baluster, domed foot, light yellow background, green feather designs, highlighted with amber iridescence, 19½" high, c. 1901-1925	1000.00	1400.00	1100.00
☐ **Vase,** Jack-in-the-Pulpit, flower face slightly ruffled, thin cylinder stem, flattened circular foot, opalescent, amber iridescent, striated green feathering, amber iridescence on foot, signed, 10¼" high, c. 1901-1925	1500.00	2000.00	1600.00
☐ **Vase,** ovoid body with vertical lobing, wide cylinder neck, slightly flaring lip, opalescent background, green and amber iridescent draping bands, applied stringing in free form design, 6¼" high, c. 1901-1925	1400.00	1600.00	1480.00
☐ **Vase,** pear shape, amber iridescent, overlaid in silver, chased with flowers and leaves, strapwork, signed, 8¾" high, c. 1905-1920	600.00	1000.00	700.00

SATIN

☐ **Bowl Vase,** decorated yellow webb with prunus blossoms and butterfly in heavy gold, trimmed in gold, 3½" high, 4¼" diameter	350.00	400.00	375.00
☐ **Bride's Bowl,** overlay of decorated pink, white on bottom, maroon flowers, green, yellow, and lavender leaves, frosted, ruffled edging, gold trim, 4½" high, 10½" x 9¼"	270.00	350.00	310.00
☐ **Ewer,** overlay of decorated, shaded pink, applied frosted handle, small flowers of white and branches of gold, three petal top, white interior, 7¾" high, 3¼" diameter	110.00	160.00	130.00

	Current Price Range		Prior Year Average

☐ **Ewer,** overlay of decorated, shaded pink, applied frosted handle, enameled flowers of white and pink, foliage of gold, white interior, 8½" high, 4¼" diameter **140.00 190.00 165.00**

☐ **Ewer,** overlay of decorated, shaded pink, frosted, applied handle, with enameled flowers of white and pink with yellow centers, three petal top, white interior, 9¼" high, 3¾" diameter **120.00 170.00 145.00**

☐ **Fairy Lamp,** Webb-like decoration, brown and tan leaves with cones on cream background, signed Clarke base, rare, 5⅜" high, 3⅞" diameter **240.00 300.00 245.00**

☐ **Lacemaker's Lamp,** shade has embossed leaves, scrolls and overlapping petals with chimney, brass handled base, 18" high, 10" diameter **520.00 570.00 530.00**

☐ **Peg Lamps,** shaded yellow, embossed completely, set in candleholders made of brass, 17" high, 6" diameter, pair **1300.00 1500.00 1350.00**

☐ **Perfume Bottle,** decorated Webb, ivory, prunus blossoms and butterfly in heavy gold, silver, hallmarked top, 3¼" high, 2⅜" diameter **260.00 300.00 275.00**

☐ **Rose Bowl,** embossed flowers of rose shaded to pink, white interior, eight crimp top, 3½" high, 4" diameter ... **130.00 180.00 155.00**

☐ **Rose Bowl,** overlay of blue diamond quilted cut velvet, four crimp, white interior, 3¼" high, 3½" diameter **175.00 220.00 185.00**

☐ **Rose Bowl,** overlay of decorated blue, egg shape, florals in cream with typical coralene foliage, frosted petal applied feet, eight crimp top, white interior, 6¼" high, 3½" diameter **150.00 200.00 155.00**

☐ **Rose Bowl,** overlay of decorated blue, flowers in white and pink with Monarch butterfly decoration, petal applied feet, four crimp top, white interior, 5½" high, 4½" diameter **150.00 200.00 155.00**

☐ **Rose Bowl,** overlay of decorated light blue, applied, frosted feet of leaf motif, enameled daisies of white and foliage of cream, center of flower has red jewel, light crimp top, white interior, 4½" high, 4½" diameter **150.00 200.00 175.00**

	Current Price Range		Prior Year Average

☐ **Rose Bowl,** overlay of decorated rose, applied, frosted petal feet, decoration of green foliage and morning glory of tan and cream, four crimp top, 5¼" high, 4½" diameter 155.00 200.00 170.00

☐ **Rose Bowl,** overlay of decorated rose shaded to pink, egg shape, mauve and yellow pansies, frosted petal applied feet, four crimp top, white lining, 5½" high, 3⅜" diameter 150.00 200.00 155.00

☐ **Vase,** circular pinched form, flared rim of petal design, 8" high 35.00 60.00 45.00

☐ **Vase,** overlay of diamond quilted, rose cut velvet, white interior, ruffled, 7¼" high, 3¼" diameter 200.00 240.00 205.00

☐ **Vases,** overlay of decorated rose shaded to pink, with enameled flowers of white, foliage of gold, white interior, 6⅞" high, 4½" diameter, pair 220.00 300.00 250.00

☐ **Water Tumbler,** decorated shaded pink overlay, enameled flowers of blue and white with green and yellow leaves, white interior, 4¼" high, 3" diameter 150.00 200.00 160.00

SPATTER

☐ **Box,** cased glass, egg shaped, decorated yellow, three applied feet in clear gold, branches and leaves of gold and white, floral decoration is blue bell shaped, 7½" high, 4½" diameter ... 260.00 300.00 270.00

☐ **Jar,** yellow, small forget-me-nots in blue, applied finial is clear, lid, 6¼" high, 3½" diameter 75.00 100.00 80.00

☐ **Finger Lamp and Chimney,** peach with white and brown spatter, clear applied handle, 6¼" high, 4¼" diameter 130.00 180.00 150.00

☐ **Vase,** Jack-In-Pulpit, ruffled, diamond quilted, green, white and peach, 9¼" high, 5½" diameter 80.00 120.00 90.00

☐ **Water Tumbler,** green and white embossed swirl, 3¾" high, 2¾" diameter 60.00 100.00 70.00

STEUBEN

☐ **Bowl,** circular shape, incurved neck and flaring rim, amber aurene and calcite, 5½" diameter, c. 1902-1932 ... 150.00 200.00 175.00

	Current Price Range		Prior Year Average
☐ **Bowl,** lobed circular, short circular foot, clear, scrolling flowers in dark blue, dark blue band at rim, 5¼" diameter, c. 1930	3500.00	4500.00	3700.00
☐ **Compote,** blue aurene and calcite, inside iridescent blue, 6" high, c. 1902-1932	200.00	400.00	210.00
☐ **Figure,** fish rising from a breaking wave, scalloped base, 5¾" high, c. 1940	3000.00	4000.00	3200.00
☐ **Finger Bowls,** bell shape, on pedestal base of selenium red, fluted body, 5" diameter, c. 1930	40.00	50.00	42.00
☐ **Flask,** flattened circular body, cylindrical neck, handles, sides have irregular air trapped bubbles, blue neck to white shoulders, signed, 10" high, c. 1925	600.00	700.00	620.00
☐ **Glasses,** wine, crystal, bell shape with fluting, long pedestal stems of selenium red, 5" high, c. 1930	40.00	50.00	43.00
☐ **Goblets,** crystal, inverted bell shape, fluted, long pedestal stem with circular base, stems selenium red, 8⅜" high, c. 1930	40.00	50.00	42.00
☐ **Vase,** baluster body, short waisted neck, spreading circular foot, amber body decorated with gold peacock feathering, signed, 8½" high	1400.00	1600.00	1480.00
☐ **Vase,** baluster shape, cylinder neck slightly flaring, knopped at bottom of base, domed and flattened circular foot, off-white background with green			

Steuben Dish, *calcite finish, gold over white, 10" diameter,* **$300.00–$350.00**

	Current Price Range		Prior Year Average
feathering, amber iridescent clinging hearts and vines, 10″ high, c. 1905-1925	1600.00	1800.00	1680.00
☐ **Vase,** beaker shape, flaring lip, short rolled base, frosted, band of leaves in green, signed, 7″ high, c. 1930	1600.00	2000.00	1700.00
☐ **Vase,** Bristol, ovoid shape, spiral ribbing, yellow, 8¼″ high, c. 1902-1930	150.00	250.00	160.00
☐ **Vase,** fan design, inverted cone flattened on two sides, knopped standard, flattened circular base, silvery-blue iridescence, stringing and hearts in bands in opalescent, green, and amber, signed, 9″ high, c. 1904-1930	600.00	1000.00	700.00
☐ **Vase,** fan shaped body pressed to a flat section, short knopped stem, circular base, blue with band of amber and opal heart and vine motifs below the rim, signed, 8¼″ high	950.00	1050.00	975.00
☐ **Vase,** flower shape, ribbed, flared sides and lip, white, with pedestal base, 7¼″ high, c. 1902-1930	400.00	500.00	420.00

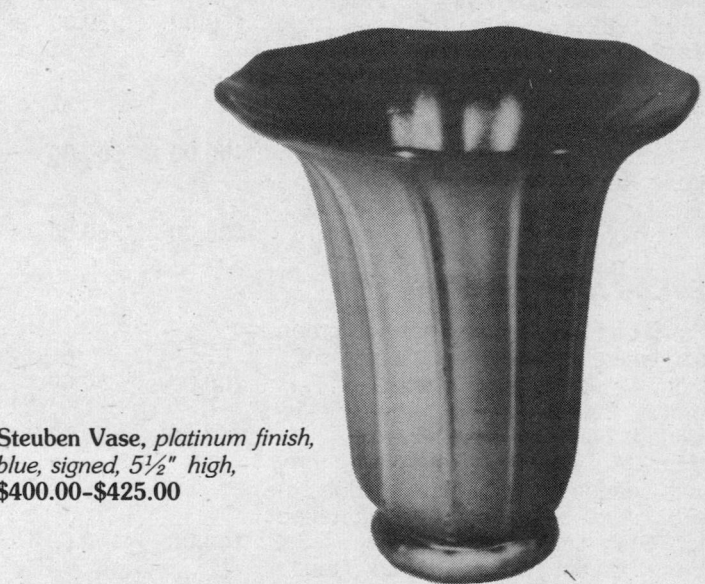

Steuben Vase, *platinum finish, blue, signed, 5½″ high,* **$400.00–$425.00**

	Current Price Range		Prior Year Average
☐ **Vase,** flower shape, ruffled neck with flaring, blue aurene iridescent, trumpet-shape stem, signed, 6¼" high, c. 1902-1930	400.00	600.00	450.00
☐ **Vase,** intarsia, inverted bell form invested with bubbles, raised circular base, pink scrolling vines on body, signed, 8¼" high, c. 1930	3200.00	3800.00	3300.00
☐ **Vase,** inverted bell shape, slightly flaring body, domed circular foot, bubbles and designs of scrolling vines encased in sides, band of pink around the rim, 8¼" high, c. 1930	3200.00	3800.00	3300.00
☐ **Vase,** ovoid shape, flaring, tinted olive green, wheel-engraved with foliage and floral designs, 8¾" high, c. 1902-1932	200.00	300.00	220.00
☐ **Vase,** ovoid shape, short flaring neck, amber aurene iridescent, signed, 8¼" high, c. 1902-1932	300.00	500.00	320.00
☐ **Vase,** ovoid shape, short flaring neck, circular base, amethyst, 6⅞" high, c. 1903-1932	150.00	250.00	175.00
☐ **Vase,** three-prong body with trumpet-shaped middle section flanked by two shorter lily-formed receptacles, circular domed foot, signed, 12¼" high, c. 1915	450.00	550.00	475.00
☐ **Vase,** trumpet shape on slightly domed circular foot, amber iridescent, signed, 8⅛" high, c. 1904-1930	400.00	500.00	410.00

STEVENS AND WILLIAMS

	Current Price Range		Prior Year Average
☐ **Fairy Lamp,** satin finish, striped green and white, base is signed Clarke, 5¼" high, 4" diameter	200.00	250.00	225.00
☐ **Plate,** Pastil, blue with fleur-de-lis, signed, 7¾" diameter	40.00	80.00	55.00
☐ **Vase,** Arboresque, frosted cranberry with opaque white, frosted, reeded applied handles and pedestal foot, ruffled top, 6⅛" high, 3⅛" diameter	140.00	180.00	145.00
☐ **Vase,** cream colored ribbed tubular body on random molded amber base, caramel Northwood pull up decoration, applied glass branches and blue flower, 5½" high	650.00	675.00	665.00

	Current Price Range		Prior Year Average
☐ **Vase,** green rib design, pinched floral form, 6″ diameter	30.00	60.00	40.00
☐ **Vase,** overlay amber applied edging around ruffle, off-white opaque with amber branches with multicolored flowers and leaves, pink interior, 6⅝″ high, 3¼″ diameter	150.00	200.00	160.00
☐ **Vase,** overlay, amber handle and branch on white background with amber plum, pink and amber leaf, square top in pink, amber edging, 8″ high, 3½″ diameter	125.00	175.00	130.00
☐ **Vase,** peachblow, applied floral decoration, long, narrow neck, bulbous shape, 8¾″ high	50.00	90.00	60.00
☐ **Vase,** white interior lining, mahogany exterior decorated with gold bordered gold and silver blossoms, jewels, one missing, 6¾″ high, decoration attributed to Oscar Pierre Erard	375.00	425.00	380.00

Stevens & Williams Vase, *cranberry, applied feet and filigree, 6¼″ high,* **$245.00–$260.00**

TIFFANY

	Current Price Range		Prior Year Average

☐ **Bottle,** scent, bulbous body, teardrop-shaped neck, short circular foot, flattened knopped stopper, silvery-blue iridescent, c. 1899-1928 .... **300.00 400.00 325.00**

☐ **Bowl,** circular with paneled sides, scalloped rim, dark blue iridescent, 7″ diameter, c. 1928 .... **5000.00 6000.00 5200.00**

☐ **Bowl,** Favrile, circular expanding towards rim, incurvate rim, clear, white paperweight flowers with orange and yellow, green leaves, signed, 4¾″ diameter, c. 1925 .... **2000.00 3000.00 2100.00**

☐ **Bread Plates,** Favrile, circular, wide flat rim with ruffling, green shading to opalescent ribbing in the center, 8″ diameter, c. 1920, set of six **600.00 700.00 625.00**

☐ **Candlestick,** elongated candle socket, openwork, green background, thin cylinder stem, flattened circular foot, 22½″ high, c. 1892-1920 .... **600.00 700.00 625.00**

☐ **Candlestick,** free form, indented swirls and flared sides, iridescent amber, signed, 9½″ high, c. 1906 .... **600.00 800.00 615.00**

☐ **Clock,** carriage, Favrile, rectangular shape, green sides overlaid with bronze filigree in grapevine pattern, angular handle at top, stepped rectangular base, 8″ high, c. 1900 .... **1400.00 1600.00 1500.00**

☐ **Compote,** circular shape, spiraling bands, scalloped rim, amber iridescent, 4⅛″ high, c. 1892-1928 .... **175.00 225.00 200.00**

☐ **Decanter and Stopper,** double-gourd shape body, circular foot, slender tapering neck, flared rim, amber-colored body, lily pad with tendrils continuing into base, flattened knopped stopper, signed, 11″ high, c. 1904 .... **800.00 900.00 815.00**

☐ **Desk Set,** includes a pair of bookends, a pen tray, a letter rack, a rocker blotter, four-corner blotter ends, a pen knife, an inkwell, a calendar holder, and a paper clip, abalone pattern, c. 1899-1920 .... **800.00 1200.00 850.00**

☐ **Inkwell** is bronze with mosaics shading from pale green to deep blue, cover is iridescent amber, 4″ high, 1902-1920 **4350.00 4900.00 4600.00**

☐ **Lamp,** cone-shaped shade, bronze cylinder standard with fluted sections, flaring circular foot, bands running ver-

	Current Price Range		Prior Year Average

tically and horizontally of striated ochre, band of opalescent turtle-back tiles in amber iridescent, 24⅜" high, c. 1899-1920 . . . . **7000.00 8000.00 7500.00**

☐ **Lamp,** desk, domed shade, irregular border, slightly domed finial with bud tip, baluster standard expanding, molded with leaves separating at base, rolled foot with openwork, five feet, shade with pattern of laburnum blossoms and leaves in yellow, ochre, green, blue, lavender and brown, 29" high, c. 1899-1920 . . . .**35000.00 45000.00 36000.00**

☐ **Lamp,** desk, domed shade, pivots on a harp-shaped support, flaring base, foot molded in petals, blue-green iridescent background, loops and trails in silvery-blue iridescence, signed, 18" high, c. 1899-1920 . . . . **1400.00 1600.00 1500.00**

☐ **Lamp,** desk, Favrile, cone-shaped shade, flattened dome finial, gilt-bronze Romanesque standard with scrolling foliage and two bands of glass bosses in green, shade with mottled yellow background and borders, graduated bands of medallions in green, blue, and red, 19¾" high, c. 1899-1920 . . . .**14000.00 16000.00 13000.00**

☐ **Lamp,** lantern-style, base is bronze, panels of glass are iridescent amber squares within an amber border, unmarked, 24¼" high, 1899-1920 . . . . . **2000.00 2400.00 2200.00**

☐ **Lamp,** desk, Favrile, domed shade, wide bell-shaped finial, cylinder flaring base in openwork honeycomb pattern of bronze, mottled blue shading to mottled green background, band of spread winged dragonflies, ochre bodies, yellow, green, and blue wings, green cabochons set above, 31" high, c. 1899-1920 . . . .**35000.00 45000.00 36000.00**

☐ **Lamp,** dome shade, emerald green background, with pattern of cherry blossoms and leaves in pink and olive green, mounted on three serpentine supports, ribbed stand in cylinder shape, circular gadroon base, five ball feet, 22" high, c. 1899-1920 . . . . **5000.00 7000.00 5200.00**

	Current Price Range		Prior Year Average

☐ **Lamp,** counter-balanced bronze base, lime-green glass shade, cut with foliage, 14¾" high, 7" wide, 1900-1920 — **2600.00 2900.00 2800.00**

☐ **Lamp,** Favrile, domed shade, cylinder standard with paneling, circular dished base, bronze standard and base, shade with design of daffodils in yellow, green opalescent background, 22" high, c. 1899-1920 . . . . — **7500.00 8500.00 7200.00**

☐ **Lamp,** Favrile, three lilies form shades, supported on three flower shaped sockets on three scrolling standards, gadrooned circular base, shade light orange streaked with green shading to opalescent, bronze base and standard, amber iridescent wash, 13¼" high, c. 1899-1920 . . . . — **1600.00 2000.00 1700.00**

☐ **Lamp,** base is bronze, shade is leaded glass, panels of white and green glass, marked, 15¼" high, c. 1910 . . . . — **475.00 525.00 500.00**

☐ **Lamp,** lily-shaped shades on stem-like supports, domed pedestal base, base and stems in bronze, three glass shades in green, 21" high, c. 1899-1920 . . . . — **6000.00 8000.00 6050.00**

☐ **Lamp,** ruffled shade in iridescent amber, mounted on column-like stem, spiraled ribbing on base, signed, 12¼" high, c. 1892-1928 . . . . — **500.00 700.00 500.00**

☐ **Lamp,** seven lily-shaped shades supported by flower-shaped sockets, thin lily-like stems, lily-pad molded base, amber iridescent, 21½" high, c. 1899-1920 . . . . — **6000.00 7000.00 6500.00**

☐ **Ornament,** moth, opalescent, body is mostly light green, wings are mottled green and gray, amber eyes, 7½" wide, 1899-1920 . . . . — **1800.00 2100.00 2000.00**

☐ **Shade,** domed-shape, domed finial with long slender pinnacle with curlicue, radiating bands of mottled ochre, band of red, white peonies and green leaves, 24" diameter, c. 1899-1920 . . **18000.00 22000.00 18500.00**

☐ **Shade,** domed shape, striated blue and green background, pattern of red, rose, lavender and mottled green peonies and leaves, 22" diameter, c. 1899-1920 . . . . **16000.00 18000.00 17000.00**

	Current Price Range		Prior Year Average

☐ **Vase,** bulbous body, brown on top shades to yellow and brown on bottom, mottled, 8¼" high, c. 1895 .... | 4300.00 | 4900.00 | 4700.00

☐ **Vase,** baluster body, waisted neck, bulbous mouth, green sides, neck and mouth are green decorated with opal and blue overlapping zigzags, blue interior, signed, 8½" high, c. 1919 .... | 2000.00 | 2300.00 | 2100.00

☐ **Vase,** baluster form, flat shoulder, waisted neck, short flaring rim, circular base, clear glass body with tan and amber vertical designs, signed, 8½" high .... | 1150.00 | 1350.00 | 1200.00

☐ **Vase,** baluster form, waisted neck, yellow body decorated with two bands of loop designs, signed, 8½" high, c. 1906 .... | 950.00 | 1150.00 | 975.00

☐ **Vase,** bulbous body, waisted, in shape of flower, opalescent, light orange, long, thin knopped stem .... | 1000.00 | 1200.00 | 1050.00

☐ **Vase,** cabinet, Favrile, spherical shape, lobed neck, waisted circular foot, light yellow background, two bands of amber and green iridescent lappets, amber iridescent wash, 4" high, c. 1892-1920 .... | 600.00 | 700.00 | 650.00

☐ **Vase,** compressed spherical body, long, slender cylinder neck expanding to slightly bulbous above body, opalescent, brown and amber lappets, pale yellow background, 11¼" high, c. 1905 .... | 1200.00 | 1600.00 | 1250.00

☐ **Vase,** cylindrical body, sloping shoulder, waisted neck, circular foot, amber body with amber and tan swirls and loop design, signed, 12" high .... | 900.00 | 1100.00 | 910.00

☐ **Vase,** cylinder shape expanding towards incurvated rim, flaring foot, clear, paperweight technique with narcissus encased in the sides, opaque flowers with yellow center, green leaves, and ochre stems, signed, 15" high, c. 1912 .... | 3500.00 | 4500.00 | 3600.00

☐ **Vase,** elongated ovoid shape, paneled sides, short circular foot, casing around neck in blue with amber and yellow iridescent design, overlapping lappets, signed, 8" high, c. 1921 .... | 3500.00 | 4500.00 | 3600.00

	Current Price Range		Prior Year Average

☐ **Vase,** elongated tulip-shaped body, triangular section, tapering to cylinder stem, slightly domed foot, opalescent, striated amber iridescent and green feathering, 6″ high, c. 1905 . . . .   **900.00 1100.00   910.00**

☐ **Vase,** Favrile, baluster body with vertical indentations around the shoulder continuing into flattened paneled sides, transparent glass sides decorated with amber and blue designs, signed, 7½″ high, c. 1900 . . . .   **1300.00 1400.00 1350.00**

☐ **Vase,** Favrile, baluster shape, opalescent shading to bright green, silvery-blue band of lappets, signed, 8½″ high, c. 1910 . . . .   **1000.00 1400.00 1100.00**

☐ **Vase,** trumpet shape, flaring, ruffled lip, amber iridescent, loop and trail designs, signed, 6¾″ high, c. 1912 . . . .   **400.00   500.00   450.00**

☐ **Vase,** trumpet shape, inverted, amber iridescent, green folds around lower body, signed, 10⅛″ high, c. 1916 . . .   **400.00   600.00   450.00**

☐ **Vase,** trumpet shape, wide flaring lip, bulbous knop at base, circular foot, amber iridescent, signed, 15¾″ high, c. 1910 . . . .   **600.00   800.00   615.00**

VASA MURRHINA

☐ **Rose Bowl,** overlay of beige with spatter of brown and pink, swirl patterned mica flakes, eight crimp top, white interior, 3¼″ high, 4″ diameter **125.00   170.00   130.00**

☐ **Rose Bowl,** overlay of rose, mica flaking, eight crimp top, white interior, 3½″ high, 3½″ diameter **120.00   170.00   125.00**

☐ **Rose Bowl,** overlay, white interior, spangled silver in coral pattern, eight crimp top, 3¾″ high, 3¾″ diameter   **110.00   150.00   125.00**

☐ **Vase,** multicolor overlay, pink and blue with spatters of maroon and mica flakes, ruffled edging, white interior, 9″ high, 4⅝″ diameter **120.00   150.00   135.00**

☐ **Vase,** pink and blue with spatters of maroon and mica flakes, ruffled edging with crystal, 7½″ high, 4½″ diameter   **140.00   180.00   155.00**

	Current Price Range		Prior Year Average

VASELINE

☐ **Cologne Bottle,** polished, cut panels, cut faceted bubble stopper, 7″ high, 2½″ diameter 110.00 150.00 115.00

☐ **Ewer,** opalescent striped, pink applique flowers with amber applied leaves and handle, flattened, bulbous shape, 8¼″ high, 4⅜″ diameter 150.00 200.00 160.00

☐ **Ewers,** opalescent, striped with pink applied flowers and clear branches, ruffled tops, clear applied handles, clear petal applied feet, pair, 13¼″ high, 4½″ diameter 680.00 710.00 685.00

☐ **Table Decoration,** Victorian, opalescent, with thorns, 6½″ long, 4½″ high 150.00 190.00 160.00

☐ **Vase,** Jack-In-Pulpit, opalescent, ruffled, 6″ high, 3⅜″ diameter 70.00 100.00 75.00

☐ **Vase,** Jack-In-Pulpit, opalescent swirl glass, ruffled top, applied ruffle around vase in pink, 7½″ high, 3¾″ diameter 100.00 120.00 110.00

☐ **Vase,** Jack-In-Pulpit, opalescent swirl with spiraled pink trim, 7¾″ high, 4¼″ diameter 120.00 170.00 125.00

☐ **Vase,** Jack-In-Pulpit, opalescent, with applied rigaree around middle, shell feet and ruffled edge, 4¾″ high, 2¼″ diameter 70.00 120.00 85.00

VERRE MOIRE

☐ **Fairy Lamp,** blue frosted with opaque loopings of white, signed Clarke insert cup, matching ruffled base, 4⅞″ high, 6⅛″ diameter 450.00 500.00 460.00

☐ **Fairy Lamp,** chartreuse green frosted, white, opaque loopings on shade and matching base, signed Clarke insert cup, 6½″ high, 7¾″ diameter 500.00 550.00 525.00

☐ **Fairy Lamp,** chartreuse green satin finish, opaque white loopings, matching ruffled base, signed Clarke insert cup, 6¼″ high, 7″ diameter 470.00 530.00 480.00

☐ **Fairy Lamp,** frosted blue, signed Clarke base, 3¾″ high, 3″ diameter 160.00 200.00 170.00

☐ **Fairy Lamp,** frosted with white, opaque loopings, matching fluted base, signed Clarke insert cup, 5¼″ high, 8¼″ diameter 475.00 520.00 480.00

	Current Price Range		Prior Year Average

☐ **Fairy Lamp,** hat shaped base, white on cranberry dome, signed Clarke, clear candle cup, 8″ wide 500.00 600.00 525.00

☐ **Vase,** satin finish of blue and white, frosted background of blue with opaque white loopings, fluted top, 3¾″ high, 3⅝″ diameter 150.00 200.00 160.00

WALTER

☐ **Bookend,** Pate de Verre, L-shaped support with a squirrel, light green shading to dark green, signed, 6″ high, c. 1920 .... 1000.00 1600.00 1100.00

☐ **Bowl,** Pate de Verre, shallow circular, blue splashed with aquamarine, inside rim molded with berries and leaves, signed, 5¾″ diameter, c. 1900 ...... 800.00 1200.00 825.00

☐ **Dish,** five-sided, molded with circular band of leaves encircling cavetto, turquoise, 5⅜″ diameter, c. 1910 ...... 300.00 400.00 325.00

☐ **Dish,** Pate de Verre, shallow oval, molded in high relief with a brown lobster at one end, mottled green background, signed, 6¾″ long, c. 1920 .. 1800.00 2200.00 1900.00

☐ **Dish,** shallow oval shape, molded salamander on one side, yellow and ochre streaked with green, signed, 6¾″ long, c. 1900 .... 3000.00 5000.00 3250.00

☐ **Pendant,** Pate de Verre, flattened arrowhead shape, green with black striations, with molded turtle in the center, 2¼″ high, c. 1920 .... 550.00 650.00 575.00

☐ **Pendant,** Pate de Verre, flattened circular, pale yellow background, brown molded moth on the center, 2½″ diameter, c. 1920 .... 1200.00 1300.00 1250.00

☐ **Plaque,** Pate de Verre, rectangular shape, mottled lavender and gray background, cast in relief Joan of Arc's profile in light green, long red hair, a halo around her head, 9″ x 6″, c. 1900 1800.00 2200.00 1900.00

☐ **Vase,** inverted helmet shape, domed foot, gray-blue background, molded with lavender holly branches and green leaves, base molded with mottled green and yellow snails, signed, 8″ high, c. 1910 .... 1500.00 2000.00 1600.00

THOMAS WEBB AND SONS

	Current Price Range		Prior Year Average

☐ **Berry Bowl and Underplate,** alexandrite, crimped edge bowl is 5″ in diameter, matching underplate is 6½″ diameter, set is 2¼″ high **1000.00** **1100.00** 1050.00

☐ **Bowl,** fruit, white opal exterior lined with thin pink glass, two tone gold decoration of bird and flowering branch, three heavy textured applied feet, 6″ high, 8″ diameter, signed with spider Webb mark over E **450.00** **550.00** 475.00

☐ **Decanter,** bell shape, paneled and tapered sides, signed, 11¾″ high **55.00** **80.00** 70.00

☐ **Bottle,** perfume, inverted teardrop shape, cylinder neck with silver, domed lid, red background, overlaid in white, cut on one side with wildflowers and leaves, the other side with ferns, 4¼ high **800.00** **1000.00** 900.00

☐ **Bottle,** perfume, squared, cylinder neck with silver, flaring rim, flattened knop, dark green background, overlaid in white, cut with blossoms and leaves, signed, 5¼″ high, c. 1901 . . . . **3000.00** **4000.00** 3300.00

☐ **Bottle,** spherical body, cylinder neck of applied silver, flattened lid, turquoise background, overlaid in white, cut with shells and underwater plants, 3⅞″ high, c. 1900 . . . . **1600.00** **2000.00** 1800.00

☐ **Bowl,** squared, lobed at lip tapering to spherical shape, short circular foot, red background, overlaid in white, cut with roses, poppies, and bowknots, floral band around lip, 6½″ diameter, c. 1895 **4000.00** **5000.00** 4100.00

☐ **Decanter,** bulbous body, long cylinder neck tapering, silver domed cover with hinge, silver neck band chased with foliage and anchored with a chain hooked to lug handle on shoulder, greenish-yellow background, overlaid in pink and white, cut with apple blossoms, 9½″ high, c. 1886 . . . . **6000.00** **8000.00** 6500.00

☐ **Plaque,** circular shape, dark brown background, overlaid in white, carved with birds perched in blossoming branches in green, pink, blue, and rust, stylized border around rim, signed, 18¼″ diameter, c. 1890 . . . . **3500.00** **4500.00** 3600.00

	Current Price Range		Prior Year Average

☐ **Potpourri Jar,** ivory satin, decorated with panels of enameled pink, blue and yellow flowers, green leaves, all outlined in gold, green bands with gold trim and decoration gold washed ormulu feet, pierced top rim and lid with hinged inside cover, very ornate, 6½" high, 4¾" diameter 500.00 700.00 550.00

☐ **Rose Bowl,** blue ground with white morning glory blossoms and foliage, reverse side has butterfly, three applied blue feet, one of which has been ground, 4" high, 6" diameter 730.00 975.00 740.00

☐ **Rose Bowl,** miniature, chartreuse green satin overlay ground with white cut to pink carved flowers and foliage, white lining, unsigned, 2½" high, 2¾" diameter 900.00 1200.00 950.00

☐ **Rose Bowl,** satin glass, peachblow, signed, 6" high 110.00 160.00 125.00

☐ **Toothpick Holder,** Alexandrite, rare, 2½" high 900.00 1000.00 925.00

☐ **Vase,** acid cut back, cream colored background, decorated with pink flowers outlined heavily in gold, gold spider in web decoration 450.00 500.00 470.00

☐ **Vase,** baluster shape, yellow background, overlaid in pink and white, cut with apple blossoms, leaves, and butterfly, 6½" high, c. 1895 . . . . 400.00 500.00 420.00

☐ **Vase,** bulbous body, acid red background with white floral decoration, narrow neck, bulbous shape, 5½" high 575.00 700.00 620.00

☐ **Vase,** bulbous body, cylinder neck, peach shading to light, overlaid in white, cut with poppies and leaves, 7½" high, c. 1895 . . . . 4000.00 6000.00 4150.00

☐ **Vase,** bulbous body, long cylinder neck, greenish-gray background, overlaid in white and pink, cut with morning glories and leaves, stylized coils around neck, 8½" high, c. 1890 . . . . 4000.00 6000.00 4300.00

☐ **Vase,** bulbous base, slender cylinder neck, red background, overlaid in white, carved with blooming apple branches, 12" high, c. 1900 . . . . 1100.00 1400.00 1150.00

☐ **Vase,** bulbous body, sloping shoulders, thin cylinder neck, yellow background, overlaid in pink and white,

Thomas Webb and Sons Vase,
Peachblow, enamel floral decor,
9½" high, **$300.00-$400.00**

	Current Price Range		Prior Year Average
carved with Star of Bethlehem blossoms, leafy branches, and a bee, band of folds around neck, 8¾" high, c. 1900	1400.00	1500.00	1450.00
☐ **Vase,** bud, bulbous body, thin cylinder neck, yellow background, overlaid in white, cut with wildflowers and leaves, band around neck, 6½" high, c. 1900	3000.00	4000.00	3100.00
☐ **Vase,** compressed spherical, cone shape neck, red and gray background, overlaid in white, cut with diamond-shaped panels with flowers in centers, double band of acanthus with arched borders, band of flowers around neck, signed, 4" high, c. 1895	4000.00	6000.00	4200.00

	Current Price Range		Prior Year Average

☐ **Vase,** egg shape body, waisted neck, flared rim, circular foot, green body overlaid in red and white and cut with chrysanthemum blossoms, leaves, a butterfly and bee, 10″ high, c. 1900 — **2500.00 3500.00   2600.00**

☐ **Vase,** elongated ovoid, tapering to cylinder neck, everted rim, turquoise background, overlaid in white, cut with bleeding hearts, leaves, and butterflies, acanthus band around neck, chevron band around foot, 8⅛″ high, c. 1900 .... **800.00 1000.00   900.00**

☐ **Vase,** elongated ovoid, waisted neck, flaring lip, ring turning around neck and foot, greenish-yellow background, overlaid in pink and white, cut with morning glories, leaves, and a butterfly, signed, 8¼″ high, c. 1900 ...... **6000.00 8000.00   6500.00**

☐ **Vase,** elongated ovoid, waisted neck, flaring lip, greenish-yellow background, overlaid in white, cut on one side with poppies and leaves and on the other side with ferns and a butterfly, ring turnings around neck and foot, 7¼″ high, c. 1895 .... **4000.00 5000.00   4100.00**

☐ **Vase,** flattened ovoid body, short cylinder neck, blue background, overlaid in white, cut with two panels on each side of body, encircling orange blossoms and butterflies on one side and cyclamens and leaves with butterflies on the other, vertical band of leaves between panels on each side, band of foliage around neck, 7¾″ high, c. 1895. .... **1800.00 2400.00   1900.00**

☐ **Vase,** miniature, chartreuse green satin overlay with white carved flowers and leaves, white leaf band around top, white lining, unsigned, 4″ high, 1¾″ diameter **700.00 900.00   725.00**

☐ **Vase,** miniature, frosted citron with white carved flowers and leaves, white bands, unsigned, 2¾″ high, 2⅛″ diameter............................. **500.00 700.00   525.00**

☐ **Vase,** miniature, rose satin overlay with white carved flowers, foliage and butterfly, white lining, unsigned, 2″ high, 2½″ diameter.................... **600.00 800.00   625.00**

	Current Price Range		Prior Year Average

☐ **Vase,** mother of pearl, quilted, diamond band, fluted rim, signed, 6½" high 130.00 180.00 150.00

☐ **Vase,** inverted trumpet shape, short circular foot, yellow background, overlaid in blue and white, carved with berries, leaves, and a bee, 8¾" high, c. 1900 .... 1500.00 2000.00 1550.00

☐ **Vase,** ovoid body, cylinder neck, red background, overlaid in white, cut with morning glories and leaves, neck trimmed with band of arrow points, 3¾" high, c. 1895 .... 600.00 800.00 630.00

☐ **Vase,** ovoid shape, short cylinder neck, stepped circular foot, yellow background, overlaid in white, cut with wildflowers, leaves, butterflies, band around neck with diagonal scrolls, signed, 6" high, c. 1895 .... 1600.00 2000.00 1700.00

☐ **Vase,** ovoid body, waisted neck, flaring lip, dark red background, overlaid in white, cut with bough with blossoms and leaves, 4½" high, c. 1900 ...... 800.00 1200.00 850.00

☐ **Vase,** ovoid shape, waisted neck, slightly flaring rim, short circular foot, off-white background, carved with sweet peas and leaves on the front, signed, c. 1890 .... 1100.00 1400.00 1200.00

☐ **Vase,** pear shape, neck cone-shaped, short flaring foot, yellow background, overlaid in red and white, cut wild rose branch and a butterfly, ring turnings around neck and foot, 5¼" high, c. 1900 .... 400.00 600.00 450.00

☐ **Vase,** pear shape, rolled shoulder, waisted neck, flaring rim with uneven scalloping, clear background, carved with irises and leaves, 11¾" high, c. 1900 .... 800.00 1000.00 850.00

☐ **Vase,** pear shape, short circular foot, clear, cut with a scene of a swamp, a bird and a tortoise, enameled in green and gilt, signed, 9¾" high, c. 1900 .. 1100.00 1400.00 1200.00

☐ **Vase,** spherical body, white cylinder neck, frosted gray background, overlaid in white and blue, cut with petunias and leaves on one side, butterfly on the opposite side, ring-turned neck, signed, 6⅛" high, c. 1900 .... 4000.00 5000.00 4500.00

	Current Price Range		Prior Year Average
☐ **Vase,** spherical body, wide cylinder neck, yellow background, overlaid in white and green, cut with leafy branches and butterflies, acanthus border around neck with floral band above, signed, 5" high, c. 1890	4000.00	6000.00	4150.00
☐ **Vase,** teardrop shape, short circular foot, yellow background, overlaid in pink and white, carved with primroses, leaves, and a butterfly, ring turnings around neck and foot, 8¼" high, c. 1900	1200.00	1400.00	1280.00
☐ **Vase,** teardrop-shaped, yellow background, overlaid in white, cut with flowers, leaves, and a butterfly, 13½" high, c. 1895	800.00	1000.00	850.00
☐ **Vase,** wide cylinder body tapering towards short cylinder neck, short circular foot, dark turquoise background, overlaid in white and grayish-blue, cut with wildflowers and leaves, ring turnings around neck and foot, 7⅛" high, c. 1900	4000.00	6000.00	4500.00
☐ **Vial,** perfume, cone shaped, screw-on cap in silver, red background, overlaid in white, cut with palms and a butterfly, 9½" long, c. 1900	700.00	800.00	720.00
☐ **Vial,** perfume, domed body with silver swelling domed lid, overlaid in white, carved ferns, a dragonfly, and a butterfly, silver collar around neck, 4¼" high, c. 1900	600.00	800.00	650.00

CARNIVAL GLASS

INTRODUCTION

The dazzling colors which capture the flamboyant varieties of the fire opal and the abalone shell characterize the most unusual glass ever produced in the history of America. Once known as Taffeta glass for its glossy, shiny appearance, Carnival glass is easily recognizable because of its bright iridescence. The chameleon colors flash exotic shades as the viewer observes it from different angles and in different light. This trait attracts the most attention.

The unusual use of colors, the ornate patterns, and the elaborate shapes—some borrowed and some original—emerged from an intermingling of styles from the past as well as ones contemporary with the period when Carnival glass was first produced. The further development of industrial mechanisms and production know-how provided the means for creating something new and different. Handcrafting combined with mass production added a distinctive flair.

During the 1800's, Americans invented practical methods for producing pressed pattern glass. By the end of the century, refinements engendered greater efficiency, thus allowing for inexpensive glass to be produced in larger quantities with a more extensive range in shapes and patterns. Eventually, pressed glass fused the geometric designs of cut glass with naturalistic motifs, culminating in an intricacy impossible fifty years earlier.

Tradition, conventionality, inhibitions, and social restraints in all areas of life were challenged and discarded at the turn of the century. A newly mechanized society with the means of providing widespread news revealed the fashions and tastes of the rich, the famous, and the avant-garde to the view of the middle class more readily than ever before. The exotic, sensuous artifacts of Art Nouveau with their sinuous lines and undulating colors fascinated the middle class, but these works were too expensive for them. As the popularity of pattern glass faded, a small group of glass producers offered a different type of glassware that was in the average person's price range, yet satisfied their desire for articles which reflected the new style so popular with the wealthy. These manufacturers devised inexpensive methods for treating intricately designed pressed glass which resulted in a surface iridescence imitative of the highly favored Tiffany glass. The masses bought this glass as it displayed a boldness and innovation in color and design indicative of the new era.

When first produced, Carnival glass provided a combination of the old coupled with an exotic originality. At times, Carnival displays the purity and perfect balance of line associated with classical pieces, such as the buttermilk goblet made by Fenton; or the naturalistic, free-flowing forms representative of the Art Nouveau style, such as the ripple vase made by Imperial. The patterns typical of cut glass in glittering green, such as the potpourri punch bowl and near-cut wreath bowl by Millersburg, offer a startling difference compared to the starkness of cut glass. Plus, the profusion of motifs common in pattern glass—floral, fruit, and animals—were freely utilized. Although the Carnival patterns and basic shapes were formed by the same methods used in pressed pattern—the molten glass was forced into a mold by being pressed with a plunger—many Carnival pieces were further worked on by hand. Craftsmen often shaped articles by ruffling, crimping, or inverting the rim of a bowl, pulling a vase into an elongated form which modified the pattern designs, or shaping some portion of an object into an asymmetric mode. One method of elongating the stem of a vase, for instance, was swinging the glass, while still molten, on the end of a pontil rod. These are still called "swung" vases. Even with this handwork, manufacturers were able to keep their production costs down. Carnival also differed from pressed in that it let less light through, although it is still transparent (with some exceptions), making raised patterns on the inside and the outside of objects possible, though the inside surface was usually left plain when the piece was made to hold liquids. Despite the borrowing of styles and motifs, and attempts to imitate art glass, Carnival glass offered the consumer a new dramatic look.

While Carnival was being produced, the manufacturers merely referred to it as iridescent pressed glass. Some advertised it as taffeta or rhodium glass. Others used names such as Etruscan or Pompeiian associating it with ancient glass which often forms a sort of iridescence from aging. During the late 1920's, Depression glass supplanted Carnival glass in popularity which led to massive amounts of the iridescent glass being sold at even lower prices to carnivals and dime stores. These businesses used the glass for promotions, prizes, and giveaways. The name Carnival evolved from many of the earlier collectors recalling how they had won a piece of this glass playing a game of chance at a carnival.

The feature of most importance to Carnival glass collectors is probably color. Color determines the value of a piece to a great extent. Rare colors, such as red, pastel yellow-green, and amber, are sought after by many collectors, commanding high prices because so few of them were made. Sometimes particular shapes and patterns often drive their prices very high. The rarest, most valuable pieces are red. Few of these were made because of the cost. Gold, copper, and selenium were necessary for producing a clear, strong red shade. Although bright colors, except for marigold, were more expensive to produce, these bright pieces were extremely popular with their original owners as well as with today's collectors.

Production and sales for marigold surpassed all other colors, partially because the orangish-yellow color set off the dark furniture common in homes during the earlier part of the century, but mostly because it was the least expensive to produce. Certain inexpensive metallic salts applied to clear glass produce iridescent marigold; whereas, agents which produced red, amethyst, blue and green were more expensive.

Intensive experimentation by a few glass manufacturers resulted in the development methods for mass producing colored glass imitative of art glass. Frank Fenton and Harry Northwood probably pioneered the majority of this experimentation. They devised a method of applying different acids and salt solutions to clear or colored pressed glass which became iridized when reheated.

The reheating process melded the various colors, allowing each color to show through in varying degrees in a wavering rainbow. Greater variety in colors and shades were possible on one piece if the base glass was colored. The base glass could be either very bright or pastel though the vivid base colors created more popular pieces.

A wide range of hues exist under each color category. For example, marigold is usually described as orange. Orange derives from the two primary colors, yellow and red. Consequently, marigold appears in shades which include the entire spectrum range of pale yellow to the deepest red; and sometimes, the entire range of colors is seen on just one piece.

Carnival was made not only in a great many colors, but the number of shades is immense, also. For example, the very popular blue pieces can be light blue, dark blue, or a stunning cobalt blue which has the sheen of peacock feathers. Purple pieces come in the lightest lavenders to a black purple. Many of the colors were also produced with a frosted iridized surface.

Experience in looking at and handling Carnival glass will enable you to distinguish the subtle differences in shades. By holding a piece close to a bright light, the base glass will be discernible from surface iridizied color. When examining rare amber pieces in such a manner, you would be able to determine that the base glass is amber with the iridized surface being brown. The best place to see this is the collar base rim.

High relief and ornateness distinguish Carnival patterns from other types of glass, also. For the most part, Carnival glass designs were made for display, and these profusive designs intensify the luminosity of hues as the numerous planes refract the light. Although color and shape attract the most collector interest, pattern designs provide the best means of identifying different Carnival pieces. But for the beginner, identification can be confusing in that there are more than a thousand patterns.

The patterns can be categorized as: near-cut or geometric patterns (many of these derived from early pressed pattern glass which attempted to imitiate cut glass); Art Nouveau motifs of flowers, leaves, foliage, fruit, birds, butterflies, and dragonflies; and scenic designs.

Manufacturers produced some patterns, such as grape and cable, and orange tree, in a large number of different pieces. Yet, the most impressive patterns are those which were designed for one particular piece only. For example, leaf swirl and small flowers, made in a compote only, displays esthetic, graceful lines not always present in more prolific patterns.

To add to the collector's confusion, some patterns have more than one name, because most pieces were named by the earlier collectors, not by the manufacturers. By reading and examining a large number of glass pieces, you'll become adept at recognizing the majority of patterns by their most descriptive name.

The grape motif appears on numerous glass pieces. All of the major manufacturers created their own versions of the grape motif: the collector can learn to distinguish each of these versions from the others. Popular with the original buyers, many collectors specialize in collecting grape patterns. The most common pattern, the grape and cable, was produced by Northwood with some fifty different types of objects having this design. New patterns continue to be discovered every once in awhile, and these new finds are invariably rarities.

Even though the shape of an object is less important than color or pattern, it can greatly influence desirability and value either due to rarity or esthetic appeal. For the most part, utility was secondary to decorativeness. So, objects suitable for display dominated. Consequently, large dinner or luncheon tableware sets were never made until after the 1920's when Depression glass table sets garnered most of the middle income buyers. During the initial popularity of Carnival glass, manufacturers created small sets. A table set included a sugar bowl, creamer, butter dish and spooner. Water sets, the most sought-after of the sets today, consisted of a pitcher and six or eight tumblers; wine sets were made up of a decanter and four or six stemmed glasses. The berry sets—one serving bowl with six small bowls—are the easiest sets to find, because large numbers were made.

Surprisingly, few plates were made in comparison to other common objects. The flat surface of a plate lends itself to the decorativeness of Carnival very well, but some may have thought a decorative plate impractical for serving food. Rarity combined with the ease of displaying plates has made these articles popular with collectors.

Don't be fooled into thinking that you have found a rare plate when you really have a low bowl in that it doesn't have the bowl's rimmed sides, and the edges of the plate are less than an inch and a quarter above the surface it sits on. It is only fair to state, however, that this is a controversial point among Carnival collectors, and that some people will accept up to two inches of space. The important thing to remember, of course, is that this becomes an important point only when a piece is changing hands. The difference in perception between buyer and seller will determine the value.

Quite often, the different types of objects produced reflect social customs and industrial development. For example, railroad transport provided the populace regularly with fresh fruit for the first time: thus, fruit bowls with some specially designed for bananas and oranges, were very popular. Since the shape of bowls allows for a fuller expression of a design, more bowls than any other object were made. For this very reason, bowls of any size or shape are highly desirable to collectors today; the larger ones are particularly prized, because the large convoluted designs radiate such brilliancy.

The opaqueness of Carnival glass made it highly suitable for flower vases—the ties holding the arrangements together and the brackish water were not visible, and florists found the glass inexpensive enough to use regularly. The rose bowl, an object produced widely in pottery and porcelain, also became quite popular.

Many other types of objects were made in Carnival glass, some which are common today, and some which are very rare. Hats and baskets, popular items in Victorian times, offer the collector with a limited budget tremendous opportunities.

Today, Carnival glass remains as concrete evidence of the yearning for the change and freedom from the heavy, overbearing Victorian era. The vibrant, pulsating colors, and the daring designs stand as a watermark of the entry of 20th century man into a new age.

BUILDING A COLLECTION

Many beginners feel overwhelmed when they read about some of the rarities of Carnival glass selling for thousands of dollars. Regardless, this is a collecting field that everyone can enjoy and still adhere to their budget. Many pieces, particularly the more common ones, sell for under $50 or $60. The newcomer needs to read and study about Carnival glass in order to develop an understanding of what characteristics influence value. Generally, supply and demand control prices. If the demand for a particular piece surpasses the supply, its value will usually soar; but, if the supply exceeds the demand, the price will stagnate or even drop. The production level of certain patterns, colors, and objects was low. Low production in itself does not drive up prices—numerous collectors must want these particular pieces. Some pieces that are plentiful are very popular, but their availability keeps the prices from rising very much.

For the most part, collectors are not interested in late Carnival glass. Whether you are or not, you need to learn how to recognize it and know how its values compare to other Carnival glass. Since the quality of these pieces is considerably less, you should never pay the same prices you would pay for the earlier pieces. Once you have compared the late Carnival with the earlier pieces, you will easily distinguish one from the other. The shapes and patterns are more typical of the 1930's—more simplistic, less busy; the patterns often lack the ornateness associated with Carnival. The iridescence on these pieces was sprayed on. These flashed-on surfaces don't match the sheen of the earlier articles, partially because the finish is not as durable. Often, the iridescence has started to wear off.

Even though the popularity for iridized pieces dissipated quickly during the late 1920's, manufcturers continued to produce some of these wares, because there was still some demand for them. Manufacturers already had molds for the earlier pieces; and since most of their cost was for designing and making molds, they could afford to produce the same old articles and still profit when selling them at exceedingly low prices. Even so, few people could afford to buy glass sheerly for decorative purposes during the Depression; besides, the popularity of Art Nouveau waned, and the public wearied of the brash, fanciful imitations.

As the Depression tableware sets became popular, table sets made of Carnival were produced. These sets are considered to be iridized Depression glass by some collectors, and late Carnival by others. Usually, the same sets are known by different names. For instance, the Carnival set called Bouquet and Lattice is known to Depression glass collectors as Normandie. Also, there have been several iridized sets produced in the last 30 years which further confuses hobbyists.

During the Depression, the time and skill necessary for producing new Carnival pieces cost the manufacturers too much. For the most part, Carnival glass production ceased until the revival of the reproductions in the 1960's.

The collecting of Carnival glass has increased tremendously over the last 20 years. Even though a large number of Carnival pieces were made, their survival rate has been low. We know that advertising pieces were made in fairly large numbers, yet out of every thousand pieces made only a half dozen exist today. These figures give us an idea of how few pieces of the Carnival have actually been saved or kept. With the increasing demand, the supply continues to dwindle.

Since the hobbyist will discover few bargains, he needs to protect himself from spending too much for an item by developing an understanding of values. You should know which colors, patterns, or articles are rare and popular, because these items will sell for thousands of dollars. For example, two-piece articles usually carry higher price tags, since it is difficult to find two pieces intact.

By studying this price guide and comparing its values for articles sold at auctions, flea markets, shops, and bazaars, you'll develop a sense or feeling as to how much a piece should sell for. You'll learn to calculate the value of a piece by weighing its rarity, popularity, esthetic appeal, and condition. If you should stumble across a piece of iridescent glass at an estate sale or a small local auction, your knowledge will enable you to spot an authentic Carnival piece and allow you to grab it up for a bargain.

Of course, no one should purchase collectibles purely as an investment, because too many unpredictable variables can affect the values adversely. You will be happiest buying what you like, so that at the very least you will have the pleasure of owning something that you enjoy. Still, anyone would be foolish to make substantial purchases without some consideration to the investment potential. The rarest pieces probably have excellent investment potential if the owner keeps them for more than five years. Most Carnival, except the most common pieces, will most likely appreciate enough to offset inflation, and any possible loss of income if the money had been invested in something else.

Although the high-priced rarities would be the best investment, even moderately scarce pieces could be profitable if the collector pays attention to quality. You should try to buy only pieces in excellent condition. The better the condition, the better chance you have for a good investment. Also, pay attention to the intensity of the iridescence, the variations in shading, esthetic appeal of the shape, the ornateness of the pattern, and any historical significance—any or all of these attributes will affect a piece's future value.

If your budget is limited, you might be wise to collect a few articles at moderately high prices. Wealthy collectors compete for the scarce objects, often driving their values out of range for most hobbyists, but the pieces just above average may be affordable for you.

As you gain more know-how, you'll become more confident about how much you should pay. You'll be able to gauge the importance of a piece to you, its suitability to your collection and how much other collectors would be willing to pay for it.

Collectors often narrow their collections by purchasing pieces by the type of object, by the manufacturers, or by the pattern. For instance, some collectors restrict their accumulations to just tumblers, or collect only marigold. But most collectors can't resist selecting pieces that include the entire range of colors available in Carnival glass.

In developing your collection, you should remain cognizant that a hodge-podge collection will have a total worth much less than that of a comparable collection that has continuity. This is true for a number of reasons. A collection is often sold en masse with the selling price being based mostly on the scarce or popular pieces. Miscellaneous, common, or poor specimens can be picked up by most avid collectors. But a collection of one motif, or all the pieces of one pattern offer the buyer something unique—something it takes time and diligence to accumulate. So, it is well worth the effort to decide on a specialized direction for your collection. Besides, a collection of all cobalt blue or all hats and baskets makes for a much more impressive visual impact.

When new Carnival pieces are made from old original molds or from molds made from old pieces, they are considered to be reproductions. Of course, there is nothing wrong with reproductions as long as they are marked appropriately, so that unsuspecting buyers don't pay prices suitable for original pieces. The Imperial Glass Company embosses an I superimposed over a G on all its reproductions; the Fenton Glass Company embosses its name within a circle. Unfortunately, other manufacturers have only placed a paper label on the base. Obviously, these labels can be easily removed, allowing pieces to be passed off as originals. Sometimes reputable dealers and collectors sell such items as originals, unaware that the labels were removed. Even the embossed pieces can be sold as originals if someone grinds the mark off. So be wary of any articles which look as if the base has been tampered with.

An original piece will normally show at least minute scratches or other signs of age. Still, scratches and dirt are sometimes added to a reproduction in order to make it look more authentic. Also, there are a number of original pieces of iridized glass that have been produced recently—not as reproductions—but as new glass with an old look.

When reproductions are first made, the prices for the originals will often decrease slightly, because a small portion of collector demand will be satisfied with these items. But, staunch collectors will insist on purchasing the original pieces, and their persistence usually brings those prices back up.

The more know-how the collector gathers and the more he handles good specimens, the more adept he'll become at spotting bogus items. Of course, buying from reputable dealers will diminish the possibility of buying reproductions.

Experience handling Carnival glass, picking up information from other collectors, reading about new developments in research—and a generous dash of your own creativity will allow you to develop an interesting, valuable collection that can bring pleasure to your family and friends as well as yourself.

CARE AND REPAIR

The condition of a piece of glass affects its value immensely. A cracked or badly damaged specimen will have very little value unless it is very rare. Minor flaws will diminish the value depending on the extent of the damage. Obviously, you should expect a higher level of condition for objects created only for decorative purposes. Articles that were used to serve food and beverages can be expected to show more wear, chips, scratches, and other imperfections. So, you should take your time and examine a piece carefully before you decide to purchase it.

Take the piece in your hand. Inspect the entire surface in a good light, carefully running your hand over it. Repaired cracks or deep scratches are not always discernible to the eye, but you should be able to feel any irregularities or roughness that indicate damage or repair. The edges and rims are the most likely spots, so pay special attention to those areas.

Next, hold the piece up to the light. Since Carnival glass is not easily transparent, mended cracks and chips are not easy to spot, particularly if they were clean breaks.

Obviously, perfect condition is ideal, but not always possible. After you've examined many pieces of glass, you'll learn to judge how many minor flaws are acceptable. Often, collectors become panicky when they find a hard-to-find item in poor condition. They're afraid they'll not get the chance to purchase it again. Just remember: numerous pieces of Carnival were produced; and there are bound to be pieces sitting forgotten in musty corners, their owners unaware of their value. Another piece will probably show up. If you do buy a damaged piece, don't pay much and keep in mind that it is merely a show piece.

Quite often, bubbles and other impurities will be visible in Carnival glass. This is nothing to be concerned with as it does not affect the value. This type of glass was made quickly and with low-quality ingredients—internal flaws are to be expected; and besides, these flaws are visible only when held up in a very strong light. In many hobbies, errors or freaks sell for much more than common specimens. This is true with Carnival collectors. In fact, many hobbyists enthusiastically snatch up any oddities which were misshapen or flawed during the manufacturing process. These are favored by some collectors not only because they are unique, but because they exemplify the difficulties faced by the glass makers.

Sometimes you will discover a piece of Carnival at a garage sale or a charity bazaar which will be very dirty from being stored away in an attic or basement. The late Carnival should be cleaned with extreme care, but the earlier pieces can be cleaned with less trepidation. The earlier pieces can be cleaned with powdered ammoniated cleaner dissolved in warm water. A soaking should remove most of the grime. If not, you could use a soft toothbrush dipped in the cleaning solution and lightly brush around the crevices of the designs. If you avoid hot water and any other strong cleaners, the iridescence will be unaffected. The late Carnival should be cleaned only in warm soapy water as the flashed-on surfaces do not hold up well to harsh or frequent washings.

If your glass is not particularly dirty, you will need only to clean it periodically with either a soap and water bath or a spray glass clearner. Be sure to dry each piece with a lint-free towel. The earlier pieces can be rubbed lightly in order to give them an extra shine.

The earlier pieces can be displayed where the sun hits them and not suffer any fading or cracking; but the late Carnival should be kept out of the sun as they can lose their coloring.

Although most advanced collectors do not advocate buying damaged pieces, don't hesitate to fix a piece that becomes damaged after you own it. It can still be used as a display piece if repaired. Special agents for gluing glass are available. Check your glass publications and local hobby and handyman shops. You'll need to devise a means of clamping the broken pieces together tightly so it mends properly. Try using elastic bands, rubber bands, and heavy string to secure the pieces while they dry.

Also, carefully consider the location you choose to store or display your Carnival. Try to keep them where they are in a light traffic area in your house. Placing them on a shelf that could be accidentally brushed by anyone who walks in is an invitation to trouble. An enclosed cabinet with special lighting is ideal—it provides a safe, clean place to keep your glass pieces where they are visible to any visitors.

THE MAJOR MANUFACTURERS

Until just recently, only four glass companies were credited with the majority of Carnival glass productions, but now two more manufacturers are recognized as being prolific producers of Carnival, also. At this time, the information as to how much these two companies produced and which pieces can be attributed to them is still not definitive.

The major manufacturers include: Northwood, Fenton, Millersburg, Imperial, Dugan/Diamond, and Westmoreland. Other glass manufacturers, such as U.S. Glass, Cambridge, and Indiana Glass and Consolidated, produced some Carnival, but they never made the extensive amount attributed to the six major glass companies.

The founder of the Northwood Glass Company, Harry Northwood, receives most of the credit for first developing a mechanized method for making iridized glass. Northwood worked in the glass industry starting in 1880 when he joined the venerable glass company of Hobbs, Brockunier and Company of Wheeling, West Virginia. After years of refining his skills, Northwood opened up his own company, locating it in Indiana, Pennsylvania. Three years later, he affiliated his company with National Glass, but broke off in 1901.

At that time, he bought the deserted plant of Hobbs, Brockunier and Company, and kept plants operating in Wheeling, West Virginia, and Indiana, Pennsylvania. In 1904, he leased the Indiana plant to Thomas E. Dugan and W.G. Minnemeyer, who had been the managers of the plant. They immediately changed the name to the Dugan Glass Company.

The date when Northwood first made iridized glass remains unknown, but he first sold iridized glass in 1908 after his former apprentice, Frank Fenton, had successfully made and sold iridized glass. It is believed that Fenton learned the secret of creating the imitation art glass while working with Northwood, and possibly learned something about making it inexpensively. Northwood's company went on to produce a large number of Carnival pieces up until the founder's death in 1921 just as the popularity for the new glass began to subside.

Frank Fenton began organizing the Fenton Glass Company in 1905, the year after leaving the Northwood Company. He located his operation at Martin's Ferry, Ohio. Starting in 1908, he introduced the first Carnival glass to the public which was received with great enthusiasm. Although the Fenton Company offered a full line of decorative wares, the Carnival glass dominated in production and popularity with almost 150 different patterns attributed to them. The company made an extensive line for 15 years.

The year after Fenton's Carnival glass had made such a splash, Frank Fenton's two brothers, John and Robert, left the company to start their own operation, the Millersburg Glass Company. Robert returned to the Fenton company in 1910.

At first, the Millersburg company produced crystal and Carnival, using the process developed by Frank Fenton. After many experiments, John Fenton developed a unique method for iridizing inexpensive glassware that is referred to as a radium finish. Shortly after offering this new glass, it was judged at a glass exposition as being the most outstanding entry at the exposition.

Although the glass was very popular and was shipped to Europe and Australia, the company was forced to declare bankruptcy in 1911, due to John Fenton's extravagance and financial mismanagement.

The Millersburg Company was bought by Samuel B. Fair, renamed the Radium Glass Company with John Fenton retained as Vice-president. Six months later, the company closed down, unable to recoup after the loss of reputation and skilled workers. Today, collectors covet any and all of the Millersburg pieces—fewer specimens were produced due to the company's short existence, and the radium process resulted in an appealing, brilliant Carnival.

The Dugan/Diamond Company produced Carnival glass as a subcontractor for Northwood, and finally, as an independent operation. Apparently, Dugan and Minnemeyer leased Northwood's Indiana, Pennsylvania plant from 1904 to 1913. It is still unclear as to how long the Dugan glass was produced for Northwood, but the plant's name was changed to Diamond in 1913, and kept making iridized glass until 1931 when it burned down. Some glass researchers feel that Dugan produced more than 80 different patterns; others feel this estimate to be too high.

The Imperial Glass Company of Bellaire, Ohio started with inexpensive pressed pattern tableware. Edward Muhleman, the founder, devised his own methods for producing iridized glass and sold these wares widely by 1910. By 1920, Imperial modified its iridized glass, making what is now referred to as late Carnival.

In the early 1960's, Imperial joined the nostalgic movement for making Carnival reproductions.

The Westmoreland Speciality Company of Grapeville, Pennsylvania issued more than 35 patterns and novelties, almost as many as Millersburg. The company began operating in 1889, creating novelties and packaging glass. It appears that Carnival was made from 1909 to 1912. The short duration may be related to the loss of their sales manager, Ed Minnemeyer in 1912. While working at Westmoreland, Ed Minnemeyer apparently was influenced by his brother, W.G. Minnemeyer, who was cofounder of the Dugan/Diamond Glass Company. As the sales manager, his views on glass were reflected in the lines which were chosen for production. It is not known if some Carnival was made after Ed Minnemeyer left to join his brother at Dugan. The Westmoreland pieces have often been attributed to Millersburg due to their similarities. The short period of production and its esthetic appeal should make these pieces highly sought-after in the near future.

Unfortunately, Northwood was the only Carnival glass manufacturer to emboss their glass with their mark, and only about half of their pieces bear one of the four marks. The marked pieces with an N inside two circles appear to have been made before 1910. Three other marks include: an N inside one circle, an N underlined, and a circle.

For their more recent reproductions, Imperial and Fenton both emboss the bases. Imperial places an I superimposed over a G on its remakes while Fenton's name is inside a circle.

ACANTHUS
Imperial

An iridescent molded glass, heavy and well detailed with a flowing swill design. The pattern has the look of a water whirlpool suddenly frozen. Most common in smoke and marigold, it can be found in a host of other colors.

	Current Price Range		Prior Year Average
Bowl, diameter 8″			
☐ purple	36.50	45.00	40.00
☐ green	36.50	45.00	40.00
☐ blue	36.50	45.00	40.00
☐ marigold	25.00	40.00	35.00
☐ smoke	48.00	60.00	50.00
Bowl, diameter 9½″			
☐ purple	36.50	45.00	40.00
☐ green	36.50	45.00	40.00
☐ blue	36.50	45.00	40.00
☐ marigold	25.00	40.00	30.00
☐ smoke	48.00	60.00	50.00
Hat Shape			
☐ marigold	22.00	35.00	24.00
☐ purple	25.00	40.00	28.00
☐ green	25.00	40.00	28.00
☐ blue	25.00	40.00	28.00
☐ amethyst	25.00	40.00	28.00
Plate, diameter 9½″			
☐ marigold	85.00	110.00	90.00
☐ purple	120.00	150.00	125.00
☐ green	120.00	150.00	125.00
☐ amethyst	120.00	150.00	125.00
☐ clear	125.00	155.00	125.00

ACORN
Fenton

A naturalistic pattern of three tiers of acorns in a round, flowing group. The branches have reliefed oak leaves. Known in the widest range of colors available to carnival glass.

	Current Price Range		Prior Year Average
Bowl, diameter 7″–8½″			
□ marigold	20.00	30.00	25.00
□ purple	28.50	50.00	30.00
□ green	28.50	50.00	30.00
□ blue	28.50	50.00	30.00
□ amethyst	28.50	50.00	30.00
□ peach opalescent	120.00	135.00	125.00
□ vaseline	110.00	125.00	115.00
□ red	225.00	325.00	260.00
Plate, diameter 9″			
□ marigold	120.00	135.00	125.00
□ purple	285.00	340.00	300.00
□ green	285.00	340.00	300.00
□ blue	285.00	340.00	300.00
□ amethyst	285.00	340.00	300.00

ACORN BURRS
Northwood

Oak leaves and acorns adorn the piece in an all-over design of finely ridged bark. The foliage is raised in relief giving the piece an interesting shape and a natural appearance. The mold is good and clean; the design is sharply engraved. Found in the full range of colors, the opalescent varieties are unusual and costly.

Acorn Burrs

	Current Price Range		Prior Year Average
Berry, bowl diameter 5″			
☐ marigold	17.00	22.00	18.00
☐ green	30.00	33.00	32.00
☐ amethyst	30.00	33.00	32.00
☐ ices	55.00	70.00	58.00
Berry, bowl diameter 10″			
☐ marigold	60.00	72.00	64.00
☐ green	115.00	120.00	117.50
☐ amethyst	115.00	120.00	117.50
☐ ices	295.00	320.00	310.00
Covered Butter			
☐ marigold	120.00	130.00	125.00
☐ green	190.00	210.00	200.00
☐ amethyst	190.00	210.00	200.00
☐ white	260.00	275.00	205.00
☐ ices	260.00	275.00	205.00
Spooner			
☐ marigold	60.00	90.00	65.00
☐ green	110.00	145.00	115.00
☐ amethyst	110.00	145.00	115.00
☐ white	150.00	200.00	160.00
☐ ice blue	150.00	200.00	160.00
☐ ice green	150.00	200.00	175.00
Tumbler			
☐ marigold	45.00	60.00	47.50
☐ green	40.00	60.00	50.00
☐ amethyst	40.00	60.00	50.00
☐ white	110.00	130.00	115.00
☐ ices	110.00	130.00	115.00
Pitcher			
☐ marigold	300.00	335.00	280.00
☐ green	360.00	460.00	375.00
☐ amethyst	350.00	450.00	375.00
☐ white	575.00	725.00	600.00
☐ ice blue	575.00	725.00	600.00
☐ ice green	575.00	725.00	600.00
Punch Bowl, two piece set			
☐ marigold	250.00	335.00	250.00
☐ purple	360.00	435.00	375.00
☐ blue	360.00	435.00	375.00
☐ green	360.00	435.00	375.00
☐ amethyst	360.00	435.00	375.00
☐ white	1000.00	1300.00	1100.00
☐ ice blue	1300.00	1600.00	1400.00
☐ ice green	1300.00	1600.00	1400.00
☐ aqua opalescent	8000.00	11,000.00	8600.00
Punch Cup			
☐ marigold	15.00	20.00	17.00

	Current Price Range		Prior Year Average
☐ purple	30.00	35.00	32.00
☐ blue	30.00	35.00	32.00
☐ green	20.00	40.00	30.00
☐ amethyst	40.00	60.00	50.00
☐ white	40.00	60.00	50.00
☐ ices	110.00	125.00	115.00
☐ aqua opalescent	240.00	260.00	250.00
Sugar Bowl			
☐ marigold	60.00	90.00	65.00
☐ purple	110.00	145.00	115.00
☐ blue	110.00	145.00	115.00
☐ green	110.00	145.00	115.00
☐ amethyst	110.00	145.00	115.00
☐ white	150.00	200.00	160.00
☐ ice blue	150.00	200.00	160.00
☐ ice green	150.00	200.00	160.00
Tumbler			
☐ marigold	35.00	50.00	40.00
☐ purple	50.00	60.00	55.00
☐ blue	50.00	60.00	55.00
☐ green	50.00	60.00	55.00
☐ amethyst	50.00	60.00	55.00
☐ white	90.00	120.00	95.00
☐ ice blue	90.00	120.00	95.00
☐ ice green	90.00	120.00	95.00

AFRICAN SHIELD

An oddly symmetrical design with a hand-crafted look highlights these pieces. Two ridged shields appear in a mirror image motif with connecting ribbons of long loops radiating out of an eight point star. The rims of the pieces are jagged in a saw tooth motif. The entire design rings of a medieval era, crude but distinctly well crafted. The facets make the wide range of colors available sharply iridescent and sparkling.

Toothpick Holder

☐ marigold	40.00	60.00	45.00

AGE HERALD
Fenton

An advertising item from the Birmingham newspaper, the plate or bowl depicts the Age Herald Building. The detail is good of the bricks and windows and the inscription is in flowing script writing. Only in amethyst, the color is rainbow-like. The rim is a modified saw tooth.

Bowl

☐ amethyst	875.00	975.00	925.00

Plate

☐ amethyst	950.00	1050.00	1000.00

AMARYLLIS
Northwood

A pattern of three full blown poppies and several buds adorn the expanded triangular shaped bowl. The colors are cobalt, marigold, and purple and the glass is nicely iridescent.

Compote	Current Price Range		Prior Year Average
☐ marigold	100.00	175.00	125.00
☐ green	80.00	100.00	90.00
☐ amethyst	75.00	120.00	90.00
Whimsey (flat top)			
☐ marigold	200.00	245.00	220.00
☐ purple	110.00	175.00	135.00

APPLE BLOSSOMS
Dugan

A prolific pattern, produced for mass-distribution at carnivals and fairs, Apple Blossom pieces can be readily obtained. The central flower is surrounded by four smaller blossoms in a circular pattern. The bowls and plates have an irregular shell shaped rim. The colors are marigold, peach and other pastels. Ocasionally the glass is white and the brighter colors are also in existence.

Bowl, diameter 7"-9"			
☐ marigold	20.00	25.00	22.00
☐ purple	25.00	30.00	27.00
☐ green	25.00	30.00	27.00
☐ blue	40.00	50.00	42.00
☐ amethyst	40.00	50.00	42.00
☐ white	60.00	80.00	65.00
☐ ices	60.00	80.00	65.00
Plate, diameter 8½"			
☐ marigold	45.00	57.50	48.50
☐ purple	65.00	85.00	70.00
☐ green	65.00	85.00	70.00
☐ blue	65.00	85.00	70.00
☐ amethyst	65.00	85.00	70.00
☐ white	95.00	120.00	105.00
☐ ice blue	95.00	120.00	105.00
☐ ice green	95.00	120.00	105.00

APPLE BLOSSOM TWIGS
Dugan

The exterior pattern on pieces with the Apple Blossom Twig design is the basket weave motif. The interior is a square of flowers and stems, sharply molded in relief, surrounding a central blossom. The edges of the piece are fluted and the colors are marigold, purple and peach.

Bowl, diameter 9"			
☐ marigold	27.00	53.00	30.00

	Current Price Range		Prior Year Average
☐ purple	38.00	42.00	40.00
☐ green	38.00	42.00	40.00
☐ blue	38.00	42.00	40.00
☐ amethyst	38.00	42.00	40.00
☐ white	80.00	90.00	85.00
☐ peach opalescent	190.00	230.00	200.00
Plate, diameter 9¼″			
☐ marigold	45.00	67.50	48.00
☐ purple	85.00	110.00	90.00
☐ green	85.00	110.00	90.00
☐ blue	85.00	110.00	90.00
☐ amethyst	85.00	110.00	90.00
☐ white	110.00	140.00	120.00
☐ peach opalescent	160.00	190.00	165.00

APPLE PANELS
Sowerly

An intaglio design of apples and leaves is set into the piece with ridged panels. Found only in sugar and creamers, the shape is simple with classic lines reminiscent of Greek urns. The glass is iridescent, colors usually green and marigold.

Creamer

☐ marigold	22.00	27.00	25.00
☐ purple	32.00	37.00	34.00
☐ blue	32.00	37.00	34.00
☐ green	32.00	37.00	34.00
Sugar Bowl			
☐ marigold	22.00	27.00	24.00
☐ purple	32.00	37.00	35.00
☐ blue	32.00	37.00	35.00
☐ green	32.00	37.00	35.00

APPLE TREE
Fenton

The all-over design of reliefed apples, twigs, and leaves is naturalistic and sharply formed. The pattern is busy and dominates the piece. The upper border is a stylized fence top. Found in water pitchers and goblets, the shape is rather typical but the top rim of the pitcher has an interesting, closely fluted design. The colors follow the wide range of bright tones.

Pitcher

☐ marigold	80.00	110.00	85.00
☐ green	200.00	275.00	215.00
☐ purple	200.00	275.00	215.00
☐ blue	200.00	275.00	215.00
☐ amethyst	200.00	275.00	215.00

	Current Price Range		Prior Year Average
☐ white	300.00	375.00	340.00
☐ ice blue	350.00	425.00	375.00
☐ ice green	350.00	425.00	375.00
Tumbler			
☐ marigold	17.50	22.00	18.00
☐ purple	32.00	37.00	34.00
☐ green	32.00	57.00	34.00
☐ blue	50.00	60.00	55.00
☐ amethyst	32.00	37.00	34.00
☐ white	40.00	50.00	45.00
☐ ices	50.00	60.00	52.00

ARCS
Imperial

Radiating half circles emanate from the circular medallion in a rather symmetrical design. Each group of arcs consists of four patterns, alternating bubbly glass with shiny smooth glass. The colors are amethyst and marigold, and less commonly green or smoke.

Bowl			
☐ marigold	18.00	22.00	19.00
☐ green	22.50	27.50	24.00
☐ amethyst	22.50	27.50	24.00
☐ smoke	45.00	55.00	50.00
Compote			
☐ marigold	18.00	22.00	19.00
☐ green	22.50	27.50	24.00
☐ amethyst	22.50	27.50	24.00
☐ smoke	32.00	42.00	36.00

Autumn Acorns

AUTUMN ACORNS
Fenton

Acorns, although only sparsely sprinkled over the piece are still the main attraction on these bowls and rare plates. The rim is bravely fluted in a vertical band, forming a frame for the sharply detailed leaves that are bunched around the interior.

Bowl	Current Price Range		Prior Year Average
☐ marigold	20.00	30.00	22.00
☐ purple	35.00	42.50	37.00
☐ green	35.00	42.50	37.00
☐ blue	35.00	42.50	37.00
☐ amethyst	35.00	42.50	37.00
Plate, diameter 7½″			
☐ marigold	40.00	55.00	42.00
☐ purple	60.00	75.00	62.00
☐ green	60.00	75.00	62.00
☐ blue	60.00	75.00	62.00
☐ amethyst	60.00	75.00	62.00

BANDED DIAMOND
Australian Manufacturer

The interest is in the shape of these pieces, created by a band of geometrically divided diamonds in an indented triangular form. The glass has a radium finish, the iridescence is mirror-like.

Tumbler			
☐ marigold	25.00	35.00	27.00
☐ purple	45.00	60.00	48.00
☐ green	45.00	60.00	48.00

Banded Diamond

	Current Price Range		Prior Year Average
☐ blue	45.00	60.00	48.00
☐ amethyst	55.00	75.00	60.00
Water Pitcher			
☐ marigold	160.00	185.00	162.00
☐ purple	350.00	400.00	360.00
☐ green	350.00	400.00	360.00
☐ blue	350.00	400.00	360.00
☐ amethyst	375.00	425.00	400.00

BANDED DRAPE
Fenton

A neat, centrally located band of ridging runs the diagonal on these water sets. The design is an enameled lily stemming from the engraved band, with its painted foliage below.

Tumbler			
☐ marigold	15.00	20.00	17.00
☐ blue	28.00	32.00	29.00
☐ amethyst	28.00	32.00	29.00
☐ ice green	35.00	41.00	37.00
☐ white	30.00	40.00	36.00
Water Pitcher			
☐ marigold	120.00	200.00	145.00
☐ blue	250.00	350.00	300.00
☐ amethyst	300.00	350.00	320.00
☐ ice green	350.00	450.00	390.00
☐ white	250.00	275.00	260.00

BASKET
Northwood

A popular pattern and shape for novelty carnival glass items, the design is woven ridges with a cane or wicker appearance. The baskets have sturdy, pudgy feet and rounded handles stemming from the upper rim. The wide range of colors include purple, cobalt, ice blue, green, aqua, white, and marigold.

Basket, flared top			
☐ marigold	47.50	52.00	49.00
☐ purple	65.00	75.00	67.00
☐ green	65.00	75.00	67.00
☐ ices	130.00	150.00	140.00
☐ aqua opalescent	110.00	120.00	115.00
☐ white	110.00	120.00	115.00
Basket, straight edge			
☐ marigold	48.50	55.00	50.00
☐ purple	65.00	70.00	67.00
☐ green	65.00	70.00	67.00
☐ ices	130.00	150.00	140.00

	Current Price Range		Prior Year Average
☐ aqua opalescent	110.00	120.00	115.00
☐ white	90.00	100.00	95.00

BASKETWEAVE
Dugan

   This popular pattern, woven wicker-like ridges, is used on many pieces that have different interior motifs as the exterior design. The pattern is in high relief with the three tiered ridges over and under bamboo-like poles. The sculpture catches the light and the iridescence is good. The colors are blue, peach, white, amethyst, and marigold.

Banana Bowl, silver footed

☐ ice green	140.00	150.00	145.00

Candy Dish

☐ marigold	22.50	30.00	25.00
☐ purple	32.50	40.00	35.00
☐ green	32.50	40.00	35.00
☐ blue	32.50	40.00	35.00
☐ amethyst	32.50	40.00	35.00
☐ white	50.00	65.00	35.00
☐ ice blue	60.00	70.00	55.00
☐ ice green	60.00	70.00	55.00

Hat Shape, plain or blackberry

☐ marigold	20.00	30.00	22.00
☐ purple	28.00	35.00	30.00
☐ green	28.00	35.00	30.00
☐ blue	28.00	35.00	30.00
☐ amethyst	28.00	55.00	30.00
☐ red	160.00	175.00	165.00

Vase

☐ white	50.00	60.00	52.00

BEADED
Northwood

   The combination of patterns connected by ribbons of beads makes this an interesting and beautiful design. The flowers, blooms, and daisies interconnected with the pearly beads are well balanced and tiered.

Bowl, diameter 8″

☐ marigold	30.00	35.00	32.00
☐ blue	37.00	42.00	40.00
☐ green	37.00	42.00	40.00
☐ purple	37.00	42.00	40.00

Bowl, diameter 9″

☐ marigold	30.00	35.00	32.00
☐ blue	37.00	42.00	35.00
☐ green	37.00	42.00	35.00
☐ purple	37.00	42.00	35.00

BEADED ACANTHUS
Imperial

The swirls of the Acanthus pattern are molded into an all-over diamond shape surrounded by pearly beads. It is found on a water pitcher with a modified scalloped rim and pronounced lip for pouring. The handle is attached in the upper middle of the piece, below the rim and above the base. Existing colors are marigold, smoke, green, and probably amethyst.

Milk Pitcher	Current Price Range		Prior Year Average
☐ marigold	40.00	55.00	42.00
☐ purple	120.00	135.00	125.00
☐ green	120.00	135.00	125.00
☐ blue	120.00	135.00	125.00
☐ amethyst	120.00	135.00	125.00
☐ smoke	60.00	75.00	62.00

BEADED BASKETS
Millersburg

A combination of the basket weaves adorn these novelty pieces, alternating a diagonally spliced weave with a parallel one. The mold work is sharp and the craftsmanship is excellent. The basket's handles rise vertically from a thumbprint rim and the base is plain and thick. The colors come in marigold, smoke, and purple; blue and green exist but are very unusual.

Basket			
☐ marigold	48.00	55.00	50.00
☐ blue	70.00	82.50	72.00
☐ green	70.00	85.00	72.00
☐ purple	60.00	70.00	62.00
☐ smoke	100.00	105.00	102.00

BEADED BULL'S EYE
Imperial

A delicate pattern seen on vases, the long, pulled look of the body is topped by a circular series of six "bull's eyes" or medallion-like imprints encapsulated by beads. The color is usually marigold, other tints are more rare.

Vase			
☐ marigold	20.00	30.00	25.00
☐ purple	32.50	37.50	35.00
☐ green	32.50	37.50	35.00
☐ blue	32.50	37.50	35.00
☐ amethyst	32.50	37.50	35.00

Beaded Cable

BEADED CABLE
Northwood

Found mostly on bowls, this is a very popular pattern with designers. Interlocking ribbons of bold glass move in a wavy design across the middle of the piece. The swirls are decorated with pearly beads of different sizes. The bowl's shape is interesting and different. It stands on pudgy round feet and the rim is rippled inward, almost closing the top. The colors are seen in the widest range of Northwood tints.

	Current Price Range		Prior Year Average
Candy Dish			
☐ marigold	22.50	30.00	25.00
☐ purple	32.50	40.00	35.00
☐ green	32.50	40.00	35.00
☐ blue	32.50	40.00	35.00
☐ amethyst	32.50	40.00	35.00
Rose Bowl			
☐ marigold	32.50	40.00	35.00
☐ purple	60.00	70.00	65.00
☐ green	45.00	60.00	50.00
☐ blue	70.00	80.00	75.00
☐ amethyst	50.00	62.50	52.00
☐ aqua opalescent	175.00	225.00	180.00
☐ ices	200.00	230.00	210.00

BEADED PANELS
Dugan

On a compote dish with a footed stem, perched on a wide, convex base, this pattern contains beads radiating upward to form the fluted edges. The stem is a series of larger beads seemingly welded together in three curved strands. Seen in marigold and peach opalescent, the iridescence is excellence.

	Current Price Range		Prior Year Average
Butter Dish			
☐ marigold	45.00	50.00	47.00
Compote			
☐ marigold	42.50	45.00	43.00
☐ purple	50.00	60.00	52.00
☐ green	50.00	60.00	52.00
☐ peach opalescence	65.00	75.00	70.00
Powder Jar			
☐ marigold	50.00	60.00	52.00

BEADED SHELL
Dugan

The shell motif is treated with strands of beads to form large nautical panels. The upper rims of the pieces are styled by the top of the shell and the base is a group of ridged shells pointing outward. The colors are blue, green, purple, marigold, and white.

Berry Bowl, footed, diameter 6½"			
☐ marigold	20.00	25.00	22.00
☐ purple	35.00	42.50	37.00
☐ green	35.00	42.50	37.00
☐ blue	35.00	42.50	37.00
☐ amethyst	35.00	42.50	37.00
Berry Bowl, footed, diameter 7½"			
☐ marigold	30.00	45.00	32.00
☐ purple	50.00	65.00	52.00
☐ green	50.00	65.00	52.00

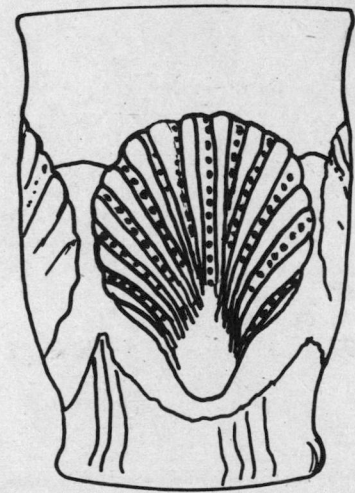

Beaded Shell

	Current Price Range		Prior Year Average
☐ blue	50.00	65.00	52.00
☐ amethyst	50.00	65.00	52.00
Berry Bowl, footed, diameter 8¾"			
☐ marigold	40.00	55.00	42.00
☐ purple	60.00	75.00	62.00
☐ green	60.00	75.00	62.00
☐ blue	60.00	75.00	62.00
☐ amethyst	60.00	75.00	62.00
Butter Dish, lidded			
☐ marigold	100.00	125.00	110.00
☐ purple	200.00	250.00	205.00
☐ green	200.00	250.00	205.00
☐ blue	200.00	250.00	205.00
☐ amethyst	200.00	250.00	205.00
Creamer, covered			
☐ marigold	55.00	65.00	60.00
☐ purple	55.00	75.00	60.00
☐ green	85.00	110.00	90.00
☐ blue	85.00	110.00	90.00
☐ amethyst	85.00	110.00	90.00
Mug			
☐ marigold	85.00	110.00	92.00
☐ purple	75.00	95.00	85.00
☐ green	60.00	75.00	62.00
☐ blue	60.00	75.00	62.00
☐ amethyst	60.00	75.00	62.00
☐ ice blue	300.00	375.00	310.00
☐ aqua opalescent	500.00	625.00	525.00
Water Pitcher			
☐ marigold	225.00	285.00	230.00
☐ purple	350.00	425.00	375.00
☐ green	350.00	425.00	375.00
☐ blue	350.00	425.00	375.00
☐ amethyst	350.00	425.00	375.00
Spooner			
☐ marigold	50.00	60.00	55.00
☐ purple	85.00	110.00	90.00
☐ green	85.00	110.00	90.00
☐ blue	85.00	110.00	90.00
☐ amethyst	85.00	110.00	90.00
Sugar Bowl, covered			
☐ marigold	40.00	50.00	42.00
☐ purple	85.00	110.00	90.00
☐ green	85.00	110.00	90.00
☐ blue	85.00	110.00	90.00
☐ amethyst	85.00	110.00	90.00
Tumbler			
☐ marigold	40.00	52.50	42.00

	Current Price Range		Prior Year Average
☐ purple	60.00	75.00	62.00
☐ green	60.00	75.00	62.00
☐ blue	60.00	75.00	62.00
☐ amethyst	60.00	75.00	62.00

BEADED SPEARS
Australian Manufacturer

A delicate and beautiful design of faceted beads ranging from perfectly round to geometrically angular. The pointed shape circles the piece with clear smooth glass between each pattern. The upper rim of the pitcher and most of the body of the water glass is a neat pattern of beads in parallel rows.

Tumbler

☐ marigold	70.00	85.00	72.00
☐ purple	85.00	95.00	87.00
☐ green	85.00	95.00	87.00
☐ blue	85.00	95.00	87.00
☐ amethyst	85.00	95.00	87.00

Water Pitcher

☐ marigold	165.00	185.00	170.00
☐ purple	225.00	250.00	240.00
☐ green	225.00	250.00	240.00
☐ blue	225.00	250.00	240.00
☐ amethyst	225.00	250.00	240.00

BELLS AND BEADS
Dugan

A finely decorated piece with swirls of bell-like flowers on stylized beaded stems. The shape has a swooping fluted edge, rolling up and down with the interior design. The colors are blue, amethyst, green, peach opalescent, and of course, marigold.

Compote

☐ marigold	12.50	18.00	14.00
☐ purple	22.50	27.50	24.00
☐ green	22.50	27.50	24.00
☐ blue	22.50	27.50	24.00
☐ amethyst	22.50	27.50	24.00

Plate, diameter 6¾"

☐ purple	40.00	50.00	42.00
☐ green	40.00	50.00	42.00
☐ blue	40.00	50.00	42.00
☐ amethyst	40.00	50.00	42.00

BIRDS AND CHERRIES
Fenton

Five birds rest among the cherry branches in the interior design of this pattern. The style is realistic and uses the techniques of high relief. The colors are amethyst, blue, green, vaseline, ice blue, and green.

	Current Price Range		Prior Year Average
Bon-Bon			
☐ amethyst	32.50	37.50	34.00
☐ blue	45.00	50.00	48.00
☐ green	45.00	52.50	49.00
☐ vaseline	60.00	75.00	62.00
☐ ices	65.00	80.00	68.00
Bowl, diameter 5″			
☐ amethyst	225.00	250.00	230.00
☐ blue	380.00	420.00	385.00
☐ green	380.00	420.00	385.00
☐ vaseline	400.00	435.00	410.00
☐ ices	425.00	450.00	430.00
Compote			
☐ amethyst	32.50	37.50	35.00
☐ blue	45.00	50.00	48.00
☐ green	45.00	52.50	48.00
☐ vaseline	60.00	75.00	63.00
☐ ices	75.00	82.00	77.00
Plate, diameter 9″			
☐ amethyst	450.00	600.00	460.00
☐ blue	600.00	750.00	625.00
☐ green	600.00	750.00	625.00
☐ vaseline	750.00	1000.00	775.00
☐ ices	800.00	1100.00	850.00
Plate, diameter 11½″			
☐ amethyst	450.00	600.00	475.00
☐ blue	600.00	750.00	625.00
☐ green	600.00	1000.00	625.00
☐ vaseline	750.00	1000.00	775.00
☐ ices	800.00	1100.00	850.00

BIRD WITH GRAPES
Dugan

A wall vase of triangular shape with an all-over matte finish and the design is smooth. The bird resembles a heron, with elongated legs and a stylized body. The grapes are of high relief and refract the light iridescently. It is marigold and amber.

Wall Vase			
☐ marigold	30.00	40.00	32.00

BLACKBERRY
Fenton

An interior pattern on many basket weave pieces, the blackberries appear on the bottom of the bowl. The colors are marigold, cobalt, amethyst, green, and red.

	Current Price Range		Prior Year Average
Bowl			
☐ marigold	25.00	30.00	27.00
☐ green	32.00	37.00	33.00
☐ amethyst	32.00	37.00	33.00
☐ cobalt	32.00	37.00	33.00
☐ green	32.00	37.00	33.00
Hat Shape			
☐ marigold	28.00	30.00	29.00
☐ green	32.50	35.00	33.00
☐ amethyst	32.50	35.00	33.00
☐ cobalt blue	32.50	35.00	33.00
☐ green	32.50	35.00	33.00
☐ ice blue	55.00	60.00	58.00
☐ red	170.00	190.00	175.00

BLACKBERRY
Northwood

An overall pattern of berries and foliage radiate out from a central medallion. The undecorated glass is clearer than most Carnival glass and usually marigold, purple, green, and white.

Compote			
☐ marigold	22.00	24.00	23.00
☐ purple	40.00	60.00	50.00
☐ green	32.00	34.00	33.00
Miniature Compote			
☐ marigold	42.00	45.00	43.00
☐ purple	63.00	70.00	64.00
☐ green	45.00	65.00	55.00
☐ white	275.00	300.00	280.00

BLACKBERRY BANDED
Fenton

Hat shaped pieces are decorated with this circular pattern of foliage and berries alternating with finely ridged vertical bands on the interior wall. The top band edge is ruffled in a large flowing rim. The colors are marigold or blue, unusual in green or smoke.

Hat Shape			
☐ marigold	17.50	21.00	20.00
☐ blue	25.00	30.00	26.00
☐ green	25.00	30.00	26.00
☐ smoke	25.00	30.00	26.00
☐ cobalt blue	30.00	35.00	32.00

Blackberry Block

BLACKBERRY BLOCK
Fenton

This piece reflects light like a mirror rainbow. The pattern is busy, in checkerboard squares up the side like a trellis with flowers and foliage. The shape is Victorian, the handle attached in the lower middle. The colors are marigold, green, and cobalt blue.

	Current Price Range		Prior Year Average
Pitcher			
☐ marigold	250.00	300.00	275.00
☐ purple	300.00	365.00	310.00
☐ green	300.00	365.00	310.00
☐ blue	300.00	365.00	310.00
☐ amethyst	300.00	365.00	310.00
☐ white	425.00	500.00	430.00
☐ cobalt blue	350.00	425.00	375.00
Tumbler			
☐ marigold	35.00	45.00	37.00
☐ purple	40.00	60.00	50.00
☐ green	60.00	72.50	62.00
☐ blue	60.00	72.50	62.00
☐ amethyst	60.00	72.50	62.00
☐ white	75.00	95.00	77.00
☐ cobalt blue	60.00	72.50	62.00

BLACKBERRY WREATH
Millersburg

The stems of the blackberry branch curve together to form a wreath, surrounding a bunch of fruit and foliage. The rim is gently scalloped and the base has a rayed star motif used on many Millersburg patterns. The exterior has wide panels of smooth glass and the colors range widely.

	Current Price Range		Prior Year Average
Bowl, diameter 5″			
☐ marigold	40.00	47.50	42.00
☐ purple	58.00	63.00	60.00
☐ blue	58.00	63.00	60.00
☐ green	58.00	63.00	60.00
Bowl, diameter 7″			
☐ marigold	63.00	70.00	65.00
☐ purple	78.00	83.00	79.00
☐ blue	78.00	83.00	79.00
☐ green	78.00	83.00	79.00
☐ ices	350.00	450.00	395.00
Bowl, diameter 9″			
☐ marigold	63.00	70.00	67.00
☐ purple	78.00	83.00	80.00
☐ blue	78.00	83.00	80.00
☐ green	78.00	83.00	80.00
☐ ices	350.00	450.00	360.00
Ice Cream Bowl, diameter 10″			
☐ marigold	90.00	120.00	95.00
☐ blue	135.00	140.00	188.00
☐ green	60.00	100.00	75.00
☐ purple	135.00	140.00	188.00
Plate, diameter 6″			
☐ marigold	460.00	490.00	470.00
☐ blue	575.00	625.00	580.00
☐ green	575.00	625.00	580.00
☐ purple	575.00	625.00	580.00
Plate, diameter 10″, very rare			
☐ marigold	1500.00	2000.00	1750.00
☐ blue	2000.00	2500.00	2200.00
☐ green	2000.00	2500.00	2200.00
☐ purple	2000.00	2500.00	2200.00
Spittoon Whimsey			
☐ marigold	700.00	900.00	750.00

BLOSSOMS AND BAND
Millersburg

The slender vases that are decorated with this pattern have long faceted prisms branded with thumbprints and a band of straightforward poppy-like flowers and foliage. The color is transparent with pinkish iridescence.

	Current Price Range		Prior Year Average
Berry Bowl, diameter 6½″			
☐ marigold	10.00	14.00	12.00
Berry Bowl, diameter 9″			
☐ marigold	20.00	25.00	22.00
Car Vase			
☐ marigold	20.00	25.00	22.00
☐ purple	37.00	43.00	40.00
☐ green	37.00	43.00	40.00
☐ blue	37.00	43.00	40.00
Lamp Shape			
☐ marigold	140.00	160.00	145.00
☐ purple	225.00	240.00	230.00
☐ green	225.00	240.00	230.00
☐ blue	225.00	240.00	230.00

BLUEBERRY
Fenton

A fabulously iridescent glass molded in a lovely design makes these pieces the favorite of many. It's gold mirror iridescence is sharp and clear, the pattern is simple and classical with a raised ridge band surrounding a bunch of pearly cherries on elongated stems. The colors are blue, marigold, and white.

Pitcher

☐ marigold	175.00	220.00	180.00
☐ purple	325.00	385.00	330.00
☐ green	325.00	385.00	330.00

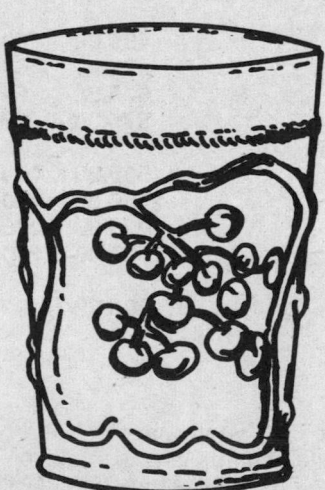

Blueberry

	Current Price Range		Prior Year Average
☐ blue	325.00	385.00	330.00
☐ amethyst	325.00	385.00	330.00
☐ white	335.00	380.00	350.00
Tumbler			
☐ marigold	27.50	35.00	30.00
☐ purple	37.50	45.00	40.00
☐ green	37.50	45.00	40.00
☐ blue	37.50	45.00	40.00
☐ amethyst	37.50	45.00	40.00
☐ white	42.00	48.00	44.00

BO PEEP
Fenton

This delightful pattern on children's ware is avidly collected because of its clear marigold color and pearly iridescence. The alphabet adorns the outside rim, surrounding Little Bo Peep with her staff and sheep.

Bowl			
☐ marigold	40.00	50.00	42.00
☐ purple	47.50	60.00	50.00
☐ green	47.50	60.00	50.00
☐ blue	47.50	60.00	50.00
☐ amethyst	47.50	60.00	50.00
Plate			
☐ marigold	65.00	85.00	68.00
☐ purple	70.00	90.00	72.00
☐ green	70.00	90.00	72.00
☐ blue	70.00	90.00	72.00
☐ amethyst	70.00	90.00	72.00
Mug			
☐ marigold	100.00	125.00	110.00
☐ purple	100.00	125.00	110.00
☐ green	100.00	125.00	110.00
☐ blue	100.00	125.00	110.00
☐ amethyst	100.00	125.00	110.00

BORDER PLANTS
Dugan

A shell motif is used to adorn this wildly patterned article. The rim follows up and down in a wavy scallop reminiscent of conch shells. The interior design resembles an eight point star fish. The colors are the darks as well as peach opalescent.

Bowl, flat			
☐ marigold	22.50	27.50	23.00
☐ purple	32.50	40.00	34.00
☐ green	32.50	40.00	34.00

	Current Price Range		Prior Year Average
☐ blue	32.50	40.00	34.00
☐ amethyst	32.50	40.00	34.00
☐ peach opalescent	60.00	80.00	70.00
Bowl, footed			
☐ marigold	22.50	27.50	23.00
☐ purple	32.50	40.00	34.00
☐ green	32.50	40.00	34.00
☐ blue	32.50	40.00	34.00
☐ amethyst	32.50	40.00	34.00
☐ peach opalescent	60.00	80.00	70.00

BOUTONNIER

This is an interesting and well conceived pattern of a central poinsettia-type flower folded in the middle, each petal emanating a stippled ray which extends to the rim.

Bon Bon			
☐ marigold	35.00	45.00	37.00
☐ purple	40.00	50.00	42.00
☐ green	40.00	50.00	42.00
☐ blue	80.00	100.00	82.00
☐ amethyst	40.00	50.00	43.00
Compote			
☐ marigold	35.00	45.00	37.00
☐ purple	40.00	50.00	42.00
☐ green	40.00	50.00	42.00
☐ blue	80.00	100.00	82.00
☐ amethyst	40.00	50.00	42.00

BROCADED ACORNS
Fostoria

These are beautifully decorated pieces, achieving the look of a satin party dress in glowing iridescence. The design is foliage and acorns, the edge is an interesting gilded rim.

Cake Tray			
☐ white	45.00	55.00	47.00
☐ ice green	57.50	70.00	60.00
☐ ice blue	57.50	70.00	60.00
Ice Bucket			
☐ white	27.50	35.00	30.00
☐ ice blue	40.00	50.00	42.00
☐ ice green	40.00	50.00	42.00

BROCADED DAFFODILS
Fostoria

Another satin-like pattern, these pieces have an intricate floral design of daffodils with foliage and stars. The motif is in low relief, the finish is perfection.

	Current Price Range		Prior Year Average
Bon Bon			
☐ ice blue	45.00	50.00	47.00
☐ ice green	45.00	50.00	47.00
☐ white	35.00	45.00	37.00
Cake Tray, handled			
☐ ice blue	70.00	80.00	73.00
☐ ice green	70.00	80.00	73.00
☐ white	60.00	70.00	62.00
Flower Set, three pieces			
☐ ice blue	100.00	120.00	110.00
☐ ice green	100.00	120.00	110.00
☐ white	90.00	110.00	92.00
Tray			
☐ ice blue	70.00	90.00	72.00
☐ ice green	70.00	90.00	72.00
☐ white	60.00	80.00	62.00
Vase			
☐ ice blue	60.00	80.00	62.00
☐ ice green	60.00	80.00	62.00
☐ white	60.00	80.00	62.00

BROKEN ARCHES
Imperial

This geometric pattern illustrates the best of the near cut achievements. The large rounded arches are divided into upwardly flairing squares, each with a thumbprint in the center. Alternating with tiny device is a half-arch decorated with rows of vertical beadwork.

Bowl, diameter 8″			
☐ purple	40.00	50.00	42.00
☐ green	40.00	50.00	42.00
☐ blue	40.00	50.00	42.00
☐ amethyst	40.00	50.00	42.00
Punch Bowl			
☐ marigold	130.00	170.00	135.00
☐ purple	325.00	375.00	335.00
☐ green	325.00	375.00	335.00
☐ blue	325.00	375.00	335.00
☐ amethyst	325.00	375.00	335.00
Punch Cup			
☐ marigold	13.00	17.00	14.00
☐ purple	22.50	27.50	25.00
☐ green	22.50	27.50	25.00
☐ blue	22.50	27.50	25.00
☐ amethyst	22.50	27.50	25.00

Butterfly Tumbler

BUTTERFLY TUMBLER
U.S. Glass

An exquisite design and all-over pattern helps to make this piece one of the most sought after pieces in the world of Carnival glass collecting. Beautifully molded butterflies are the central motif on the band of the tumbler with stipled diamonds and upside down leaves directly under the rim. The design on the base of the glass, matching the upper rim, is molded circles in relief.

	Current Price Range		Prior Year Average
Tumbler			
☐ marigold	4000.00	6000.00	4500.00

BUTTERFLY AND BERRY
Fenton

The butterfly and berry is a pleasing all-over pattern, the exterior being dominated with wide panels of each motif. The berries are in a triangular shape with the stem and leaves below; the butterfly is a large monarch in high relief. The rim is saw-toothed and the foot has a porcelain look. The colors are cobalt, green, white, and amethyst, unusual in red.

Berry Bowl, footed, diameter 8¼"			
☐ marigold	30.00	40.00	32.00
☐ purple	47.50	65.00	50.00
☐ green	47.50	65.00	50.00
☐ blue	47.50	65.00	50.00
☐ amethyst	47.50	65.00	50.00

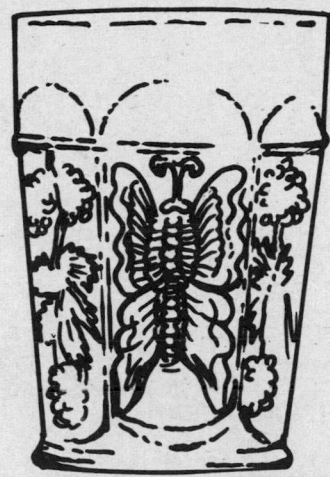

Butterfly and Berry

	Current Price Range		Prior Year Average
☐ red	60.00	75.00	57.00
Butter Dish, lidded			
☐ marigold	110.00	140.00	115.00
☐ purple	160.00	185.00	170.00
☐ green	160.00	185.00	170.00
☐ blue	160.00	185.00	170.00
☐ amethyst	160.00	185.00	170.00
☐ red	180.00	200.00	185.00
Cuspidor			
☐ purple	650.00	850.00	660.00
☐ green	650.00	850.00	660.00
☐ blue	650.00	850.00	660.00
☐ amethyst	650.00	850.00	660.00
☐ red	680.00	900.00	720.00
Hatpin Holder			
☐ marigold	500.00	650.00	525.00
☐ purple	500.00	650.00	525.00
☐ green	500.00	650.00	525.00
☐ blue	500.00	650.00	525.00
☐ amethyst	525.00	675.00	575.00
Pitcher			
☐ marigold	100.00	150.00	125.00
☐ purple	250.00	325.00	275.00
☐ green	425.00	500.00	450.00
☐ blue	250.00	325.00	275.00
☐ amethyst	250.00	325.00	275.00
Tumbler			
☐ marigold	18.00	23.00	20.00

	Current Price Range		Prior Year Average
☐ purple	40.00	55.00	43.00
☐ green	40.00	55.00	43.00
☐ blue	40.00	55.00	43.00
☐ amethyst	40.00	55.00	43.00
☐ red	60.00	80.00	65.00
Vase			
☐ marigold	22.50	27.50	23.00
☐ purple	32.50	40.00	33.00
☐ green	32.50	40.00	33.00
☐ blue	32.50	40.00	33.00
☐ amethyst	32.50	40.00	33.00
☐ red	130.00	175.00	140.00

BUTTERFLY AND FERN
Fenton

A mirror iridescent molded pattern that refracts light in all the hues. Wide butterfly panels decorate the long sides with wreaths of foliage around them. The rim is an unusual shape of irregular flutes, the handles are sunk low past the middle. Colors are gold, amethyst, cobalt, and green.

Pitcher

☐ marigold	180.00	215.00	190.00
☐ purple	375.00	450.00	400.00
☐ green	375.00	450.00	400.00
☐ blue	375.00	450.00	400.00
☐ amethyst	375.00	450.00	400.00

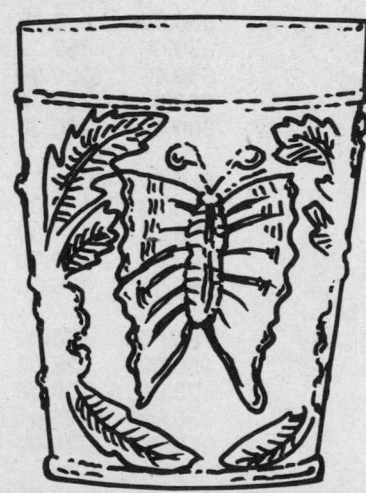

Butterfly and Fern

	Current Price Range		Prior Year Average

Tumbler
☐ marigold	30.00	40.00	32.00
☐ purple	35.00	47.50	37.00
☐ green	35.00	47.50	37.00
☐ blue	35.00	47.50	37.00
☐ amethyst	35.00	47.50	37.00

BUTTERFLY ORNAMENT
Fenton

A small giveaway for visitors to the Fenton factory, the novelty is shaped like a moth butterfly, simple in line with beaded decoration. The colors are marigold, ice blue, cobalt, white, green, and amethyst.

Butterfly Shaper
☐ marigold	45.00	60.00	50.00
☐ cobalt blue	60.00	80.00	65.00
☐ green	50.00	70.00	65.00
☐ amethyst	50.00	70.00	65.00
☐ white	50.00	70.00	65.00
☐ ices	65.00	80.00	70.00

BUTTERMILK GOBLET
Fenton

A very plain and simple glass on a long stem and pedestal foot. The mark that makes it Carnival glass is its glowing iridescence on the interior. Colors are in a wide range especially in green and amethyst.

Goblet
☐ marigold	37.00	43.00	40.00
☐ green	45.00	50.00	48.00
☐ purple	45.00	50.00	48.00
☐ blue	45.00	50.00	48.00
☐ amethyst	45.00	50.00	48.00

BUTTON AND DAISY

The top hat shape and the iridescent faceted glass make this novelty a top collectible. The pattern is all over, and almost resembles cut glass. The daisies are geometrically stylized and alternate with round medallion shapes. A wide range of colors is available.

Hat
☐ ice blue	70.00	80.00	68.00
☐ ice green	70.00	80.00	68.00
☐ aqua	62.00	70.00	64.00
☐ vaseline	62.00	70.00	64.00
☐ clambroth	62.00	70.00	64.00

Slipper
☐ ice blue	80.00	90.00	84.00

	Current Price Range		Prior Year Average
☐ ice green	80.00	90.00	84.00
☐ aqua	72.00	80.00	76.00
☐ vaseline	72.00	80.00	76.00
☐ clambroth	72.00	80.00	76.00

CANE
Imperial

The same cane pattern seen on chair backs and seats is repeated here with a molded band around the center of the bowl interior. The outer rim resembles a full blown blossom. The colors are clear, usually marigold, and seen in smoke and amethyst.

Bowl, diameter 7½"

☐ marigold	27.00	33.00	30.00
☐ smoke	35.00	40.00	38.00
☐ amethyst	35.00	40.00	38.00

Bowl, diameter 10"

☐ marigold	27.00	33.00	30.00
☐ smoke	35.00	40.00	36.00
☐ amethyst	35.00	40.00	36.00

Dish, oval

☐ marigold	27.00	30.00	29.00
☐ smoke	35.00	40.00	37.00
☐ amethyst	35.00	40.00	37.00

Wine Goblet

☐ marigold	22.00	27.00	24.00
☐ amethyst	22.00	27.00	24.00
☐ smoke	22.00	27.00	24.00

CAPTIVE ROSE
Fenton

An extremely busy pattern covers the entire surface of the shallow bowl. Tiers of diamonds, circles, and scales encircle a wide ribbon of carefully spaced roses in full bloom. The colors are cobalt, green, amethyst, smoke, and marigold.

Bowl, diameter 8⅝"

☐ marigold	22.50	27.50	24.00
☐ purple	32.50	40.00	34.00
☐ green	32.50	40.00	34.00
☐ blue	32.50	40.00	34.00
☐ amethyst	32.50	40.00	34.00
☐ aqua opalescent	150.00	200.00	175.00

Compote

☐ marigold	22.50	27.50	24.00
☐ purple	32.50	40.00	34.00
☐ green	50.00	60.00	55.00
☐ blue	32.50	40.00	34.00

	Current Price Range		Prior Year Average
☐ amethyst	32.50	40.00	34.00
Plate, diameter 6½"			
☐ marigold	27.50	35.00	29.00
☐ purple	35.00	47.50	38.00
☐ green	35.00	47.50	38.00
☐ blue	35.00	47.50	38.00
☐ amethyst	35.00	47.50	38.00
Plate, diameter 8"			
☐ marigold	45.00	60.00	48.00
☐ purple	70.00	95.00	72.00
☐ green	70.00	95.00	72.00
☐ blue	70.00	95.00	72.00
☐ amethyst	70.00	95.00	72.00

CAROLINA DOGWOOD
Fenton

A smooth opaque pattern with dogwood blossoms, suggested all over the piece. Six sprays radiate from the central single bloom. Colors are varied.

Bowl, diameter 8½"			
☐ amethyst	15.00	25.00	20.00
☐ green	40.00	45.00	42.00
☐ purple	40.00	45.00	42.00
☐ blue	40.00	45.00	42.00
☐ peach opalescent	75.00	100.00	78.00
Plate			
☐ marigold	27.50	35.00	30.00
☐ peach opalescent	40.00	50.00	42.00
☐ green	37.50	45.00	39.00
☐ purple	37.50	45.00	39.00
☐ blue	37.50	45.00	39.00
☐ amethyst	37.50	45.00	40.00

CATHEDRAL
Davisons of Gateshead

A beautiful pattern with many motifs that complement each other. The base is simple, but working upward, the first panel of ridged studs starts the busy design. Next going up is diamonds containing flowers, then a flying "V" form surrounding a crown motif. The colors are blue, amethyst and marigold.

Butter, diameter 10"			
☐ marigold	33.50	37.00	35.00
☐ amethyst	45.00	52.00	46.00
☐ blue	45.00	52.00	46.00
Butter Dish			
☐ marigold	135.00	150.00	140.00

	Current Price Range		Prior Year Average
Chalice, height 7″			
☐ marigold	67.50	80.00	70.00
☐ amethyst	75.00	90.00	80.00
☐ blue	75.00	90.00	80.00
Compote			
☐ marigold	38.50	42.00	40.00
☐ amethyst	45.00	55.00	47.00
☐ blue	45.00	55.00	47.00
Creamer			
☐ marigold	38.50	45.00	40.00
Epergne			
☐ marigold	435.00	450.00	440.00
Flower Holder			
☐ marigold	55.00	75.00	60.00

CATTAILS AND WATER LILIES
Fenton

A nice simple pattern highlights the iridescence on the many pieces of this design. Along the bottom is a hint of a basketweave forming the soil for the well molded cattails and the pretty water lilies. The glass is heavy and nearly opaque.

Berry Bowl, diameter 9″			
☐ marigold	22.50	27.50	24.00
☐ purple	32.50	40.00	34.00
☐ green	32.50	40.00	34.00
☐ blue	32.50	40.00	34.00
☐ amethyst	32.50	40.00	34.00
Bowl, oval, footed			
☐ marigold	60.00	75.00	62.00
☐ purple	85.00	110.00	90.00
☐ green	85.00	110.00	90.00
☐ blue	85.00	110.00	90.00
☐ amethyst	85.00	110.00	90.00
Creamer			
☐ marigold	30.00	40.00	32.00
☐ purple	30.00	40.00	32.00
☐ green	30.00	40.00	32.00
☐ blue	30.00	40.00	32.00
☐ amethyst	30.00	40.00	32.00
Spooner			
☐ marigold	30.00	40.00	32.00
☐ purple	30.00	40.00	32.00
☐ green	30.00	40.00	32.00
☐ blue	30.00	40.00	32.00
☐ amethyst	30.00	40.00	32.00
Toothpick			
☐ marigold	32.50	40.00	33.00

	Current Price Range		Prior Year Average
☐ purple	32.50	40.00	33.00
☐ blue	32.50	40.00	33.00
☐ green	32.50	40.00	33.00
☐ amethyst	32.50	40.00	33.00
Tumbler			
☐ marigold	12.50	18.00	15.00
☐ purple	27.50	35.00	28.00
☐ blue	27.50	35.00	28.00
☐ green	27.50	35.00	28.00
☐ amethyst	27.50	35.00	28.00
Water Pitcher			
☐ marigold	65.00	85.00	70.00
☐ purple	130.00	165.00	135.00
☐ green	130.00	165.00	135.00
☐ blue	130.00	165.00	135.00
☐ amethyst	140.00	175.00	145.00

CHATELAINE
Imperial

The design is tasteful and executed beautifully. The mold is sharp; the color vibrant and iridescent to the maximum degree. This water pitcher commands a staggering price when it changes hands, which is rarely. The central motif is a beaded cascade reminiscent of April showers. The wide panels just off center are made up of two angular medallions topped by a ridged fan design. The shape is classical, with a bullet rim and beaded handle. The detail is magnificent. Deep purple is the only existent color.

Pitcher
☐ marigold	1100.00	1450.00	1200.00

Chatelaine

	Current Price Range		Prior Year Average

Tumbler
☐ marigold	200.00	265.00	220.00

CHERRY
Millersburg

The cherries among intricate foliage form the exterior panels on many shapes of Millersburg products. The relief is high and the moldwork is excellent. The branches and leaves are stippled and the cherries are round, glossy glass. The iridescence is mirror-like and the colors found in the wide range.

Bowl, diameter 5½″
☐ marigold	18.00	23.00	20.00
☐ purple	26.00	32.00	28.00
☐ green	26.00	32.00	28.00
☐ blue	50.00	65.00	52.00
☐ amethyst	26.00	32.00	28.00

Bowl, diameter 9¼″
☐ marigold	40.00	60.00	45.00
☐ purple	60.00	75.00	62.00
☐ green	60.00	75.00	62.00
☐ blue	120.00	150.00	125.00
☐ amethyst	60.00	75.00	62.00

Butter Dish, lidded
☐ marigold	30.00	40.00	32.00
☐ purple	30.00	40.00	32.00
☐ green	30.00	40.00	32.00
☐ blue	30.00	40.00	32.00
☐ amethyst	30.00	40.00	32.00

Compote
☐ marigold	450.00	525.00	475.00
☐ purple	460.00	535.00	485.00
☐ green	460.00	535.00	485.00
☐ blue	850.00	1000.00	870.00
☐ amethyst	460.00	535.00	485.00

Creamer
☐ marigold	40.00	50.00	42.00
☐ purple	85.00	110.00	90.00
☐ green	85.00	110.00	90.00
☐ blue	85.00	110.00	90.00
☐ amethyst	85.00	110.00	90.00

Plate, diameter 6″
☐ marigold	225.00	275.00	232.00

Plate, diameter 6½″
☐ marigold	57.50	75.00	62.00
☐ purple	57.50	75.00	62.00
☐ green	57.50	75.00	62.00
☐ blue	57.50	75.00	62.00
☐ amethyst	57.50	75.00	62.00

	Current Price Range		Prior Year Average
Water Pitcher			
☐ marigold	375.00	450.00	400.00
☐ purple	575.00	675.00	600.00
☐ green	575.00	675.00	600.00
☐ blue	1200.00	1500.00	1400.00
☐ amethyst	575.00	675.00	600.00
Powder Jar			
☐ purple	425.00	500.00	450.00
☐ green	425.00	500.00	450.00
☐ blue	850.00	975.00	900.00
☐ amethyst	425.00	500.00	450.00
Pitcher			
☐ marigold	180.00	215.00	190.00
☐ purple	360.00	430.00	375.00
☐ green	360.00	430.00	375.00
☐ blue	360.00	430.00	375.00
☐ amethyst	360.00	430.00	375.00
Spooner			
☐ marigold	40.00	50.00	42.00
☐ purple	85.00	110.00	90.00
☐ green	85.00	110.00	90.00
☐ blue	85.00	110.00	90.00
☐ amethyst	85.00	110.00	90.00
Sugar Bowl			
☐ marigold	40.00	50.00	45.00
☐ purple	85.00	110.00	90.00
☐ green	85.00	110.00	90.00
☐ blue	85.00	110.00	90.00
☐ amethyst	85.00	110.00	90.00
Tumbler			
☐ marigold	100.00	130.00	120.00
☐ purple	130.00	160.00	140.00
☐ green	180.00	200.00	190.00
☐ blue	250.00	325.00	260.00
☐ amethyst	130.00	160.00	140.00

CHERRY
Northwood

A circular spray of cherries on branches adorns the interior of bowls, the fruit forming the center medallion. The rims of the bowls are ruffled in wide waves, the base can be flat or footed. The colors are often deep and dark but pieces can be found in almost all the Carnival colors.

Bowl, flat, diameter 6″			
☐ marigold	16.00	19.00	17.00
☐ purple	23.00	28.00	24.00
☐ green	23.00	28.00	24.00
☐ blue	23.00	28.00	24.00
☐ amethyst	23.00	28.00	24.00

Cherry

	Current Price Range		Prior Year Average
Bowl, footed, diameter 8″			
☐ marigold	25.00	32.00	24.00
☐ purple	37.00	45.00	38.00
☐ green	37.00	45.00	38.00
☐ blue	37.00	45.00	38.00
☐ amethyst	37.00	45.00	38.00
☐ peach opalescent	55.00	70.00	54.00
Bowl, flat, diameter 9″			
☐ marigold	25.00	32.00	28.00
☐ purple	50.00	65.00	51.00

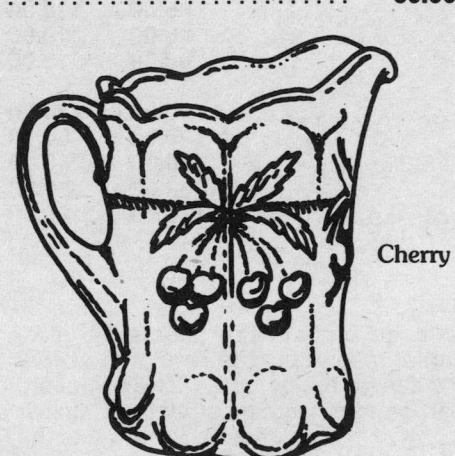

Cherry and Cable

CHERRY AND CABLE
Northwood

Architectural panels frame the background, with symmetrical bunches of cherries dropping from a stylized leave bow. This pattern repeats, giving the pieces an octagonal shape. The color is a deep marigold with opaque iridescence.

	Current Price Range		Prior Year Average
Berry Bowl, 9″			
☐ marigold	55.00	75.00	60.00
Butter Dish, lidded			
☐ marigold	175.00	225.00	180.00
Creamer			
☐ marigold	70.00	90.00	75.00
Pitcher			
☐ marigold	550.00	675.00	560.00
Sugar Bowl, lidded			
☐ marigold	100.00	125.00	120.00
Spooner			
☐ marigold	70.00	90.00	75.00
Tumbler			
☐ marigold	75.00	95.00	80.00

CHERRY CHAIN

The pattern is busy and covers the entire bowl, the central motif being five bunches of cherries connected by an ornate chain. One single bunch forms the central medallion with a hint of the intricate chain network used as a round frame. The colors are blue, green, white, marigold, and amethyst.

	Current Price Range		Prior Year Average
Bon Bon			
☐ marigold	20.00	25.00	22.00
☐ purple	25.00	30.00	27.00
☐ green	25.00	30.00	27.00
☐ blue	25.00	30.00	27.00
☐ white	35.00	40.00	27.00
☐ amethyst	35.00	40.00	27.00
Bowl, diameter, 8⅞″			
☐ marigold	30.00	40.00	35.00
☐ purple	40.00	55.00	45.00
☐ green	40.00	55.00	45.00
☐ blue	40.00	55.00	45.00
☐ amethyst	40.00	55.00	45.00
☐ white	42.50	55.00	45.00
☐ ice green	50.00	70.00	60.00
☐ ice blue	50.00	70.00	60.00

CHERRY CIRCLES
Fenton

An all-over pattern with dropping cherries in groups of three forming a wide central band, surrounded by wreaths of foliage. The central medallion is ornate fish scales; the outer rim has a houndstooth ridging. Colors are marigold, white, amethyst, green, and cobalt.

	Current Price Range		Prior Year Average
Bon Bon			
☐ marigold	30.00	40.00	35.00
☐ amethyst	25.00	30.00	27.00
☐ green	25.00	30.00	27.00
☐ cobalt blue	25.00	30.00	27.00
☐ red	235.00	250.00	240.00
Bowl			
☐ marigold	35.00	45.00	37.50
☐ amethyst	42.00	50.00	43.00
☐ green	42.00	50.00	43.00
☐ cobalt blue	42.00	50.00	43.00
☐ red	475.00	525.00	480.00
Compote			
☐ marigold	78.00	82.00	80.00
☐ amethyst	85.00	92.00	87.00
☐ green	85.00	92.00	87.00
☐ blue	85.00	92.00	87.00

CHERRY WREATH
Northwood

Butter Dish, lidded			
☐ marigold, cherries	65.00	85.00	70.00
☐ marigold, red cherries	75.00	97.50	80.00
☐ purple	135.00	170.00	140.00
☐ purple, red cherries	150.00	190.00	155.00
☐ green	135.00	170.00	140.00
☐ green, red cherries	150.00	190.00	160.00
☐ blue	135.00	170.00	140.00
☐ blue, red cherries	150.00	190.00	155.00
☐ amethyst	135.00	170.00	140.00
☐ amethyst, red cherries	150.00	190.00	160.00
☐ white	175.00	225.00	190.00
Creamer			
☐ marigold	50.00	60.00	52.00
☐ marigold, red cherries	57.50	70.00	56.00
☐ purple	85.00	110.00	86.00
☐ purple, red cherries	100.00	135.00	110.00
☐ green	85.00	110.00	86.00
☐ green, red cherries	100.00	135.00	110.00
☐ blue	85.00	110.00	86.00
☐ blue, red cherries	100.00	135.00	110.00
☐ amethyst	85.00	110.00	86.00

	Current Price Range		Prior Year Average
☐ amethyst, red cherries	100.00	135.00	110.00
☐ white	130.00	175.00	140.00
Cuspidor			
☐ marigold	875.00	1000.00	900.00
Pitcher			
☐ marigold	110.00	140.00	115.00
☐ purple	200.00	250.00	225.00
☐ green	200.00	250.00	225.00
☐ blue	200.00	250.00	225.00
☐ amethyst	200.00	250.00	225.00
☐ white	370.00	440.00	375.00
Sugar Bowl			
☐ marigold	50.00	60.00	55.00
☐ marigold, red cherries	57.50	70.00	60.00
☐ purple	85.00	110.00	80.00
☐ purple, red cherries	100.00	135.00	110.00
☐ green	85.00	110.00	90.00
☐ green, red cherries	100.00	135.00	110.00
☐ blue	85.00	110.00	90.00
☐ blue, red cherries	100.00	135.00	110.00
☐ amethyst	85.00	110.00	90.00
☐ amethyst, red cherries	100.00	135.00	110.00
Spooner			
☐ marigold	50.00	60.00	55.00
☐ marigold, red cherries	57.50	70.00	60.00
☐ purple ....,	85.00	110.00	90.00
☐ purple, red cherries	100.00	135.00	110.00
☐ green	85.00	110.00	90.00
☐ green, red cherries	100.00	135.00	110.00
☐ blue	85.00	110.00	90.00
☐ blue, red cherries	100.00	135.00	110.00
☐ amethyst	85.00	110.00	90.00
☐ amethyst, red cherries	100.00	135.00	110.00
☐ white	120.00	160.00	150.00
Tumbler			
☐ marigold	27.50	35.00	30.00
☐ purple	40.00	50.00	42.00
☐ green	40.00	50.00	42.00
☐ blue	40.00	50.00	42.00
☐ amethyst	40.00	50.00	42.00
☐ white	65.00	90.00	80.00

CHRYSANTHEMUM
Fenton

A busy pattern with boats, buildings, and blossoms covers the interior of the pieces. Four sprays of chrysanthemums form a cross that frames the scenes. The large bowls have ruffled rims and can be flat or footed. Colors are red, ice green, white, marigold, and blue.

	Current Price Range		Prior Year Average
Bowl, flat, diameter 10″			
☐ marigold	33.00	37.00	35.00
☐ blue	47.00	55.00	50.00
☐ green	47.00	55.00	50.00
☐ ice green	95.00	110.00	100.00
☐ white	95.00	110.00	100.00
☐ red	500.00	600.00	550.00
Bowl, footed, diameter 10″			
☐ marigold	70.00	90.00	80.00
☐ blue	47.00	55.00	50.00
☐ green	47.00	55.00	50.00
☐ ice green	95.00	110.00	100.00
☐ white	95.00	110.00	100.00
☐ red	500.00	600.00	525.00

CIRCLE SCROLL
Dugan

A rather modernistic pattern containing broad ridges all of a sudden swirled in an elongated circular motion. The top rim is gently scalloped. The colors are marigold, purple, and others.

Bowl			
☐ marigold	17.50	22.50	19.00
☐ purple	27.50	32.50	30.00
☐ green	27.50	32.50	30.00
☐ blue	27.50	32.50	30.00
☐ amethyst	27.50	32.50	30.00

Circle Scroll

	Current Price Range		Prior Year Average
Butter Dish, lidded			
☐ marigold	60.00	72.50	62.00
☐ purple	85.00	110.00	90.00
☐ green	85.00	110.00	90.00
☐ blue	85.00	110.00	90.00
☐ amethyst	85.00	110.00	90.00
Creamer			
☐ marigold	22.50	27.50	25.00
☐ purple	30.00	40.00	32.00
☐ green	30.00	40.00	32.00
☐ blue	30.00	40.00	32.00
☐ amethyst	30.00	40.00	32.00
Pitcher			
☐ marigold	360.00	450.00	375.00
☐ purple	540.00	675.00	560.00
☐ green	540.00	675.00	560.00
☐ blue	540.00	675.00	560.00
☐ amethyst	540.00	675.00	560.00
Spooner			
☐ marigold	22.50	27.50	24.00
☐ purple	30.00	40.00	32.00
☐ green	30.00	40.00	32.00
☐ blue	30.00	40.00	32.00
☐ amethyst	30.00	40.00	32.00
Sugar Bowl			
☐ marigold	22.50	27.50	25.00
☐ purple	30.00	40.00	32.00
☐ green	30.00	40.00	32.00
☐ blue	30.00	40.00	32.00
☐ amethyst	30.00	40.00	32.00
Tumbler			
☐ marigold	50.00	60.00	55.00
☐ purple	75.00	95.00	80.00
☐ green	75.00	95.00	80.00
☐ blue	75.00	95.00	80.00
☐ amethyst	75.00	95.00	80.00
Vase			
☐ marigold	27.50	32.50	30.00
☐ purple	40.00	50.00	42.00
☐ green	40.00	50.00	42.00
☐ blue	40.00	50.00	42.00
☐ amethyst	40.00	50.00	42.00

COIN DOT
Fenton

A straightforward pattern of radiating coin forms of various sizes adorns the entire piece. The round shapes are stippled and the wavy ruffled rim adds interest to the piece. Colors are marigold, cobalt, red, green, and amethyst.

	Current Price Range		Prior Year Average
Bowl, diameter 6″			
☐ marigold	22.00	26.00	24.00
☐ purple	32.00	40.00	38.00
☐ green	32.00	40.00	38.00
☐ blue	32.00	40.00	38.00
☐ aqua opalescent	160.00	190.00	165.00
Bowl, diameter 9″			
☐ marigold	22.50	27.50	24.00
☐ purple	30.00	40.00	32.00
☐ green	30.00	40.00	32.00
☐ blue	30.00	40.00	32.00
☐ amethyst	30.00	40.00	32.00
☐ aqua opalescent	200.00	250.00	225.00
Pitcher			
☐ marigold	110.00	160.00	115.00
Rose Bowl			
☐ marigold	25.00	30.00	26.00
☐ purple	32.50	40.00	34.00
☐ green	32.50	40.00	34.00
☐ blue	32.50	40.00	34.00
☐ amethyst	32.50	40.00	34.00
Tumbler			
☐ marigold	27.50	35.00	30.00
☐ purple	27.50	35.00	30.00
☐ green	27.50	35.00	30.00
☐ blue	27.50	35.00	30.00
☐ amethyst	27.50	35.00	30.00

COIN SPOT
Dugan

The exterior pattern of this wide rimmed compote is a series of stippled ovals alternating with flat panels. The rim is opened all the way with a wavy ruffled shape. The base is a plain disk while the stem is ornate with a balloon waist. Colors come in the wide range of Carnival iridescent.

Basket			
☐ marigold	42.00	50.00	46.00
☐ purple	48.00	60.00	49.00
☐ green	48.00	60.00	49.00
☐ blue	48.00	60.00	49.00
☐ amethyst	48.00	60.00	49.00

	Current Price Range		Prior Year Average
Bowl, diameter 8"			
☐ marigold	17.50	22.50	19.00
☐ purple	27.50	35.00	30.00
☐ green	27.50	35.00	30.00
☐ blue	27.50	35.00	30.00
☐ amethyst	27.50	35.00	30.00
Compote			
☐ marigold	20.00	24.00	22.00
☐ purple	32.00	40.00	34.00
☐ green	32.00	40.00	34.00
☐ blue	32.00	40.00	34.00
☐ amethyst	32.00	40.00	34.00
☐ peach opalescent	37.00	45.00	40.00
☐ white	45.00	57.50	46.00
☐ ice blue	45.00	57.50	46.00
☐ ice green	45.00	57.50	46.00

COLONIAL
Imperial

A simple pattern formed more by the shape of the piece than the decoration, the architectural style of the pieces is distinguished by wide arched panels. The colors are marigold, purple, and green with a clear iridescence.

	Current Price Range		Prior Year Average
Candlesticks			
☐ marigold	80.00	95.00	82.00
Creamer			
☐ marigold	32.00	37.00	34.00
☐ purple	38.00	42.00	40.00
☐ green	38.00	42.00	40.00
☐ red	85.00	95.00	57.00
Sugar Bowl			
☐ marigold	32.00	37.00	34.00
☐ purple	38.00	42.00	40.00
☐ green	38.00	42.00	40.00
☐ red	85.00	95.00	87.00
Tumbler			
☐ red	160.00	200.00	185.00
Vase			
☐ marigold	35.00	45.00	37.00
☐ purple	35.00	45.00	37.00
☐ green	35.00	45.00	37.00
Water Pitcher			
☐ red	2000.00	3000.00	2200.00

CONCORD
Fenton

A netting effect covers the entire surface of these pieces, providing the background for reliefed grapes and stippled leaves. The body is ruffled from the center and the rim is formed by a sawtooth edging. Colors come in blue, amethyst, amber, marigold, and green.

Bowl, diameter 8″	Current Price Range		Prior Year Average
☐ marigold	57.50	70.00	60.00
☐ purple	87.50	100.00	90.00
☐ green	87.50	100.00	90.00
☐ blue	87.50	100.00	90.00
☐ amethyst	87.50	100.00	90.00
Plate, diameter 9″			
☐ marigold	225.00	275.00	250.00
☐ purple	330.00	380.00	350.00
☐ green	330.00	380.00	350.00
☐ blue	330.00	380.00	350.00
☐ amethyst	330.00	380.00	350.00

CONSTELLATION
Dugan

The form of this compote is its unique feature—the rim is pulled from the center creating a ruffle and ridges. The exterior pattern is a stippled swirling design and the interior is glossy, smooth glass. Colors also come in white and peach opalescence.

Compote			
☐ marigold	20.00	25.00	22.00
☐ purple	30.00	38.00	32.00
☐ green	30.00	38.00	32.00
☐ red	30.00	38.00	32.00
☐ white	70.00	90.00	80.00
☐ ice blue	42.00	55.00	45.00
☐ ice green	42.00	55.00	45.00
☐ peach opalescence	37.00	45.00	40.00

CORAL
Fenton

A floral and fruitful wide band decorates the interior of this piece, radiating all the way out to the irregularly fluted edge. The glass is clear, and the colors are varied.

Bowl, diameter 8¾″			
☐ marigold	45.00	55.00	47.00
☐ purple	70.00	100.00	75.00
☐ green	70.00	100.00	75.00
☐ blue	70.00	100.00	75.00
☐ amethyst	70.00	100.00	75.00

	Current Price Range		Prior Year Average

Compote
☐ marigold	30.00	40.00	32.00
☐ purple	50.00	65.00	52.00
☐ green	50.00	65.00	52.00
☐ blue	50.00	65.00	52.00
☐ amethyst	50.00	65.00	52.00

Plate, diameter 8¼"
☐ marigold	160.00	200.00	180.00
☐ purple	275.00	325.00	300.00
☐ green	275.00	325.00	300.00
☐ blue	275.00	325.00	300.00

CORINTH
Dugan

Long, broad ridges, resembling reaching fingers form the shape of these pieces. The base is indented and the glass is smooth and glossy, iridized on the inside only. The colors are seen in green, marigold, amethyst, and peach opalescent.

Bowl, diameter 8"
☐ marigold	22.50	27.50	25.00
☐ aqua opalescent	85.00	110.00	89.00

Banana Plate
☐ marigold	27.00	34.00	30.00
☐ purple	40.00	50.00	42.00
☐ green	40.00	50.00	42.00
☐ blue	40.00	50.00	42.00
☐ amethyst	40.00	50.00	42.00
☐ peach opalescent	32.00	39.00	36.00

Vase, height 7"
☐ marigold	16.00	20.00	18.00
☐ purple	25.00	30.00	27.00
☐ green	25.00	30.00	27.00
☐ blue	25.00	30.00	27.00
☐ peach opalescent	28.00	35.00	30.00
☐ white	35.00	45.00	37.00
☐ ice blue	35.00	45.00	37.00
☐ ice green	35.00	45.00	37.00

CORN BOTTLE
Imperial

The corn husk motif is used again in this bottle with a cork stopper. The individual niblets are sharply molded, the glass has a mirror-like quality. Colors exist in green, amethyst, smoke, and marigold.

Bottle
☐ marigold	160.00	180.00	165.00

	Current Price Range		Prior Year Average
☐ green	190.00	210.00	200.00
☐ amethyst	190.00	210.00	200.00
☐ smoke	190.00	210.00	200.00

CORN VASE
Northwood

A half an ear of corn with its husk forms the body of this vase, stuck into a rather simple pedestal foot. The geometrical niblets are sharply molded, the lines on the husk are slightly stylized with wavy lines. The colors are ice green, ice blue, white, and marigold.

Vase

☐ marigold	450.00	500.00	475.00
☐ green	230.00	300.00	250.00
☐ blue	230.00	300.00	250.00
☐ white	200.00	250.00	225.00

Vase, pulled husk base

☐ purple	1500.00	3000.00	1600.00
☐ green	1500.00	3000.00	1600.00
☐ blue	1500.00	3000.00	1600.00

CORNUCOPIA

Candlestick

☐ marigold	70.00	90.00	74.00
☐ white	70.00	90.00	74.00

Vase, height 5″

☐ marigold	27.50	32.50	30.00
☐ white	50.00	60.00	55.00

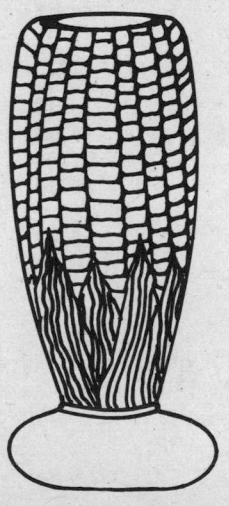

Corn Vase

COSMOS
Millersburg

One huge poppy-like flower adorns the entire surface of the interior of this piece, resolving in a rippled rim that follows the petal of the flower. The center of the flower, which is the base of the piece, is stippled in high relief. Green is the usual color with a sharp radium finish.

	Current Price Range		Prior Year Average
Bowl, diameter 8½"			
☐ marigold	32.50	40.00	36.00
☐ purple	50.00	60.00	52.00
☐ green	50.00	60.00	52.00
☐ blue	50.00	60.00	52.00
☐ amethyst	50.00	60.00	52.00
Compote			
☐ marigold	20.00	27.50	22.00
☐ purple	25.00	32.50	27.00
☐ green	25.00	32.50	27.00
☐ blue	25.00	32.50	27.00
☐ amethyst	25.00	32.50	27.00
Plate, diameter 9"			
☐ marigold	50.00	60.00	52.00
☐ purple	70.00	100.00	74.00
☐ green	70.00	100.00	74.00
☐ blue	70.00	100.00	74.00
☐ amethyst	70.00	100.00	74.00

Cosmos and Cane

COSMOS AND CANE
Imperial

A prolific pattern found on many pieces, the combination of different motifs complement each other in a satisfying, balanced way. Along the long side, ferns reach up toward a bond of flowers directly below the rim. The central long panel on each side is stylized crystals in a diagonal trellis-work. The colors are white marigold, and the ices.

Berry Bowl, diameter 8″	Current Price Range		Prior Year Average
☐ marigold	25.00	30.00	28.00
☐ white	60.00	70.00	65.00
Butter Dish, covered			
☐ marigold	100.00	125.00	110.00
☐ white	160.00	190.00	170.00
☐ ice blue	160.00	190.00	170.00
☐ ice green	160.00	190.00	170.00
Compote			
☐ marigold	60.00	75.00	62.00
☐ white	80.00	100.00	84.00
☐ ice blue	85.00	110.00	90.00
☐ ice green	85.00	110.00	90.00
Creamer			
☐ marigold	40.00	50.00	42.00
☐ white	75.00	100.00	77.00
☐ ice green	75.00	100.00	77.00
☐ ice blue	75.00	100.00	77.00
Pitcher			
☐ marigold	450.00	550.00	475.00
☐ white	675.00	825.00	700.00
Spooner			
☐ marigold	40.00	50.00	46.00
☐ white	75.00	100.00	80.00
☐ ice green	75.00	100.00	80.00
☐ ice blue	75.00	100.00	80.00
Sugar Bowl			
☐ marigold	40.00	50.00	42.00
☐ white	75.00	100.00	80.00
☐ ice green	75.00	100.00	80.00
☐ ice blue	75.00	100.00	80.00
Tumbler			
☐ marigold	45.00	55.00	47.00
☐ white	85.00	110.00	90.00

COUNTRY KITCHEN
Millersburg

An exterior pattern of faceted flowers, triangular ridges, and fan-like bands adorns these pieces. The emphasis is on the sharp molding that has the look of cut glass. The rims are saw toothed. The pieces are available in the wide range of Millersburg tints.

	Current Price Range		Prior Year Average
Bowl			
☐ marigold	40.00	50.00	42.00
☐ purple	60.00	75.00	64.00
☐ green	60.00	75.00	64.00
☐ blue	120.00	150.00	130.00
☐ amethyst	60.00	75.00	64.00
Butter Dish, lidded			
☐ marigold	250.00	320.00	275.00
☐ purple	275.00	325.00	300.00
☐ green	275.00	325.00	300.00
☐ blue	500.00	650.00	525.00
☐ amethyst	275.00	325.00	300.00
Creamer			
☐ marigold	125.00	165.00	140.00
☐ purple	160.00	195.00	170.00
☐ green	160.00	195.00	170.00
☐ blue	325.00	375.00	340.00
☐ amethyst	160.00	195.00	170.00
Cuspidor			
☐ purple	2500.00	2900.00	2600.00
☐ green	2500.00	2900.00	2600.00
☐ blue	2500.00	2900.00	2600.00
☐ amethyst	2500.00	2900.00	2600.00
Pitcher			
☐ marigold	700.00	900.00	725.00
☐ green	900.00	1250.00	925.00
☐ purple	900.00	1250.00	925.00
☐ amethyst	900.00	1250.00	925.00
Spittoon			
☐ purple	2200.00	2900.00	2250.00
☐ green	2200.00	2900.00	2250.00
☐ blue	4500.00	5500.00	4750.00
☐ amethyst	2200.00	2900.00	2250.00
Spooner			
☐ marigold	125.00	165.00	130.00
☐ purple	160.00	195.00	165.00
☐ green	160.00	195.00	165.00
☐ blue	325.00	375.00	350.00
☐ amethyst	160.00	195.00	165.00
Sugar Bowl			
☐ marigold	65.00	85.00	70.00
☐ purple	100.00	125.00	110.00
☐ blue	100.00	125.00	110.00
☐ green	100.00	125.00	110.00
☐ amethyst	100.00	125.00	110.00
Tumbler			
☐ marigold	75.00	95.00	90.00
☐ purple	100.00	130.00	110.00

	Current Price Range		Prior Year Average
☐ green	100.00	130.00	110.00
☐ amethyst	100.00	130.00	110.00
☐ blue	200.00	275.00	225.00

CRAB CLAW
Imperial

An interlocking pattern of various motifs, including beadwork, hexagons, diamonds, and crystals, give these pieces a cut glass appearance. The design is all over and busy with a saw toothed, scalloped rim. The color is seen in marigold, amethyst, and green.

Berry Bowl, diameter 5″

☐ marigold	13.50	18.00	15.00
☐ purple	22.50	30.00	24.00
☐ blue	22.50	30.00	24.00
☐ green	22.50	30.00	24.00
☐ amethyst	22.50	30.00	24.00

Berry Bowl, diameter 8¼″

☐ marigold	20.00	25.00	22.00
☐ purple	40.00	47.50	42.00
☐ green	40.00	47.50	42.00
☐ blue	40.00	47.50	42.00
☐ amethyst	40.00	47.50	42.00

Pitcher

☐ marigold	200.00	250.00	225.00

Tumbler

☐ marigold	75.00	85.00	77.00

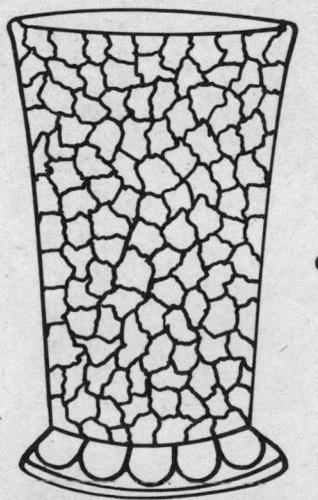

Crackle

CRACKLE

A flat pattern resembling cracked ice, this design is found on thousands of pieces and on all shapes of Carnival glass. It was mass produced for premium giveaways so it is easy to find on the collector's market. The colors run the full gamut of carnival tints.

	Current Price Range		Prior Year Average
Auto Vase			
☐ marigold	14.00	16.00	15.00
☐ purple	18.00	22.00	19.00
☐ green	18.00	22.00	19.00
☐ blue	18.00	22.00	19.00
Berry Bowl, diameter 5″			
☐ marigold	7.00	10.00	8.00
☐ purple	11.00	13.00	12.00
☐ green	11.00	13.00	12.00
☐ blue	11.00	13.00	12.00
Candy Jar, covered			
☐ marigold	22.50	27.00	25.00
Plate, diameter 7″			
☐ marigold	20.00	25.00	22.00
Punch Bowl			
☐ marigold	40.00	60.00	42.00
☐ purple	60.00	70.00	63.00
☐ blue	60.00	70.00	63.00
☐ green	60.00	70.00	63.00
Punch Cup			
☐ marigold	12.00	16.00	14.00
☐ purple	12.00	16.00	14.00
☐ blue	12.00	16.00	14.00
☐ green	12.00	16.00	14.00
Tumbler			
☐ marigold	9.00	11.50	10.00
☐ purple	9.00	11.50	10.00
☐ blue	9.00	11.50	10.00
☐ green	9.00	11.50	10.00

CURVED STARS

A ruffled edge turned upward distinguishes this pattern. The cut glass band just under the rim is reminiscent of country kitchen and other styles utilizing sunburst and curved spear motifs. The colors that exist are blue, green, marigold, and purple.

Bowl, diameter 4½″			
☐ marigold	22.50	27.50	24.00
☐ purple	30.00	40.00	32.00
☐ green	30.00	40.00	32.00
☐ blue	30.00	40.00	32.00
☐ amethyst	30.00	40.00	32.00
Candlestick			
☐ marigold	32.50	40.00	35.00

	Current Price Range		Prior Year Average
Chalice			
☐ marigold	110.00	120.00	115.00
☐ purple	140.00	160.00	145.00
☐ green	140.00	160.00	145.00
☐ blue	140.00	160.00	145.00
☐ amethyst	140.00	160.00	145.00
Creamer			
☐ marigold	40.00	45.00	42.00
☐ purple	65.00	70.00	67.00
☐ green	65.00	70.00	67.00
☐ blue	65.00	70.00	67.00
☐ amethyst	65.00	70.00	67.00
Flower Holder			
☐ marigold	69.00	80.00	75.00

CUT COSMOS

An arched panel is the background for this floral and vine design. The moldwork is sharp and the pattern is pleasing because of its restraint. The rim and edge are plain, smooth glass. The color is marigold and is iridescent.

Pitcher			
☐ marigold	200.00	250.00	225.00
Tumbler			
☐ marigold	40.00	50.00	42.00

CUT CRYSTAL
Australian Manufacturer

A cut glass fan design is the central motif on this pattern. There are a variety of motifs interwoven including beadwork ferns and stylized flowers. The upper rim is ruffled and the base is a simple pedestal and stem. Marigold is the usual color.

Carafe			
☐ marigold	130.00	160.00	135.00

CUT FLOWERS
Jenkins

An intaglio design of dogwood flowers on stalks and leaves. The pattern is deeply cut into the long straight sides and the stang shapes that make up the ridge band catch the light beneath the surface. Colors are generally pastel or smoke.

Vase			
☐ marigold	32.00	38.00	34.00
☐ peach	32.00	38.00	34.00
☐ smoke	39.00	52.00	40.00

CUT OVALS
Fenton

Incised ovals in intaglio and iridescence make the pattern on these pieces. They follow a geometrical line up the long sides of the piece, creating a simple and classic effect. The colors are clearly iridescent.

Candlesticks, pair	Current Price Range		Prior Year Average
☐ marigold	32.00	38.00	34.00
☐ ice blue	40.00	45.00	42.00
☐ ice green	40.00	45.00	42.00

DAISY
Fenton

Sprays of daisies on stems jet diagonally around a central bloom. The edge is a small saw tooth and bowls are usually footed. Blue is the color most often found.

Bon Bon			
☐ marigold	30.00	35.00	32.00
☐ purple	45.00	55.00	47.00
☐ blue	45.00	55.00	47.00

DAISY AND DRAPE
Northwood

An interesting downward swooping motion accompanies this pattern, as the curved ridges radiate toward the footed base. The upper band directly under the moderately ruffled rim is a line of realistic daisies. The colors range widely and the iridescence is excellent.

Butter Dish			
☐ marigold	85.00	110.00	86.00
☐ purple	130.00	170.00	135.00
☐ green	130.00	170.00	135.00
☐ blue	130.00	170.00	135.00
☐ aqua opalescent	175.00	225.00	180.00
☐ white	100.00	125.00	110.00

DAISY AND PLUME
Northwood

Wide panels of relief daisies with beadwork framing them tightly on either side of this main motif. Long branches with fern-like leaves appear to grow from the base. The upper rim is pushed inward in a tight flute. The colors are generally in the dark iridescent range, yet white is known to exist.

Candy Dish			
☐ marigold	17.00	23.00	18.00
☐ purple	28.00	35.00	30.00
☐ green	28.00	35.00	30.00

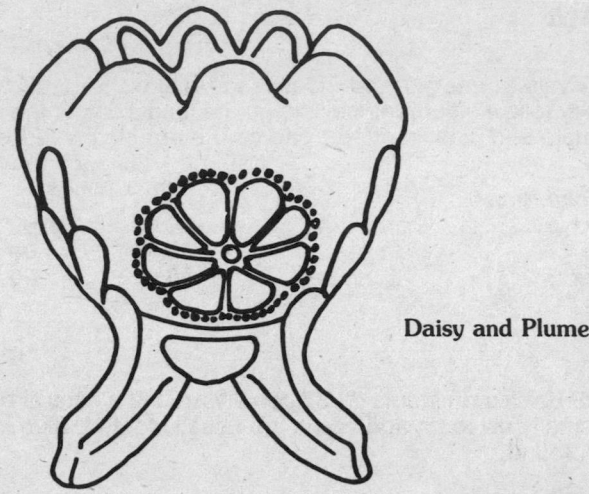

Daisy and Plume

	Current Price Range		Prior Year Average
☐ blue	28.00	35.00	30.00
☐ amethyst	28.00	35.00	30.00
☐ white	50.00	60.00	52.00
☐ ice green	60.00	70.00	62.00
Rose Bowl			
☐ marigold	25.00	32.00	26.00
☐ purple	40.00	50.00	42.00
☐ green	55.00	75.00	60.00
☐ blue	40.00	50.00	42.00
☐ amethyst	40.00	50.00	42.00
☐ white	50.00	70.00	52.00
☐ ice blue	60.00	80.00	52.00
☐ ice green	60.00	80.00	52.00

DAISY BASKET
Imperial

The elongated basket shape with a tall upright handle is decorated with plenty of blossoms, covering the piece. The relief is high and the mold work is sharp. It was produced in marigold and smoke only.

Basket

☐ marigold	20.00	25.00	22.00
☐ smoke	30.00	35.00	32.00

DAISY BLOCK ROWBOAT
Sowerby

A stationary piece for holding writing implements, the interior pattern is vertical ridges in a simple line meeting at the pointed bottom of the piece. The exterior motif is blocked daisies formed by beadwork. The overall shape suggest a thin rowboat such as the kind in which men court their ladies. Marigold, amethyst, and aqua are the colors.

	Current Price Range		Prior Year Average
Rowboat			
☐ marigold	200.00	255.00	240.00
☐ amethyst	200.00	255.00	240.00
☐ aqua opalescent	295.00	350.00	315.00

DAISY CUT BELL
Fenton

The diamond trellis frames the well-molded daisy in this close design. The pattern is intaglio with the sharp cuts all achieved under the surface of the bell. The handle of the bell is decorated with curvy beadwork. Marigold is the standard color.

Bell			
☐ marigold	465.00	500.00	475.00

DAISY SQUARES
Millersburg

Squared-off flowers of low relief form an all-over pattern on these rose bowls and compotes. The upper edge is tightly banded, then flared out in an irregular ruffle. The base is plain for the ornateness of the body. The colors green, amethyst, gold, and marigold.

Rose Bowl			
☐ marigold	225.00	250.00	230.00
☐ green	225.00	250.00	230.00
☐ amethyst	225.00	250.00	230.00
☐ gold	250.00	300.00	260.00

DAISY WREATH
Fenton

A star-shaped bowl is decorated with shadowy, elongated daisies in a circular design. The central medallion is a lone large daisy overlapping the circular base. The color marigold is over milk glass.

Bowl, diameter 9″			
☐ marigold	22.00	28.00	24.00
☐ ice blue	80.00	110.00	82.00
☐ aqua opalescent	180.00	220.00	190.00

Dandelion

DANDELION
Northwood

A bold dandelion and foliage is the central motif on pieces of this design. The background is an arched panel design with a plain upper rim. The colors come in the full range of Northwood colors.

	Current Price Range		Prior Year Average
Mug, lettered			
☐ marigold	200.00	250.00	225.00
☐ purple	250.00	300.00	275.00
☐ green	130.00	160.00	135.00
☐ blue	130.00	160.00	135.00
☐ amethyst	130.00	160.00	135.00
Mug, unlettered			
☐ marigold	60.00	75.00	65.00
☐ purple	75.00	100.00	80.00
☐ green	75.00	100.00	80.00
☐ blue	75.00	100.00	80.00
☐ aqua opalescent	250.00	300.00	275.00
Pitcher, tankard style			
☐ marigold	140.00	165.00	145.00
☐ purple	325.00	375.00	330.00
☐ green	325.00	375.00	330.00
☐ blue	325.00	375.00	330.00
☐ ice blue	500.00	600.00	525.00
☐ ice green	500.00	600.00	525.00
Tumbler			
☐ marigold	40.00	50.00	45.00
☐ purple	50.00	70.00	60.00
☐ green	60.00	75.00	62.00
☐ blue	60.00	75.00	62.00

	Current Price Range		Prior Year Average
☐ ice blue	120.00	160.00	110.00
☐ ice green	120.00	160.00	110.00

DEEP GRAPE COMPOTE
Millersburg

Bunches of grapes tumble in high relief covering the convex exterior with the fruit and foliage. The stem is plain with base and the upper rim gently scalloped. It was produced in marigold, amethyst, vaseline, and green.

Bowl, diameter 8″

☐ marigold	650.00	750.00	675.00
☐ vaseline	2500.00	3000.00	2600.00
☐ green	950.00	1100.00	100.00
☐ amethyst	950.00	1100.00	1000.00

DIAMOND AND DAISY CUT
Jenkins

A swirling band of diamond trellising sweeps along the tops of these pieces. Just below, shadowy daisies decorate the rest of the body. The shape is modern and clean with long lines. Colors are amethyst and marigold.

Compote

☐ marigold	32.00	38.00	36.00

Pitcher

☐ marigold	135.00	170.00	140.00

Pitcher

☐ marigold	37.00	44.00	40.00

DIAMOND AND SUNBURST
Fenton

A diamond frame surrounds a stylized sunburst, closely decorating the entire body of the piece. The shape of the different pieces is angular to follow the geometric shapes of the diamonds. Colors come in purple, amber, green, and marigold.

Bowl

☐ marigold	22.00	28.00	24.00

Decanter

☐ marigold	36.00	45.00	38.00

Pitcher

☐ marigold	110.00	140.00	115.00
☐ purple	160.00	190.00	170.00
☐ green	160.00	190.00	170.00
☐ blue	160.00	190.00	170.00

	Current Price Range		Prior Year Average
Tumbler			
☐ marigold	22.00	27.00	23.00
☐ purple	30.00	38.00	32.00
☐ green	30.00	38.00	32.00
☐ blue	30.00	38.00	32.00
Wine Glass			
☐ marigold	14.00	17.00	16.00
☐ purple	40.00	50.00	42.00
☐ green	40.00	50.00	42.00
☐ blue	40.00	50.00	42.00
☐ ice blue	90.00	120.00	92.00

DIAMOND LACE
Heisey

A stained glass window is what this pattern is reminiscent of, with its long diagonal frameworks containing a starburst. The pattern never ceases, with filler work of tiny beads and stippling. The only colors seem to be marigold, purple, and white.

Berry Bowl, diameter 5½″			
☐ marigold	15.00	20.00	16.00
☐ purple	20.00	25.00	22.00
☐ white	18.00	23.00	21.00
Berry Bowl, diameter 9″			
☐ marigold	30.00	45.00	32.00
☐ purple	65.00	75.00	70.00
☐ white	60.00	70.00	68.00
Fruit Bowl, diameter 10½″			
☐ marigold	35.00	70.00	38.00
☐ purple	65.00	85.00	70.00
☐ white	60.00	80.00	65.00

Diamond Lace

	Current Price Range		Prior Year Average
Pitcher			
☐ marigold	160.00	200.00	175.00
☐ purple	160.00	250.00	200.00
☐ white	300.00	325.00	370.00
Tumbler			
☐ marigold	30.00	38.00	32.00
☐ purple	50.00	60.00	55.00
☐ white	50.00	60.00	55.00

DIAMOND POINT COLUMNS
Imperial

The columns are made of rows of diamond shaped checkerboard alternating with plain panels. It is a classically simple design, well-balanced and pleasing to the eye. The pattern is known in a wide range of shapes.

Butter Dish			
☐ marigold	55.00	75.00	60.00
Compote			
☐ marigold	14.00	17.00	16.00
Creamer			
☐ marigold	20.00	25.00	22.00
Plate			
☐ marigold	22.00	28.00	24.00
Spooner			
☐ marigold	27.00	34.00	30.00
Sugar Bowl			
☐ marigold	27.00	34.00	30.00
Vase			
☐ marigold	22.00	28.00	24.00

DIAMOND POINT BASKETS
Fenton

The basket is of an odd shape, the handles reaching out of the sides with a heavy triangularly fluted rim. The pattern is diamond-shaped trelliswork with a fill-in pattern of large beadwork. The colors are purple, cobalt, and blue.

Basket			
☐ marigold	270.00	290.00	275.00
☐ purple	325.00	375.00	330.00
☐ cobalt blue	325.00	375.00	330.00
☐ blue	325.00	375.00	330.00

DIAMOND RING
Imperial

This design is highlighted by swirling ribbons surrounding diamond prisms in an all-over pattern. The interior is smooth, glossy iridescent glass reaching out in a widely ruffled rim. The color are smoke and marigold.

	Current Price Range		Prior Year Average
Berry Bowl, diameter 4½"			
☐ marigold	15.00	20.00	16.00
☐ smoke	20.00	30.00	22.00
Berry Bowl, diameter 9"			
☐ marigold	25.00	28.00	26.00
☐ smoke	32.00	40.00	34.00
Fruit Bowl, diameter 8½"			
☐ marigold	23.00	29.00	24.00
☐ smoke	55.00	60.00	58.00

DIAMONDS
Millersburg

Stretched out diamonds in an all-over pattern take up most of the exterior space on pieces with this style. The shapes are outlined in beadwork and the upper rim is resolved by gentle scalloping. The colors are deeply iridescent and come in a full range of colors.

Pitcher			
☐ purple	500.00	700.00	550.00
☐ green	500.00	700.00	550.00
☐ blue	900.00	1250.00	950.00
☐ amethyst	500.00	700.00	550.00
Tumbler			
☐ marigold	27.00	35.00	30.00
☐ purple	33.00	40.00	35.00
☐ green	33.00	40.00	35.00
☐ blue	65.00	80.00	70.00

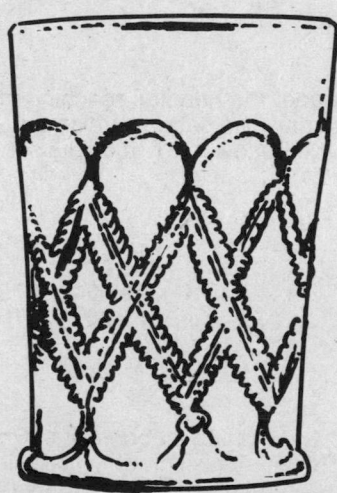

Diamonds

	Current Price Range		Prior Year Average
☐ amethyst	33.00	40.00	35.00
☐ white	45.00	60.00	47.00
☐ ice blue	55.00	65.00	55.00
☐ ice green	55.00	65.00	55.00

DOGWOOD SPRAYS
Dugan

The circular wreath of dogwood blossoms and foliage gracefully decorates the interior of these wide bowls with ruffled edges. The rest of the piece is glossy smooth glass found in purple and peach.

Banana Bowl

☐ purple	80.00	100.00	90.00
☐ green	80.00	100.00	90.00
☐ blue	80.00	100.00	90.00
☐ ice blue	100.00	125.00	110.00
☐ ice green	100.00	125.00	110.00
☐ peach	100.00	125.00	100.00

Bowl, footed, diameter 9″

☐ marigold	30.00	40.00	35.00
☐ purple	40.00	50.00	45.00
☐ green	40.00	50.00	45.00
☐ blue	40.00	50.00	45.00
☐ peach opalescent	60.00	80.00	65.00

Compote

☐ marigold	18.00	23.00	20.00
☐ purple	27.00	34.00	30.00
☐ green	27.00	34.00	30.00
☐ blue	27.00	34.00	30.00
☐ peach opalescent	40.00	60.00	50.00

DOLPHINS COMPOTE
Millersburg

Very playful dolphins pause on the exterior of this stately compote, forming the pedestal feet. They seem to be smiling, perhaps because they support one of the finest crafted bowls in Carnival glass. The interior, with the Rosalind pattern, is molded beautifully with stippled glass alternating in arches with smooth, glossy glass. The edge is gently scalloped.

Compote

☐ marigold	400.00	500.00	425.00
☐ purple	450.00	550.00	475.00
☐ green	450.00	550.00	475.00
☐ blue	800.00	1000.00	850.00
☐ amethyst	450.00	550.00	475.00

DOUBLE DOLPHIN
Fenton

Large expanses of smooth, almost opaque glass, shimmeringly iridescent, make up this pattern. The decoration is the scaled dolphins flipping
their tails in high relief off the side of the glass. It is a simple but effective
pattern, an excellent addition to any collection.

	Current Price Range		Prior Year Average
Bowl, diameter 8″			
☐ purple	55.00	70.00	58.00
☐ green	55.00	70.00	58.00
☐ blue	55.00	70.00	58.00
☐ ice blue	70.00	90.00	72.00
☐ ice green	70.00	90.00	72.00
Cake Plate			
☐ purple	27.00	34.00	28.00
☐ green	27.00	34.00	28.00
☐ blue	27.00	34.00	28.00
☐ ice blue	35.00	45.00	37.00
☐ ice green	35.00	45.00	37.00
Candlesticks, pair			
☐ ice blue	45.00	55.00	48.00
☐ ice green	45.00	55.00	48.00
Compote			
☐ ice blue	55.00	60.00	58.00
☐ ice green	55.00	60.00	58.00
☐ topaz	55.00	60.00	58.00
☐ tangerine	55.00	60.00	58.00

DOUBLE FAN

Fan motifs made up of cut glass ridges form an all-over design on this
beautiful tumbler. The glass is heavy and clear, the iridescence is excellent.

Tumbler			
☐ marigold	85.00	100.00	90.00

DOUBLE DUTCH
Imperial

A lovely, well-perspected scene graces the wide plate. The huge oak
in the foreground gives way to water and a windmill in the rear. The rim
is ridged and resolves in a gently fluted edge. Commonly in marigold, also
in amethyst, green, and smoke.

Bowl, diameter 9″			
☐ marigold	22.00	28.00	24.00
☐ purple	36.00	44.00	38.00
☐ green	36.00	44.00	38.00
☐ blue	36.00	44.00	38.00
☐ smoke	36.00	44.00	38.00
☐ amethyst	36.00	44.00	38.00

DOUBLE LOOP
Northwood

A fine simple pattern of straight-sided arches with a slightly bulging waist adorn these creamers and sugars. The colors are green, purple, aqua opalescent, and cobalt.

Chalice	Current Price Range		Prior Year Average
☐ marigold	30.00	37.00	32.00
☐ purple	45.00	50.00	47.00
☐ green	45.00	50.00	47.00
☐ blue	45.00	50.00	47.00
☐ peach opalescent	170.00	200.00	175.00

DOUBLE SCROLL
Imperial

A spindled design with scrolls of glass attached on the side make this otherwise plain pattern distinctive. The glass is heavy and the iridescence is mirror-like and refractory. The colors are green, smoke, amethyst, and marigold.

Bowl, dome foot			
☐ marigold	22.00	25.00	23.00
☐ purple	35.00	40.00	37.00
☐ green	35.00	40.00	37.00
☐ blue	35.00	40.00	37.00
Bowl, oval			
☐ marigold	17.00	22.00	18.00
☐ purple	32.00	38.00	33.00
☐ green	32.00	38.00	33.00
☐ blue	32.00	38.00	33.00
Candlestick			
☐ marigold	17.00	22.00	18.00
☐ purple	32.00	38.00	33.00
☐ green	32.00	38.00	33.00
☐ blue	32.00	38.00	33.00

DOUBLE STAR

An excellent, well-balanced geometrical design is formed by various motifs working well together. The central design is a small radiating star with whirling etchings framed with deep slashes in a broken arch. The bottom band is reminiscent of Egyptian markings with a rising sun and small stars surrounding. The colors are marigold, amethyst and, most commonly, green.

Pitcher			
☐ marigold	325.00	400.00	330.00
☐ purple	250.00	325.00	275.00
☐ green	250.00	325.00	275.00
☐ blue	250.00	325.00	275.00

	Current Price Range		Prior Year Average
Tumbler			
☐ marigold	45.00	60.00	47.00
☐ purple	40.00	55.00	42.00
☐ green	40.00	55.00	42.00
☐ blue	40.00	55.00	42.00

DOUBLE-STEM ROSE
Dugan

The fully-bloomed rose is the center point of this pattern, in high relief surrounded by petals. The midband is made up of a half dozen small roses and the rest of the piece remains smooth and clear. The colors are lavender, blue, green, amethyst, and marigold.

	Current Price Range		Prior Year Average
Bowl			
☐ marigold	27.00	34.00	28.00
☐ purple	40.00	50.00	42.00
☐ green	40.00	50.00	42.00
☐ blue	40.00	50.00	42.00
☐ peach opalescent	85.00	95.00	90.00
Plate, dome foot			
☐ peach opalescent	150.00	175.00	160.00

DRAGON AND LOTUS
Fenton

Another busy, overall pattern with a distinctly oriental flair. The center point resembles a dragonfly while the outer wide bands contain alternating portraits of winged dragons and beautiful lotus blossoms. All of the colors are represented in this prolific pattern by Fenton.

	Current Price Range		Prior Year Average
Bowl			
☐ marigold	40.00	50.00	45.00
☐ purple	50.00	60.00	55.00
☐ green	50.00	60.00	55.00
☐ blue	50.00	60.00	55.00
☐ peach opalescent	220.00	280.00	225.00
Plate			
☐ marigold	180.00	230.00	185.00
☐ purple	260.00	350.00	270.00
☐ green	260.00	350.00	270.00
☐ blue	260.00	350.00	270.00
☐ amethyst	260.00	350.00	270.00

DRAGON AND STRAWBERRY

Stylized dragons with wings in attack position alternate with groups of three innocent strawberries. The oriental influence is evident especially in the central starburst which contains the dragon on a bed of the berries.

	Current Price Range		Prior Year Average
Bowl, flat, diameter 9″			
☐ marigold	160.00	190.00	170.00

	Current Price Range		Prior Year Average
☐ purple	235.00	310.00	240.00
☐ green	235.00	310.00	240.00
☐ blue	235.00	310.00	240.00
☐ amethyst	235.00	310.00	240.00
Bowl, footed, diameter 9″			
☐ marigold	130.00	160.00	140.00
☐ purple	190.00	230.00	200.00
☐ green	190.00	230.00	200.00
☐ blue	190.00	230.00	200.00
☐ amethyst	190.00	230.00	200.00
Dragonfly Lamp Shade			
☐ white	600.00	700.00	615.00

DRAPERY
Northwood

The lines are graceful and full bodied, reminding one of the draperies in a Renaissance painting. It is an all-over design, and the shape is a flowing swirl itself. The colors come in the widest range of Carnival tints.

Candy Dish			
☐ marigold	22.00	28.00	24.00
☐ purple	30.00	40.00	32.00
☐ green	30.00	40.00	32.00
☐ blue	30.00	40.00	32.00
☐ amethyst	30.00	40.00	32.00
☐ white	42.00	55.00	44.00
☐ ice blue	50.00	60.00	54.00
☐ ice green	50.00	60.00	54.00
Pitcher			
☐ ice blue	270.00	345.00	295.00
☐ ice green	270.00	345.00	295.00
☐ white	250.00	325.00	275.00
Rose Bowl			
☐ marigold	35.00	45.00	27.00
☐ purple	80.00	100.00	90.00
☐ green	46.00	54.00	48.00
☐ blue	46.00	54.00	48.00
☐ amethyst	46.00	54.00	48.00
☐ white	70.00	85.00	72.00
☐ ice blue	90.00	110.00	95.00
☐ ice green	90.00	110.00	95.00
☐ aqua opalescent	175.00	220.00	180.00
Tumbler			
☐ white	60.00	75.00	62.00
☐ ice green	70.00	90.00	77.00
☐ ice blue	70.00	90.00	77.00
Vase			
☐ marigold	18.00	24.00	20.00
☐ purple	35.00	42.00	37.00

	Current Price Range		Prior Year Average
☐ green	35.00	42.00	37.00
☐ blue	35.00	42.00	37.00
☐ peach opalescent	38.00	45.00	40.00
☐ marigold	40.00	55.00	42.00
☐ white	38.00	45.00	40.00
☐ ice blue	45.00	55.00	50.00
☐ ice green	45.00	55.00	50.00

ELKS
Fenton

An Elks Club souvenir from three years, 1910, 1911 and 1914, the pattern is dominated by an inscribed ribbon. The outer band is of stippled stars with three tiered flutes to follow the design. The color is spectacular with a rich cobalt and green with a radium luster.

Bowl, Detroit

☐ purple	325.00	375.00	330.00
☐ green	325.00	375.00	330.00
☐ blue	325.00	375.00	330.00
☐ amethyst	325.00	375.00	330.00

Bowl, Parkersburg

☐ purple	350.00	425.00	360.00
☐ green	350.00	425.00	360.00
☐ blue	350.00	425.00	360.00
☐ amethyst	350.00	425.00	360.00

EMBROIDERED MUMS
Northwood

The central medallion is a giant multi-petaled mum framed by a thin band of wreathed foliage. The design continues out with a number of various sized flowers and a lot of branches and leaves. It is an overall pattern, reaching out to its saw toothed rim. Known in many Northwood colors.

Bowl, diameter 9"

☐ marigold	45.00	55.00	50.00
☐ purple	70.00	80.00	75.00
☐ green	36.00	46.00	37.00
☐ blue	36.00	46.00	37.00
☐ amethyst	36.00	46.00	37.00
☐ white	60.00	75.00	62.00
☐ ice blue	70.00	90.00	70.00
☐ ice green	70.00	90.00	70.00
☐ aqua opalescent	200.00	250.00	225.00

Plate

☐ marigold	50.00	65.00	52.00
☐ purple	85.00	110.00	90.00
☐ green	85.00	110.00	90.00

	Current Price Range		Prior Year Average
☐ blue	85.00	110.00	90.00
☐ amethyst	85.00	110.00	90.00
☐ white	70.00	90.00	72.00
☐ ice blue	80.00	90.00	84.00
☐ ice green	80.00	90.00	84.00

FAN
Northwood

A classic design and a restrained, tasteful pattern make these pieces quite distinctive. The bottom decoration is a tightly scrolled and flowered relief design, the rest of the body remains smooth and glossy. The upper rim is gently and widely ruffled, mimicking the tiny waves of scrolls that rise occasionally off the edge. Peach, purple, and marigold are existing colors.

Sauce Dish
☐ marigold	18.00	22.00	20.00
☐ purple	32.00	38.00	36.00
☐ green	32.00	38.00	36.00
☐ blue	32.00	38.00	36.00
☐ amethyst	32.00	38.00	36.00
☐ peach	32.00	38.00	36.00

FAN-TAILS
Fenton

Motion is the key to what this pattern attempts to achieve by radiating six well-detailed peacock feathers out from the center. The mold work is good and the rest of the body is glossy and smooth. Colors are white, green, cobalt, and marigold.

Bowl, diameter 5"
☐ marigold	20.00	25.00	22.00
☐ cobalt	31.00	34.00	32.00
☐ green	31.00	34.00	32.00
☐ white	27.00	30.00	28.00

Bowl, diameter 9"
☐ marigold	50.00	57.00	52.00
☐ cobalt	63.00	67.00	65.00
☐ green	63.00	67.00	65.00
☐ white	60.00	65.00	63.00

Compote
☐ marigold	32.00	35.00	34.00
☐ cobalt	42.00	47.00	43.00
☐ green	42.00	47.00	43.00
☐ white	40.00	45.00	41.00

Fanciful

FANCIFUL
Dugan

The basketweave exterior pattern complements the busy, overall design of the interior. Many motifs are used, dominated by foliage and beadwork. The colors are peach, white, purple, and marigold.

	Current Price Range		Prior Year Average
Bowl, diameter 7½″			
☐ marigold	40.00	50.00	42.00
☐ purple	60.00	75.00	62.00
☐ green	60.00	75.00	62.00
☐ blue	60.00	75.00	62.00
☐ amethyst	60.00	75.00	62.00
☐ white	80.00	110.00	82.00
☐ ice blue	90.00	120.00	100.00
☐ ice green	90.00	120.00	100.00
Bowl, diameter 8½″			
☐ marigold	25.00	32.00	21.00
☐ purple	40.00	55.00	42.00
☐ green	40.00	55.00	42.00
☐ blue	40.00	55.00	42.00
☐ amethyst	40.00	55.00	42.00
☐ white	57.50	70.00	60.00
☐ ice blue	57.50	70.00	60.00
☐ ice green	57.50	70.00	60.00
☐ peach opalescent	70.00	90.00	80.00
Plate			
☐ marigold	80.00	100.00	82.00
☐ purple	100.00	130.00	110.00
☐ green	100.00	130.00	110.00
☐ blue	100.00	130.00	110.00
☐ amethyst	100.00	130.00	110.00

	Current Price Range		Prior Year Average

Plate, diameter 8″
☐ marigold	70.00	85.00	72.00
☐ purple	90.00	110.00	95.00
☐ green	90.00	110.00	95.00
☐ blue	90.00	110.00	95.00
☐ amethyst	90.00	110.00	95.00
☐ white	160.00	190.00	165.00
☐ ice blue	170.00	200.00	165.00
☐ ice green	170.00	200.00	165.00

FARMYARD

Two large roosters are placed back to back in a symmetrical way. The mold work is sharp and the detail on the chickens Is excellent, and in high relief. Known to be one of the ten wonders of Carnival, these pieces rarely trade hands, and when they do, the price is sky high. Green, purple, peach opalescent, and amethyst are the colors.

Bowl, circular, diameter 10″
☐ green	2000.00	3000.00	2200.00
☐ purple	1500.00	2500.00	1775.00
☐ peach	7500.00	8200.00	7800.00
☐ amethyst	8200.00	8500.00	8400.00

Bowl, squared, diameter 10″
☐ green	2200.00	3000.00	2300.00
☐ purple	2200.00	3000.00	2300.00
☐ peach	7500.00	8200.00	7700.00
☐ amethyst	8200.00	8500.00	8400.00

FASHION
Imperial

A common and prolific pattern, pieces with this design were mass produced throughout the Carnival era. It's an overall style, with diamonds, jewels, sunburst, and beadwork swirls filled in with stippling. The colors are green, purple, smoke, and marigold.

Creamer
☐ marigold	32.00	38.00	33.00
☐ purple	85.00	110.00	90.00
☐ green	85.00	110.00	90.00
☐ blue	85.00	110.00	90.00
☐ amethyst	85.00	110.00	90.00

Pitcher
☐ marigold	85.00	110.00	90.00
☐ purple	600.00	700.00	650.00
☐ green	650.00	850.00	675.00
☐ blue	650.00	850.00	675.00
☐ amethyst	650.00	850.00	675.00

Punch Bowl
☐ marigold	90.00	110.00	100.00

	Current Price Range		Prior Year Average
☐ purple	500.00	600.00	525.00
☐ green	500.00	600.00	525.00
☐ blue	500.00	600.00	525.00
☐ amethyst	500.00	600.00	525.00
Punch Cup			
☐ marigold	14.00	17.00	15.00
☐ purple	40.00	50.00	42.00
☐ green	40.00	50.00	42.00
☐ blue	40.00	50.00	42.00
☐ amethyst	40.00	50.00	42.00
Spooner			
☐ marigold	32.00	38.00	34.00
☐ purple	85.00	110.00	87.00
☐ green	85.00	110.00	87.00
☐ blue	85.00	110.00	87.00
☐ amethyst	85.00	110.00	87.00
Sugar Bowl			
☐ marigold	32.00	38.00	34.00
☐ purple	85.00	110.00	87.00
☐ green	85.00	110.00	87.00
☐ blue	85.00	110.00	87.00
☐ amethyst	85.00	110.00	87.00
Tumbler			
☐ marigold	18.00	23.00	17.00
☐ purple	100.00	145.00	110.00
☐ green	100.00	145.00	110.00
☐ blue	100.00	145.00	110.00
☐ amethyst	100.00	145.00	110.00

FEATHERED
Fenton

The interior design is a twirl of feathered scrolls in a wide upper band. The central medallion is four plumes radiating out from the connection in the middle. Blue, green, marigold, and amethyst are the existing colors.

Berry Bowl, diameter 9″

☐ marigold	45.00	60.00	55.00
☐ purple	50.00	60.00	52.00
☐ green	50.00	60.00	52.00
☐ blue	50.00	60.00	52.00
☐ amethyst	50.00	60.00	52.00
Bowl, diameter 5″			
☐ marigold	14.00	18.00	15.00
☐ purple	22.00	28.00	27.00
☐ green	22.00	28.00	27.00
☐ blue	40.00	55.00	42.00
☐ amethyst	22.00	28.00	27.00
Fruit Bowl, diameter 10½″			
☐ marigold	26.00	34.00	27.00

	Current Price Range		Prior Year Average
☐ purple	40.00	50.00	42.00
☐ green	40.00	50.00	42.00
☐ blue	40.00	50.00	42.00
☐ amethyst	40.00	50.00	42.00
Plate			
☐ marigold	60.00	70.00	62.00
☐ purple	110.00	140.00	115.00
☐ green	110.00	140.00	115.00
☐ blue	225.00	290.00	230.00
☐ amethyst	110.00	140.00	115.00

FENTONIA
Fenton

A pleasing diamond on the diagonal pattern, Fentonia is made up of beadwork frames surrounding scales and stitchery. Marigold, amethyst, green, and blue are the standard colors.

Berry Bowl, diameter 9″			
☐ marigold	32.00	37.00	34.00
☐ purple	60.00	75.00	62.00
☐ green	60.00	75.00	62.00
☐ blue	60.00	75.00	62.00
☐ amethyst	60.00	75.00	62.00
Butter Dish, lidded			
☐ marigold	100.00	125.00	110.00
☐ purple	135.00	170.00	140.00
☐ green	135.00	170.00	140.00
☐ blue	135.00	170.00	140.00
☐ amethyst	135.00	170.00	140.00
Creamer			
☐ marigold	60.00	80.00	70.00
☐ purple	75.00	100.00	80.00
☐ green	75.00	100.00	80.00
☐ blue	75.00	100.00	80.00
☐ amethyst	75.00	100.00	80.00
Pitcher			
☐ marigold	325.00	375.00	330.00
☐ purple	450.00	550.00	460.00
☐ green	450.00	550.00	460.00
☐ blue	450.00	550.00	460.00
☐ amethyst	450.00	550.00	460.00
Spooner			
☐ marigold	40.00	50.00	42.00
☐ purple	75.00	100.00	80.00
☐ green	75.00	100.00	80.00
☐ blue	75.00	100.00	80.00
☐ amethyst	75.00	100.00	80.00
Sugar Bowl			
☐ marigold	40.00	50.00	42.00

	Current Price Range		Prior Year Average
☐ purple	75.00	100.00	78.00
☐ green	75.00	100.00	78.00
☐ blue	75.00	100.00	78.00
☐ amethyst	75.00	100.00	78.00
Tumbler			
☐ marigold	30.00	40.00	32.00
☐ purple	60.00	72.00	64.00
☐ green	60.00	72.00	64.00
☐ blue	60.00	72.00	64.00
☐ amethyst	60.00	72.00	64.00
Bowl, footed, diameter 7½″			
☐ marigold	30.00	38.00	32.00
☐ purple	58.00	70.00	60.00
☐ green	58.00	70.00	60.00
☐ blue	58.00	70.00	60.00
☐ amethyst	58.00	70.00	60.00
Tumbler			
☐ marigold	80.00	110.00	82.00
☐ purple	120.00	150.00	125.00
☐ green	120.00	150.00	125.00
☐ blue	120.00	150.00	125.00
☐ amethyst	120.00	150.00	125.00

FERN
Northwood

An interior pattern consisting of a series of ferns alternating with delicate branches growing out of the center. The rest of the interior body is clear of decoration although usually the exterior contains some pattern. The colors are sharp and iridescent and range widely.

Bowl, diameter 7″			
☐ marigold	22.00	28.00	24.00
☐ purple	35.00	44.00	37.00
☐ green	35.00	44.00	37.00
☐ blue	35.00	44.00	37.00
☐ amethyst	35.00	44.00	37.00
Bowl, diameter 8¼″			
☐ marigold	18.00	22.00	20.00
☐ purple	26.00	35.00	27.00
☐ green	26.00	35.00	27.00
☐ blue	26.00	35.00	27.00
☐ amethyst	26.00	35.00	27.00
☐ white	40.00	50.00	42.00
☐ ice blue	50.00	60.00	52.00
☐ ice green	50.00	60.00	52.00
Compote			
☐ marigold	14.00	17.00	15.00
☐ purple	18.00	23.00	19.00

	Current Price Range		Prior Year Average
☐ green	18.00	23.00	19.00
☐ blue	18.00	23.00	19.00
☐ amethyst	18.00	23.00	19.00
Hat			
☐ marigold	10.00	14.00	11.00
☐ purple	14.00	18.00	15.00
☐ green	14.00	18.00	15.00
☐ blue	14.00	18.00	15.00
☐ amethyst	14.00	18.00	15.00
☐ white	22.00	30.00	23.00
☐ ice blue	25.00	35.00	27.00
☐ ice green	25.00	35.00	27.00

FIELD FLOWER
Imperial

An overall pattern of incredible intricacy is achieved by a simple spray of stylized flowers with feathered foliage, framed by classical, architectural arches and filled in with a flat stippling. The colors are purple, green, and marigold.

Milk Pitcher

	Current Price Range		Prior Year Average
☐ marigold	60.00	85.00	62.00
☐ purple	110.00	145.00	115.00
☐ green	110.00	145.00	115.00
☐ blue	110.00	145.00	115.00
☐ amethyst	110.00	145.00	115.00
Tumbler			
☐ marigold	22.00	28.00	24.00

Field Flower

	Current Price Range		Prior Year Average
☐ purple	42.00	52.00	44.00
☐ green	42.00	52.00	44.00
☐ blue	42.00	52.00	44.00
☐ amethyst	42.00	52.00	44.00
Water Pitcher			
☐ marigold	160.00	190.00	165.00
☐ purple	175.00	215.00	180.00
☐ green	175.00	215.00	180.00
☐ blue	175.00	215.00	180.00
☐ amethyst	175.00	215.00	180.00

FIELD THISTLE
U.S. Glass

An intaglio design of an overall pattern is created by swirling foliage radiating out to daisies and blooms with an impressionistic aura. The center medallion is a clear glass daisy, the color picked up with the circular foliage band. Marigold and green are the usual colors and ice blue is known.

Butter Dish, lidded			
☐ marigold	65.00	85.00	70.00
Creamer			
☐ marigold	26.00	34.00	27.00
Plate, diameter 9″			
☐ marigold	150.00	200.00	175.00
Pitcher			
☐ marigold	175.00	225.00	180.00
Spooner			
☐ marigold	55.00	65.00	60.00
Sugar Bowl			
☐ marigold	26.00	34.00	28.00
Tumbler			
☐ marigold	40.00	50.00	42.00

FILE
Imperial

A delightful pattern formed by a series of rounded panels decorated by ridged files. The central band divides the two wide rows of files, consisting of pyramid shaped jewels. The iridescence is excellent and golden; the colors come in green, smoke, amethyst, and marigold.

Bowl, diameter 9″			
☐ marigold	18.00	23.00	20.00
☐ purple	25.00	35.00	27.00
☐ green	25.00	35.00	27.00
☐ blue	25.00	35.00	27.00
☐ amethyst	25.00	35.00	27.00
Compote			
☐ marigold	18.00	23.00	20.00

	Current Price Range		Prior Year Average
☐ purple	25.00	35.00	27.00
☐ green	25.00	35.00	27.00
☐ blue	25.00	35.00	27.00
☐ amethyst	25.00	35.00	27.00

FINE CUT AND ROSES
Northwood

A pleasing rose pattern with foliage in high relief is underscored with an interesting, diamond-etched band swirling up the sides in a reverse arc. The rose bowl is footed with clear stumpy glass and the inwardly fluted rim resolves with opaque color. All the Northwood colors are represented.

Candy Dish, footed
☐ marigold	28.00	36.00	50.00
☐ purple	60.00	80.00	70.00
☐ green	55.00	75.00	60.00
☐ blue	40.00	50.00	42.00
☐ amethyst	40.00	50.00	42.00
☐ white	130.00	160.00	145.00
☐ ice blue	70.00	85.00	75.00

Rose Bowl
☐ marigold	45.00	65.00	50.00
☐ purple	60.00	80.00	70.00
☐ green	50.00	65.00	52.00
☐ blue	50.00	65.00	52.00
☐ amethyst	65.00	80.00	70.00
☐ white	90.00	115.00	95.00
☐ ice blue	100.00	135.00	115.00
☐ ice green	100.00	135.00	115.00
☐ aqua opalescent	500.00	600.00	550.00

FINE PRISMS AND DIAMONDS
English Manufacturer

A low wide band of elongated diamond trelliswork adorns the piece along the bottom near the base. The rest of the body is finely ridged with delicate prisms. The glass is heavy and the iridescence is good.

Vase, height 13½"
☐ marigold	16.00	20.00	18.00
☐ purple	22.00	28.00	24.00
☐ blue	22.00	28.00	24.00
☐ green	22.00	28.00	24.00

FINE RIB
Northwood

A simple ribbed design of vertical ridges covers the exterior of these pieces, influencing the interior shape. The iridescence is excellent because the ripples refract the light. The colors are marigold, purple and, less commonly, green.

	Current Price Range		Prior Year Average
Banana Dish			
☐ peach opalescent	60.00	75.00	62.00
Bowl, diameter 5″			
☐ purple	23.00	29.00	24.00
☐ green	23.00	29.00	24.00
☐ blue	23.00	29.00	24.00
☐ amethyst	23.00	29.00	24.00
Bowl, diameter 10″			
☐ purple	45.00	65.00	48.00
☐ green	45.00	65.00	48.00
☐ blue	45.00	65.00	48.00
☐ amethyst	45.00	65.00	48.00
Plate, diameter 8″			
☐ marigold	14.00	17.00	15.00
☐ purple	22.00	28.00	23.00
☐ green	22.00	28.00	23.00
☐ blue	22.00	28.00	23.00
☐ amethyst	22.00	28.00	23.00
☐ peach opalescent	40.00	50.00	42.00
Vase			
☐ marigold	16.00	20.00	18.00
☐ purple	25.00	34.00	26.00
☐ green	35.00	45.00	40.00
☐ blue	25.00	34.00	26.00
☐ amethyst	25.00	34.00	26.00
☐ aqua peach opalescent	27.50	37.00	30.00
☐ white	35.00	42.00	37.00
☐ ice blue	35.00	42.00	37.00
☐ ice green	35.00	42.00	37.00

FISH SCALE AND BEADS

Bon Bon			
☐ marigold	26.00	35.00	28.00
☐ purple	20.00	25.00	22.00
☐ green	20.00	25.00	22.00
☐ blue	20.00	25.00	22.00
☐ amethyst	20.00	25.00	22.00
Bowls			
☐ marigold	23.00	28.00	24.00
☐ purple	18.00	20.00	19.00
☐ green	18.00	20.00	19.00
☐ blue	18.00	20.00	19.00
☐ amethyst	18.00	20.00	19.00

	Current Price Range		Prior Year Average
Plate, diameter 7″			
☐ marigold	22.00	28.00	24.00
☐ purple	40.00	50.00	42.00
☐ green	40.00	50.00	42.00
☐ blue	40.00	50.00	42.00
☐ amethyst	40.00	50.00	42.00
☐ peach opalescent	75.00	100.00	80.00

FLEUR DE LIS
Millersburg

The formal interior design of carefully placed fleur de lis is well balanced with alternating blossoms. The ridges are fluted in a sawtooth pattern, both the upper edge and on the base. It is seen in a wide range of colors.

	Current Price Range		Prior Year Average
Bowl, flat			
☐ marigold	45.00	55.00	47.00
☐ purple	70.00	80.00	72.00
☐ green	70.00	80.00	72.00
☐ blue	125.00	150.00	130.00
☐ amethyst	70.00	80.00	72.00
Bowl, footed			
☐ marigold	50.00	60.00	55.00
☐ purple	85.00	110.00	90.00
☐ green	85.00	110.00	90.00
☐ blue	185.00	240.00	200.00
☐ amethyst	200.00	300.00	250.00

FLORAL AND GRAPE
Fenton

A mass-produced design seen on many pieces, the pattern is an overall style of grapes and different blooms, all in high relief. The top band is a diagonally ridged bracelet broken here and there by blossoms. Colors are amethyst, marigold, cobalt, green, and rarely white.

	Current Price Range		Prior Year Average
Pitcher			
☐ marigold	85.00	110.00	90.00
☐ purple	175.00	225.00	180.00
☐ green	250.00	350.00	300.00
☐ blue	175.00	225.00	180.00
☐ amethyst	175.00	225.00	180.00
☐ white	225.00	300.00	270.00
☐ ice blue	250.00	300.00	275.00
☐ ice green	250.00	300.00	275.00
Tumbler			
☐ marigold	22.00	28.00	24.00
☐ purple	20.00	30.00	25.00
☐ green	32.00	40.00	34.00
☐ blue	32.00	40.00	34.00

	Current Price Range		Prior Year Average
☐ amethyst	32.00	40.00	34.00
☐ white	40.00	50.00	45.00
☐ ice blue	50.00	60.00	55.00
☐ ice green	50.00	60.00	55.00

FLORAL OVAL

Bowl, diameter 7½"
☐ marigold	18.00	22.00	20.00

Creamer
☐ marigold	40.00	50.00	42.00

Plate, diameter 7"
☐ marigold	30.00	40.00	32.00

Sugar Bowl
☐ marigold	30.00	40.00	32.00

FLORAL AND WHEAT
Dugan

Compote
☐ marigold	14.00	16.00	15.00
☐ purple	22.00	27.00	23.00
☐ green	22.00	27.00	23.00
☐ blue	22.00	27.00	23.00
☐ amethyst	22.00	27.00	23.00
☐ white	32.00	40.00	33.00
☐ ice blue	40.00	60.00	50.00
☐ ice green	40.00	60.00	50.00
☐ peach opalescent	80.00	95.00	85.00

FLOWERING DILL
Fenton

Made in the hat shape, this exterior pattern is delicate and alive with blossoms in line art. It is an all-over design, swirling and curving over the body to the wide fluted rim.

Hat Shape
☐ marigold	14.00	18.00	16.00
☐ purple	18.00	25.00	19.00
☐ green	18.00	25.00	19.00
☐ blue	18.00	25.00	19.00
☐ amethyst	18.00	25.00	19.00
☐ aqua opalescent	85.00	110.00	90.00

FLOWERS AND FRAMES
Dugan

The frames in question are arches of stippled glass, containing tall daisy-like flowers, also stippled. The upper rim is worked out into a squared ruffle and the base is plain. Colors are purple, green, marigold, and, most commonly, peach opalescent.

Flowers and Frames

	Current Price Range		Prior Year Average
Bowl			
☐ marigold	20.00	30.00	24.00
☐ purple	40.00	50.00	42.00
☐ green	40.00	50.00	42.00
☐ blue	40.00	50.00	42.00
☐ amethyst	40.00	50.00	42.00

FLUFFY PEACOCK
Fenton

The high iridescence is the main feature on these pieces. They have a gold rainbow quality no matter what colors they are in. The design is long peacock feathers alternating with the figure of the birds prancing on the side. Colors are marigold, green, amethyst, and cobalt.

	Current Price Range		Prior Year Average
Pitcher			
☐ marigold	375.00	450.00	400.00
☐ purple	425.00	500.00	450.00
☐ green	425.00	500.00	450.00
☐ blue	850.00	1000.00	875.00
☐ amethyst	425.00	500.00	450.00
Tumbler			
☐ marigold	28.00	35.00	30.00
☐ purple	35.00	42.00	37.00
☐ green	35.00	42.00	37.00
☐ blue	70.00	90.00	72.00
☐ amethyst	35.00	42.00	37.00

FLUTE
English Manufacturer

A rather triangular series of flutes, wide at the top just below the plain rim and tapering toward the stem and pedestal base. The foot mimicks the panels with thumbprints. Color is marigold with a clear iridescence.

	Current Price Range		Prior Year Average
Compote			
☐ marigold	37.50	40.00	39.00

FLUTE #3
Imperial

Wide fluted panels, similar to the Millersburg pattern make up the body of these pieces. The base is resolved by angular out sweeps mounted on a plain circular base. The glass is very heavy and the rim looks lipped, slightly pouting.

	Current Price Range		Prior Year Average
Bowl, diameter 5″			
☐ purple	62.00	72.00	65.00
☐ green	62.00	72.00	65.00
☐ blue	62.00	72.00	65.00
☐ amethyst	62.00	72.00	65.00
Bowl, diameter 10″			
☐ purple	190.00	225.00	200.00
☐ green	190.00	225.00	200.00
☐ blue	190.00	225.00	200.00
☐ amethyst	190.00	225.00	200.00
Butter Dish, covered			
☐ marigold	170.00	200.00	190.00
☐ purple	195.00	225.00	200.00
☐ green	195.00	225.00	200.00
☐ blue	195.00	225.00	200.00
☐ amethyst	195.00	225.00	200.00
Celery Dish			
☐ purple	200.00	250.00	210.00
☐ green	200.00	250.00	210.00
☐ blue	200.00	250.00	210.00
☐ amethyst	200.00	250.00	210.00
Creamer			
☐ marigold	80.00	90.00	85.00
☐ purple	90.00	100.00	95.00
☐ green	90.00	100.00	95.00
☐ blue	90.00	100.00	95.00
☐ amethyst	90.00	100.00	95.00
Pitcher			
☐ marigold	200.00	250.00	210.00
☐ gold	500.00	550.00	525.00
Punch Bowl, base			
☐ marigold	250.00	275.00	240.00
☐ purple	450.00	550.00	475.00
☐ green	450.00	550.00	475.00

	Current Price Range		Prior Year Average
☐ blue	450.00	550.00	475.00
☐ amethyst	450.00	550.00	475.00
Punch Cup			
☐ marigold	25.00	32.00	30.00
☐ purple	32.00	36.00	34.00
☐ green	32.00	36.00	34.00
☐ blue	32.00	36.00	34.00
☐ amethyst	32.00	36.00	34.00
Toothpick Holder, handled			
☐ marigold	50.00	70.00	52.00
☐ purple	65.00	75.00	70.00
☐ green	65.00	75.00	70.00
☐ blue	65.00	75.00	70.00
☐ amethyst	65.00	75.00	70.00
☐ aqua opalescent	100.00	110.00	105.00
Toothpick Holder, unhandled			
☐ marigold	45.00	55.00	47.00
☐ purple	50.00	65.00	52.00
☐ green	50.00	65.00	52.00
☐ blue	50.00	65.00	52.00
☐ amethyst	50.00	65.00	52.00
☐ smoke	75.00	95.00	77.00
Tumbler			
☐ marigold	40.00	60.00	42.00
☐ purple	75.00	95.00	77.00
☐ green	75.00	95.00	77.00
☐ blue	75.00	95.00	77.00
☐ amethyst	75.00	95.00	77.00

FLUTE
Millersburg

A series of thin flutes form sixteen panels on these pieces, resolved by creating the fluted upper edge. The glass is well colored, deep and iridescent. It comes in a wide range of Millersburg colors.

Berry Bowl, diameter 10″			
☐ marigold	100.00	125.00	110.00
Berry Sauce Dish, diameter 5″			
☐ marigold	15.00	17.50	16.00
Bowl, diameter 4″			
☐ purple	38.00	42.00	40.00
☐ green	38.00	42.00	40.00
☐ blue	38.00	42.00	40.00
Creamer			
☐ marigold	45.00	55.00	48.00
☐ purple	65.00	85.00	40.00
☐ green	65.00	85.00	40.00
☐ blue	65.00	85.00	40.00

	Current Price Range		Prior Year Average
Punch Bowl			
☐ marigold	150.00	200.00	160.00
☐ purple	210.00	225.00	240.00
☐ green	210.00	225.00	240.00
☐ blue	210.00	225.00	240.00
☐ amethyst	210.00	225.00	240.00
Punch Cup			
☐ marigold	17.00	22.00	18.00
☐ purple	23.00	28.00	24.00
☐ green	23.00	28.00	24.00
☐ blue	23.00	28.00	24.00
☐ amethyst	23.00	28.00	24.00
Sugar Bowl, covered			
☐ marigold	45.00	65.00	50.00
☐ purple	70.00	75.00	72.00
☐ green	70.00	75.00	72.00
☐ blue	70.00	75.00	72.00
☐ amethyst	70.00	75.00	72.00

FLUTE
Northwood

A prolific design on many pieces, the wide panels are made up of ridged flutes or arched designs. It is simple but effective because of the way the slightly concave panels refract the iridescence. It comes in the complete range of Northwood colors.

Bowl, diameter 5″

☐ purple	30.00	38.00	32.00
☐ green	30.00	38.00	32.00
☐ blue	30.00	38.00	32.00

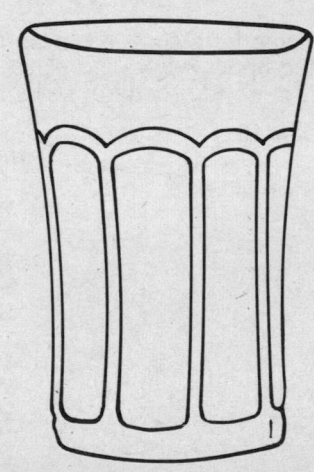

Flute

	Current Price Range		Prior Year Average
☐ amethyst	30.00	38.00	32.00
Bowl, diameter 10"			
☐ purple	55.00	62.00	57.00
☐ green	55.00	62.00	57.00
☐ blue	55.00	62.00	57.00
☐ amethyst	55.00	62.00	57.00
Creamer			
☐ marigold	30.00	40.00	32.00
☐ purple	70.00	85.00	75.00
☐ green	70.00	85.00	75.00
☐ blue	70.00	85.00	75.00
☐ amethyst	70.00	85.00	75.00
Pitcher			
☐ marigold	350.00	400.00	375.00
☐ purple	475.00	525.00	400.00
☐ green	475.00	525.00	400.00
☐ blue	475.00	525.00	400.00
☐ amethyst	475.00	525.00	400.00
Ring Tree			
☐ marigold	150.00	165.00	160.00
Salt Dip, footed			
☐ marigold	30.00	40.00	34.00
☐ purple	55.00	70.00	60.00
☐ green	55.00	70.00	60.00
☐ blue	55.00	70.00	60.00
☐ amethyst	55.00	70.00	60.00
Sherbert			
☐ marigold	17.00	38.00	18.00
Spooner			
☐ marigold	30.00	40.00	32.00
☐ purple	70.00	85.00	74.00
☐ green	70.00	85.00	74.00
☐ blue	70.00	85.00	74.00
☐ amethyst	70.00	85.00	74.00
Sugar Bowl			
☐ marigold	40.00	50.00	42.00
☐ purple	85.00	95.00	90.00
☐ green	85.00	95.00	90.00
☐ blue	85.00	95.00	90.00
☐ amethyst	85.00	95.00	90.00
Tumbler			
☐ marigold	22.00	28.00	23.00
☐ purple	40.00	50.00	42.00
☐ green	40.00	50.00	42.00
☐ blue	40.00	50.00	42.00
☐ amethyst	40.00	50.00	42.00

FLUTE AND CANE *Imperial*	Current Price Range		Prior Year Average
Goblet			
☐ marigold	30.00	40.00	32.00
☐ purple	50.00	65.00	52.00
☐ green	50.00	65.00	52.00
☐ blue	50.00	65.00	52.00
☐ amethyst	50.00	65.00	52.00
Milk Pitcher			
☐ marigold	80.00	110.00	90.00
Wine Glass			
☐ marigold	22.00	28.00	27.00

FORMAL
Dugan

The pattern is a chain alternating with a beadwork panel ending with a horizontal band of circles in high relief. The base is etched with a geometric design and the body has a flower-shaped rim. The colors come in purple, marigold, and other pastels.

Jack in the Pulpit Vase			
☐ marigold	40.00	50.00	42.00
☐ purple	52.00	65.00	55.00
☐ ice blue	65.00	70.00	67.00
☐ ice green	65.00	70.00	67.00
☐ peach opalescent	65.00	70.00	67.00

FROSTED BLOCK
Imperial

An excellent paneled pattern of stippled glass separated into panels by beadwork columns. It comes in a wide realm of shapes and the colors are marigold and a lovely, pearly clambroth.

Bowl, diameter 8″			
☐ marigold	12.00	17.00	13.00
Butter Dish, lidded			
☐ marigold	40.00	50.00	42.00
Creamer			
☐ marigold	18.00	23.00	19.00
Plate, diameter 9″			
☐ marigold	22.00	28.00	24.00
Rose Bowl			
☐ marigold	32.00	40.00	33.00
Spooner			
☐ marigold	18.00	23.00	20.00

FRUITS AND FLOWERS
Northwood

An overall pattern of fruit, including grapes and berries, is interspersed among blossoms, with well-detailed foilage. The pattern covers the interior, with a basketweave exterior. The rim is modified saw tooth. Several Northwood colors are represented.

	Current Price Range		Prior Year Average
Berry Bowl, diameter 9″			
☐ marigold	40.00	50.00	42.00
☐ purple	35.00	47.00	37.00
☐ green	35.00	47.00	37.00
☐ blue	35.00	47.00	37.00
☐ amethyst	35.00	47.00	37.00
☐ white	50.00	70.00	55.00
☐ ice blue	60.00	80.00	65.00
☐ ice green	60.00	80.00	65.00
Bowl, footed, diameter 8″			
☐ marigold	22.00	28.00	24.00
☐ purple	32.00	40.00	36.00
☐ green	32.00	40.00	36.00
☐ blue	32.00	40.00	36.00
☐ amethyst	32.00	40.00	36.00
☐ aqua opalescent	100.00	140.00	120.00
Bowl, diameter 9″			
☐ marigold	35.00	42.00	37.00
☐ purple	55.00	65.00	60.00
☐ green	50.00	60.00	55.00
☐ blue	50.00	60.00	55.00
☐ amethyst	50.00	60.00	55.00
☐ white	65.00	85.00	68.00
☐ ice blue	75.00	90.00	80.00
☐ ice green	75.00	90.00	80.00
Plate, diameter 7″			
☐ marigold	30.00	38.00	32.00
☐ purple	55.00	70.00	58.00
☐ green	55.00	70.00	58.00
☐ blue	55.00	70.00	58.00
☐ amethyst	55.00	70.00	84.00
☐ white	80.00	115.00	84.00
☐ ice blue	95.00	125.00	100.00
☐ ice green	95.00	125.00	100.00
Plate, diameter 8″			
☐ marigold	40.00	50.00	42.00
☐ purple	75.00	100.00	80.00
☐ green	75.00	100.00	80.00
☐ blue	75.00	100.00	80.00
☐ amethyst	75.00	100.00	80.00
☐ white	100.00	130.00	110.00
☐ ice blue	115.00	150.00	130.00

	Current Price Range		Prior Year Average
☐ ice green	115.00	150.00	130.00
Plate, diameter 9″			
☐ marigold	50.00	70.00	55.00
☐ purple	65.00	85.00	70.00
☐ green	65.00	85.00	70.00
☐ blue	65.00	85.00	70.00
☐ amethyst	65.00	85.00	70.00

GAY 90's
Millersburg

Considered to be among the most finely crafted water sets ever made, Gay 90's has a well-balanced geometrical pattern and a wonderfully detailed finish. The design resembles a dropping curtain, covering the body from the snug waist to just above the base. The rest of the glass is smooth and glossy, showing off the incredible iridescence achieved in spite of its transparency.

Pitcher

☐ purple	4000.00	6000.00	4100.00
☐ green	4000.00	6000.00	4100.00
☐ amethyst	4000.00	6000.00	4100.00
Tumbler			
☐ marigold	450.00	550.00	460.00
☐ purple	425.00	525.00	450.00
☐ green	425.00	525.00	450.00
☐ blue	800.00	1000.00	850.00
☐ amethyst	425.00	525.00	450.00

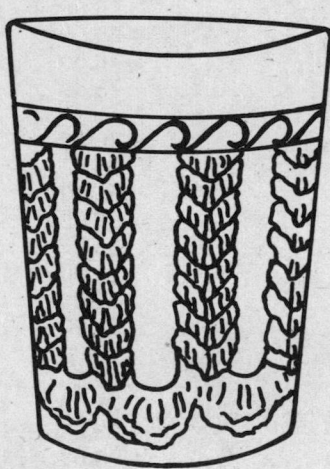

Gay 90's

GODDESS OF HARVEST
Fenton

The lovely lady that graces the center of this plate has hair made up of flowers, foliage and leaves. Her sharply molded profile is framed with a serpentine chain of fine ridging with an occasional spray of flowers to balance the design. Colors exist in blue, amethyst, and marigold.

Bowl	Current Price Range		Prior Year Average
☐ purple	2100.00	3000.00	2200.00
☐ green	2100.00	3000.00	2200.00
☐ blue	2100.00	3000.00	2200.00

GOLDEN GRAPE
Dugan

A well-molded pattern of alternating leaves and grapes, both large and equally dominant. The band is playfully framed by a meandering vine. The rest of the body is smooth but the pattern is followed by the long flutes on the rim. Marigold is the only reported color.

Butter Dish

☐ marigold	24.00	32.00	26.00
☐ purple	28.00	36.00	30.00
☐ green	28.00	36.00	30.00
☐ blue	50.00	70.00	52.00
☐ amethyst	28.00	36.00	30.00
☐ white	32.00	45.00	36.00
☐ ice blue	45.00	65.00	50.00
☐ ice green	45.00	65.00	50.00

Rose Bowl

☐ marigold	30.00	50.00	40.00
☐ white	45.00	55.00	47.00
☐ ice blue	55.00	70.00	60.00
☐ ice green	55.00	70.00	60.00

GOLDEN HARVEST
U.S. Glass

An overall pattern of a stylized wheat sheaf, starts out naturalistically and emanates into a fountain of geometrical shapes. This alternates with bunches of grapes in high relief. The colors are amethyst and white.

Wine Decanter

☐ marigold	90.00	120.00	100.00
☐ purple	220.00	280.00	225.00
☐ green	220.00	280.00	225.00
☐ blue	220.00	280.00	225.00
☐ amethyst	220.00	280.00	225.00

Wine Glass, stemmed

☐ marigold	27.00	37.00	30.00
☐ purple	32.00	38.00	35.00
☐ green	32.00	38.00	35.00

	Current Price Range		Prior Year Average
☐ blue	32.00	38.00	35.00
☐ amethyst	32.00	38.00	35.00

GOLDEN HONEY COMB
Imperial

Reminiscent of the coin dot pattern, this design covers the piece with row after row of squared off circles resembling a honey comb. The large central medallion is a starburst that covers the base. It is a deep marigold and the iridescence is successfully refracted by the honey combs.

Bon Bon, diameter 5″			
☐ marigold	42.00	50.00	44.00
Bowl, diameter 5″			
☐ marigold	12.50	17.00	13.00
Compote			
☐ marigold	17.00	20.00	19.00
Creamer			
☐ marigold	27.00	32.00	30.00
Plate, diameter 7″			
☐ marigold	22.50	30.00	28.00
Sugar Bowl			
☐ marigold	27.00	32.00	28.00

GOOD LUCK
Northwood

The dominant theme on this piece is the inscription with the horseshoe shaped with stippled glass. Surrounding this central medallion is a wreath of flowers and foliage that meanders toward the rim which is ruffled sharply. The pattern is prolific and comes in the full range of Carnival glass colors.

Butter Dish			
☐ marigold	60.00	75.00	65.00
☐ purple	100.00	130.00	110.00
☐ green	100.00	130.00	110.00
☐ blue	100.00	130.00	110.00
☐ amethyst	100.00	130.00	110.00
☐ ice blue	400.00	500.00	425.00
☐ aqua opalescent	475.00	575.00	500.00
Plate, diameter 9″			
☐ marigold	110.00	140.00	115.00
☐ purple	165.00	200.00	175.00
☐ green	165.00	200.00	175.00
☐ blue	165.00	200.00	175.00
☐ amethyst	165.00	200.00	175.00
☐ aqua opalescent	325.00	400.00	330.00
☐ white	175.00	250.00	200.00

	Current Price Range		Prior Year Average
☐ ice blue	220.00	275.00	225.00
☐ ice green	220.00	275.00	225.00

GOOSEBERRY SPRAY

Berry Bowl, diameter 5″

☐ marigold	22.00	28.00	24.00
☐ purple	30.00	42.00	32.00
☐ green	30.00	42.00	32.00
☐ blue	30.00	42.00	32.00
☐ amethyst	30.00	42.00	32.00
☐ white	42.00	55.00	44.00
☐ ice blue	55.00	65.00	56.00
☐ ice green	55.00	65.00	56.00

Berry Bowl, diameter 9″

☐ marigold	26.00	32.00	28.00
☐ purple	36.00	47.00	38.00
☐ green	36.00	47.00	38.00
☐ blue	36.00	47.00	38.00
☐ amethyst	36.00	47.00	38.00
☐ white	46.00	52.00	47.00
☐ ices	55.00	65.00	56.00

Compote

☐ purple	90.00	110.00	95.00
☐ green	90.00	110.00	95.00
☐ blue	90.00	110.00	95.00
☐ ices	130.00	140.00	125.00
☐ white	100.00	130.00	110.00

Grape

GRAPE
Imperial

The relief is high, the detail intricate, the pattern a delight. The design of grapes, vines, and leaves rambles all over the piece, filled in with stippling. The handle is edged in a bark motif resembling an old grape vine. All the shapes and colors were used with this pattern.

	Current Price Range		Prior Year Average
Berry Bowl, diameter 5″			
☐ marigold	11.00	14.00	12.00
☐ purple	22.00	30.00	23.00
☐ green	22.00	30.00	23.00
☐ blue	22.00	30.00	23.00
Berry Bowl, diameter 10″			
☐ marigold	22.00	30.00	23.00
☐ purple	36.00	40.00	37.00
☐ green	36.00	40.00	37.00
☐ blue	36.00	40.00	37.90
Compote			
☐ marigold	22.00	26.00	24.00
☐ blue	32.00	36.00	35.00
☐ green	32.00	36.00	35.00
☐ purple	32.00	36.00	35.00
☐ amethyst	32.00	36.00	35.00
Cup and Saucer			
☐ marigold	50.00	60.00	52.00
☐ blue	70.00	75.00	72.00
☐ green	70.00	75.00	72.00
☐ purple	70.00	75.00	72.00
☐ amethyst	70.00	75.00	72.00
Cuspidor			
☐ blue	600.00	750.00	620.00
☐ green	600.00	750.00	620.00
☐ purple	60.00	75.00	62.00
☐ amethyst	600.00	750.00	625.00
Goblet			
☐ marigold	25.00	35.00	30.00
☐ blue	58.00	65.00	60.00
☐ green	58.00	65.00	60.00
☐ purple	58.00	65.00	60.00
☐ amethyst	58.00	65.00	60.00
Pitcher			
☐ marigold	100.00	120.00	110.00
☐ purple	225.00	260.00	230.00
☐ green	225.00	260.00	230.00
☐ blue	225.00	260.00	230.00
☐ amethyst	225.00	260.00	230.00
☐ smoke	335.00	370.00	340.00
Punch Bowl			
☐ marigold	135.00	150.00	145.00

	Current Price Range		Prior Year Average
☐ purple	185.00	220.00	200.00
☐ green	185.00	220.00	200.00
☐ blue	185.00	220.00	200.00
☐ amethyst	185.00	220.00	200.00
Punch Cup			
☐ marigold	17.00	20.00	19.00
☐ purple	20.00	24.00	22.00
☐ green	20.00	24.00	22.00
☐ blue	20.00	24.00	22.00
☐ amethyst	20.00	24.00	22.00
☐ smoke	28.00	34.00	30.00
Shade			
☐ marigold	35.00	40.00	37.00
Tumbler			
☐ marigold	16.00	20.00	18.00
☐ purple	45.00	52.00	47.00
☐ green	45.00	52.00	47.00
☐ blue	45.00	52.00	47.00
☐ amethyst	45.00	52.00	47.00
Water Bottle			
☐ marigold	90.00	110.00	95.00
☐ purple	125.00	140.00	130.00
Wine Decanter			
☐ marigold	38.00	46.00	40.00
☐ purple	85.00	96.00	90.00
☐ green	85.00	96.00	90.00
☐ blue	85.00	96.00	90.00
☐ amethyst	85.00	96.00	90.00
Wine Glass			
☐ marigold	20.00	24.00	22.00
☐ purple	26.00	30.00	28.00
☐ green	26.00	30.00	28.00
☐ blue	26.00	30.00	28.00
☐ amethyst	26.00	30.00	28.00

GRAPE AND CABLE
Fenton

The cable is a reverse diagonal series of ridges, curving up and down just below the rim, and is intertwined with delicate grape vines. Attached to this vining are vertical bunches of heavy grapes alternating with big veined leaves. The upper edge follows the meandering vine. Colors come in amethyst, marigold, green, blue, and red.

Bowl, diameter 7″

☐ marigold	50.00	60.00	55.00
☐ purple	35.00	45.00	36.00
☐ green	35.00	45.00	36.00
☐ blue	35.00	45.00	36.00
☐ amethyst	35.00	45.00	36.00

Grape and Cable

	Current Price Range		Prior Year Average
☐ red	350.00	400.00	375.00
Orange Bowl			
☐ marigold	85.00	110.00	90.00
☐ purple	130.00	170.00	135.00
☐ green	130.00	170.00	135.00
☐ blue	130.00	170.00	135.00
☐ amethyst	130.00	170.00	135.00
Plate, footed			
☐ marigold	50.00	65.00	55.00
☐ purple	65.00	85.00	70.00
☐ green	65.00	85.00	70.00
☐ blue	65.00	85.00	70.00
☐ amethyst	65.00	85.00	70.00
☐ red	300.00	400.00	310.00
Salad Bowl			
☐ marigold	120.00	150.00	125.00
☐ purple	170.00	215.00	175.00
☐ green	170.00	215.00	175.00
☐ blue	170.00	215.00	175.00
☐ amethyst	170.00	215.00	175.00

GRAPE AND CABLE
Northwood

The moldwork is superior in high relief. Bunches of grapes form the center, raised so that almost three quarters of their round little bodies are exposed. The surrounding leaves are sharp and detailed with veins. The base band is formed by concave coin dots alternating with teardrop shapes. The edges, when fluted, are in a saw tooth pattern. The colors range in all of the Northwood tints.

	Current Price Range		Prior Year Average
Banana Boat, footed, diameter 12″			
☐ marigold	100.00	150.00	125.00
☐ purple	250.00	300.00	275.00
☐ green	250.00	300.00	275.00
☐ blue	250.00	300.00	275.00
☐ amethyst	225.00	275.00	250.00
☐ white	300.00	400.00	370.00
☐ ice blue	320.00	420.00	400.00
☐ ice green	320.00	420.00	400.00
Berry Bowl, diameter 5″			
☐ marigold	14.00	18.00	15.00
☐ purple	22.00	28.00	24.00
☐ green	22.00	28.00	24.00
☐ amethyst	22.00	28.00	24.00
☐ white	40.00	50.00	42.00
☐ ice blue	50.00	60.00	52.00
☐ ice green	50.00	60.00	52.00
Berry Bowl, diameter 10″			
☐ marigold	70.00	100.00	85.00
☐ purple	55.00	75.00	60.00
☐ green	55.00	75.00	60.00
☐ blue	55.00	75.00	60.00
☐ amethyst	55.00	75.00	60.00
☐ white	90.00	110.00	95.00
☐ ice blue	100.00	130.00	105.00
☐ ice green	100.00	130.00	105.00
Bowl, scalloped edge, diameter 7″			
☐ marigold	35.00	45.00	37.00
☐ purple	62.00	80.00	65.00
☐ green	62.00	80.00	65.00
☐ blue	62.00	80.00	65.00
☐ amethyst	62.00	80.00	65.00
☐ white	75.00	95.00	80.00
☐ ice blue	85.00	115.00	95.00
☐ ice green	85.00	115.00	95.00
Bowl, footed, diameter 8¼″			
☐ marigold	45.00	65.00	50.00
☐ purple	42.00	49.00	45.00
☐ green	42.00	49.00	45.00
☐ blue	42.00	49.00	45.00
☐ amethyst	42.00	49.00	45.00
Breakfast Set			
☐ marigold	75.00	100.00	80.00
☐ purple	125.00	175.00	150.00
☐ green	90.00	140.00	95.00
☐ blue	90.00	140.00	95.00
☐ amethyst	90.00	140.00	95.00

	Current Price Range		Prior Year Average

Butter Dish

☐ marigold	140.00	175.00	150.00
☐ purple	100.00	130.00	115.00
☐ green	140.00	185.00	145.00
☐ blue	140.00	185.00	145.00
☐ amethyst	140.00	185.00	145.00
☐ white	200.00	230.00	210.00
☐ ice blue	225.00	275.00	210.00
☐ ice green	225.00	275.00	210.00

Candlestick

☐ marigold	80.00	110.00	85.00
☐ purple	120.00	155.00	130.00
☐ green	120.00	155.00	130.00
☐ blue	120.00	155.00	130.00
☐ amethyst	120.00	155.00	130.00
☐ white	160.00	175.00	165.00
☐ ice blue	175.00	210.00	165.00
☐ ice green	175.00	210.00	165.00

Candlesticks, pair

☐ marigold	150.00	190.00	160.00
☐ purple	230.00	290.00	240.00
☐ green	230.00	290.00	240.00
☐ blue	230.00	290.00	240.00
☐ amethyst	230.00	290.00	240.00
☐ white	360.00	420.00	370.00
☐ ice blue	390.00	460.00	370.00
☐ ice green	390.00	460.00	370.00

Centerpiece, footed

☐ marigold	250.00	325.00	260.00
☐ purple	340.00	420.00	350.00
☐ green	340.00	420.00	350.00
☐ blue	340.00	420.00	350.00
☐ amethyst	340.00	420.00	350.00
☐ white	450.00	525.00	460.00
☐ ice blue	470.00	570.00	460.00
☐ ice green	470.00	570.00	460.00

Compote, large, lidded

☐ marigold	180.00	250.00	190.00
☐ purple	300.00	400.00	310.00
☐ green	300.00	400.00	310.00
☐ blue	300.00	400.00	310.00
☐ amethyst	475.00	525.00	500.00

Compote, large, unlidded

☐ marigold	400.00	500.00	425.00
☐ purple	320.00	375.00	340.00
☐ blue	320.00	375.00	340.00
☐ amethyst	320.00	375.00	340.00
☐ white	500.00	560.00	575.00

	Current Price Range		Prior Year Average
☐ ice blue	550.00	650.00	575.00
☐ ice green	550.00	650.00	575.00
Cookie Jar			
☐ marigold	175.00	220.00	190.00
☐ purple	150.00	200.00	175.00
☐ green	220.00	280.00	225.00
☐ blue	220.00	280.00	225.00
☐ amethyst	220.00	280.00	225.00
☐ white	450.00	550.00	525.00
☐ ice blue	500.00	600.00	525.00
☐ ice green	500.00	600.00	525.00
☐ aqua opalescent	2500.00	3000.00	2750.00
Creamer			
☐ marigold	50.00	60.00	55.00
☐ purple	70.00	85.00	75.00
☐ green	70.00	85.00	75.00
☐ blue	70.00	85.00	75.00
☐ amethyst	225.00	275.00	250.00
☐ white	95.00	125.00	115.00
☐ ice blue	110.00	140.00	115.00
☐ ice green	110.00	140.00	115.00
Cup and Saucer			
☐ marigold	130.00	170.00	140.00
☐ purple	135.00	175.00	150.00
☐ green	135.00	175.00	150.00
☐ blue	135.00	175.00	150.00
☐ amethyst	135.00	175.00	150.00
Cuspidor			
☐ marigold	1800.00	2800.00	1900.00
☐ purple	1800.00	2800.00	1900.00
☐ green	1800.00	2800.00	1900.00
☐ blue	1800.00	2800.00	1900.00
☐ amethyst	1800.00	2800.00	1900.00
Dresser Tray			
☐ marigold	120.00	160.00	125.00
☐ purple	160.00	215.00	175.00
☐ green	160.00	215.00	175.00
☐ blue	160.00	215.00	175.00
☐ amethyst	160.00	215.00	175.00
☐ white	250.00	320.00	275.00
☐ ice blue	250.00	320.00	275.00
☐ ice green	250.00	320.00	275.00
Fernery, footed			
☐ marigold	1200.00	1500.00	1400.00
☐ purple	700.00	900.00	750.00
☐ green	700.00	900.00	750.00
☐ blue	700.00	900.00	750.00
☐ amethyst	700.00	900.00	750.00

	Current Price Range		Prior Year Average
☐ ice blue	2200.00	2875.00	2250.00
Hat Pin Holder			
☐ marigold	110.00	125.00	115.00
☐ purple	100.00	200.00	150.00
☐ green	160.00	200.00	170.00
☐ blue	160.00	200.00	170.00
☐ amethyst	160.00	200.00	170.00
☐ white	150.00	200.00	175.00
☐ ice blue	280.00	345.00	275.00
☐ ice green	280.00	345.00	275.00
☐ aqua opalescent	1800.00	2300.00	2000.00
Ice Cream Bowl, diameter 4″			
☐ marigold	25.00	30.00	28.00
☐ purple	32.00	36.00	30.00
☐ green	32.00	36.00	30.00
☐ blue	32.00	36.00	30.00
☐ amethyst	32.00	36.00	30.00
☐ white	75.00	90.00	80.00
☐ ice blue	80.00	90.00	80.00
☐ ice green	80.00	90.00	80.00
Ice Cream Bowl, diameter 11″			
☐ marigold	80.00	100.00	85.00
☐ purple	160.00	200.00	170.00
☐ green	160.00	200.00	170.00
☐ blue	160.00	200.00	170.00
☐ amethyst	160.00	200.00	170.00
☐ white	220.00	270.00	225.00
☐ ice blue	230.00	270.00	225.00
☐ ice green	230.00	270.00	225.00
Lampshade			
☐ marigold	160.00	220.00	180.00
☐ purple	140.00	180.00	160.00
☐ green	140.00	180.00	160.00
☐ blue	140.00	180.00	160.00
☐ amethyst	140.00	180.00	160.00
Nappy			
☐ marigold	55.00	75.00	65.00
☐ purple	75.00	90.00	80.00
☐ green	75.00	90.00	80.00
☐ blue	75.00	90.00	80.00
☐ amethyst	75.00	90.00	80.00
☐ white	110.00	140.00	115.00
☐ ice blue	110.00	140.00	115.00
☐ ice green	110.00	140.00	115.00
Occasional, diameter 7″			
☐ marigold	20.00	28.00	25.00
☐ purple	30.00	40.00	32.00
☐ green	30.00	40.00	32.00

	Current Price Range		Prior Year Average
☐ blue	30.00	40.00	32.00
☐ amethyst	30.00	40.00	32.00
☐ white	60.00	75.00	65.00
☐ ice blue	70.00	85.00	75.00
☐ ice green	70.00	85.00	75.00
Orange Bowl, footed			
☐ marigold	110.00	140.00	115.00
☐ purple	145.00	175.00	160.00
☐ green	155.00	185.00	160.00
☐ blue	155.00	185.00	160.00
☐ amethyst	155.00	185.00	160.00
☐ ice green	1200.00	1500.00	1300.00
☐ aqua opalescent	2400.00	2875.00	2600.00
Pin Tray			
☐ marigold	100.00	125.00	125.00
☐ purple	130.00	180.00	135.00
☐ green	130.00	180.00	135.00
☐ blue	130.00	180.00	135.00
☐ amethyst	130.00	180.00	135.00
☐ white	180.00	250.00	230.00
☐ ice blue	200.00	275.00	225.00
☐ ice green	200.00	275.00	225.00
Plate, diameter 7½"			
☐ marigold	60.00	75.00	62.00
☐ purple	70.00	85.00	75.00
☐ green	70.00	85.00	75.00
☐ blue	70.00	85.00	75.00
☐ amethyst	70.00	85.00	75.00
☐ white	90.00	120.00	95.00
☐ ice green	100.00	120.00	110.00
☐ ice blue	100.00	120.00	110.00
☐ aqua opalescent	375.00	450.00	400.00
Plate, footed			
☐ marigold	70.00	85.00	75.00
☐ purple	80.00	100.00	88.00
☐ green	80.00	100.00	88.00
☐ blue	80.00	100.00	88.00
☐ amethyst	80.00	100.00	88.00
☐ white	105.00	150.00	105.00
☐ ice blue	115.00	165.00	120.00
☐ ice green	115.00	165.00	120.00
Powder Jar, lidded			
☐ marigold	65.00	85.00	75.00
☐ purple	60.00	75.00	65.00
☐ green	75.00	95.00	85.00
☐ blue	60.00	75.00	65.00
☐ amethyst	75.00	95.00	85.00
☐ aqua opalescent	270.00	335.00	280.00

	Current Price Range		Prior Year Average

Punch Bowl, small, with base

☐ marigold	250.00	350.00	275.00
☐ purple	360.00	450.00	275.00
☐ green	360.00	450.00	275.00
☐ blue	360.00	450.00	275.00
☐ amethyst	360.00	450.00	275.00
☐ white	440.00	550.00	500.00
☐ ice blue	475.00	575.00	500.00
☐ ice green	475.00	575.00	500.00

Punch Bowl, banquet size, with base

☐ marigold	1275.00	1750.00	1400.00
☐ purple	1850.00	2350.00	2000.00
☐ aqua opalescent	7000.00	9000.00	7500.00
☐ white	3400.00	4000.00	3800.00
☐ ice blue	3400.00	4000.00	3800.00
☐ ice green	3400.00	4000.00	3800.00

Punch Cup

☐ marigold	12.00	17.00	15.00
☐ purple	22.00	28.00	24.00
☐ green	22.00	28.00	24.00
☐ blue	22.00	28.00	24.00
☐ amethyst	22.00	28.00	24.00
☐ white	35.00	45.00	37.00
☐ ice blue	45.00	60.00	50.00
☐ ice green	45.00	60.00	50.00
☐ aqua opalescent	170.00	225.00	150.00

Shot Glass

☐ marigold	140.00	170.00	170.00
☐ purple	160.00	210.00	170.00
☐ green	160.00	210.00	170.00
☐ blue	160.00	210.00	170.00
☐ amethyst	160.00	210.00	170.00

Spittoon

☐ marigold	4500.00	5250.00	4650.00
☐ purple	6750.00	7750.00	7000.00

Spooner

☐ marigold	60.00	70.00	65.00
☐ purple	120.00	165.00	125.00
☐ green	130.00	170.00	140.00
☐ blue	120.00	165.00	125.00
☐ amethyst	120.00	165.00	125.00
☐ white	170.00	210.00	180.00
☐ ice blue	175.00	230.00	190.00
☐ ice green	175.00	230.00	190.00

Spooner

☐ marigold	50.00	60.00	57.00
☐ purple	70.00	85.00	75.00
☐ green	70.00	85.00	75.00

	Current Price Range		Prior Year Average
☐ blue	70.00	85.00	75.00
☐ amethyst	70.00	85.00	75.00
☐ white	110.00	140.00	117.00
☐ ice blue	120.00	150.00	123.00
☐ ice green	120.00	150.00	123.00
Sugar Bowl, lidded			
☐ marigold	70.00	85.00	75.00
☐ purple	140.00	185.00	145.00
☐ green	80.00	120.00	95.00
☐ blue	140.00	185.00	145.00
☐ amethyst	140.00	185.00	145.00
☐ white	210.00	275.00	220.00
☐ ice blue	220.00	275.00	230.00
☐ ice green	220.00	275.00	230.00
Sugar Bowl, unlidded			
☐ marigold	50.00	60.00	55.00
☐ purple	70.00	85.00	75.00
☐ green	70.00	85.00	75.00
☐ blue	70.00	85.00	75.00
☐ amethyst	70.00	85.00	75.00
☐ white	110.00	140.00	115.00
☐ ice blue	120.00	160.00	130.00
☐ ice green	120.00	160.00	130.00
Sweetmeat Dish, lidded			
☐ marigold	380.00	460.00	390.00
☐ purple	225.00	275.00	240.00
☐ green	225.00	275.00	240.00
☐ blue	225.00	275.00	240.00
☐ amethyst	225.00	275.00	240.00
Sweetmeat Compote			
☐ marigold	600.00	700.00	610.00
☐ purple	150.00	190.00	170.00
☐ green	150.00	190.00	170.00
☐ blue	150.00	190.00	170.00
☐ amethyst	150.00	190.00	170.00
☐ cobalt	300.00	385.00	320.00
Tobacco Jar, lidded			
☐ marigold	350.00	420.00	375.00
☐ purple	375.00	430.00	400.00
☐ green	375.00	430.00	400.00
☐ blue	375.00	430.00	400.00
☐ amethyst	375.00	430.00	400.00
Tankard Pitcher			
☐ marigold	800.00	975.00	810.00
☐ purple	725.00	850.00	760.00
☐ green	725.00	850.00	760.00
☐ blue	725.00	850.00	760.00
☐ amethyst	725.00	850.00	760.00

	Current Price Range		Prior Year Average
☐ white	900.00	1100.00	1000.00
☐ ice blue	1000.00	1250.00	1100.00
☐ ice green	2500.00	3000.00	2775.00
Tumbler, small			
☐ marigold	45.00	70.00	60.00
☐ purple	30.00	50.00	40.00
☐ green	40.00	60.00	50.00
☐ blue	50.00	65.00	52.00
☐ amethyst	30.00	50.00	40.00
☐ white	65.00	80.00	67.00
☐ ice blue	70.00	90.00	70.00
☐ ice green	70.00	90.00	70.00
Tumbler, large			
☐ marigold	45.00	55.00	47.00
☐ purple	65.00	80.00	69.00
☐ green	65.00	80.00	69.00
☐ blue	65.00	80.00	69.00
☐ amethyst	65.00	80.00	69.00
☐ white	85.00	110.00	88.00
☐ ice blue	90.00	115.00	92.00
☐ ice green	90.00	115.00	92.00
Water Pitcher			
☐ marigold	250.00	320.00	260.00
☐ purple	350.00	420.00	375.00
☐ green	350.00	420.00	375.00
☐ blue	350.00	420.00	375.00
☐ amethyst	350.00	420.00	375.00
☐ white	350.00	400.00	400.00
☐ ice blue	375.00	445.00	400.00
☐ ice green	375.00	445.00	400.00
Whiskey Decanter			
☐ marigold	800.00	950.00	850.00
☐ purple	900.00	1100.00	950.00
☐ green	900.00	1100.00	950.00
☐ blue	900.00	1100.00	950.00
☐ amethyst	900.00	1100.00	1000.00

GRAPE AND CHERRY
Sowerby

An intaglio design, achieved from the exterior, grape bunches alternate with cherries attached to their branches with leaves. Separating the two large motifs is a design of a flaming torch rising out of scrolls. Colors are clearly iridescent and come in cobalt and marigold.

Bowl, large			
☐ marigold	65.00	70.00	67.50
☐ blue	145.00	160.00	150.00

Grape and Gothic Arches

GRAPE AND GOTHIC ARCHES
Northwood

The architectural background resembles a picket fence—the panels are separated by reliefed ridges, and run the length of the side, terminating in a triangular arch. The grape bunches interrupt this pattern, more geometrical than most grape designs with leaves flanking.

	Current Price Range		Prior Year Average
Berry Bowl, large			
☐ marigold	30.00	42.00	32.00
☐ purple	50.00	65.00	52.00
☐ green	50.00	65.00	52.00
☐ blue	50.00	65.00	52.00
☐ amethyst	50.00	65.00	52.00
Bowl, diameter 5″			
☐ marigold	20.00	25.00	22.00
☐ purple	35.00	42.00	37.00
☐ green	35.00	42.00	37.00
☐ blue	35.00	42.00	37.00
☐ amethyst	35.00	42.00	37.00
Butter Dish, lidded			
☐ marigold	65.00	85.00	67.00
☐ purple	85.00	110.00	87.00
☐ green	85.00	110.00	87.00
☐ blue	85.00	110.00	87.00
☐ amethyst	85.00	110.00	87.00
Creamer			
☐ marigold	35.00	45.00	37.00

	Current Price Range		Prior Year Average
☐ purple	50.00	60.00	52.00
☐ green	50.00	60.00	52.00
☐ blue	50.00	60.00	52.00
☐ amethyst	50.00	60.00	52.00
Spooner			
☐ marigold	35.00	45.00	37.00
☐ purple	50.00	60.00	52.00
☐ green	50.00	60.00	52.00
☐ blue	50.00	60.00	52.00
☐ amethyst	50.00	60.00	52.00
Sugar Bowl, lidded			
☐ marigold	45.00	55.00	47.00
☐ purple	60.00	75.00	62.00
☐ green	60.00	75.00	62.00
☐ blue	60.00	75.00	62.00
☐ amethyst	60.00	75.00	62.00
Tumbler			
☐ marigold	22.00	30.00	25.00
☐ purple	30.00	42.00	32.00
☐ green	30.00	42.00	32.00
☐ blue	30.00	42.00	32.00
☐ amethyst	30.00	42.00	32.00
Water Pitcher			
☐ marigold	170.00	210.00	175.00
☐ purple	260.00	330.00	275.00
☐ green	260.00	330.00	275.00
☐ blue	260.00	330.00	275.00
☐ amethyst	260.00	330.00	275.00

GRAPE DELIGHT
Dugan

Grape bunches in relief high enough to resemble marbles are superimposed on intricately detailed leaves. The viney branches wind around the body. There is no filler pattern. The shapes are usually small bowls with the unique six footed base. The colors range widely.

Nut Bowl			
☐ purple	60.00	75.00	62.00
Rose Bowl			
☐ marigold	40.00	50.00	42.00
☐ purple	50.00	65.00	52.00
☐ green	50.00	65.00	52.00
☐ blue	50.00	65.00	52.00
☐ amethyst	50.00	65.00	52.00
☐ white	60.00	75.00	62.00

GRAPE VINE LATTICE
Dugan

An overall pattern of a barked trellis without further decoration dominates the interior on these pieces. Although the design is not intricate, it manages to be busy because of the diamond pattern created by the vines.

	Current Price Range		Prior Year Average
Bowl, diameter 7½"			
☐ marigold	20.00	27.00	22.00
☐ purple	35.00	43.00	37.00
☐ green	35.00	43.00	37.00
☐ blue	35.00	43.00	37.00
☐ amethyst	35.00	43.00	37.00
☐ white	45.00	55.00	47.00
Plate, diameter 7½"			
☐ marigold	35.00	45.00	37.00
☐ purple	55.00	67.50	57.00
☐ green	55.00	67.50	57.00
☐ blue	55.00	67.50	57.00
☐ amethyst	55.00	67.50	57.00
☐ white	60.00	75.00	62.00
Tankard Pitcher			
☐ marigold	160.00	215.00	165.00
☐ purple	360.00	450.00	365.00
☐ green	360.00	450.00	365.00
☐ blue	360.00	450.00	365.00
☐ amethyst	360.00	450.00	365.00
☐ white	350.00	410.00	360.00
Tumbler			
☐ marigold	32.00	38.00	36.00
☐ purple	50.00	60.00	52.00
☐ green	50.00	60.00	52.00
☐ blue	50.00	60.00	52.00
☐ amethyst	50.00	60.00	52.00
☐ white	45.00	55.00	47.00

GREEK KEY
Northwood

A pattern repeated often in architecture, mold work, jewelry, and other decorative arts, the Greek key works well on these glass pieces. The central band is made up of the maze-like design, surrounding a starburst of fine rays and framed by a delicate row of bead work. This pattern was used often and the colors vary widely.

Bowl, flat, diameter 9"			
☐ marigold	40.00	50.00	45.00
☐ purple	55.00	60.00	58.00
☐ blue	55.00	60.00	58.00
☐ green	55.00	60.00	58.00

	Current Price Range		Prior Year Average
Bowl, footed, diameter 9″			
☐ marigold	40.00	47.00	42.00
☐ purple	55.00	60.00	58.00
☐ blue	55.00	60.00	58.00
☐ green	55.00	60.00	58.00
Pitcher			
☐ marigold	450.00	500.00	475.00
☐ purple	225.00	250.00	230.00
☐ blue	225.00	250.00	230.00
☐ green	225.00	250.00	230.00
☐ red	600.00	750.00	625.00
Plate			
☐ marigold	110.00	135.00	115.00
☐ purple	230.00	240.00	235.00
☐ blue	230.00	245.00	235.00
☐ green	260.00	300.00	270.00
Tumbler			
☐ marigold	40.00	60.00	42.00
☐ purple	85.00	100.00	92.00
☐ blue	60.00	80.00	62.00
☐ green	80.00	100.00	90.00

HATTIE
Imperial

An extremely busy pattern, an all-over design of various motifs decorates these pieces. The central medallion is a plainly petaled flower resembling a daisy surrounded by the rest of the design made up of flowers in triangular ridges. The colors are marigold, green, amethyst, and smoke.

	Current Price Range		Prior Year Average
Bowl, diameter 9″			
☐ marigold	30.00	50.00	32.00
☐ green	45.00	60.00	47.00
☐ amethyst	45.00	60.00	47.00
☐ smoke	62.00	70.00	64.00
Plate, diameter 9″			
☐ marigold	72.00	80.00	75.00
☐ green	123.00	133.00	128.00
☐ amethyst	123.00	133.00	128.00
☐ smoke	136.00	145.00	140.00
Rose Bowl			
☐ marigold	58.00	65.00	60.00

HEADDRESS
Imperial

A busy overall pattern of high relief feathers composed of radiating ridges in an arched design. The center is a lobed petal flower, each feather radiating out of a section of the bloom. The colors vary widely.

Bowl, diameter 9″			
☐ marigold	16.00	18.00	17.00
☐ purple	25.00	30.00	28.00
☐ green	25.00	30.00	28.00
☐ blue	25.00	30.00	28.00
☐ ice blue	40.00	50.00	46.00
☐ ice green	40.00	50.00	46.00
☐ vaseline	38.00	42.00	40.00
☐ clambroth	38.00	42.00	40.00

HEART AND VINE
Fenton

Heart shapes grow out of a large spread-out wreath of foliage and vine. The center is clear of decoration other than the lower leaves that dip toward the middle. The glass is heavy, the iridescence good, the colors green, blue, white, amethyst, and marigold.

Bowl, diameter 9″			
☐ marigold	25.00	28.00	26.00
☐ green	40.00	45.00	42.00
☐ blue	40.00	45.00	42.00
☐ amethyst	40.00	45.00	42.00
☐ white	60.00	80.00	62.00
Plate, diameter 8″			
☐ marigold	80.00	95.00	82.00
☐ green	130.00	135.00	132.00
☐ blue	130.00	135.00	132.00
☐ amethyst	130.00	135.00	132.00
☐ white	140.00	160.00	142.00

HEARTS AND FLOWERS
Northwood

A detailed overall design of heart-shaped scrolls surrounding petaled leaves form the pattern on these pieces. The center is defined by a diamond-work band framing the central medallion. The colors and shapes run the gamut of Northwood productions.

	Current Price Range		Prior Year Average
Bowl, diameter 9″			
☐ marigold	35.00	45.00	37.00
☐ purple	60.00	75.00	62.00
☐ green	60.00	75.00	62.00
☐ blue	60.00	75.00	62.00
☐ amethyst	60.00	75.00	62.00
☐ white	70.00	90.00	72.00
☐ ice blue	80.00	90.00	76.00
☐ ice green	80.00	90.00	76.00
☐ aqua opalescent	235.00	290.00	42.00
Compote			
☐ marigold	40.00	50.00	70.00
☐ purple	70.00	90.00	80.00
☐ green	65.00	87.50	70.00
☐ blue	65.00	87.50	70.00
☐ amethyst	65.00	87.50	70.00
☐ white	80.00	100.00	82.00
☐ ice blue	175.00	225.00	200.00
☐ ice green	175.00	225.00	200.00
☐ aqua opalescent	260.00	300.00	270.00
Plate, diameter 9½″			
☐ marigold	110.00	140.00	115.00
☐ purple	220.00	280.00	225.00
☐ green	220.00	280.00	225.00
☐ blue	220.00	280.00	225.00
☐ amethyst	220.00	280.00	225.00
☐ white	220.00	270.00	280.00
☐ ice blue	250.00	320.00	275.00
☐ ice green	250.00	320.00	275.00

HEARTSTONE TREES
Fenton

Large knobby stipples serve as the ground for this many-motifed pattern. Beadwork, hearts of triple ridges and trees growing out of a chain-link band adorn the pieces in an all-over design. The colors are green, marigold, blue, and amethyst.

Bowl, diameter 8″			
☐ marigold	130.00	150.00	140.00
☐ green	145.00	155.00	150.00
☐ blue	145.00	155.00	150.00
☐ amethyst	145.00	155.00	150.00

	Current Price Range		Prior Year Average
Compote			
☐ marigold	30.00	42.00	32.00
☐ green	45.00	52.00	47.00
☐ blue	45.00	52.00	47.00
☐ amethyst	45.00	52.00	47.00
Pitcher			
☐ marigold	120.00	135.00	130.00
☐ green	135.00	140.00	137.00
☐ blue	135.00	140.00	137.00
☐ amethyst	135.00	140.00	137.00
Plate, diameter 9″			
☐ marigold	40.00	45.00	42.00
☐ green	45.00	52.00	46.00
☐ blue	45.00	52.00	46.00
☐ amethyst	45.00	52.00	46.00
Tumbler			
☐ marigold	40.00	45.00	42.00
☐ green	45.00	52.00	46.00
☐ blue	45.00	52.00	47.00
☐ amethyst	45.00	52.00	47.00

HEAVY GRAPE
Imperial

The central decoration is the thick, high relief grape bunch surrounded by foliage and backgrounded with stippling. The rest of the piece is smooth but notched in huge thumbprints which pick up the light and show off the incredible iridescence. The colors come in green, purple, amber, blue, marigold, and amethyst.

Berry Bowl, diameter 5″			
☐ marigold	20.00	25.00	22.00
☐ green	25.00	30.00	27.00
☐ purple	25.00	30.00	27.00
☐ blue	25.00	30.00	27.00
☐ amethyst	25.00	30.00	27.00
☐ amber	45.00	60.00	47.00
Berry Bowl, diameter 9″			
☐ marigold	40.00	60.00	42.00
☐ green	72.00	80.00	75.00
☐ purple	72.00	80.00	75.00
☐ blue	72.00	80.00	75.00
☐ amethyst	72.00	80.00	75.00
☐ amber	80.00	100.00	84.00
Chop Plate, diameter 12″			
☐ marigold	180.00	210.00	185.00
☐ green	300.00	325.00	310.00
☐ purple	300.00	325.00	310.00
☐ blue	300.00	325.00	310.00
☐ amethyst	300.00	325.00	310.00

	Current Price Range		Prior Year Average
☐ amber	360.00	400.00	275.00
Plate, diameter 7"			
☐ marigold	40.00	60.00	42.00
☐ green	65.00	80.00	67.00
☐ purple	65.00	80.00	67.00
☐ blue	65.00	80.00	67.00
☐ amethyst	65.00	80.00	67.00
☐ amber	90.00	100.00	94.00

HEAVY GRAPE
Millersburg

The design is sharply molded, almost resembling cut or engraved glass. The grape bunches in high relief alternate with oak leaves, connected with narrow branches and surrounding the central medallion of leaf over grapes. The pattern has a golden iridescence; colors are varied.

Bowl

☐ marigold	75.00	90.00	80.00
☐ purple	110.00	155.00	115.00
☐ green	110.00	155.00	115.00
☐ blue	225.00	300.00	230.00
☐ amethyst	110.00	155.00	120.00

HEAVY IRIS
Dugan

The detail is in such high relief it appears to be sculptured. The design is stylized blooms on long stems with foliage and flora. The upper rim is fluted in a wide ruffle on the pitcher, the tumbler has a wide ridged band of smooth glass atop the design. The colors are marigold, white, and purple.

Pitcher

☐ marigold	400.00	500.00	425.00
☐ purple	700.00	825.00	725.00
☐ green	700.00	825.00	725.00
☐ blue	700.00	825.00	725.00
☐ amethyst	700.00	825.00	725.00
☐ white	750.00	875.00	760.00

Tumbler

☐ marigold	40.00	50.00	42.00
☐ purple	55.00	67.50	60.00
☐ green	55.00	67.50	60.00
☐ blue	55.00	67.50	60.00
☐ amethyst	55.00	67.50	60.00
☐ white	75.00	95.00	80.00

HEAVY PRISM
Davisons

This is a tasteful design of balanced bands, lozenge style on the upper and lower portions of the body. The middle ground is heavily paneled with chunky prisms in high relief. The upper rim is a beaded strip the base is decidedly plain. The colors are blue, marigold, and amethyst.

		Current Price Range		Prior Year Average
Celery Dish				
☐ marigold		40.00	50.00	42.00
☐ blue		52.00	60.00	55.00
☐ amethyst		52.00	60.00	55.00

HEAVY SHELL
Dugan

The pattern here refers to the modern stylized shell shape, heavily ruffled like nautical fingers. The iridescence is sharply delineated by the almost transparent glass.

Shell				
☐ white		90.00	100.00	95.00

HEAVY WEB
Dugan

These pieces, again, resemble a conch shell, because the richly opalescent peach color, combined with the draped ridges of the web pattern has the look of the sea. The iridescent glass is rainbow-like, the colors peach, green, and purple.

Bowl, diameter 10″				
☐ peach opalescent		100.00	150.00	110.00
☐ green		250.00	350.00	275.00
☐ purple		250.00	350.00	275.00
Plate, diameter 12″				
☐ peach opalescent		225.00	300.00	275.00
☐ green		135.00	150.00	140.00
☐ purple		135.00	150.00	140.00

HERON
Dugan

This is a straightforward design, realistically portrayed, of a heron standing proudly among the marsh growth. The frame on the upper and lower rim is a corded band of diagonal ridges. The pattern decorates only one side, the rest of the mug is of smooth glossy iridescence. Colors are marigold and amethyst.

Mug				
☐ marigold		70.00	90.00	72.00
☐ amethyst		100.00	120.00	110.00

HOBNAIL
Millersburg

Often seen in other types of glass, iridized Carnival glass takes to this pattern well. The glossy knobs are perfectly suited to refracting the rainbows on these deeply colored pieces. The shapes and colors vary widely.

Bowl	Current Price Range		Prior Year Average
☐ cherries, marigold	550.00	675.00	560.00
☐ purple	460.00	550.00	475.00
☐ green	460.00	550.00	475.00
☐ blue	850.00	1000.00	875.00
☐ amethyst	460.00	550.00	475.00

Heron

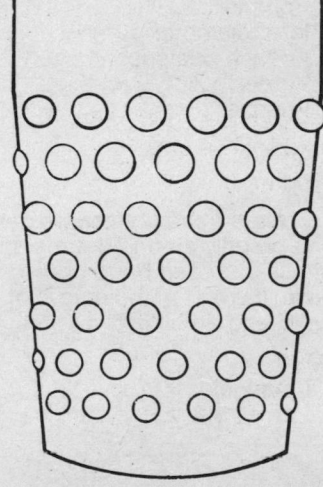

Hobnail

	Current Price Range		Prior Year Average
Butter Dish			
☐ purple	225.00	275.00	240.00
☐ green	225.00	275.00	240.00
☐ blue	450.00	550.00	475.00
☐ amethyst	225.00	275.00	240.00
Creamer			
☐ purple	110.00	150.00	115.00
☐ green	110.00	150.00	115.00
☐ amethyst	225.00	300.00	240.00
☐ amethyst	110.00	150.00	115.00
Pitcher			
☐ marigold	1250.00	1700.00	1400.00
☐ purple	1800.00	2200.00	1950.00
☐ green	1800.00	2200.00	1950.00
☐ blue	3500.00	5000.00	3750.00
☐ amethyst	1800.00	2200.00	1950.00
Rose Bowl			
☐ marigold	85.00	110.00	90.00
☐ purple	110.00	130.00	115.00
☐ green	110.00	130.00	115.00
☐ blue	200.00	275.00	225.00
☐ amethyst	110.00	130.00	115.00
Spittoon			
☐ marigold	225.00	275.00	250.00
☐ purple	275.00	325.00	300.00
☐ green	275.00	325.00	300.00
☐ blue	500.00	650.00	525.00
☐ amethyst	275.00	325.00	300.00
Spooner			
☐ purple	110.00	150.00	115.00
☐ green	110.00	150.00	115.00
☐ blue	225.00	300.00	230.00
☐ amethyst	110.00	150.00	115.00
Tumbler			
☐ marigold	275.00	325.00	300.00
☐ purple	325.00	375.00	340.00
☐ green	325.00	375.00	340.00
☐ blue	650.00	850.00	675.00
☐ amethyst	325.00	375.00	340.00
Vase			
☐ purple	110.00	155.00	115.00
☐ green	110.00	155.00	115.00
☐ blue	200.00	275.00	225.00
☐ amethyst	110.00	155.00	115.00

Hobstar

HOBSTAR
Imperial

It looks like cut glass; the pattern is geometrical and faceted. The diamond banding surrounds a mum-like central motif, repeated around the piece. The design is over all, the background is filled in with fan shaped ridges. The colors are marigold, purple, and green.

	Current Price Range		Prior Year Average
Butter Dish			
☐ marigold	60.00	75.00	62.00
☐ purple	160.00	200.00	165.00
☐ green	160.00	200.00	165.00
☐ blue	160.00	200.00	165.00
☐ amethyst	160.00	200.00	165.00
Cracker Jar			
☐ marigold	60.00	75.00	62.00
Creamer			
☐ marigold	18.00	23.00	20.00
☐ purple	85.00	110.00	90.00
☐ green	85.00	110.00	90.00
☐ blue	85.00	110.00	90.00
☐ amethyst	85.00	110.00	90.00
Pickle Castor			
☐ marigold	300.00	375.00	325.00
Spooner			
☐ marigold	18.00	23.00	20.00
☐ purple	85.00	110.00	90.00
☐ green	85.00	110.00	90.00
☐ blue	85.00	110.00	90.00
☐ amethyst	85.00	110.00	90.00

	Current Price Range		Prior Year Average

Sugar Bowl

☐ marigold	18.00	23.00	20.00
☐ purple	85.00	110.00	90.00
☐ green	85.00	110.00	90.00
☐ blue	85.00	110.00	90.00
☐ amethyst	85.00	110.00	90.00

HOBSTAR AND ARCHES
Imperial

The hobstar flower, still the central design, is surrounded and almost obscured by a busy overall pattern. Beadwork arches, broken at the matrix and forming a tent-shaped form, sweep over the piece in continuous motion. The colors are marigold, amethyst, green, and smoke.

Bowl, diameter 9"

☐ marigold	32.00	36.00	34.00
☐ amethyst	42.00	46.00	43.00
☐ green	42.00	46.00	43.00
☐ smoke	52.00	66.00	54.00

Fruit Bowl, two piece

☐ marigold	70.00	85.00	73.00
☐ amethyst	90.00	100.00	94.00
☐ green	90.00	100.00	94.00
☐ smoke	110.00	120.00	115.00

HOBSTAR AND CUT TRIANGLES
English manufacturer

This is a bizarre pattern of sharp counterpoints. Lozenged triangles, slightly convex but very angular and geometrical, are spaced between flat planes of iridescent glass. The effect is good because it is so different. The shapes are varied, the colors are marigold, green, and amethyst.

Bowl

☐ marigold	45.00	65.00	47.00
☐ green	65.00	80.00	67.00
☐ amethyst	65.00	80.00	67.00

Compote

☐ marigold	45.00	65.00	47.00
☐ green	65.00	80.00	67.00
☐ amethyst	65.00	80.00	67.00

Plate

☐ marigold	45.00	65.00	50.00
☐ green	60.00	80.00	65.00
☐ amethyst	60.00	80.00	65.00

Rose Bowl

☐ marigold	45.00	65.00	50.00
☐ green	60.00	80.00	65.00
☐ amethyst	60.00	80.00	65.00

HOBSTAR AND FEATHER
Millersburg

A heavy, chunky pattern on thick glass distinguishes this style. The feathers are arranged around the hobstar which is deeply cut with a marble-like center. The rim is bullet-edged and scalloped, the bottom base is banded with a lozenge motif. The pedestal's edge is also bullet-rimmed. The shapes vary widely and the colors are green, marigold, and amethyst.

	Current Price Range		Prior Year Average
Punch Bowl			
☐ marigold	1600.00	2000.00	1800.00
☐ purple	2500.00	3000.00	2600.00
☐ green	2500.00	3000.00	2600.00
☐ amethyst	2500.00	3000.00	2600.00
Punch Cup			
☐ marigold	100.00	200.00	125.00
☐ purple	110.00	240.00	150.00
☐ green	110.00	240.00	150.00
☐ blue	160.00	240.00	200.00
☐ amethyst	110.00	240.00	150.00
Vase			
☐ purple	1500.00	1900.00	1600.00
☐ green	1500.00	1900.00	1600.00
☐ amethyst	1500.00	1900.00	1600.00

HOBSTAR BAND
Imperial

This interesting pattern is made up of elongated petals, on the lower half containing vertical rows of beadwork, the upper pointed ovals contain the hobstar. The clear glass has a diamond-like iridescence shown off in marigold.

Pitcher			
☐ marigold	190.00	210.00	195.00
Tumbler			
☐ marigold	40.00	45.00	42.00

HOBSTAR FLOWER
Northwood

This is a pleasing pattern of fruit and flower, spaced by triangular cuts framed by beaded strips. The flower or hobstar that forms the central motif is a sun-like shape of proportionately large size. It is found in marigold and amethyst.

Compote			
☐ marigold	55.00	65.00	57.00
☐ amethyst	70.00	85.00	72.00

HOBSTAR REVERSED
Davisons

This is a similar pattern to Hobstar panels, but the elongated panels which contain a simple light sided hobstar have a gentler curve, a pointed oval shape. The glass is transparent but the colors are good; in amethyst, marigold, and blue.

	Current Price Range		Prior Year Average
Butter Dish			
☐ marigold	45.00	55.00	47.00
☐ blue	50.00	65.00	52.00
☐ amethyst	50.00	65.00	52.00
Frog, with base			
☐ marigold	45.00	60.00	47.00
Spooner			
☐ marigold	40.00	60.00	42.00

HOLLY
Fenton

This is an overall foliage pattern in high relief. The vines and leaves are presented delicately radiating out from the center in a broad circular pattern. The pattern is prolific, used on almost all the shapes and comes in all of the Fenton colors including: amethyst and variations, different shades of marigold, green, blue, and their icy counterparts; also red, white, and vaseline.

Bowl, diameter 7¼"			
☐ marigold	16.00	20.00	18.00
☐ green	32.00	40.00	36.00
☐ blue	32.00	40.00	36.00
☐ amethyst	32.00	40.00	36.00
☐ ice blue	65.00	80.00	70.00
☐ ice green	65.00	80.00	70.00
☐ vaseline	50.00	65.00	52.00
☐ white	50.00	65.00	52.00
☐ red	575.00	600.00	580.00
Bowl, diameter 10"			
☐ marigold	16.00	20.00	18.00
☐ green	32.00	40.00	34.00
☐ blue	32.00	40.00	34.00
☐ amethyst	32.00	40.00	34.00
☐ ices	65.00	80.00	70.00
☐ vaseline	50.00	65.00	52.00
☐ white	50.00	65.00	52.00
☐ red	575.00	600.00	580.00
Compote, small			
☐ marigold	12.00	18.00	14.00
☐ green	32.00	36.00	34.00
☐ blue	32.00	36.00	34.00
☐ amethyst	32.00	36.00	34.00

	Current Price Range		Prior Year Average
☐ ices	50.00	60.00	53.00
☐ vaseline	40.00	50.00	42.00
☐ white	40.00	50.00	42.00
☐ red	150.00	200.00	160.00
Compote			
☐ marigold	16.00	19.00	17.00
☐ green	25.00	30.00	26.00
☐ blue	25.00	30.00	26.00
☐ amethyst	25.00	30.00	26.00
☐ ices	50.00	60.00	53.00
☐ vaseline	40.00	45.00	42.00
☐ white	40.00	45.00	42.00
☐ red	160.00	185.00	165.00
Hat Shape			
☐ marigold	14.00	16.00	16.00
☐ green	20.00	25.00	22.00
☐ blue	20.00	25.00	22.00
☐ amethyst	20.00	25.00	22.00
☐ ices	50.00	60.00	53.00
☐ vaseline	40.00	44.00	42.00
☐ white	40.00	44.00	42.00
☐ red	250.00	350.00	300.00
Plate			
☐ marigold	50.00	55.00	52.00
☐ green	65.00	72.00	67.00
☐ blue	65.00	72.00	67.00
☐ amethyst	65.00	72.00	67.00
☐ ices	110.00	120.00	115.00
☐ vaseline	100.00	120.00	110.00
☐ white	130.00	150.00	140.00
☐ red	600.00	750.00	625.00

HOLLY AND BERRY
Dugan

The central medallion is a sprig of holly and berries, sharply and delicately molded. The design then continues around the interior in a wide band of foliage and fruits. The colors are purple, blue, green, marigold, and peach opalescent.

Bowl

☐ marigold	30.00	40.00	34.00
☐ purple	45.00	55.00	46.00
☐ green	45.00	55.00	46.00
☐ blue	45.00	55.00	46.00
☐ amethyst	45.00	55.00	46.00
☐ peach opalescent	80.00	100.00	90.00
Nappy, handled			
☐ marigold	40.00	50.00	42.00
☐ purple	60.00	75.00	62.00

	Current Price Range		Prior Year Average
☐ green	60.00	75.00	62.00
☐ blue	60.00	75.00	62.00
☐ amethyst	60.00	75.00	62.00
☐ peach opalescent	85.00	95.00	87.00

HOLLY SPRIG
Millersburg

This is a basic holly pattern, with the sharply pointed leaves twisting in a wreath shape around the waist, interspersed with berries. The rim is ruffled irregularly in an indented pattern. Colors are marigold, amethyst, and green.

Bowl

☐ marigold	35.00	45.00	37.00
☐ purple	55.00	65.00	57.00
☐ green	55.00	65.00	57.00
☐ blue	100.00	130.00	110.00
☐ amethyst	55.00	65.00	57.00

Nappy

☐ marigold	35.00	45.00	37.00
☐ purple	45.00	55.00	47.00
☐ green	45.00	55.00	47.00
☐ blue	90.00	100.00	95.00
☐ amethyst	45.00	55.00	47.00
☐ white	40.00	50.00	42.00
☐ ice green	50.00	65.00	55.00
☐ ice blue	50.00	65.00	55.00

Sauce Dish

☐ marigold	110.00	150.00	115.00
☐ purple	120.00	160.00	125.00
☐ green	120.00	160.00	125.00
☐ blue	250.00	300.00	275.00
☐ amethyst	120.00	160.00	130.00

HONEYCOMB ROSEBOWL
Dugan

High relief ridges make up this straightforward pattern. The hexagonal shape appears almost intaglio because the heightened ridges are over the piece in its entirety. The shape of the piece is simply rounded, all together an effective design. Colors are marigold and peach.

Rose Bowl

☐ marigold	100.00	125.00	115.00
☐ peach opalescent	150.00	175.00	160.00

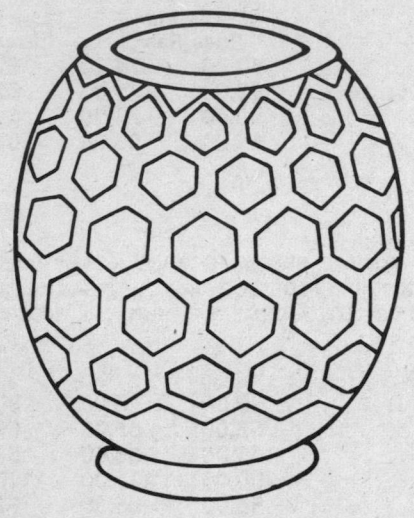

Honeycomb Rosebowl

HORSE'S HEAD
Fenton

A band of beadwork ovals framing the bust of a spirited horse rounds the interior of pieces with this pattern. The ground between these cameos is scale-like, covering the majority of the bowl. The colors are blue, green, white, vaseline, aqua, and marigold.

	Current Price Range		Prior Year Average
Bowl, flat, diameter 7″			
☐ marigold	50.00	60.00	52.00
☐ blue	72.00	80.00	75.00
☐ green	72.00	80.00	75.00
☐ vaseline	125.00	130.00	126.00
☐ aqua opalescent	140.00	160.00	145.00
Bowl, footed, diameter 7″			
☐ marigold	58.00	62.00	60.00
☐ blue	58.00	62.00	60.00
☐ green	62.00	70.00	64.00
☐ vaseline	125.00	150.00	130.00
☐ aqua opalescent	140.00	160.00	145.00
Plate, diameter 6½″			
☐ marigold	82.00	95.00	65.00
☐ green	110.00	130.00	115.00
☐ blue	110.00	130.00	115.00
☐ vaseline	140.00	160.00	145.00
☐ aqua opalescent	150.00	165.00	160.00
Rose Bowl			
☐ marigold	90.00	95.00	92.00
☐ green	100.00	110.00	105.00
☐ blue	100.00	110.00	105.00

	Current Price Range		Prior Year Average
☐ vaseline	185.00	200.00	190.00
☐ aqua opalescent	190.00	210.00	200.00

ILLINOIS DAISY
Davisons of Gateshead

The daisies on the surface of this pattern are rounded and plump. The center is a marble circle in high relief. The framework that separates each flower is scroll-like, twisting and turning, interconnected. The glass is heavy, resembling cut glass; the color is marigold.

Bon-Bon
☐ marigold	42.00	50.00	45.00
Bowl			
☐ marigold	60.00	75.00	62.00

ILLUSION
Fenton

The pattern is an interesting combination of straightforward flora and foliage and a central medallion of Escher-like shapes. The connection between the blooms and the geometrics creates quite a different perspective. The colors are marigold and blue.

Bon Bon
☐ marigold	42.00	50.00	45.00
☐ blue	62.00	80.00	65.00
Bowl			
☐ marigold	62.00	80.00	65.00
☐ blue	82.00	100.00	85.00

INDIANA STATE HOUSE
Fenton

This is a souvenir plate with the center motif a well-detailed building. The rest of the pattern is devoid of decoration but is richly iridized. The rim is an irregular scallop with a bullet edge. The color is marigold.

Plate
☐ marigold	1500.00	2000.00	1600.00

INTAGLIO DAISY
Sowerby

Horizontal and vertical panels of angular ridges frame deep cut branches and intricately lined flowers. This combination of geometry and tradition makes a neat intaglio pattern. The color is marigold.

Bowl, diameter 4″
☐ marigold	20.00	25.00	22.00
Bowl, diameter 7¾″			
☐ marigold	20.00	25.00	22.00

INVERTED STRAWBERRY
Cambridge

This is a lovely intaglio pattern of stylized fruit and foliage, dancing in motion over the piece. The strawberries are made up of tiny fretwork rows of diamonds, dainty and sharply cut. The branches and leaves are understated, showing off a glossy, smooth background. The colors are marigold, amethyst, green, and blue.

	Current Price Range		Prior Year Average
Berry Bowl, diameter 5″			
☐ marigold	30.00	37.00	32.00
☐ amethyst	50.00	60.00	52.00
☐ green	50.00	60.00	52.00
☐ blue	50.00	60.00	52.00
Berry Bowl, diameter 9″			
☐ marigold	60.00	70.00	62.00
☐ amethyst	90.00	100.00	93.00
☐ green	90.00	100.00	93.00
☐ blue	90.00	100.00	93.00
Butter Dish, with cover			
☐ marigold	200.00	225.00	210.00
☐ amethyst	275.00	310.00	300.00
☐ green	275.00	310.00	300.00
☐ blue	275.00	310.00	300.00
Candlesticks			
☐ marigold	120.00	130.00	125.00
☐ amethyst	160.00	180.00	175.00
☐ green	160.00	180.00	175.00
☐ blue	160.00	180.00	175.00
Compote			
☐ marigold	160.00	185.00	175.00
☐ amethyst	225.00	260.00	230.00
☐ green	225.00	260.00	230.00
☐ blue	225.00	260.00	230.00
Creamer			
☐ marigold	70.00	90.00	72.00
☐ amethyst	95.00	115.00	100.00
☐ green	95.00	115.00	100.00
☐ blue	95.00	115.00	100.00
Cuspidor			
☐ marigold	900.00	1100.00	950.00
☐ amethyst	900.00	1100.00	950.00
☐ green	900.00	1100.00	950.00
☐ blue	900.00	1100.00	950.00
Milk Pitcher			
☐ amethyst	1200.00	1400.00	1250.00
☐ green	1200.00	1400.00	1250.00
☐ blue	1200.00	1400.00	1250.00
Pitcher			
☐ marigold	575.00	700.00	600.00
☐ amethyst	850.00	1000.00	860.00

	Current Price Range		Prior Year Average
☐ green	850.00	1000.00	860.00
☐ blue	850.00	1000.00	860.00

INVERTED THISTLE
Cambridge

Another intaglio pattern from the English innovators, this design is tasteful and classic. The flowers of the thistle are made up of the same fretwork as inverted strawberry, the branches and leaves are stylized into scrolls, the upper half of the bloom suggests a crown. The colors are marigold, amethyst, green and, less commonly, blue.

Butter Dish, with cover
☐ marigold	320.00	335.00	325.00
☐ amethyst	425.00	475.00	450.00
☐ green	425.00	475.00	450.00
☐ blue	425.00	475.00	450.00

Creamer
☐ marigold	120.00	135.00	125.00
☐ amethyst	180.00	195.00	190.00
☐ green	180.00	195.00	190.00
☐ blue	180.00	195.00	190.00

Pitcher
☐ marigold	2500.00	3000.00	2600.00
☐ amethyst	2500.00	3000.00	2600.00
☐ green	2500.00	3000.00	2600.00
☐ blue	2500.00	3000.00	2600.00

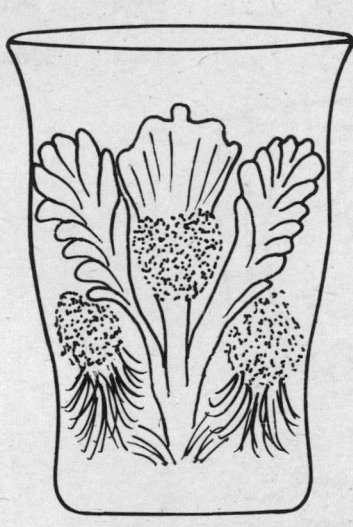

Inverted Thistle

	Current Price Range		Prior Year Average
Spooner			
☐ marigold	120.00	135.00	125.00
☐ amethyst	180.00	195.00	190.00
☐ green	180.00	195.00	190.00
☐ blue	180.00	195.00	190.00
Sugar Bowl			
☐ marigold	120.00	135.00	125.00
☐ amethyst	180.00	195.00	190.00
☐ green	180.00	195.00	190.00
☐ blue	180.00	195.00	190.00
Tumbler			
☐ marigold	325.00	375.00	340.00
☐ amethyst	325.00	375.00	340.00
☐ green	325.00	375.00	340.00
☐ blue	325.00	375.00	340.00

JEWELED HEART
Dugan

The heart is made up of scrolls facing each other in a kiss, the background of the heart is stippled, giving a gem-like appearance. In the center of each panel is a football shape, suggesting an oval jewel. The upper rim is beaded. The colors are marigold, purple, and peach.

Berry Bowl, diameter 5″			
☐ peach opalescent	30.00	35.00	32.00
Berry Bowl, diameter 10″			
☐ peach opalescent	80.00	95.00	82.00
Pitcher			
☐ marigold	600.00	675.00	625.00

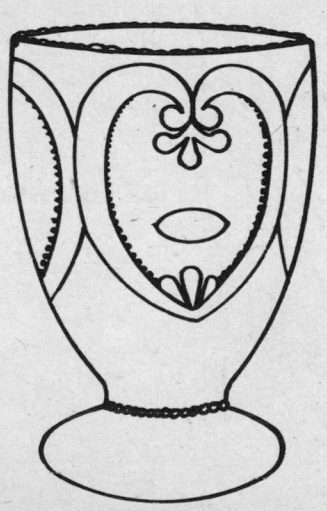

Jeweled Heart

	Current Price Range		Prior Year Average
☐ purple	725.00	850.00	750.00
☐ green	725.00	850.00	750.00
☐ blue	725.00	850.00	750.00
☐ amethyst	725.00	850.00	750.00
Tumbler			
☐ marigold	70.00	100.00	72.00
☐ purple	80.00	115.00	84.00
☐ green	80.00	115.00	84.00
☐ blue	80.00	115.00	84.00
☐ amethyst	80.00	115.00	84.00

JOCKEY CLUB
Northwood

The interior of the bowl is inscribed "Jockey Club" in elongated cursive, winding around a horseshoe. The floral pattern below is a neat bloom on a foliaged stem, with a tiny duplicate right above the inscription. The iridescence is lavish, the color amethyst and other dark tints.

Plate			
☐ purple	110.00	140.00	115.00
☐ green	110.00	140.00	115.00
☐ blue	110.00	140.00	115.00
☐ amethyst	110.00	140.00	115.00

KINGFISHER
Australian Manufacturer

The bird is perched proudly in the center. He sits on delicate branches surrounded with a wreath of foliage. The central medallion is stippled, the rest of the glass smooth. A variant adds berries to the foliage. The color is purple or marigold.

Kingfisher

	Current Price Range		Prior Year Average

Bowl, diameter 9″

☐ marigold	120.00	130.00	125.00
☐ purple	160.00	180.00	170.00

KITTENS
Fenton

Originally children's glass, this pattern found on many bowls and other shapes and is a favorite with collectors. It shows a series of kittens falling over each other to drink from a long oval bowl. The rest of the glass is smooth and the iridescence magnificent. The colors are vaseline, marigold, and cobalt.

Bowl, oval

☐ marigold	62.00	70.00	64.00
☐ cobalt blue	83.00	90.00	84.00
☐ vaseline	90.00	100.00	92.00

Bowl, upswept sides

☐ marigold	67.00	75.00	70.00
☐ cobalt blue	80.00	90.00	82.00
☐ vaseline	175.00	200.00	190.00

Cereal Bowl

☐ marigold	82.00	90.00	84.00
☐ cobalt blue	95.00	100.00	90.00
☐ vaseline	115.00	125.00	120.00

Cup and Saucer

☐ marigold	145.00	160.00	150.00
☐ cobalt blue	190.00	210.00	195.00

Spooner

☐ marigold	100.00	150.00	125.00
☐ cobalt blue	200.00	250.00	225.00
☐ vaseline	100.00	110.00	105.00

Vase, height 3¼″

☐ marigold	125.00	150.00	130.00
☐ cobalt blue	125.00	150.00	130.00
☐ vaseline	160.00	175.00	165.00

KIWI
Australian Manufacturer

This is an interesting pattern of the New Zealand birds in the foreground, a mountain range in good perspective in the background. This scene makes up the central medallion, the rest of the piece is covered with delicate, etched ferns. The colors are dark, marigold, and purple.

Bowl, diameter 10″

☐ marigold	60.00	80.00	62.00
☐ purple	80.00	90.00	85.00

KNOTTED BEADS
Fenton

This is a modernistic pattern consisting of stretched beads grouped in oval shapes and connected in big bows. The pattern is not directly vertical, it twists diagonally from the base to the upper rim which is ruffled irregularly. The colors are blue, green, white, vaseline, and marigold.

	Current Price Range		Prior Year Average
Vase			
☐ marigold	40.00	60.00	42.00
☐ blue	20.00	30.00	25.00
☐ green	30.00	50.00	40.00
☐ vaseline	70.00	80.00	72.00
☐ white	70.00	80.00	72.00

KOOKABURRA
Australian Manufacturer

Looking like the Kingfisher, the little Australian bird is perched in the center on a thick horizontal branch. The outer pattern which rims the interior is a busy, varied design of different blooms and stylized foliage. As with the Kingfisher, there is a variant which is distinguished by a large stippled medallion.

Butter Dish			
☐ marigold	75.00	90.00	77.00
☐ purple	90.00	110.00	92.00
☐ blue	90.00	110.00	92.00
☐ green	90.00	110.00	92.00

Lattice and Daisy

LATTICE AND DAISY
Dugan

The lattice is a wide banded lozenge just under the smooth rim. Just below is a diagonally angled daisy on detailed foliage. The glass is nearly opaque, the iridescence is rainbow-like and the colors are marigold and cobalt.

	Current Price Range		Prior Year Average
Butter Dish			
☐ marigold	7.00	9.00	7.50
Berry Bowl, diameter 9″			
☐ marigold	20.00	25.00	22.00
Tankard Pitcher			
☐ marigold	80.00	90.00	82.00
☐ cobalt blue	310.00	340.00	315.00
Tumbler			
☐ marigold	17.00	30.00	19.00
☐ cobalt blue	30.00	32.00	31.00

LEA
Sowerby

This is a simple, tasteful design made up of stippled bands horizontally alternating with vertical ridging. The interior is smooth but reflects the exterior design in an interesting effect. The colors are amethyst and marigold.

Bowl, oval, footed			
☐ marigold	25.00	27.00	26.00
☐ amethyst	38.00	40.00	39.00
Bowl, round, footed			
☐ marigold	22.00	25.00	23.00
☐ amethyst	32.00	36.00	34.00
Creamer, footed			
☐ marigold	20.00	25.00	22.00
☐ amethyst	30.00	40.00	32.00

Leaf and Beads

LEAF AND BEADS
Northwood

This prolific pattern is found on many shapes in various types of glass. In Carnival, it has a wonderful iridescence on opaque color. The design is a row of leaves growing out of the base, terminating a quarter of the way up in a bead band that continues to the rim. The background is smooth and shows of the rainbow effect. The colors available are the wides range of Northwood tints.

Candy Bowl	Current Price Range		Prior Year Average
☐ marigold	35.00	43.00	37.00
☐ purple	50.00	60.00	52.00
☐ green	50.00	60.00	52.00
☐ blue	50.00	60.00	52.00
☐ amethyst	50.00	60.00	52.00
☐ white	80.00	110.00	85.00
☐ ice green	90.00	120.00	95.00
☐ ice blue	90.00	120.00	95.00
☐ aqua opalescent	160.00	210.00	175.00
Rose Bowl, footed			
☐ marigold	40.00	50.00	42.00
☐ purple	60.00	90.00	70.00
☐ green	57.50	72.50	60.00
☐ blue	57.50	72.50	60.00
☐ amethyst	57.50	72.50	60.00
☐ white	85.00	100.00	87.00
☐ ice green	90.00	110.00	87.00
☐ ice blue	90.00	110.00	87.00
☐ aqua opalescent	180.00	235.00	187.00

LEAF CHAIN
Fenton

This overall design is common on many types of articles. It is made up of a snowflake medallion taking up the center in an intricate scrolled design. This motif is continued around the edge in panels surrounded by a scale background and curvy scrolls. Colors run the gamut available to Carnival glass.

Bon Bon			
☐ marigold	18.00	22.00	19.00
☐ purple	32.00	40.00	34.00
☐ green	32.00	40.00	34.00
☐ blue	32.00	40.00	34.00
☐ amethyst	32.00	40.00	34.00
Bowl			
☐ marigold	18.00	20.00	17.00
☐ purple	30.00	40.00	32.00
☐ green	30.00	40.00	32.00
☐ blue	30.00	40.00	32.00
☐ amethyst	30.00	40.00	32.00

	Current Price Range		Prior Year Average

Plate
☐ marigold	42.00	35.00	43.00
☐ green	70.00	80.00	72.00
☐ blue	70.00	80.00	72.00
☐ purple	70.00	80.00	72.00
☐ amethyst	70.00	80.00	72.00
☐ ices	100.00	110.00	105.00

LEAF COLUMN
Northwood

This pattern is a series of vertical bands made up of fern-like leaves. They curve around the vase framed with a reversed arch rather resembling twigs or branches. The iridescence is good and the colors range widely.

Lamp Shade
☐ white	80.00	110.00	85.00
☐ ice green	80.00	110.00	85.00
☐ ice blue	80.00	110.00	85.00

Vase
☐ marigold	25.00	32.00	27.00
☐ purple	30.00	40.00	32.00
☐ green	30.00	40.00	32.00
☐ blue	30.00	40.00	32.00
☐ amethyst	30.00	40.00	32.00
☐ white	80.00	110.00	82.00
☐ ice green	90.00	120.00	82.00
☐ ice blue	90.00	120.00	82.00
☐ peach opalescent	45.00	65.00	47.00

LEAF SWIRL
Millersburg

Again geometry combines with naturalistic design to create this pattern. Leaves grow out of the pedestal base, each framed with a diagonally curved panel that continues up the side, terminating at the widely ruffled rim. The colors are excellent, and range widely.

Bowl
☐ marigold	20.00	22.00	21.00
☐ purple	28.00	32.00	30.00
☐ green	28.00	32.00	30.00
☐ blue	28.00	32.00	30.00
☐ amethyst	28.00	32.00	30.00
☐ white	35.00	40.00	37.00
☐ ices	50.00	60.00	52.00

Compote
| ☐ marigold | 35.00 | 45.00 | 37.00 |

	Current Price Range		Prior Year Average
☐ purple	38.00	47.50	39.00
☐ green	38.00	47.50	39.00
☐ blue	65.00	85.00	67.00
☐ amethyst	38.00	47.50	39.00
☐ white	38.00	47.50	39.00
☐ ice blue	44.00	60.00	50.00
☐ ice green	44.00	60.00	50.00

LEAF SWIRL AND FLOWER
Fenton

The pattern is etched into the piece, not quite intaglio but in low relief. It is a lovely, delicate design of flowers and foliage and it covers the piece sparingly. The colors available are marigold and other pastels.

Vase

☐ marigold	25.00	40.00	27.00
☐ ices	35.00	50.00	37.00

LEAF TIERS
Sowerly

The leaves are set in rows overlapping around the piece, creating an interesting perspective. It is a straightforward, overall pattern that shows off the iridescence nicely. The most common color is marigold, then purple, green, and blue.

Berry Bowl, diameter 5½"

☐ marigold	14.00	16.00	15.00

Berry Bowl, diameter 9"

☐ marigold	30.00	35.00	32.00

Butter Dish

☐ marigold	10.00	15.00	12.00

Creamer

☐ marigold	42.00	46.00	44.00

Spooner

☐ marigold	42.00	46.00	44.00

Sugar Bowl

☐ marigold	42.00	46.00	44.00

Tumbler

☐ marigold	45.00	50.00	47.00
☐ purple	80.00	90.00	82.00
☐ green	80.00	90.00	82.00
☐ blue	80.00	90.00	82.00

Water Pitcher

☐ marigold	300.00	325.00	315.00
☐ purple	600.00	650.00	610.00
☐ green	600.00	650.00	610.00
☐ blue	600.00	650.00	610.00

LILY OF THE VALLEY
Fenton

This is a well-balanced pattern of flowers, neatly geometrical leaf work, and beaded bands. Three motifs are used, horizontally rounding the pieces in wide bands. All of the bands contain tiny bell-like flowers. The iridescence is very fine, found in marigold and cobalt.

	Current Price Range		Prior Year Average
Pitcher			
☐ marigold	1500.00	1700.00	1550.00
☐ cobalt............................	2000.00	2200.00	2100.00
Tumbler			
☐ marigold	50.00	70.00	52.00
☐ cobalt............................	80.00	100.00	85.00

LINED LATTICE
Dugan

This is an offbeat pattern of elongated diamond work curving asymmetrically around the piece. Each shape is filled in by vertical ridge which refracts the light to a great degree. Colors come in marigold, amethyst, peach opalescent, blue, white, and green.

Vase			
☐ marigold	17.00	20.00	18.00
☐ blue	22.00	25.00	23.00
☐ green	22.00	25.00	23.00
☐ amethyst	22.00	25.00	23.00
☐ white	35.00	45.00	37.00
☐ peach opalescent	50.00	70.00	60.00

Lion

LION
Fenton

A series of four panels, each made up of a full figured lion in a roaring gallop, round the wide middle of these pieces. The lions seem to be chasing each other tail to tail. They are framed with natural looking trees topped with foliage, growing out of the central medallion of misplaced flowers. The colors are marigold and blue.

	Current Price Range		Prior Year Average
Bowl, diameter 5¼"			
☐ marigold	70.00	80.00	72.00
☐ blue	95.00	110.00	100.00
Bowl, diameter 8½"			
☐ marigold	70.00	80.00	72.00
☐ blue	95.00	110.00	100.00

LITTLE FISHES
Fenton

The fishes are swimming around, practically obscured by a busy combination of geometry and natural designs. There are berries, flowers, leaves, and vines interspersed among diamonds and, most distinctively, "X" shapes. The colors are marigold, purple, green, blue, and amethyst.

Pitcher			
☐ marigold	65.00	80.00	67.00
☐ purple	90.00	110.00	92.00
☐ green	90.00	110.00	92.00
☐ blue	90.00	110.00	92.00
☐ amethyst	90.00	110.00	92.00
Bowl, footed			
☐ marigold	85.00	95.00	87.00
☐ purple	100.00	120.00	110.00
☐ green	100.00	120.00	110.00
☐ blue	100.00	120.00	110.00
☐ amethyst	100.00	120.00	110.00
Plate			
☐ purple	500.00	600.00	520.00
☐ green	500.00	600.00	520.00
☐ blue	500.00	600.00	520.00
☐ amethyst	500.00	600.00	520.00
☐ ices	800.00	850.00	825.00

LITTLE FLOWERS
Fenton

The center is a large flower, widely petaled around a stippled center. The interior band which frames the center is a row of smaller flowers of a different variety, the background is smooth. The colors are green, blue, red, amber, aqua, vaseline, marigold, and amethyst.

Berry Bowl, diameter 5"			
☐ marigold	25.00	28.00	26.00

	Current Price Range		Prior Year Average
☐ green	28.00	32.00	27.00
☐ blue	28.00	32.00	27.00
☐ amethyst	28.00	32.00	27.00
☐ amber	90.00	100.00	95.00
☐ aqua	90.00	100.00	95.00
☐ vaseline	90.00	100.00	95.00
☐ red	600.00	700.00	625.00
Berry Bowl, diameter 9″			
☐ marigold	75.00	110.00	90.00
☐ green	50.00	60.00	52.00
☐ blue	50.00	60.00	52.00
☐ amethyst	50.00	60.00	52.00
☐ amber	100.00	110.00	105.00
☐ aqua	100.00	110.00	105.00
☐ vaseline	110.00	125.00	115.00
Plate			
☐ marigold	100.00	110.00	105.00
☐ green	120.00	135.00	125.00
☐ blue	120.00	135.00	125.00
☐ amethyst	120.00	135.00	125.00
☐ amber	130.00	140.00	135.00
☐ aqua	130.00	140.00	135.00
☐ vaseline	130.00	140.00	135.00

LOGANBERRY
Imperial

This pattern is considered to be one of the greatest in Carnival glass. The mold work is exceptional, tiny berries and foliage in high relief decorating the entire body of the piece, terminating in smooth, arched panels which resolve the neck. The iridation is as glowing and as rainbow as any piece in Carnival. Colors are purple, green, amber, smoke, and marigold.

Vase

☐ marigold	90.00	110.00	95.00
☐ purple	120.00	130.00	125.00
☐ green	130.00	150.00	140.00
☐ amber	170.00	200.00	175.00
☐ smoke	170.00	200.00	175.00

LONG THUMBPRINT
Dugan

This is a simple design of rows of concave ovals in various sizes, eventually stretched out to an airy thinness. The glass is nearly transparent, the colors are blue, green, and amethyst.

Bowl

☐ blue	14.00	16.00	15.00

	Current Price Range		Prior Year Average
☐ green	14.00	16.00	15.00
☐ amethyst	14.00	16.00	15.00
Compote			
☐ blue	15.00	17.00	16.00
☐ green	15.00	17.00	16.00
☐ amethyst	15.00	17.00	16.00
Creamer			
☐ blue	12.00	15.00	14.00
☐ green	12.00	15.00	14.00
☐ amethyst	12.00	15.00	14.00
Sugar Bowl			
☐ blue	12.00	15.00	13.00
☐ green	12.00	15.00	13.00
☐ amethyst	12.00	15.00	13.00

LOTUS AND GRAPE
Fenton

This pattern is distinctive because of the well-molded relief flowers and grapes which are raised nicely but flattened across the surface. The design is all encompassing, covering all of the available space. The colors are green, blue, red, white, amethyst, and marigold.

Bon Bon			
☐ marigold	17.00	20.00	18.00
☐ green	50.00	60.00	55.00
☐ blue	38.00	42.00	40.00
☐ amethyst	38.00	42.00	40.00
☐ white	70.00	75.00	72.00
Bowl			
☐ marigold	17.00	20.00	18.00
☐ green	22.00	25.00	23.00
☐ blue	22.00	25.00	23.00
☐ amethyst	22.00	25.00	23.00
Plate			
☐ marigold	45.00	65.00	47.00
☐ green	90.00	110.00	92.00
☐ blue	90.00	110.00	92.00
☐ amethyst	90.00	110.00	92.00
☐ white	145.00	165.00	150.00

LOUISA
Fenton

Round panels of sparsely decorated flora are made up of vines and leaves. The rest of the ground is filled in with tiny leaves that resemble scales the way they overlap. The colors are marigold, green, blue, and amethyst.

	Current Price Range		Prior Year Average
Bowl, diameter 9″			
☐ marigold	11.00	14.00	12.00
☐ green	17.00	21.00	18.00
☐ blue	17.00	21.00	18.00
☐ amethyst	17.00	21.00	18.00
Bowl, footed			
☐ green	19.00	24.00	20.00
☐ blue	19.00	24.00	20.00
☐ amethyst	19.00	24.00	20.00
Rose Bowl			
☐ marigold	25.00	40.00	27.00
☐ amethyst	40.00	60.00	50.00
☐ green	35.00	50.00	37.00
☐ blue	35.00	50.00	37.00
Sauce Dish			
☐ marigold	6.00	8.00	7.00
☐ amethyst	11.00	13.00	12.00
☐ green	11.00	13.00	12.00
☐ blue	11.00	13.00	12.00

LUSTRE AND CLEAR
Imperial

A simple pattern of pillars resolved at the rim by matching flutes shows off the glowing iridescence. As the name implies, the glass is rather transparent and the color is marigold.

Bowl			
☐ marigold	11.00	13.00	12.00
Butter Dish			
☐ marigold	5.00	6.00	7.00
Creamer			
☐ marigold	16.00	20.00	17.00
Milk Pitcher			
☐ marigold	25.00	28.00	26.00
Nappy			
☐ marigold	7.00	9.00	7.50
Plate			
☐ marigold	8.00	11.00	9.00
Pitcher			
☐ marigold	120.00	130.00	125.00
Sugar Bowl			
☐ marigold	16.00	20.00	18.00
Tumbler			
☐ marigold	18.00	22.00	20.00

Lustre Flute

LUSTRE FLUTE
Northwood

A plain pattern of pillars topped by a lozenge band adorns these pieces. It was made in many shapes and a variety of colors.

	Current Price Range		Prior Year Average
Bowl			
☐ marigold	16.00	20.00	18.00
☐ purple	22.00	28.00	24.00
☐ green	22.00	28.00	24.00
☐ blue	22.00	28.00	24.00
☐ amethyst	22.00	28.00	24.00
Compote			
☐ purple	25.00	32.00	26.00
☐ green	25.00	32.00	26.00
☐ blue	25.00	32.00	26.00
☐ amethyst	25.00	32.00	26.00
Creamer			
☐ marigold	30.00	38.00	32.00
☐ purple	35.00	45.00	37.00
☐ green	35.00	45.00	37.00
☐ blue	35.00	45.00	37.00
☐ amethyst	35.00	45.00	37.00
Nappy			
☐ marigold	18.00	23.00	20.00
☐ purple	25.00	32.00	27.00
☐ blue	25.00	32.00	27.00
☐ amethyst	25.00	32.00	27.00
Punch Bowl, with base			
☐ purple	150.00	180.00	160.00
☐ green	150.00	180.00	160.00
☐ blue	150.00	180.00	160.00
☐ amethyst	150.00	180.00	160.00
Sugar Bowl			
☐ marigold	30.00	38.00	32.00
☐ blue	35.00	45.00	37.00
☐ amethyst	35.00	45.00	37.00

Lustre Rose

LUSTRE ROSE
Imperial

Another favorite among collectors, Lustre Rose was one of Imperial's first patterns. The quality is excellent, the moldwork sharp and the iridescence, of course, wonderful. The design is an intricate band of roses among foliage and thorns. The pattern was made in many shapes and the colors are green, purple, amber, smoke, clambroth, and marigold.

	Current Price Range		Prior Year Average
Berry Bowl, diameter 5″			
☐ marigold	9.00	11.00	10.00
☐ green	18.00	22.00	20.00
☐ purple	18.00	22.00	20.00
Berry Bowl, diameter 9″			
☐ marigold	9.00	11.00	10.00
☐ green	18.00	22.00	20.00
☐ purple	18.00	22.00	20.00
Bowl, flat			
☐ marigold	20.00	24.00	22.00
☐ green	30.00	35.00	32.00
☐ purple	30.00	35.00	32.00
☐ amber	35.00	40.00	37.00
☐ smoke	35.00	40.00	37.00
☐ clambroth	35.00	40.00	37.00
Bowl, footed			
☐ marigold	50.00	60.00	52.00
☐ green	70.00	80.00	72.00
☐ purple	70.00	80.00	72.00
☐ amber	90.00	100.00	95.00
☐ smoke	90.00	100.00	95.00
☐ clambroth	90.00	100.00	95.00

	Current Price Range		Prior Year Average

Fernery

☐ marigold	30.00	40.00	32.00
☐ green	50.00	60.00	55.00
☐ purple	50.00	60.00	55.00
☐ amber	60.00	70.00	65.00
☐ smoke	60.00	70.00	65.00
☐ clambroth	60.00	70.00	65.00

Plate

☐ marigold	17.00	22.00	19.00
☐ green	38.00	45.00	40.00
☐ purple	38.00	45.00	40.00
☐ amber	50.00	60.00	52.00
☐ smoke	50.00	60.00	52.00
☐ clambroth	50.00	60.00	52.00

Tumbler

☐ marigold	20.00	40.00	30.00
☐ green	20.00	30.00	25.00
☐ purple	30.00	35.00	32.00
☐ amber	40.00	45.00	42.00
☐ smoke	40.00	45.00	42.00
☐ clambroth	40.00	45.00	42.00

Water Pitcher

☐ marigold	50.00	60.00	52.00
☐ green	190.00	210.00	200.00
☐ purple	190.00	210.00	200.00
☐ amber	190.00	210.00	200.00
☐ smoke	190.00	210.00	200.00
☐ clambroth	190.00	210.00	200.00

MALAGA
Dugan

It's a new twist on the many grape patterns that exist. The central motif is one big bunch of grapes nestled on leaves like a fruit salad on lettuce. It is framed by a series of rectangular panels, set off at an angle and terminating into a stippled background. The colors are marigold, purple, and green.

Bowl, diameter 9"

☐ marigold	55.00	65.00	57.00
☐ purple	60.00	65.00	62.00
☐ green	60.00	65.00	62.00

MANY FRUITS
Dugan

As the name implies, the overall pattern consists of a great variety of fruits and foliage. The distinctive quality is the sharp moldwork combined with the achievement of wonderful iridescent coloring that makes these pieces a treasure. The colors, which are luminescent, come in green, blue, purple, marigold, and white.

	Current Price Range		Prior Year Average
Punch Bowl, with base			
☐ marigold	175.00	200.00	195.00
☐ purple	400.00	500.00	450.00
☐ blue	275.00	325.00	300.00
☐ white	500.00	600.00	525.00
Punch Cup			
☐ purple	23.00	29.00	25.00
☐ green	23.00	29.00	25.00
☐ amethyst	23.00	29.00	25.00
☐ white	50.00	60.00	52.00

MAPLE LEAF
Dugan

This is an interesting pattern. The geometric mosaic shapes are formed by ridges in high relief and are the background for maple leaf panels that are on the same surface as the ridging. This gives the background an appearance of intaglio design while the panels show in relief. The combination works well as the iridescence is highlighted by these illusions. The colors are blue, green, purple, and marigold.

Butter Dish, with cover			
☐ marigold	75.00	100.00	80.00

Maple Leaf

	Current Price Range		Prior Year Average
☐ purple	100.00	125.00	110.00
☐ green	100.00	125.00	110.00
☐ blue	100.00	125.00	.110.00
☐ amethyst	100.00	125.00	110.00
Creamer			
☐ marigold	35.00	42.00	37.00
☐ purple	45.00	55.00	47.00
☐ green	45.00	55.00	47.00
☐ blue	45.00	55.00	47.00
☐ amethyst	45.00	55.00	47.00
Ice Cream Bowl, stemmed			
☐ marigold	50.00	60.00	52.00
☐ purple	100.00	125.00	115.00
☐ green	100.00	125.00	115.00
☐ blue	100.00	125.00	115.00
☐ amethyst	100.00	125.00	115.00
Pitcher			
☐ marigold	100.00	150.00	145.00
☐ purple	190.00	240.00	210.00
☐ green	250.00	325.00	260.00
☐ blue	250.00	325.00	260.00
☐ amethyst	180.00	230.00	200.00
Spooner			
☐ marigold	35.00	42.00	37.00
☐ purple	45.00	57.50	47.00
☐ green	45.00	57.50	47.00
☐ blue	45.00	57.50	47.00
☐ amethyst	45.00	57.50	47.00

Marilyn

MARILYN
Millersburg

The pattern is a combination of rosettes and fanned ridges framed by X shapes and double arches. The background is smooth, the design balanced and tasteful. The glass is very heavy, well radiated, and the colors are almost opaque in the darker colors.

Pitcher	Current Price Range		Prior Year Average
☐ marigold	600.00	750.00	625.00
☐ purple	775.00	950.00	800.00
☐ green	775.00	950.00	800.00
☐ blue	1500.00	1750.00	1600.00
☐ amethyst	775.00	950.00	800.00
Tumbler			
☐ marigold	25.00	50.00	35.00
☐ purple	130.00	175.00	140.00
☐ green	130.00	175.00	140.00
☐ blue	250.00	325.00	275.00
☐ amethyst	130.00	175.00	140.00

MARY ANN
Dugan

A loving-cup shape, with three shallow handles made up of beadwork jewels, is decorated with a sparse design of foliage and flowers in low relief. The overall effect is a delicate and elegant piece. The iridescence is golden and reflects the highest at the rim.

Vase, three handled			
☐ marigold	70.00	90.00	75.00
☐ purple	180.00	200.00	190.00
☐ green	180.00	200.00	190.00
☐ blue	180.00	200.00	190.00
☐ amethyst	180.00	200.00	190.00

Mayan

MAYAN
Millersburg

A unique pattern consisting of a large feathery flower bloom over three quarters of the surface. It is surrounded by a beaded band which is framed by panels of gentle flutes. The glass is very heavy; iridescence good.

	Current Price Range		Prior Year Average
Bowl			
☐ marigold	30.00	35.00	32.00
☐ purple	50.00	100.00	75.00
☐ green	40.00	47.50	42.00
☐ blue	80.00	100.00	82.00
☐ amethyst	40.00	47.50	42.00
Plate			
☐ purple	350.00	400.00	375.00
☐ green	350.00	400.00	375.00
☐ blue	375.00	400.00	390.00
☐ amethyst	375.00	400.00	390.00

MEMPHIS
Northwood

Berry Bowl			
☐ marigold	50.00	70.00	55.00
☐ purple	75.00	100.00	80.00
☐ green	75.00	100.00	80.00
☐ blue	75.00	100.00	80.00
☐ amethyst	75.00	100.00	80.00
Compote			
☐ purple	100.00	125.00	110.00
☐ green	100.00	125.00	110.00
☐ blue	100.00	125.00	110.00
☐ amethyst	100.00	125.00	110.00
Fruit Bowl, with base			
☐ marigold	100.00	125.00	110.00
☐ purple	140.00	175.00	145.00
☐ green	140.00	175.00	145.00
☐ blue	140.00	175.00	145.00
☐ amethyst	140.00	175.00	145.00
☐ ice blue	475.00	535.00	500.00
Punch Bowl, with base			
☐ marigold	140.00	180.00	145.00
☐ purple	400.00	500.00	450.00
☐ green	210.00	275.00	230.00
☐ blue	210.00	275.00	230.00
☐ amethyst	210.00	275.00	230.00
☐ ice blue	540.00	625.00	550.00
Punch Cup			
☐ marigold	20.00	25.00	25.00
☐ purple	30.00	36.00	32.00
☐ green	30.00	36.00	32.00
☐ blue	30.00	36.00	32.00

	Current Price Range		Prior Year Average
☐ amethyst	30.00	36.00	32.00
☐ ice blue	37.00	45.00	40.00

MIRRORED LOTUS

The central medallion is plain smooth glass, surrounded by the first of many radiating panels, each one of pine cone-like foliage. A geometric panel follows and then a repeat of the foliage in reverse. The colors are green, blue, and marigold.

Bon Bon

☐ marigold	18.00	22.00	19.00
☐ green	28.00	34.00	30.00
☐ blue	28.00	34.00	30.00

Bowl, diameter 8″

☐ marigold	23.00	27.00	24.00
☐ green	37.00	40.00	38.00
☐ blue	37.00	40.00	38.00

Plate, diameter 7″

☐ marigold	40.00	45.00	42.00

Rose Bowl

☐ marigold	60.00	75.00	62.00
☐ green	75.00	90.00	77.00
☐ blue	75.00	90.00	77.00

MOONPRINT
Sowerby

This is a tasteful, well-balanced pattern, simply conceived of orbs in intaglio alternating with four pointed stars. These geometric panels cover the body of the piece, the rim is smooth and gently scalloped. The pedestal base has a starburst motif. The color is marigold—transparent and beautifully irridescent.

Banana Boat

☐ marigold	60.00	80.00	62.00

Bowl, diameter 8″

☐ marigold	30.00	40.00	32.00

Compote

☐ marigold	35.00	50.00	37.00

Covered Jar

☐ marigold	35.00	50.00	37.00

Creamer

☐ marigold	20.00	25.00	22.00

Milk Pitcher

☐ marigold	60.00	80.00	62.00

Sugar Bowl

☐ marigold	20.00	25.00	22.00

Vase

☐ marigold	20.00	25.00	22.00

MORNING GLORY
Millersburg

	Current Price Range		Prior Year Average
Pitcher			
☐ marigold	5000.00	7000.00	5500.00
☐ purple	6000.00	8000.00	6500.00
☐ green	6000.00	8000.00	6500.00
☐ amethyst	6000.00	8000.00	6500.00
Tumbler			
☐ marigold	350.00	425.00	375.00
☐ purple	425.00	525.00	440.00
☐ green	700.00	800.00	750.00
☐ blue	850.00	1000.00	875.00
☐ amethyst	425.00	525.00	450.00

MULTI FRUITS AND FLOWERS
Millersburg

Many motifs have been used together in this pattern and although it is an overall design, it is not busy. The relief is high and sharply molded, the glass is heavy and almost opaque.

	Current Price Range		Prior Year Average
Dessert Dish			
☐ purple	80.00	100.00	85.00
☐ green	80.00	100.00	85.00
☐ blue	150.00	200.00	160.00
☐ amethyst	80.00	100.00	85.00
Pitcher			
☐ marigold	4500.00	5750.00	4800.00
☐ purple	4750.00	5750.00	4800.00
☐ green	4750.00	5750.00	4800.00
☐ blue	10000.00	12000.00	11000.00
☐ amethyst	4750.00	5750.00	5000.00
Punch Bowl			
☐ marigold	500.00	650.00	525.00
☐ purple	550.00	650.00	575.00
☐ blue	1000.00	1300.00	1100.00
☐ amethyst	550.00	650.00	575.00
Punch Cup			
☐ marigold	25.00	32.00	26.00
☐ green	30.00	40.00	32.00
☐ blue	60.00	80.00	45.00
☐ amethyst	30.00	40.00	32.00

NAUTILUS
Northwood

This is an artistic pattern of curving ridges radiating out of the middle of the rim in outward sweeps. The ridges are rounded and have suggestions of knobs spaced around.

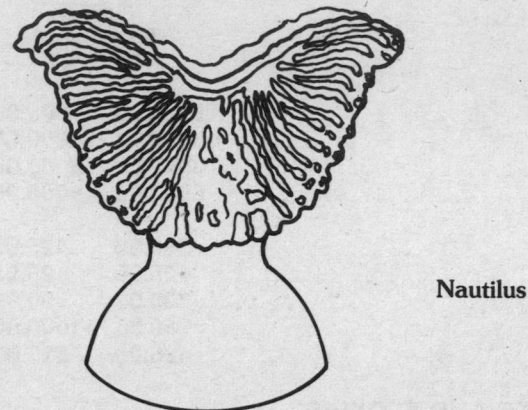

Nautilus

		Current Price Range		Prior Year Average
Dish				
☐ purple	....	160.00	225.00	175.00
☐ green	....	160.00	225.00	175.00
☐ blue	....	160.00	225.00	175.00
☐ amethyst	....	160.00	225.00	175.00
☐ peach opalescent	....	135.00	170.00	145.00

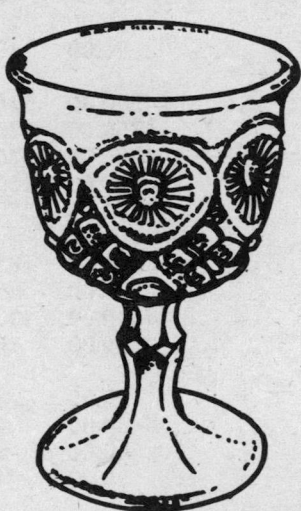

Near Cut

NEAR CUT
Northwood

The hobstar motif is treated this time with a teardrop shaped frame in a wide band accross the middle. There are triangular shapes of lozenge, placed together to form a diamond. The rest of the glass is smooth, highly iridescent and the colors are purple and marigold.

	Current Price Range		Prior Year Average
Compote			
☐ purple	80.00	100.00	90.00
Goblet			
☐ marigold	70.00	90.00	72.00
☐ purple	100.00	125.00	110.00
Pitcher			
☐ marigold	1200.00	1600.00	1400.00

NESTING SWAN
Millersburg

A swan on a glossy pond in good perspective is surrounded by diagonally placed sprays of foliage and flowers. The rim is resolved in fan-like ridges that form the scalloped edge. The colors are marigold, green, amber, blue, and amethyst.

Bowl			
☐ marigold	170.00	220.00	180.00
☐ purple	325.00	425.00	330.00
☐ green	325.00	425.00	330.00
☐ blue	650.00	850.00	675.00
☐ amethyst	325.00	425.00	330.00
Spittoon			
☐ purple	550.00	625.00	575.00
☐ green	550.00	625.00	575.00
☐ blue	1000.00	1250.00	1100.00
☐ amethyst	550.00	625.00	575.00

NEW ORLEANS CHAMPAGNE
U.S. Glass

A souvenir from the Mardi Gras of 1910, this piece is an excellent representation of the essence of Carnival glass. Besides the clear glass and high iridescence, the design of a bearded king with a well-detailed crown in high relief is typical to this era. The funny face is flanked by molded alligators attached vertically to the side of the body.

Glass			
☐ clear iridescent	50.00	60.00	52.00

NIGHT STARS
Millersburg

The central medallion is a big-faceted star, surrounded by a band of similar shapes, smaller and separated by tear drops. The background is all stippled. The rim of the bowl is gently fluted and waved in and out. The finish is fine and radiated.

	Current Price Range		Prior Year Average
Bon Bon			
☐ purple	225.00	250.00	230.00
☐ green	225.00	250.00	230.00
☐ blue	250.00	300.00	240.00
☐ amethyst	225.00	250.00	230.00
Card Tray			
☐ purple	125.00	175.00	130.00
☐ green	125.00	175.00	130.00
☐ blue	250.00	325.00	275.00
☐ amethyst	125.00	175.00	130.00

NUMBER 4
Imperial

This is a simple pattern, actually suggested rather than apparent, of diamond bands rowed vertically from rim to base. The upper rim is bullet edged and waved. The colors are marigold and smoke.

Bowl			
☐ marigold	20.00	30.00	22.00
☐ smoke	30.00	40.00	32.00
Compote			
☐ marigold	25.00	30.00	27.00

NUMBER 5
Imperial

Bundles of curvy ridges are tied together in the middle of the sheaf, form a pattern that resembles Siamese fans. The exterior design is in low relief, the glass is clear, the color amber or marigold.

Bowl			
☐ amber	50.00	60.00	52.00
☐ marigold	40.00	50.00	42.00

NUMBER 9
Imperial

This geometric pattern suggests stylized grape bunches, arranged in ice cream cone shapes around broken arches. The central medallion is a rayed star. The colors are smoke, marigold, and green.

Bowl			
☐ marigold	25.00	35.00	27.00
☐ smoke	40.00	50.00	42.00
☐ green	50.00	60.00	52.00

NUMBER 270
Sowerly

The shape creates this pattern, a series of molded flutes wave over the body of these pieces. The glass is otherwise devoid of decoration, smooth and glossy with good iridescence. The colors are aqua and peach.

	Current Price Range		Prior Year Average
Bowl			
☐ aqua opalescent	30.00	40.00	32.00
☐ peach opalescent	40.00	50.00	42.00

OCTAGON
Imperial

A prolific pattern made in many shapes; this geometric design was very popular. It is a variation on a theme used in many types of glass—light, near cut panels of vertical stars, diamonds, lozenge and beadwork. The panels alternate in a broken arch and cathedral shape with concave sides. Colors come in marigold and rarely in purple and other dark colors.

Butter Dish, with cover			
☐ marigold	75.00	85.00	80.00
☐ purple	145.00	155.00	150.00
Creamer			
☐ marigold	35.00	45.00	37.00
☐ purple	55.00	65.00	60.00
Goblet			
☐ marigold	40.00	50.00	42.00
Spooner			
☐ marigold	35.00	45.00	37.00
☐ purple	55.00	65.00	57.00
Sugar Bowl, with cover			
☐ marigold	40.00	50.00	42.00
☐ purple	60.00	70.00	62.00

Octagon

	Current Price Range		Prior Year Average
Toothpick			
☐ marigold	90.00	110.00	92.00
Tumbler			
☐ marigold	25.00	30.00	28.00
☐ purple	60.00	70.00	62.00
Water Pitcher			
☐ marigold	75.00	125.00	77.00
☐ purple	200.00	250.00	210.00
Wine Decanter			
☐ marigold	80.00	110.00	85.00
☐ purple	225.00	275.00	240.00
Wine Glass			
☐ marigold	15.00	25.00	20.00
☐ purple	30.00	50.00	40.00

OCTET
Northwood

A tasteful, simply conceived pattern of intaglio marbles indented in a row, radiating from the central medallion. This is composed of a faceted petaled flower, deep cut and well molded. The shape of the body mimics the bloom shape with a gently scalloped rim. The colors are purple, green, ice green, and white.

Bowl, footed, diameter 9″

☐ marigold	35.00	43.00	37.00
☐ purple	50.00	60.00	52.00
☐ green	50.00	60.00	52.00
☐ blue	50.00	60.00	52.00
☐ amethyst	50.00	60.00	52.00
☐ white	60.00	75.00	62.00
☐ ice green	70.00	80.00	72.00

Octet

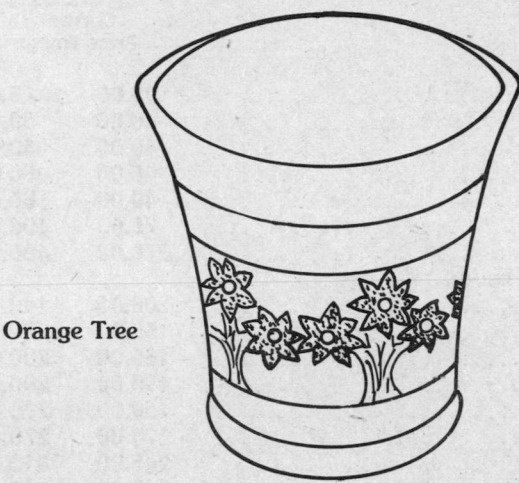

Orange Tree

ORANGE TREE
Fenton

An extremely pleasing pattern, an asset to any collection. The fruit trees are wonderfully stylized, three branches on a thick trunk with a topping of funny orange blossoms with a stippled center. The upper band is a border of delicate ridges forming a bullhorn-shaped chain. This is repeated on the base. This pattern was made in many shapes and colors.

	Current Price Range		Prior Year Average
Berry Bowl, diameter 5″			
☐ marigold	10.00	15.00	11.00
☐ purple	15.00	20.00	16.00
☐ green	15.00	20.00	16.00
☐ blue	15.00	20.00	16.00
☐ amethyst	15.00	20.00	16.00
☐ white	35.00	40.00	37.00
Berry Bowl, diameter 9″			
☐ marigold	20.00	25.00	22.00
☐ purple	45.00	50.00	47.00
☐ green	45.00	50.00	47.00
☐ blue	45.00	50.00	47.00
☐ amethyst	45.00	50.00	47.00
☐ white	70.00	80.00	72.00
Bowl, flat			
☐ marigold	30.00	40.00	32.00
☐ amethyst	60.00	75.00	62.00
☐ purple	60.00	75.00	62.00
☐ green	60.00	75.00	62.00
☐ white	60.00	75.00	62.00
☐ red	400.00	500.00	425.00
☐ milk glass	125.00	175.00	130.00

	Current Price Range		Prior Year Average
Bowl, footed			
☐ marigold	20.00	25.00	22.00
☐ purple	40.00	50.00	42.00
☐ green	40.00	50.00	42.00
☐ blue	40.00	50.00	42.00
☐ amethyst	40.00	50.00	42.00
☐ white	75.00	100.00	85.00
☐ red	370.00	400.00	375.00
Butter Dish, lidded			
☐ marigold	100.00	140.00	110.00
☐ purple	150.00	200.00	155.00
☐ green	150.00	200.00	155.00
☐ blue	150.00	200.00	155.00
☐ amethyst	150.00	200.00	155.00
☐ white	220.00	270.00	230.00
☐ ice blue	245.00	310.00	250.00
☐ ice green	245.00	310.00	250.00
Centerpiece, footed, diameter 12″			
☐ purple	400.00	500.00	425.00
☐ green	400.00	500.00	425.00
☐ blue	400.00	500.00	425.00
☐ amethyst	400.00	500.00	425.00
Creamer			
☐ marigold	60.00	75.00	62.00
☐ purple	50.00	75.00	60.00
☐ green	80.00	115.00	82.00
☐ blue	80.00	115.00	82.00
☐ amethyst	80.00	115.00	82.00
☐ white	110.00	130.00	110.00
☐ ice blue	120.00	150.00	125.00
☐ ice green	120.00	150.00	125.00
Hat Pin Holder			
☐ marigold	120.00	130.00	125.00
☐ purple	140.00	160.00	145.00
☐ green	275.00	300.00	290.00
☐ blue	140.00	160.00	145.00
☐ amethyst	140.00	160.00	145.00
Mug			
☐ marigold	20.00	30.00	25.00
☐ purple	30.00	40.00	32.00
☐ green	30.00	40.00	32.00
☐ blue	30.00	40.00	32.00
☐ amethyst	30.00	40.00	32.00
☐ white	400.00	500.00	425.00
Pitcher, footed			
☐ marigold	140.00	160.00	145.00
☐ purple	220.00	240.00	225.00
☐ green	220.00	240.00	225.00

	Current Price Range		Prior Year Average
☐ blue	220.00	240.00	225.00
☐ amethyst	220.00	240.00	225.00
☐ white	400.00	500.00	425.00
Plate, diameter 9″			
☐ marigold	50.00	60.00	52.00
☐ purple	90.00	110.00	95.00
☐ green	90.00	110.00	95.00
☐ blue	90.00	110.00	95.00
☐ amethyst	90.00	110.00	95.00
☐ white	350.00	450.00	375.00
Powder Jar, with cover			
☐ marigold	65.00	85.00	75.00
☐ purple	70.00	80.00	72.00
☐ green	70.00	80.00	72.00
☐ blue	70.00	80.00	72.00
☐ amethyst	70.00	80.00	72.00
Punch Bowl, with base			
☐ marigold	100.00	120.00	110.00
☐ purple	150.00	175.00	155.00
☐ blue	150.00	175.00	155.00
☐ green	150.00	175.00	155.00
☐ amethyst	150.00	175.00	155.00
☐ white	300.00	350.00	310.00
Punch Cup			
☐ marigold	10.00	15.00	11.00
☐ purple	20.00	25.00	22.00
☐ green	20.00	25.00	22.00
☐ blue	20.00	25.00	22.00
☐ amethyst	20.00	25.00	22.00
☐ white	30.00	40.00	32.00
Shaving Mug			
☐ marigold	30.00	40.00	32.00
☐ purple	35.00	45.00	37.00
☐ green	35.00	45.00	37.00
☐ blue	35.00	45.00	37.00
☐ amethyst	35.00	45.00	37.00
Spooner			
☐ marigold	65.00	75.00	67.00
☐ purple	80.00	115.00	85.00
☐ green	80.00	115.00	85.00
☐ blue	80.00	115.00	85.00
☐ amethyst	80.00	115.00	85.00
☐ white	110.00	130.00	115.00
☐ ice blue	120.00	150.00	125.00
☐ ice green	120.00	150.00	125.00
Sugar Bowl			
☐ marigold	65.00	75.00	67.00
☐ purple	70.00	100.00	85.00

	Current Price Range		Prior Year Average
☐ green	80.00	115.00	85.00
☐ blue	80.00	115.00	85.00
☐ amethyst	80.00	115.00	85.00
☐ white	110.00	130.00	125.00
☐ ice blue	120.00	150.00	125.00
☐ ice green	120.00	150.00	125.00
Tumbler, footed			
☐ marigold	30.00	35.00	32.00
☐ purple	40.00	50.00	42.00
☐ green	40.00	50.00	42.00
☐ blue	40.00	50.00	42.00
☐ amethyst	40.00	50.00	42.00
☐ white	60.00	70.00	42.00
Wine Glass			
☐ marigold	20.00	30.00	22.00
☐ purple	30.00	40.00	32.00
☐ blue	30.00	40.00	32.00
☐ green	30.00	40.00	32.00
☐ amethyst	30.00	40.00	32.00

ORANGE TREE AND SCROLL
Fenton

This pattern is a work of art. The orange trees are more naturally represented than in other patterns, but the fruit laden branches seem to be out of the Garden of Eden. The wide bottom band is scroll work rows with a green iridescence that bring to mind the planted hills of Florida. The upper band is a series of eight serpentine scrolls catching and reflecting the radium finish. The colors are green, marigold, and amethyst.

Pitcher

☐ marigold	250.00	300.00	275.00
☐ green	350.00	450.00	360.00
☐ amethyst	350.00	450.00	360.00
Tumbler			
☐ marigold	40.00	45.00	42.00
☐ green	55.00	65.00	57.00
☐ amethyst	55.00	65.00	57.00

ORIENTAL POPPY
Northwood

This is a wonderful pattern with an Oriental influence. The long panels of poppies are sharply molded, decorated with deeply-cut foliage and leaves, and framed with curvy beadwork. The bottom rim is a series of rounded horizontal ridging. The colors are green, purple, white, ice blue, green, and marigold.

Tankard Pitcher

☐ marigold	200.00	250.00	225.00

	Current Price Range		Prior Year Average
☐ purple	500.00	600.00	550.00
☐ green	425.00	575.00	450.00
☐ blue	425.00	575.00	450.00
☐ amethyst	425.00	575.00	450.00
☐ white	650.00	800.00	700.00
☐ ice blue	800.00	1000.00	850.00
Tumbler			
☐ marigold	37.00	47.00	40.00
☐ purple	35.00	45.00	37.00
☐ green	45.00	60.00	50.00
☐ blue	35.00	45.00	37.00
☐ amethyst	35.00	45.00	37.00
☐ white	70.00	90.00	85.00
☐ ice blue	80.00	100.00	85.00

PANSY
Imperial

This lovely pattern has a stippled background that covers the piece to just below the rim providing a setting for a dancing bouquet of flowers. The wide detailed pansies are of smooth panelled glass and are arranged among branches and foliage.

Bowl			
☐ marigold	20.00	30.00	22.00
☐ purple	40.00	50.00	45.00
Creamer			
☐ marigold	15.00	25.00	17.00
☐ purple	25.00	35.00	27.00

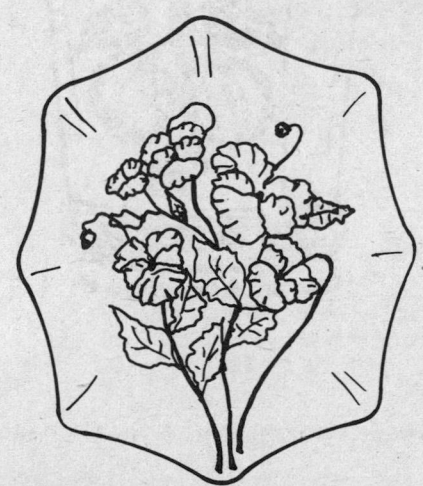

Pansy

	Current Price Range		Prior Year Average
Dresser Tray			
☐ marigold	30.00	40.00	32.00
☐ purple	80.00	100.00	85.00
Relish Tray			
☐ marigold	10.00	20.00	14.00
☐ purple	25.00	30.00	27.00

PANTHER
Fenton

	Current Price Range		Prior Year Average
Berry Bowl, footed, diameter 5″			
☐ marigold	60.00	75.00	62.00
☐ purple	100.00	125.00	110.00
☐ green	100.00	125.00	110.00
☐ amethyst	100.00	125.00	110.00
☐ white	600.00	700.00	625.00
Berry Bowl, footed, diameter 9″			
☐ marigold	20.00	25.00	22.00
☐ purple	30.00	40.00	32.00
☐ green	30.00	40.00	32.00
☐ amethyst	30.00	40.00	32.00
☐ white	120.00	140.00	130.00
☐ red	300.00	350.00	310.00

Peach

PEACH
Northwood

This is a pattern in high relief, expertly molded with lifelike representation. On each side of the piece a bunch of plump peaches hang suspended from leaf clusters, superimposed over panels of parallel ridges. The upper and lower horizontal framing is beadwork. The glass is heavy and glossy, the iridescence excellent. The colors are cobalt and white.

	Current Price Range		Prior Year Average
Berry Bowl, diameter 5″			
☐ white	30.00	50.00	32.00
Berry Bowl, diameter 9″			
☐ white	100.00	125.00	110.00
Butter Dish, with cover			
☐ white	170.00	200.00	170.00
Creamer			
☐ white	60.00	70.00	65.00
Pitcher			
☐ cobalt blue	300.00	400.00	325.00
☐ white	275.00	375.00	320.00
Spooner			
☐ white	60.00	70.00	65.00
Sugar Bowl			
☐ white	60.00	70.00	65.00
Tumbler			
☐ cobalt blue	50.00	70.00	60.00
☐ white	40.00	45.00	42.00

PEACOCK
Millersburg

A peacock struts in a royal setting, with a Grecian pillar behind and a spray of ferns at his foot. The detail is magnificent, each feather molded in relief, the body of the bird roughly stippled. The scene is framed by a wreath of elegant foliage stopping before the wide glossy band that ruffles along the edge. The colors are marigold, amethyst, green, and clambroth.

Bowl, diameter 6⅜″			
☐ marigold	30.00	35.00	32.00
☐ purple	45.00	55.00	47.00
☐ green	45.00	55.00	47.00
☐ blue	90.00	120.00	95.00
☐ amethyst	45.00	55.00	47.00
Bowl, diameter 8″			
☐ marigold	75.00	95.00	77.00
☐ purple	140.00	175.00	145.00
☐ green	140.00	175.00	145.00
☐ blue	275.00	350.00	300.00
☐ amethyst	140.00	175.00	150.00
Bowl, diameter 9″			
☐ marigold	60.00	80.00	65.00

	Current Price Range		Prior Year Average
☐ purple	75.00	100.00	80.00
☐ green	75.00	100.00	80.00
☐ blue	75.00	100.00	80.00
☐ amethyst	75.00	100.00	80.00
☐ aqua opalescent	250.00	320.00	265.00
☐ white	170.00	195.00	175.00
☐ ice blue	170.00	195.00	175.00
☐ ice green	170.00	195.00	175.00
Chop Plate			
☐ marigold	800.00	1000.00	900.00
Plate, diameter 6″			
☐ purple	150.00	225.00	175.00
☐ green	150.00	225.00	175.00
☐ blue	300.00	450.00	325.00
☐ amethyst	150.00	225.00	160.00

PEACOCK AND GRAPES
Fenton

Similar to the Peacock and Dahlia in style but not execution, this pattern is busier. The medallion motif is used again, but this one resembles a huge flower, each section a petal. The alternating grapes and peacocks, again in full dress, round the middle section of the interior, surrounding a cobweb center. The colors are blue, green, aqua, white, red, peach, opalescent, vaseline, marigold, and amethyst.

Bowl, footed			
☐ marigold	30.00	40.00	32.00
☐ blue	45.00	50.00	47.00
☐ green	45.00	50.00	47.00
☐ amethyst	45.00	50.00	47.00
☐ aqua opalescent	225.00	275.00	250.00
Bowl, flat			
☐ marigold	30.00	50.00	40.00
☐ blue	45.00	50.00	47.00
☐ green	60.00	80.00	70.00
☐ amethyst	45.00	50.00	47.00
☐ aqua opalescent	225.00	275.00	235.00
☐ red	400.00	500.00	425.00
Plate			
☐ marigold	90.00	110.00	95.00
☐ blue	200.00	250.00	210.00
☐ green	225.00	275.00	250.00
☐ amethyst	205.00	260.00	230.00

PEACOCK AND URN
Millersburg

The difference between this pattern and the Millersburg Peacock is the stylized bee in the bird's beak. Also, the ridgework on the urn is more rigid as opposed to the scrollwork on the one above. The quality workmanship is evident in both. Colors are green, amethyst, and marigold.

	Current Price Range		Prior Year Average
Bowl, diameter 9"			
☐ marigold	75.00	95.00	80.00
☐ purple	120.00	150.00	125.00
☐ green	225.00	275.00	250.00
☐ blue	250.00	300.00	275.00
☐ amethyst	120.00	150.00	125.00
Compote			
☐ marigold	45.00	55.00	47.50
☐ purple	45.00	55.00	47.50
☐ green	45.00	55.00	47.50
☐ blue	85.00	100.00	87.50
☐ amethyst	45.00	55.00	47.50
Spittoon			
☐ purple	1750.00	2250.00	1800.00
☐ green	1750.00	2250.00	1800.00
☐ blue	3750.00	4750.00	4000.00
☐ amethyst	1750.00	2250.00	1800.00

PEACOCK AND URN
Northwood

Although this design is similar to Millersburg, there are apparent differences in the foliage wreath that make it easy to tell them apart. The circle of leaves has less detail and has lots of glossy space between. The flowers appear only on the inside of the band and the whole pattern stops well within the inside of the body. The colors run the gamut of Northwood tints.

	Current Price Range		Prior Year Average
Bowl, diameter 7"			
☐ purple	30.00	40.00	32.00

Peacock and Urn

	Current Price Range		Prior Year Average
☐ green	40.00	50.00	42.00
☐ blue	40.00	50.00	42.00
☐ amethyst	40.00	50.00	42.00
☐ ice blue	50.00	60.00	52.00
☐ ice green	50.00	60.00	52.00
Chop Plate			
☐ purple	600.00	700.00	620.00
☐ green	600.00	700.00	620.00
☐ blue	600.00	700.00	620.00
☐ amethyst	600.00	700.00	620.00
Ice Cream Bowl, diameter 7″			
☐ marigold	30.00	40.00	32.00
☐ purple	42.00	52.00	44.00
☐ green	42.00	52.00	44.00
☐ blue	42.00	52.00	44.00

PEACOCK AT THE FOUNTAIN
Northwood

An elegant design, this is one of the collectors' favorites. The design consists of a large bird in marvelous detail with a wavy ridged tail and eight body feathers. He is standing on a brick pedestal with a single daisy growing out of the masonry. Behind him stands a stylized fruit tree with ray-like branches. There's a fountain with its flow represented by closely lined ridges and other details, all with an Oriental flair. The colors and shapes vary widely.

Berry Bowl

☐ marigold	55.00	65.00	57.00
☐ purple	80.00	100.00	82.00
☐ green	80.00	100.00	82.00

Peacock at the Fountain

	Current Price Range		Prior Year Average
☐ blue	80.00	100.00	82.00
☐ amethyst	80.00	100.00	82.00
☐ white	120.00	160.00	150.00
☐ ice blue	145.00	185.00	150.00
☐ ice green	145.00	185.00	150.00
Butter Dish			
☐ marigold	80.00	110.00	82.00
☐ purple	130.00	160.00	140.00
☐ green	130.00	160.00	140.00
☐ blue	130.00	160.00	140.00
☐ amethyst	130.00	160.00	140.00
☐ white	140.00	200.00	170.00
☐ ice blue	160.00	220.00	170.00
☐ ice green	160.00	220.00	170.00
Compote			
☐ marigold	120.00	150.00	130.00
☐ purple	200.00	260.00	220.00
☐ green	200.00	260.00	220.00
☐ blue	200.00	260.00	220.00
☐ amethyst	200.00	265.00	220.00
☐ aqua opalescent	260.00	320.00	275.00
☐ white	200.00	255.00	240.00
☐ ice green	230.00	280.00	240.00
☐ ice blue	230.00	280.00	240.00
Creamer			
☐ marigold	45.00	55.00	50.00
☐ purple	60.00	80.00	62.00
☐ green	60.00	80.00	62.00
☐ blue	60.00	80.00	62.00
☐ amethyst	60.00	80.00	62.00
☐ white	70.00	100.00	82.00
☐ ice blue	80.00	110.00	82.00
☐ ice green	80.00	110.00	82.00
Orange Bowl			
☐ marigold	100.00	140.00	110.00
☐ purple	155.00	195.00	160.00
☐ green	155.00	195.00	160.00
☐ blue	155.00	195.00	160.00
☐ amethyst	155.00	195.00	160.00
☐ white	330.00	410.00	375.00
☐ ice blue	360.00	450.00	375.00
Pitcher			
☐ marigold	210.00	260.00	220.00
☐ purple	350.00	420.00	375.00
☐ white	450.00	550.00	525.00
☐ ice blue	500.00	600.00	525.00
☐ ice green	500.00	600.00	525.00

	Current Price Range		Prior Year Average
Punch Bowl, with base			
☐ marigold	140.00	170.00	160.00
☐ purple	270.00	340.00	275.00
☐ green	270.00	340.00	275.00
☐ blue	270.00	340.00	275.00
☐ amethyst	270.00	340.00	275.00
☐ aqua opalescent	3000.00	4000.00	3250.00
☐ white	310.00	400.00	375.00
☐ ice blue	360.00	435.00	375.00
☐ ice green	360.00	435.00	375.00
Punch Cup			
☐ marigold	16.00	20.00	18.00
☐ purple	23.00	30.00	25.00
☐ green	23.00	30.00	25.00
☐ blue	23.00	30.00	25.00
☐ amethyst	23.00	30.00	25.00
☐ aqua opalescent	135.00	165.00	140.00
☐ white	27.00	35.00	34.00
☐ ice blue	32.00	40.00	34.00
☐ ice green	32.00	40.00	34.00

PEACOCK GARDEN VASE
Northwood

This overall design consists of the peacock with his long sweeping tail swirling around the piece from bottom to top. He is perched on a dogwood branch which appears to have no trunk, stretching vine like around the body. The moldwork is sharp and the color exceptional. Colors vary, marigold is common.

Vase			
☐ marigold	30.00	40.00	32.00
☐ purple	60.00	70.00	64.00
☐ green	60.00	70.00	65.00
☐ blue	60.00	70.00	62.00
☐ amethyst	60.00	70.00	64.00
☐ ices	75.00	80.00	78.00

PEACOCK TAIL
Fenton

The interior of the body is shaped in wavy flutes of peacock feathers, radiating out of the center from a star shaped medallion. The scroll work is excellent, arching around over and over, covering the available space. The colors come in marigold, amethyst, amber, blue, and green.

Bowl, diameter 9″			
☐ marigold	22.00	32.00	34.00
☐ blue	32.00	42.00	36.00
☐ green	32.00	42.00	36.00

	Current Price Range		Prior Year Average
☐ amethyst	32.00	42.00	36.00
Compote			
☐ marigold	20.00	30.00	22.00
☐ blue	30.00	40.00	32.00
☐ green	30.00	40.00	32.00
Hat Shape			
☐ marigold	20.00	30.00	22.00
☐ purple	30.00	40.00	32.00
☐ green	50.00	40.00	32.00
☐ amethyst	30.00	40.00	32.00
Tri-Corner Dish			
☐ marigold	17.00	20.00	18.00
☐ purple	25.00	30.00	27.00
☐ green	25.00	30.00	27.00
☐ amethyst	25.00	30.00	27.00

PEACOCKS
Northwood

Two peacocks flirt with each other, surrounded by flowers and foliage. The male is in full plume, the female stretches out on a basket, well-detailed with lozenge patterns. The mold work is sharp, the coloring magnificent. The colors run the gamut of Northwood tints.

Plate, diameter 9″

☐ marigold	90.00	115.00	95.00
☐ purple	120.00	155.00	125.00
☐ green	120.00	155.00	125.00
☐ blue	120.00	155.00	125.00
☐ amethyst	120.00	155.00	125.00
☐ aqua opalescent	300.00	420.00	330.00

PERFECTION
Millersburg

A large heavy piece, sharply molded with a distinctive pattern, shows off iridescence in true carnival form. The design is ovals in a row, just under the neck of pitcher, made up of beadwork and lined with deep ridges. The bottom body is filled with feather-like columns, disappearing to airy nothingness by the base. These ovals are repeated in a delicate, elongated style up the neck, divided by maple leaves. The colors are marigold and the deep, vivid shades.

Pitcher

☐ marigold	1750.00	2250.00	1800.00
☐ purple	2600.00	3400.00	2800.00
☐ green	2600.00	3400.00	2800.00
☐ blue	2600.00	3400.00	2800.00

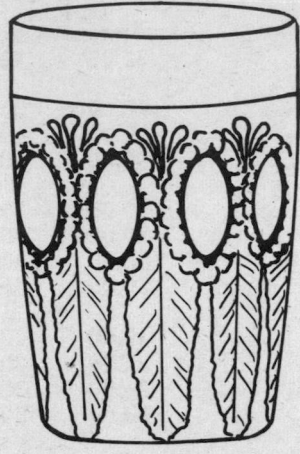

Perfection

Tumbler	Current Price Range		Prior Year Average
☐ marigold	250.00	335.00	270.00
☐ purple	350.00	450.00	360.00
☐ green	350.00	450.00	360.00
☐ blue	700.00	900.00	750.00
☐ amethyst	350.00	450.00	360.00

PERSIAN MEDALLION
Fenton

This is a prolific Fenton pattern consisting of flowery medallions with an offbeat Oriental flair. The shapes vary widely but they all carry a band of these petaled circles containing teardrops and eggshapes formed by delicate ridges. The colors are marigold, green, amethyst, amber, red, white, and blue.

Bon Bon			
☐ marigold	25.00	32.00	27.00
☐ green	35.00	40.00	36.00
☐ blue	35.00	40.00	36.00
☐ amethyst	35.00	40.00	36.00
☐ white	75.00	85.00	77.00
☐ amber	70.00	80.00	72.00
Bowl, diameter 5″			
☐ marigold	14.00	17.00	15.00
☐ green	20.00	25.00	21.00
☐ blue	20.00	25.00	21.00
Bowl, diameter 10″			
☐ marigold	40.00	50.00	42.00
☐ green	50.00	60.00	55.00
☐ blue	50.00	60.00	55.00

	Current Price Range		Prior Year Average
Bowl, collar base, diameter 10″			
☐ marigold	40.00	50.00	42.00
☐ green	50.00	60.00	52.00
☐ blue	50.00	60.00	52.00
Compote			
☐ marigold	30.00	40.00	32.00
☐ blue	40.00	50.00	43.00
☐ green	40.00	50.00	43.00
Plate, diameter 6″			
☐ marigold	30.00	40.00	32.00
☐ blue	40.00	50.00	44.00
☐ green	40.00	50.00	44.00
Plate, diameter 9″			
☐ marigold	70.00	90.00	75.00
☐ blue	120.00	140.00	130.00
☐ green	240.00	280.00	260.00
Rose Bowl			
☐ marigold	40.00	45.00	42.00
☐ blue	45.00	65.00	47.50
☐ green	45.00	65.00	46.50
☐ amber	45.00	65.00	46.50
☐ white	120.00	140.00	115.00

PETER RABBIT
Fenton

This pattern consists of a series of bands, alternating design with smooth, glossy glass. The center is clear, the next band made up of ridging that resembles pine needles separated with four shapes. The next larger band has Peter, a rotund rabbit hopping at a mad pace around the piece, divided by two leafy trees. The band which stretches the diameter of rim is a repeat of the first band. The colors are blue, green, marigold and amethyst. Although all pieces are difficult to find, amethyst is the scarcest.

Bowl			
☐ marigold	500.00	600.00	550.00
☐ blue	600.00	700.00	650.00
☐ green	600.00	700.00	650.00
☐ amethyst	650.00	750.00	700.00
Plate			
☐ marigold	1200.00	1600.00	1250.00
☐ blue	1400.00	2000.00	1450.00
☐ green	1400.00	2000.00	1450.00
☐ amethyst	1450.00	2100.00	1550.00

PINEAPPLE
Sowersby

Six well-defined pineapples grace the corner panels on these pieces, creating an unusual fluted shape. The detail work is excellent, each fruit made up of row after geometric row of triangular lozenges, separated by fan-like ridging. The colors are marigold, blue, and purple.

	Current Price Range		Prior Year Average
Bowl			
☐ marigold	50.00	60.00	45.00
☐ purple	60.00	70.00	65.00
☐ blue	60.00	70.00	65.00
Compote			
☐ purple	60.00	70.00	65.00
☐ blue	60.00	70.00	65.00
Creamer			
☐ marigold	50.00	60.00	55.00
☐ purple	60.00	70.00	65.00
☐ blue	60.00	70.00	65.00

PINECONE
Fenton

This pattern makes excellent use of texture, stippling, and tiny beads. The clump of pine cones dangles from long fern-like leaves, some with feather-like scrolls. The background is smooth, accentuating the low-relief. Colors are marigold and dark shades.

Bon Bon			
☐ marigold	25.00	30.00	27.50
☐ purple	35.00	40.00	37.50
☐ blue	35.00	40.00	37.50
☐ green	35.00	40.00	37.50
☐ amethyst	35.00	40.00	37.50
Bowl			
☐ marigold	35.00	40.00	37.00
☐ purple	40.00	45.00	40.00
☐ blue	40.00	45.00	40.00
☐ green	40.00	45.00	40.00
☐ amethyst	40.00	45.00	40.00
Plate, diameter 8″			
☐ marigold	80.00	90.00	85.00
☐ purple	100.00	125.00	110.00
☐ blue	100.00	125.00	110.00
☐ green	100.00	125.00	110.00
☐ amethyst	100.00	125.00	110.00
Plate, diameter 6″			
☐ marigold	80.00	90.00	85.00
☐ purple	100.00	125.00	110.00
☐ blue	100.00	125.00	110.00
☐ green	100.00	125.00	110.00
☐ amethyst	60.00	85.00	70.00

PLAID
Fenton

This is a neat pattern of ray-like ridges, closely spaced and emanating from the center point. There is a series of bands that circle the piece creating the plaid effect. The outer rim is ruffled and bullet edged. The colors are cobalt, purple, and a rare red.

Bowl	Current Price Range		Prior Year Average
☐ marigold	20.00	30.00	25.00
☐ purple	40.00	50.00	45.00
☐ cobalt	40.00	50.00	45.00
Plate			
☐ marigold	80.00	100.00	85.00
☐ purple	100.00	120.00	110.00
☐ cobalt	100.00	120.00	110.00

PLUME PANELS
Fenton

This is an elegant design of long stretched panels with a feathery look. The upper panel is resolved by scrolls in arch shape, the bottom starts from under the base. The panels are separated by clear glass strips. The color is luminous, in marigold, amethyst, blue, and rare in red.

Vase			
☐ marigold	30.00	35.00	35.00
☐ blue	35.00	40.00	37.00
☐ amethyst	35.00	40.00	37.00
☐ red	150.00	200.00	160.00

POINSETTIA
Imperial

This is quite a spectacular design, a flower that is as alive as fireworks. The eight petalled flowers form the wide band at the top, the stem and branches comprise the bottom three-quarters of the body. The foliage is the focal point comprised of wonderful jewel-like beadwork in sweeping arches. The colors are marigold and smoke, less common in green and purple.

Milk Pitcher			
☐ marigold	45.00	85.00	64.00
☐ green	60.00	80.00	70.00
☐ purple	140.00	200.00	150.00
☐ smoke	120.00	140.00	130.00

POINSETTIA
Fenton

This is an entirely different approach to the same motif as the Imperial pattern. Here the flower is treated naturalistically, winding around the face of the piece on a basketweave or trellis background. The mold work is sharp, the iridescence marvelous, the colors green, purple, white, marigold, and amethyst.

Bowl	Current Price Range		Prior Year Average
☐ marigold	75.00	95.00	78.00
☐ purple	120.00	150.00	125.00
☐ green	120.00	150.00	125.00
☐ blue	120.00	150.00	125.00
☐ amethyst	120.00	150.00	125.00
☐ white	160.00	200.00	165.00

POPPY
Northwood

Poppies are placed sparingly in low relief on a stippled background. The pattern starts out naturalistically, getting more elaborate as it reaches for the feathery scrolled border. The detail work is good, the design well-executed, the colors are blue, purple, peach, white, and marigold.

Bowl			
☐ marigold	20.00	30.00	22.00
☐ purple	30.00	40.00	32.00
☐ green	30.00	40.00	32.00
☐ blue	30.00	40.00	32.00
☐ amethyst	30.00	40.00	32.00
Relish Dish			
☐ marigold	45.00	55.00	47.00
☐ purple	52.00	67.50	53.00
☐ green	52.00	67.50	53.00
☐ blue	52.00	67.50	53.00
☐ amethyst	52.00	67.50	53.00
☐ white	65.00	85.00	67.00
☐ ice green	65.00	85.00	67.00
☐ ice blue	65.00	85.00	67.00

PREMIUM
Imperial

This is a pattern distinguished by shape rather than decoration. The iridescence is highlighted by the smooth glossy finish, clear in places and highly luminescent in others. The colors are purple, green, smoke, marigold, and clambroth.

Bowl			
☐ marigold	60.00	70.00	65.00
☐ purple	90.00	110.00	95.00
☐ green	90.00	110.00	95.00

	Current Price Range		Prior Year Average
☐ clambroth	80.00	90.00	85.00
Candlesticks			
☐ marigold	20.00	30.00	25.00

PRIMROSE
Millersburg

This is a simple pattern of flowers growing out of a leafy center. Each spray consists of two six-petalled flowers with snake-like leaves steming out of the branches. The iridescence is excellent; the colors—marigold, amethyst, purple, and a rare frosty blue.

Bowl

☐ marigold	80.00	120.00	100.00
☐ purple	80.00	110.00	85.00
☐ blue	150.00	200.00	160.00
☐ amethyst	150.00	200.00	160.00

PRISMS
Northwood

An intaglio design of bead-worked prisms, all in a row and over the entire space. They terminate on the fluted upper edge and appear from under the base. The bottom design is a huge multi-rayed star. The colors are amethyst, marigold, and green.

Compote

☐ marigold	50.00	60.00	55.00
☐ purple	65.00	85.00	60.00
☐ green	65.00	85.00	60.00
☐ blue	65.00	85.00	60.00
☐ amethyst	65.00	85.00	60.00
☐ aqua	90.00	115.00	95.00

PUZZLE
Dugan

This is another interior design whose central feature is the stippled background. The scrolly designs that dot the piece intermittently resemble upside down lilies or bells. The colors vary widely including purple, blue, green, marigold, and peach opalescent.

Bon Bon

☐ marigold	40.00	50.00	45.00
☐ purple	30.00	50.00	40.00
☐ blue	20.00	30.00	25.00
☐ green	20.00	30.00	25.00
☐ peach opalescent	50.00	60.00	55.00
Compote			
☐ purple	20.00	30.00	22.00

	Current Price Range		Prior Year Average
☐ blue	30.00	40.00	32.00
☐ green	30.00	40.00	32.00
☐ peach opalescent	50.00	60.00	55.00

RAGGED ROBIN
Fenton

The outstanding feature on these pieces is the irregular "ragged" rim that takes up almost half of the plate. The design, in low relief, is a wreath of foliage surrounding a central medallion of a bird perched among the flora. The colors are marigold, purple, blue, green, and white.

Bowl

☐ marigold	40.00	45.00	45.00
☐ purple	45.00	55.00	48.00
☐ blue	45.00	55.00	48.00
☐ green	45.00	55.00	48.00
☐ white	76.00	82.00	77.00

RAMBLER ROSE
Dugan

An overall foliage and flower design in low relief refracts the excellent iridescence on these pieces. The central motif is a well detailed rose nestled in leaves, this design is repeated on most of the available space. The colors are marigold, purple, green, and blue.

Pitcher

☐ marigold	130.00	160.00	140.00
☐ purple	250.00	320.00	275.00
☐ green	250.00	320.00	275.00

Rambler Rose

	Current Price Range		Prior Year Average
☐ blue	250.00	320.00	275.00
☐ amethyst	250.00	320.00	275.00
Tumbler			
☐ marigold	22.00	27.00	24.00
☐ purple	32.00	42.00	34.00
☐ green	32.00	42.00	34.00
☐ blue	32.00	42.00	34.00
☐ amethyst	40.00	60.00	50.00

RAYS AND RIBBONS
Millersburg

This is a neat pattern of alternating glossy spears and stippled rays emanating out of a central medallion of a starburst. The outer border is an interesting pattern of connected spades. The glass is heavy and iridescence good. The colors are marigold, green, vaseline, and amethyst.

Bowl			
☐ marigold	22.00	30.00	24.00
☐ purple	50.00	75.00	60.00
☐ green	70.00	100.00	85.00
☐ blue	60.00	80.00	62.00
☐ amethyst	30.00	40.00	32.00
Plate, ruffled			
☐ purple	160.00	190.00	180.00
☐ green	160.00	190.00	180.00
☐ blue	300.00	375.00	315.00
☐ amethyst	160.00	190.00	175.00

RIBBON TIE
Fenton

The basic, underlying pattern is circular ridges covering the entire piece. They are boldly interrupted by curvy sprays of diagonally placed ridges creating a whirling comet effect. The colors are blue, red, green, amethyst, and marigold.

Bowl			
☐ marigold	45.00	70.00	55.00
☐ blue	40.00	50.00	45.00
☐ green	40.00	50.00	45.00
☐ amethyst	40.00	50.00	45.00
☐ red	1400.00	1600.00	1450.00
Plate			
☐ marigold	60.00	70.00	65.00
☐ blue	70.00	80.00	75.00
☐ green	70.00	80.00	75.00
☐ amethyst	70.00	80.00	75.00

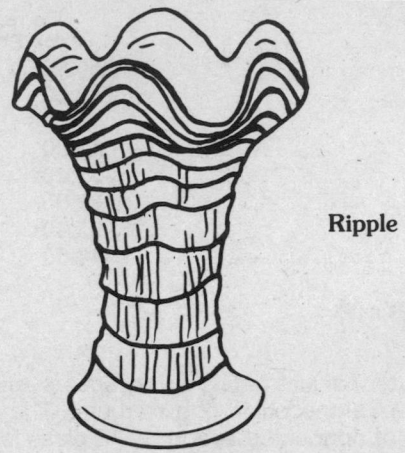

Ripple

RIPPLE
Imperial

This delicate vase is practically devoid of decoration because it is pulled to an airy thinness. Where the design remains, it appears as a suggested series of vertical ridges, rippling on the piece, showing off the iridescence. The colors are marigold and amethyst.

	Current Price Range		Prior Year Average
Vase, height 14″			
☐ marigold	20.00	30.00	25.00
☐ amethyst	30.00	40.00	35.00
Vase, height 20″			
☐ marigold	120.00	140.00	125.00
☐ amethyst	200.00	300.00	210.00

ROBIN
Imperial

This delicate, elegant pattern was well-conceived and remains one of the most popular in Carnival glass. The pretty bird warbles perched on a branch with foliage around. Although the design is detailed and sharply molded, it covers the pieces sharply and tastefully. The color is marigold.

Mug			
☐ marigold	40.00	60.00	50.00
Pitcher			
☐ marigold	275.00	325.00	300.00

Robin

ROSALIND
Millersburg

Also known as Drape and Tie, this pattern consists of one huge rosette that covers the entire interior space. The burst has the look of a kaleidoscope alternating curvy arches with scale-like panels all radiating out of a well-molded center. The colors vary widely.

	Current Price Range		Prior Year Average
Bowl			
☐ purple	100.00	110.00	105.00
☐ blue	80.00	90.00	85.00
☐ amethyst	80.00	90.00	85.00
Plate			
☐ green	200.00	225.00	215.00
☐ purple	200.00	225.00	215.00
☐ blue	200.00	225.00	215.00

ROSE COLUMN
Millersburg

This difficult pattern is successfully molded in good detail. Roses, lined in six vertical columns, cover the piece, extraordinary because they are hollow in high relief. Each row stems some sharply molded foliage, balancing out the design and adding interest to the widely ruffled edge. The iridescence is wonderful; the colors are blue, green, marigold, and amethyst.

Vase			
☐ marigold	800.00	900.00	815.00
☐ blue	600.00	700.00	625.00
☐ green	600.00	700.00	625.00

	Current Price Range		Prior Year Average
☐ amethyst	600.00	700.00	625.00
☐ vaseline	1800.00	2000.00	1900.00

ROSE GARDEN
English Manufacturer

The roses alternate with geometric rosettes in panel around the exterior of these pieces. The interesting detail on the flowers is comprised of vertical ridging, a new twist to a widely used design. The effect of this all-intaglio design is a surprising combination of flora and geometry, traditional versus modern, executed beautifully in high iridescence and a variety of colors.

Butter Dish, with cover

☐ marigold	120.00	125.00	130.00
☐ blue	250.00	275.00	260.00
☐ green	250.00	275.00	260.00
☐ amethyst	250.00	275.00	260.00
☐ purple	250.00	275.00	260.00

Creamer

☐ marigold	40.00	50.00	45.00
☐ blue	80.00	90.00	85.00
☐ green	80.00	90.00	85.00
☐ amethyst	80.00	90.00	85.00

Milk Pitcher

☐ marigold	300.00	400.00	315.00
☐ blue	500.00	600.00	515.00
☐ green	500.00	600.00	515.00
☐ purple	500.00	600.00	515.00
☐ amethyst	500.00	600.00	515.00

Spooner

☐ marigold	40.00	50.00	42.00
☐ blue	80.00	90.00	84.00
☐ green	80.00	90.00	84.00
☐ purple	80.00	90.00	84.00
☐ amethyst	80.00	90.00	84.00

Sugar Bowl

☐ marigold	40.00	50.00	42.00
☐ blue	80.00	90.00	84.00
☐ green	80.00	90.00	84.00
☐ purple	80.00	90.00	84.00
☐ amethyst	80.00	90.00	84.00

Vase

☐ blue	170.00	200.00	175.00
☐ green	170.00	200.00	175.00
☐ purple	170.00	200.00	175.00
☐ amethyst	170.00	200.00	175.00

ROSE SHOW
Northwood

The background for the bouquet of fully blooming roses is a quiet basketweave, covering all of the interior. The moldwork is excellent and the representation is very naturalistic. Each flower is nestled in foliage, pointed and detailed leaves in high relief. A wide range of colors was produced.

Bowl, diameter 8"	Current Price Range		Prior Year Average
☐ marigold	125.00	150.00	130.00
☐ blue	150.00	175.00	160.00
☐ purple	150.00	175.00	160.00
☐ ices	180.00	200.00	190.00
☐ white	180.00	200.00	190.00
☐ aqua opalescent	350.00	400.00	375.00
Plate			
☐ marigold	200.00	250.00	225.00
☐ green	300.00	350.00	315.00
☐ amethyst	300.00	350.00	315.00
☐ ices	325.00	375.00	330.00
☐ white	325.00	375.00	330.00
☐ milk glass	800.00	1000.00	850.00

ROSE TREE
Fenton

This intricate pattern, covering most of the surface, manages to look elegant rather than busy. There are four wide panels of rose blooms and branches, lots of leaves in a graceful, symmetrical design. The center medallion is smooth, glossy glass with just the tips of the dangling leaves dipping toward the middle. The colors are marigold and cobalt blue.

Bowl			
☐ marigold	16.00	22.00	18.00
☐ cobalt blue	20.00	30.00	22.00

Rosette

ROSETTE
Northwood

The central medallion is a large rayed sunburst taking up most of the bottom of the interior. It is simply conceived of alternating smooth and stippled rays, surrounded by a band of flowery rosettes against a stippled background. The last band is simple vertical ridge work that reaches halfway to the wavy ruffled rim. Colors are marigold and amethyst.

Bowl	Current Price Range		Prior Year Average
☐ marigold	17.00	21.00	18.00
☐ amethyst	20.00	25.00	22.00

RUFFLED RIB SPITTOON
Northwood

This is a simple pattern of rounded, interior ridges, vertically covering the body of the piece. They are made of smooth, glossy iridescence and terminate under the angularly ruffled rim. The colors are marigold, purple, blue, green, and amethyst.

Bowl, 4″			
☐ marigold	20.00	24.00	25.00
☐ purple	14.00	18.00	16.00
☐ blue	14.00	18.00	16.00
☐ green	14.00	18.00	16.00
☐ amethyst	14.00	18.00	16.00

S-Repeat

S-REPEAT
Dugan

A continuing row of serpentine scrolls in high relief and decorated with beadwork covers the entire available exterior space on these pieces. The voluptuous swirls are molded beautifully, the design is elegant. The color in Carnival glass is marigold.

	Current Price Range		Prior Year Average
Creamer			
☐ marigold	60.00	70.00	65.00
Punch Bowl			
☐ marigold	450.00	600.00	460.00
Punch Cup			
☐ marigold	30.00	40.00	35.00
Toothpick			
☐ marigold	200.00	225.00	215.00

SAILBOATS
Fenton

Wide panels framed with ridged ribbons contain a floating sailboat on rippling water. This motif repeats around the piece, showing motion. It is a sparse and tasteful pattern with excellent iridescence. Colors are blue, green, amber, vaseline, marigold, and red.

Bowl			
☐ marigold	17.00	22.00	18.00
☐ blue	32.00	35.00	33.00
☐ green	32.00	35.00	33.00
☐ amber	32.00	35.00	33.00
☐ vaseline	40.00	55.00	42.00
☐ red	200.00	250.00	215.00
Goblet			
☐ marigold	130.00	175.00	140.00
☐ blue	200.00	250.00	215.00
☐ green	200.00	250.00	215.00
Plate			
☐ marigold	40.00	60.00	45.00
☐ blue	120.00	130.00	125.00
☐ green	120.00	130.00	125.00
☐ purple	120.00	130.00	125.00
☐ amethyst	120.00	130.00	125.00
Wine Glass			
☐ marigold	22.00	27.00	24.00
☐ blue	40.00	50.00	42.00
☐ green	40.00	50.00	42.00
☐ purple	40.00	50.00	42.00
☐ amethyst	40.00	50.00	42.00

SCALES
Northwood

This interior design is a simple overall effect of fish scales, radiating out of a central medallion made up of a rosette with scaly petals. It is sparsely decorated and the big scales resemble upside-down arches. The colors vary; the glass is transparent.

Bowl	Current Price Range		Prior Year Average
☐ marigold	20.00	22.00	22.00
☐ purple	25.00	28.00	27.00
☐ green	25.00	28.00	27.00
☐ blue	25.00	28.00	27.00
☐ amethyst	25.00	28.00	27.00
☐ ices	30.00	35.00	32.00
☐ milk white	125.00	145.00	130.00
☐ peach opalescent	20.00	25.00	22.00
☐ aqua opalescent	175.00	225.00	180.00
Plate			
☐ marigold	20.00	25.00	22.00
☐ purple	30.00	35.00	32.00
☐ green	30.00	35.00	32.00
☐ blue	30.00	35.00	32.00
☐ amethyst	30.00	35.00	32.00
☐ ices	45.00	60.00	47.00
☐ peach opalescent	60.00	70.00	65.00
☐ milk	125.00	170.00	130.00

SCROLL AND FLOWERS PANELS
Imperial

Another intricate, elegant design reminiscent of Victorian drawing rooms, the scroll work is the eye catcher. The swirling serpentines frame the feathery petalled flower which occupies the middle ground. Gentle arches terminate the pattern just under the bulleted rim. Colors are purple, green, and marigold.

Vase			
☐ marigold	60.00	70.00	65.00
☐ purple	175.00	225.00	190.00
☐ green	175.00	225.00	190.00

SCROLL EMBOSSED
Imperial

This marvelous pattern consists of a central series of circles in glossy ribbing, surrounded by four round panels arranged in a cross design. Alternating stippled glass with glossy adds to the sparkle on these grandly iridescent pieces. The colors are purple, marigold, green, and smoke.

Bowl			
☐ marigold	20.00	25.00	22.00

	Current Price Range		Prior Year Average
☐ purple	30.00	35.00	32.00
☐ green	30.00	35.00	32.00
☐ smoke	30.00	35.00	32.00
Plate			
☐ marigold	40.00	45.00	42.00
☐ purple	70.00	80.00	75.00
☐ green	70.00	80.00	75.00
☐ smoke	70.00	80.00	75.00

SEA GULLS VASE
English Manufacturer

The sea gulls are represented with wide wings and diving in an impressionistic manner. The wings are geometric wide ridges, the bird's stalking body is made up of arched ribbing. The sky and clouds, as well as the earth below, is almost surreal, very modernistic. The color is iridescent and marigold.

Vase

☐ marigold	60.00	80.00	65.00

SHELL
Imperial

A straightforward pattern, perfect for Carnival glass, this design is a band of eight ridged shells taking up most of the outer edge and surrounding a center motif that resembles a sand dollar. The long rays that make up the middle design are voluptuously rounded in high relief. The colors are green, purple, marigold, amber, and smoke.

Bowl

☐ marigold	30.00	38.00	32.00
☐ green	40.00	45.00	42.00
☐ purple	40.00	45.00	42.00
☐ amethyst	40.00	45.00	42.00
Plate			
☐ marigold	70.00	80.00	75.00
☐ green	120.00	140.00	125.00
☐ purple	120.00	140.00	125.00
☐ amethyst	120.00	140.00	125.00

SHELL AND JEWEL
Westmoreland

The shells are massive arches fluted widely and centered by a nice, simple flower. The background which takes up most of the body is roughly stippled. The upper rim has an interesting drapework with beaded decoration. The colors are green, amethyst, and marigold.

Creamer, lidded

☐ marigold	30.00	40.00	32.00

Shell and Jewel

	Current Price Range		Prior Year Average
☐ green	40.00	50.00	42.00
☐ amethyst	40.00	50.00	42.00
Sugar Bowl			
☐ marigold	40.00	50.00	42.00
☐ green	40.00	50.00	42.00
☐ amethyst	40.00	50.00	42.00

SMOOTH PANELS

It is the lack of design or decoration that is the achievement here. The smooth, slightly convex panels ripple over the piece like a breath of wind. The effect is that the color and the iridescence are showcased—both are of superior craftsmanship. Colors are marigold, amethyst, green, smoke, purple, and amber.

Pitcher			
☐ marigold	70.00	80.00	75.00
☐ green	150.00	175.00	160.00
Tumbler			
☐ crystal opalescent	35.00	45.00	37.00
Vase			
☐ marigold	30.00	40.00	32.00
☐ green	45.00	50.00	47.00
☐ purple	45.00	50.00	47.00
☐ amethyst	45.00	50.00	47.00
☐ smoke	180.00	200.00	185.00
☐ amber	180.00	200.00	185.00

Springtime

SPRINGTIME
Northwood

Basketweave borders the bottom and top of these panelled pieces. The floral pattern in high relief that sits in the middle of the body is made up of daisy in chain, all stippled and nicely molded. The colors are rich and luminous, in the pastels as well as green, marigold, and amethyst.

	Current Price Range		Prior Year Average
Berry Bowl, diameter 4½"			
☐ green	30.00	40.00	32.00
☐ amethyst	30.00	40.00	32.00
Berry Bowl, diameter 7½"			
☐ green	80.00	100.00	82.00
☐ amethyst	80.00	100.00	82.00
Butter Dish, with cover			
☐ marigold	160.00	180.00	170.00
☐ green	225.00	260.00	230.00
☐ amethyst	225.00	260.00	230.00
Creamer			
☐ marigold	50.00	60.00	52.00
☐ green	85.00	95.00	86.00
☐ amethyst	85.00	95.00	86.00
Pitcher			
☐ marigold	250.00	300.00	275.00
☐ green	375.00	400.00	395.00
☐ amethyst	375.00	400.00	395.00
☐ ices	580.00	610.00	590.00
Spooner			
☐ marigold	55.00	65.00	58.00
☐ green	90.00	110.00	95.00

	Current Price Range		Prior Year Average
☐ amethyst	90.00	110.00	95.00
Sugar Bowl			
☐ marigold	60.00	75.00	65.00
☐ green	85.00	95.00	90.00
☐ amethyst	85.00	95.00	90.00
Tumbler			
☐ marigold	40.00	60.00	42.00
☐ green	45.00	65.00	47.00

STAR MEDALLION
Imperial

This pattern makes use of contrasts—the sharply cut stars in a wide band around the piece are multi-rayed and splayed outward. The background is a neat vertical and horizontal row of heavy round knobs covering the piece. The overall effect is one of eyecatching balances. The glass is very heavy, the colors rich in marigold and smoke.

Bowl, round, diameter 7″			
☐ marigold	14.00	17.00	15.00
☐ smoke	17.00	25.00	19.00
Bowl, square, diameter 7″			
☐ marigold	14.00	17.00	18.00
☐ smoke	17.00	25.00	19.00
Bowl, square, diameter 9″			
☐ marigold	14.00	17.00	18.00
☐ smoke	17.00	25.00	17.00

Star Medallion

	Current Price Range		Prior Year Average
Butter Dish, with lid			
☐ marigold	70.00	80.00	72.00
Compote			
☐ marigold	25.00	35.00	27.00
Creamer			
☐ marigold	25.00	30.00	27.00
Goblet			
☐ marigold	30.00	40.00	32.00
Pitcher			
☐ marigold	42.00	50.00	44.00
Punch Bowl			
☐ marigold	70.00	80.00	72.00
Punch Cup			
☐ marigold	10.00	20.00	11.00
Spooner			
☐ marigold	25.00	35.00	24.00
Sugar Bowl			
☐ marigold	25.00	30.00	27.00
Tumbler			
☐ marigold	25.00	30.00	27.00

STAR OF DAVID
Imperial

The Star of David is the centerpiece made up of braided ribbons with a smooth background. From the tips of these rays starts a busy many rayed pattern that covers the rest of the piece. The ribbing that makes up the rays seems stretched in the motion of reflecting light. Under the vertical panels on the exterior are contrasting horizontal arcs in a wave pattern. The glass is sharply molded, the colors green with silver finish, marigold, smoke, and purple.

Bowl			
☐ marigold	40.00	60.00	42.00
☐ purple	70.00	80.00	72.00
☐ green	70.00	80.00	72.00
☐ smoke	90.00	100.00	95.00

STIPPLED RAYS
Fenton

Alternating rays of glossy smooth glass and stippled spears are used once again, this time on an Interior pattern. It is a simple, effective design, especially suited to iridescent Carnival glass. The central medallion is a thousand rayed star in deep cut. The colors are marigold, green, blue, amethyst and, rarely, red.

Bon Bon			
☐ marigold	20.00	30.00	25.00
☐ green	35.00	45.00	37.00

	Current Price Range		Prior Year Average
☐ blue	35.00	45.00	37.00
☐ amethyst	35.00	45.00	37.00
☐ red	300.00	400.00	315.00
Bowl			
☐ green	25.00	30.00	27.00
☐ blue	35.00	45.00	37.00
☐ amethyst	35.00	45.00	37.00
☐ red	270.00	300.00	275.00
Compote			
☐ marigold	25.00	30.00	27.00
☐ green	35.00	45.00	37.00
☐ blue	35.00	45.00	37.00
☐ amethyst	35.00	45.00	37.00
Creamer			
☐ marigold	20.00	30.00	22.00
☐ green	25.00	35.00	26.00
☐ blue	25.00	35.00	26.00
☐ amethyst	25.00	35.00	26.00
☐ red	280.00	320.00	285.00
Plate			
☐ marigold	25.00	35.00	27.00
☐ green	40.00	50.00	42.00
☐ blue	40.00	50.00	42.00
☐ amethyst	40.00	50.00	42.00
☐ red	320.00	350.00	325.00

STIPPLED RAYS
Northwood

Another interior pattern of mildly fluted panels, stipples and glossies decorate the whole of the piece. They radiate from a central medallion of tightly ridged rays. The colors are varied as are the shapes.

Bon Bon			
☐ marigold	16.00	18.00	17.00
☐ blue	20.00	30.00	22.00
☐ purple	20.00	30.00	22.00
☐ green	20.00	30.00	22.00
☐ amethyst	20.00	30.00	22.00
Bowl			
☐ marigold	17.00	21.00	18.00
☐ blue	25.00	32.00	27.00
☐ purple	25.00	32.00	27.00
☐ green	25.00	32.00	27.00
☐ amethyst	25.00	32.00	27.00
Compote			
☐ blue	60.00	70.00	62.00
☐ purple	60.00	70.00	62.00
☐ green	60.00	70.00	62.00
☐ amethyst	60.00	70.00	62.00

STORK ABC PLATE
Imperial

A children's plate with the ABC's on the outside band in low stippling, and the numbers one through ten frame a knobby design of a stork. The background is glossy and smooth, the iridescence high and the marigold is clear.

	Current Price Range		Prior Year Average
Plate, diameter 7"			
☐ marigold	60.00	70.00	62.00

STRAWBERRY
Millersburg

Perhaps this is a later pattern, as the workmanship and coloring seem to be at the peak of quality on these pieces. The design consists of foliage and strawberries, the fruit having a well-detailed stippling. The glass is heavy and glossy, highlighting the pattern's high relief. There is a multi-rayed star at the base that shines through, seeming to illuminate the foliage wreath.

Bon Bon

☐ marigold	17.00	22.00	18.00
☐ purple	23.00	30.00	24.00
☐ blue	23.00	30.00	24.00
☐ green	23.00	30.00	24.00
☐ amethyst	23.00	30.00	24.00
☐ ices	28.00	35.00	29.00

Strawberry

STRAWBERRY
Fenton

This sparsely decorated interior pattern shows off an excellent iridescence. The wreath is foliage and strawberries in low relief, stippling around the edge of the bowl. The rest of the piece is clear of design but luminescent. The colors are green, cobalt, amethyst, marigold, red, and amberina.

Bon Bon

	Current Price Range		Prior Year Average
☐ marigold	25.00	30.00	28.00
☐ green	50.00	60.00	52.00
☐ cobalt blue	60.00	70.00	62.00
☐ amethyst	60.00	70.00	62.00
☐ amberina	210.00	220.00	215.00
☐ red	300.00	350.00	310.00

STRAWBERRY
Northwood

This deep intaglio pattern is a swirl of fruit and well-detailed leaves on vines covering most of the body of the piece. There are two versions of the pattern, plain glossy background or stippled throughout. The colors are widely varied, as are the shapes.

Bowl, diameter 4½"

☐ marigold	20.00	25.00	22.00
☐ purple	28.00	32.00	29.00
☐ green	28.00	32.00	29.00
☐ blue	28.00	32.00	29.00
☐ amethyst	28.00	32.00	29.00
☐ white	110.00	160.00	115.00

Bowl, diameter 8½"

☐ marigold	40.00	50.00	42.00
☐ purple	55.00	65.00	56.00
☐ green	55.00	65.00	56.00
☐ blue	55.00	65.00	56.00
☐ amethyst	55.00	65.00	56.00
☐ ices	65.00	80.00	70.00

Plate, diameter 7"

☐ marigold	70.00	80.00	72.00
☐ purple	85.00	100.00	86.00
☐ blue	85.00	100.00	86.00
☐ green	85.00	100.00	86.00
☐ amethyst	85.00	100.00	86.00

Plate, diameter 7"

☐ marigold	80.00	90.00	82.00
☐ purple	90.00	110.00	92.00
☐ blue	90.00	110.00	92.00
☐ green	90.00	110.00	92.00
☐ amethyst	90.00	110.00	92.00
☐ ices	150.00	180.00	160.00

STRAWBERRY EPERGNE
Northwood

	Current Price Range		Prior Year Average

Epergne Set

☐ green	300.00	400.00	325.00
☐ purple	300.00	400.00	325.00
☐ blue	300.00	400.00	325.00
☐ amethyst	300.00	400.00	325.00

STRAWBERRY INTAGLIO
Northwood

The design is under the thick glass, swirling beneath the surface in fruit and foliage.

Bowl, diameter 5″

☐ marigold	18.00	22.00	19.00

Bowl, diameter 9½″

☐ purple	35.00	45.00	37.00

STRAWBERRY SCROLL
Fenton

Bordering on art glass, this is one of Fenton's outstanding achievements. It consists of three wide horizontal bands. The bottom, which covers almost half of the piece, is a lovely floral design of reeds and flowers. The middle band is ridged on both sides and contains scrolls and feathers. The upper band, just under the plain rim, has the strawberries in high relief. The outstanding feature is the golden iridescence, and colors are marigold and purple.

Pitcher

☐ marigold	800.00	950.00	825.00
☐ purple	1300.00	1500.00	1400.00

Tumbler

☐ marigold	180.00	200.00	190.00
☐ purple	280.00	320.00	290.00

STREAM OF HEARTS
Fenton

Bowl, diameter 9½″

☐ marigold	60.00	80.00	62.00
☐ purple	80.00	100.00	82.00
☐ green	80.00	100.00	82.00
☐ blue	80.00	100.00	82.00
☐ amethyst	80.00	100.00	82.00

Compote

☐ marigold	45.00	60.00	47.00
☐ ices	65.00	75.00	68.00

SUNFLOWER PINTRAY
Millersburg

The shape of this tray is the special feature, formed like a swirling petaled flower, with a distinctive looped handle with bark ridges. The detail is magnificent, the color sharp in purple, green, amethyst, and marigold.

Pintray	Current Price Range		Prior Year Average
☐ marigold	320.00	355.00	330.00
☐ purple	310.00	320.00	320.00
☐ green	310.00	320.00	320.00
☐ amethyst	310.00	320.00	320.00
☐ marigold	310.00	320.00	320.00

SUNKEN HOLLYHOCK

Another lamp of impressive height, the iridescent bulbous glass is separated by nicely crafted brass fittings. The pattern suggests intaglio (although it isn't), with wide vertical panels raised high off the surface, the holly and foliage indented within. Each panel is framed by a braided ridge, which stems from the base and terminates over the rim. The colors are marigold and red.

Lamp			
☐ marigold	2000.00	2200.00	2100.00
☐ red	3500.00	4000.00	3600.00

SWAN
Dugan

A swan-shaped novelty in heavy glass, these pieces are nicely detailed and beautifully iridescent. The feathers are represented by low relief beads, the body is roughly stippled. The colors range widely.

Swan Shape			
☐ marigold	60.00	70.00	62.00
☐ green	90.00	100.00	92.00
☐ blue	90.00	100.00	92.00
☐ amethyst	90.00	100.00	92.00
☐ ices	35.00	45.00	37.00
☐ peach opalescent	110.00	130.00	115.00

SWIRL HOBNAIL
Millersburg

Rose Bowl			
☐ marigold	135.00	165.00	140.00
☐ purple	260.00	320.00	270.00
☐ green	260.00	320.00	270.00
☐ blue	500.00	650.00	525.00
☐ amethyst	260.00	320.00	270.00
Spittoon			
☐ purple	420.00	480.00	425.00

	Current Price Range		Prior Year Average
☐ green	420.00	480.00	425.00
☐ blue	900.00	1100.00	910.00
☐ amethyst	420.00	480.00	425.00

TAFFETA LUSTRE
Fostoria

A simple knobbed design on these chunky candlesticks is enhanced by the luxurious iridescent lustre. The finish is smooth and radiated, the colors are blue, green, amber, and orchid.

Bowl, diameter 10″

☐ blue	110.00	130.00	115.00
☐ green	110.00	130.00	115.00
☐ amber	90.00	110.00	95.00
☐ orchid	90.00	110.00	95.00

Candlesticks

☐ blue	250.00	260.00	255.00
☐ green	250.00	260.00	255.00
☐ amber	230.00	240.00	235.00
☐ orchid	230.00	240.00	235.00

TEN MUMS
Fenton

This pattern shows off mold work and coloring in a most tasteful and well-balanced way. The central medallion is a multi-petalled mum resting between two fern-like branches. The surrounding wreath is interconnected leaves, showcasing the ten half mums that appear from the fluted edge. The glass is heavy, the colors are green, cobalt, marigold, peach opalescent, and white.

Ten Mums

	Current Price Range		Prior Year Average
Bowl			
☐ marigold	70.00	80.00	75.00
☐ green	90.00	100.00	95.00
☐ blue	90.00	100.00	95.00
☐ white	120.00	140.00	125.00
Compote			
☐ marigold	40.00	50.00	45.00
☐ green	50.00	60.00	55.00
☐ blue	50.00	60.00	55.00
Pitcher			
☐ marigold	400.00	425.00	405.00
☐ green	700.00	900.00	750.00
☐ blue	700.00	900.00	750.00
☐ white	1100.00	1200.00	1150.00
Plate			
☐ green	370.00	400.00	375.00
☐ blue	370.00	400.00	375.00
Tumbler			
☐ marigold	65.00	85.00	70.00
☐ green	90.00	100.00	95.00
☐ blue	90.00	100.00	95.00
☐ white	170.00	200.00	175.00

THISTLE
Fenton

Naturalistically depicted in the art glass tradition, the thistles and foliage grace the interior in an all-over design. The detail has been documented with care, and the background left smooth to showcase the pattern. The colors are blue, marigold, amethyst, and green.

	Current Price Range		Prior Year Average
Bowl, diameter 7″			
☐ marigold	30.00	40.00	32.00
☐ amethyst	40.00	50.00	42.00
☐ blue	40.00	50.00	42.00
☐ green	40.00	50.00	42.00
Compote			
☐ marigold	40.00	50.00	42.00
☐ amethyst	50.00	60.00	52.00
☐ blue	50.00	60.00	52.00
☐ green	60.00	70.00	65.00
Plate, diameter 8½″			
☐ purple	350.00	375.00	360.00
☐ green	350.00	375.00	360.00
Horlacher Bowl			
☐ marigold	60.00	80.00	62.00
☐ amethyst	80.00	100.00	82.00
☐ blue	80.00	100.00	82.00
☐ green	80.00	100.00	82.00

THISTLE AND THORN
English Manufacturer

This pattern of foliage and thistles is an overall design but much room has been left to show off the glossy iridescence on the smooth background. The upper border resembles a chain of twigs, pointing toward the gently scalloped rim. The color is marigold.

	Current Price Range		Prior Year Average
Bowl			
☐ marigold	30.00	40.00	35.00
Creamer			
☐ marigold	20.00	30.00	25.00
Nut Bowl			
☐ marigold	20.00	40.00	30.00
Plate			
☐ marigold	120.00	130.00	125.00

THISTLE BANANA BOAT
Fenton

This is an elegant pattern, consisting of thistles and an interesting cane-like border on the interior and water lilies and cattails on the outside. Every detail has been taken care of, everywhere you look on these pieces, you see quality of mold work. The glass is extraordinarily heavy, the iridescence rainbow-like, the colors are cobalt blue, marigold, and green.

Banana Bowl			
☐ marigold	80.00	90.00	82.00
☐ cobalt blue	110.00	120.00	115.00
☐ green	110.00	120.00	115.00

Three Fruits

THREE FRUITS
Northwood

This delicate overall pattern is well conceived as a series of branches, twining around the outside band, framing three fruits: a well-molded pair of pears, a spray of cherries, and double apples. The pattern is filled in with stippling, creating a very unified look. The colors are widely varied.

	Current Price Range		Prior Year Average
Berry Bowl, diameter 5″			
☐ marigold	20.00	30.00	22.00
☐ purple	25.00	35.00	27.00
☐ blue	25.00	35.00	27.00
☐ green	25.00	35.00	27.00
☐ amethyst	25.00	35.00	27.00
☐ aqua opalescent	100.00	125.00	110.00
☐ ices	50.00	65.00	55.00
Berry Bowl, diameter 10″			
☐ marigold	40.00	50.00	42.00
☐ purple	45.00	55.00	47.00
☐ blue	45.00	55.00	47.00
☐ green	45.00	55.00	47.00
☐ amethyst	45.00	55.00	47.00
☐ aqua opalescent	340.00	375.00	350.00
☐ ices	75.00	90.00	80.00
Bon Bon			
☐ marigold	40.00	50.00	42.00
☐ purple	50.00	60.00	52.00
☐ blue	50.00	60.00	52.00
☐ green	50.00	60.00	52.00
☐ amethyst	50.00	60.00	52.00
☐ aqua opalescent	100.00	125.00	110.00
☐ ices	125.00	135.00	127.00
Plate			
☐ marigold	70.00	80.00	72.00
☐ blue	100.00	120.00	110.00
☐ green	100.00	120.00	110.00
☐ amethyst	100.00	120.00	110.00
☐ aqua opalescent	450.00	500.00	475.00
☐ ices	150.00	160.00	175.00

THREE FRUITS

The same theme is given a different treatment here, a central spray of cherries on a smooth background is framed by a wreath of foliage and dangling fruit. The design is sparsely planted around the plate, showing off a golden iridescence. The colors vary.

Plate			
☐ marigold	90.00	100.00	95.00
☐ purple	110.00	120.00	115.00
☐ green	110.00	120.00	115.00

	Current Price Range		Prior Year Average
☐ blue	110.00	120.00	115.00
☐ amethyst	110.00	120.00	115.00
☐ ices	150.00	170.00	160.00

TREE OF LIFE

Similar to crackle, this overall pattern of mosaic shapes has smooth glossy glass as the finish and filler. The shapes are framed by low-relief ridges, giving the piece a nice texture and a good ground for light refraction. The color is marigold.

Perfume
☐ marigold	35.00	45.00	37.00

Pitcher
☐ marigold	55.00	60.00	58.00

Plate
☐ marigold	25.00	35.00	27.00

Tumbler
☐ marigold	15.00	25.00	16.00

TREE TRUNK
Northwood

The tree bark texture is given a new twist with high-relief knobs dotting each elongated diamond shape. The moldwork is sharp, the glass slightly clear. The colors are green, blue, purple, and marigold.

Vase
☐ marigold	10.00	20.00	15.00

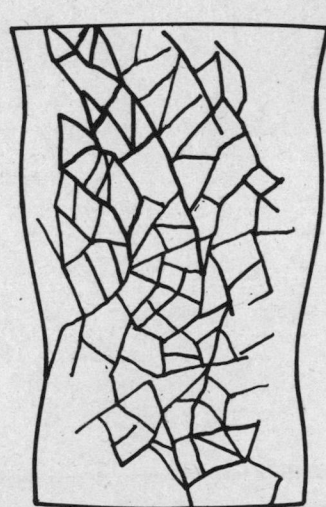

Tree of Life

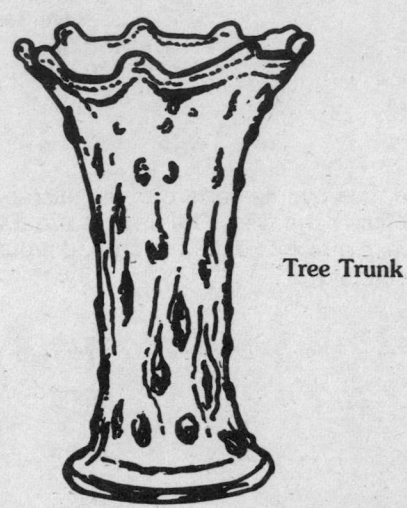

Tree Trunk

	Current Price Range		Prior Year Average
☐ purple	70.00	90.00	80.00
☐ green	35.00	40.00	37.00
☐ blue	35.00	40.00	37.00
☐ white	45.00	50.00	47.00
Whimsey			
☐ marigold	120.00	130.00	125.00
☐ purple	220.00	230.00	225.00
☐ green	220.00	230.00	225.00
☐ blue	220.00	230.00	225.00

TROUT AND FLY
Millersburg

Bowl			
☐ marigold	220.00	300.00	245.00
☐ purple	160.00	200.00	170.00
☐ green	160.00	200.00	170.00
☐ blue	325.00	400.00	330.00
☐ amethyst	325.00	400.00	330.00
Plate			
☐ purple	3750.00	4500.00	4000.00
☐ blue	3750.00	4500.00	4000.00
☐ amethyst	3750.00	4500.00	4000.00

TWINS
Imperial

This geometric, symetrical pattern consists of vaguely pointed arches, made up of high-relief ridges and separated by teardrop-shaped rosettes arranged in a wide band wreath around a central sunburst. The color is clearly iridescent, the mold work is excellent.

	Current Price Range		Prior Year Average
Berry Bowl, diameter 4½″			
☐ marigold	8.00	10.00	9.00
☐ green	8.00	10.00	9.00
Berry Bowl, diameter 9″			
☐ marigold	17.00	20.00	18.00
☐ green	17.00	20.00	18.00
Bowl, diameter 8″			
☐ marigold	16.00	20.00	17.00
☐ smoke	35.00	50.00	40.00
Bride's Basket			
☐ marigold	60.00	70.00	62.00
Fruit Bowl, with base			
☐ marigold	35.00	40.00	37.00
Punch Bowl, with base			
☐ marigold	35.00	40.00	37.00
Punch Cup			
☐ marigold	16.00	20.00	18.00

TWO FLOWERS
Fenton

An overall pattern nicely arranged from the rim to the floral center, contains foliage, waterlilies, and cattails. The background is smooth glossy glass, heavy molded, and the outer rim is a wavy scale band. The finish is radiated.

Bon Bon			
☐ marigold	10.00	13.00	11.00
☐ blue	19.00	21.00	20.00
☐ green	19.00	21.00	20.00
☐ amethyst	19.00	21.00	20.00
☐ white	28.00	32.00	29.00
Bowl			
☐ marigold	37.00	42.00	39.00
☐ blue	37.00	42.00	39.00
☐ green	37.00	42.00	39.00
☐ amethyst	37.00	42.00	39.00
☐ white	48.00	52.00	49.00

URN VASE
Imperial

The pattern is a fine grain stippling, the shape is the interesting feature. The bulbous body curves from the high neck, uninterrupted to under the rim. The handles are short and elliptical, from the base of the neck to the rim. The glass is heavy and frosty, the iridescence is excellent.

Vase	Current Price Range		Prior Year Average
□ marigold	25.00	30.00	28.00
□ white	25.00	30.00	28.00

VINTAGE
Fenton

A straightforward, utilitarian pattern, Vintage is a grape and leaf design. The motif is sparsely sprinkled over the surface, the moldwork is in low relief.

Berry Bowl, diameter 4″
□ marigold	9.00	11.00	9.50
□ green	14.00	16.00	15.00
□ blue	14.00	16.00	15.00
□ purple	14.00	16.00	15.00
□ amethyst	14.00	16.00	15.00
□ amber	17.00	20.00	16.00

Berry Bowl, diameter 8″
□ marigold	17.00	20.00	16.00
□ green	30.00	32.00	21.00
□ blue	30.00	32.00	21.00
□ purple	30.00	32.00	21.00
□ amethyst	30.00	32.00	21.00
□ amber	33.00	37.00	30.00

Bon Bon
□ marigold	17.00	20.00	18.00
□ green	25.00	30.00	26.00
□ blue	25.00	30.00	26.00
□ purple	25.00	30.00	26.00
□ amethyst	25.00	30.00	26.00
□ amber	28.00	33.00	29.00

Bowl, flat
□ marigold	15.00	18.00	16.00
□ purple	24.00	28.00	26.00
□ blue	24.00	28.00	26.00
□ green	24.00	28.00	26.00
□ amethyst	24.00	28.00	26.00
□ amber	28.00	33.00	29.00

Bowl, footed
□ marigold	20.00	24.00	22.00
□ purple	25.00	30.00	26.00
□ blue	25.00	30.00	26.00

	Current Price Range		Prior Year Average
☐ green	25.00	30.00	26.00
☐ amethyst	25.00	30.00	26.00
☐ amber	28.00	33.00	29.00
Compote			
☐ marigold	30.00	34.00	31.00
☐ purple	36.00	40.00	37.00
☐ blue	36.00	40.00	37.00
☐ green	36.00	40.00	37.00
☐ amethyst	36.00	40.00	37.00
☐ amber	40.00	44.00	41.00
Dresser Tray			
☐ marigold	80.00	90.00	82.00
Epergne			
☐ marigold	100.00	125.00	110.00
☐ purple	95.00	100.00	99.00
☐ blue	95.00	100.00	99.00
☐ green	95.00	100.00	99.00
☐ amethyst	95.00	100.00	99.00
☐ amber	100.00	110.00	102.00
Ice Cream Bowl			
☐ purple	160.00	180.00	165.00
☐ green	160.00	180.00	165.00
☐ blue	160.00	180.00	165.00
☐ amethyst	160.00	180.00	165.00
☐ amber	165.00	180.00	165.00
Nut Bowl, trifoot			
☐ marigold	20.00	30.00	25.00
☐ purple	38.00	45.00	39.00
☐ green	38.00	45.00	39.00
☐ blue	38.00	45.00	39.00
☐ amethyst	38.00	45.00	39.00
☐ amber	42.00	49.00	42.00
Nut Bowl, six footed			
☐ marigold	35.00	40.00	37.00
☐ purple	70.00	80.00	72.00
☐ green	70.00	80.00	72.00
☐ blue	70.00	80.00	72.00
☐ amethyst	70.00	80.00	72.00
☐ amber	75.00	85.00	77.00
Orange Bowl, footed			
☐ marigold	60.00	70.00	62.00
☐ purple	80.00	100.00	82.00
☐ green	80.00	100.00	82.00
☐ blue	80.00	100.00	82.00
☐ amethyst	80.00	100.00	82.00
☐ amber	80.00	110.00	85.00
Plate, flat			
☐ marigold	48.00	55.00	50.00

	Current Price Range		Prior Year Average
☐ purple	60.00	70.00	62.00
☐ blue	60.00	70.00	62.00
☐ green	60.00	70.00	62.00
☐ amethyst	60.00	70.00	62.00
☐ amber	65.00	70.00	67.00
Plate, footed			
☐ marigold	38.00	42.00	40.00
☐ purple	60.00	70.00	62.00
☐ blue	60.00	70.00	62.00
☐ green	60.00	70.00	62.00
☐ amethyst	60.00	70.00	62.00
☐ amber	65.00	75.00	67.00
Powder Jar			
☐ marigold	40.00	50.00	45.00
Punch Bowl			
☐ marigold	110.00	140.00	115.00
☐ purple	130.00	150.00	140.00
☐ blue	130.00	150.00	140.00
☐ green	130.00	150.00	140.00
☐ blue	130.00	150.00	140.00
☐ amber	135.00	160.00	140.00
Punch Cup			
☐ marigold	8.00	10.00	9.00
☐ purple	13.00	16.00	14.00
☐ blue	13.00	16.00	14.00
☐ green	13.00	16.00	14.00
☐ blue	13.00	16.00	14.00
☐ amber	16.00	20.00	17.00
Rose Bowl			
☐ marigold	50.00	60.00	52.00
☐ purple	70.00	80.00	72.00
☐ green	70.00	80.00	72.00
☐ blue	70.00	80.00	72.00
☐ amethyst	70.00	80.00	72.00
☐ amber	75.00	85.00	78.00
☐ amberina	90.00	100.00	92.00
Sandwich			
☐ marigold	40.00	50.00	45.00
☐ amberina	60.00	70.00	62.00
Wine Glass			
☐ marigold	16.00	18.00	17.00
☐ purple	30.00	40.00	32.00
☐ green	30.00	40.00	32.00
☐ blue	30.00	40.00	32.00
☐ amethyst	30.00	40.00	32.00
☐ amber	35.00	45.00	37.00

WAFFLE BLOCK

	Current Price Range		Prior Year Average
Basket			
☐ marigold	20.00	30.00	22.00
☐ ice blue	45.00	60.00	47.00
☐ ice green	45.00	60.00	47.00
☐ white	40.00	50.00	42.00
Parfait Glass			
☐ marigold	10.00	15.00	12.00
☐ ice blue	40.00	50.00	45.00
☐ ice green	40.00	50.00	45.00
☐ white	28.00	32.00	30.00
Punch Cup			
☐ marigold	10.00	14.00	12.00
☐ blue	14.00	16.00	15.00
☐ green	14.00	16.00	15.00
☐ purple	14.00	16.00	15.00
☐ amethyst	14.00	16.00	15.00
Tumbler			
☐ marigold	38.00	42.00	39.00
Vase, diameter 9"			
☐ marigold	14.00	17.00	15.00
☐ ice blue	42.00	50.00	46.00
☐ ice green	42.00	50.00	46.00
☐ white	38.00	42.00	40.00

WIDE PANEL
Imperial

A simple, elegant look in iridized glass catches the eye; these pieces use their iridescence to show off their style. The wide panels take up three quarters of the body, gently convex and terminated by a three rim band that horizontally rims the upper edge. The glass is almost opaque and heavy.

	Current Price Range		Prior Year Average
Compote			
☐ marigold	9.00	11.00	10.00
☐ ice blue	25.00	35.00	22.00
☐ ice green	25.00	35.00	22.00
☐ vaseline	20.00	30.00	22.00
☐ pink	20.00	30.00	22.00
Console Set			
☐ marigold	50.00	65.00	52.00
☐ ice blue	75.00	87.00	72.00
☐ ice green	75.00	87.00	72.00
☐ vaseline	70.00	80.00	72.00
☐ pink	70.00	80.00	72.00
Epergne			
☐ marigold	150.00	175.00	160.00
☐ purple	375.00	425.00	400.00
☐ ices	495.00	510.00	505.00

	Current Price Range		Prior Year Average
☐ vaseline	495.00	510.00	505.00
☐ white	495.00	510.00	505.00
Goblet, small			
☐ marigold	14.00	16.00	15.00
Goblet, large			
☐ marigold	30.00	40.00	35.00
Lemonade Pitcher, handled			
☐ marigold	22.00	26.00	24.00
Plate, diameter 10″			
☐ marigold	25.00	30.00	27.00
☐ ices	35.00	40.00	37.00
☐ vaseline	35.00	40.00	37.00
☐ white	35.00	40.00	37.00
Punch Bowl			
☐ marigold	60.00	70.00	62.00
Punch Cup			
☐	6.00	7.00	6.50

WILD ROSE
Northwood

This exterior pattern is a draped wreath of an eight-petaled rose and holly-like leaves. The background is smooth and glossy, the glass is opaque, the iridescence is good.

Bowl, flat			
☐ marigold	16.00	18.00	17.00
☐ green	28.00	30.00	29.00
☐ amethyst	28.00	30.00	29.00
☐ ices	38.00	40.00	39.00
Bowl, open work edge, fluted			
☐ marigold	50.00	60.00	55.00
☐ green	45.00	65.00	50.00
☐ amethyst	40.00	50.00	42.00
☐ ices	50.00	60.00	52.00
Bride's Basket			
☐ marigold	90.00	110.00	95.00
☐ ices	120.00	135.00	125.00

WILD STRAWBERRY
Northwood

This is an interesting, swirling pattern, full of action and movement. The foliage wreath is arranged diagonally in a curve around the outer band, lightly detailed strawberries separate the sprays of foliage.

Bowl, flat, diameter 8½″			
☐ purple	60.00	70.00	65.00
☐ green	60.00	70.00	65.00

	Current Price Range		Prior Year Average

Plate, handgrip, diameter 7″
☐ purple 60.00 70.00 65.00
☐ green 60.00 70.00 65.00

WINDMILL
Imperial

The windmill motif is treated with high relief, framed by poplar trees and surrounded by a ridged oval, creating a picture effect. The rest of the body has blossoms raining down the stippled paneled sides. The color is glimmering, the glass almost opaque.

Berry Bowl, diameter 4″
☐ marigold 6.00 8.00 7.00
☐ green 30.00 35.00 32.00
☐ purple 30.00 35.00 32.00
Berry Bowl, diameter 8″
☐ marigold 15.00 17.00 16.00
☐ green 30.00 35.00 32.00
☐ purple 30.00 35.00 32.00
Fruit Bowl
☐ marigold 16.00 18.00 17.00
☐ green 30.00 35.00 32.00
☐ purple 30.00 35.00 32.00
Milk Pitcher
☐ marigold 30.00 35.00 32.00
☐ purple 60.00 70.00 62.00
☐ green 60.00 70.00 62.00
Pickle Dish
☐ marigold 13.00 17.00 14.00

Windmill

	Current Price Range		Prior Year Average
☐ purple	30.00	40.00	32.00
☐ green	30.00	40.00	32.00
Pitcher			
☐ marigold	40.00	50.00	42.00
☐ purple	170.00	180.00	175.00
☐ green	170.00	180.00	175.00
Tray			
☐ marigold	30.00	40.00	32.00
☐ purple	40.00	50.00	42.00
☐ green	40.00	50.00	42.00

WISHBONE AND SPADES

This well-ridged pattern is primarily centered in the middle of these pieces. A large voluptuous eight sided bloom is the most striking motif, covering over three quarters of the body and framed by smart little blossoms that radiate out of the petals. The background is smooth but the detail is stippled, giving a contrasting texture.

Bowl, diameter 6″			
☐ purple	35.00	40.00	37.00
☐ green	40.00	50.00	42.00
☐ peach opalescent	50.00	60.00	55.00
Plate, diameter 6″			
☐ purple	55.00	60.00	57.00
☐ green	55.00	60.00	57.00
☐ peach opalescent	65.00	76.00	67.00
Plate, diameter 9″			
☐ purple	120.00	160.00	140.00
☐ green	270.00	300.00	275.00

Wishbone and Spades

WREATHS OF ROSES
Fenton

	Current Price Range		Prior Year Average
Basket			
☐ marigold	60.00	70.00	62.00
☐ green	40.00	50.00	42.00
☐ blue	40.00	50.00	42.00
☐ amethyst	40.00	50.00	42.00
Bon Bon, flat			
☐ marigold	18.00	20.00	19.00
☐ green	30.00	35.00	32.00
☐ blue	30.00	35.00	32.00
☐ amethyst	30.00	35.00	32.00
☐ peach opalescent	55.00	70.00	46.00
☐ white	45.00	50.00	46.00
Bon Bon, footed			
☐ marigold	35.00	40.00	37.00
☐ green	45.00	55.00	47.00
☐ blue	45.00	55.00	47.00
☐ amethyst	45.00	55.00	47.00
☐ peach opalescent	90.00	100.00	92.00
☐ white	80.00	90.00	82.00
Compote			
☐ marigold	20.00	25.00	22.00
☐ green	35.00	40.00	37.00
☐ blue	35.00	40.00	37.00
☐ amethyst	35.00	40.00	37.00
☐ peach opalescent	50.00	60.00	52.00
☐ white	45.00	50.00	46.00
Punch Bowl			
☐ marigold	210.00	225.00	215.00
☐ green	250.00	275.00	260.00
☐ blue	250.00	275.00	260.00
☐ amethyst	250.00	275.00	260.00
Punch Cup			
☐ marigold	13.00	16.00	14.00
☐ green	17.00	19.00	18.00
☐ blue	17.00	19.00	18.00
☐ amethyst	17.00	19.00	18.00
Rose Bowl			
☐ marigold	30.00	40.00	32.00
☐ green	50.00	60.00	52.00
☐ blue	50.00	60.00	52.00
☐ amethyst	50.00	60.00	52.00

WREATHED CHERRY
Dugan

The cherries are not only molded in high relief, they are usually treated with a different and darker color. The result is an interesting pattern with an eye catching motif. The wreath is a slight band of draped ridges in gentle scallops and it frames the three cherry bunch.

	Current Price Range		Prior Year Average
Berry Bowl, diameter 4″			
☐ marigold	14.00	18.00	15.00
☐ amethyst	25.00	30.00	28.00
☐ purple	25.00	30.00	28.00
☐ white	38.00	40.00	39.00
Berry Bowl, diameter 8″			
☐ marigold	60.00	70.00	62.00
☐ amethyst	120.00	125.00	122.00
☐ purple	120.00	125.00	122.00
☐ white	290.00	300.00	295.00
Butter Dish			
☐ marigold	90.00	100.00	92.00
☐ amethyst	150.00	170.00	160.00
☐ purple	150.00	170.00	160.00
☐ white	180.00	200.00	185.00
Creamer			
☐ marigold	35.00	40.00	37.00
☐ amethyst	40.00	50.00	42.00
☐ purple	60.00	70.00	65.00
☐ white	70.00	80.00	72.00
Pitcher			
☐ marigold	135.00	145.00	140.00
☐ amethyst	260.00	270.00	265.00
☐ purple	260.00	270.00	265.00
☐ white	375.00	425.00	400.00
Spooner			
☐ marigold	35.00	40.00	37.00
☐ amethyst	40.00	50.00	42.00
☐ purple	40.00	50.00	42.00
☐ white	70.00	80.00	72.00
Sugar Bowl			
☐ marigold	35.00	40.00	37.00
☐ amethyst	40.00	50.00	42.00
☐ purple	40.00	50.00	42.00
☐ white	70.00	80.00	72.00
Toothpick			
☐ amethyst	180.00	220.00	190.00
Tumbler			
☐ marigold	20.00	30.00	22.00
☐ amethyst	40.00	50.00	42.00
☐ purple	40.00	50.00	42.00
☐ white	60.00	70.00	62.00

ZIPPERED HEART

This exterior pattern consists of a wide band of hearts, formed by pearly beadwork with rosette lobes. The scrolls are cut into the sides of the piece, influencing the shape and creating distinct panels. The color is magnificent, the iridescence mirrorlike.

	Current Price Range		Prior Year Average
Berry Bowl, diameter 9″			
☐ marigold	45.00	50.00	46.00
☐ purple	80.00	90.00	85.00
Pitcher			
☐ marigold	225.00	250.00	230.00
☐ purple	700.00	800.00	725.00
Tumbler			
☐ marigold	40.00	50.00	42.00
☐ purple	120.00	130.00	125.00
Vase			
☐ purple	575.00	625.00	600.00

CUT GLASS

THE BRILLIANT PERIOD

The cut glass dealt with in this book is the American cut glass produced from 1876 to 1914 which has come to be known as the Brilliant Period. This glass was made for the wealthy class in America who desired something more distinctive than the pattern glass which was by that time in widespread use throughout middle-class American homes. However, despite the excellent quality and fine workmanship of American cut glass, it had to compete with European imports which were preferred in this country by the upper classes.

The glass making industry in America fought a hard battle to educate the public on the beauty of domestic cut glass, utilizing the Centennial Exposition of 1876 and the Columbian World's Fair of 1892–93. W.L. Libbey and Sons Company built and operated a complete cut glass factory at the Columbian Exposition and dazzled fair goers with the glittering results.

With the battle against European glass finally won, the Brilliant Period of cut glass flourished until the Art Nouveau period began to wane and was replaced by the more streamlined Art Deco movement. At that time brilliant cut glass was considered too fussy and elaborate to be in good taste and the American glass cutters turned their skills toward the war effort of World War I.

THE MAKING OF CUT GLASS

The making of cut glass was a time consuming process requiring the patience and talent of master craftsmen. The glass was handblown of the finest 35–45% lead crystal and poured into molds to produce the shaped piece, called a blank. These blanks were anywhere from ¼" to ½" thick in order to achieve the deep cutting which distinguished this glass from later periods. The resulting finished product was therefore exceedingly heavy.

The cutting and polishing was accomplished in four steps. The first step involved making the desired pattern on the blank with crayons or paint. Next the deepest cuts were made by rough cutting. This was accomplished by pressing the blank on an abrasive cutting wheel of metal or stone which was lubricated by a small stream of water and sand. In the third step, the rough cuts were smoothed with a finer stone wheel and water only. Finally, polishing or "coloring" was done on a wooden wheel with putty powder or pumice, in order to produce the gleaming brilliant finish.

BUYING CUT GLASS

In building a collection of cut glass, it is important to buy the very best quality you can afford. If you are a novice in this field, the best way to acquire the skills needed to buy successfully is to see as much cut glass as you can. Go to museums, galleries, antique shops, and shows. Look at the glass and handle it whenever possible. Using the criteria which will follow later, evaluate the glass you see without buying it. After you have seen a great deal of good cut glass you will be better equipped to make good purchases.

Another point to be stressed is the importance of buying from reputable dealers. Later, as your expertise increases, you may buy successfully at auctions and from other collectors. In the meantime, you will need to rely on the expert advice of ethical professionals who are prepared to stand behind what they sell. This is a field where you generally get what you pay for. Therefore it will pay you to deal with people you can trust. If you are considering the purchase of a very expensive piece, ask the dealer if you may have it appraised. A reputable dealer will not be offended by this and, if a lot of money is involved, it may be wise.

Probably the two factors which affect price the most are quality and scarcity. In determining the quality of a piece, first judge the workmanship involved. Appraise each piece carefully, asking yourself certain questions. Is the glass crystal clear? Is it uniformly thick and heavy? Does it gleam from hand polishing or does it have the high gloss, unnatural shine produced by acid polishing? Are there any traces of cloudiness? Does it refract the light well? When tapped with your fingernail, does it ring with a clear bell-like sound?

Now look at the cutting. Are the cuts deep and true and is the pattern balanced and aesthetically pleasing? Do the surface cuts feel sharp to the touch?

Consider now the condition of the piece. Has it been deeply scratched, or badly chipped? Is the glass itself sick, grayish looking, or cloudy? Are there any repaired areas? The condition of the glass is extremely important. Value is lowered drastically by any real damage no matter how rare the piece itself may otherwise be. However, you must use common sense in this area. Nicks, scratches, small chips and the like are to be expected on old cut glass. They are simply the result of many years of normal use and do not seriously detract from the value of any piece.

Scarcity is of course a factor in the price of glass. This is an area which requires some study, however. Consult the bibliography at the end of the book and do some serious reading in this area. Some of the most beautiful patterns have become scarce due to their appeal to the collector based on their beauty. The "Russian" pattern is a classic example of this. It is one of the very most detailed and exquisite patterns ever developed. There were thousands of pieces produced and because of their incredible beauty they have been collected to the point of scarcity. However, not all scarce glass is beautiful and therefore scarcity doesn't necessarily contribute to the value of a piece.

If a piece is an oddity; that is if it has an unusual shape and function, it may be more valuable than a more standard piece of the same pattern.

Signed pieces are tricky. Just because a piece is signed doesn't always mean a great deal. First of all, it depends on who signed it and the condition of the glass. Also, unfortunately, forgeries of backstamps are not uncommon in the cut glass world. In addition, many famous companies did not sign all of their glass for one reason or another. Some retailers preferred that the glass was unsigned because in the early days the American product was passed off as the preferred European imported glass. Also, many companies produced glass for years before they registered a trademark.

The history of the glass can also affect its price. If a piece has the significance of having been owned by a notable person its value is naturally increased. Whether or not you wish to pay considerably more for a piece because of prior ownership is a very personal matter. Some people specialize in these items, building whole collections on this premise.

Naturally, value is also affected by current economic conditions. Therefore, there are certain things to keep in mind while considering the purchase of any piece of cut glass. Are you collecting for the pleasure of the hobby or do you view cut glass as an investment? Do you want to build an important collection of valuable pieces, one which can be sold later on? Are you interested in long term profits or a short term turnover? Or are you interested only in collecting? The best rule of thumb is to always buy the very best quality you can and also to purchase only those pieces you really like. By doing so your collection will always be a source of pleasure and pride for however long you keep it.

REPAIRING CUT GLASS

Since glass is so fragile it is prone to breakage and other types of damage caused by temperature and various chemical reactions. Some of these problems can be repaired successfully, others just cannot be dealt with satisfactorily.

The easiest repair to make concerns the abrasions on the bottom of a piece caused by wear. These can be removed by fine polishing but it is important to find the right person for this job. You need a master craftsman who has been affiliated with a cutting shop specializing in cut glass wares. This is a dying trade and you shouldn't procrastinate indefinitely for there are no master glass cutters being trained these days.

Small nicks which occur in the rims of stemmed glasses and tumblers can be reground and reshaped by experts also. This will run from $10 to $30 per glass, depending on the piece itself.

If the sawtooth or scalloped edges of a bowl have been nicked or knocked off repairs can sometimes be made by reshaping and polishing.

Cracks present an insurmountable problem. They cannot be removed and it is inadvisable to use the piece for anything other than display. If an object breaks into several pieces it can be cemented together but the cemented line will show.

Various liquids, including water, can also damage brilliant cut glass leaving gray, cloudy areas. There are chemicals which can clean up this damage to a degree but there is no known method of complete restoration.

Here are some hard and fast rules concerning the care of cut glass:

1. Remember that even though it is very heavy, cut glass is not strong; it is very fragile. The deep cutting actually weakens the glass structurally. There are many bizarre stories concerning breakage. For example, one heartsick woman reported that while an insistent dinner guest was helping her clear the table the guest inadvertently dropped a very small paper thin crystal cordial glass. The weightless cordial glass fell to the table, glancing off the corner of an heirloom cut glass bread tray. To everyone's horror, the bread tray shattered into a million pieces. To further add insult to injury, the thin, lightweight cordial glass suffered no damage whatsoever. By all means, use your lovely tableware, but be very careful when you do.

2. Wash your cut glass in warm sudsy water with a very mild detergent. First line the sink with several layers of toweling. Then fill with warm water and mild detergent. Cover the end of the water spout with a rubber guard which can be purchased from a hardware store. As a further safeguard, move the spout out of the way. Wash carefully with a flannel cloth using a large soft sable artist's brush for cleaning into the cutting. Rinse carefully, dry with a lint-free cloth, and immediately put the glass away. Never put more than one piece of glass in the sink at a time!

3. When displaying your glass do not make the mistake of crowding. The pieces should never touch one another. Above all, never stack your cut glass. This can cause much damage including abrasion, chipping, and cracking.

4. Do not attempt any repairs on your own such as cementing or smoothing away scratches or nicks. You will only make matters worse and cause serious damage. ALWAYS HAVE AN EXPERIENCED PERSON DO All REPAIRS.

5. Never arrange fresh flowers in an antique cut glass vase without using a container or liner for protection. The water and the stems cause a chemical reaction which can cause permanent discoloration of the glass.

MAJOR MANUFACTURERS OF THE BRILLIANT PERIOD

C. DORFLINGER AND SONS

Christian Dorflinger learned glassmaking in St. Louis, France, before coming to America with his family in 1846. He worked in Pennsylvania and New Jersey before starting the Long Island Flint Glass Works in Brooklyn, New York in 1852. He started from scratch and eventually built three glassworks before his health forced him into retirement in 1863. While recuperating in Pennsylvania, Dorflinger decided to settle there and farm out the rest of his days. This didn't last long, however, and soon he was building a new glassworks in the Pennsylvania countryside. It wasn't long before he expanded to two glassworks; the latter, in White Mills,

Pennsylvania, moved quickly into full production. Several more factories were added over the years and Christian Dorflinger's sons came to work with their father in 1881.

Dorflinger glass was sold in all the finest stores of its day, including Tiffany's of New York. However, after his death in 1915 and the depression of World War I, Dorflinger's closed.

Dorflinger's glass was used by Presidents Lincoln, Grant, Harrison, Wilson, and many of the crowned heads of Europe.

Among the many patterns patented by Dorflinger were:

> PARISIAN — May 4, 1886
> FLORENTINE — November 13, 1888
> RATTAN — March 22, 1892
> COLONIAL — July 4, 1893
> LORRAINE — November 13, 1894

H. C. FRY GLASS CO.

Henry Clay Fry began producing glass in the 1860's. Over the years he was associated with several companies including Fry and Scott, and the Rochester Tumbler Company. In 1901 he organized the H. C. Fry Glass Co., and manufactured blown and pressed blanks, glassware (including etched glass), cut glass, and various novelty items.

Fry glass was known for its exceptionally high lead content and for the floral designs that became fashionable at the end of the Brilliant Period.

Fry obtained many patents, among them are:

> ASTER — May 18, 1909
> DAISY — November 25, 1913
> FLOWER BASKET — February 20, 1917
> PRISM, PRISM AND FLUTE — March 20, 1917

The H. C. Fry Glass Company manufactured glass until 1925 when it closed its doors, reopening briefly in 1933. This lasted only one year and in 1934 H. C. Fry Glass Company permanently ceased operation.

J. HOARE AND CO.

James Hoare was born in Cork, Ireland where he learned the glass cutting trade. His son, John, also was a glass cutter, and when the family moved to Birmingham, England they worked for various prestigious glass manufacturers. The Hoare family moved to the United States, first to Philadelphia and then to Brooklyn, New York where they established the Brooklyn Flint Glass Co. Then they traveled to Corning, New York and formed the very successful Corning Glass Works.

The succeeding generations of the Hoare family were in the glass cutting business for many years. Numerous partnerships with many notable glass cutters were formed, among them Amory Houghton Sr., Amory Houghton Jr., Thomas G. Hawkes, George L. Abbott, Rome Bixby, William Langendorfer, and others. At various times they operated glassworks in Philadelphia, Pennsylvania, New York City, Corning, New York, and Wellsboro, Pennsylvania.

T. J. HAWKES AND CO.

Thomas Gibbons Hawkes, a glass cutter from Ireland, was brought to America to work for John Hoare. Indeed, he lived with the Hoares in Corning, New York before going into business for himself with Samuel Hawkes, Townsend de M. Haukes, and Frederick Carder, establishing the Steuben Glass Company. This company produced some of the finest cut glass patterns of the Brilliant Period, among them the dazzling "Russian" pattern. Thousands of pieces of Hawkes glass have been used in the White House by Presidents Grover Cleveland, Benjamin Harrison, Theodore Roosevelt, Franklin D. Roosevelt, Harry S. Truman, and Dwight D. Eisenhower.

Hawkes cut glass was exhibited at many world's fairs and expositions, always creating a stir and winning prizes for excellence.

The cut glass of T. J. Hawkes and Co. was purchased by the rich and famous of the day including European royalty such as the Prince of Sweden and also the legendary empire building families of the Astors, Rockefellers, Vanderbilts, Whitneys, and DuPonts.

Hawkes patents include:

RUSSIAN — January 20, 1882
RUSSIAN AND PIIIAR — October 25, 1887
GRECIAN — October 25, 1887
STAR ROSETTE — April 24, 1888
OLD FASHIONED HOBNAIL — April 24, 1888
DEVONSHIRE — May 8, 1888
LOUIS XIV — May 21, 1889
BRAZILIAN — May 28, 1889
VENETIAN — June 3, 1890
MALTESE CROSS — September 2, 1890
CHRYSANTHEMUM — November 4, 1890
CORONET — June 12, 1892
VALENCIAN — January 17, 1893
ABERDEEN — April 14, 1896
NAUTIIUS — August 18, 1896
NELSON — March 9, 1897
FESTOON — March 9, 1897
PANEL — August 3, 1909
CARNATION — November 21, 1909
GRAVIC FLORAL — November 2, 1909
TIGER FLOWER — November 29, 1910
LATTICED ROSETTES AND RIBBONS — February 7, 1911

Their trademark, registered on March 3, 1903 shows a trefoil enclosing a fleur de lis with two hawks toward the bottom.

MANUFACTURERS' MARKS

Abraham & Straus Inc.

American Wholesale Corp.

C.G. Alford & Co.

M.J. Averback

Almay & Thomas

T.B. Clark & Co.

J.D. Bergen Co.

House of Birks

Buffalo Cut Glass Co.

George L. Borden & Co.

Burley & Tyrrell Co.

George Borgfeldt & Co.

Conlow-Dorworth Co.

Corona Cut Glass Co.

Crown Cut Glass Co.

SILVART

Deidrick Glass Co.

Crystal Cut Glass Co.

Diamond Cut Glass Works

FLORAL CRYSTAL
Duncan Dithridge

Crystolyne Cut Glass Co.

C. Dorflinger & Sons

Geo. Drake Cut Glass Co.

VESTALIA
Eska Mfg. Co.

O.F. Egginton Co.

H.C. Fry Glass Co.

Empire Cut Glass Co.

Gowans, Kent, & Co., Ltd.

Gundy-Clapperton Co.

T.G. Hawkes & Co.

BALTIC
BILTMORE
BRESLIN
BRESLIN SPECIAL
DIAMOND POINSETTA
FUSHIA
PANAMA
TACOMA
TEXAS
TEXAS SPECIAL
VICTORIA
W.P. Hitchcock Co.

A.H. Heisey & Co.

J. Hoare & Co.

L. Hinsberger Cut Glass

Hobbs Glass Co.

Hobbs, Brockunier & Co.

Honesdale Decorating Co.

Imperial Glass Co.

Hope Glass Works

Iorio Glass Shop

Hunt Glass Co.

Irving Cut Glass Co.

Jewel Cut Glass Co.

PEERLESS
Kelly & Steinman

Edward J. Kock & Co.

Keystone Cut Glass Co., Ltd.

TRADE MARK
Krantz, Smith & Co. Inc.

MARS
STRAND
Kings Co. Rich Cut Glass Works

Lackawanna Cut Glass Co.

Laurel Cut Glass Co.

W.L. Libbey & Son

LOWELL CUT GLASS CO.
LOWELL MASS

Lowell Cut Glass Co.

Wm. H. Lum

Joseph Locke & Sons

Luzerne Cut Glass Co.

Lotus Cut Glass Co.

Lyons Cut Glass Co.

McKanna Cut Glass Co.

Maple City Glass Co.

PRESCUT

McKee-Jeannette Glass Works

Meriden Cut Glass Co.

Majestic Cut Glass Co.

Kelva C.F. Monroe Co.

Moses, Swan & McLawee Co.

Roden Bros., Ltd.

H.P. Sinclair & Co.

Seattle Cut Glass Co.

Standard Cut Glass Co.

Signet Glass Co.

Sterling Glass Co.

Steuben Glass Works

L. Straus & Sons

Tuthill Cut Glass Co.

Taylor Brothers Co.

Unger Bros.

Thatcher Bros. & Co.

United States Glass Co.

Van Heusen, Charles Co.

PATTERN MOTIFS

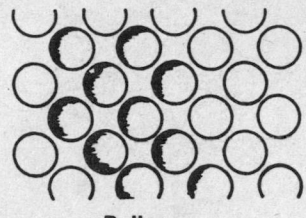

Bullseye

Cross Hatching

Buzz Star

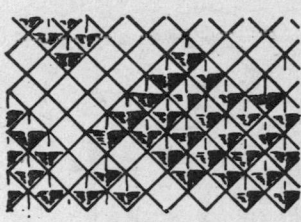

Diamond Point

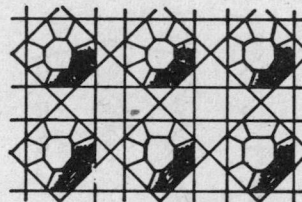

Cane/Chair Bottom

Fan-Feathered Fan

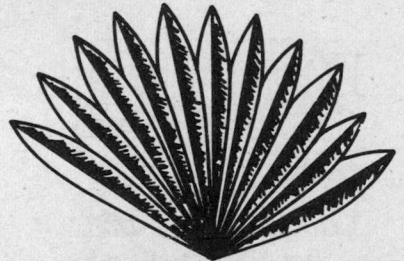

Flashed Fan

Flashed Rosette

Hobstar

Fluting

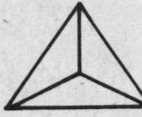

Mitered Diamond Cutting

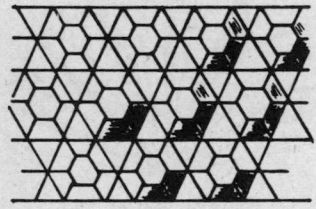

Hobnail

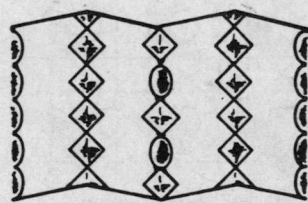

Notched Prismatic Panel

Octagon Diamond Design

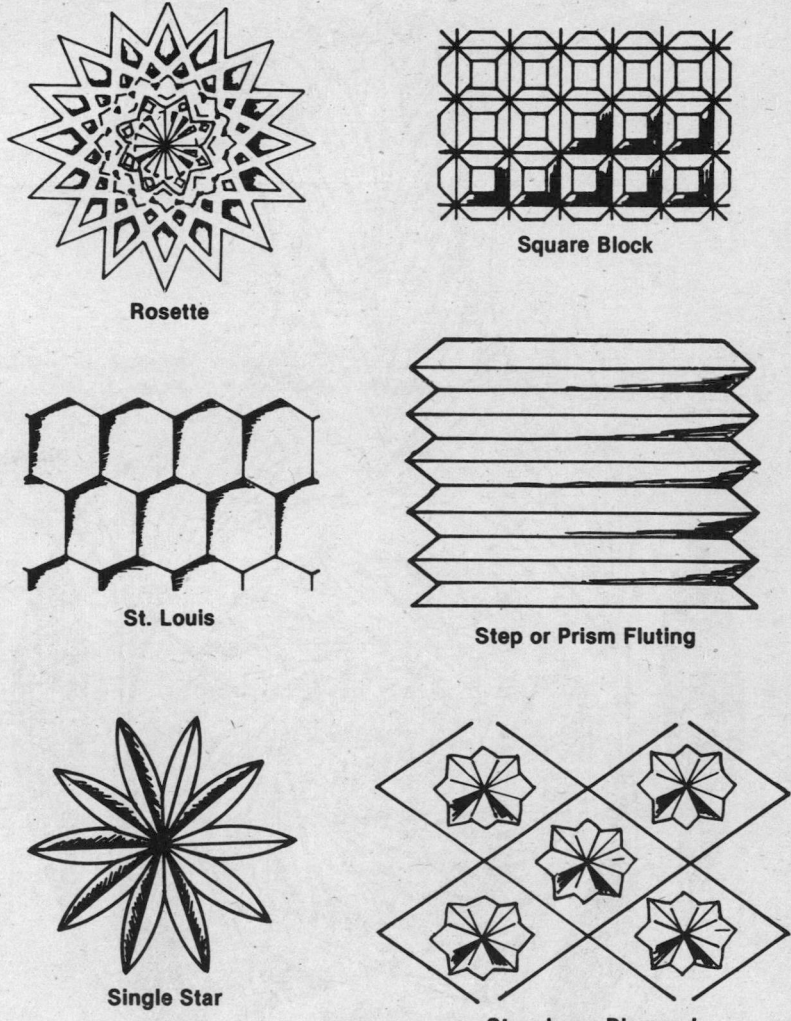

Rosette

Square Block

St. Louis

Step or Prism Fluting

Single Star

Strawberry Diamond

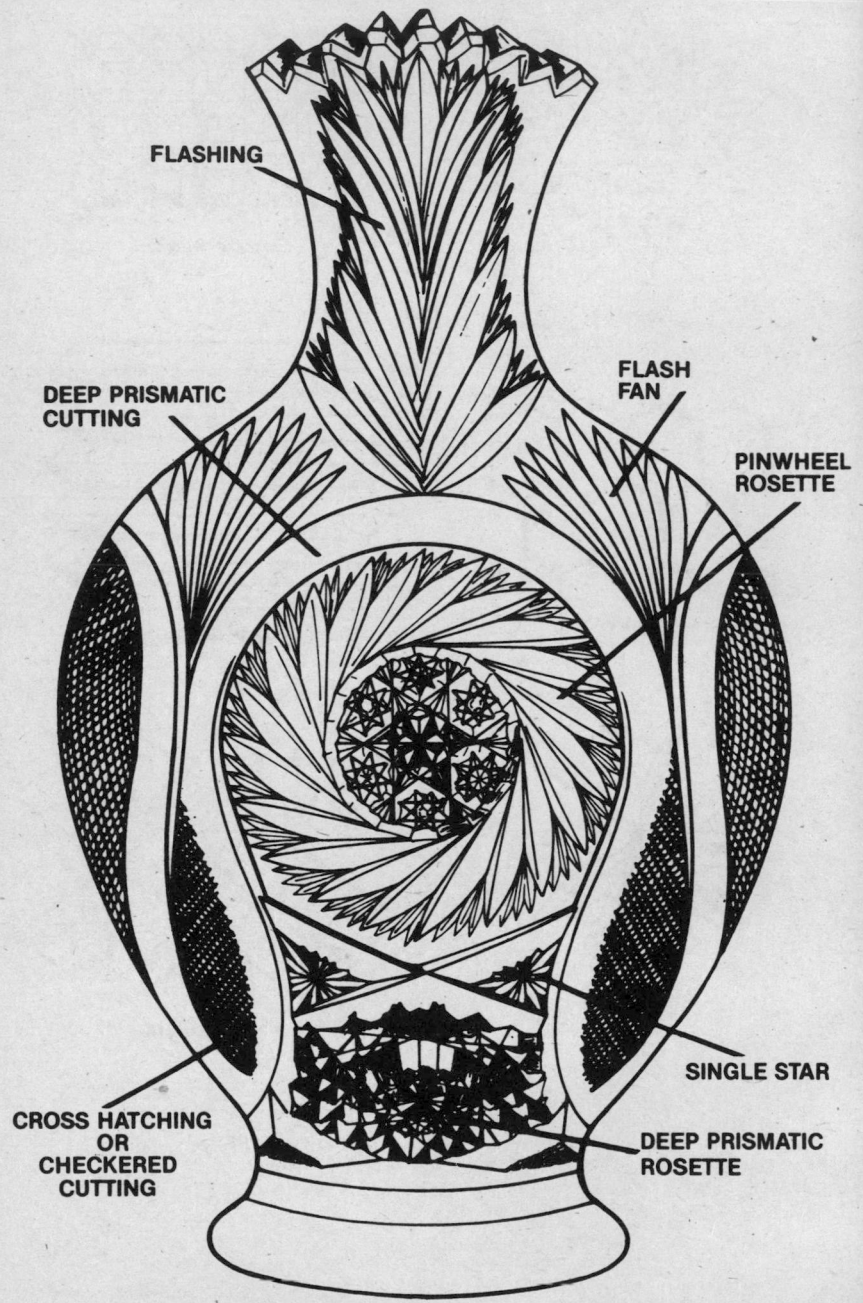

FLASHING

DEEP PRISMATIC
CUTTING

FLASH
FAN

PINWHEEL
ROSETTE

CROSS HATCHING
OR
CHECKERED
CUTTING

SINGLE STAR

DEEP PRISMATIC
ROSETTE

	Current Price Range		Prior Year Average

BASKET

☐ **Rope Motif Handle,** alternating flashed rosettes with deep cut fan, sawtooth scalloped rim 215.00 240.00 225.00

☐ **Thumbprint Handled,** flash fans, notched prismatic panel, deep cut caned star, by Pitkin and Brooks 300.00 400.00 325.00

☐ **Thumbprint Handled,** deep prismatic cutting underneath flash fans, pinwheel rosettes surround deep prismatic cutting, rectangular base, scalloped rim, diameter 8" 295.00 325.00 310.00

☐ **Thumbprint Handled,** pinwheel rosettes surround deep prismatic cut panels, footed, diameter, 8" 290.00 315.00 300.00

☐ **Twisted Handle,** large hobstars with flashed fanning, scalloped edge, by David Walsh 125.00 140.00 130.00

BELL

☐ **Cross Hatching,** all of bell except for a small portion of handle is crosshatched, some fans on the very bottom, handle is knopped and ends in a knob, height 6" 150.00 165.00 155.00

☐ **Paneled Handle,** with diamond cut band around top, hobstar and light prism cuts, Premier, by J.D. Bergen, height 7½" 185.00 200.00 190.00

☐ **Paneled Handle,** most of bell is crosshatched, four panels of deep hobstar cutting surround bell, handle comes to sharp point, height 7" 170.00 190.00 180.00

☐ **Pinwheel Rosette,** alternated with deep prismatic cutting, paneled handle, handle comes to a sharp point, height 7" 140.00 165.00 150.00

BON BON DISH

☐ **Boat Shape,** simple fern motif with frozen ball rim, Hiawatha, by Pitkin and Brooks 120.00 140.00 125.00

☐ **Heart Shape,** lightly cut single stars among cross hatching, feathered fans and prism cuts, Emblem, by J.D. Bergen 60.00 80.00 65.50

	Current Price Range		Prior Year Average

☐ **Hexagon,** mitered diamond center, surrounded by cross-hatching and rosette cutting, length 8" 80.00 90.00 85.00

☐ **Lidded,** deep cut daisy with prism stems and thumbprints, garland, by Pitkin and Brooks, diameter 4" 60.00 80.00 65.00

☐ **Lidded,** deeply cut daisy on top of lid, cross hatching on side of lid and on side of base, diameter 10" 345.00 400.00 385.00

☐ **Modified Triangle Shape,** tiny rosette center, caning, cross hatching, dogwood blossom shaped deep prism cuts, diameter 6¾" 95.00 115.00 97.50

☐ **Oval Shape,** lightly cut single star surrounded by deep cross hatching, feathered fans form the rim, length 8" 160.00 180.00 167.00

☐ **Oval Shape,** fans on either end, prism cutting, towards the middle borders a deeply cut single fan, Bedford by J.D. Bergen, diameter 7" 55.00 70.00 63.00

☐ **Sawtooth Rim,** single star base framed by triangle mitered diamond cuts, feathered fans and rosette, Thelma, by J.D. Bergen, length 9" ... 95.00 110.00 90.00

☐ **Sawtooth Rim,** single star base surrounded by mitered diamonds and feathered fans, St. George, by T.B. Clarke and Company 65.00 75.00 67.50

☐ **Sawtooth Rim,** five panels of mitered diamonds surrounded by cross-hatching, c-shaped handle, diameter 6½" 55.00 65.00 60.00

☐ **Scalloped Rim,** rosette in deep cut triangle framed by flashed rosette, cross hatching on fans, Myrtle, by Pitkin and Brooks 45.00 55.00 47.50

☐ **Scalloped Sawtooth Rim,** strawberry diamond panels between rosettes, fan motifs form rim, Dorrance, by T.B. Clark 80.00 95.00 82.50

☐ **Square Shape,** overall deep cut hobstars framed by prism cut, feathered fan filler, sawtooth rim 60.00 80.00 62.50

☐ **Square Shape,** deep prismatic rosette center, mitered diamonds surround the center, rim is made of feather fans, slightly scalloped, length 5½" 62.00 76.00 68.00

BOTTLE	Current Price Range		Prior Year Average
☐ **Buzz Star Motif,** scalloped handle, height 8″	45.00	53.00	48.00
☐ **Cane Bottom,** to fan border, flat stopper, height 8″	26.00	32.00	27.50
☐ **Diamond Motif,** notched prism cut, faceted lid, height 3″	30.00	35.00	32.00
☐ **Hobnail Stars,** chair bottom, diamonds, by Stage, height 9″	90.00	120.00	100.00
☐ **Humidor,** heavy stopper, with sponge, hobstar and fans, height 7″	150.00	200.00	165.00
☐ **Octagon Diamond,** flashed fans, faceted stopper, height 7″	40.00	48.00	43.00
☐ **Star Design,** with flashed fanning and deep prism cuts, by Clark	30.00	36.00	33.00
☐ **Star and Diamond Motif,** step prism cut at neck, scalloped handle, faceted stopper, height 9″	65.00	78.00	68.00
☐ **Water,** fluted neck, bull's eyes and ovals, star bottom	30.00	40.00	32.50

BOWL

	Current Price Range		Prior Year Average
☐ **Allover Cut Patterns,** wide scallop rim, heavy cut glass, by Libbey	285.00	360.00	295.00
☐ **Allover Cut,** with scallop, serrated rim, Sabre, by Libbey, signed, diameter 8″	325.00	400.00	330.00
☐ **Berry,** Marlboro, by Dorflinger, diameter 8″	150.00	200.00	175.00
☐ **Berry,** with tray, overall rosette pattern with cross hatch filler and occasional single stars, tray and bowl have sawtooth rim, Peerless, by Higgins and Seiter	195.00	210.00	200.00
☐ **Buzz Star,** deep prism cut, cross hatching, diameter 8″	55.00	70.00	60.00
☐ **Butterfly Cut,** with feathered fan, scalloped edges, Butterfly, by Niland, height 5″	45.00	55.00	48.00
☐ **Chair Bottom,** band across top, floral design, diameter 8″	110.00	132.00	115.00
☐ **Collar Base,** widely flared rim, deep cut mitered diamond, draping, diameter 7″	140.00	160.00	145.00
☐ **Cut Leaves,** leaves touch lightly at the top of bowl, leaves alternate with deep cut single stars and mitered diamonds, rim is scalloped diameter 7″	80.00	95.00	86.00

	Current Price Range		Prior Year Average
diameter 8"	95.00	115.00	105.00
diameter 9"	115.00	130.00	120.00
diameter 10"	125.00	145.00	135.00
☐ **Diamond Cut Base,** miter cut flowers, leaves and stems, signed, by Edenhall, diameter 9"	140.00	168.00	150.00
☐ **Diamond Cut Center,** flower is miter cut, prism cut, double handled, Poinsettia, by McKanna	20.00	25.00	22.00
☐ **Diamond Cut,** scalloped edge, prism cut stem, by Franklin Flint, diameter 9"	120.00	145.00	125.00
☐ **Diamond Point,** with deep prismatic cuts, scalloped edge, cross hatchings, prism cuts in base, by Frizlen, height 3⅞"	100.00	120.00	105.00
☐ **Diamond Point,** with flash fanning and deep prismatic cutting, Caldonia, by Pairpoint	75.00	90.00	80.00
☐ **Engraved Butterfly,** surrounded by leaf and flower designs, Garland, by Pairpoint	160.00	190.00	170.00
☐ **Feathered and Flashed Fan Designs,** scalloped edge, by Thatcher Brothers, diameter 8¼"	65.00	80.00	70.00
☐ **Flared Side,** rim is alternating intaglio rosette with step cut outlines, ragged spears, deep cut, form triangle teeth on rim, diameter 10"	140.00	160.00	145.00
☐ **Flashed Rosettes,** scalloped edge, Maywood, by Richter, diameter 10" ..	150.00	175.00	155.00
☐ **Hearts and Flowers,** miter cut, diamond point cut, hearts and flowers—rose, Elite, diameter 8", height 7½"	60.00	80.00	65.00
☐ **Hobnail,** deep prism cuts, footed, by Washington	65.00	78.00	70.00
☐ **Hobnail,** fine miter cuts, flower center is cross hatchings, scalloped edge, diameter 8"	110.00	132.00	115.00
☐ **Hobstar Center,** deep cut, mitered diamond triangular panels radiating from center alternating with feathered fans, scalloped and sawtooth rim			
diameter 7"	75.00	90.00	80.00
diameter 8"	90.00	115.00	97.00
diameter 9"	115.00	137.00	125.00
☐ **Hobstars,** diamond point cut, cross hatchings, scalloped edges, by Enterprise	100.00	120.00	105.00

	Current Price Range		Prior Year Average

☐ **Hobstars,** flashed fan, deep prism cuts, scalloped edge, signed, by Libbey 140.00 168.00 150.00

☐ **Hobstars,** scalloped edge, eight sided, diameter 9" 130.00 156.00 135.00

☐ **Inverted Edge,** mitered rosettes alternate with fancy feathered sunburst, diameter 8" 135.00 145.00 138.50

☐ **Large Feathered Fan Design,** with prismatic cutting, scalloped edge, signed, by Libbey, diameter 10¾", height 3½" 240.00 290.00 245.00

☐ **Large Rosette,** with strawberry diamond cuttings, square blocks, oval, strawberry, by Dorflinger, length 10" 50.00 60.00 55.00

☐ **Leaf and Single Star Design,** lightly cut single stars alternated with mitered diamond leaves, diameter 10" 125.00 145.00 132.50

☐ **Oval,** flared rim, feathered fans, mitered diamonds and cross hatching, Roosevelt, by Averbeck, diameter 11½" 200.00 225.00 205.00

☐ **Oval Shape,** deep cut rosettes alternating with lightly cut single stars, cross-hatching at the bottom of the bowl, length 10" 155.00 180.00 170.00

☐ **Oval,** hobstar and fine checkering, by Eggington, length 10" 285.00 300.00 290.00

☐ **Pedestal Base,** swirled prism panel, rosette band around rim, Orient, by T.B. Clark, diameter 9" 325.00 360.00 350.00

☐ **Pinwheel Rosette,** rim is made of fans alternating with the pinwheel rosette design, deep diagonal cuts border the rosette, rim is scalloped, diameter 7" 90.00 110.00 97.50

☐ **Pinwheel Rosette,** alternates with feathered fan design, base is cross-hatched, Tornado, by Higgins & Seiter, diameter 8" 95.00 120.00 110.00

diameter 9" 120.00 130.00 125.00

☐ **Rose-Colored,** six flowers on stems with etched centers and leaf veins, diameter 5⅝" 50.00 60.00 55.00

☐ **Roses,** mitered cut, rosettes, hobnail cuttings, Rose, by Figueroa, diameter 8" 65.00 75.00 70.00

☐ **Rose Miter Cut,** stars, cross hatching, scalloped edge, Rose, by Keystone, diameter 9", height 4½" 55.00 66.00 60.00

	Current Price Range		Prior Year Average

☐ **Rosettes and Buttons,** with deep prismatic cuts, star, by Enterprise, diameter 7½" 50.00 60.00 55.00

☐ **Rosettes,** cross hatchings, deep prism cuts, scalloped edge, trefoil shape, diameter 9½", by Western 120.00 145.00 125.00

☐ **Rosettes,** cross hatchings, diamond cuts, footed, scalloped edge, by Figueroa, height 6½" 95.00 115.00 100.00

☐ **Rosettes,** deep prism cuts, diamond, scalloped edge, Imperial, by Heinz, diameter 8" 100.00 120.00 105.00

☐ **Rosettes,** flashed fans, cross hatching, deep prism cuts, Rose, by Gibbs, diameter 10½" 125.00 150.00 130.00

☐ **Rosettes,** hobnail, deep prismatic cuts, scalloped rim, by Lesch, diameter 8", height 3½" 125.00 150.00 130.00

☐ **Rosettes,** hobnail designs, scalloped edge, signed, by Lyons, height 5" ... 75.00 90.00 80.00

☐ **Rosettes,** rose mitered cut, scalloped edge, Rose, by Elite, diameter 9", height 4½" 45.00 55.00 47.00

☐ **Rosettes,** stars, deep prismatic cuts, scalloped edge, diameter 9¼" 150.00 180.00 155.00

☐ **Rosettes,** with square block and prism cuttings, signed, by Taylor Brothers, diameter 8" 135.00 160.00 140.00

☐ **Round,** four feet, scalloped edge, shell motif with silver deposit, diameter 10½" 24.00 28.00 26.50

☐ **Sawtooth and Scalloped Rim,** flashed rosette, deep prism cuttings and feathered fans, Golf, by J.D. Bergen, diameter 9" 90.00 110.00 92.50

☐ **Sawtooth Edge,** rosette base, caning, hobstar, and fan, Desdemona, by T.B. Clark and Company, diameter 10" ... 200.00 250.00 225.00

☐ **Sawtooth Rim,** rosette with deep cut prisms forming long petals with a thin banded background, cross hatching, caning with a polished ground, Goldenrod, by J.D. Bergen, diameter 9" 120.00 130.00 122.50

☐ **Scalloped Sawtooth Rim,** hobstar base, rosettes with deep cut prisms, cross hatching, Florida, by Higgins and Seiter, length 13½" 120.00 140.00 125.00

	Current Price Range		Prior Year Average

☐ **Scalloped Rim,** deep cut hobnail center bordered by feathered fans and crosshatching

diameter 8″	120.00	140.00	132.00
diameter 10″	170.00	195.00	180.00

☐ **Scalloped Edge,** diamond cut center, surrounded by feathered fans, diameter 8½″ ... **115.00 130.00 120.00**

☐ **Scalloped Rim,** salad bowl, feathered fans swirl around a design of a single cut star surrounded by mitered diamonds, diameter 8″ ... **110.00 135.00 117.50**

☐ **Shallow,** by Windsor, diameter 9″ ... **250.00 300.00 260.00**

☐ **Single Stars,** feathered fan, cross hatchings, rosettes, scalloped edge, by Kellner and Munro ... **50.00 60.00 55.00**

☐ **Single Star Pattern,** single stars separated by small cross-hatched panels, rim is scalloped

diameter 8″	92.00	107.50	100.00
diameter 9″	100.00	115.00	110.00
diameter 10″	135.00	155.00	145.00

☐ **Square Block Design,** with rosettes, flashed fanning, deep prism cuts, by Dorflinger, height 5½″ ... **80.00 100.00 85.00**

☐ **Star,** cross hatchings, prism cuts, scalloped edge, diameter 8″ ... **150.00 175.00 155.00**

☐ **Stars,** diamond, deep prism cuts, scalloped edge, Amore, by Dorflinger, diameter 8″ ... **75.00 90.00 80.00**

☐ **Star Motif,** flashed fan, diamond cut, by Clark ... **25.00 30.00 27.00**

☐ **Steep Sided,** jagged edge, caned rosette, inverted fan, step cuts in a long triangle, Keystone, by J.D. Bergen, diameter 8″ ... **110.00 115.00 112.50**

☐ **Steep Sided,** rim is sawtooth curves alternating with sharp triangle panels, long, wide cross hatch panels frame hobstars, Webster, by Averbeck, diameter 9″ ... **115.00 135.00 120.00**

☐ **Steep Sided,** scalloped edge, vertical prism cut band, rosettes and mitered diamonds, Kenwood, by J.D. Bergen, diameter 10″ ... **210.00 250.00 215.00**

☐ **Sterling Rim,** hobstar, cane, fine checkering, signed Gorham, 1904 mark, diameter 9″ ... **300.00 350.00 310.00**

	Current Price Range		Prior Year Average

☐ **Straight Rim,** flashed hobstar and miter cut rosettes, polished background 75.00 85.00 77.50

☐ **Strawberry Diamond Cuttings,** cross hatchings, deep prismatic cuts, feathered fan design at rim, Encore, by Benjamin Davies, square, height 8" 60.00 72.00 65.00

☐ **Strawberry,** fine miter cut, hobstar, cross hatchings, scalloped rim, diameter 8" 160.00 190.00 165.00

☐ **Three Legged,** scalloped rim, Gravic Wild Rose, by Hawkes, diameter 8¼" 300.00 400.00 325.00

☐ **Three Legged,** flared rim, cross hatching and caning 85.00 90.00 87.50

☐ **Tri-Foil Shape,** wide fluted rim, long beaded leaf-like designs from center of bowl extending to fluted rim, ribbed base with rayed center, length 1½" 35.00 45.00 40.00

☐ **Two Ring Handles,** cross hatched background with deep cut rosette, flat shape, diameter 6" 135.00 145.00 148.50

☐ **Undulating Sawtooth Rim,** deep cut diamond rosettes framed by caned spears, prism cuts, American Beauty by Averbeck, diameter 8" 110.00 115.00 111.00

☐ **Undulating Sawtooth Rim,** feathered fans form upper edge, cross hatching, deep prism cuts, single star center, diameter 9" 185.00 200.00 190.00

☐ **Undulating Sawtooth Rim,** rosette center, strawberry diamond alternating with fan rim, diameter 9" 130.00 150.00 135.00

☐ **Undulating Scalloped Edge,** single stars around rim, banana shaped caning, flatten caned hobstar, Genoa, by Averbeck, diameter 10" 140.00 160.00 145.00

☐ **Undulating Scalloped Rim,** caned daisy blossom base, with feathered fan fillers, large rosette border around waist, Carnation, by T.B. Clarke, diameter 9" 210.00 240.00 215.00

☐ **Vertical Cuts,** medial horizontal band of cut diamonds, bottom half of bowl is a single star design surrounded by mitered diamonds
Round
diameter 7" 110.00 125.00 117.00
diameter 8" 125.00 145.00 135.00
diameter 9" 160.00 180.00 170.00

	Current Price Range		Prior Year Average
diameter 10″	190.00	225.00	207.50
Oblong			
length 10½″	172.00	195.00	183.00

BUTTER DISH

☐ **One Loop Handle,** steep sided, deep vertical prism cuts decorated with twisted ribbons, mitered rosette base, diameter 6″ ....

130.00   150.00   135.00

☐ **Rosettes,** cross hatchings, diamond cuts, prism cuts on lid, scalloped base, Zella, by Irving, diameter 8″ ....

100.00   120.00   105.00

☐ **Rosettes,** prismatic panels, scalloped edge, by Willson, height 6½″ ....

115.00   138.00   120.00

☐ **Rosettes,** with scalloped underplate, cover is decorated by cut leaves alternated with single stars, cross-hatched near bottom, diameter 8″ ....

125.00   145.00   135.00

☐ **Six Pointed Star Design,** alternated with triangular panel surrounding hobstar, with scalloped rim underplate, handle of cover is knobbed, plate diameter 6″, cover height 5¼″ ....

250.00   280.00   265.00

☐ **Square Block and Cross Hatching Cuts,** leaves and roses are miter cut, prism cut lid, signed, Rose Combination, by Irving, height 6″ ....

75.00   95.00   80.00

CANDLESTICK

☐ **Hollow Heavy Cut,** flutes and hobstars, height 9½″ ....

130.00   150.00   140.00

☐ **Metal Inserts,** to hold candle, teardrop center, flute and flashed star, by Libbey ....

300.00   350.00   320.00

☐ **Single Light,** mitered rosettes above feather fans form base, diamond shaped rosettes, height 10″ ....

180.00   235.00   195.00

☐ **Three Light,** high polished ground with single rosette bands, inverted fan around base ....

260.00   350.00   275.00

☐ **Wheel Cut Base,** by Hawkes, height 2¾″ ....

50.00   60.00   52.00

☐ **Wide Flared Base,** made up of rosettes, strawberry diamonds and cross hatching, sawtooth edge, height 8″ ..

135.00   140.00   137.50

CARAFE	Current Price Range		Prior Year Average
☐ **Bulbous Body,** unusual design, panel neck, flaring rim, scalloped foot, two rows of feathered fans separated by a medial band of plain glass, fans alternate with triangular panels of mitered diamonds, height 10″	205.00	235.00	220.00
☐ **Flared Pedestal Base,** alternating mitered diamond triangles with fans, panels and cross hatching, height 8½″	210.00	240.00	215.00
☐ **Flashed Fan,** cross hatchings, beaded neck, slightly scalloped edge, Montauk, capacity one quart	90.00	110.00	95.00
☐ **Flashed Rosette,** star, vertical beaded neck, capacity one quart	65.00	70.00	68.00
☐ **Globular Body,** fluted neck, flaring rim, one row of feathered fans with a pattern of cut diamonds underneath, plain base, height 9½″	60.00	85.00	70.00
☐ **Oval Shaped Bowl,** with short, paneled neck, flashed hobstar, alternating cross hatching and feathered fans, height 7″	95.00	115.00	97.50
☐ **Ovoid Body,** long fluted neck, flaring rim, lightly cut hobstar alternated with triangular panels of mitered diamonds topped by flaring fans, height 10″ ...	105.00	130.00	120.00
☐ **Ovoid Body,** long fluted neck, flaring rim, deep vertical cutting alternating with single row of cut diamonds topped with fans, height 11¼″	130.00	150.00	135.00
☐ **Rosettes,** flashed fan, deep prism cuts, vertical beaded neck, by William Volker	75.00	80.00	77.00
☐ **Round Bowl,** with flared neck, flashed hobstar and feathered fans, height 8½″	110.00	115.00	112.00
☐ **Round Bowl,** with heavily paneled neck, starburst motif with stippled rays, polished center, Sunburst by Pitkin and Brooks, height 8½″	155.00	165.00	158.50
☐ **Round Bowl,** paneled neck with stippled ridges, rosette in deep cut diamond, deep prisms with cut out scallops, Bedford by J.D. Bergen, height 10″	85.00	110.00	87.50
☐ **Round Bowl,** tall thin neck, thumbprint border above deep cut rosettes and strawberry diamonds, height 8″	95.00	110.00	97.50

	Current Price Range		Prior Year Average

☐ **Squat Bowl,** widely flared mouth, thumbprints around feathered star, height 7½" 90.00 95.00 92.50

☐ **Squat Bowl,** with patrician neck, vertical prism cuts with twisted ribboning, diamond mitering, height 6½" 125.00 140.00 127.50

☐ **Squat Shape Bowl,** with long neck, starburst motif with bull's eye behind, caned panels, Goldenrod by J.D. Bergen, height 8" 220.00 250.00 225.00

☐ **Thumbprint Design,** surrounding a flared fan design bisected by a single vertical cut, ovoid body, paneled neck, slightly flared rim, height 8" 85.00 105.00 92.00

☐ **Urn Shaped Bowl,** with heavy paneled neck, thumbprints above and below starburst band, high polished glass, height 8" 85.00 115.00 87.50

☐ **Urn Shaped Bowl,** feathered fans, diamond mitering, cross hatching, deep cut prisms surround each design, height 7¼" 120.00 140.00 125.00

CELERY

☐ **Boat Shape,** cut diamonds on either end, single star in the middle, length 11½" 110.00 130.00 115.00

☐ **Double Helix Pattern Center,** with hobstars on either end, length 13" .. 125.00 150.00 135.00

☐ **Figure Eight Shape,** deep prism cuts with cross hatched diamonds, three rosettes along the bottom, Halle by Pitkin and Brooks, length 11½" 110.00 140.00 115.00

☐ **Figure Eight Shape,** vertical prism cuts with stepped panels, beadwork eight shaped cut around bottom, length 12" 115.00 125.00 117.50

☐ **Flared Sawtooth Rim,** rosettes along side are framed by deep prism cut vaulted arches with cross hatched filler, length 11½" 185.00 195.00 190.00

☐ **Oval,** lightly undulating sawtooth rim, cross hatching, mitered rosettes surrounding a wild starburst, length 11" 125.00 145.00 130.00

☐ **Oval Shape,** cross hatched at either end with a pinwheel rosette center, scalloped rim, length 12" 100.00 135.00 125.00

	Current Price Range		Prior Year Average

☐ **Oval Shape,** fans alternate with hobstars, prism cutting along bottom, length, 11½" **105.00 130.00 115.00**

☐ **Rounded,** deep prism cuts decorated with caning and beadwork, rosettes at four corners **145.00 165.00 150.00**

☐ **Six Pointed Star Center,** surrounded by deep radiating cuts, deep prism cutting on either side, oval shaped with small protrusions near ends, length 10¾" **125.00 150.00 135.00**

☐ **Twisted Dough Shape,** bulbous to either side on the ends, oval prism cuts containing rosettes across bottom, length 11" **145.00 155.00 150.00**

☐ **Undulating Sawtooth Rim,** formed by alternating rosettes and fans, St. Cloud, by Higgins and Seiter, length 11½" **85.00 95.00 87.50**

CIGAR JAR

☐ **Beaded Vertical Cutting,** ball stopper with fan design **175.00 200.00 185.00**

☐ **Deep Prism Cutting,** with fan design on stopper, slightly waisted, hollow top
white **170.00 195.00 182.00**
green **190.00 220.00 200.00**

☐ **Fitted Cover,** cross hatched triangles in a low border, stars and starbursts around middle, fans at the top, height 6½" **210.00 250.00 215.00**

☐ **Flashed Fans,** prism cuts, rosettes, Kennelworth, by Stage, length 10¼" **160.00 180.00 170.00**

☐ **Light Vertical Cuts** in varying lengths along side of bottle, fan design on stopper, slightly waisted, hollow top, Renaissance, by Higgins & Seiter
white **170.00 195.00 180.00**
green **200.00 220.00 205.00**

☐ **Hollow Top,** thumbprint band, wide panel prism cuts, by Higgins and Seiter **165.00 185.00 175.00**

COLOGNE BOTTLE

☐ **Buzz Star,** size 4 oz. **40.00 45.00 42.00**

☐ **Cross Hatchings,** with deep prism cuts, flashed fanning, by Clark **20.00 25.00 22.00**

	Current Price Range		Prior Year Average

☐ **Flower,** flashed fan, eaves are miter cut, faceted stopper **50.00** **55.00** **52.00**

☐ **Genie Style,** pointed stopper with beadwork decor, twisted prism cuts along waist down to thumbprints, height 9½″ **55.00** **65.00** **57.50**

☐ **Honeycomb Stopper,** short neck, deep vertical prism cuts with scalloped trim, Prism, by J.D. Bergen, height 8″ **52.00** **56.00** **54.50**

☐ **Honeycomb Stopper,** square cut neck on rim, rosettes bordered by angular cuts with cross hatched filler, height 4½″ **40.00** **50.00** **42.50**

☐ **Honeycomb Stopper,** vertical cane panel strips, polished elongated thumbprints, 8 oz. **40.00** **45.00** **42.50**

☐ **Rosette,** notched prism cut, faceted stopper, height 6″ **55.00** **63.00** **58.00**

☐ **Tower Style,** pointed honeycomb stopper, fruit thumbprints around middle, diamond stars below, 5 oz. **40.00** **60.00** **45.00**

COMPOTE

☐ **Attached Underplate,** star bottom, cross cut with half moon cut rim **28.00** **35.00** **28.50**

☐ **Boat Shape,** c-scroll handles on either side, prism cutting, fans at either end, smooth stem, wide foot.
    height 6″ **205.00** **227.00** **210.00**
    height 7″ **220.00** **245.00** **230.00**

☐ **Chalice Shape,** triangular panels of cut diamonds alternated with squares of cross hatching, feathered fans along top of bowl, thick stem, partly beaded, wide foot, height 6″ **105.00** **135.00** **120.00**

☐ **Chalice Shape,** honeycomb knobbed cover, cross hatching separating rosettes, fan upper border **275.00** **325.00** **280.00**

☐ **Champagne Shape,** wide foot, beaded stem, scalloped rim, hobstar design, alternated with fans, height 8″ **135.00** **160.00** **147.00**

☐ **Concave Panel,** scalloped rim, Colonial, by Heisey, diameter 4″ **16.00** **18.00** **16.50**

☐ **Flat Bowl,** feathered fan along side of bowl, thick stem, plain edge, height 5″ **100.00** **110.00** **104.00**

	Current Price Range		Prior Year Average

☐ **Funnel Shape,** feathered fan surrounding cross hatched square, alternated with mitered diamond panels, beaded stem with medial stepped band, scalloped rim, height 8″ **180.00 210.00 190.00**

☐ **Funnel Shape,** hobstar base, hobstars, fans and fine checkering, diameter 9½″ **375.00 400.00 380.00**

☐ **High Loop Handles,** sawtooth rim, feathered fans on the sides, deep cut V's on bottom of bowl, height 6″ **200.00 300.00 225.00**

☐ **Hobnail Motif,** with diamond and prismatic cuttings, scalloped edge, by Figueroa, height 8″ **115.00 140.00 120.00**

☐ **Hobstar,** cross hatchings, scalloped edge, beaded stem, height 5″, diameter 6″ **85.00 100.00 85.00**

☐ **Hobstars,** flashed fanning, deep prism cut in base, scalloped rim, diameter 8″, height 9¾″ **300.00 360.00 320.00**

☐ **Rosette,** hobstars alternated with pinwheel rosette, thick stem, wide foot, height 8″ **90.00 120.00 100.00**

☐ **Rosette,** flashed fan, notched prism cut in stem and base, scalloped edge, height 5½″, diameter 6½″ **60.00 72.00 63.00**

☐ **Rosette Motif,** cross hatching, flashed fan, scalloped edge, by Wilson, height 9″, diameter 9½″ **125.00 150.00 130.00**

☐ **Small Bowl,** tall stem, strawberry motif with feathered fan top, sawtoothed arch, heart by Pitkin and Brooks, height 9″ **190.00 250.00 200.00**

☐ **Square Molded Design,** irregular scallop and pointed rims, blue, Valleystall France, 4″ square base, height 6½″ **75.00 100.00 80.00**

☐ **Tulip Shaped Bowl,** rosette between deep prism cuts, plain base, height 7½″ **220.00 350.00 25.00**

☐ **Wide Flat Bowl,** squared tooth rim, vertical deep prism cuts, height 7″ .. **145.00 165.00 150.00**

☐ **Wide Flat Bowl,** with thick flared base, deep cut fans in border around waist, height 5″ **80.00 90.00 85.50**

☐ **Wide Tray Bowl,** octagon shaped stem, ridged base, rosettes and fans, height 7½″ **175.00 250.00 185.00**

CREAMER

	Current Price Range		Prior Year Average

☐ **Elongated Shape,** sawtooth rim, three rosettes across middle, fern shaped prism cuts in a row below . . . . — 160.00 — 180.00 — 165.00

☐ **Looped Handles,** deeply flared spout, thumbprint and rosettes separated by starburst, 8 oz. — 60.00 — 80.00 — 65.00

☐ **Low Scooped Spout,** overall star and mitered diamonds, slightly scalloped rim, Venus, by T.B. Clarke . . . . — 185.00 — 210.00 — 195.00

☐ **Middle Loop Handle,** mitered hobstar motif, sawtooth edge . . . . — 75.00 — 80.00 — 77.50

☐ **Pinwheel Rosette,** cross-hatching, high c-scroll handle . . . . — 50.00 — 62.00 — 57.00

☐ **Sawtooth Rim,** high loop handle, step cutting on spout, flashed hobstar, 8 oz. — 50.00 — 60.00 — 55.00

☐ **Star Cut,** fine nobnails, diamond points, floral cut bottom . . . . — 35.00 — 40.00 — 36.50

☐ **Thumbprint Design,** alternated with pinwheel rosettes, c-scroll handles .. — 60.00 — 70.00 — 64.00

CREAM AND SUGAR SET

☐ **Buzz Star,** diamond, scalloped rim and handles . . . . — 90.00 — 110.00 — 95.00

☐ **Buzz Star,** scalloped edge, diameter of both 3″ . . . . — 75.00 — 90.00 — 80.00

☐ **Cut Floral Design,** Virginia, by McKee — 45.00 — 55.00 — 50.00

☐ **Deep Prismatic,** rosette, flashed, fan, scalloped edge, diameter of both 3″ — 50.00 — 75.00 — 55.00

☐ **Diamond Motif,** scalloped handle and edges, diameter of sugar 4¼″, diameter of cream 4″ . . . . — 175.00 — 210.00 — 180.00

☐ **Flashed Rosette,** flashed fan, scalloped edge . . . . — 80.00 — 95.00 — 85.00

☐ **Flowers and Chain of Hobstars,** by Tuthill diameter 3″, height 3″ . . . . — 290.00 — 310.00 — 295.00

☐ **Flower Miter Cut,** cross hatching, scalloped edge, creamer has double handle, by Clinton, height 2¾″ . . . . . . — 55.00 — 66.00 — 60.00

☐ **Hobnail Design,** with deep prismatic cuts, sugar bowl has two handles, both have scalloped edges, by Frontier . . . — 65.00 — 85.00 — 70.00

☐ **Hobnail Motif,** both have two handles, creamer has two pouring lips, Romeo, by Keystone, height 4½″ . . . . — 90.00 — 120.00 — 95.00

☐ **Hobstar,** flashed fan, beaded spout on creamer, both are three legged, scalloped rim . . . . — 150.00 — 180.00 — 155.00

	Current Price Range		Prior Year Average

☐ **Rosettes,** cross hatchings, deep prism cuts, scalloped edge, by Richter, height 4" **65.00 80.00 70.00**

☐ **Rosettes,** cross hatchings, deep prism cuts, scalloped rim, handle, by Irving, height 4" **75.00 95.00 80.00**

☐ **Rosettes,** feathered fans, scalloped edge, feathered star, by Heinz, height 2⅝" **60.00 75.00 65.00**

☐ **Star and Diamond Motif,** diameter of sugar 3¼", diameter of creamer 4" **90.00 120.00 100.00**

CRUET

☐ **Beaded Vertical Cuts,** high arched handle with thumbprint, height 8" ... **80.00 100.00 87.00**

☐ **Cross-Hatched** with pointed stopper, plain handle, height 6" **80.00 105.00 90.00**

☐ **Diamond Cut,** cross hatching, beaded neck, prism cut stopper, by Gibbs, Kelly & Co., height 6½" **30.00 36.00 32.00**

☐ **Flashed Rosette,** faceted stopper, height 7" **60.00 68.00 63.00**

☐ **Flat Bowl,** tall prism cuts around flat stopper, thumbprint, and wheat sheaf decor, height 6" **35.00 45.00 37.50**

☐ **Flatten Bowl,** with arch shaped panels, thumbprints above, honeycomb stopper, jagged handle, height 7" ... **45.00 55.00 47.50**

☐ **Flower and Leaves,** miter cut, diamond, prism cut stopper, by Wayne **35.00 40.00 37.00**

☐ **Handled,** tapered straight sides, horizontal accordion ribbed neck, hobstars, flowers and leaves, height 8" **12.00 16.00 12.50**

☐ **Hobstars,** slightly bulbous body, flashed fans at bottom, thumbprint design on handle, height 7" **90.00 120.00 100.00**

☐ **Honeycomb Stopper,** floral and thumbprint with etched foliage **50.00 60.00 52.50**

☐ **Short Bowl,** with tall honeycomb stopper, pineapple motif formed by caning and feathered fans, height 7" **125.00 145.00 130.00**

☐ **Star Design,** surrounded by diamond cuttings, flash fanning, and prismatic cuttings, by Hope, height 5" **40.00 48.00 43.00**

☐ **Stretched Shape,** honeycomb stopper, flared lip spout, satin finished plain background with lightly etched thumbprints **25.00 35.00 27.50**

	Current Price Range		Prior Year Average

☐ **Tall Honeycombed Stopper,** plain background with vertical prism cuts, 8 oz. 40.00 50.00 42.50

☐ **Tall,** thin, with small waisted stopper, angular cuts with smooth polished background, height 9¾″ 36.00 40.00 37.50

☐ **Thumbprint Design** on body, with cut floral design, arched handles, wide base, height 6″ 77.00 95.00 84.00

CUP

☐ **Butterfly Design,** with feathered fan and flash fan cuttings, prism cuttings on base, butterfly, by Niland 40.00 50.00 45.00

☐ **Flashed Fans** alternated with triangular panels of mitered diamonds, plain rim, plain c-scroll handle 40.00 52.00 45.00

☐ **Flashed Rosette,** flashed fan, stars, deep prism cut 45.00 55.00 50.00

☐ **Hobnail Design,** with flashed fanning, by Clark 12.00 15.00 12.50

☐ **Hobstar,** flashed fan, deep prism cuts, by Clark 18.00 22.00 19.00

☐ **Hobstar Design** alternated with flashed fans, plain rim, plain c-scroll handle 30.00 37.50 33.00

☐ **Hobstars,** cross-hatching, plain rim, plain c-scroll handle 25.00 33.00 29.00

☐ **Large Fans,** hobstars, fine checkering, flared top, three handled, height 6″, diameter 5″ 550.00 590.00 555.00

☐ **Pinwheel Rosettes** alternated with fans and cross-hatching, plain rim, plain c-scroll handle 31.00 39.00 35.00

☐ **Punch Cup,** fans and fine checkering, by Dorflinger 45.00 50.00 47.50

☐ **Rounded Bowl,** low loop handle, fans and hobstars 40.00 50.00 42.50

☐ **Sawtooth Rim,** punch cup, flashed fans alternated with triangular patterns of cross-hatching, with underplate, no handle 64.00 76.00 68.00

☐ **Small Rosettes,** with prismatic cutting, scalloped base, by Libbey 70.00 85.00 75.00

☐ **Tapered Sides,** loop handle with scalloped edge, strawberry formed by fans and feathers 65.00 75.00 67.50

DECANTER

	Current Price Range		Prior Year Average

☐ **Bulbous Bottom,** honeycomb stopper, mitered diamond cuts alternating across waist with feathered fans, 32 oz. 115.00 120.00 117.50

☐ **Butterfly Design,** with flashed fan and rosettes, clear stopper, prism cut neck, Butterfly, by Niland, height 10" 85.00 100.00 90.00

☐ **Elongated Rectangle Shape,** single stars and foliage, thumbprints around border, Delmar, by Pitkin and Brooks 150.00 175.00 165.00

☐ **Flashed Rosette,** flashed fans, deep prism cuts, vertical beaded neck, faceted stopper, capacity one quart ..:. 180.00 210.00 190.00

☐ **Handled,** honeycomb stopper, step cuts on underside of lip, hobstar and cross hatching, 32 oz. 215.00 300.00 230.00

☐ **Handled,** stepped cuts on neck, fernlike cross hatched spears around rosettes, 32 oz. 225.00 250.00 230.00

☐ **Hobstars** alternated with flashed fans, thumbprint design on arched handle, short beaded neck, faceted stopper, capacity 32 oz..................... 220.00 250.00 230.00

☐ **Hobstars** surrounded by checkering, long paneled neck, flat stopper, capacity 32 oz. 170.00 195.00 180.00

☐ **Hobstar,** flashed fan, cross hatchings, notched prism cut, faceted stopper, Winthrop, capacity one quart. 250.00 280.00 260.00

☐ **Hobstar,** flashed fans, handle, prism cut, Star and Big Four, by O'Connor 175.00 210.00 180.00

☐ **Honeycomb Stopper,** octagonal neck, thumbprint around middle waist, rosettes with cross-hatched ground, 32 oz. 240.00 260.00 245.00

☐ **Pinwheel Rosette** on body; long neck, waisted; flaring rim, faceted stopper, capacity 32 oz..................... 210.00 235.00 215.00

☐ **Pinwheel Rosettes** alternated with flashed fans and fine checkering, long neck, paneled and beaded, no spout, faceted stopper, capacity 32 oz. 128.00 150.00 140.00

☐ **Thumbprint Design** with floral and garland design, long paneled neck, no spout, paneled flat stopper 140.00 175.00 157.00

DISH

	Current Price Range		Prior Year Average
☐ **Buzz Star,** hobnail, diamond, scalloped rim, diameter 5″	80.00	90.00	85.00
☐ **Deep,** polished bottom, floral, leaf and swag polished cuttings, diameter 7½″	20.00	30.00	25.00
☐ **Deep,** prismatic cuttings surrounded by hobstar and diamond designs, cross hatchings, scalloped rim, signed, by C.G. Alferd, length 12″	85.00	95.00	90.00
☐ **Deep,** prismatic rosette, flashed fans, deep prism cuts, diameter 6″	60.00	80.00	65.00
☐ **Diamond Motif,** flashed fan, deep prism cut, scalloped edge, length 8″	75.00	90.00	80.00
☐ **Diamond and Star Motif,** rosettes, length 7¾″	70.00	84.00	75.00
☐ **Flashed Rosette,** diamond, flashed fan, deep prism cut, scalloped edge, length 12″	95.00	115.00	100.00
☐ **Four Compartments,** two handles, large hobstars, zipper cutting, thumbprint, length 11″	165.00	200.00	175.00
☐ **French Stars,** silver diamond, pinwheel star, by Stage, diameter 8″	60.00	75.00	65.00
☐ **Hobstars,** with deep flashed fans, ring of leaves in miter cut around rim, by Sinclaire & Co., diameter 9″	125.00	150.00	130.00
☐ **Lidded,** four footed, square mitered corners, high finial, deep cut cross hatching	42.00	50.00	42.50
☐ **Rosettes,** deep prism cuts, scalloped edge, by Hawkes, diameter 8″	45.00	55.00	50.00
☐ **Rosettes,** deep prismatic curts, scalloped edge, heart shaped, by Western	25.00	30.00	27.00
☐ **Rosettes,** stars, deep prism cuts, covered, heart shaped	80.00	90.00	85.00
☐ **Spade Dish,** handled, flowers with heavy brilliant cut around rim, height 7½″	85.00	115.00	90.00
☐ **Star Cut Design,** hobstars, deep prismatic cuts, diameter 7″	40.00	50.00	44.00
☐ **Stars,** flashed fans, scalloped edge, deep prism cuts, by Western, length 13″	80.00	100.00	85.00
☐ **Triangular Shape,** with lid, three footed, spike finial, cut hobstars, pinwheels, cross hatched	13.00	16.00	13.50

GOBLET

	Current Price Range		Prior Year Average
☐ **Champagne Style,** large single stars with small rosettes, ridged stem	60.00	70.00	65.00
☐ **Concave Paneled,** scalloped rim, cut bottom, Colonial, by Heisey, 2½ oz.	8.00	10.00	8.50
☐ **Flared Body,** barbell shaped stem, fan forms sunrise on upper rim, Florida, by Averbeck	70.00	90.00	75.00
☐ **Funnel Shape,** paneled and beaded, footed, hobstars in square panels surrounded by fine checkering, flaring rim	66.00	85.00	74.00
☐ **Pinwheel Rosette,** alternated with flashed fans, footed, paneled and beaded stem	62.00	77.00	70.00
☐ **Rounded Sides,** paneled stem, square hobstar with cross hatching	50.00	60.00	55.00
☐ **Starburst Design** with faceted stem, footed, checkering on foot	55.00	65.00	60.00
☐ **Tapered Sides** with starburst design, plain stem, wide foot	27.00	41.00	36.00
☐ **Strawberry Diamond Cuttings,** flashed fan with prismatic cuts, beaded stem, Encore, by Benjamin Davies . .	55.00	66.00	60.00
☐ **Tapered Straight Sides,** flashed hobstar with deep cut fans, Golf, by J.D. Bergen	45.00	55.00	47.50

ICE BUCKET

☐ **Flared Top,** loop handle thumbprint around scalloped edge, ridged tray, diameter 7¾"	200.00	250.00	225.00
☐ **High Handled,** diamond canes and rosettes, cross hatching and fans	160.00	180.00	165.00
☐ **Hobstar,** cross hatchings, deep prism cuts, diameter 7"	195.00	215.00	200.00
☐ **Sawtooth Rim,** low c-scroll handles with thumbprint design, long beaded vertical cuts, height 6"	200.00	220.00	207.00
☐ **Tab Handles,** overall deep cuts, rosettes and hobstars, Amazon, by J.D. Bergen	250.00	350.00	275.00
☐ **Three Handles,** vertical mitered cut with two long stars on the sides, fans form sawtooth rim, height 9"	115.00	130.00	120.00

JAR

☐ **Large Rosettes,** hobnail, flashed fanning and deep prismatic cuttings, by Majestic, height 9½"	125.00	150.00	130.00

	Current Price Range		Prior Year Average
☐ **Dresser,** rectangular, floral motif with stylized foliage, diamond caning around border, length 11″	260.00	300.00	275.00
☐ **Dresser,** round, rosette lid, deep cut prisms with beadwork decor, polished insides	55.00	65.00	57.00
☐ **Single Stars,** cross hatchings, deep prismatic cuttings, chair bottom by Kellmer and Munro, height 8″	85.00	100.00	90.00

JUG

☐ **Cross Hatchings,** deep prism cuts, sterling silver top, height 4″	75.00	85.00	78.00
☐ **Star and Diamond Motif,** notched prism cuts at neck, capacity one quart	100.00	120.00	105.00
☐ **Star Motif,** feathered fanning, prism cut, silver top, by Wayne	50.00	60.00	45.00
☐ **Tall,** slender, vertically cut neck with one band of thumbprints, rosettes on bottom, cross hatching scalloped handle	320.00	340.00	325.00
☐ **Tapered Straight Sides,** mitered diamonds, diamond caning and fans, 32 oz.	120.00	130.00	125.00
☐ **Wide Mouth,** flared lip, fans and caning, high handle, 32 oz.	140.00	166.00	145.00

KNIFE REST

☐ **Barbell Shape,** rosette alternating with deep prism cuts, sawtooth edges, length 5″	62.00	75.00	65.50
☐ **Fine Checkering,** faceted stem in between is also checkered, length 5″ ..	25.00	30.00	27.00
☐ **Rosettes,** with faceted stem in between, length 4½″	47.00	60.00	54.00

LAMP

☐ **Bulls Eye,** beaded and peanut pattern, diameter 6¾″	100.00	120.00	105.00
☐ **Greek Key,** beaded peanut pattern, 9½″ high, diameter 7¼″ at base	100.00	120.00	105.00
☐ **Hurricane,** prismatic panel, rosettes, cross hatching, height 22″	14.00	16.00	1450.00
☐ **Hurricane Style,** rosettes, caning, fans, hobstars and cross hatching, height 24″	1200.00	1400.00	1300.00

	Current Price Range		Prior Year Average
☐ **Open Poppy Design,** red, height 22¼"	195.00	245.00	185.00
☐ **Prism Style,** overall swirl and floral pattern, scalloped bottom, height 17" ...	1200.00	1500.00	1350.00
☐ **Red,** 4½" diameter of base, base to oil fount cap, height 6"	22.50	25.00	20.00
☐ **Spade Shape,** caning, prismatic panel, waisted, flared base, height 26"	1500.00	1700.00	1550.00

MAYONNAISE BOWL AND PLATE SET

☐ **Rosette,** stars, feathered fans, diameter of bowl 6", diameter of plate 7¼"	150.00	167.00	155.00
☐ **Rosettes,** stars, scalloped edge on both, diameter of plate 7", diameter of bowl 5"	175.00	210.00	180.00
☐ **Star and Diamond Motif,** feathered fans, oval, length of bowl 6¼", length of plate 7½"	160.00	195.00	165.00
☐ **Waisted Bowl,** with tray, thumbprint around middle with fans forming border sawtooth rim on bowl and tray, diameter 6"	110.00	125.00	115.00

MUSTARD POT

☐ **Notched Prism Cut,** stars, faceted top	35.00	40.00	37.00
☐ **Prism Knobbed Handle,** flutes and border of single stars	35.00	50.00	40.00
☐ **Round,** hexagonal knob, thumbprints around waist	35.00	45.00	37.50
☐ **Tapering Sides,** mitered diamonds and single star	35.00	45.00	37.50

NAPPY

☐ **Blossom Bottom,** cane filler, hobstars around border, sawtooth, diameter 6"	90.00	110.00	95.00
☐ **Circular,** hobstars alternated with flashed fans, cut diamonds in square panel in center, diameter 9"	87.00	105.00	95.00
☐ **Diamond Cut,** leaves, flowers are miter cut, handle, Poinsettia, by McKanna	25.00	30.00	27.00
☐ **Dual Hobstars,** fans and single stars on other side, diameter 8"	85.00	95.00	87.50
☐ **Five Sided,** fluted border with cross hatching in the corners, rosette center, length 8"	160.00	180.00	165.00

	Current Price Range		Prior Year Average

☐ **Flashed Fans,** alternated with triangular panels of cut diamonds, no handles on sugar, sawtooth rim .... 105.00 | 120.00 | 110.00

☐ **Heart Shape,** alternated with vertical beaded cuts, sawtooth rim, thumbprint design on handles .... 140.00 | 160.00 | 150.00

☐ **Hexagon Shape,** hobstar center surrounded by deep prism cutting, no handle, diameter 5½" .... 90.00 | 115.00 | 100.00

☐ **Loop Handle,** rolled edge, rosette center, diamond circle, prism cuts, diameter 6" .... 70.00 | 80.00 | 75.00

☐ **One Loop Handle,** undulating sawtooth rim, hobstar versus deep prism cuts, diameter 6" .... 50.00 | 60.00 | 55.00

☐ **Pinwheel Fans,** with lightly cut diamonds, diameter 8" .... 78.00 | 95.00 | 86.00

☐ **Pinwheel Rosette,** with feathered fan design, sawtooth rim, thumbprint design on handles .... 125.00 | 140.00 | 130.00

☐ **Pinwheel Rosette** with beaded vertical cuts, sawtooth rim, thumbprint design on handles .... 90.00 | 110.00 | 100.00

☐ **Round,** rosette center, flashed foliage, scalloped edge, diameter 8" .... 110.00 | 120.00 | 115.00

☐ **Rosette Center,** prism cut triangle frame, feathered fan, diameter 8" ... 60.00 | 70.00 | 65.00

☐ **Sawtooth Edge,** flashing fans alternated with mitered diamonds and hobstars

diameter 8" .... 121.00 | 137.00 | 127.00
diameter 9" .... 145.00 | 167.00 | 157.00
diameter 10" .... 195.00 | 220.00 | 205.00

☐ **Scalloped Edge,** hobstar in triangular panel, cross-hatching, c-scroll handle on either side, diameter 6" .... 50.00 | 67.00 | 57.00

☐ **Six-Pointed Star Design,** alternated with flashed fans, thumbprint design on handles .... 95.00 | 120.00 | 110.00

☐ **Star Design,** hobstars, prism cuttings, handle, signed, by Taylor Brothers, diameter 6" .... 50.00 | 60.00 | 55.00

☐ **Sunburst Design,** surrounded by hobstars, deep prism cutting, c-scroll handle

diameter 5" .... 66.00 | 80.00 | 72.00
diameter 6" .... 80.00 | 97.00 | 89.00

☐ **Two Tab Handles,** dual flashed hobstars, deep cut diamonds, diameter 6" 70.00 | 80.00 | 75.00

PITCHER

	Current Price Range		Prior Year Average

☐ **Bulbous Body,** hobstar bordered by mitered diamonds and beaded prism cuts, beaded c-scroll handle, sawtooth rim, capacity 64 oz. . . . . | 300.00 | 340.00 | 325.00

☐ **Bulbous Bottom,** flared lip, high handle, petal base, rosettes and fans, Desdemona, by T.B. Clarke . . . . | 400.00 | 500.00 | 425.00

☐ **Buzz Star,** flashed fan, beaded spout, fine miter cut, scalloped handle and rim, by William Volker, capacity two pints . . . . | 140.00 | 160.00 | 145.00

☐ **Clear Applied Handle,** 38 rayed base, three bunches of engraved grapes on front, one bunch on each side . . . . . . | 55.00 | 70.00 | 60.00

☐ **Cut,** all over except plain panel on back where handle is applied, base has 24 rays, three areas have buttorn cutting, by Libbey, height 9½″, diameter 5½″ | 325.00 | 400.00 | 350.00

☐ **Deep Cut Diamonds** in pentagonal panel, alternated with cross-hatching and flashed fans, scalloped rim, high arched handle, thumbprint design, capacity 48 oz. . . . . | 185.00 | 200.00 | 190.00

☐ **Flowers and Brilliant Cut Hobstars,** signed Tuthill, height 9¾″ . . . . | 475.00 | 525.00 | 485.00

☐ **Flowers Miter Cut,** leaves prism cut, Carnation, by Irving, height 9″ . . . . . . | 70.00 | 90.00 | 75.00

☐ **Hobnail Cuts,** cross hatching, flashed fan, by Dorflinger, height 7½″ . . . . . . | 80.00 | 100.00 | 85.00

☐ **Hobstar Design,** tapered straight sides, flashed fans, drapery, capacity 32 oz. . . . . | 150.00 | 170.00 | 160.00

☐ **Hobstars,** cross hatchings, deep prismatic cuttings, Sunburst, by Enterprise, height 8″ . . . . | 100.00 | 120.00 | 105.00

☐ **Hobstars,** flashed fans, cross hatching, bottom is notched prism panel, height 8″ . . . . | 120.00 | 144.00 | 130.00

☐ **Juice,** English cut strawberry diamond and fan, optic swirl, silver applied rim, applied handle, 32-rayed base . . . . . . | 50.00 | 60.00 | 55.00

☐ **Mitered Diamond Design,** tapered straight sides, scalloped rim, fans
    capacity 32 oz. . . . . | 125.00 | 147.00 | 132.00
    capacity 48 oz. . . . . | 140.00 | 165.00 | 150.00

☐ **Notched Handle,** gently scalloped rim, flared lip, deep cut rosette, caning, height 10½″ . . . . | 230.00 | 260.00 | 235.00

	Current Price Range		Prior Year Average

☐ **Patterned Handles,** Gravic Grapes and Leaves, by Hawkes, height 10½″ — 475.00 / 525.00 / 500.00

☐ **Pedestal Type Base,** by Tuthill, height 8½″ .... — 860.00 / 875.00 / 865.00

☐ **Petals of Flowers and Stem,** miter cut, Daisy, by Enterprise, height 7″ .. — 60.00 / 72.00 / 65.00

☐ **Pinwheel Rosette,** deep vertical cutting, beading, high handle, scalloped edge, capacity 16 oz. .... — 100.00 / 125.00 / 110.00

☐ **Pinwheel Rosettes,** with cross hatchings and deep prismatic cuts, one handle, scalloped edge, beaded spout, by Frizlen, height 12¾″ .... — 125.00 / 150.00 / 130.00

☐ **Rosettes,** diamond cuts, flashed fanning, scalloped edge, Imperial, by Enterprise, height 13½″ .... — 175.00 / 210.00 / 180.00

☐ **Rosettes,** with notched prismatic designs, by Hope, height 4½″ .... — 55.00 / 65.00 / 60.00

☐ **Rosette,** flashed fans, cross hatchings, prism cuts, by Wilson, height 10″ — 100.00 / 120.00 / 105.00

☐ **Rosettes,** prism cuts, hobnail, cross hatching, scalloped rim, handle, Alicia, by Krantz, Smith & Co. .... — 145.00 / 170.00 / 150.00

☐ **Scalloped Edge,** buzz-star design, deep prism cuts, cross-hatching near base, capacity 48 oz. .... — 90.00 / 115.00 / 100.00

☐ **Stars,** hobnail motif, by Sell and Co., height 11″ .... — 150.00 / 180.00 / 155.00

☐ **Star Motif,** capacity three pints ..... — 30.00 / 35.00 / 33.00

☐ **Step Cutting and Flowers,** signed, by Sinclair, height 8½″ .... — 860.00 / 885.00 / 865.00

☐ **Strawberry Diamond,** with deep prism cuts, flowers and leaves are miter cut, by Clark, height 11″ .... — 120.00 / 144.00 / 125.00

☐ **Sunburst Design,** alternated with double thumbprints, one row of hobstars in diamond panels circling bottom of vessel; a similar, but smaller row circles top; sawtooth rim made by fans, low handle, capacity 64 oz. .... — 250.00 / 275.00 / 260.00

☐ **Tall,** slender, vertical deep prism cuts with rosettes and cross hatching around middle, flared rim with fanning, 48 oz. .... — 315.00 / 400.00 / 330.00

☐ **Tankard Shape,** Brilliant by Libbey, height 8¼″ .... — 250.00 / 300.00 / 275.00

☐ **Tapered Straight Sides,** overall mitered diamonds, fans form scalloped rim, 48 oz. .... — 120.00 / 130.00 / 125.00

	Current Price Range		Prior Year Average

☐ **Tapered Straight Side,** prism cuts with beadwork, rosettes around mouth, sawtooth rim, 32 oz. **160.00 180.00 170.00**

☐ **Tapered Sides,** hobstars surrounded by deep prism cuts, low handle, scalloped rim, capacity 48 oz. **125.00 145.00 135.00**

☐ **Thumbprint,** six-pointed stars in diamond panels circle the vessel, fans border the panels, handle is high and arched, some beading and paneling near top of vessel, scalloped rim, capacity 48 oz. **145.00 165.00 153.00**

☐ **Wide Mouth,** flared lip, gently scalloped rim, hobstar, mitered diamond cuts and fans, 16 oz. **85.00 95.00 87.50**

PLATE

☐ **Center of Flower,** hatch cutting, leaves and stem are miter cut, scalloped edges, Rambler Rose, by Enterprise, diameter 8¼" **90.00 110.00 95.00**

☐ **Cake,** deep prismatic rosette, scalloped edge, diameter 8" **135.00 157.00 140.00**

☐ **Cake,** notched prism cut, feathered fan, diameter 6¾" **45.00 55.00 50.00**

☐ **Dessert,** Russian, by Cleveland, set of ten, diameter 7" **750.00 1000.00 775.00**

☐ **Diamond Shape,** ribbon cut with beadwork interior, hobnail borders, length 9" **200.00 225.00 205.00**

☐ **Flashed Fanning,** hobstars, diamond cuts, cross hatchings, prismatic cuts, scalloped edge, signed, by Van Heusen, Charles Co., diameter 6" ... **60.00 70.00 65.00**

☐ **Flashed Hobstar,** on medallion, and around border under fans, diameter 5" **55.00 65.00 57.50**

☐ **Hobstar,** deep prism cut, diameter 3¼" **30.00 35.00 32.00**

☐ **Hobstar,** flashed fan, deep prism cuts, diameter 3¼" **25.00 30.00 27.00**

☐ **Hobstar,** flashed rosette, cross hatchings, scalloped rim, by William Volker, diameter 6" **50.00 60.00 55.00**

☐ **Large and Small Rosettes,** deep prismatic cuttings, cross hatchings, scalloped edges, signed, by C. G. Alferd, diameter 7¼" **65.00 75.00 70.00**

	Current Price Range		Prior Year Average

☐ **Modified Triangle Shape,** deep cuts form stars, cross hatch ground, diameter 9″ **275.00 300.00 280.00**

☐ **Rolled Edge,** flashed hobstars, cross hatch triangles, smooth ground, diameter 6″ **48.00 62.00 47.50**

☐ **Roses and Leaf,** designs with cross hatchings, hobstar and diamond cuts, scalloped edge, Wild Rose, by Tuthill, diameter 13″ **375.00 450.00 380.00**

☐ **Rosette,** flashed fanning, cross hatching, deep prism cuts, scalloped edge, by Krantz, Smith and Co., diameter 7″ **45.00 55.00 50.00**

☐ **Scalloped Edge,** fan border, single star center, deep cut, diameter 7″ ... **85.00 95.00 90.00**

☐ **Star Bottom,** pin wheel and cross hatch, diameter 6½″ **10.00 12.00 10.50**

☐ **Star Cut,** with feathered fan design, Carnation, by diameter 7″ **75.00 90.00 80.00**

☐ **Stars,** hobstars, cross hatchings, flashed fan, strawberry diamonds, scalloped edge, signed, by Tuthill, diameter 7″ **125.00 150.00 130.00**

☐ **Wreath and Floral Cut,** star in middle, Virginia, by McKee, diameter 12″ **185.00 220.00 190.00**

PUNCH BOWL

☐ **Central Medallion,** unusual jagged cuts framed with stippling and fans, cross hatched spears around outside, height 10″ **450.00 500.00 475.00**

☐ **Feathered Fan Design,** sawtooth edge, large fans bordered by small mitered diamond cuts, scalloped foot, short stem, Manhattan, by T.B. Clark
    diameter 8″ **160.00 180.00 167.50**
    diameter 9″ **195.00 220.00 210.00**

☐ **Fine Checkering Design** in a square panel bordered by fans, alternated with hobstars, sawtooth edge; same design on foot, foot also sawtooth, neck is collared with prism cutting and cut diamonds, height 14″ **650.00 700.00 670.00**

☐ **Flared Base,** diamond cross hatched center with geometrical cross hatching around and five point stars emanating, height 14″ **650.00 850.00 675.00**

	Current Price Range		Prior Year Average
☐ **Flared Base,** heavy cut hobstar, cross hatching, decorated flute with scalloped rim, Kenwood, by J.D. Bergen	1500.00	1700.00	1600.00
☐ **Flared Pedestal,** hobstar and fans, framed by swooping deep cuts, height 12″	450.00	650.00	475.00
☐ **Flared,** scalloped base, large sunburst covering whole side, undulating sawtooth rim, height 12″	600.00	700.00	625.00
☐ **Flowers Miter Cut,** rosettes, cross hatching, stars, height 10″	375.00	450.00	390.00
☐ **Large Rosettes,** hobnails, deep prismatic cuttings, Majestic, by Enterprise	350.00	420.00	360.00
☐ **Pedestal,** collared base, flashed hobstars with additional feathering, inverted fans, height 14″	600.00	700.00	650.00
☐ **Pinwheel Fans** surrounding large hobstar, faceted neck, same design on foot, sawtooth rim, height 14″	575.00	645.00	605.00
☐ **Pinwheel Rosette,** alternated with fans and prism cutting, sawtooth edge, same pattern on foot, collared neck, height 13″	600.00	650.00	620.00
☐ **Rosette,** flash fan and cross hatch design in body and base, scallop edge, signed, by Bergen, height 16⅛″	700.00	840.00	710.00
☐ **Scalloped Edge and Base,** several rosettes, deep prismatic cuts, by Libbey, diameter 25″, height 24″	4,300.00	5,100.00	4,350.00
☐ **Scalloped Foot,** sawtooth rim made up mostly by fans, cut diamonds, hobstars, cross-hatching, small rope motif neck			
height 12″	445.00	480.00	460.00
height 15″	475.00	505.00	490.00
☐ **Sunburst Design,** alternated with fans, small hobstars, and lightly cut diamonds, sawtooth edge, footed, rope motif neck, height 14″	360.00	405.00	380.00
☐ **Tall Chalice Style,** diamond cane, fluting, cross hatching, diamond rosettes, height 14″	600.00	700.00	625.00
☐ **Undulating Scalloped Rim,** vaulted mitered cut rosettes, diamonds, height 14″	510.00	540.00	515.00

SALAD BOWL

	Current Price Range		Prior Year Average

☐ **Deeply Curved Sawtooth,** prism cut rosettes alternating with cross hatched prism cuts, arranged in a triangle, diameter 9" **115.00 120.00 117.00**

☐ **Rounded Sawtooth Rim,** four panels alternating hobstar with feathered fan, prism cuts, diameter 9" **90.00 100.00 95.00**

☐ **Undulating Scalloped Rim,** flashed hobstar alternating with feathered fans, deep prism cuts, polished ground, diameter 9" **115.00 125.00 118.50**

☐ **Undulating Scalloped Rim,** rosette and feathered fans, triangular cross hatching Nellore, by Pitkin and Brooks, diameter 8" **80.00 100.00 85.00**

SALT

☐ **Concave Flutes,** ridged panels **40.00 50.00 42.50**

☐ **Crosscut,** strawberry diamonds, fans, 24 point star bottom **15.00 20.00 17.50**

☐ **Diamond Point,** notched prismatic design scalloped rim, by Dethridge Flint Co., height 2¼" **12.00 15.00 13.00**

☐ **Etched Sterling Fittings,** cross hatching and single star **30.00 40.00 32.00**

☐ **Octagonal Shape,** smooth, highly polished by Pitkin and Brooks, length 2½" **18.00 22.00 19.50**

☐ **Oval,** concave sides, deep prism cuts with sawtooth edges, diameter 1¾" **20.00 25.00 22.50**

☐ **Rosette and Trio of Flutes,** thumbprints **40.00 60.00 42.50**

☐ **Square,** plain, polished, edges shorn, length 2" **12.00 18.00 13.50**

☐ **Squared Shape,** rosette and fluting .. **25.00 30.00 27.50**

☐ **Step Cut Vertical Panels,** with diamond mitering **25.00 30.00 27.50**

☐ **Sterling Fittings,** cross hatch and hobnail **60.00 80.00 65.00**

☐ **Tab Handled,** round, rosette, cross hatching, sawtooth rim, diameter 2½" **40.00 50.00 42.50**

☐ **Teardrop Diamond Miters,** step cuttings **28.00 32.00 28.50**

☐ **Vertical Deep Prism Cuts,** shaped scallop on thin side, polished glass, diameter 1½" **25.00 30.00 27.50**

SALT AND PEPPER SHAKERS

	Current Price Range		Prior Year Average
☐ **Bulbous Body,** prism cutting on bottom of vessel, paneled at the top, sterling silver top . . . . : .	35.00	42.00	37.50
☐ **Cut Diamonds** with fine checkering and fans, sterling silver top	62.00	70.00	64.00
☐ **Diamond Cut,** step prism cut	12.00	16.00	13.00
☐ **Diamond Cut,** vessel tapers towards top, sterling silver top	18.00	22.00	20.00
☐ **Notched Prism Cut,** at base, diamond cut in middle, fine notched prism cut on lid	10.00	15.00	12.00
☐ **Ovoid Body,** mitered diamond design, height 2″	21.00	26.00	24.00
☐ **Ovoid Body,** beaded prism cutting on top part of vessel, bottom part is diamond shaped faceting, sterling silver top	26.00	34.00	29.00
☐ **Pepper,** sterling silver top, opposed fans, diamond mitering	100.00	125.00	115.00
☐ **Prism Cutting** alternated with beaded vertical cuts, sterling silver top	19.00	24.00	21.50
☐ **Salt,** faceted body, sterling silver top	35.00	40.00	37.00
☐ **Salt or Pepper,** diamond, flashed fan, sterling silver tops, step prism cut at neck, height 2⅞″	35.00	42.00	37.00
☐ **Salt or Pepper,** star design, sterling silver tops	40.00	48.00	42.00
☐ **Strawberry Diamond Design,** with flash fanning, by Mt. Washington	40.00	50.00	45.00

SPOONER

☐ **Cross Design,** fan bottoms, hobstar on each corner	60.00	80.00	65.00
☐ **Egg Shape,** triple hobstar across bottom, flutes and prism cuts, length 7½″	60.00	80.00	65.00
☐ **Flashed Fan,** diamond, stars, hobstars, deep prism cut, scalloped edge, Carmen, height 4½″	150.00	180.00	155.00
☐ **Square,** with hobstar ends that form edges	70.00	80.00	75.00

SUGAR BOWL

☐ **Covered,** cross hatching, feathered fan design on body and lid, circular base, height 8⅝″	250.00	300.00	255.00
☐ **Loving Cup Shape,** rosette and diamond caning, thin fans in opposition, notched handles	80.00	90.00	85.00

	Current Price Range		Prior Year Average

☐ **Round,** overall deep cut hobstars, shield shapes, height 3″ .... | 175.00 | 200.00 | 185.00

☐ **Sawtooth Rim,** two high loop handles, buzz star with deep prism cuts as framing, Golf, by J.D. Bergen .... | 67.00 | 80.00 | 70.00

☐ **Sawtooth Rim,** loop handles, deep prism cuts around starburst, Magnet, by J.D. Bergen .... | 55.00 | 65.00 | 57.50

☐ **Starcut and Fine Hobnails,** diamond points, floral cut bottom .... | 35.00 | 40.00 | 36.50

☐ **Tapered Side,** with flat handles, prism cuts with beadwork borders, diamond cross hatching around top .... | 140.00 | 150.00 | 145.00

☐ **Thumbprint Handle,** star base, pinwheels and deep mitre cuts, sawtooth rim .... | 45.00 | 55.00 | 47.50

☐ **Three-Handled,** star design with flash fanning and cross hatching, by Libbey | 75.00 | 90.00 | 80.00

☐ **Two Low Handles,** buzz star with vertical prism cuts .... | 95.00 | 105.00 | 100.00

☐ **Two Handles,** thumbprint, lightly etched flowers, deep cut rows, height 5¼″ .... | 210.00 | 250.00 | 225.00

SUGAR SIFTER

☐ **Diamond,** deep prism cuts, flashed fans .... | 50.00 | 55.00 | 52.00

☐ **Flashed Fans,** stars, deep prism cut on lid, height 4¼″ .... | 50.00 | 60.00 | 55.00

☐ **Sterling Silver Top,** diamond mitering, fans, height 3″ .... | 130.00 | 150.00 | 135.00

TANKARD

☐ **Convex Tapered Sides,** with slightly flared lip, double buzz stars, caning and deep cut prisms, 64 oz. .... | 250.00 | 300.00 | 275.00

☐ **Flared Lip,** smooth neck with beadwork ridges, flashed hobstar alternating with V motif containing cross hatching and single stars, 64 oz. .... | 150.00 | 170.00 | 160.00

☐ **Heart Shaped Body,** overall hobstar and rosettes, caning and cross hatch filler, 64 oz. .... | 250.00 | 275.00 | 260.00

TOOTHPICK HOLDER

☐ **Barrel Shaped,** stars, fans, notched ribs .... | 20.00 | 40.00 | 22.50

	Current Price Range		Prior Year Average
☐ **Bulbous Shaped,** diamond faceted base, flared thistle cut top, serrated rim	12.00	15.00	12.50
☐ **Faceted Base,** waisted middle with step prism cuts, diamond and feathered fan around top	25.00	34.00	30.00
☐ **Faceted Bottom,** rosettes, flashed fan, diamond	20.00	25.00	22.00
☐ **Hobstar,** flashed fan, scalloped edge, height 2¾"	25.00	30.00	27.00
☐ **Honeycomb Pattern,** overall, height 2"	27.50	32.50	30.00
☐ **Rosette,** flashed fan, deep prism cuts, scalloped edge	15.00	20.00	18.00
☐ **Square,** diamond miters and fans, height 2½"	25.00	30.00	27.50

TRAY

	Current Price Range		Prior Year Average
☐ **Butterfly and Floral Motif,** fine miter cutting, hobstars, scalloped edge, length 8"	90.00	110.00	95.00
☐ **Calling Tray,** Brazilian, by Hawkes, diameter 5"	100.00	125.00	110.00
☐ **Center-Star Cut,** flashed rosettes, diamond, length 8"	60.00	68.00	63.00
☐ **Colonial Pattern,** by Libbey, diameter 17½", height 10"	765.00	795.00	770.00
☐ **Deep Prismatic Rosette,** Buzz star, deep prism cuts, length 13¾"	300.00	340.00	310.00
☐ **Egg Shaped,** flashed hobstars surrounded by mitered diamond cuts, length 18"	450.00	650.00	475.00
☐ **Flashed Rosette,** flashed fan, cross hatching, deep prism cut, scalloped rim, length 10½"	90.00	110.00	95.00
☐ **Hobstars,** cross hatching, flashed fan, length 11¼"	80.00	95.00	85.00
☐ **Hob Star,** cross hatching, scalloped edge, length 10½"	100.00	120.00	105.00
☐ **Hobstar Cut,** center of flower, leaves are miter cut, scalloped edge, Rose, by Enterprise, diameter 12½"	45.00	55.00	50.00
☐ **Ice Cream Tray,** Colonade, Libbey, length 17½"	850.00	950.00	875.00
☐ **Knobbed Cover,** rosettes and vaulted arches formed by deep cut prisms, Webster, by Higgins and Seiter	285.00	325.00	290.00

	Current Price Range		Prior Year Average

☐ **Meat Tray,** oval, moons around rim with leaf and ivy motif in center, Pattern No. 2 by Sinclair, length 12″ 200.00   250.00   225.00

☐ **Miter and Lattice Pattern,** sterling frame holds tray 450.00   485.00   455.00

☐ **Mt. Washington Ox-Bow Pattern,** diameter 12″ 530.00   545.00   535.00

☐ **Modified Rectangle,** parallel deep cuts with cane background, length 16″   450.00   500.00   475.00

☐ **Oval,** overall hobstar motif separated by deep prism cuts, length 15″ 460.00   500.00   450.00

☐ **Petal Shape,** deep cut circles with hobstar centers, diameter 12″ 260.00   275.00   265.00

☐ **Rosettes,** flashed fans, hobstar, deep prism cuts, scalloped edge, Winthop, length 11½″ 180.00   205.00   190.00

☐ **Serving Tray,** engraved No. 134, by Mount Washington 175.00   200.00   180.00

☐ **Spade Shaped,** deep miter cuts, caning, hobstars in four corners, length 13″ 500.00   600.00   550.00

☐ **Square,** rosettes in four corners, plaited deep cut caning, step cuts, length 11″ 300.00   400.00   325.00

☐ **Star,** hobnail, cross hatchings, deep prism cuts, scalloped edge, length 11¼″ 140.00   170.00   145.00

TUMBLER

☐ **Buzz Star,** diamond point, flashed fan, deep prism cuts, height 3⅞″ 25.00   30.00   27.00

☐ **Cut Diamonds** in diamond-shaped panel, feathered fans 17.00   22.00   19.00

☐ **Diamond Point,** with flashed fanning, deep prismatic cutting on base and body, by Blackmer 60.00   75.00   65.00

☐ **Double Thumbprint Pattern,** alternated with starburst pattern, flared shape 24.00   28.00   24.00

☐ **Flashed Fan,** hobstar, miter cut, deep prism cut in base, height 4¾″ 55.00   60.00   57.00

☐ **Flashed Rosette,** deep prism cuts, by Owanda 15.00   18.00   16.00

☐ **Flashed Rosette,** flashed fans, deep prism cuts, height 3¼″ 20.00   25.00   22.00

☐ **Flowers and Brilliant Cut Hobstars,** signed Tuthill, height 9¾″ 200.00   300.00   225.00

	Current Price Range		Prior Year Average
☐ **Flower Miter Cut,** deep prism cuts, beaded stem, by Wayne	20.00	25.00	22.00
☐ **Hobstar,** feathered fan, prism cuts in base, height 4½"	50.00	60.00	55.00
☐ **Hobstar,** flashed fan, cross hatchings, by William Volker	25.00	30.00	27.00
☐ **Juice,** strawberry, diamond and star, by Clark	35.00	50.00	37.50
☐ **Leaves and Water Lilies,** miter cut, Kalana Lily, by Dorflinger, height 4½"	25.00	30.00	27.00
☐ **Pinwheel Rosette,** surrounded by fans, flared shape, height 5¼"	62.00	80.00	70.00
☐ **Pinwheel Rosette,** with prism cutting	22.00	26.00	23.00
☐ **Prism Cutting,** body and base, Spiral by Dorflinger	45.00	55.00	50.00
☐ **Rosette,** fine miter cut, flashed fan, height 4½"	20.00	24.00	22.00
☐ **Rosettes,** with cross hatching, feathered fanning and deep prismatic cutting, Columbia, by Blackmer	60.00	75.00	65.00
☐ **Square Block Cuttings,** with flashed fanning, beaded stem, prism cuts on base, Exeter, by Dorflinger	35.00	42.00	37.00
☐ **Star Design,** with cross hatchings and deep prismatic cuttings, signed, by Unger, height 4"	25.00	30.00	27.00
☐ **Straight Side,** mitered diamond up to center, fan border	25.00	30.00	27.00
☐ **Straight Sides,** sprinkling of single stars, lightly etched	35.00	50.00	37.50
☐ **Strawberries,** square block design, leaves are prism cuts, by Clark	25.00	30.00	27.00
☐ **Tapered Sides,** flashed hobstar with prism cuts, Golf, by J.D. Bergen	60.00	80.00	65.00
☐ **Tapered Sides,** single star with prism cuts, height 4"	30.00	50.00	35.00
☐ **Thumbprint Pattern,** with six-pointed stars, mitered diamonds, height 4½"	38.00	43.50	40.00
☐ **Whiskey,** Jubilee, by Hawkes	45.00	55.00	47.50

VASE

	Current Price Range		Prior Year Average
☐ **Butterfly Design,** diamond, step prism cut, scallop edge, height 12"	250.00	300.00	265.00
☐ **Buzz Star,** cross hatching, fine miter cut, scalloped edge, height 8"	70.00	80.00	73.00
☐ **Chair Bottom,** scalloped edge, by Stage, height 14"	80.00	95.00	85.00

	Current Price Range		Prior Year Average

☐ **Cross Hatchings,** feathered fan, deep prism cuts, by Washington, height 10″ — 70.00 — 95.00 — 75.00

☐ **Corset Shape,** star bottom floral and leaf cut, cone and cross hatch band at rim, height 6″ .... — 45.00 — 55.00 — 45.50

☐ **Corset Shape,** star bottom, deep cut polished leaves and unpolished daisies, cross hatch mitred band, height 10″ .... — 115.00 — 135.00 — 120.00

☐ **Corset Shape,** star bottom, floral and leaf cut top and bottom with mitred cross hatch around waist, height 12″ — 85.00 — 95.00 — 87.50

☐ **Cylinder Shape,** slightly waisted, sawtooth rim, starburst design
height 8″ .... — 80.00 — 92.00 — 84.00
height 9″ .... — 91.00 — 105.00 — 97.00

☐ **Diamond Cut,** scalloped edge, by Franklin Flint .... — 75.00 — 90.00 — 80.00

☐ **Flaring Top,** scalloped base, hobstar medallion with overall deep cut prisms, height 14″ .... — 300.00 — 400.00 — 325.00

☐ **Flash Fan and Flower Design,** by Boston and Sandwich, height 6½″ .. — 125.00 — 150.00 — 130.00

☐ **Flashed Rosette,** flashed fan, strawberry diamond, scalloped edge, height 12″ .... — 160.00 — 180.00 — 170.00

☐ **Flashed Star Pattern,** brilliant cut, height 12″, by Tuthill .... — 315.00 — 325.00 — 320.00

☐ **Floral Design,** chain bottom, star, miter cut, height 12″ .... — 150.00 — 180.00 — 160.00

☐ **Globular Body,** long flaring neck, diamond cutting on body, feathered fans on neck, height 14″ .... — 230.00 — 255.00 — 240.00

☐ **Hobstar,** cross hatching, deep prismatic cuttings, scalloped edge, signed, by Taylor Brothers, height 8″ .... — 75.00 — 90.00 — 80.00

☐ **Hobnail Design,** with cross hatching and deep prismatic cutting, scalloped rim, by Thatcher Brothers, height 10½″ .... — 75.00 — 90.00 — 80.00

☐ **Hobstars,** flashed fanning with deep prismatic cutting, large rosette on base, signed, by Hoare & Company, height 18″ .... — 425.00 — 510.00 — 435.00

☐ **Hobstar Base,** hobstar border around rim, zipper cuttings down side, Brunswick by Hawkes, height 12″ .... — 275.00 — 300.00 — 285.00

	Current Price Range		Prior Year Average
☐ **Large Rosettes,** diamond cuts, cross hatchings, deep prismatic cuts on base, by Enterprise, height 13"	300.00	360.00	320.00
☐ **Large Rosettes,** surrounded by deep prismatic cutting, cross hatching, and diamond point designs, Constellation, by Blackmer, height 8"	250.00	300.00	260.00
☐ **Notched Prismatic Panel,** flashed fan design with single stars and deep prismatic cutting, by Thatcher Brothers, height 13"	180.00	215.00	185.00
☐ **Ovoid Body,** long beaded neck, flaring rim, sawtooth edge, fans on body, height 10"	182.00	200.00	190.00
☐ **Palm Motif,** hobstar, scalloped edge, height 6"	50.00	55.00	52.00
☐ **Rosettes,** cross hatchings, deep prismatic cuts, scalloped edge, Ogontz by Drake, height 9"	70.00	84.00	75.00

WATERFORD

Waterford, the most famous Irish glass, was made from 1783 until 1850. Produced at the Waterford Glass House, an establishment formed by brothers George and William Penrose, Waterford is known for its fine cutting, lovely clarity, and design.

Blank items were cut by a revolving iron wheel combined with sand and a water trickle. Cuts were then polished with a soft powder. After 1800 glass cutters used a wider variety of cutting strokes to make an even more brilliant product. Manufacturers most often marked their glass with raised words under the base; Waterford items are marked "Penrose Waterford." The color of Waterford is much whiter than other Irish glass, though it is often mistakenly thought to have a blue tinge.

Much Waterford was imported from 1790 to 1850 and popular import items were decanters, glasses, lamps, chandeliers, candlesticks and candelabra. However, the characteristic Waterford items most often associated with Ireland and Irish glass, include covered vases and jars for food, large serving bowls, oil and vinegar bottles, glasses, jugs, and salts.

A new company was started at Waterford in the late 1940's. Along with a variety of fine cut glass items, they also make some copies of the original Waterford pieces. The Waterford crystal listed here was produced during this period.

	Current Price Range		Prior Year Average
☐ **Ashtray,** vesicas on sides, starcut base, 1¼" high, 7" diameter	20.00	60.00	35.00

	Current Price Range		Prior Year Average

☐ **Bowl,** fruit, spiked diamond panels flank cut fans in reserves, notched rim, cut crescents, signed, 3½" high, 8" diameter **110.00 150.00 130.00**

☐ **Bowl,** fruit, spiked diamonds with panels and thumbprints, tapered sides, signed, 4½" high, 12" diameter **70.00 130.00 100.00**

☐ **Bowl,** fruit, tapered sides, cut vesicas on sides and base, round shape, 3½" high, 8" long **80.00 110.00 90.00**

☐ **Bowl,** fruit, tapered sides, cut stars within a square design, notched rim, round shape, signed, 4" high, 7¾" diameter **45.00 85.00 65.00**

☐ **Bowl,** notched diamonds, notched and paneled edge, starcut design on base, oblong shape, signed, 4¼" high, 13½" long **80.00 130.00 100.00**

☐ **Bowl,** salad, cut diamond design, notched edge, starcut base on tapered base, signed, 4¼" high, 10" diameter **80.00 130.00 100.00**

☐ **Bowl,** salad, marquise shape with daisy and button motif, flared rim, cylindrical shape, signed, 3¾" high, 9" diameter **80.00 110.00 90.00**

☐ **Bowl,** salad, slanted sides, cut zigzag vesicas, starcut design on base, round, signed, 4" high, 8½" diameter **80.00 110.00 90.00**

☐ **Bowl,** wide diamond cut band, pinwheel cut in pedestal base, signed, 3" high, 10¼" diameter **80.00 120.00 90.00**

☐ **Candlesticks,** starcut design on bases, 6" high, ... **55.00 80.00 65.00**

☐ **Compote,** spiked diamond band, cut fans around scalloped rim, starcut design on base, signed, 5½" high, 5½" diameter **80.00 110.00 90.00**

☐ **Compote,** spiked diamond band with thumbprint band, round, notched rim, notched base, signed, 6" high, 7½" diameter **130.00 160.00 140.00**

☐ **Compotes,** pair, notched thumbprint, lid has spiral finials, base is six-sided, 14½" high **150.00 250.00 200.00**

☐ **Decanter,** cut diamonds with sunburst design, thumbprints, notched neck, starcut design stopper, signed **65.00 90.00 75.00**

☐ **Decanter,** paneled neck, base has cut sawtooth band, signed, 11½" high . . **80.00 110.00 95.00**

	Current Price Range		Prior Year Average
☐ **Dish,** round shape spiked diamond bands, ball finial, starcut design on base, signed, 6″ high, 6″ diameter ..	55.00	80.00	65.00
☐ **Dishes,** pair, star design in center, 3½″ diameter	35.00	50.00	40.00
☐ **Jar,** marmalade, pedestal base, 6″ high	55.00	75.00	60.00
☐ **Jar,** starcut design on lid, cut crosses and panels, signed, 3¾″ high	90.00	165.00	125.00
☐ **Mug,** notched sides, 4½″ high	55.00	70.00	60.00
☐ **Mugs,** marquise shapes alternate with cane design in reserves, starcut design on base, signed, set of four, 4½″ high	90.00	160.00	120.00
☐ **Napkin Ring,** cut diamond pattern ...	20.00	30.00	25.00
☐ **Vase,** cut diamond design, cylindrical shape, 6″ high	35.00	55.00	40.00
☐ **Vase,** cut diamond panels with tapered sides, cylindrical shape, 10″ high	80.00	130.00	100.00
☐ **Vase,** fine panels of double shield form notching, cylindrical shape, signed, 8″ high	40.00	80.00	55.00
☐ **Vase,** trumpet shape, grid design formed from cut vesicas, starburst design on base, signed, 10″ high	110.00	150.00	130.00

DEPRESSION GLASS

INTRODUCTION

In the years from 1925 through the 1940's, American glass manufacturers produced inexpensive lines of clear and colored glass dinnerware which has come to be termed Depression glass. The new glass manufacturing technique of tank molding permitted automatic pressing and pattern etching and tooling using acid. These fancy designs not only added to the attractiveness of this dinnerware, they also served to cover up the many bubbles and flaws caused by the pressing process itself.

The scope of the glass referred to as Depression has been evolving steadily over recent years and now also includes the expensive, high quality glassware made by Cambridge, Fostoria, Hiesey, and others during the Depression era and continuing through the 1950's. This glassware was sold in fine jewelry and department stores unlike traditional Depression glass which was given away as a premium at gas stations, theatres, store openings, and in boxes of breakfast cereal and laundry detergent. Old Sears, Roebuck and Company catalogs feature complete sets for $1.99.

In reference books you will often find that Depression glass is grouped according to motif design. The earliest patterns had etched designs. Other classifications include raised, geometric, cut glass, opaque, and pressed pattern. Manufacturers rarely marked the inexpensive wares with more than a pattern label. Some of the primary manufacturers of depression glass were:

Anchor Hocking Glass
    Company
Belmont Tumbler Company
Cambridge Glass Company
Diamond Glass Company
Federal Glass Company
Fostoria Glass Company
Hazel Atlas Glass Company
A. H. Heisey And Company
Hocking Glass Company
Imperial Glass Company
Indiana Glass Company
Jeannette Glass Company

L. B. Smith Glass Company
Lancaster Glass Company
Liberty Works
Macbeth Evans Glass
    Company
McKee Glass Company
New Martinsville Glass
    Company
Paden City Glass Company
Tiffin Glass Company
U.S. Glass Company
Westmoreland Glass
    Company

While Depression glass is most often collected by pattern, this is by no means the only approach taken. For example, there are a number of people who specialize in cobalt blue glass and include pieces of Depression glass, art glass, pattern glass, Victorian colored glass, modern glass, and bottles in their collectibles. Many Depression glass enthusiasts have broadened their interest to include kitchenware and ceramic tableware of the 1930's, 1940's and 1950's. In fact, most advanced collectors acquire at least a few pieces of these Depression era wares to round out their collections.

Speaking of Depression glass collectors, you won't find a better informed group of hobbyists anywhere in the collecting world. They are extremely well organized due to the network of dynamic local Depression glass clubs which are found all over the country. It is these local clubs which sponsor the shows and sales which are the very core of the Depression glass world. At these shows a much wider variety of glassware is made available to collectors providing them with access to pieces they might not be able to find in local shops. As a result, prices of Depression glass tend to be more specific and uniform throughout the country. Of course regional differences in supply and demand do occur but they have been minimized by mail order dealers who advertise in collector publications like *The Depression Glass Daze*. These classified ads provide collectors with the opportunity to acquire pieces which may be unavailable in their particular area. It is this harmonious blend of shows and mail order business which is undoubtedly responsible for stabilizing prices throughout the country.

We have previously stated that Depression glass collectors are a very knowledgeable, well-informed group. They have been educated to a large extent by Hazel Marie Weatherman, Gene Florence, and Nora Koch, who is editor of *The Depression Glass Daze*.

The contribution of Hazel Marie Weatherman cannot be overstated. Ms. Weatherman has painstakingly researched Depression glass and is considered to be the foremost authority in the field. It is largely through her efforts that documentation of companies, patterns, colors, and pieces produced has been achieved. Her many books on the subject of Depression glass are listed in the bibliography of this book.

Former teacher Gene Florence of Lexington, Kentucky, is an author and dealer who devotes most of his time to researching and writing Depression glass books. He is perhaps best known for *The Collector's Encyclopedia of Depression Glass* now in its sixth edition. Mr. Florence has also written books on Akro Agate, Occupied Japan, and Depression-era kitchenware. His books are listed in the bibliography found in the back of this book.

The Depression glass collector is fortunate indeed because one of the finest of all collector publications is devoted to depression glass. This publication is, of course, *The Depression Glass Daze*, known to its subscribers simply as "The Daze." It is an indispensable source of information on every aspect of Depression glass and dinnerware. Informative articles, old catalog reprints, club news, reproduction alerts—in short, everything of interest pertaining to Depression glass is covered in detail. The driving force behind The Daze is its editor, Nora Koch, who has imprinted this publication with her inimitable warmth and enthusiasm. Of special interest are the classified ads where readers may buy and sell Depression era glass and dinnerware with confidence.

BUYING AND SELLING

In order to buy successfully, you must develop a certain instinct for Depression glass. To acquire this instinct you must study the glass first-hand. There simply is no substitute for seeing Depression glass in person. When viewing it, ask yourself the following questions. Are the colors of the glass true to the pattern? Are there small bubbles and impurities in the glass? Is the surface etching or relief worn with age and are there scratches caused by the use of utensils? Remember that this glass was used every day and should show the normal signs of wear. Does the pattern look too sharp and new? Reissues and reproductions are the main pitfalls in Depression glass. Only a firm knowledge of true Depression glass can help you avoid mistakes.

In addition to seeing as many good specimens of glass as possible, subscribe to periodicals and newspapers on Depression glass. Many of these publications exist for today's glass collector and they are listed in the bibliography of this book. Publications like *The Depression Glass Daze* provide tremendous help to beginning collectors as well as to the more advanced hobbyist. Not only do they contain informative articles and news of glass shows and sales, they usually have an extensive ad section for both buying and selling purposes. Reading the ads will also give you a good idea of the general availability of any particular pattern and piece. This is very helpful since certain patterns are more plentiful in some parts of the country than they might be in others.

Shopping by mail provides you with the opportunity to acquire pieces which may be difficult to find in your immediate area and therefore more expensive when they do appear on the local market. The ads are taken out by reputable sellers and generally the seller is excellent with most dealers offering a ten day return privilege. They will often provide complete lists of their inventory if you send them a SASE (self-addressed stamped envelope). Prices are quoted per piece and postage, insurance, and handling are extra.

If you are looking for a special piece and have had no success in locating it, you can place an ad stating that you want to purchase that particular item. Response to the "want" ads is generally excellent and the chances are good that you will find the piece you are looking for.

When selling your glass to a dealer you will be offered 40–70% of the retail price depending on many factors. These include condition, popularity of pattern and color, whether it's highly sought by collectors, and how much of this particular pattern he has in inventory. Basically, supply and demand will determine the offer he makes.

REPRODUCTIONS

Depression glass, along with most other antiques and collectibles, has its share of reproductions. Those that are advertised and sold as reproductions pose no threat to the Depression glass collector. In fact, some pieces may make a nice addition to a Depression glass table setting.

Not all reproductions are labeled as such, however, and unknowing collectors may buy it and think they have originals. To arm against such buying, the collector must have a firm knowledge of reproductions and their characteristics.

Color is a major point of comparison. Reproduction shades vary greatly from the original colors, and sometimes reproductions are made in colors not originally used. The design on a reproduction is often more vague and undefined than an original piece.

Reproductions of Adam have been made by the St. Louis Importing Company of Korea. Most of the new items, including a butter dish, have poor mold lines and a glossy pink color.

In 1974, Avocado was reproduced by Indiana Glass Company Tiara Exclusive Lines. Items were made in pink, yellow, blue, and amethyst. None of these colors, except pink, was originally made, so reproductions are easy to spot. The new pink is a different shade than the original pink. Reproduction Avocado was made using the original molds.

Cameo has new salt and pepper shakers and children's dishes. The dishes don't pose a problem because they weren't originally made. The salt and pepper shakers are of poor quality and are fairly easy to detect.

Many manufacturers have reproduced Cherry Blossom. New pieces have been made in pink, green, cobalt, blue, and red, and include such items as a two handled tray, cake plate, cereal bowl, plate, cup, saucer, butter dish, and salt and pepper shakers. Children's dishes were first made in 1973. The new pitcher has only seven cherries on the bottom, while the original has nine. The new background has a rough finish with no plain glass, and new pieces tend to crack easily.

Westmoreland has made some reproduction pieces of English Hobnail. It is difficult to tell the old from the new because the new was made with the original molds and in the original shade of red.

Vase and candy bottom reproductions of Iris have been reproduced. However the new pieces have mold numbers on the bottom and the original pieces don't.

June stems in crystal as well as four other colors have been reproduced by Fostoria. The new June stems have been signed on the bottom.

Mayfair reproduction shot glasses in pink, green, blue, and cobalt were first made in 1977, and cookie jars in pink and green were first made in 1982. Originally shot glasses were only in pink, so the reproductions are easy to spot. The old cookie jars have a distinct raised design, while the pattern on the reproduction is more vague.

Reproduction Miss America has been made in crystal, green, pink, blue, and red amberina. Items made include butter dishes, salt and pepper shakers, tumblers, and pitchers.

Pineapple and Floral, No. 618, was made in the avocado color in the late 1960's. Avocado was not used before the 1960's.

Anchor Hocking has reproduced some Royal Ruby, but the new items contain Anchor Hocking's trademark. The company has also reproduced their Sandwich cookie jar. New ones are easy to detect because they are much larger than the original ones.

Sandwich has been reproduced by the Indiana Glass Company Tiara Exclusive Line since 1969. Reproduction colors include blue, amber, red, and crystal. There is very little difference between new and old crystal pieces.

Sharon was first reproduced in 1976 in blue, green, pink, and dark orange. New items include butter dishes and cheese dishes. Both are made of thicker glass than the original dishes. The new cream and sugar is in a lighter shade of pink than the original, while the new salt and pepper lacks design detail.

Recollection, a reproduction of Madrid, was made in 1976 by Federal Glass. It was not made from old molds and those made in 1976 bear that year. However Indiana Glass Company acquired the molds for Recollection and their pieces do not carry the year.

Since this summary only includes a few of the reproduced Depression glass patterns, the best way to learn how to spot the differences is to compare an original piece to a reproduction. When it is not possible to compare the two in person, photographs of the glass may help the collector learn how to detect differences.

MANUFACTURERS' MARKS

Anchor Hocking Glass Co.

Hazel Atlas Glass Co.

VITROCK

Hocking Glass Co., Vitrock

Hazel Atlas Glass Co.

D.C. Jenkins Glass Co.

Imperial Glass Co.

Federal Glass Co.

Imperial Glass Co.

Indiana Glass Co.

McKee Glass Co.

Jeannette Glass Co.

New Martinsville Glass Co.

L.E. Smith Glass Co.

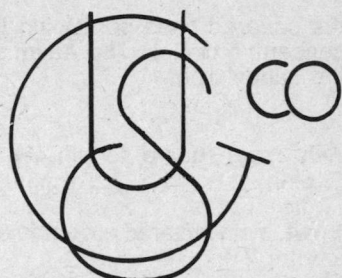

United States Glass Co.

Maryland Glass Corporation

Westmoreland Specialty Co.

Adam

ADAM
Jeannette

   This pattern is usually found in pink and green, but occasionally yellow and crystal pieces can be collected. A typical piece is square in shape and of a medium thick weight, with a central floral motif and a string of flowers around the border. Adam water pitchers were issued with both the squared base containing the motif and the rounded base featuring concentric circles. The Adam sugar lid is interchangeable with the lid of the candy dish.

	Current Price Range		Prior Year Average
Ash Tray, square, length 4¾"			
☐ pink	18.00	21.00	19.00
☐ green	15.00	17.50	16.00
Bowl, plain squared rim, paneled body, diameter 7½"			
☐ pink	12.00	14.00	13.00
☐ green	12.50	14.50	13.50
Bowl, oval, length 10"			
☐ pink	13.50	17.00	14.00
☐ green	15.50	19.00	16.50
Butter Dish and Cover, Sierra mold, Adam motif			
☐ pink	65.00	69.00	67.00
☐ green	210.00	222.00	215.00
Cake Stand, footed, diameter 9⅞"			
☐ pink	11.50	13.50	12.00
☐ green	14.00	17.00	15.50
Candlesticks, pair, squared base, with a goblet-shaped body, height 3⅞"			
☐ pink	46.00	50.00	47.50
☐ green	66.00	70.00	67.50
Candy Jar and Cover, diameter 2½"			
☐ pink	49.00	54.00	51.00
☐ green	56.00	60.00	57.00
Cereal Bowl, diameter 5¾"			
☐ pink	20.00	23.00	21.50
☐ green	18.00	22.00	19.50
Coaster, diameter 3¾"			
☐ pink	12.00	15.00	13.00
☐ green	10.50	13.00	11.50
Covered Bowl, wide squared edge, round body, diameter 9½", with a domed lid bearing the Adam motif and a bell-like finial			
☐ pink	35.00	39.00	36.50
☐ green	55.00	58.00	56.50
Creamer, paneled sides, with the leaf and flower design on the top border, and a plain handle straight at the top and swooping downwards, height 3¾"			
☐ pink	9.50	12.50	10.50
☐ green	10.50	13.50	11.50

	Current Price Range		Prior Year Average

Cup, rounded, paneled sides, with the leaf and flower design on the top border and a straight topped handle that sweeps downwards

☐ pink	14.00	18.00	15.50
☐ green	13.00	16.50	14.00
☐ yellow	92.00	98.00	94.00

Dessert Bowl, diameter 4¾″

☐ pink	8.50	11.50	9.50
☐ green	8.00	11.00	9.00

Dinner Plate, squared, length 9″

☐ pink	13.00	16.00	14.00
☐ green	12.00	15.00	13.00

Lamp, made from a sherbet dish which is frosted and notched to accommodate a switch

☐ pink	90.00	100.00	93.00
☐ green	90.00	100.00	93.00

Pitcher, with a wide, bordered top section bearing the leaf and flower design, the body of which tapers, with close paneled sides, to a square footed base decorated with the leaves and flowers, 32 oz., height 8″

☐ pink	22.00	25.00	23.00
☐ green	30.00	35.00	31.50

Pitcher, with a wide, plain bordered top section, the body of which tapers, with close paneled sides, to a round footed base with concentric rings, 32 oz., height 8″

☐ pink	33.00	39.00	34.50

Platter, length 11⅝″

☐ pink	9.50	12.00	10.00
☐ green	10.00	13.00	11.00

Relish Plate, 8″, oblong, 2-part tab handles

☐ pink	7.00	10.00	8.50
☐ green	9.00	12.00	10.50

AMERICAN SWEETHEART
Macbeth Evans

A highly manufactured line, produced from 1930 through 1936. Colors include pink, monax, cherry, red, ritz blue, and smoke. This pattern's popularity is increasing dramatically as many new items are being found.

Berry Bowl, round, 9½″

☐ pink	10.00	13.00	12.00

	Current Price Range		Prior Year Average
☐ monax	20.00	24.00	22.00
Bread and Butter Plate, 6"			
☐ pink	2.25	3.75	3.00
☐ monax	2.60	3.90	3.40
☐ smoke	3.00	5.00	3.90
Cereal Bowl, flat, 5½"			
☐ pink	2.00	4.50	3.00
☐ monax	3.00	5.00	4.00
Chop Plate, 11"			
☐ monax	6.00	8.25	7.00
☐ cherry red	60.00	70.00	64.00
☐ ritz blue	60.00	70.00	64.00
Console Bowl, flange rim, 18"			
☐ monax	110.00	130.00	117.50
☐ cherry red	205.00	235.00	210.00
☐ ritz blue	205.00	235.00	210.00
Creamer, oval, footed			
☐ pink	3.00	5.75	4.10
☐ monax	6.00	8.00	7.00
☐ cherry red	42.00	52.00	48.00
☐ ritz blue	44.00	54.00	49.00
☐ smoke	10.00	16.00	13.00
Cup			
☐ pink	2.00	5.00	3.00
☐ monax	4.00	6.00	5.00
Dinner Plate, 9½"			
☐ monax	4.00	5.25	4.60
Dinner Plate, 10"			
☐ pink	2.00	4.00	3.25
Luncheon Plate, 9"			
☐ pink	3.00	4.75	3.90
☐ monax	4.00	5.00	4.60
☐ smoke	5.00	5.75	5.50
Oval Bowl, flange rim, 11"			
☐ pink	10.00	13.00	12.00
☐ monax	20.00	24.00	22.00
Pitcher, ice guard, bulbous, 8", 60 oz.			
☐ pink	56.00	67.00	62.00
Pitcher, ice guard, bulbous, 8", 80 oz.			
☐ pink	70.00	75.00	72.00
Platter, oval, flange rim, 13"			
☐ pink	12.00	15.00	14.00
☐ monax	18.00	22.00	20.00
☐ cherry red	65.00	75.00	69.00
☐ ritz blue	63.00	73.00	68.00
Salt and Pepper, footed			
☐ pink	20.00	27.00	24.00
☐ monax	45.00	52.00	49.00

	Current Price Range		Prior Year Average
☐ cherry red	110.00	130.00	120.00
☐ ritz blue	110.00	130.00	120.00
☐ smoke	44.00	50.00	48.00
Salver Plate, 12″			
☐ monax	7.00	10.00	8.25
☐ cherry red	90.00	105.00	95.00
☐ ritz blue	90.00	105.00	95.00
Saucer			
☐ pink	1.00	2.10	1.40
☐ monax	2.00	3.25	2.60
☐ cherry red	25.00	35.00	30.00
☐ ritz blue	22.00	32.00	29.00
☐ smoke	3.75	5.25	4.50
Serving Plate, 16″			
☐ monax	18.00	24.00	19.00
☐ cherry red	115.00	120.00	115.00
☐ ritz blue	115.00	120.00	115.00
Sherbet, footed, 4″			
☐ pink	3.00	3.75	3.35
☐ monax	4.00	4.75	4.60
Soup Bowl, 2 handled, 4½″			
☐ pink	4.00	6.50	5.25
☐ monax	6.50	8.75	7.25
Soup bowl, flat, 9½″			
☐ pink	3.00	5.50	3.50
☐ monax	7.00	9.50	8.00
Sugar, unlidded, oval, footed			
☐ pink	2.75	5.00	3.75
☐ monax	5.50	7.00	6.00
☐ cherry red	40.00	50.00	44.00
☐ ritz blue	40.00	50.00	44.00
☐ smoke	10.00	16.00	13.00
Tid-bit Set, 8″ and 12″ plates on two tiers, metal handle in the middle			
☐ monax	29.00	37.00	34.00
☐ cherry red	200.00	265.00	230.00
☐ ritz blue	200.00	265.00	230.00
Tid-bit Set, 8″, 12″ & 16″ plates on three tiers, metal handle in the middle			
☐ monax	12.00	17.00	14.50
Tumbler, 4″			
☐ pink	8.00	9.00	8.60

ANNIVERSARY
Jeannette

Originally, this glass line was produced in pink, but crystal and the sprayed-on iridescent types were made as late as 1970. It is not truly Depression glass, having been made in the late forties, but is included here

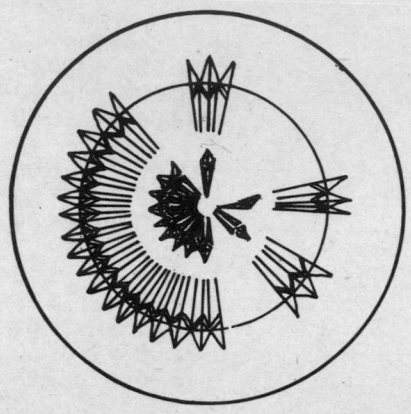

Anniversary

due to the rising interest of Depression glass collectors in this pattern. The most recent name for Anniversary was Diamond Cut, which suggests the sharp, geometric motif, a series of spiked lines emanating outwards from the base of, say, a plate or bowl, with a central medallion of the same lines separated from the outer design by a plain, circular border.

	Current Price Range		Prior Year Average
Berry Bowl, diameter 4⅞″			
☐ pink	1.50	3.00	2.00
☐ crystal	.75	2.50	1.00
Butter Dish and Cover			
☐ pink	36.00	44.00	38.00
☐ crystal	19.00	25.00	21.00
Cake Plate, diameter 12½″			
☐ pink	6.00	10.00	7.50
☐ crystal	3.50	6.00	4.50
Cake Plate and Cover			
☐ pink	11.00	14.00	11.50
☐ crystal	8.00	12.00	9.00
Candlesticks, pair, 4⅞″			
☐ crystal	10.00	14.00	11.50
Candy Jar and Cover, with a pointed finial on the lid			
☐ pink	21.00	29.00	23.00
☐ crystal	15.00	19.00	16.00
Compote, open, 3 legged			
☐ pink	5.50	8.50	6.00
☐ crystal	2.00	4.00	2.50
Creamer, with a handle pointed on the top edge, footed on a round base			
☐ pink	4.50	8.00	5.50
☐ crystal	2.00	4.00	2.50

	Current Price Range		Prior Year Average

Cup
| ☐ pink .... | 2.50 | 5.50 | 3.50 |
| ☐ crystal .... | 1.00 | 3.00 | 1.50 |

Dinner Plate, diameter 9″
| ☐ pink .... | 3.50 | 5.50 | 4.00 |
| ☐ crystal .... | 2.50 | 4.50 | 3.00 |

Fruit Bowl, diameter 9″
| ☐ pink .... | 9.00 | 13.00 | 10.00 |
| ☐ crystal .... | 6.00 | 9.00 | 6.50 |

Pickle Dish, diameter 9″
| ☐ pink .... | 4.00 | 8.00 | 5.00 |
| ☐ crystal .... | 2.00 | 4.00 | 2.50 |

Relish Dish, diameter 8″
| ☐ pink .... | 5.00 | 8.00 | 5.75 |
| ☐ crystal .... | 3.75 | 5.50 | 4.00 |

Sandwich Server Plate, diameter 12½″
| ☐ pink .... | 5.00 | 8.00 | 6.00 |
| ☐ crystal .... | 3.00 | 6.00 | 3.50 |

Saucer
| ☐ pink .... | 1.00 | 2.00 | 1.25 |
| ☐ crystal .... | .50 | 1.50 | .75 |

Sherbet, stub stem, footed on a round base
| ☐ pink .... | 3.00 | 5.50 | 4.00 |
| ☐ crystal .... | 1.00 | 3.50 | 1.75 |

Sherbet Plate, diameter 6¼″
| ☐ pink .... | 1.00 | 3.00 | 1.50 |
| ☐ crystal .... | .75 | 1.75 | 1.00 |

Sugar, open, with two handles pointed on the top edge
| ☐ pink .... | 3.50 | 5.50 | 4.00 |
| ☐ crystal .... | 1.00 | 3.00 | 1.75 |

Sugar Covers, with a pointed finial
| ☐ pink .... | 3.00 | 5.00 | 3.50 |
| ☐ crystal .... | 2.00 | 4.00 | 2.50 |

Vase, with a scalloped rim, height 6½″
| ☐ pink .... | 8.00 | 11.00 | 8.50 |
| ☐ crystal .... | 4.50 | 7.50 | 5.00 |

Vase, wall pin-up
| ☐ pink .... | 13.00 | 17.00 | 14.00 |
| ☐ crystal .... | 8.00 | 12.00 | 9.00 |

Wine Glass, footed on a round base, 2¾″ oz.
| ☐ pink .... | 7.00 | 9.50 | 7.50 |
| ☐ crystal .... | 4.00 | 7.00 | 4.50 |

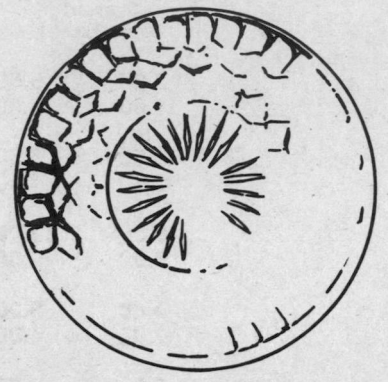

Aunt Polly

AUNT POLLY
U.S. Glass

Available in blue, green, and iridescent, this line features a basic diamond pattern, usually (as on the bowls, tumblers, pitchers, etc.) rising from the edge of the base and culminating almost midway into a series of arched panels that do not quite reach the rim, creating a scalloped effect against the smooth top border. The circular base contains a starburst motif.

	Current Price Range		Prior Year Average
Berry Bowl, diameter 4⅜"			
☐ green	3.50	6.00	4.00
☐ blue	4.50	7.50	5.00
Berry Bowl, diameter 7⅞"			
☐ green	9.00	13.00	10.00
☐ blue	15.00	20.00	16.00
Bowl, height 2", diameter 4½"			
☐ green	7.00	10.00	7.50
☐ blue	9.00	13.00	10.00
Bowl, oval, length 8½"			
☐ green	17.50	22.00	18.50
☐ blue	29.00	35.00	31.00
Butter Dish and Cover			
☐ green	175.00	190.00	180.00
☐ blue	143.00	155.00	145.00
Candy Jar, with a pointed finial on the cover, and two flat, thumbprint topped handles			
☐ green	30.00	40.00	33.00
☐ blue	43.00	55.00	45.00
Creamer, with a flat, thumbprint topped handle			
☐ green	14.00	20.00	15.00
☐ blue	22.00	29.00	23.00
Luncheon Plate, diameter 8"			
☐ blue	7.00	10.00	8.00

	Current Price Range		Prior Year Average

Pickle Bowl, oval, with two flat, thumb-print topped handles, diameter 7½"

☐ green	7.50	11.00	8.50
☐ blue	10.50	14.50	11.00

Pitcher, with a scalloped rim and plain handle, 48 oz., height 8"

☐ blue	112.00	125.00	114.00

Salt and Pepper Shakers

☐ blue	138.00	155.00	143.00

Sherbet, smooth stub stem on a plain round base

☐ green	6.00	9.00	7.00
☐ blue	7.00	10.00	8.00

Sherbet Plate, diameter 6"

☐ green	2.00	4.00	2.50
☐ blue	3.00	6.00	3.50

Sugar, with two flat, thumbprint topped handles

☐ green	9.50	13.00	10.25
☐ blue	13.00	18.00	14.50

Sugar Cover, with a pointed finial

☐ green	25.00	32.00	26.50
☐ blue	36.00	44.00	38.00

Tumbler, 8 oz., height 3⅝"

☐ blue	11.00	15.00	12.00

Vase, slightly flared body, footed on a round, decorated base, height 6½"

☐ green	20.00	26.00	21.00
☐ blue	24.00	30.00	26.00

Aurora

AURORA
Hazel Atlas

This breakfast line was issued primarily in cobalt blue, but sometimes is found in platonite and pale pink. It is characterized by continuous band of vertical raised pleats or ribs around the object, with a horizontal band encircling the rim.

	Current Price Range		Prior Year Average
Cereal Bowl, diameter 5¼"			
☐ cobalt	3.00	5.00	3.50
Cup			
☐ cobalt	3.50	6.00	4.50
Milk Pitcher, 4" high			
☐ cobalt	6.75	9.50	7.50
Plate, diameter 6½"			
☐ cobalt	2.50	4.50	3.00
☐ pink	2.50	4.50	3.00
Saucer			
☐ cobalt	1.50	3.50	2.00
Tumbler, 10 oz., height 4¾"			
☐ cobalt	7.25	9.75	8.25
☐ pink	7.25	9.75	8.25

AVOCADO, NO. 601
Indiana

This high relief fruit pattern was mostly produced in pink and green, but can be found in crystal. The central motif is composed of two pears surrounded by a profusion of leaves that gather to the outer edge, giving the piece an irregular shape.

Bowl, two-handled, with an oval shape, diameter 8"			
☐ pink	12.50	15.00	13.50
☐ green	17.00	21.00	17.50

Avocado, No. 601

	Current Price Range		Prior Year Average

Bowl, two-handled, diameter 5¼″
☐ pink 18.00   22.00   19.00
☐ green 20.00   24.00   21.00
Bowl, height 3″, diameter 9½″
☐ pink 54.00   61.00   55.75
☐ green 74.00   81.00   76.00
Cake Plate, two-handled, diameter 10¼″
☐ pink 20.00   24.00   21.00
☐ green 30.00   34.00   31.00
Creamer, footed
☐ pink 23.00   27.00   24.00
☐ green 27.00   31.00   28.00
Cup, footed, on a round base
☐ pink 25.00   28.00   25.75
☐ green 26.00   29.00   26.75
Luncheon Plate, diameter 8¼″
☐ pink 11.00   15.00   12.00
☐ green 13.00   17.00   14.00
Pitcher, cone-shaped, footed on a round, smooth-edged base that contains a single row of leaves, but with the typical pear and leaf design on the body and the ragged top rim, 64 oz.
☐ pink 280.00   315.00   290.00
☐ green 475.00   520.00   490.00
Saucer
☐ pink 18.00   22.00   19.00
☐ green 20.50   24.50   21.50
Tumbler, cone-shaped, slightly flared rim, on a round base
☐ pink 67.00   73.00   68.00
☐ green 96.00   104.00   98.00
Sherbert
☐ pink 44.00   49.00   45.50
☐ green 49.00   54.00   51.00
Sherbet Plate, diameter 6¼″
☐ pink 8.00   11.50   9.00
☐ green 9.00   13.00   10.00
Sugar, two-handled, footed
☐ pink 22.00   27.00   23.50
☐ green 27.00   32.00   28.25

BANDED RINGS
Hocking

Whether painted or plain, the series of rings that run from the top to the bottom of these pieces is well-molded and attractively arranged. Three ridges alternate with a clear panel and get successively wider as they move toward the bottom. On some pieces, the colored rings alternate in the complementary shades.

	Current Price Range		Prior Year Average
Berry Bowl, diameter 4⅞"			
☐ crystal	1.00	3.00	1.50
☐ green	2.00	4.00	2.50
☐ decorated	2.00	4.00	2.50
Berry Bowl, diameter 8"			
☐ crystal	3.00	5.00	3.50
☐ green	4.50	7.00	5.00
☐ decorated	4.50	7.00	5.00
Butter Tub, tab handled			
☐ crystal	7.00	11.00	7.75
☐ green	11.00	15.00	12.00
☐ decorated	11.00	15.00	12.00
Cocktail Glass, pedestal foot			
☐ crystal	3.00	5.00	3.50
☐ green	3.50	5.75	4.00
☐ decorated	3.50	5.75	4.00
Cocktail Shaker			
☐ crystal	6.00	9.00	6.75
☐ green	11.00	15.00	12.00
☐ decorated	11.00	15.00	12.00
Creamer			
☐ crystal	2.00	4.50	3.00
☐ green	3.00	5.50	4.00
☐ decorated	3.00	5.50	4.00
Cup			
☐ crystal	1.00	3.00	1.50
☐ green	2.25	5.00	3.00
☐ decorated	2.25	5.00	3.00
Decanter, faceted stopper			
☐ crystal	12.50	16.00	13.50
☐ green	21.00	28.00	22.50
☐ decorated	21.00	28.00	22.50
Goblet, stemmed, 9 oz. height 7¼"			
☐ crystal	3.00	6.50	4.00
☐ green	8.00	11.50	9.00
☐ decorated	8.00	11.50	9.00
Ice Bucket			
☐ crystal	7.00	10.00	8.00
☐ green	10.00	14.00	11.00
☐ decorated	10.00	14.00	11.00
Ice Tea Glass, pedestal foot, height 6½"			
☐ crystal	4.00	6.00	4.50

	Current Price Range		Prior Year Average
☐ green	7.00	10.00	8.00
☐ decorated	7.00	10.00	8.00
Juice Tumbler, 5 oz. height 3½"			
☐ crystal	1.50	4.00	2.25
☐ green	2.50	5.00	3.00
☐ decorated	2.50	5.00	3.00
Pitcher, 60 oz. height 8"			
☐ crystal	7.00	10.00	8.00
☐ green	13.00	17.00	14.00
☐ decorated	13.00	17.00	14.00
Pitcher, 80 oz., height 8½"			
☐ crystal	8.75	12.00	9.25
☐ green	15.00	19.00	16.00
☐ decorated	15.00	19.00	16.00
Plate, diameter 6"			
☐ crystal	.75	2.50	1.00
☐ green	2.50	4.50	3.00
☐ decorated	2.50	4.50	3.00
Plate, diameter 6½"			
☐ crystal	.75	2.25	1.00
☐ green	1.50	3.50	2.00
☐ decorated	1.50	3.50	2.00
Plate, diameter 8½"			
☐ crystal	.75	2.25	1.00
☐ green	1.25	3.25	2.00
☐ decorated	1.25	3.25	2.00
☐ red	15.00	19.00	16.00
☐ blue	20.00	24.00	21.00
Salt and Pepper Shakers, height 3"			
☐ crystal	10.00	14.50	11.00
☐ green	54.00	59.00	55.50
☐ decorated	20.00	25.00	21.00
Sandwich Tray, center handle			
☐ crystal	8.00	11.00	9.00
☐ green	15.00	19.00	16.25
☐ decorated	15.00	19.00	16.25
Saucer			
☐ crystal	.75	2.00	1.00
☐ green	1.00	3.00	1.50
☐ decorated	1.00	3.00	1.50
Sherbet, pedestal foot, height 4½"			
☐ crystal	3.00	5.00	3.50
☐ green	3.50	5.50	4.25
☐ decorated	3.50	5.50	4.25
Sugar Bowl, pedestal foot, height 5"			
☐ crystal	2.00	4.00	2.50
☐ green	3.00	5.00	3.50
☐ decorated	3.00	5.00	3.50

	Current Price Range		Prior Year Average
Tumbler, 5 oz. height 3½"			
☐ crystal	1.75	3.50	2.00
☐ green	2.50	4.50	3.00
☐ decorated	2.50	4.50	3.00
Tumbler, 9 oz. height 4½"			
☐ crystal	2.50	4.50	3.00
☐ green	3.50	5.50	4.00
☐ decorated	3.50	5.50	4.00
Tumbler, 12 oz. height 5½"			
☐ crystal	3.00	5.00	3.50
☐ green	3.50	5.50	4.00
☐ decorated	3.50	5.50	4.00
Water Glass, height 5½"			
☐ crystal	2.50	4.50	3.00
☐ green	3.50	5.50	4.00
☐ decorated	3.50	5.50	4.00

BEADED BLOCK
Imperial

Similar to an older "Pattern" glass, this line was issued in pink, green, crystal, ice blue, vaseline, iridescent amber, and opalescent colors. A typical plate or bowl, for example, features two continuous rows of blocks, one on top of the other, the top row of blocks being somewhat wider and longer, following the natural contour of the object. Blocks are smooth and lined on all sides by a sharply contrasting jewel-like border. The outer rim is softly scalloped, and on footed pieces, such as the vase or creamer, the round base is rayed, terminating in a scalloped edge. The center contains a sunburst design. Unlike most Depression glass, some hand work was involved in creating this line, as was necessary, for example, in the fluting of some of the bowls and in the making of those bowls which were made by turning up the edges of the plates.

Beaded Block

	Current Price Range		Prior Year Average

Bowl, for jelly, with two pointed, sharply curved handles, diameter 4″
□ pink	5.00	7.00	5.50
□ opalescent	11.00	14.00	12.00

Bowl, round, lily, diameter 4½″
□ pink	7.00	10.00	8.00
□ opalescent	13.00	17.00	14.00

Bowl, squared shape, length 5½″
□ pink	5.00	7.00	5.50
□ opalescent	7.00	10.00	8.00

Bowl, one handle, pointed, sharply curved, diameter 5¼″
□ pink	5.50	8.00	6.00
□ opalescent	7.00	10.00	8.00

Bowl, round, deep, diameter 6″
□ pink	7.00	10.00	8.00
□ opalescent	13.00	16.00	14.00

Bowl, round shape, flared, diameter 7¼″
□ pink	6.50	9.50	7.25
□ opalescent	13.00	16.00	14.00

Bowl, round, fluted edges, diameter 7½″
□ pink	15.00	20.00	16.00
□ opalescent	18.00	22.00	19.00

Bowl, round, diameter 6¼″
□ pink	5.00	8.00	6.00
□ opalescent	11.00	15.00	12.00

Bowl, round, diameter 6½″
□ pink	5.00	8.00	6.00
□ opalescent	11.00	15.00	12.00

Bowl, round, with a plain edge, diameter 7½″
□ pink	6.00	9.00	7.00
□ opalescent	12.50	16.00	13.50

Celery Bowl, with a design featuring a single row of blocks, diameter 8¼″
□ pink	8.00	12.00	9.00
□ opalescent	13.00	17.00	14.00

Creamer, with a stub stem on a round decorative base, and a milky, scalloped top rim with wide-lipped spout
□ pink	8.50	11.50	9.25
□ opalescent	15.00	19.00	16.50

Jelly Dish, with a plain stem on a round, decorative base, diameter 4¼″
□ pink	6.50	9.50	7.25
□ opalescent	13.00	16.00	14.00

	Current Price Range		Prior Year Average

Jelly Dish, with a flared top and a plain stem on a round, decorative base, diameter 4¼″

☐ pink	7.00	10.00	8.00
☐ opalescent	14.00	18.00	15.00

Pitcher, pint jug, with a wide-lipped spout and the characteristic pointed and sharply curved handle, diameter 5″

☐ pink	105.00	130.00	112.00

CAMEO
Hocking

This ornate, romantic pattern was cast in green, yellow, crystal with or without platinum rims, and pink. Collectors often descriptively refer to this line as "ballerina" or "dancing girl," as the basic motif is a side view of a dancing figure enclosed within a curving, ribboned frame which forms a kind of lantern shape, and which is decorated with a bow-knot that drops from the center point of the bottom, tassled on either side of the pointed top and bottom ends. These figure motifs are well-spaced on the object and strung together by floral, ribbon-tied festoons that loop once, fall into a central V-shape, than loop again to complete the connection. Often, as on the plates, this design is trimmed overall with a scrolled ribbon border about the rim. In the center of some bowls and plates, the garland extends to form a multipointed star decorated with rosebuds on the tips and containing a floral design within. Sometimes there is a definite variation in the etched trim, or in the handles or sizes. The pitchers, for example, are found with and without the rope trims. The 7-inch round saucer with an indented ring is a most unusual item. No doubt one reason for the popularity of this pattern is the variety of pieces that are available, in addition to its other appealing qualities.

Berry Bowl, diameter 8¼″

☐ green	21.00	27.00	22.50

Butter Dish, lidded

☐ green	115.00	140.00	121.00

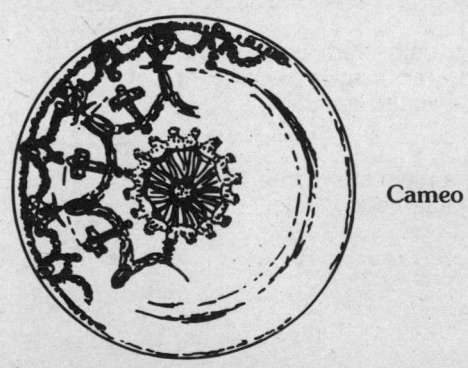

Cameo

	Current Price Range		Prior Year Average
☐ yellow	590.00	640.00	610.00

Cake Plate, three legs, diameter 10″

☐ green	12.00	16.00	13.00

Cake Plate, without legs, diameter 10½″

☐ green	50.00	65.00	53.00

Candlesticks, pair, height 4″

☐ green	60.00	80.00	70.00

Candy Jar, cover, height 4″

☐ green	33.00	45.00	38.00
☐ yellow	45.00	55.00	47.00
☐ pink	325.00	375.00	340.00

Candy Jar, cover, height 6½″

☐ green	85.00	95.00	97.00

Cereal Bowl, diameter 5½″

☐ green	19.00	24.00	20.50
☐ yellow	20.00	24.50	21.00
☐ crystal	2.00	4.00	2.50

Cocktail Shaker, metal lid

☐ crystal	300.00	335.00	315.00

Console Bowl, tri-legged, diameter 11″

☐ green	35.00	45.00	37.00
☐ yellow	47.00	57.00	50.00
☐ pink	15.00	19.00	16.50

Cookie Jar, lidded

☐ green	32.00	40.00	35.00

Creamer, height 3¼″

☐ green	15.00	19.00	15.75
☐ yellow	10.50	14.00	11.50

Creamer, height 4¼″

☐ green	14.00	18.00	15.00

Cup

☐ green	9.00	13.00	10.00
☐ yellow	5.50	7.50	6.00
☐ pink	47.00	53.00	49.00

Decanter, stoppered, height 10″

☐ green	75.00	90.00	79.00

Dinner Plate, diameter 9½″

☐ green	12.00	15.00	13.00
☐ yellow	5.00	7.00	5.50
☐ pink	25.00	35.00	27.50

Grill Plate diameter 10½″

☐ green	6.00	8.00	6.50
☐ yellow	5.00	7.00	5.50
☐ pink	29.00	34.00	31.00

Grill Plate, closed handles, diameter 10½″

☐ green	44.00	54.00	45.50
☐ yellow	4.00	6.50	5.00

	Current Price Range		Prior Year Average
Ice Bowl, diameter 5½"			
☐ green	93.00	105.00	95.00
☐ pink	380.00	420.00	390.00
☐ crystal	160.00	200.00	170.00
Jam Jar, lidded, height 2"			
☐ green	82.00	95.00	85.00
Juice Pitcher, 36 oz., height 6"			
☐ green	35.00	45.00	37.00
Juice Tumbler, 5 oz. height 3¾"			
☐ green	16.00	20.00	17.50
☐ pink	55.00	65.00	67.00
Luncheon Plate, diameter 8"			
☐ green	6.00	8.00	6.50
☐ yellow	1.50	3.50	2.00
☐ pink	20.00	26.00	21.50
☐ crystal	2.50	4.50	3.00
Mayonnaise Bowl, wide, diameter 5"			
☐ green	17.00	21.00	18.00
Plate, with closed handles, diameter 11½"			
☐ green	5.50	7.50	6.00
☐ yellow	4.00	6.00	4.50
Platter, closed handles, length 12"			
☐ green	12.00	15.00	13.00
☐ yellow	12.00	15.00	13.00
Relish Dish, three compartments, footed, diameter 7½"			
☐ green	14.00	17.00	15.00
Salad Bowl, square, diameter 7¼"			
☐ green	21.00	28.00	22.50
Salad Plate, diameter 7"			
☐ crystal	2.00	4.00	2.50
Salt and Pepper Shakers, footed, height 7½"			
☐ green	45.00	55.00	47.00
☐ pink	475.00	525.00	490.00
Sandwich Plate, diameter 10"			
☐ green	8.00	11.50	9.00
☐ pink	27.00	33.00	29.00
Sauce Bowl, diameter 4½"			
☐ crystal	3.00	5.00	3.50
Saucer, cup ring			
☐ green	71.00	78.00	72.50
Sherbet, diameter 3⅛"			
☐ green	9.50	12.50	10.50
☐ yellow	13.00	17.00	13.50
☐ pink	21.00	27.00	22.50

	Current Price Range		Prior Year Average
Sherbet, diameter 5″			
☐ green	20.00	25.00	21.50
☐ yellow	20.00	25.00	21.50
Sherbet Plate, diameter 6″			
☐ crystal	1.00	2.50	1.25
☐ green	2.00	4.00	2.50
☐ yellow	1.00	3.00	1.50
☐ pink	41.00	48.00	42.00
Soup Bowl, diameter 4¾″			
☐ green	40.00	47.00	41.50
Soup Bowl, rimmed, diameter 9″			
☐ green	27.00	33.00	29.00
Sugar Bowl, diameter 3¼″			
☐ green	9.00	13.00	10.50
Sugar Bowl, diameter 4¼″			
☐ green	15.00	18.00	16.00
☐ pink	47.00	53.00	49.00
Syrup Pitcher, 20 oz., height 5¾″			
☐ green	128.00	142.00	133.00
☐ yellow	165.00	185.00	170.00
Tray, with indentations, length 7″			
☐ green	60.00	75.00	64.00
Tray, without indentations, length 7″			
☐ pink	140.00	155.00	143.00
☐ crystal	80.00	95.00	84.00
Tumbler, footed, 9 oz., height 5″			
☐ green	18.00	22.00	19.00
☐ yellow	9.00	13.50	10.50
☐ pink	70.00	80.00	73.00
Tumbler, flat, 10 oz., height 4¾″			
☐ green	18.00	22.00	19.00
Tumbler, footed, 11 oz., height 5¾″			
☐ green	32.00	37.00	33.00
Tumbler, 15 oz., height 5¼″			
☐ green	32.00	42.00	35.00
Tumbler, footed, 15 oz., height 6⅜″			
☐ green	140.00	160.00	147.00
Vase, height 5¾″			
☐ green	85.00	95.00	90.00
Vase, height 8″			
☐ green	16.00	20.50	17.00
Vegetable Bowl, oval length 10″			
☐ green	12.00	14.50	13.00
☐ yellow	18.00	22.00	19.00
Water Bottle, cork stopper			
☐ green	16.00	20.50	17.00
Water Goblet, height 6″			
☐ green	32.00	38.00	33.50
☐ pink	103.00	115.00	107.00

CHERRY BLOSSOM
Jeannette

This pattern was produced from 1930 to 1938. The colors were pink, green, delfite (opaque blue), and a few pieces in crystal. It has always been a very popular pattern. Green was taken out of production in 1935; it is more scarce than pink and delfite. Very little crystal exists. The 10½" fruit bowl is available in jadeite (opaque green).

	Current Price Range		Prior Year Average
Bowl, 9"			
☐ pink	17.00	21.00	18.25
☐ green	18.00	22.00	19.25
☐ delfite	14.00	18.00	15.35
Butter Dish and Cover			
☐ pink	55.00	63.00	58.00
☐ green	60.00	65.00	63.00
Butter Dish, bottom			
☐ pink	16.00	20.00	17.00
☐ green	18.00	24.00	19.00
Butter Dish, top			
☐ pink	42.00	50.00	46.00
☐ green	47.00	55.00	53.00
Cake Plate, 10½"			
☐ pink	13.00	15.25	14.00
☐ green	16.00	18.25	17.00
Creamer			
☐ pink	10.00	12.00	11.00
☐ green	11.00	13.25	12.25
☐ delfite	15.00	17.50	16.00
Dinner Plate, 9"			
☐ pink	11.00	14.00	12.50
☐ green	13.00	16.00	14.00
☐ delphite	11.00	15.00	13.25
Fruit Bowl, 10½"			
☐ pink	32.00	40.00	35.00
☐ green	32.00	40.00	35.00
☐ delphite	50.00	60.00	54.00
☐ jadeite	125.00	175.00	147.50
Grill Plate, 9"			
☐ pink	14.00	17.00	15.00
☐ green	13.50	16.00	14.50
Grill Plate, 10"			
☐ pink	15.00	18.00	16.25
☐ green	15.00	18.00	16.25
Nappy, 4¾"			
☐ pink	7.00	10.00	8.00
☐ green	7.75	10.75	9.00
☐ delfite	8.00	10.50	8.50
Nappy, 5¾"			
☐ pink	19.00	23.00	18.00
☐ green	18.00	22.00	17.50

	Current Price Range		Prior Year Average
Nappy, 8½"			
☐ pink	17.00	21.00	18.50
☐ green	16.00	20.00	17.75
☐ delfite	27.50	32.50	30.00
Oval Bowl, vegetable, 9"			
☐ pink	17.00	21.00	18.25
☐ green	18.00	22.00	19.25
☐ delfite	30.00	34.00	31.00
Platter, 11"			
☐ pink	19.00	25.50	21.00
☐ green	19.00	25.50	21.00
☐ delfite	30.00	40.00	33.00
Platter, 13"			
☐ pink	30.00	35.00	32.00
☐ green	30.00	36.00	32.50
Platter, divided, 13"			
☐ pink	30.00	35.00	32.00
☐ green	32.00	36.00	32.50
Salad Plate, 7"			
☐ pink	11.00	14.25	12.50
☐ green	11.00	14.25	12.50
Sherbet Plate, 6"			
☐ pink	5.00	8.00	6.00
☐ green	4.00	7.00	5.00
☐ delfite	6.00	9.00	7.50
Soup Bowl, 7¾"			
☐ pink	32.00	37.00	34.00
☐ green	32.00	37.00	34.00
Tray, handled, 10½"			
☐ pink	14.00	17.00	15.00
☐ green	15.00	18.00	16.00
Tumbler, 12 oz., 5"			
☐ pink	24.00	28.00	26.00
☐ green	24.00	28.00	26.00
Tumbler, 9 oz. 4⅛"			
☐ pink	14.00	16.00	15.00
☐ green	16.00	18.00	15.00
Tumbler, footed, 9 oz., 4⅜"			
☐ pink	19.00	24.00	21.00
☐ green	20.00	25.50	21.00
Tumbler, 5 oz., 3⅜"			
☐ pink	11.00	15.00	12.25
☐ green	11.00	15.00	12.25
Tumbler, footed, 4 oz. juice, 3½"			
☐ pink	12.00	16.00	13.50
☐ green	12.00	16.00	13.50

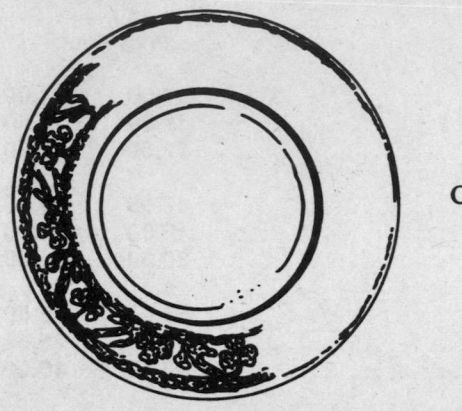

Cloverleaf

CLOVERLEAF
Hazel Atlas

This line is identifiable by the simple, stylized cloverleaf border that trails close to the rim on bowls and other vessels, such as the conical shaped and footed tumblers. The saucer does not bear the design in the center, as do the other plates and dishes. It can be found in pink, green, yellow, crystal, and the relatively scarce but striking black.

	Current Price Range		Prior Year Average
Ashtray, with match holder, diameter 4"			
☐ black	50.00	60.00	52.00
Bowl, deep, diameter 8"			
☐ green	37.00	47.00	39.00
Candy Dish, with cover			
☐ yellow	90.00	100.00	93.00
☐ green	34.00	43.00	36.00
Cereal Bowl, straight sides, diameter 5"			
☐ yellow	18.00	23.00	19.00
☐ green	13.00	17.00	14.00
Creamer, footed, height 4⅝"			
☐ yellow	11.00	14.00	11.50
☐ black	11.00	14.00	11.50
☐ green	6.00	8.50	6.50
Cup			
☐ black	8.00	11.00	8.50
☐ pink	4.00	6.00	4.50
☐ green	4.50	6.50	5.00
Dessert Bowl, diameter 4"			
☐ green	11.00	14.00	11.50
☐ yellow	14.00	18.00	15.00
Grill Plate, diameter 10¼"			
☐ green	13.00	17.00	14.00
☐ yellow	15.00	19.00	16.00
Luncheon Plate, diameter 8"			
☐ green	4.00	6.00	4.50

	Current Price Range		Prior Year Average
☐ pink	4.00	6.00	4.50
☐ yellow	8.00	12.00	9.00
☐ black	8.50	12.50	9.50
Salad Bowl, deep, diameter 7″			
☐ green	20.00	25.00	21.00
☐ yellow	33.00	40.00	35.00
Salt and Pepper Shakers			
☐ green	20.00	25.00	21.00
☐ yellow	75.00	85.00	78.00
☐ black	48.00	55.00	50.00
Saucer			
☐ yellow	2.00	4.00	2.50
☐ black	2.00	4.00	2.50
☐ pink	1.00	3.00	1.50
☐ green	1.50	3.50	2.00
Sherbet, footed, diameter 3″			
☐ green	3.50	5.50	4.00
☐ pink	4.00	6.00	4.50
☐ yellow	7.00	10.00	8.00
☐ black	11.00	14.00	12.00
Sugar Bowl, footed, diameter 3½″			
☐ green	6.00	8.50	6.50
☐ yellow	11.00	14.00	12.00
☐ black	11.00	14.00	12.00
Tumbler, flat, 9 oz., height 4″			
☐ green	22.00	32.00	26.00

COLONIAL
Hocking

This elegant pattern is markedly similar to the Early American pressed Knife and Fork, also referred to as Pillar Optic or Colonial Design. The sides are composed of alternating arched columns, with a sunburst design

Colonial

in the center of plates, bowls, etc. Stemmed ware terminates in a round base decorated with an emanating petal design that stops short of the rim, breaking into a smooth border. It appears primarily in pink, green and crystal, although opaque white may occasionally be found.

	Current Price Range		Prior Year Average
Berry Bowl, diameter 4½″			
☐ crystal	2.50	4.50	3.00
☐ green	7.00	10.00	8.00
☐ pink	5.00	8.00	6.00
Berry Bowl, diameter 9″			
☐ crystal	7.00	10.00	7.75
☐ pink	11.00	14.00	12.00
☐ green	16.00	19.00	17.00
Butter Dish, with cover			
☐ pink	430.00	470.00	440.00
☐ green	38.00	46.00	40.00
Celery Holder			
☐ pink	72.00	82.00	74.00
☐ green	80.00	90.00	83.00
Cereal Bowl, diameter 5½″			
☐ pink	21.00	26.00	22.00
☐ green	32.00	40.00	34.50
Cheese Dish			
☐ green	72.00	82.00	74.00
Claret Glass, 4 oz., height 5¼″			
☐ green	16.00	19.00	17.00
Cocktail Glass, 3 oz., height 4″			
☐ green	16.00	19.00	17.00
Cordial Goblet, 1 oz., height 3¾″			
☐ green	21.00	25.00	22.00
Cup			
☐ pink	4.50	7.50	5.25
☐ green	7.00	10.00	8.00
☐ milk glass	5.50	8.50	6.25
Dinner Plate, diameter 10″			
☐ pink	20.00	25.00	21.00
☐ green	36.00	45.00	37.00
Grill Plate, diameter 10″			
☐ pink	13.00	17.00	14.00
☐ green	16.00	19.00	17.00
Iced Tea Glass, 12 oz.			
☐ pink	18.00	22.00	19.00
☐ green	27.00	33.00	29.00
Juice Glass, 5 oz., height 3″			
☐ pink	7.50	11.50	8.25
☐ green	13.00	17.00	14.00
Luncheon Plate, diameter 8½″			
☐ pink	4.00	6.50	5.00
☐ green	4.50	7.00	5.50

	Current Price Range		Prior Year Average

Mug, 12 oz., height 4½"
☐ pink 140.00 160.00 145.00
Pitcher, 54 oz., height 7"
☐ pink 29.00 34.50 31.50
Pitcher, ice lip, 54 oz., height 7"
☐ pink 29.00 34.50 31.50
☐ green 31.00 38.00 32.50
Pitcher, ice lip, 68 oz., height 7¾"
☐ pink 32.00 38.00 33.50
☐ green 43.00 51.00 45.00
Pitcher, 68 oz., height 7¾"
☐ pink 32.00 38.00 33.50
☐ green 43.00 51.00 45.00
Platter, oval, length 12"
☐ pink 11.00 15.00 12.00
☐ green 13.00 16.50 14.00
Salt and Pepper Shakers
☐ pink 95.00 105.00 97.00
☐ green 104.00 114.00 105.50
Saucer
☐ pink 2.50 4.50 3.00
☐ green 2.50 4.50 3.00
☐ milk glass 2.00 4.00 2.50
Sherbet Bowl
☐ pink 4.00 6.50 4.50
☐ green 8.00 12.00 9.00
Soup Bowl, diameter 4½"
☐ pink 27.00 31.00 27.50
☐ green 32.00 37.00 33.50
Soup Bowl, shallow, diameter 7"
☐ pink 22.00 27.00 23.00
☐ green 32.00 37.00 33.00
Sugar Bowl, diameter 5"
☐ pink 8.50 11.50 9.00
☐ green 9.50 12.50 10.00
Tumbler, 10 oz.,
☐ pink 12.00 15.00 13.00
☐ green 15.00 19.00 16.50
Tumbler, footed, 10 oz. height 5¼"
☐ pink 12.00 17.00 13.50
☐ green 18.00 22.00 19.00
Tumbler, 15 oz.
☐ pink 25.00 30.00 26.00
☐ green 53.00 63.00 55.00
Tumbler, footed, 3 oz., height 3¼"
☐ pink 8.50 11.50 9.25
☐ green 13.00 17.00 14.00

	Current Price Range		Prior Year Average
Tumbler, footed, 5 oz., height 4"			
☐ pink	11.00	14.50	12.00
☐ green	16.00	22.00	17.00
Vegetable Bowl, oval, length 10"			
☐ pink	12.00	15.00	13.00
☐ green	16.50	20.50	17.50
Water Glass, 9 oz., height 4"			
☐ pink	7.00	10.50	8.00
☐ green	13.00	17.00	14.00

COLONIAL FLUTED, ROPE
Federal

This line was generally issued in green, but is also occasionally found in crystal. It is typified by a fluted panel design with a roping effect along the edge. Plates are round and bowls are slightly flared at the mouth. There is a modified ball finial on the domed sugar cover.

	Current Price Range		Prior Year Average
Berry Bowl, diameter 4"			
☐ green	3.00	5.00	3.50
Berry Bowl, diameter 7½"			
☐ green	7.50	10.50	8.25
Cereal Bowl, diameter 6"			
☐ green	4.00	6.00	4.50
Creamer			
☐ green	3.50	5.50	4.00
Cup			
☐ green	2.50	4.50	3.00
Luncheon Plate, diameter 8"			
☐ green	2.00	4.00	2.50
Salad Bowl, deep diameter 6½"			
☐ green	7.50	10.50	8.25
Saucer			
☐ green	.75	2.50	1.00
Sherbet Bowl			
☐ green	3.50	5.50	4.00

Colonial Fluted, Rope

	Current Price Range		Prior Year Average
Sherbet Plate, diameter 6″			
☐ green	.75	2.50	1.00
Sugar Bowl			
☐ green	2.50	4.50	3.00

COLUMBIA
Federal

One can easily understand why collectors refer to this pattern as Oyster and Pearl, as it is composed of alternating rays of recessed "pearls" that radiate from a central pearled ring. This ring encircles a rayed circle within a circle of pearls, with a single pearl in the center. The sides of some of the plates and bowls are somewhat squared, relieved by an undulating corner line. The tops of the butter dishes are often decorated with flashed-on colors, such as blue, red, purple, and green. The pattern itself was issued in crystal and pink.

	Current Price Range		Prior Year Average
Bowl, ruffled rim, diameter 10½″			
☐ crystal	11.00	14.00	11.75
Bread and Butter Plate, diameter 6″			
☐ crystal	.75	2.50	1.00
☐ pink	2.50	4.50	3.00
Butter Dish, lid			
☐ crystal	12.00	16.00	13.00
Cereal Bowl, diameter 5″			
☐ crystal	6.00	9.00	7.00
Cup			
☐ crystal	2.50	4.50	3.00
☐ pink	6.00	9.00	7.00
Luncheon Plate, diameter 9½″			
☐ crystal	2.50	4.50	3.00
☐ pink	11.00	14.50	12.00

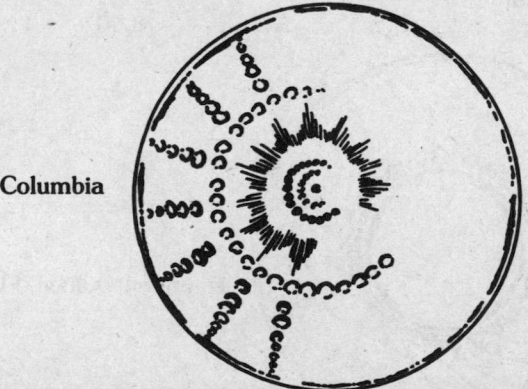

Columbia

	Current Price Range		Prior Year Average
Plate, diameter 11¾"			
☐ crystal	4.00	6.50	4.75
Salad Bowl, diameter 8½"			
☐ crystal	7.00	10.00	8.00
Saucer			
☐ crystal	.50	1.75	.75
☐ pink	4.00	7.00	5.00
Soup Bowl, shallow, diameter 8"			
☐ crystal	7.00	10.50	8.00

DIAMOND QUILTED, FLAT DIAMOND
Imperial

This overall diamond motif is the flattest of all the other quilted diamond patterns. The centers of bowls and plates are plain. The edges of some items are smooth, crimped, or rolled. Candlesticks may be either round and flat, or large and ripple edged. The blue and black pieces generally have the quilting effect on the inside of the dish; the black plate has a smooth exterior with the pattern underneath. This pattern also appears in pink, green, and crystal.

Bowl, handle, diameter 5¾"			
☐ green	4.50	6.50	5.00
☐ pink	4.50	6.50	5.00
☐ blue	7.00	10.00	8.00
☐ black	7.00	10.00	8.00
Bowl, diameter 7¼"			
☐ green	4.50	6.50	5.00
☐ pink	4.50	6.50	5.00
Cake Salver, height 10"			
☐ green	24.00	30.00	25.00
Candlesticks			
☐ green	8.00	11.50	9.00

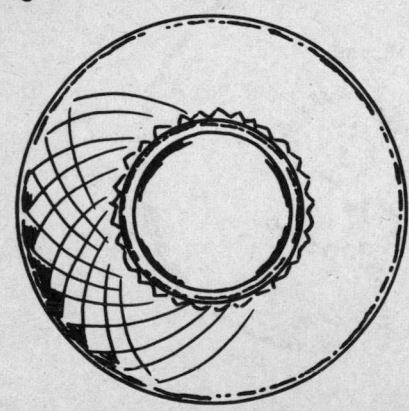

Diamond Quilted, Flat Diamond

	Current Price Range		Prior Year Average
☐ pink	8.00	11.50	9.00
☐ blue	18.00	24.00	19.00
☐ black	18.00	24.00	19.00
Candy Jar, lidded, footed			
☐ green	15.00	19.00	16.00
☐ pink	15.00	19.00	16.00
Cereal Bowl, diameter 5″			
☐ green	3.50	5.50	4.00
☐ pink	3.50	5.50	4.00
☐ blue	6.00	9.00	7.00
☐ black	6.00	9.00	7.00
Compote, with lid, diameter 11″			
☐ pink	34.00	44.00	36.00
Console Bowl, rolled edge			
☐ pink	12.00	15.50	13.00
☐ blue	22.00	29.00	23.00
☐ black	22.00	29.00	23.50
Cordial Goblet			
☐ green	4.00	7.00	5.00
☐ pink	4.00	7.00	5.00
Creamer			
☐ green	4.50	7.50	5.25
☐ pink	4.50	7.50	5.25
☐ blue	8.00	11.50	9.00
☐ black	8.00	11.50	9.00
Cup			
☐ green	3.00	5.00	3.50
☐ pink	3.00	5.00	3.50
☐ blue	4.50	7.50	5.25
☐ black	4.50	7.50	5.25
Ice Bucket, with tongs			
☐ green	33.00	41.00	35.00
☐ pink	33.00	41.00	35.00
☐ blue	52.00	58.00	53.00
☐ black	52.00	58.00	53.50
Lunch Plate, diameter 8″			
☐ green	3.00	5.00	3.50
☐ pink	3.00	5.00	3.50
Iced Tea Glass, 12 oz.			
☐ green	6.00	9.00	7.00
☐ pink	6.00	9.00	7.00
Mayonnaise Set, three piece			
☐ green	15.00	19.50	16.25
☐ pink	15.00	19.50	16.25
Pitcher, 64 oz.			
☐ green	24.00	31.00	25.50
☐ pink	24.00	31.00	25.50

	Current Price Range		Prior Year Average
Salad Plate, diameter 7"			
☐ green	3.00	5.00	3.50
☐ pink	3.00	5.00	3.50
Sandwich Plate, diameter 14"			
☐ pink	13.00	17.00	14.00
☐ green	13.00	17.00	14.00
Saucer			
☐ green	1.00	3.00	1.50
☐ pink	1.00	3.00	1.50
Sherbet Plate, diameter 6"			
☐ green	1.50	3.50	2.00
☐ pink	1.50	3.50	2.00
Soup Bowl, diameter 4½"			
☐ green	5.00	8.00	6.00
☐ pink	5.00	8.00	6.00
Sugar Bowl			
☐ green	4.50	7.50	5.25
☐ pink	4.50	7.50	5.25
Tumbler, footed, 6 oz.			
☐ green	4.50	7.50	5.25
☐ pink	5.00	7.50	5.25
Water Tumbler, footed, 9 oz.			
☐ green	5.00	8.00	5.75
☐ pink	4.00	8.00	5.75
Whiskey Glass, jigger			
☐ green	5.00	8.00	5.75
☐ pink	5.00	8.00	5.75
Wine Glass, 2 oz.			
☐ green	4.50	6.50	5.00
☐ pink	4.50	6.50	5.00

CORONATION
Hocking

This pattern was manufactured in crystal and pink in 1936; in Royal Ruby in 1940. It was originally thought to be called "Saxon," but most catalogues list it as "Coronation." Although not produced in large numbers, it is not difficult to find. The bowls are the most available pieces.

Cup			
☐ crystal	2.25	3.50	2.90
☐ pink	2.25	3.50	2.90
☐ royal ruby	3.50	4.60	4.10
Fruit Bowl, 4¼"			
☐ crystal	2.00	3.00	2.40
☐ pink	2.00	3.00	2.40
☐ royal ruby	3.00	4.00	3.40
Luncheon Plate, 8½"			
☐ crystal	2.25	3.75	2.70

	Current Price Range		Prior Year Average
☐ pink	2.25	3.75	2.70
☐ royal ruby	4.35	5.50	4.90
Nappy, 6½"			
☐ crystal	3.00	4.00	3.50
☐ pink	3.00	4.00	3.50
☐ royal ruby	4.00	8.00	6.00
Nappy, 8"			
☐ crystal	6.00	8.00	6.75
☐ pink	6.00	8.00	6.75
☐ royal ruby	8.00	10.00	9.00
Sherbet Plate, 6"			
☐ crystal	1.00	2.60	1.90
☐ pink	1.00	2.60	1.90
Sherbet, footed, 5¾ oz.			
☐ crystal	2.00	4.60	3.00
☐ pink	2.00	4.60	3.00
☐ royal ruby	4.60	5.75	5.10
Tumbler, 10 oz., footed, 5"			
☐ crystal	6.25	8.00	6.75
☐ pink	6.50	8.50	7.10

DAISY
Indiana

This pattern has been manufactured several times. First in crystal in 1933; second in amber in 1940; third in milk white and olive green in the 1980's. It originally was unnamed, but collectors coined the term "Daisy." Amber is not too easy to find, but crystal is available. Prices for milk white are the same as olive green.

Berry Bowl, 4½"			
☐ crystal	2.25	3.25	2.60
☐ amber	3.50	4.50	3.90
☐ olive green	2.00	3.00	2.50
Berry Bowl, deep, 9⅜"			
☐ crystal	5.50	6.50	6.00
☐ amber	16.00	19.00	17.25
☐ olive green	4.75	5.75	5.10
Cake Plate, 11½"			
☐ crystal	5.00	7.00	6.00
☐ amber	7.00	8.50	7.50
☐ olive green	4.50	5.50	5.00
Cereal Bowl, 6"			
☐ crystal	4.75	6.25	5.35
☐ amber	15.00	17.50	16.00
☐ olive green	4.50	5.75	5.10
Creamer			
☐ crystal	2.25	3.25	2.65
☐ amber	5.00	6.00	5.50
☐ olive green	1.85	2.85	1.95

	Current Price Range		Prior Year Average
Cream Soup Bowl, 4½"			
☐ crystal	2.65	3.65	3.00
☐ amber	4.25	5.75	5.00
☐ olive green	2.25	3.25	2.65
Cup			
☐ crystal	2.35	3.10	2.80
☐ amber	3.00	3.65	3.45
☐ olive green	2.00	2.60	2.20
Bowl, deep, 7½"			
☐ crystal	4.00	6.00	5.00
☐ amber	13.00	16.00	14.25
☐ olive green	3.50	4.75	4.20
Dinner Plate, 9⅜"			
☐ crystal	2.65	3.65	3.00
☐ amber	4.45	5.45	5.10
☐ olive green	2.35	3.35	2.85
Grill Plate, 10¼"			
☐ crystal	3.50	4.50	4.00
☐ amber	8.50	9.65	9.00
☐ olive green	3.00	4.00	3.50
Luncheon Plate, 8⅜"			
☐ crystal	1.75	2.75	2.25
☐ amber	3.10	4.10	3.60
☐ olive green	1.25	2.25	1.75
Oval Vegetable Bowl, 10"			
☐ crystal	4.75	5.75	5.25
☐ amber	8.00	10.00	9.00
☐ olive green	4.35	5.35	4.80
Salad Plate, 7⅜"			
☐ crystal	1.75	2.75	2.25
☐ amber	3.10	4.10	3.60
☐ olive green	1.25	2.25	1.75
Saucer			
☐ crystal	1.25	2.00	1.55
☐ amber	1.75	2.35	2.00
☐ olive green	1.00	1.60	1.30
Sherbet			
☐ crystal	2.75	3.50	3.00
☐ amber	3.75	5.00	4.45
☐ olive green	2.30	3.10	2.80
Sherbet Plate, 6"			
☐ crystal	1.35	2.00	1.50
☐ amber	1.50	2.20	1.65
☐ olive green	1.00	1.50	1.20
Sugar			
☐ crystal	2.00	3.00	2.60
☐ amber	3.50	4.25	3.85
☐ olive green	1.65	2.35	2.00

	Current Price Range		Prior Year Average

Tumbler, footed, 12 oz.
☐ crystal	7.00	9.00	8.00
☐ amber	17.00	22.00	18.50
☐ olive green	6.25	8.50	7.50

Tumbler, footed, 9 oz.
☐ crystal	5.50	6.50	6.00
☐ amber	13.50	15.75	14.75
☐ olive green	5.00	6.00	5.50

DIANA
Federal

One discovers a variety of swirling patterns in Depression glass; however, this particular pattern not only features outside ribs (swirling and sharp) but center or base ribbing, too. It was issued in pink, amber, and crystal.

Ashtray, diameter 3½"
☐ pink	2.00	4.00	2.50
☐ crystal	1.00	3.00	1.50

Bowl, diameter 11"
☐ amber	6.50	9.50	7.25

Bowl, scalloped rim, diameter 12"
☐ pink	6.00	9.00	7.00
☐ crystal	3.50	5.50	4.00
☐ amber	7.00	10.50	8.00

Bread and Butter, diameter 6"
☐ pink	.75	2.25	1.00
☐ crystal	.50	2.00	.75
☐ amber	.75	2.25	1.00

Candy Jar, circular, with lid
☐ pink	18.00	22.00	19.00
☐ crystal	10.50	13.50	11.25
☐ amber	20.00	25.00	21.50

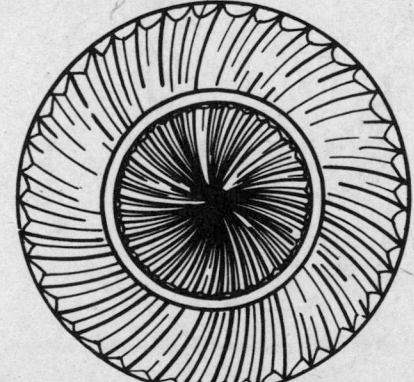

Diana

	Current Price Range		Prior Year Average
Cereal Bowl, diameter 5″			
☐ pink	2.50	4.50	3.00
☐ crystal	1.50	3.50	2.00
Coaster, diameter 3½″			
☐ pink	2.50	4.50	3.00
☐ crystal	1.00	3.00	1.50
Cup			
☐ pink	2.50	4.50	3.00
☐ crystal	1.50	3.50	2.00
☐ amber	2.50	4.50	3.00
Dinner Plate, diameter 9″			
☐ pink	4.00	4.50	3.00
☐ crystal	3.00	5.00	3.50
☐ amber	5.00	8.00	5.75
Plate, diameter 5″			
☐ pink	2.50	4.50	3.00
☐ crystal	1.00	3.00	1.50

DOGWOOD
Macbeth-Evans

In the early 1930's this pattern was promoted as Wild Rose and Wild-rose Design. Plates, bowls, etc., carry an overall flower and leaf motif in etched effect, the flower consisting of only four petals, with a half round bite out of each petal. The glass is thin and appears in pink, green, crystal, monax, cremax, and yellow.

Berry Bowl, diameter 8½″			
☐ pink	29.00	34.00	30.50
☐ green	65.00	75.00	67.50

Dogwood

	Current Price Range		Prior Year Average
Bread and Butter Plate, diameter 6″			
☐ pink	3.00	5.00	3.50
☐ green	4.00	6.00	4.50
Cake Plate, diameter 11″			
☐ pink	147.00	157.00	150.00
Cake Plate, diameter 13″			
☐ pink	57.00	67.00	59.50
☐ green	47.00	57.00	49.50
Cereal Bowl, diameter 5″			
☐ pink	12.00	16.00	13.00
☐ green	15.00	19.00	16.00
Creamer, diameter 2½″			
☐ pink	9.50	12.50	10.00
☐ green	31.00	39.00	33.00
Cup			
☐ pink	7.50	10.50	8.25
☐ green	13.00	17.00	14.00
Dinner Plate, diameter 9¼″			
☐ pink	15.50	19.50	16.25
Lunch Plate, diameter 8″			
☐ pink	3.00	5.00	3.50
☐ green	4.00	6.00	4.50
Pitcher, decorated, height 8″			
☐ pink	123.00	133.00	126.00
☐ green	430.00	465.00	440.00
Platter, oval, diameter 12″			
☐ pink	235.00	260.00	240.00
Salver Plate, diameter 12″			
☐ pink	16.50	20.50	17.50
Saucer			
☐ pink	3.00	5.00	3.50
☐ green	4.00	6.00	4.50

DORIC
Jeannette

Issued in pink, green, delphite, and yellow, this pattern has wide paneled sides with a band of alternating plain and snowflake decorated squares that encircles the top section of a piece, stopping short of the rim which is slightly flared on bowls and other items. The base of plates is characterized by pie-cut paneling with a central diamond shaped snowflake design, and with the alternating plain and decorated square pattern on the rim.

	Current Price Range		Prior Year Average
Berry Bowl, diameter 4⅞″			
☐ pink	4.00	6.00	4.50
☐ green	4.50	7.00	5.00
☐ delphite	22.00	30.00	24.00
Berry Bowl, diameter 8¼″			
☐ pink	8.00	11.00	9.00

Doric

	Current Price Range		Prior Year Average
☐ green	10.00	14.00	11.50
☐ delphite	73.00	83.00	75.00
Bowl, twin handled, diameter 9″			
☐ pink	8.00	11.50	9.00
☐ green	8.00	11.50	9.00
Butter Dish, with lid			
☐ pink	52.00	58.00	53.50
☐ green	63.00	73.00	65.00
Cake Plate, tri-legged, diameter 10″			
☐ pink	10.50	13.50	11.25
☐ green	10.00	13.00	10.75
Candy Dish, with lid, diameter 8″			
☐ pink	22.00	28.00	23.50
☐ green	22.00	28.00	23.50
Coaster, diameter 3″			
☐ pink	8.00	11.00	8.75
☐ green	9.50	12.50	10.25
Creamer, diameter 4″			
☐ pink	6.00	9.00	7.00
☐ green	7.00	10.00	8.00
Cup			
☐ pink	4.00	7.00	5.00
☐ green	5.00	8.00	6.00
Dinner Plate, diameter 9″			
☐ pink	6.00	9.00	7.00
☐ green	8.00	11.00	9.00
Grill Plate, diameter 9″			
☐ pink	6.00	9.00	7.00

	Current Price Range		Prior Year Average
☐ green	8.50	11.50	9.00
Pitcher, collar base, 36 oz., height 6″			
☐ pink	22.00	28.00	23.50
☐ green	24.00	33.00	26.00
☐ delphite	368.00	385.00	373.00
Platter, oval, length 11″			
☐ pink	9.50	12.50	10.25
☐ green	10.50	13.50	11.25
Relish Tray			
☐ pink	4.00	6.00	4.50
☐ green	6.00	9.00	7.00
Salt and Pepper Shakers			
☐ pink	21.00	27.00	22.50
☐ green	24.00	31.00	25.50
Salad Plate, diameter 7″			
☐ pink	11.00	14.00	12.00
☐ green	10.00	13.00	11.00
Saucer			
☐ pink	1.00	3.00	1.50
☐ green	1.50	3.50	2.00
Serving Tray, length 8″			
☐ pink	6.00	9.00	7.00
☐ green	6.00	9.00	7.00
Sherbet, footed			
☐ pink	6.00	9.00	7.00
☐ green	7.00	10.00	8.00
Sherbet Plate, diameter 6″			
☐ pink	1.50	3.50	2.00
☐ green	2.00	4.00	2.50
Soup Bowl, diameter 5″			
☐ green	122.00	132.00	124.00
Sugar Bowl			
☐ pink	7.00	10.00	8.00
☐ green	8.00	11.00	9.00
Tray, handled, length 10″			
☐ pink	6.00	9.00	7.00
☐ green	8.00	11.00	9.00
Tumbler, height 5″			
☐ pink	32.00	38.00	32.50
☐ green	34.00	41.00	36.00
Vegetable Bowl, oval, diameter 9″			
☐ pink	9.00	13.00	10.00
☐ green	10.50	14.50	11.50

Doric and Pansy

DORIC AND PANSY
Jeannette

The difference between this pattern and Doric, which is made of the same mold, is that in the alternating open squares a pansy is featured in full bloom. It was cast in pink, crystal, and green ultramarine.

	Current Price Range		Prior Year Average
Berry Bowl, diameter 4½"			
☐ ultramarine	8.00	11.00	9.00
☐ crystal	5.00	7.00	5.50
☐ pink	5.00	7.00	5.50
Berry Bowl, diameter 8"			
☐ ultramarine	54.00	64.00	55.50
☐ crystal	15.00	19.00	16.50
☐ pink	15.00	19.00	16.50
Bowl, handled, diameter 9"			
☐ ultramarine	22.00	28.00	24.00
☐ crystal	8.00	11.00	9.00
☐ pink	8.00	11.00	9.00
Butter Dish, lidded			
☐ ultramarine	520.00	600.00	540.00
Creamer			
☐ ultramarine	150.00	185.00	158.00
☐ pink	52.00	62.00	55.00
☐ crystal	52.00	62.00	55.00
Cup			
☐ ultramarine	13.00	17.00	14.00
☐ pink	6.00	9.00	7.00
☐ crystal	6.00	9.00	7.00
Dinner Plate, diameter 9"			
☐ ultramarine	17.00	21.00	18.00
☐ pink	3.50	6.50	4.25
☐ crystal	3.50	6.50	4.25
Salad Plate, diameter 7"			
☐ ultramarine	23.00	33.00	25.00

	Current Price Range		Prior Year Average
Salt and Pepper			
☐ ultramarine	385.00	415.00	393.00

FLORAL
Jeannette

This pattern was produced from 1930 through 1935. It was made in emerald green, pink, topaz, and crystal. The topaz was only experimental so very few of those items can be found in the market. Crystal is the most common. The Jeannette Co. used the Adam molds for the candlesticks.

Berry Bowl, individual, 4⅛″			
☐ crystal	3.00	3.75	3.50
☐ pink	3.00	3.75	3.50
☐ emerald green	3.25	3.90	3.60
Candlesticks, ea., 4″			
☐ crystal	10.00	12.00	11.00
☐ pink	10.00	12.00	11.00
☐ emerald green	11.00	12.50	11.50
Candy Jar, with cover			
☐ crystal	10.00	13.00	12.00
☐ pink	10.00	13.00	12.00
☐ emerald green	10.50	13.50	12.50
Creamer			
☐ crystal	3.75	5.25	4.75
☐ pink	3.75	5.25	4.75
☐ emerald green	4.00	5.50	5.00
Cup			
☐ crystal	2.50	3.25	2.90
☐ pink	2.50	3.25	2.90
☐ emerald green	2.65	3.40	3.00
Dinner Plate, 8⅞″			
☐ crystal	3.00	3.90	3.60
☐ pink	3.00	3.90	3.60
☐ emerald green	3.25	4.10	3.75
Pitcher, 32 oz. water, footed, 8″			
☐ crystal	18.00	22.00	20.00
☐ pink	18.00	22.00	20.00
☐ emerald green	19.00	23.00	21.00
Pitcher, lemonade, footed, 10¼″			
☐ crystal	30.00	40.00	36.00
☐ pink	30.00	40.00	36.00
☐ emerald green	32.00	42.00	37.00
Platter, oval, 10¾″			
☐ crystal	6.00	8.00	7.25
☐ pink	6.00	8.00	7.25
☐ emerald green	7.00	9.00	8.00
Relish Dish, oval, two handles, 5″			
☐ crystal	5.00	6.00	5.00

	Current Price Range		Prior Year Average
☐ pink	5.00	6.00	5.00
☐ emerald green	5.50	6.50	6.50
Salad Bowl, 7½"			
☐ crystal	6.00	9.00	7.25
☐ pink	6.00	9.00	7.25
☐ emerald green	6.50	9.25	7.60
Salt and Pepper, footed, pair, 4"			
☐ crystal	10.00	14.00	11.00
☐ pink	10.00	14.00	11.00
☐ emerald green	11.00	15.00	12.00
Saucer			
☐ crystal	1.00	2.00	1.50
☐ pink	1.00	2.00	1.50
☐ emerald green	1.15	2.15	1.60
Sherbet, 5 oz., 3"			
☐ crystal	2.00	3.25	2.65
☐ pink	2.00	3.25	2.65
☐ emerald green	2.25	3.50	2.85
Sherbet Plate, 6"			
☐ crystal	1.60	2.75	2.40
☐ pink	1.60	2.75	2.40
☐ emerald green	1.75	2.85	2.50
Spice Shakers, pair, 6"			
☐ crystal	15.00	20.00	18.00
☐ pink	15.00	20.00	18.00
☐ emerald green	17.00	21.00	18.75
Tumbler, 9 oz., footed, 5¼"			
☐ crystal	5.00	6.75	5.75
☐ pink	5.00	6.75	5.75
☐ emerald green	5.25	7.00	6.00
Tumbler, 7 oz., footed, 4¾"			
☐ crystal	4.50	5.50	5.00
☐ pink	4.50	5.50	5.00
☐ emerald green	4.75	5.75	5.25
Tumbler, 5 oz., juice, footed, 4"			
☐ crystal	3.75	4.75	4.30
☐ pink	3.75	4.75	4.30
☐ emerald green	3.90	4.90	4.40

HARP
Jeannette

The main feature of this pattern is harps, combined with stippling and scrolls. Most of the pieces are decorated with a gold rim. It was generally issued in crystal with a gray cast to the glass, and in ice blue crystal.

Ashtray			
☐ crystal	3.00	5.00	3.50
Cake Tray, diameter 8½"			
☐ crystal	10.00	12.00	11.00

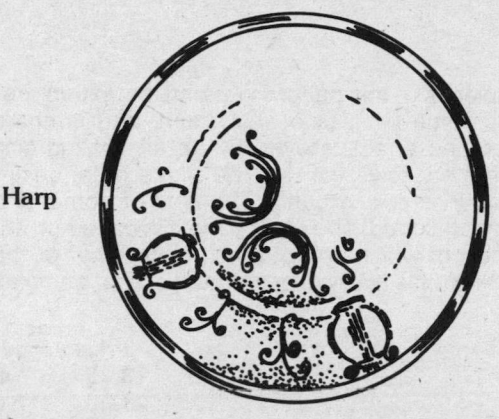

Harp

	Current Price Range		Prior Year Average
Coaster, diameter 3½"			
☐ crystal	2.00	3.00	2.50
Cup			
☐ crystal	2.00	3.00	2.50
Plate, diameter 7"			
☐ crystal	2.00	3.00	2.50
Saucer			
☐ crystal	1.00	4.00	1.25
Vase, height 6"			
☐ crystal	6.00	8.00	6.50

Heritage

HERITAGE
Federal

Occasional pieces of this pattern were made up into the 1960's. It was cast in crystal, some pink, blue and green, and is characterized by a pearled background effect relieved by an alternating single and three-petal design that encircles the rim, the single petal being topped by an extended, two-part scrolling band. The rims of some of the plates and bowls are softly scalloped. The central motif is based on an eight-petaled, flower, the petals of which do not touch each other or the flower's eye. A plain border encircles this, with a serrated border completing the central frame.

	Current Price Range		Prior Year Average
Berry Bowl, diameter 5″			
☐ crystal	3.75	4.75	4.25
☐ blue	28.00	31.00	29.50
☐ green	28.00	31.00	29.50
☐ pink	14.25	15.25	14.75
Berry Bowl, diameter 8″			
☐ crystal	11.75	12.75	12.25
☐ blue	56.00	58.00	57.00
☐ green	56.00	58.00	57.00
☐ pink	38.00	41.00	39.50
Creamer, pedestal foot			
☐ crystal	10.75	11.75	11.25
Cup			
☐ crystal	2.75	3.75	3.25
Dinner Plate, diameter 9″			
☐ crystal	5.75	6.75	6.25
Fruit Bowl			
☐ crystal	11.75	12.75	12.25
Lunch Plate, diameter 8″			
☐ crystal	4.25	5.25	4.75
Sandwich Plate, diameter 12″			
☐ crystal	7.75	8.75	8.25
Saucer			
☐ crystal	.75	1.50	1.00
Sugar Bowl			
☐ crystal	8.25	10.25	9.25

HEXAGON OPTIC
Jeannette

Also referred to as "Elongated Honeycomb," this line is characterized by an overall honeycomb pattern consisting of rows of hexagons. The plates, for example, are made up of three rows of hexagons with a plain center. The utility pitcher features a sunflower embossed bottom, a typical Jeannette trademark. The handles on all but the footed pitcher are characteristically closed. This is a heavy pressed glass and was cast in green and pink, the pink of which often has a salamander orange hue.

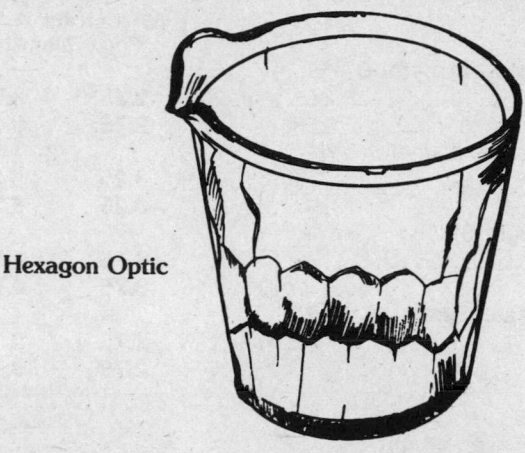

Hexagon Optic

	Current Price Range		Prior Year Average
Berry Bowl, rippled rim			
☐ pink	1.75	2.75	2.25
☐ green	1.75	2.75	2.25
Butter Dish, rectangular, lidded			
☐ pink	33.00	36.00	34.50
Creamer			
☐ pink	3.25	4.25	3.75
☐ green	3.25	4.25	3.75
Cup			
☐ pink	1.75	3.00	2.50
☐ green	1.75	3.00	2.00
Ice Bucket, chrome fittings			
☐ pink	9.00	15.00	10.00
☐ green	9.00	15.00	10.00
Lunch Plate, diameter 9″			
☐ pink	3.25	5.25	4.25
☐ green	3.25	5.25	4.25
Mixing Bowl, diameter 8¾″			
☐ pink	13.25	14.25	13.75
Pitcher, footed, 48 oz., diameter 9″			
☐ pink	26.00	28.00	27.00
☐ green	26.00	28.00	27.00
Platter, diameter 11″			
☐ pink	5.00	4.25	5.25
☐ green	5.00	4.25	5.25
Refrigerator Set			
☐ pink	28.00	31.00	29.00
☐ green	28.00	31.00	29.00
Salt and Pepper			
☐ green	16.00	18.00	17.00

	Current Price Range		Prior Year Average
Sherbert Plate, diameter 6″			
☐ pink	2.75	3.75	3.25
☐ green	2.75	3.75	3.25
Tumbler, footed, diameter 5¾″			
☐ pink	3.25	5.25	4.25
☐ green	3.25	5.25	4.25
Tumbler, height 5″			
☐ pink	3.75	4.75	4.25
☐ green	3.75	4.75	4.25
Whiskey Glass, jigger, height 2″			
☐ pink	2.75	3.75	3.25
☐ green	2.75	3.75	3.25

HOBNAIL
Hocking

Rows of hobnails encircle a piece in this pattern that was cast in both crystal and pink. On the pitchers, goblets, cups and some other items, the design terminates in a narrow ribbed border followed by a plain rim. Sometimes this pattern can also be found with fired-on red trim around rims and the base of footed items. In the center and on the base of footed pieces, there is a many-rayed star in relief, the rays of which are rounded at the tip, like flower petals.

	Current Price Range		Prior Year Average
Cereal Bowl, diameter 5½″			
☐ crystal	1.75	2.75	2.25
Cordial Glass, height 3½″			
☐ crystal	3.25	4.25	3.75

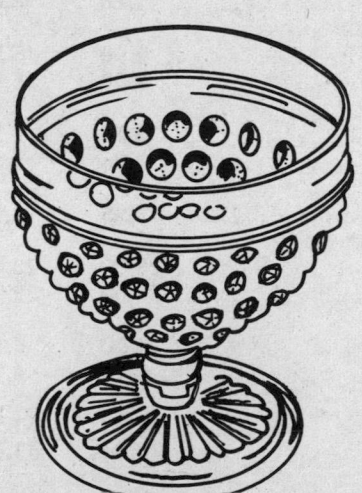

Hobnail

	Current Price Range		Prior Year Average
Creamer, pedestal foot			
☐ crystal	1.75	2.75	2.25
Cup, collar base			
☐ pink	1.75	2.75	2.25
☐ crystal	1.75	2.75	2.25
Decanter, with stopper, bulbous			
☐ crystal	10.00	13.00	12.00
Iced Tea Glass, collar base, height 8″			
☐ crystal	4.25	5.25	4.75
Iced Tea Glass, pedestal foot, 13 oz.			
☐ crystal	4.25	5.25	4.75
Juice Glass, height 3½″			
☐ crystal	2.25	3.25	2.75
Lunch Plate, diameter 8″			
☐ crystal	1.25	2.25	1.75
Milk Pitcher, 18 oz.			
☐ crystal	11.75	12.75	12.25
Salad Bowl, diameter 7″			
☐ crystal	1.25	2.25	1.75
Saucer, diameter 6″			
☐ pink	1.00	2.50	1.50
☐ crystal	.50	1.25	.75
Sherbet Plate, diameter 6″			
☐ pink	.50	1.25	.75
☐ crystal	.75	1.50	1.25
Sugar Bowl, pedestal base			
☐ pink	1.75	2.75	2.25
☐ crystal	1.75	2.75	2.25
Water Goblet, stemmed, 10 oz.			
☐ crystal	3.75	4.75	4.25
Water Tumbler, collar base			
☐ crystal	3.75	4.75	4.25
Whiskey Glass, jigger, 1½ oz.			
☐ crystal	3.25	4.25	3.75
Wine Glass, pedestal and stem			
☐ crystal	4.25	5.25	4.75

HOBNAIL AND PANEL
Imperial

This pattern was manufactured from 1931 through 1935. The colors were crystal, green, and pink. Crystal is by far the most common; the green and pink are not impossible to find, but they are scarce.

Cake Plate			
☐ crystal	4.25	5.00	4.90
☐ green	7.00	8.25	7.60
☐ pink	7.00	8.25	7.60
Creamer, footed			
☐ crystal	2.00	3.00	2.60

	Current Price Range		Prior Year Average
☐ green	4.00	5.00	4.60
☐ pink	4.00	5.00	4.60
Cup, 7 oz.			
☐ crystal	1.35	1.90	1.50
☐ green	2.00	3.00	2.55
☐ pink	2.00	3.00	2.55
Salad Plate, 8″			
☐ crystal	1.50	2.25	2.00
☐ green	2.00	2.70	2.45
☐ pink	2.00	2.70	2.45
Saucer, 5½″			
☐ crystal	1.35	2.00	1.65
☐ green	1.60	2.10	1.75
☐ pink	1.60	2.10	1.75
Stemware, cocktail, 3 oz.			
☐ crystal	1.75	2.75	2.30
☐ green	3.50	4.40	4.10
☐ pink	3.50	4.40	4.10
Stemware, goblet, 9 oz.			
☐ crystal	2.40	3.10	2.80
☐ green	5.00	6.00	5.40
☐ pink	5.00	6.00	5.40
Stemware, sherbet, high stem, 5 oz.			
☐ crystal	1.90	2.90	2.55
☐ green	4.00	5.00	4.60
☐ pink	4.00	5.00	4.60
Stemware, sherbet, footed, 5 oz.			
☐ crystal	1.00	1.75	1.55
☐ green	2.00	3.00	2.50
☐ pink	2.00	3.00	2.50
Tumbler, iced tea, 12 oz.			
☐ crystal	1.65	2.65	2.20
☐ green	4.20	5.00	4.60
☐ pink	4.20	5.00	4.60
Tumbler, 9 oz.			
☐ crystal	2.00	3.00	2.50
☐ green	4.00	5.00	4.50
☐ pink	4.00	5.00	4.50

HOLIDAY
Jeannette

It is easy to understand why this radiant pattern is referred to as "Buttons and Bows," for it consists of consecutive rows of faceted rectangular sections with a recessed "button" center at the top of each shaped section. The rims are either smooth or serrated. The centers of most pieces bear a rayed motif, encircled by a pointed petal border. This pattern was originally cast in pink.

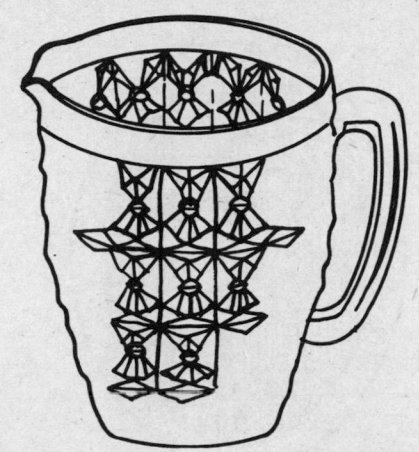

Holiday

	Current Price Range		Prior Year Average
Berry Bowl			
☐ pink	6.25	7.25	6.75
Butter Dish			
☐ pink	32.00	36.00	34.00
Candlesticks, pair			
☐ pink	47.00	51.00	49.00
Creamer			
☐ pink	5.25	6.25	5.75
Cup and Saucer			
☐ pink	7.25	8.25	7.75
Plate, diameter 9″			
☐ pink	8.75	9.75	9.25
Pitcher, diameter 7″			
☐ pink	23.00	26.00	24.50
Sherbet, footed			
☐ pink	2.25	3.25	2.75
Sugar and Creamer			
☐ pink	10.00	13.00	11.50
Tumbler, footed, diameter 4″			
☐ pink	23.00	26.00	24.50

HOMESPUN
Jeannette

This pattern is similar to the Hazel Atlas Fine Rib Beverage Set, although that was cast in cobalt blue and crystal, whereas Homespun was issued in pink and crystal, including a child's tea set. The main difference between the patterns, however, is that this pattern is characterized by a

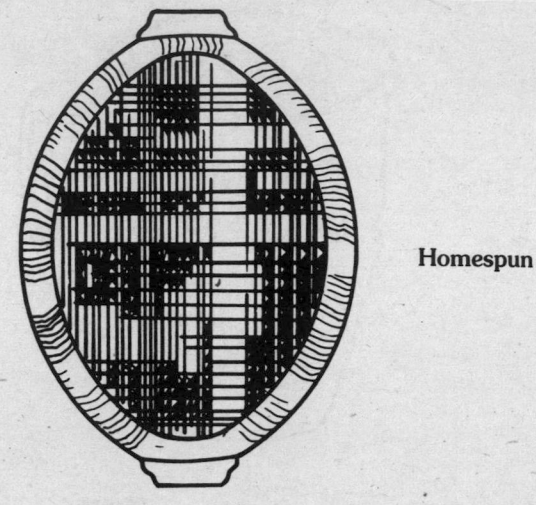

Homespun

waffle quilt motif in the base or center of each item, unlike Fine Rib by other companies. Also, it features both vertical and horizontal lines in its basic design, rather like the weave in homespun cloth.

	Current Price Range		Prior Year Average
Ashtray			
☐ pink	4.25	5.25	4.75
☐ crystal	4.25	5.25	4.75
Bowl, tab handle, diameter 4″			
☐ pink	3.75	4.75	4.25
☐ crystal	3.75	4.75	4.25
Butter Dish, with cover			
☐ pink	37.00	41.00	39.00
☐ crystal	37.00	41.00	39.00
Cereal Bowl, diameter 5″			
☐ pink	6.75	7.75	7.25
☐ crystal	6.75	7.75	7.25
Creamer, footed			
☐ pink	5.75	6.75	6.25
☐ crystal	5.75	6.75	6.25
Cup			
☐ pink	3.25	4.25	3.75
☐ crystal	3.25	4.25	3.75
Plate, diameter 6″			
☐ pink	1.25	2.25	1.75
Tumbler, footed, 4″			
☐ pink	6.75	7.75	7.25

INDIANA CUSTARD
Indiana

This lovely and delicate pattern is found in ivory or custard only, although in the 1950's a version appeared in white. It is called "Flower and Leaf Band" after the decorative motif that encircles the squarely scalloped rim of plates and bowls, or the mid-section of other items. To actually qualify as custard glass, a piece contains a certain amount of uranium which will cause it to fluoresce under blacklight, and it must also produce a ring when struck, rather than a dull thud.

	Current Price Range		Prior Year Average
Berry Bowl, diameter 4⅞"			
☐ ivory	4.00	6.00	5.00
Berry Bowl, diameter 8¾"			
☐ ivory	17.00	21.00	19.00
Bread and Butter Plate, diameter 5¾"			
☐ ivory	3.00	5.00	4.00
Butter Dish, with lid			
☐ ivory	50.00	53.00	51.50
Cereal Bowl, diameter 5¾"			
☐ ivory	11.25	13.25	12.25
Creamer			
☐ ivory	11.25	13.25	12.25
Cup			
☐ ivory	27.50	31.50	29.50
Dinner Plate, diameter 9¾"			
☐ ivory	12.00	14.00	13.00
Luncheon Plate, diameter 8⅞"			
☐ ivory	7.25	9.25	8.25
Platter, oval, length 11½"			
☐ ivory	21.00	23.00	22.00
Salad Bowl, diameter 7½"			
☐ ivory	15.25	17.25	16.25
Saucer			
☐ ivory	5.25	6.25	5.75
Sherbet			
☐ ivory	60.00	70.00	65.00
Soup Bowl, flat, diameter 7½"			
☐ ivory	7.00	9.00	8.00
Sugar Bowl, with lid			
☐ ivory	20.00	23.00	21.50
Vegetable Bowl, diameter 9½"			
☐ ivory	18.00	21.00	19.50

IRIS, IRIS AND HERRINGBONE
Jeannette

This pattern was periodically made through 1970, and features a stippled ray background with a prominent iris floral motif. The footed items will be found with rayed bases, or the iris floral motif. The rim is identifiable by the two-part scallop that alternates with a sloping valley, although some pieces (such as the goblets, pitchers, etc.) have a plain band encir-

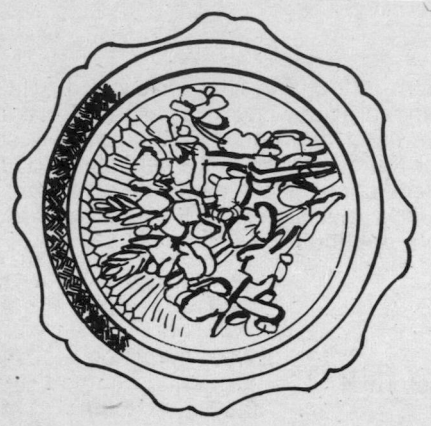

Iris, Iris and Herringbone

cling the rim. It was cast in crystal, iridescent, and some pink, with the milk white and red-yellow and blue-green combinations being of recent origin.

	Current Price Range		Prior Year Average
Berry Bowl, beaded edge, diameter 4½"			
☐ crystal	27.00	31.00	29.00
☐ iridescent	5.00	7.00	6.00
Berry Bowl, diameter 8"			
☐ crystal	8.00	10.00	9.00
☐ iridescent	7.00	9.00	8.00
Bowl, ruffled rim, 5"			
☐ crystal	4.00	6.00	5.00
☐ iridescent	4.25	5.25	4.75
Butter Dish, with cover			
☐ crystal	27.00	31.00	29.00
☐ iridescent	30.00	33.00	31.50
Candlesticks, pair			
☐ crystal	16.00	18.00	17.50
☐ iridescent	20.00	24.00	22.00
Candy Jar, with cover			
☐ crystal	60.00	70.00	65.00
Cereal Bowl, diameter 5"			
☐ crystal	20.00	30.00	25.00
Coaster			
☐ crystal	30.00	33.00	31.50
Creamer, footed			
☐ crystal	6.25	7.25	6.75
☐ iridescent	6.75	8.75	7.75
Cup			
☐ crystal	7.00	9.00	8.00
☐ iridescent	6.75	8.75	7.75

	Current Price Range		Prior Year Average
Demitasse Cup, with saucer			
☐ crystal	13.50	15.50	14.50
☐ iridescent	47.00	52.00	49.50
Dinner Plate, diameter 9″			
☐ crystal	27.00	31.00	29.00
☐ iridescent	16.25	18.25	17.25
Fruit Bowl, diameter 11″			
☐ crystal	28.00	31.00	29.50
Fruit Bowl, ruffled rim, diameter 11″			
☐ crystal	7.00	9.00	8.00
☐ iridescent	5.25	6.25	5.75
Goblet, 4 oz., height 5¾″			
☐ crystal	13.00	15.00	14.00
Goblet, 8 oz., height 5¾″			
☐ crystal	13.00	16.00	14.50
Luncheon Plate, diameter 8″			
☐ crystal	30.00	33.00	31.50
Pitcher, footed, height 9½″			
☐ crystal	17.00	21.00	19.00
☐ iridescent	23.00	26.00	24.50
Salad Bowl, diameter 9″			
☐ crystal	7.00	9.00	8.00
☐ iridescent	6.50	8.50	7.50
Sandwich Plate, diameter 11¾″			
☐ crystal	10.00	13.00	11.50
☐ iridescent	9.50	11.50	10.50
Sherbet Bowl, footed, diameter 2½″			
☐ crystal	12.00	14.00	13.00
☐ iridescent	7.00	10.00	8.50
Sherbet Bowl, footed, diameter 4″			
☐ crystal	9.00	12.00	10.50
Sherbet Plate, diameter 5½″			
☐ crystal	9.00	5.25	6.25
☐ iridescent	4.25	5.25	4.75
Soup Bowl, diameter 7½″			
☐ crystal	60.00	70.00	65.00
☐ iridescent	17.00	21.00	19.00
Sugar Bowl, with lid			
☐ crystal	12.00	14.00	13.00
☐ iridescent	10.00	15.00	11.50
Tumbler, flat, height 4″			
☐ crystal	40.00	50.00	45.00
Tumbler, footed, height 6″			
☐ crystal	10.00	12.00	11.00
☐ iridescent	10.00	12.00	11.00
Tumbler, footed, height 7″			
☐ crystal	13.25	14.25	13.75
☐ iridescent	12.00	14.00	13.00

	Current Price Range		Prior Year Average
Vase, height 9″			
☐ crystal	14.25	15.25	14.75
☐ iridescent	13.25	14.25	13.75
Wine Glass, height 4″			
☐ crystal	11.25	13.25	12.25
☐ iridescent	12.25	14.25	13.25
Wine Goblet, height 4½″			
☐ crystal	11.00	13.00	12.00

JUBILEE
Lancaster

Found only in a golden yellow color, this pattern is composed of a single chain of etched flowers and leaves which encircles the rim of a plate or the mid-section of a cup or other vessel. The plates feature a six-point scallop. Centers are plain.

	Current Price Range		Prior Year Average
Cake Tray, open handle, diameter 11″			
☐ yellow	17.00	21.00	19.00
Cheese and Cracker Set			
☐ yellow	27.00	31.00	29.00
Creamer			
☐ yellow	15.00	17.00	16.00
Cup			
☐ yellow	10.00	12.00	11.00
Fruit Bowl, open handle, diameter 8½″			
☐ yellow	30.00	33.00	31.50
Goblet, stem and pedestal, height 6″			
☐ yellow	20.00	23.00	21.50
Goblet, stem and pedestal, height 6¼″			
☐ yellow	23.00	26.00	24.50
Lunch Plate, diameter 8½″			
☐ yellow	7.00	9.00	8.00
Mayonnaise Compote, with ladle			
☐ yellow	55.00	65.00	60.00
Salad Plate, diameter 7¼″			
☐ yellow	5.00	7.00	6.00
Sandwich Plate, diameter 13″			
☐ yellow	17.00	21.00	19.00
Sandwich Tray, center open handle			
☐ yellow	23.00	26.00	24.50
Saucer			
☐ yellow	2.25	3.25	2.75
Sugar Bowl			
☐ yellow	14.50	16.50	15.50

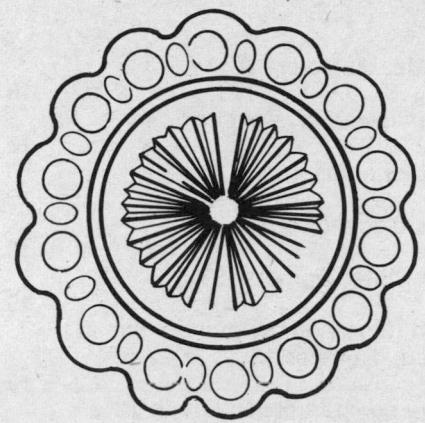

Lace Edge

LACE EDGE
Hocking

This pattern is also called "Open Lace," alluding to the scalloped, open work rim on plates, bowls and other items. The body is either rayed or plain, with a rayed center and, on footed items, a round, rayed base. The pattern can be found in pink, and occasionally crystal. Many other companies made lace edged pieces, so if you have blue, green, yellow, or black pieces with a laced edge, you can be sure it does not belong to this particular pattern.

	Current Price Range		Prior Year Average
Bowl, plain, diameter 9½"			
☐ pink	10.00	13.00	11.50
Bowl, ribbed, diameter 9½"			
☐ pink	10.00	13.00	11.50
Bowl, three-legged, diameter 10½"			
☐ pink	120.00	130.00	125.00
Butter Dish, with cover			
☐ pink	43.00	46.00	44.50
Candlesticks, pair			
☐ pink	110.00	120.00	115.00
Cereal Bowl, diameter 6⅜"			
☐ pink	11.00	13.00	12.00
Comport, diameter 7"			
☐ pink	13.00	16.00	14.50
Comport, with cover, footed			
☐ pink	20.00	30.00	25.00
Cookie Jar, with cover			
☐ pink	32.00	42.00	37.00
Creamer			
☐ pink	13.00	15.00	14.00
Cup			
☐ pink	14.50	16.50	15.50

	Current Price Range		Prior Year Average
Dinner Plate, diameter 10½"			
☐ pink	16.00	18.00	17.00
Flower Vase, with crystal frog			
☐ pink	15.00	17.00	16.00
Fish Bowl, one gallon and 8 oz.			
☐ crystal	13.00	16.00	14.50
Grill Plate, diameter 10½"			
☐ pink	10.00	12.00	11.00
Luncheon Plate, diameter 8¾"			
☐ pink	10.00	13.00	11.50
Plate, with four compartments, rim in closed Lace, diameter 13"			
☐ pink	15.00	18.00	16.50
Platter, five compartments, length 13¾"			
☐ pink	15.00	17.00	16.00
Platter, length 13¾"			
☐ pink	16.00	18.00	17.00
Relish Dish, three compartments, deep, diameter 7½"			
☐ pink	30.00	40.00	35.00
Relish Tray, three compartments, diameter 10½"			
☐ pink	16.00	18.00	17.00
Salad Bowl, diameter 7¾"			
☐ pink	12.00	14.00	13.00
Salad Plate, diameter 7¼"			
☐ pink	11.00	13.00	12.00
Saucer			
☐ pink	6.00	8.00	7.00
Sherbet Bowl, footed			
☐ pink	40.00	50.00	45.00
Sugar Bowl			
☐ pink	13.00	15.00	14.00
Tumbler, flat, height 3½"			
☐ pink	6.00	8.00	7.00

Laced Edge

LACED EDGE

Laced Edge, made by Imperial Glass Company, is also called Katy Blue. It is distinguished by the white opalescent edges on the rims of various pieces. The glass also features a series of tiny triangular designs. The opalescent rims feature an open design. Laced Edge was mostly made in blue, though some green was also made.

	Current Price Range		Prior Year Average
Bread and Butter Plate, 6½"			
☐ blue	6.50	9.50	7.50
Candleholder, double branch			
☐ blue	27.00	33.00	28.00
Creamer			
☐ blue	13.00	17.00	14.00
Cup			
☐ blue	13.00	17.00	14.00
Dinner Plate, 10"			
☐ blue	18.00	22.00	19.00
Fruit Bowl, 4½"			
☐ blue	7.50	10.50	8.25
Salad Plate, 8"			
☐ blue	10.50	13.50	11.50
Saucer			
☐ blue	3.00	5.00	3.50
Soup Bowl, 7"			
☐ blue	13.00	17.00	14.00
Sugar			
☐ blue	13.00	17.00	14.00
Tumbler, 9 oz.			
☐ blue	18.00	22.00	19.00
Tumbler, water, footed			
☐ blue	18.00	22.00	19.00
Vase, 5½"			
☐ blue	20.00	25.00	21.00
Vegetable Bowl, 9"			
☐ blue	27.00	33.00	28.00

LAKE COMO
Hocking

This scenic pattern is white with blue decoration and can be identified by its depiction of a lakeside garden. Guarded steps lead to a platform featuring three Greek columns in perspective; the top pedestal of the stairway is mounted with a large, decorative urn. A sailboat is seen in the distance against a backdrop of rolling hills and clouds. Plate rims are encircled with five consecutive blue bands of white flowers, five to each grouping.

Cereal Bowl, diameter 5¼"			
☐ white	4.00	6.00	4.50
Creamer, pedestal base			
☐ white	7.00	9.00	8.00

	Current Price Range		Prior Year Average

Cup
- [ ] white 6.00   8.00   7.00

Dinner Plate, diameter 9½"
- [ ] white 8.00   10.00   9.00

Platter, diameter 11"
- [ ] white 13.00   16.00   14.50

Salad Plate, diameter 7½"
- [ ] white 4.00   6.00   4.50

Salt and Pepper Shakers
- [ ] white 21.00   23.00   22.00

Saucer
- [ ] white 2.00   4.00   2.50

Sugar Bowl, pedestal foot
- [ ] white 7.00   9.00   8.00

Vegetable Bowl, diameter 9¼"
- [ ] white 11.00   13.00   12.00

LAUREL
McKee

A continuous laurel trim, consisting of a band of berries with stippled leaves, encircles the rim of these items which were cast in French ivory, jade green, white opal, and very rarely, poudre (powder) blue. The child's sets feature fired-on rims of either orange, red, blue, or green. In another motif, a Scottie dog is fired on under the glass. The colored band rim can be found on some of the adult items.

Berry Bowl, diameter 5"
- [ ] ivory 3.25   5.25   4.25
- [ ] white 2.75   3.75   3.25
- [ ] jade 2.75   3.75   3.25
- [ ] blue 5.00   7.00   6.00

Berry Bowl, diameter 9"
- [ ] ivory 11.00   13.00   12.00
- [ ] white 8.00   10.00   9.00
- [ ] jade 8.00   10.00   9.00
- [ ] blue 15.00   18.00   16.50

Bowl, three-legged, diameter 6"
- [ ] ivory 7.00   9.00   7.50
- [ ] white 5.00   7.00   6.00
- [ ] jade 5.00   7.00   6.00

Bowl, three-legged, diameter 10½"
- [ ] ivory 23.00   26.00   24.50
- [ ] white 17.00   21.00   19.00
- [ ] jade 17.00   21.00   19.00
- [ ] blue 30.00   33.00   31.50

Bowl, diameter 11"
- [ ] ivory 24.00   28.00   26.00
- [ ] white 15.00   17.00   16.00

	Current Price Range		Prior Year Average
☐ jade	15.00	17.00	16.00
☐ blue	24.00	28.00	26.00
Candlesticks, pair, height 4″			
☐ ivory	19.00	23.00	21.00
☐ white	15.00	17.00	16.00
☐ jade	15.00	17.00	16.00
☐ blue	19.00	23.00	21.00
Cereal Bowl, diameter 6″			
☐ ivory	4.50	6.00	4.75
☐ white	3.00	5.00	4.00
☐ jade	3.00	5.00	4.00
☐ blue	7.25	8.25	7.75
Cheese Dish, with cover			
☐ ivory	40.00	50.00	45.00
☐ white	30.00	40.00	35.00
☐ jade	30.00	40.00	35.00
Creamer, small			
☐ ivory	6.00	8.00	7.00
☐ white	5.00	7.00	6.00
☐ jade	5.00	7.00	6.00
Creamer, large			
☐ ivory	7.00	9.00	8.00
☐ white	6.00	8.00	7.00
☐ jade	6.00	8.00	7.00
☐ blue	11.00	13.00	12.00
Cup			
☐ ivory	4.00	6.00	4.50
☐ white	3.00	5.00	3.50
☐ jade	3.00	5.00	3.50
☐ blue	10.00	12.00	10.50
Dinner Plate, diameter 9⅛″			
☐ ivory	3.50	5.50	4.50
☐ white	3.00	5.00	4.00
☐ jade	3.00	5.00	4.00
☐ blue	8.00	10.00	9.00
Grill Plate, diameter 9⅛″			
☐ ivory	3.00	5.00	4.00
☐ white	3.00	4.00	3.25
☐ jade	3.00	4.00	3.25
☐ blue	6.00	8.00	7.00
Platter, oval, length 10¾″			
☐ ivory	15.00	17.00	16.00
☐ white	12.00	15.00	13.00
☐ jade	12.00	15.00	13.00
☐ blue	18.00	21.00	19.50
Salad Plate, diameter 7½″			
☐ ivory	4.50	5.50	4.75
☐ white	2.50	3.50	2.75

	Current Price Range		Prior Year Average
☐ jade	2.50	3.50	2.75
☐ blue	6.00	8.00	7.00
Salt and Pepper Shakers			
☐ ivory	34.00	36.00	34.50
☐ white	43.00	46.00	44.50
☐ jade	43.00	46.00	44.50
Saucer			
☐ ivory	2.00	3.00	2.50
☐ white	2.00	3.00	2.50
☐ jade	2.00	3.00	2.50
☐ blue	4.00	6.00	4.50
Sherbet Dish			
☐ ivory	8.00	10.00	9.00
☐ white	5.00	7.00	6.00
☐ jade	5.00	7.00	6.00
Sherbet Plate, diameter 6″			
☐ ivory	3.00	4.00	3.25
☐ white	2.00	3.00	2.25
☐ jade	2.00	3.00	2.25
☐ blue	3.00	5.00	4.00
Sugar Bowl, small			
☐ ivory	6.00	8.00	7.00
☐ white	5.00	7.00	6.00
☐ jade	5.00	7.00	6.00
☐ blue	11.00	13.00	12.00
Sugar Bowl, large			
☐ ivory	7.00	9.00	7.50
☐ white	6.00	8.00	7.00
☐ jade	6.00	8.00	7.00
☐ blue	12.00	14.00	13.00

Lorain

LORAIN
Indiana

This decorative pattern features a scroll and garland design, alternating with a basket motif about which is draped a chain of flowers. The plates, for example, are squared on four sides with scalloped corners; the basket motif is contained in the corners with the two-part scroll and garland finishing the side rims. The center is octagonal and carries further ornamentation, with a "crown of thorns" outer trim, broken into eight undulating lines and enclosing a buckle border that contains the central cross-shaped curlicue and floral design. It appears in green, yellow, and occasionally crystal.

	Current Price Range		Prior Year Average
Berry Bowl, diameter 8"			
☐ green	59.00	69.00	60.00
☐ yellow	90.00	100.00	95.00
Cereal Bowl, diameter 6"			
☐ green	20.00	30.00	21.00
☐ yellow	37.00	41.00	39.00
Creamer, footed			
☐ green	9.00	12.00	10.00
☐ yellow	16.00	18.00	16.50
Cup			
☐ green	7.00	10.00	8.00
☐ yellow	9.00	12.00	10.00
Dinner Plate, diameter 9⅜"			
☐ green	25.00	30.00	26.00
☐ yellow	37.00	41.00	39.00
Dinner Plate, diameter 10¼"			
☐ green	30.00	35.00	31.00
☐ yellow	35.00	40.00	36.00
Luncheon Plate, diameter 8⅜"			
☐ green	11.00	13.00	12.00
☐ yellow	18.00	21.00	19.00
Platter, length 11½"			
☐ green	16.00	20.00	17.00
☐ yellow	26.00	28.00	27.00
Relish Bowl, four compartments, diameter 8"			
☐ green	12.00	16.00	13.00
☐ yellow	18.00	23.00	19.00
Salad Bowl, diameter 7¼"			
☐ green	27.00	31.00	28.00
☐ yellow	37.00	41.00	39.00
Salad Plate, diameter 7¾"			
☐ green	6.00	8.00	6.50
☐ yellow	9.00	12.00	10.00
Saucer			
☐ green	3.00	5.00	3.25
☐ yellow	4.00	5.00	4.25

	Current Price Range		Prior Year Average
Sherbet Dish, footed			
☐ green	12.00	15.00	13.00
☐ yellow	20.00	27.00	23.50
Sherbet Plate, diameter 5½"			
☐ green	3.00	5.00	3.50
☐ yellow	5.00	7.00	5.75
Sugar Bowl, footed			
☐ green	10.00	12.00	10.50
☐ yellow	13.00	15.00	18.00
Vegetable Bowl, oval, length 9¾"			
☐ green	24.00	29.00	26.00
☐ yellow	35.00	39.00	36.00

LOUISA
Jeannette

	Current Price Range		Prior Year Average
Ashtray, diameter 4"			
☐ iridescent	4.00	6.00	4.50
Bowl, square, diameter 4½"			
☐ iridescent	3.00	5.00	3.00
Butter Dish, with cover, oblong			
☐ iridescent	14.00	16.00	15.00
Candlesticks, pair			
☐ iridescent	27.00	32.00	28.00
Candy Dish, footed, diameter 5¼"			
☐ iridescent	3.00	5.00	4.00
Candy Dish, with cover, diameter 6¾"			
☐ iridescent	28.00	33.00	29.00
Creamer			
☐ iridescent	5.00	7.00	5.50
Cup			
☐ iridescent	3.00	5.00	3.50
Butter Dish, with cover, round			
☐ iridescent	30.00	38.00	33.00
Cereal Bowl, round, diameter 5½"			
☐ iridescent	15.00	18.00	16.00
Dinner Plate, diameter 8½"			
☐ iridescent	15.00	17.00	16.00
Fruit Bowl, ruffled rim, diameter 5½"			
☐ iridescent	3.00	5.00	3.25
Fruit Bowl, ruffled rim, diameter 8½"			
☐ iridescent	3.00	5.00	4.00
Fruit Bowl, ruffled rim, diameter 12"			
☐ iridescent	5.00	8.00	6.00
Pitcher, 64 oz.			
☐ iridescent	20.00	26.00	21.00
Platter, diameter 11¼"			
☐ iridescent	12.00	16.00	13.00

	Current Price Range		Prior Year Average

Salad Bowl, deep, diameter 9½"
☐ iridescent .... 23.00 · 28.00 · 24.00
Salt and Pepper Shakers
☐ iridescent .... 32.00 · 38.00 · 33.00
Saucer, diameter 5¼"
☐ iridescent .... 4.00 · 6.00 · 4.50
Sherbet Dish, footed
☐ iridescent .... 7.00 · 9.00 · 7.50
Sherbet Plate, diameter 5¾"
☐ iridescent .... 4.00 · 6.00 · 4.50
Sugar Bowl, with cover
☐ iridescent .... 10.00 · 14.00 · 11.00
Tray, length 13½"
☐ iridescent .... 12.00 · 15.00 · 13.00
Tumbler, footed, 10 oz.
☐ iridescent .... 10.00 · 13.00 · 11.00
Tumbler, footed, 11 oz.
☐ iridescent .... 12.00 · 14.00 · 13.00
Tumbler, footed, 15 oz.
☐ iridescent .... 38.00 · 45.00 · 40.00
Vase
☐ iridescent .... 70.00 · 80.00 · 75.00

LYDIA RAY
Hazel Atlas

This pattern was produced sometime between 1930 and 1936. The colors were: crystal, burgundy, green, and blue. The 9 oz. tumbler was also made in pink.

Ash Tray, 5½"
☐ crystal .... 22.00 · 27.00 · 23.50
☐ green .... 22.00 · 27.00 · 23.50
Butter Dish, with cover
☐ crystal .... 32.00 · 40.00 · 35.00
☐ green .... 32.00 · 40.00 · 35.00
Butter, top
☐ crystal .... 17.00 · 23.00 · 18.00
☐ green .... 17.00 · 23.00 · 18.00
Casserole Bowl, with cover, 9"
☐ crystal .... 37.50 · 45.00 · 40.00
☐ green .... 37.50 · 45.00 · 40.00
Casserole Bowl, with cover, 9"
☐ crystal .... 27.00 · 35.00 · 29.50
☐ green .... 27.00 · 35.00 · 29.50
Cocktail Goblet, 3¼ oz.
☐ crystal .... 10.00 · 12.50 · 11.25
☐ green .... 10.00 · 12.50 · 11.25
Cream Soup Bowl
☐ crystal .... 6.00 · 10.00 · 6.75

	Current Price Range		Prior Year Average
☐ green	6.00	10.00	6.75
Creamer			
☐ crystal	5.00	7.50	6.00
☐ green	5.00	7.50	6.00
Cup			
☐ crystal	4.00	6.50	4.90
☐ green	4.00	6.50	4.90
Decanter, with stopper			
☐ crystal	32.00	37.00	33.00
☐ green	32.00	37.00	33.00
Dinner Plate, 10″			
☐ crystal	7.00	11.00	8.50
☐ green	7.00	11.00	8.50
Grill Plate, 10″			
☐ crystal	6.50	10.00	7.25
☐ green	6.50	10.00	7.25
Luncheon Plate, 8½″			
☐ crystal	5.00	7.00	5.75
☐ green	5.00	7.00	5.75
Nappy, 4½″			
☐ crystal	4.75	5.75	5.00
☐ green	4.75	5.75	5.00
Nappy, 4½″			
☐ crystal	4.50	5.75	4.90
☐ green	4.50	5.75	4.90
Nappy, 8″			
☐ crystal	7.00	10.00	8.00
☐ green	7.00	10.00	8.00
Pitcher, 60 oz., with ice lip, 7¾″			
☐ crystal	22.00	27.00	23.50
☐ green	22.00	27.00	23.50
☐ burgundy	24.00	29.00	25.00
☐ blue	24.00	29.00	25.00
Pitcher, 60 oz. without ice lip, 7¾″			
☐ crystal	22.00	27.00	23.50
☐ green	22.00	27.00	23.50
☐ burgundy	24.00	29.00	25.00
☐ blue	24.00	29.00	25.00
Pitcher, 80 oz., with ice lip, 8¼″			
☐ crystal	24.00	28.00	25.00
☐ green	24.00	28.00	25.00
☐ burgundy	27.00	30.00	28.00
☐ blue	27.00	30.00	28.00
Pitcher, 80 oz., without ice lip, 8¼″			
☐ crystal	24.00	28.00	25.00
☐ green	24.00	28.00	25.00
☐ burgundy	27.00	30.00	28.00
☐ blue	27.00	30.00	28.00

	Current Price Range		Prior Year Average
Salad Plate, 7⅛″			
☐ crystal	4.50	6.50	5.25
☐ green	4.50	6.50	5.25
Saucer			
☐ crystal	1.75	2.50	1.90
☐ green	1.75	2.50	1.90
Sherbet			
☐ crystal	4.50	5.50	5.00
☐ green	4.50	5.50	5.00
Sherbet Plate, 6″			
☐ crystal	2.25	3.25	2.75
☐ green	2.25	3.25	2.75
Sugar, cover			
☐ crystal	7.50	10.00	8.50
☐ green	7.50	10.00	8.50
Sugar			
☐ crystal	3.75	4.75	4.20
☐ green	3.75	4.75	4.20
Sugar, with cover			
☐ crystal	10.00	12.00	11.00
☐ green	10.00	12.00	11.00
Tumbler, 9 oz., footed, 4⅞″			
☐ crystal	8.00	10.00	9.00
☐ green	8.00	10.00	9.00
Tumbler, 9 oz., 4″			
☐ crystal	6.00	8.75	7.25
☐ green	6.00	8.75	7.25
☐ pink	6.75	9.75	8.00
Tumbler, 10 oz., 5″			
☐ crystal	6.00	8.75	7.25
☐ green	6.00	8.75	7.25
Tumbler, 12 oz., 5¼″			
☐ crystal	10.00	12.50	11.00
☐ green	10.00	12.50	11.00
☐ burgundy	10.50	13.50	11.50
☐ blue	10.50	13.50	11.50
Tumbler, 5 oz., 3½″			
☐ crystal	4.00	8.00	5.50
☐ green	4.00	8.00	5.50
☐ burgundy	5.00	9.00	6.25
☐ blue	5.00	8.00	6.25
Tumbler, 5 oz., footed, 4″			
☐ crystal	8.00	11.00	9.00
☐ green	8.00	11.00	9.00
Wine Goblet, 2½ oz.			
☐ crystal	10.00	12.50	11.25
☐ green	10.00	12.50	11.25

MADRID
Federal

Sometimes called "Meandering Vine," this pattern consists of a dainty and scrolling leafy trim which is generally, but not always, set about a prominent diamond design. It was cast from the same molds used to make Parrot. The round knob on the butter cover is a Federal trademark. It can be found in green, pink, amber, crystal, and "madonna" blue.

	Current Price Range		Prior Year Average
Ashtray, fluted rim, square, length 6"			
□ green	75.00	80.00	75.00
□ amber	120.00	125.00	121.00
□ crystal	120.00	125.00	121.00
Berry Bowl, diameter 9½"			
□ pink	15.00	20.00	16.00
□ amber	12.00	15.00	13.00
□ crystal	12.00	15.00	13.00
Butter Dish, with lid			
□ green	60.00	70.00	65.00
□ amber	58.00	62.00	59.00
□ crystal	58.00	62.00	59.00
Candlesticks, pair, height 2½"			
□ pink	12.00	15.00	13.00
□ amber	13.00	16.00	14.00
□ crystal	13.00	16.00	14.00
Cake Plate, diameter 12"			
□ green	15.00	17.00	16.00
□ pink	7.00	9.00	8.00
□ amber	7.00	9.00	8.00
□ crystal	140.00	150.00	145.00
Cookie Jar, with lid			
□ pink	23.00	28.00	24.00
□ amber	30.00	34.00	31.00
□ crystal	30.00	34.00	31.00
Console Bowl, diameter 11"			
□ pink	7.00	9.00	8.00
□ amber	9.00	13.00	11.00
□ crystal	9.00	13.00	11.00
Creamer, pedestal foot			
□ green	7.00	9.00	7.50
□ blue	10.00	12.00	11.00
□ crystal	5.00	7.00	6.00
□ amber	5.00	7.00	6.00
Cup			
□ green	5.00	7.00	5.50
□ pink	5.00	7.00	5.50
□ blue	9.00	12.00	9.50
□ amber	4.00	6.00	4.50
□ crystal	4.00	6.00	4.50
Dinner Plate, diameter 11"			
□ green	24.00	28.00	25.00

	Current Price Range		Prior Year Average
☐ blue	30.00	40.00	35.00
☐ amber	22.00	26.00	23.00
☐ crystal	22.00	26.00	23.00
Gelatin Mold, height 2½″			
☐ crystal	7.00	9.00	8.00
☐ amber	7.00	9.00	8.00
Gravy Boat, with platter			
☐ amber	625.00	800.00	840.00
☐ crystal	625.00	800.00	840.00
Grill Plate, diameter 11″			
☐ green	12.00	15.00	12.50
☐ amber	7.00	9.00	7.50
☐ crystal	7.00	9.00	7.50
Hot Plate			
☐ green	25.00	30.00	26.00
☐ crystal	23.00	26.00	24.00
☐ amber	23.00	26.00	24.00
Hot Plate, with spoon holder			
☐ green	25.00	30.00	26.00
☐ crystal	25.00	30.00	26.00
☐ amber	25.00	30.00	26.00
Jelly Dish, diameter 6½″			
☐ green	11.00	15.00	12.00
☐ blue	20.00	25.00	21.00
☐ amber	14.00	17.00	15.00
☐ crystal	14.00	17.00	15.00
Juice Pitcher, height 5″			
☐ crystal	140.00	150.00	145.00
☐ amber	27.00	32.00	29.00
Lunch Plate, diameter 9″			
☐ green	7.00	9.00	7.50
☐ pink	5.00	7.00	5.50
☐ blue	11.00	13.00	11.50
☐ amber	4.50	6.50	5.00
☐ crystal	4.50	6.50	5.00
Pitcher, ice lip, height 9″			
☐ green	170.00	190.00	175.00
☐ amber	45.00	55.00	47.50
☐ crystal	45.00	55.00	47.50
Pitcher, rounded body, height 9″			
☐ green	170.00	190.00	175.00
☐ crystal	45.00	55.00	47.00
☐ amber	45.00	55.00	47.00
Pitcher, squared body, height 8″			
☐ green	110.00	120.00	113.00
☐ pink	30.00	33.00	31.00
☐ blue	135.00	145.00	137.00
☐ amber	35.00	40.00	36.00

	Current Price Range		Prior Year Average
☐ crystal	35.00	40.00	36.00

Platter, oval, length 12″
☐ pink	8.00	10.00	9.00
☐ green	11.00	14.00	12.00
☐ blue	16.00	19.00	17.00
☐ amber	9.00	11.00	9.50
☐ crystal	9.00	11.00	9.50

Relish Plate, two compartments, length 11″
☐ green	8.00	11.00	9.00
☐ pink	7.00	9.00	8.00
☐ amber	7.00	9.00	8.00
☐ crystal	7.00	9.00	8.00

Salad Bowl, diameter 8″
☐ green	14.00	16.00	14.50
☐ blue	21.00	24.00	21.50
☐ amber	10.00	13.00	11.00
☐ crystal	10.00	13.00	11.00

Salad Bowl, steep sided, diameter 9″
☐ amber	17.00	20.00	18.00
☐ crystal	17.00	20.00	18.00

Salad Plate, diameter 7″
☐ green	7.00	9.00	7.50
☐ pink	7.00	9.00	7.50
☐ blue	11.00	13.00	11.50
☐ amber	7.00	9.00	7.50
☐ crystal	7.00	9.00	7.50

Salt and Pepper Shakers, flat, height 3¼″
☐ green	50.00	60.00	55.00
☐ amber	30.00	35.00	32.00
☐ crystal	35.00	40.00	36.00

Salt and Pepper Shakers, footed, height 3¼″
☐ green	70.00	80.00	75.00
☐ blue	105.00	115.00	108.00
☐ amber	50.00	60.00	55.00
☐ crystal	50.00	60.00	55.00

Sauce Bowl, diameter 5″
☐ green	5.00	6.00	5.50
☐ pink	4.50	6.50	5.00
☐ blue	6.00	8.00	7.00
☐ amber	4.00	6.00	5.00

Saucer
☐ green	3.00	4.00	3.50
☐ pink	2.00	3.00	2.50
☐ blue	4.00	5.00	4.50
☐ amber	2.00	3.00	2.50

	Current Price Range		Prior Year Average
☐ crystal	2.00	3.00	2.50
Sherbet Dish, stemmed			
☐ green	6.00	8.00	6.50
☐ blue	9.00	10.00	9.50
☐ amber	6.00	8.00	6.00
☐ crystal	6.00	8.00	6.00
Sherbet Plate, diameter 6"			
☐ green	2.50	3.50	2.75
☐ pink	2.50	3.50	2.75
☐ blue	5.50	7.50	6.00
☐ amber	2.00	3.00	2.25
Soup Bowl, diameter 4½"			
☐ amber	9.00	11.00	9.50
☐ crystal	9.00	11.00	9.50
Soup Bowl, diameter 7"			
☐ green	9.00	11.00	9.50
☐ blue	10.00	13.00	11.00
☐ amber	9.00	11.00	9.25
☐ crystal	9.00	11.00	9.25
Sugar Bowl			
☐ green	7.00	9.00	7.50
☐ blue	9.00	11.00	9.50
☐ amber	6.00	8.00	6.50
☐ crystal	6.00	8.00	6.50
Sugar Lid			
☐ green	22.00	26.00	23.00
☐ blue	65.00	75.00	70.00
☐ amber	22.00	26.00	23.00
☐ crystal	22.00	26.00	23.00
Tumbler, height 4"			
☐ green	26.00	29.00	27.00
☐ blue	15.00	20.00	16.00
☐ amber	10.00	12.00	11.00
☐ crystal	10.00	12.00	11.00
Tumbler, height 4½"			
☐ green	16.00	20.00	17.00
☐ pink	10.00	12.00	11.00
☐ blue	16.00	20.00	17.00
☐ amber	10.00	12.00	11.00
☐ crystal	10.00	12.00	11.00
Tumbler, height 5½"			
☐ green	20.00	25.00	22.00
☐ blue	18.00	22.00	19.00
☐ amber	15.00	17.00	16.00
☐ crystal	15.00	17.00	16.00
Tumbler, pedestal foot, height 4"			
☐ green	31.00	33.00	31.50
☐ amber	16.00	18.00	17.00

	Current Price Range		Prior Year Average
☐ crystal	16.00	18.00	17.00
Tumbler, pedestal foot, height 5½"			
☐ green	28.00	32.00	29.00
☐ amber	18.00	22.00	19.00
☐ crystal	18.00	22.00	19.00
Vegetable Bowl, egg shape, length 10"			
☐ green	12.00	14.00	13.00
☐ blue	18.00	22.00	19.00
☐ pink	10.00	13.00	11.00
☐ amber	10.00	14.00	12.00
☐ crystal	10.00	14.00	12.00

MANHATTAN
Anchor Hocking

This heavy glass is remarkable for its large, well-defined horizontal ribs, characteristically somewhat sharp to the touch, unlike the more rounded ribs of some other similar patterns. It was cast in pink, crystal, and infrequently, green and ruby.

Ashtray, diameter 4"			
☐ crystal	4.00	6.00	5.00
Berry Bowl, handled, diameter 5"			
☐ crystal	4.00	6.00	5.00
☐ pink	5.00	7.00	6.00
Bowl, tab handled, diameter 8"			
☐ crystal	10.00	12.00	10.50
☐ pink	12.00	14.00	12.25
Candlesticks, pair, height 4"			
☐ crystal	8.00	11.00	8.50
Candy Dish, flat, with cover			
☐ crystal	18.00	22.00	19.00

Manhattan

	Current Price Range		Prior Year Average
Candy Dish, tri-legged			
☐ crystal	4.00	6.00	4.50
☐ pink	5.00	7.00	5.50
Coaster, diameter 3½″			
☐ crystal	1.50	2.50	1.75
☐ pink	2.50	3.50	2.75
Comport, height 5½″			
☐ crystal	7.00	9.00	8.00
☐ pink	9.00	11.00	9.50
Creamer, egg shape			
☐ crystal	3.00	5.00	3.50
☐ pink	5.00	7.00	5.50
Cup			
☐ crystal	6.00	8.00	6.50
Fruit Bowl, diameter 9″			
☐ crystal	14.00	16.00	14.50
☐ pink	15.00	17.00	15.50
Pitcher, 40 oz.			
☐ crystal	12.00	16.00	13.00
☐ pink	20.00	30.00	21.00
Pitcher, tilt, 50 oz.			
☐ crystal	18.00	20.00	19.00
☐ pink	30.00	40.00	31.00
Relish Tray, four compartments, length 14″			
☐ crystal	6.00	8.00	6.50
☐ pink	8.00	10.00	7.00
Relish Tray, five compartments, length 14″			
☐ crystal	8.00	10.00	8.50
☐ pink	13.00	15.00	14.00
Relish Tray Bowls			
☐ crystal	3.00	4.00	3.50
☐ pink	4.00	5.00	4.50
☐ ruby	2.00	3.00	2.50
Salad Bowl, diameter 9″			
☐ crystal	8.00	10.00	9.00
☐ pink	8.00	11.00	9.00
Sauce Bowl, diameter 4½″			
☐ crystal	4.00	5.00	4.50
☐ pink	5.00	6.00	5.50
Sherbet Plate, diameter 6″			
☐ crystal	2.00	3.00	2.50
Sugar Bowl, oval			
☐ crystal	3.00	5.00	3.25
☐ pink	5.00	7.00	5.50
Tumbler, pedestal foot, height 6½″			
☐ crystal	6.00	8.00	6.50
☐ pink	7.00	10.00	7.50

	Current Price Range		Prior Year Average
Vase, height 8″			
☐ crystal	7.00	9.00	8.00
Wine Glass, stemmed, height 3″			
☐ crystal	6.00	8.00	6.50

MAYFAIR
Federal

This intricate pattern is in the Cabbage Rose family. The same molds were used in the production of Rosemary (Dutch Rose). Plates can be identified by a small rayed center enclosed in a large, circular diamond-grill design. Many items have scalloped rims, but even if smooth, feature a scalloped-effect with a top section consisting of diamond-grill Gothic arches alternating with rounded arch panels containing two roses and leaves. Three are variations in this basic design, with some of the pieces lacking the diamond-grill in the alternate panel, although the roses are always featured. On these pieces, the "triple arch" effect is most noticeable. This pattern was issued in crystal, yellow amber, and mint green.

	Current Price Range		Prior Year Average
Cereal Bowl, diameter 6″			
☐ green	12.00	14.00	13.00
☐ amber	11.00	13.00	11.50
☐ crystal	5.00	7.00	5.50
Creamer, pedestal foot			
☐ green	7.00	11.00	8.00
☐ amber	11.00	14.00	12.00
☐ crystal	8.00	10.00	8.50
Cup			
☐ green	5.00	8.00	6.00
☐ amber	4.00	6.00	4.50
☐ crystal	3.00	4.00	3.25
Dinner Plate, diameter 9″			
☐ green	7.00	9.00	7.50

Mayfair

	Current Price Range		Prior Year Average
☐ amber	8.00	11.00	9.00
☐ crystal	5.00	7.00	5.50
Grill Plate, diameter 10″			
☐ green	7.00	9.00	6.50
☐ amber	8.00	10.00	8.50
☐ crystal	6.00	8.00	6.50
Platter, oval, length 11″			
☐ green	13.00	15.00	13.00
☐ amber	11.00	13.00	11.50
☐ crystal	8.00	10.00	8.50
Salad Plate, diameter 6½″			
☐ green	3.50	5.50	4.00
☐ amber	3.00	4.00	3.25
☐ crystal	1.75	2.75	2.00
Sauce Bowl, diameter 4½″			
☐ green	4.00	6.00	4.50
☐ amber	3.00	4.00	3.25
☐ crystal	1.75	2.75	2.00
Saucer			
☐ green	1.50	2.50	1.75
☐ amber	1.50	2.50	1.75
☐ crystal	1.00	2.00	1.00
Soup Bowl, diameter 5″			
☐ green	11.50	13.50	12.00
☐ amber	11.50	13.50	12.00
☐ crystal	8.00	10.00	8.50
Sugar Bowl, pedestal foot			
☐ green	7.00	9.00	8.00
☐ amber	8.00	10.00	8.50
☐ crystal	6.00	8.00	6.50
Tumbler, height 4″			
☐ green	12.50	14.50	13.00
☐ amber	9.00	11.00	9.50
☐ crystal	5.00	8.00	6.00
Vegetable Bowl, oval, length 10″			
☐ green	12.00	14.00	13.00
☐ amber	11.50	13.50	12.00

MAYFAIR
Hocking

This delicate and widely popular pattern is characterized by a wide panel containing wild roses relieved by graceful flutings on either side. It can be found in azure blue, frosted pink, true pink, green, crystal, and topaz. Hand-painted flowers are featured on some of the items. Rims are either smooth or slightly ruffled or scalloped.

Bowl, shallow, diameter 11″			
☐ green	18.00	22.00	19.00

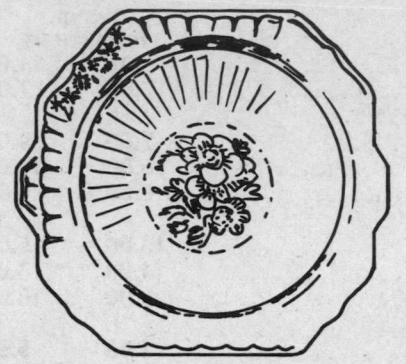

Mayfair

	Current Price Range		Prior Year Average
☐ yellow	75.00	85.00	80.00
☐ blue	40.00	48.00	44.00
☐ pink	31.00	37.00	34.00
Butter Dish, with cover, diameter 6⅞"			
☐ green	875.00	925.00	885.00
☐ yellow	875.00	925.00	885.00
☐ blue	190.00	210.00	195.00
☐ pink	40.00	50.00	42.00
Cake Plate, handles, diameter 12"			
☐ green	22.00	26.00	24.00
☐ blue	37.00	42.00	38.50
☐ pink	23.00	26.00	24.00
Cake Plate, pedestal foot, diameter 10"			
☐ green	47.00	52.00	49.00
☐ blue	38.00	42.00	39.00
☐ pink	15.00	20.00	16.50
Candy Dish, with lid			
☐ green	400.00	450.00	410.00
☐ yellow	285.00	320.00	290.00
☐ blue	120.00	140.00	125.00
☐ pink	32.00	38.00	34.00
Celery Bowl, two compartments, length 9"			
☐ green	95.00	105.00	97.50
☐ yellow	95.00	105.00	97.50
Celery Dish, two compartments, length 10"			
☐ green	80.00	90.00	85.00
☐ yellow	80.00	90.00	85.00
☐ blue	25.00	30.00	26.00
☐ pink	65.00	70.00	67.00
Cereal Bowl, diameter 5¼"			
☐ green	47.00	53.00	49.00

	Current Price Range		Prior Year Average
☐ yellow	47.00	53.00	49.00
☐ blue	28.00	32.00	29.00
☐ pink	13.00	15.00	14.00

Cocktail Glass, height 4″

☐ green	225.00	275.00	230.00
☐ pink	48.00	54.00	50.00

Console Bowl, tri-legged, diameter 8⅞″

☐ pink	1850.00	2100.00	1900.00

Cookie Jar, with cover

☐ green	440.00	460.00	450.00
☐ yellow	475.00	525.00	485.00
☐ blue	140.00	150.00	145.00
☐ pink	28.00	32.00	29.00

Cordial Glass, height 3½″

☐ green	340.00	350.00	345.00
☐ pink	340.00	350.00	345.00

Creamer, pedestal foot

☐ green	145.00	155.00	147.50
☐ yellow	145.00	155.00	147.50
☐ pink	13.00	15.00	14.00
☐ blue	45.00	50.00	46.00

Cup

☐ green	120.00	130.00	122.50
☐ yellow	120.00	130.00	122.50
☐ blue	33.00	38.00	34.00
☐ pink	11.00	13.00	12.00

Decanter, with glass stopper

☐ pink	85.00	95.00	90.00

Dinner Plate, diameter 9″

☐ green	95.00	100.00	97.00
☐ yellow	95.00	100.00	97.00
☐ blue	40.00	43.00	41.00
☐ pink	38.00	42.00	39.00

Fruit Bowl, fluted edge, deep sides, diameter 12¼″

☐ green	20.00	25.00	22.00
☐ yellow	85.00	95.00	87.50
☐ blue	48.00	53.00	49.00
☐ pink	35.00	40.00	36.50

Goblet, cylindrical, height 7¼″

☐ blue	95.00	100.00	96.50
☐ pink	125.00	130.00	126.50

Goblet, stemmed, height 4″

☐ pink	70.00	75.00	71.00

Grill Plate, diameter 9″

☐ green	50.00	55.00	52.00
☐ yellow	50.00	55.00	52.00
☐ blue	20.00	25.00	22.00
☐ pink	20.00	25.00	22.00

	Current Price Range		Prior Year Average
Grill Plate, tab handles, diameter 11"			
☐ yellow	78.00	83.00	79.00
Iced Tea Glass, footed, height 6"			
☐ green	175.00	180.00	176.50
☐ blue	78.00	83.00	79.50
☐ pink	26.00	30.00	27.50
Iced Tea Glass, height 5½"			
☐ blue	83.00	88.00	84.00
☐ pink	27.00	32.00	28.50
Juice Glass, height 3¾"			
☐ blue	60.00	70.00	62.00
☐ pink	20.00	25.00	22.00
Juice Tumbler, pedestal foot, height 3"			
☐ pink	50.00	54.00	52.00
Lunch Plate, diameter 8"			
☐ green	55.00	60.00	56.50
☐ yellow	55.00	60.00	56.50
☐ blue	23.00	26.00	24.00
☐ pink	14.50	16.50	15.00
Pitcher, bulbous body, 80 oz., height 8¼"			
☐ green	355.00	360.00	356.50
☐ yellow	355.00	360.00	356.50
☐ blue	125.00	130.00	127.00
☐ pink	62.00	67.00	64.00
Pitcher, 37 oz., height 6"			
☐ green	355.00	360.00	356.50
☐ yellow	355.00	360.00	356.50
☐ blue	85.00	90.00	87.00
☐ pink	28.00	33.00	29.50
Pitcher, 60 oz., height 8"			
☐ green	315.00	320.00	316.50
☐ yellow	315.00	320.00	316.50
☐ blue	33.00	37.00	34.00
☐ pink	950.00	1000.00	965.00
Plate, diameter 5¾"			
☐ green	65.00	70.00	67.00
☐ yellow	65.00	70.00	67.00
☐ blue	12.50	14.50	13.00
☐ pink	7.00	9.00	8.00
Plate, spoon holder, diameter 6½"			
☐ green	60.00	65.00	61.50
☐ blue	22.00	26.00	24.00
☐ pink	38.00	42.00	39.50
Platter, oval, lip handles, diameter 12½"			
☐ yellow	155.00	160.00	156.50
Platter, oval, open handles, length 12"			
☐ green	115.00	120.00	116.50
☐ yellow	115.00	120.00	116.50

	Current Price Range		Prior Year Average
☐ blue	33.00	37.00	34.50
☐ pink	14.00	18.00	14.50
Relish, four compartments, length 8½″			
☐ green	96.00	100.00	97.00
☐ yellow	93.00	97.00	94.50
☐ blue	28.00	33.00	29.50
☐ pink	16.00	19.00	17.00
Salt and Pepper, flat			
☐ green	575.00	625.00	590.00
☐ yellow	575.00	625.00	590.00
☐ blue	170.00	180.00	172.50
☐ pink	37.00	43.00	38.50
Salt and Pepper, pedestal foot			
☐ pink	1900.00	2100.00	1950.00
Sandwich Server, central loop handle			
☐ green	19.00	21.00	19.50
☐ yellow	80.00	90.00	85.00
☐ blue	43.00	47.00	44.00
☐ pink	25.00	30.00	26.50
Saucer			
☐ pink	16.00	20.00	17.00
Sherbet Dish, flat, diameter 2½″			
☐ blue	50.00	55.00	52.00
☐ pink	85.00	90.00	87.50
Sherbet Dish, footed, height 3″			
☐ pink	11.50	13.50	12.00
Sherbet Dish, pedestal foot, diameter 4½″			
☐ green	120.00	130.00	125.00
☐ yellow	120.00	130.00	125.00
☐ blue	45.00	50.00	46.50
☐ pink	53.00	58.00	54.00
Sherbet Plate, diameter 6¼″			
☐ pink	8.00	10.00	8.50
Sherry Glass, height 5½″			
☐ green	360.00	390.00	375.00
☐ pink	360.00	390.00	375.00
Soup Bowl, diameter 5″			
☐ pink	28.00	33.00	29.00
Sugar Bowl, pedestal foot			
☐ yellow	145.00	155.00	147.50
☐ green	145.00	155.00	147.50
☐ blue	42.00	46.00	43.00
☐ pink	14.00	16.00	14.50
Tumbler, pedestal foot, height 5″			
☐ blue	65.00	70.00	66.50
☐ pink	20.00	25.00	22.00

	Current Price Range		Prior Year Average
Vase			
☐ green	145.00	155.00	147.50
☐ blue	60.00	68.00	62.00
☐ pink	120.00	128.00	122.00
Vegetable Bowl, oval, length 9″			
☐ green	70.00	80.00	72.00
☐ yellow	70.00	80.00	72.00
☐ blue	30.00	40.00	32.00
☐ pink	15.00	17.00	15.50
Vegetable Bowl, diameter 10″			
☐ yellow	85.00	90.00	86.50
☐ pink	12.00	15.00	12.50
☐ blue	37.00	43.00	38.50
Vegetable Bowl, with cover, diameter 10″			
☐ yellow	220.00	230.00	222.50
☐ blue	70.00	80.00	72.50
☐ pink	58.00	63.00	58.50
Water Glass, height 4″			
☐ blue	60.00	65.00	61.50
☐ pink	18.00	22.00	19.00
Water Glass, height 5″			
☐ green	150.00	160.00	155.00
☐ blue	82.00	88.00	83.50
☐ pink	85.00	90.00	86.50
Water Glass, stemmed, height 6″			
☐ green	250.00	260.00	255.00
☐ pink	38.00	43.00	39.00
Whiskey Glass, jigger, height 2″			
☐ pink	50.00	60.00	55.00
Wine Glass, stemmed, height 4″			
☐ green	250.00	260.00	255.00
☐ pink	50.00	55.00	51.00

MISS AMERICA
Hocking

This diamond pattern features sunburst centers, uniform in circle. The rays form an elongated oval on such elongated pieces as the platters. Stemmed items are mounted on square bases, with a rayed finish. It was mostly cast in crystal and pink, although some green, ice blue, and red pieces can be found.

Berry Bowl, diameter 5″			
☐ green	6.00	8.00	6.50
Berry Bowl, diameter 6½″			
☐ green	8.00	10.00	8.50
☐ pink	12.00	14.00	13.00
☐ crystal	5.00	7.00	5.75

Miss America

	Current Price Range		Prior Year Average
Butter Dish, with lid			
☐ pink	360.00	400.00	370.00
☐ crystal	185.00	190.00	185.00
Candy Jar, with lid, height 11″			
☐ pink	95.00	100.00	96.50
☐ crystal	45.00	50.00	46.50
Cake Plate, pedestal foot, height 8″			
☐ pink	25.00	30.00	26.50
☐ crystal	15.00	18.00	16.00
Celery Dish, oval, length 10″			
☐ pink	14.00	16.00	14.50
☐ crystal	6.00	8.00	7.00
Coaster, diameter 5½″			
☐ pink	17.00	20.00	17.50
☐ crystal	11.00	13.00	12.00
Comport, height 5″			
☐ pink	13.00	16.00	14.00
☐ crystal	9.00	11.00	9.50
Creamer, pedestal foot			
☐ pink	11.00	13.00	12.00
☐ crystal	5.50	7.50	6.00
Cup			
☐ green	7.00	9.00	7.50
☐ pink	14.00	16.00	14.50
☐ crystal	6.50	8.50	7.00
Dinner Plate, diameter 10¼″			
☐ pink	16.50	19.50	17.00
☐ crystal	8.00	10.00	9.00
Fruit Bowl, steep sided			
☐ pink	35.00	40.00	37.00
☐ crystal	20.00	25.00	21.50

	Current Price Range		Prior Year Average

Grill Plate, diameter 10″
☐ pink 11.00 14.00 12.00
☐ crystal 6.00 8.00 6.50
Iced Tea Glass, height 7″
☐ pink 45.00 50.00 46.50
☐ crystal 19.00 22.00 20.00
Juice Glass, height 4½″
☐ red 145.00 155.00 147.50
☐ pink 45.00 50.00 46.50
☐ crystal 14.00 17.00 14.50
Juice Tumbler, height 4″
☐ pink 30.00 40.00 32.00
☐ crystal 12.00 15.00 12.00
Pitcher, height 8″
☐ pink 80.00 90.00 85.00
☐ crystal 48.00 53.00 49.50
Pitcher, ice lip, height 8½″
☐ pink 90.00 95.00 92.00
☐ crystal 55.00 60.00 56.50
Plate, diameter 6½″
☐ green 5.00 7.00 5.50
Platter, oblong, length 12″
☐ pink 14.00 16.00 14.50
☐ crystal 9.00 11.00 9.50
Relish Dish, four compartments, length 8½″
☐ pink 12.00 14.00 13.00
☐ crystal 6.00 9.00 7.00
Relish Dish, round, two compartments, diameter 11″
☐ pink 120.00 130.00 122.50
☐ crystal 10.00 13.00 11.00
Rose Bowl, diameter 8″
☐ pink 40.00 50.00 42.50
☐ red 275.00 325.00 290.00
☐ crystal 28.00 33.00 29.00
Salad Plate, diameter 8½″
☐ red 50.00 60.00 51.00
☐ green 7.00 9.00 7.50
☐ pink 13.00 15.00 13.50
☐ crystal 4.00 6.00 4.50
Salt and Pepper
☐ green 250.00 260.00 255.00
☐ pink 40.00 44.00 42.00
☐ crystal 20.00 25.00 21.50
Saucer
☐ pink 3.50 5.50 4.00
☐ crystal 2.00 3.00 2.25

	Current Price Range		Prior Year Average
Sherbet Dish			
☐ pink	11.50	13.50	12.00
☐ crystal	5.50	7.50	6.00
Sherbet Plate, diameter 5½″			
☐ green	4.00	6.00	4.50
☐ pink	4.00	6.00	4.50
☐ crystal	2.50	3.50	2.75
Sugar Bowl			
☐ pink	11.00	14.00	12.00
☐ crystal	5.00	7.00	5.50
☐ red	120.00	130.00	122.50
Vegetable Bowl, oval, length 10″			
☐ pink	15.50	17.50	16.00
☐ crystal	9.00	11.00	9.50
Water Glass, height 5¾″			
☐ red	145.00	155.00	147.50
☐ pink	35.00	40.00	36.50
☐ crystal	16.50	18.50	17.00
Water Tumbler, height 4½″			
☐ green	12.50	14.50	13.00
☐ pink	22.00	26.00	23.00
☐ crystal	10.00	13.00	11.00
Wine Glass, height 3½″			
☐ red	145.00	155.00	147.50
☐ pink	45.00	50.00	46.50
☐ crystal	13.00	15.00	13.50

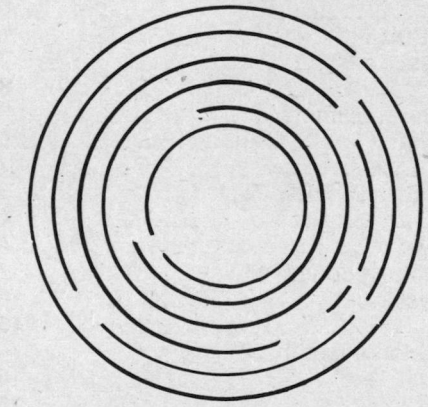

Moderntone

MODERNTONE
Hazel Atlas

This simple but elegant pattern is also known as "Wedding Band," which may allude to the characteristic horizontal bands which encircle each piece. Centers are plain. It appears in cobalt blue, amethyst, and some crystal, pink and platonite fired-on colors.

	Current Price Range		Prior Year Average
Ashtray, with match holder, height 7½"			
☐ cobalt	83.00	93.00	85.00
Berry Bowl, diameter 4¾"			
☐ cobalt	11.00	15.50	12.50
☐ amethyst	5.00	8.50	5.75
Berry Bowl, diameter 8½"			
☐ amethyst	15.00	20.00	16.25
☐ cobalt	20.00	25.00	21.50
Butter Dish, metal cover			
☐ cobalt	53.00	60.00	55.00
Cereal Bowl, diameter 6"			
☐ amethyst	22.00	27.00	23.50
☐ cobalt	29.00	35.00	30.50
Cheese Dish, diameter 7"			
☐ cobalt	64.00	71.00	65.50
Creamer			
☐ amethyst	5.00	7.00	5.50
☐ cobalt	6.00	9.00	7.00
Cup			
☐ amethyst	5.00	7.00	5.50
☐ cobalt	6.00	9.00	7.00
Custard Cup			
☐ amethyst	7.50	10.50	8.25
☐ cobalt	8.00	11.00	8.75
Dinner Plate, diameter 9"			
☐ amethyst	5.50	7.50	6.00
☐ green	7.50	10.50	8.25
Lunch Plate, diameter 7½"			
☐ cobalt	4.00	6.00	4.50
☐ amethyst	4.00	6.00	4.50
Platter, oblong, length 11"			
☐ amethyst	10.00	13.00	10.75
☐ cobalt	15.00	20.00	16.50
Platter, oblong, length 12"			
☐ amethyst	16.00	20.00	17.00
☐ cobalt	22.00	28.00	22.50
Salad Plate, diameter 6½"			
☐ amethyst	3.50	5.50	4.50
☐ cobalt	5.00	8.00	5.50
Salt and Pepper Shakers, pair			
☐ amethyst	22.00	28.00	23.50
☐ cobalt	22.00	28.00	23.50

	Current Price Range		Prior Year Average
Sandwich Plate, diameter 10″			
☐ amethyst	8.50	11.50	9.25
☐ cobalt...........................	13.00	17.00	14.00
Saucer			
☐ amethyst	1.00	3.00	1.50
☐ cobalt...........................	1.00	3.00	1.50
Sherbet Plate, diameter 5½″			
☐ amethyst	5.00	8.00	6.00
☐ cobalt...........................	6.00	9.00	7.00
Soup Bowl, diameter 4″			
☐ cobalt...........................	9.50	13.00	10.00
☐ amethyst	8.00	11.00	9.00
Soup Bowl, diameter 7″			
☐ amethyst	23.00	27.00	24.00
☐ cobalt...........................	29.00	35.00	30.50
Soup Bowl, scalloped rim, diameter 5″			
☐ cobalt...........................	13.00	17.00	14.00
☐ amethyst	10.00	13.00	10.50
Sugar Bowl			
☐ amethyst	5.50	7.50	6.00
☐ cobalt...........................	6.00	9.00	7.00
Tumbler, height 8″			
☐ cobalt...........................	13.00	17.00	14.00
Whiskey Glass, jigger, height 1½″			
☐ cobalt...........................	10.00	13.00	11.00

MOONSTONE
Anchor Hocking

This striking crystal glassware features opalescent trim on rims and hobnails. It was issued from the Hobnail molds, and can be distinguished from other Hobnail patterns by the many-rayed star in relief in the center and/or on the feet of most items.

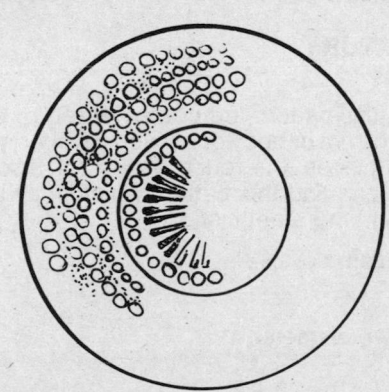

Moonstone

	Current Price Range		Prior Year Average
Berry Bowl, diameter 5"			
☐ opalescent crystal	5.50	8.50	6.50
Bon Bon, heart shape			
☐ opalescent crystal	5.50	8.50	6.25
Bowl, flat, diameter 7½"			
☐ opalescent crystal	6.50	9.50	7.25
Bowl, fluted edge, diameter 9"			
☐ opalescent crystal	11.00	14.00	12.00
Bowl, fluted rim, with handle			
☐ opalescent crystal	5.50	8.50	6.25
Bud Vase, height 5"			
☐ opalescent crystal	7.00	10.00	8.00
Candlesticks, pair			
☐ opalescent crystal	13.00	17.00	14.00
Candy Jar, with lid, diameter 5"			
☐ opalescent crystal	16.00	18.50	16.75
Cigarette Bowl, with lid			
☐ opalescent crystal	13.00	16.00	13.75
Creamer			
☐ opalescent crystal	4.50	7.50	5.25
Cup			
☐ opalescent crystal	4.50	7.50	5.25
Dessert Bowl, fluted rim, diameter 5"			
☐ opalescent crystal	4.50	7.50	5.25
Goblet, height 5½"			
☐ opalescent crystal	13.00	16.00	14.00
Lunch Plate, diameter 8"			
☐ opalescent crystal	7.00	9.50	8.00
Puff Box, with lid, diameter 4½"			
☐ opalescent crystal	13.00	17.00	14.00
Relish Bowl, two compartments, diameter 7"			
☐ opalescent crystal	6.00	9.00	7.00

NEW CENTURY
Hazel Atlas

Items in this pattern are characterized by a banded ribbon design that encircles the rim or body of a piece, finished with a concentric ring border. On footed pieces, the round bases are also ringed. Centers are rayed. Collectors can find this pattern abundantly in green, but also in crystal, pink, cobalt, and amethyst.

	Current Price Range		Prior Year Average
Ashtray, diameter 5⅜"			
☐ crystal	23.00	27.00	24.00
☐ green	23.00	27.00	24.00
Berry Bowl, diameter 4½"			
☐ crystal	3.50	5.50	4.00
☐ green	3.50	5.50	4.00

New Century

	Current Price Range		Prior Year Average
Butter Dish, with cover			
☐ crystal	44.00	54.00	55.50
☐ green	44.00	54.00	55.50
Casserole Bowl, with cover, diameter 9″			
☐ crystal	40.00	50.00	43.00
☐ green	40.00	50.00	43.00
Cocktail Glass, 3¼ oz.			
☐ crystal	11.00	14.00	12.00
☐ green	11.00	14.00	12.00
Creamer			
☐ crystal	4.50	6.50	5.00
☐ green	4.50	6.50	5.00
Cup			
☐ crystal	3.50	5.50	4.00
☐ green	3.50	5.50	4.00
Decanter, with stopper			
☐ crystal	33.00	41.00	35.00
☐ green	33.00	41.00	35.00
Dinner Plate, diameter 10″			
☐ crystal	8.00	11.50	9.00
☐ green	8.00	11.50	9.00
Grill Plate, diameter 10″			
☐ crystal	6.00	9.00	7.00
☐ green	6.00	9.00	7.00
Plate, diameter 7⅛″			
☐ green	4.50	6.50	5.00
☐ crystal	4.50	6.50	5.00
Platter, oval, length 11″			
☐ crystal	8.50	11.50	9.00
☐ green	8.50	11.50	9.00
Pitcher, with ice lip, 60 oz., height 7¾″			
☐ crystal	23.00	27.00	24.00

	Current Price Range		Prior Year Average
☐ green	23.00	27.00	24.00
Pitcher, without ice lip, 60 oz., height 7¾"			
☐ crystal	23.00	27.00	24.00
☐ green	23.00	27.00	24.00
Pitcher, with ice lip, 80 oz., height 8"			
☐ crystal	25.00	30.00	26.00
☐ green	25.00	30.00	26.00
Pitcher, without ice lip, 80 oz., height 8"			
☐ crystal	25.00	30.00	26.00
☐ green	25.00	30.00	26.00
Salad Plate, diameter 8½"			
☐ crystal	4.50	6.50	5.00
☐ green	4.50	6.50	5.00
Salt and Pepper Shakers			
☐ crystal	22.00	27.00	23.00
☐ green	22.00	27.00	23.00
Saucer			
☐ crystal	1.00	3.00	1.50
☐ green	1.00	3.00	1.50
Sherbet Dish, diameter 3"			
☐ crystal	4.00	6.00	4.50
☐ green	4.00	6.00	4.50
Sherbet Plate, diameter 6"			
☐ crystal	1.00	3.00	1.50
☐ green	1.00	3.00	1.50
Soup Bowl, diameter 4¾"			
☐ crystal	7.00	10.00	8.00
☐ green	7.00	10.00	8.00
Wine Glass, 2½ oz.			
☐ crystal	10.00	13.00	10.50
☐ green	10.00	13.00	10.50

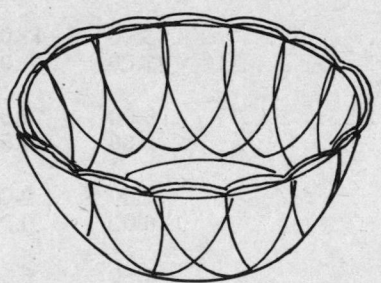

Newport

NEWPORT
Hazel Atlas

In this pattern, hairpin lines are pressed into the glass, creating an interconnected series of undulating, triangular motifs that follow the contour of a piece. Plate edges and bowls are slightly scalloped and centers are generally plain. It can be collected in cobalt blue, amethyst, pink, and white.

	Current Price Range		Prior Year Average
Berry Bowl, diameter 4¼"			
☐ cobalt	6.50	9.50	7.00
☐ amethyst	6.00	9.00	7.00
Berry Bowl, diameter 8¼"			
☐ cobalt	20.00	25.00	21.50
☐ amethyst	18.00	22.00	19.00
Cereal Bowl, diameter 5¼"			
☐ cobalt	15.50	19.50	16.25
☐ amethyst	11.00	14.00	12.00
Creamer			
☐ cobalt	8.00	11.00	9.00
☐ amethyst	6.50	9.50	7.00
Cup			
☐ cobalt	5.00	8.00	6.00
☐ amethyst	4.00	6.00	4.50
Luncheon Plate, diameter 8½			
☐ cobalt	5.00	7.00	5.50
☐ amethyst	5.50	7.50	6.00
Platter, oval, length 11¾"			
☐ cobalt	20.00	25.00	21.50
☐ amethyst	16.00	20.00	19.00
Salt and Pepper Shakers			
☐ cobalt	29.00	35.00	31.00
☐ amethyst	27.00	32.00	28.50
Sandwich Plate, diameter 11½"			
☐ cobalt	17.00	22.00	18.00
☐ amethyst	12.00	16.00	13.00
Saucer			
☐ cobalt	1.50	3.50	2.00
☐ amethyst	1.50	3.50	2.00

NORMANDIE
Federal

This pattern was manufactured from 1933 to 1939. The colors are pink, amber, crystal, green, and "Sunburst" (an imitation of carnival glass). Pink is the most common of the standard colors; Sunburst was produced in huge numbers and used by the Great Northern Products Co. as a premium.

Bread and Butter Plate, 6"			
☐ pink	2.50	4.00	3.00

	Current Price Range		Prior Year Average
☐ crystal	2.00	3.50	2.50
☐ amber	2.00	3.50	2.50
☐ sunburst	1.75	2.50	2.00
Cup			
☐ pink	5.50	7.00	6.00
☐ crystal	4.50	6.00	5.00
☐ amber	4.50	6.00	5.00
☐ sunburst	4.00	6.00	4.50
Dinner Plate, 10½"			
☐ pink	27.00	31.00	25.00
☐ crystal	12.00	16.00	11.00
☐ amber	12.00	16.00	11.00
☐ green	22.00	26.00	23.00
☐ sunburst	15.00	18.00	16.00
Grill Plate, 10½"			
☐ pink	10.00	14.00	11.00
☐ crystal	6.00	8.00	6.50
☐ amber	6.00	8.00	6.50
☐ sunburst	5.00	7.00	5.50
Nappy, 5"			
☐ pink	5.00	7.00	5.00
☐ crystal	4.00	6.00	4.50
☐ amber	4.00	6.00	4.50
☐ sunburst	4.00	6.00	4.50
Nappy, 8½"			
☐ pink	13.50	16.00	14.50
☐ crystal	12.00	14.00	12.50
☐ amber	12.00	14.00	12.50
☐ sunburst	11.00	13.00	11.50
Pitcher, 8"			
☐ pink	65.00	75.00	67.50
☐ crystal	45.00	55.00	50.00
☐ amber	45.00	55.00	50.00
Platter, 11¾"			
☐ pink	14.00	17.00	15.00
☐ crystal	12.50	15.50	13.00
☐ amber	12.50	15.50	13.00
☐ sunburst	13.00	15.50	13.50
Salad Plate, 8"			
☐ pink	7.50	9.50	8.00
☐ crystal	5.00	7.50	5.00
☐ amber	5.00	7.50	5.00
☐ sunburst	4.50	6.50	5.00
Salt and Pepper			
☐ pink	42.00	46.00	41.00
☐ crystal	28.00	32.00	29.00
☐ amber	28.00	32.00	29.00

	Current Price Range		Prior Year Average

Saucer
- ☐ pink .... 2.00 | 3.00 | 2.00
- ☐ crystal .... 1.75 | 2.75 | 1.75
- ☐ amber .... 1.75 | 2.75 | 1.75
- ☐ sunburst .... 3.00 | 4.00 | 3.00

Sherbet
- ☐ pink .... 5.50 | 8.00 | 6.00
- ☐ crystal .... 5.00 | 7.00 | 5.00
- ☐ amber .... 5.00 | 7.00 | 5.00
- ☐ sunburst .... 4.50 | 6.50 | 5.00

Sugar
- ☐ pink .... 7.00 | 9.00 | 7.00
- ☐ crystal .... 6.00 | 8.00 | 6.00
- ☐ amber .... 5.00 | 8.00 | 6.00
- ☐ sunburst .... 5.00 | 7.00 | 5.00

Sugar and Cover
- ☐ pink .... 77.50 | 87.50 | 79.00
- ☐ crystal .... 70.00 | 80.00 | 72.00
- ☐ amber .... 70.00 | 80.00 | 72.00

Tumbler, 4″
- ☐ pink .... 22.00 | 27.00 | 23.50
- ☐ crystal .... 14.00 | 18.00 | 15.00
- ☐ amber .... 14.00 | 18.00 | 15.00

Tumbler, 4½″
- ☐ pink .... 16.00 | 19.50 | 17.00
- ☐ crystal .... 10.00 | 13.00 | 11.00
- ☐ amber .... 10.00 | 13.00 | 11.00

Vegetable Bowl, oval, 9½″
- ☐ pink .... 17.00 | 21.00 | 18.00
- ☐ crystal .... 10.00 | 13.00 | 11.00
- ☐ amber .... 10.00 | 13.00 | 11.00
- ☐ sunburst .... 13.00 | 16.00 | 14.50

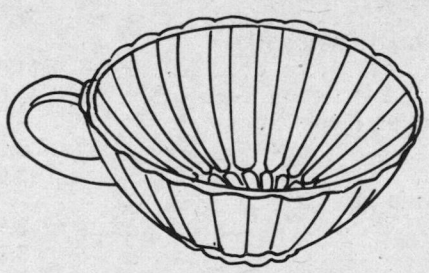

Old Cafe

OLD CAFE
Hocking

This geometric pattern is made up of bunches of flutes, grouped together in two's, separated by a wider, thickly molded panel. These vertical panels are arranged in three horizontal bands nesting into each other from the center. The mold work is voluptuously rounded.

	Current Price Range		Prior Year Average
Berry Bowl, diameter 3½"			
□ pink	1.00	3.00	1.50
□ red	3.00	5.00	3.50
□ crystal	1.00	3.00	1.50
Bowl, loop handle, diameter 5"			
□ pink	2.00	4.00	2.50
□ crystal	2.00	4.00	2.50
Bowl, tab handled, diameter 9"			
□ pink	6.00	9.00	7.00
□ red	9.00	13.00	10.00
□ crystal	6.00	9.00	7.00
Bowl, two loop handles, diameter 5"			
□ pink	2.00	4.00	2.50
□ crystal	2.00	4.00	2.50
Candy Dish, shallow, diameter 8"			
□ pink	4.00	6.00	4.50
□ red	8.50	11.50	9.00
□ crystal	4.00	6.00	5.50
Cereal Bowl, diameter 5"			
□ pink	3.00	5.00	3.50
□ red	7.00	10.00	8.00
□ crystal	3.00	5.00	3.50
Cup			
□ pink	2.00	4.00	2.50
□ red	4.50	7.50	5.00
□ crystal	2.00	4.00	2.50
Dinner Plate, diameter 10"			
□ pink	11.00	14.00	12.00
□ crystal	11.00	14.00	12.00
Juice Tumbler, height 3"			
□ pink	3.00	5.00	3.50
□ crystal	3.00	5.00	3.50
Juice Tumbler, 3"			
□ crystal	3.50	4.50	3.75
□ pink	3.50	4.50	3.75
□ royal ruby	5.75	8.00	5.50
Lamp			
□ pink	8.00	11.00	9.00
□ red	15.00	20.00	16.00
□ crystal	8.00	11.00	9.00
Olive Dish, oval, length 6"			
□ pink	3.00	5.00	3.50

	Current Price Range		Prior Year Average
☐ crystal	3.00	5.00	3.50
Pitcher, height 6″			
☐ pink	43.00	51.00	45.00
☐ crystal	43.00	51.00	45.00
Pitcher, height 8″			
☐ pink	63.00	73.00	65.00
☐ crystal	63.00	73.00	65.00
Saucer			
☐ pink	1.00	3.00	1.50
☐ crystal	1.00	3.00	1.50
Sherbet Dish, footed			
☐ pink	3.00	5.00	3.50
☐ crystal	3.00	5.00	3.50
Sherbet Plate, diameter 6″			
☐ pink	.75	2.00	1.00
☐ crystal	.75	2.00	1.00
Tumbler, 4″			
☐ crystal	5.00	7.00	5.50
☐ pink	5.00	7.00	5.50
☐ royal ruby	5.50	8.00	6.00

OVIDE
Hazel Atlas

These opaque pieces are durable and heat resistant, hence they were often used in the restaurants and full sets are hard to find. This Art Deco pattern comes in a variety of bright colors with a simple contrasting band around the outside. Often the table service is seen with an interesting oblique design, futuristic in conception, and consisting of black and white rays resembling the skyline of New York, occasionally overshadowed by red, yellow, and green suns.

Berry Bowl, diameter 5″			
☐ decorated	5.00	8.00	6.00

Ovide

	Current Price Range		Prior Year Average
☐ black	5.00	8.00	6.00
Berry Bowl, diameter 8″			
☐ decorated	12.00	15.00	13.00
☐ black	12.00	15.00	13.00
Candy Dish, cover			
☐ decorated	20.00	25.00	21.00
☐ black	20.00	25.00	21.00
☐ green	13.00	15.50	14.00
Cereal Bowl, diameter 6″			
☐ decorated	5.00	8.00	6.00
☐ black	5.00	8.00	6.00
Creamer			
☐ decorated	6.00	9.00	7.00
☐ black	6.00	9.00	7.00
☐ green	1.50	3.50	2.00
Dinner Plate, diameter 9″			
☐ decorated	6.00	9.00	7.00
☐ black	6.00	9.00	7.00
Fruit Bowl, pedestal foot			
☐ decorated	5.00	8.00	6.00
☐ black	5.00	8.00	6.00
☐ green	.75	2.00	1.00
Luncheon Plate, diameter 8″			
☐ decorated	4.00	6.00	4.50
☐ black	4.00	6.00	4.50
☐ green	.75	2.50	1.00
Platter, length 11″			
☐ decorated	8.00	11.00	9.00
☐ black	8.00	11.00	9.00
Salt and Pepper Shakers, pair			
☐ decorated	18.00	22.00	19.00
☐ black	18.00	22.00	19.00
☐ green	6.00	9.00	7.00
Saucer			
☐ decorated	2.00	4.00	2.50
☐ black	2.00	4.00	2.50
☐ green	.75	2.25	1.00
Sherbet Dish			
☐ decorated	5.00	8.00	5.50
☐ black	5.00	8.00	5.50
☐ green	.75	2.50	1.00
Sherbet Plate, diameter 6″			
☐ decorated	1.50	3.50	2.00
☐ black	1.50	3.50	2.00
☐ green	.50	1.75	.75
Sugar Bowl			
☐ decorated	6.00	9.00	7.00
☐ black	6.00	9.00	7.00
☐ green	1.50	3.50	2.00

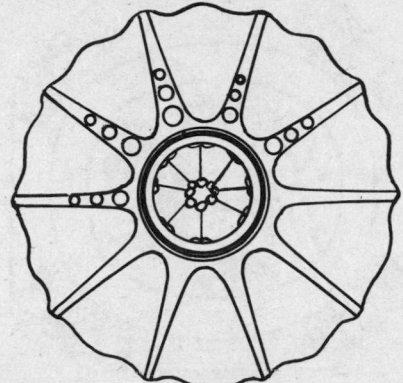

Oyster and Pearl

OYSTER AND PEARL
Anchor Hocking

Found in opaque and transparent glass Oyster and Pearl is decorated with a spindly ten-rayed star with a mandala center. The rays climb the sides of the pieces and are resolved over the gently fluted rims. There are beadwork decorations and nicely molded panels.

	Current Price Range		Prior Year Average
Bowl, heart shape, tab handle, diameter 5″			
☐ pink	4.00	6.00	4.50
☐ opaque pink	4.00	6.00	4.50
☐ opaque green	4.00	6.00	4.50
☐ crystal	4.00	6.00	4.50
Bowl, tab handle, steep sides, diameter 6″			
☐ pink	6.50	10.00	7.00
☐ crystal	6.50	10.00	7.00
Candleholders, pair, height 3″			
☐ pink	13.00	17.00	14.00
☐ ruby	26.00	33.00	27.50
☐ opaque pink	11.00	14.00	12.00
☐ opaque green	11.00	14.00	12.00
☐ crystal	13.00	17.00	14.00

PARROT, SYLVAN
Federal

Three engaging parrots chatter in the center of these pieces, well-molded and nicely detailed, and perched in a tropical scene. The bamboo and fern-like foliage is interesting and repeated in four sprays on the corners of the plates and bowls. On glasses and other vessels, the parrot motif is panelized and repeats around the sides. The glass is wonderfully colored and delicately molded.

Parrot, Sylvan

	Current Price Range		Prior Year Average
Berry Bowl, diameter 5″			
☐ green	11.00	14.00	12.00
☐ amber	8.50	11.50	9.00
Berry Bowl, diameter 8″			
☐ green	45.00	50.00	46.00
☐ amber	46.00	54.00	48.00
Butter Dish, with cover			
☐ green	215.00	240.00	220.00
☐ amber	530.00	570.00	543.00
Creamer, footed			
☐ green	18.00	22.00	19.00
☐ amber	20.00	25.00	21.00
Cup			
☐ green	20.00	25.00	21.00
☐ amber	20.00	25.00	21.00
Dinner Plate, diameter 9″			
☐ green	24.00	31.00	26.00
☐ amber	22.00	28.00	23.00
Grill Plate, round, diameter, 10½″			
☐ green	15.00	21.00	16.50
Grill Plate, square, diameter 10½″			
☐ amber	14.00	18.00	15.00
Plate, square, length 10¼″			
☐ green	30.00	35.00	31.00
☐ amber	30.00	35.00	31.00
Platter, oblong, length 11¼″			
☐ green	24.00	31.00	26.00
☐ amber	37.00	43.00	39.00
Pitcher, 80 oz., height 8½″			
☐ green	730.00	770.00	740.00
Salad Plate, diameter 7½″			
☐ green	12.00	16.00	13.00

	Current Price Range		Prior Year Average
Salt and Pepper Shakers			
☐ green	160.00	190.00	170.00
Saucer			
☐ green	7.00	10.00	8.00
☐ amber	7.00	10.00	8.00
Sherbet Dish, footed			
☐ green	14.50	18.50	15.50
☐ amber	14.50	18.50	15.50
Sherbet Dish, height 4¼"			
☐ green	120.00	135.00	123.00
Sherbet Plate, diameter 5¾"			
☐ green	8.50	11.50	9.00
☐ amber	8.50	11.50	9.00
Soup Bowl, diameter 7"			
☐ green	22.00	28.00	23.00
☐ amber	22.00	28.00	23.00
Sugar Bowl, with cover			
☐ green	18.00	22.00	19.00
☐ amber	17.50	21.50	18.50
Tumbler, 10 oz., height 4¼"			
☐ green	73.00	81.00	75.00
☐ amber	73.00	81.00	75.00
Tumbler, 12 oz., diameter 5¾"			
☐ green	93.00	103.00	95.00
☐ amber	93.00	103.00	95.00
Tumbler, footed, 14 oz., height 5¾"			
☐ green	83.00	95.00	85.00
☐ amber	85.00	97.00	87.00
Vegetable Bowl, diameter 10"			
☐ green	32.00	39.00	33.00
☐ amber	37.00	44.00	38.00

PATRICIAN

The beadwork that runs the perimeter of the outside rim is the framework for a star and drape band that points toward the central medallion. A gentle dogwood is shaped by the same kind of beading that circles the middle body, surrounding a frolicking rosette that graces the center. The rims of the bowls and plates have a gentle wave and flute.

Berry Bowl, diameter 5"			
☐ green	6.00	9.00	7.00
☐ pink	8.00	11.00	9.00
☐ amber	6.00	9.00	7.00
☐ crystal	6.00	9.00	7.00
Berry Bowl, diameter 8½"			
☐ green	16.00	19.00	17.00
☐ pink	16.00	19.00	17.00
☐ amber	22.00	28.00	24.00
☐ crystal	22.00	28.00	24.00

Patrician

	Current Price Range		Prior Year Average
Butter Dish, with cover			
☐ green	85.00	95.00	87.00
☐ pink	180.00	220.00	190.00
☐ amber	62.00	72.00	65.00
Cereal Bowl, diameter 6″			
☐ green	15.50	19.50	16.50
☐ pink	15.50	19.50	16.50
☐ amber	13.00	17.00	14.00
☐ crystal	13.00	17.00	14.00
Cookie Jar, with cover			
☐ green	250.00	300.00	265.00
☐ amber	48.00	55.00	50.00
☐ crystal	48.00	55.00	50.00
Creamer, footed			
☐ green	8.00	11.00	9.00
☐ pink	7.00	10.00	8.00
☐ amber	5.00	8.00	6.00
☐ crystal	5.00	8.00	6.00
Cup			
☐ green	6.50	9.50	7.50
☐ pink	6.00	9.00	7.00
Dinner Plate, diameter 10½″			
☐ green	18.00	22.00	19.00
☐ pink	14.00	18.00	15.00
☐ amber	4.00	6.00	4.50
☐ crystal	4.00	6.00	4.50
Grill Plate, diameter 10½″			
☐ green	8.00	11.00	9.00

	Current Price Range		Prior Year Average
☐ pink	8.00	11.00	9.00
☐ amber	6.00	9.00	7.00
☐ crystal	6.00	9.00	7.00
Luncheon Plate, diameter 9″			
☐ green	5.00	8.00	6.00
☐ pink	5.00	8.00	6.00
☐ amber	5.50	8.50	6.50
☐ crystal	5.50	8.50	6.50
Platter, oval, length 11½″			
☐ green	10.50	14.50	11.50
☐ pink	8.50	11.50	9.50
☐ amber	8.50	11.50	9.50
☐ crystal	8.50	11.50	9.50
Pitcher, 75 oz., height 8″			
☐ green	75.00	85.00	78.00
☐ pink	93.00	105.00	95.00
☐ amber	93.00	82.00	75.00
☐ crystal	73.00	82.00	75.00
Pitcher, 75 oz., height 8¼″			
☐ green	83.00	95.00	85.00
☐ pink	93.00	105.00	95.00
☐ amber	72.00	84.00	75.00
☐ crystal	72.00	84.00	75.00
Salad Plate, diameter 7½″			
☐ green	8.00	11.00	9.00
☐ pink	11.00	14.00	12.00
☐ amber	8.00	11.00	9.00
☐ crystal	8.00	11.00	9.00
Salt and Pepper Shakers			
☐ green	38.00	46.00	40.00
☐ pink	70.00	80.00	73.00
☐ amber	36.00	44.00	38.00
☐ crystal	36.00	44.00	38.00
Saucer			
☐ green	4.00	6.00	4.50
☐ pink	4.00	6.00	4.50
☐ amber	4.00	6.00	4.50
☐ crystal	4.00	6.00	4.50

PRINCESS
Hocking

This pattern was produced between 1931 and 1934. The colors were green, pink, and "topaz." A large number of tumblers are available on the market today. Interestingly, they are made of thinner glass than the rest of the pattern.

Creamer

☐ pink	6.00	8.00	7.00
☐ green	6.50	7.50	6.50

	Current Price Range		Prior Year Average
☐ topaz	7.00	9.00	7.50
Cup			
☐ pink	4.00	6.50	4.50
☐ green	6.50	8.50	7.00
☐ topaz	4.50	6.50	5.00
Dinner Plate, 9″			
☐ pink	11.00	13.50	12.00
☐ green	18.50	21.00	19.00
☐ topaz	10.00	12.00	10.50
Dinner Plate, 9½″			
☐ pink	11.50	14.00	12.50
☐ green	19.00	21.50	19.50
☐ topaz	10.50	12.50	11.00
Grill Plate, 9½″			
☐ pink	9.00	11.50	9.50
☐ green	11.00	14.00	11.50
☐ topaz	5.00	7.00	5.50
Grill Plate, with handle, 11½″			
☐ pink	9.00	11.00	9.50
☐ green	9.50	11.50	10.00
Nappy, 4½″			
☐ pink	11.00	14.50	12.00
☐ green	17.00	19.50	17.50
☐ topaz	27.00	33.00	29.00
Orange Bowl, 9½″			
☐ pink	15.00	20.00	16.50
☐ green	21.50	26.00	22.50
☐ topaz	60.00	67.00	60.00
Platter, 12″			
☐ pink	11.00	13.50	12.00
☐ green	11.00	15.00	12.50
☐ topaz	37.50	42.50	40.00
Salad Bowl, 9″			
☐ pink	20.00	24.00	21.00
☐ green	20.00	24.00	21.00
☐ topaz	55.00	65.00	60.00
Salad Plate, 8″			
☐ pink	7.00	9.00	7.50
☐ green	7.50	9.50	8.00
☐ topaz	5.50	7.50	6.00
Saucer			
☐ pink	2.50	3.50	3.00
☐ green	3.25	4.25	3.50
☐ topaz	1.50	2.50	2.00
Sherbet Plate, 6″			
☐ pink	3.00	4.00	3.00
☐ green	3.50	4.50	3.50
☐ topaz	2.00	3.00	2.50

		Current Price Range		Prior Year Average
Sherbet				
☐ pink		9.00	11.00	10.00
☐ green		10.00	12.00	11.00
☐ topaz		10.00	12.00	11.00
Tumbler, 5 oz, 3½″				
☐ pink		13.00	16.00	14.00
☐ green		17.00	19.00	18.00
☐ topaz		15.50	18.50	16.00
Tumbler, 9 oz., 4″				
☐ pink		13.00	16.00	14.50
☐ green		15.00	17.00	15.50
☐ topaz		13.00	15.50	14.00
Tumbler, 10 oz., 5¼″				
☐ pink		15.50	18.00	16.00
☐ green		18.00	23.00	19.00
☐ topaz		16.00	19.00	16.50
Tumbler, 12½ oz., ice tea, 5″				
☐ pink		15.00	18.00	16.00
☐ green		16.50	19.00	17.00
☐ topaz		18.00	21.00	19.00
Tumbler, 12½ oz., footed, 6½″				
☐ pink		20.00	25.00	21.00
☐ green		39.00	44.00	40.00
Vase, 8″				
☐ pink		17.00	21.00	19.00
☐ green		17.50	21.50	19.00
Vegetable Bowl, oval				
☐ pink		12.00	14.00	13.00
☐ green		12.00	14.00	13.00
☐ topaz		32.00	35.00	32.00

S Pattern, Strippled Rose Band

S PATTERN, STIPPLED
ROSE BAND
MacBeth-Evans

Stippling is the small dot work used as a filler behind main motifs adding depth and dimension and a certain elegance. In this case the central medallion has a wide rose surrounded by wonderfully curved foliage, with a stippled background. The outer rim is a band of these roses and leaves decorated above and below with "S" shaped scrolls. The entire effect is quite pleasing and artistic.

	Current Price Range		Prior Year Average
Berry Bowl, diameter 8½"			
☐ crystal	5.00	7.00	6.25
☐ crystal with trim	11.50	13.50	12.00
☐ yellow	11.50	13.50	12.00
☐ amber	11.50	13.50	12.00
Cake Plate, diameter 11"			
☐ crystal	28.00	33.00	29.00
☐ crystal with trim	20.00	34.00	31.50
☐ yellow	30.00	34.00	31.50
☐ amber	30.00	34.00	31.50
Cake Plate, diameter 13"			
☐ crystal	45.00	50.00	46.00
☐ crystal with trim	50.00	60.00	52.00
☐ yellow	50.00	60.00	52.00
☐ amber	75.00	80.00	76.50
Cereal Bowl, diameter 5½"			
☐ crystal	2.00	3.00	2.50
☐ crystal with trim	3.00	5.00	3.50
☐ yellow	3.00	5.00	3.50
☐ amber	3.00	5.00	3.50
Creamer			
☐ crystal	3.00	5.00	3.50
☐ crystal with trim	4.50	6.50	5.00
☐ yellow	4.50	6.50	5.00
☐ amber	4.50	6.50	5.00
Cup			
☐ crystal	2.00	3.00	2.25
☐ crystal with trim	3.00	5.00	3.25
☐ yellow	3.00	5.00	3.25
☐ amber	3.00	5.00	3.25
Dinner Plate, diameter 9¼"			
☐ crystal	3.00	5.00	3.25
☐ crystal with trim	4.00	6.00	4.25
☐ yellow	4.00	6.00	4.25
☐ amber	4.00	6.00	4.25
Grill Plate			
☐ crystal	2.00	3.00	2.35
☐ crystal with trim	4.00	6.00	4.25
☐ yellow	4.00	6.00	4.25
☐ amber	4.00	6.00	4.25

	Current Price Range		Prior Year Average
Pitcher, 80 oz.			
☐ crystal	35.00	40.00	36.50
☐ crystal with trim	65.00	70.00	66.00
☐ yellow	65.00	70.00	66.00
☐ amber	65.00	70.00	66.00
☐ green	490.00	500.00	492.50
Sandwich Plate, diameter 8″			
☐ crystal	2.00	3.00	2.00
☐ crystal with trim	2.00	3.00	2.25
☐ yellow	2.00	3.00	2.25
☐ amber	2.00	3.00	2.25
Saucer			
☐ crystal	1.00	3.00	1.25
☐ crystal with trim	1.00	3.00	1.25
☐ yellow	1.00	3.00	1.25
☐ amber	1.00	3.00	1.25
Sherbet Dish, footed			
☐ crystal	3.00	5.00	3.25
☐ crystal with trim	4.00	6.00	4.25
☐ yellow	4.00	6.00	4.25
☐ amber	4.00	6.00	4.25
Sherbet Plate, diameter 6″			
☐ crystal	1.00	3.00	1.25
☐ crystal with trim	1.50	2.50	1.75
☐ yellow	1.50	2.50	1.75
Sugar Bowl			
☐ crystal	3.00	5.00	3.25
☐ crystal with trim	5.00	7.00	5.25
☐ yellow	5.00	7.00	5.25
☐ amber	5.00	7.00	5.25
Tumbler, 9 oz., height 4″			
☐ crystal	3.00	5.00	3.25
☐ crystal with trim	5.00	7.00	5.25
☐ yellow	5.00	7.00	5.25
☐ amber	5.00	7.00	5.25
☐ green	55.00	60.00	56.50
Tumbler, 10 oz., height 4¼″			
☐ crystal	3.00	5.00	3.50
☐ crystal with trim	5.00	7.00	5.50
☐ yellow	5.00	7.00	5.50
☐ amber	5.00	7.00	5.50
Tumbler, 12 oz., height 5″			
☐ crystal	4.00	6.00	4.25
☐ crystal with trim	6.00	7.00	6.25
☐ yellow	6.00	7.00	6.25
☐ amber	6.00	7.00	6.25

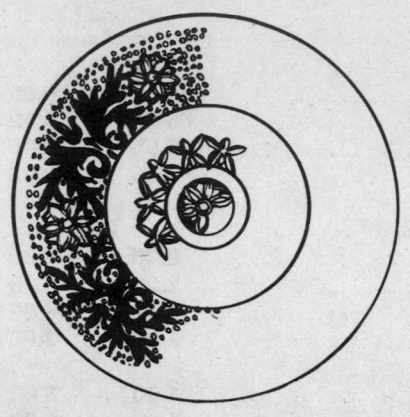

Sandwich

SANDWICH
Anchor Hocking

This is another pattern which has been reissued, so take care when collecting this design. It is an all encompassing decoration consisting of a multi-petalled flower medallion in the center surrounded by a band of interesting star shapes that resemble bees. The wide band which runs the perimeter of the outside alternates rosettes with scroll and foliage panels, all filled in with stippling. The design is well balanced and refrains from being busy.

	Current Price Range		Prior Year Average
Berry Bowl, diameter 4⅞″			
☐ crystal	2.50	3.50	2.75
☐ pink	2.00	3.00	2.25
☐ red	8.00	10.00	8.50
☐ amber	2.00	3.00	2.25
☐ green	1.00	3.00	1.25
Bowl, diameter 6½″			
☐ crystal	4.00	6.00	4.25
☐ amber	5.00	7.00	5.25
☐ green	18.00	23.00	19.00
Bowl, scalloped rim, diameter 6½″			
☐ crystal	4.00	6.00	4.50
☐ amber	5.00	7.00	5.25
☐ green	18.00	23.00	19.00
Bowl, diameter 8″			
☐ crystal	5.00	7.00	6.00
☐ pink	6.00	8.00	7.00
☐ red	28.00	33.00	29.00
☐ green	33.00	38.00	34.00
Bowl, scalloped rim, diameter 8″			
☐ crystal	5.00	7.00	6.00
☐ pink	6.00	8.00	7.00
☐ red	28.00	33.00	29.00
☐ green	33.00	38.00	34.00

	Current Price Range		Prior Year Average
Butter Dish			
☐ crystal	30.00	35.00	31.50
Cereal Bowl, diameter 6″			
☐ crystal	11.00	14.00	12.00
☐ amber	5.00	7.00	5.00
Cookie Jar, with cover			
☐ crystal	28.00	33.00	29.00
☐ gold	25.00	30.00	26.00
Creamer			
☐ crystal	3.50	4.50	3.75
☐ green	13.50	15.50	14.00
Cup			
☐ crystal	1.00	3.00	1.25
☐ amber	3.00	5.00	3.50
☐ green	12.00	13.00	12.25
Custard Cup			
☐ crystal	3.00	4.00	3.25
☐ green	1.00	2.00	1.50
Dessert Plate, diameter 7″			
☐ crystal	5.00	7.00	5.50
☐ amber	2.00	3.00	2.50
Dinner Plate, diameter 9″			
☐ crystal	8.00	10.00	8.50
☐ amber	3.50	4.50	3.75
☐ green	33.00	38.00	34.00
Juice Glass, 5 oz.			
☐ crystal	4.00	6.00	4.25
☐ green	1.50	2.50	1.75
Pitcher, height 6″			
☐ crystal	43.00	48.00	44.00
☐ green	90.00	95.00	91.50
Pitcher, ice lip, 64 oz.			
☐ crystal	40.00	45.00	41.50
☐ green	160.00	170.00	162.50
Salad Bowl, diameter 7″			
☐ crystal	5.00	7.00	6.00
☐ green	28.00	33.00	29.00
Sandwich Plate, diameter 12″			
☐ crystal	6.50	8.50	6.75
☐ amber	6.50	8.50	6.75
Saucer			
☐ crystal	1.00	3.00	1.25
☐ amber	2.50	3.50	2.75
☐ green	3.50	5.50	4.00
Serving Bowl, oval, length 8¼″			
☐ crystal	4.00	6.00	4.75
Sherbet Dish, footed			
☐ crystal	5.00	7.00	5.50

	Current Price Range		Prior Year Average
Sugar Bowl			
☐ crystal, with lid	11.50	13.50	12.00
☐ green, no lid	13.50	15.50	14.00
Tumbler, footed, 9 oz.			
☐ crystal	13.00	14.00	13.25
Water Glass, 9 oz.			
☐ crystal	6.00	7.00	6.25
☐ green	2.00	3.00	2.25

SANDWICH

This Sandwich pattern was made by Indiana, though other companies also made Sandwich patterns. The all-over design features flowers, scroll work and crossed diamond designs. The colors pink, green, amber, and crystal were made beginning in the 1920s, and teal, green, and red were made from the 1930s.

Sandwich is still made today with the original molds and colors. It is very hard to tell the old from the new.

Berry Bowl, 4¼"			
☐ crystal	1.50	3.50	2.00
☐ pink	2.00	4.00	2.50
☐ green	2.00	5.00	2.50
Bowl, 6"			
☐ pink	2.50	4.50	3.00
☐ green	2.50	4.50	3.00
Bowl, six sided, 6"			
☐ crystal	2.00	4.00	2.50
☐ teal	6.00	9.00	7.00
Bread and Butter Plate, 7"			
☐ crystal	3.00	5.00	3.50
☐ pink	2.50	4.50	3.00
☐ green	2.50	4.50	3.00

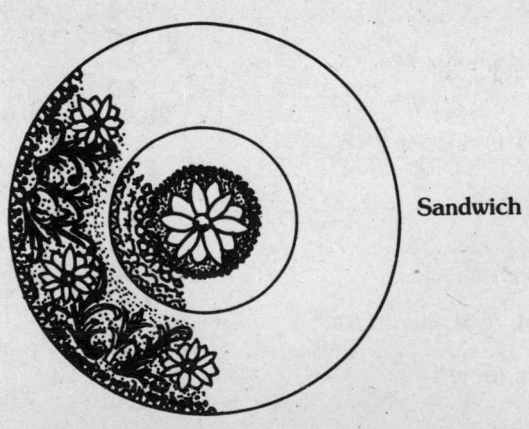

Sandwich

	Current Price Range		Prior Year Average
Butter Dish, with cover			
☐ pink	145.00	165.00	150.00
☐ green	145.00	165.00	150.00
☐ teal	180.00	210.00	190.00
Candlesticks, 3½"			
☐ crystal	9.00	11.50	10.00
☐ pink	13.00	17.00	14.00
☐ green	13.00	17.00	14.00
Cocktail Tumbler, footed, 3 oz.			
☐ pink	13.00	17.00	14.00
☐ green	13.00	17.00	14.00
Creamer			
☐ pink	5.00	8.00	6.00
☐ green	5.00	8.00	6.00
Cup			
☐ pink	3.50	5.50	4.00
☐ green	3.50	5.50	4.00
☐ teal	3.50	5.50	4.00
☐ red	18.00	22.00	19.00
Decanter, with stopper			
☐ pink	70.00	85.00	73.00
☐ green	70.00	85.00	73.00
Goblet, 9 oz.			
☐ pink	13.00	17.00	14.00
☐ green	13.00	17.00	14.00
Iced Tea Tumbler, footed, 12 oz.			
☐ pink	20.00	25.00	21.00
☐ green	20.00	25.00	21.00
Luncheon Plate, 8⅜"			
☐ crystal	2.00	4.00	2.50
☐ pink	3.50	5.50	4.00
☐ green	3.50	5.50	4.00
Pitcher, 68 oz.			
☐ pink	75.00	85.00	77.00
☐ green	75.00	85.00	77.00
Sandwich Plate, 13"			
☐ pink	11.00	14.00	12.00
☐ green	11.00	14.00	12.00
Sandwich Serving Plate, handle in center			
☐ crystal	20.00	25.00	21.00
☐ pink	25.00	30.00	26.00
☐ green	25.00	30.00	26.00
Saucer			
☐ pink	1.50	3.50	2.00
☐ green	1.50	3.50	2.00
☐ teal	2.50	4.50	3.00
☐ red	4.50	7.50	5.00

	Current Price Range		Prior Year Average
Sherbet			
☐ crystal	2.50	4.50	3.00
☐ pink	4.00	6.00	4.50
☐ green	4.00	6.00	4.50
☐ teal	4.50	7.50	5.00
Sherbet Plate, 6″			
☐ pink	1.50	3.50	2.00
☐ green	1.50	3.50	2.00
☐ teal	3.50	5.50	4.00
Water Tumbler, 8 oz.			
☐ pink	11.00	14.00	12.00
☐ green	11.00	14.00	12.00
Wine Goblet, 4 oz.			
☐ pink	15.00	20.00	16.00
☐ green	15.00	20.00	16.00

SHARON
Federal

This interesting and elegant pattern has sustained through the decades and emerged as one of the most popular collectibles in Depression glass. The design consists of a half spray of flower, flirtatiously arranged on one side of the center. The wide outer band is a series of floral panels separated by gentle indentations and resolved on the smooth rims. The shapes are straightforward, the glass clear and the colors mild.

Berry Bowl, diameter 5″			
☐ pink	6.00	8.00	7.00
☐ amber	5.00	7.00	5.50
☐ green	6.00	8.00	7.00

Sharon

	Current Price Range		Prior Year Average

Berry Bowl, diameter 8½
☐ pink	15.00	17.00	15.50
☐ amber	3.50	5.50	4.00
☐ green	18.00	22.00	19.00

Bread and Butter Plate, diameter 6″
☐ pink	3.00	5.00	4.00
☐ amber	2.00	4.00	3.00
☐ green	3.00	5.00	4.00

Butter Dish, with cover
☐ pink	40.00	45.00	41.50
☐ amber	38.00	43.00	39.50
☐ green	65.00	70.00	67.00

Cake Plate, footed, diameter 11½″
☐ pink	23.00	28.00	24.00
☐ amber	15.00	17.00	16.00
☐ green	43.00	48.00	44.00

Candy Jar, with cover
☐ pink	38.00	43.00	39.50
☐ amber	33.00	38.00	34.00
☐ green	115.00	120.00	116.50

Cereal Bowl, diameter 6″
☐ pink	14.00	15.00	14.25
☐ amber	9.00	11.00	9.75
☐ green	11.50	13.50	12.00

Cheese Dish, with cover
| ☐ pink | 575.00 | 625.00 | 585.00 |
| ☐ amber | 155.00 | 160.00 | 156.50 |

Creamer, footed
☐ pink	9.00	11.00	13.00
☐ amber	9.00	10.00	9.25
☐ green	13.00	14.00	13.25

Cup
☐ pink	9.00	11.00	9.50
☐ amber	7.00	9.00	8.00
☐ green	9.00	11.00	10.00

Dinner Plate, diameter 9½″
☐ pink	11.00	13.00	11.50
☐ amber	8.50	10.50	9.00
☐ green	11.00	13.00	11.50

Fruit Bowl, diameter 10″
☐ pink	23.00	28.00	24.00
☐ amber	14.00	16.00	15.00
☐ green	20.00	25.00	22.00

Jam Dish, diameter 7½″
☐ pink	78.00	83.00	79.00
☐ amber	22.00	28.00	23.00
☐ green	30.00	35.00	32.00

	Current Price Range		Prior Year Average
Pitcher, 80 oz.			
☐ pink	95.00	105.00	97.50
☐ amber	93.00	98.00	93.50
☐ green	315.00	325.00	317.50
Pitcher, with ice lip, 80 oz.			
☐ pink	100.00	110.00	103.50
☐ amber	90.00	95.00	92.00
☐ green	290.00	310.00	295.00
Platter, oval, length 12½			
☐ pink	12.00	16.00	13.00
☐ amber	10.00	12.00	11.00
☐ green	15.00	17.00	15.50
Salad Plate, diameter 7½″			
☐ pink	14.00	15.00	14.25
☐ amber	9.00	11.00	9.50
☐ green	12.50	14.50	13.00
Salt and Pepper Shakers			
☐ pink	35.00	40.00	36.50
☐ amber	30.00	35.00	32.00
☐ green	53.00	58.00	54.00
Saucer			
☐ pink	4.50	6.50	5.00
☐ amber	3.50	4.50	3.75
☐ green	4.50	6.50	4.75
Sherbet Dish, footed			
☐ pink	9.00	11.00	9.50
☐ amber	7.50	9.50	8.00
☐ green	18.00	22.00	19.00
Soup Bowl, diameter 5″			
☐ pink	28.00	33.00	29.00
☐ amber	15.50	17.50	16.00
☐ green	30.00	35.00	31.00
Soup Bowl, diameter 7½″			
☐ pink	25.00	30.00	26.50
☐ amber	20.00	25.00	22.00
Sugar Bowl, with lid			
☐ pink	30.00	35.00	31.00
☐ amber	20.00	25.00	21.00
☐ green	23.00	28.00	24.00
Tumbler, 9 oz., height 4⅛″			
☐ pink	18.00	22.00	19.00
☐ amber	17.00	20.00	18.00
☐ green	38.00	43.00	39.00
Tumbler, 12 oz., height 5¼″, thin			
☐ pink	30.00	34.00	32.00
☐ amber	20.00	25.00	22.00
☐ green	63.00	68.00	64.00

	Current Price Range		Prior Year Average
Tumbler, footed, 15 oz., height 6½"			
☐ pink	32.00	38.00	33.00
☐ amber	45.00	50.00	46.00
Vegetable Bowl, oval, lenghth 9½"			
☐ pink	15.00	17.00	16.00
☐ amber	9.00	11.00	9.50

SIERRA
Jeannette

These pieces have the look of glass fused together in panels, geometrically arranged, with this shape taking on the characteristics of the slats. The rims are continuations of these panels giving them a squared tooth appearance. The central medallion is an all encompassing starburst with elongated triangular rays.

Berry Bowl, diameter 8½"			
☐ pink	9.00	11.00	9.50
☐ green	12.00	15.00	13.00
Butter Dish, with cover			
☐ pink	43.00	48.00	44.00
☐ green	45.00	50.00	46.00
Cereal Bowl, diameter 5½"			
☐ pink	5.00	7.00	5.00
☐ green	6.00	8.00	6.00
Creamer			
☐ pink	7.50	9.50	7.75
☐ green	11.50	13.50	12.00
Cup			
☐ pink	5.00	7.00	5.50
☐ green	7.50	9.50	8.00
Dinner Plate, diameter 9"			
☐ pink	8.50	10.50	9.00
☐ green	9.00	11.50	13.50

Sierra

	Current Price Range		Prior Year Average
Pitcher, 32 oz., height 6½″			
☐ pink	35.00	40.00	36.50
☐ green	60.00	65.00	62.00
Platter, oval, length 11″			
☐ pink	11.50	13.50	12.00
☐ green	14.00	16.00	14.50
Salt and Pepper Shakers, pair			
☐ pink	23.00	28.00	24.00
☐ green	25.00	30.00	26.00
Saucer			
☐ pink	2.50	4.50	3.00
☐ green	3.00	5.00	3.50

SUNFLOWER
Jeannette

The sunflowers are vaguely reminiscent of Van Gogh with their wavy foliage arranged in a wide outer band. The center of the flower is made up of stippling, the center medallion is a multi-petalled flower with fern-like foliage. Whether in transparent glass or opaque, the colors are pretty and pastel.

Ashtray, diameter 5″			
☐ pink	6.00	8.00	6.50
☐ green	6.00	8.00	6.50
Cake Plate, three-legged, diameter 10″			
☐ pink	8.00	10.00	8.50
☐ green	8.00	10.00	8.50
Creamer			
☐ pink	7.00	9.00	8.00
☐ green	7.00	9.00	8.00

Sunflower

	Current Price Range		Prior Year Average
Cup			
☐ pink	6.00	8.00	7.00
☐ green	6.00	8.00	7.00
Dinner Plate, diameter 9″			
☐ pink	9.00	11.00	9.50
☐ green	9.00	11.00	9.50
Saucer			
☐ pink	2.50	3.50	2.75
☐ green	2.50	3.50	2.75
Sugar Bowl			
☐ pink	8.00	9.00	8.25
☐ green	8.00	9.00	8.25
Trivet, three-legged, length 7″			
☐ pink	105.00	115.00	107.50
☐ green	105.00	115.00	107.50
Tumbler, footed 8 oz., height 4¾″			
☐ pink	12.50	14.50	13.00
☐ green	12.50	14.50	13.00

SWANKY SWIGS

Promotional items that contained Kraft Cheese products, Swanky Swigs were made from the 1930's to the 1950's. Different designs were used on the swigs, and once empty they had many uses.

	Current Price Range		Prior Year Average
Antique Clock and Coal Scuttle, 3¾″			
☐ brown	.50	2.50	1.25
Antique Coffee Grinder and Plate, 3¾″			
☐ green	.50	2.50	1.25
Antique Coffee Pot and Trivet, 3¾″			
☐ black	.50	2.50	1.25
Antique Lamp and Kettle, 3¾″			
☐ blue	.50	2.50	1.25
Band Number 1, 3⅜″			
☐ red and black	1.00	3.00	1.75
☐ red and blue	1.50	3.50	2.25
☐ blue	2.00	4.00	2.75
Band Number 2, 4¾″			
☐ red and black	2.50	4.50	3.25
Band Number 2, 3⅜″			
☐ red and black	1.50	3.50	2.25
Bear and Pig Kiddie Kup, 3¾″			
☐ blue	.50	2.50	1.25
Bird and Elephant Kiddie Kup, 3¾″			
☐ red	.50	2.25	1.50
Cat and Rabbit Kiddie Kup, 3¾″			
☐ green	.50	2.25	1.25
Carnival, 3½″			
☐ blue	2.00	4.00	2.75

	Current Price Range		Prior Year Average
☐ red	2.00	4.00	2.75
☐ green	5.00	9.00	6.50
☐ yellow	5.00	9.00	6.50
Checkerboard, 3½″			
☐ blue	14.00	18.00	15.50
☐ red	14.00	18.00	15.50
☐ green	16.00	21.00	17.00
Cornflower Number 2, 3½″			
☐ blue	1.00	3.00	1.75
☐ red	1.00	3.00	1.75
☐ yellow	1.00	3.00	1.75
Daisy, 3¾″			
☐ red and white	.50	2.00	1.00
☐ red, white and green	.50	2.00	1.00
Dog and Rooster Kiddie Kup, 3¾″			
☐ orange	.50	2.50	1.25
Forget-Me-Not, 3½″			
☐ blue	.50	2.50	1.25
☐ red	.50	2.50	1.25
☐ yellow	.50	2.50	1.25
☐ yellow with decale	2.50	4.50	3.25
Sailboat, 3½″			
☐ blue	7.00	12.00	8.50
☐ green	7.00	12.00	8.50
Sailboat, 4½″			
☐ blue	9.00	16.00	11.00
☐ red	8.00	13.00	10.00
☐ green	8.00	13.00	10.00
Star, 3½″			
☐ blue	2.00	4.00	2.75
☐ red	2.00	4.00	2.75
☐ green	2.00	4.00	2.75
☐ black	2.00	4.00	2.75
Star, 4¾″			
☐ blue	3.50	5.50	4.25
Tulip Number 1, 3½″			
☐ blue	2.00	4.00	2.75
☐ red	2.00	4.00	2.75
Tulip Number 1, 4½″			
☐ blue	4.00	7.00	5.50
☐ red	4.00	7.00	5.50

SWIRL
Jeannette

This swirl pattern has a gentler curve, the flutes wide and flat and motioned counterclockwise. The central medallion is a bull's eye pattern made up of nesting ridges. The plates and bowls have a fluted edge, the pedestals are made up of the bull's eye design.

Swirl

	Current Price Range		Prior Year Average
Ashtray, diameter 5⅜″			
☐ pink	5.00	7.00	5.50
Bowl, footed, tab handles, diameter 10″			
☐ aquamarine	20.00	25.00	21.00
Bowl, footed, diameter 10½″			
☐ pink	12.00	15.00	13.00
☐ aquamarine	17.50	19.50	18.00
Butter Dish			
☐ pink	125.00	135.00	128.50
☐ aquamarine	190.00	200.00	195.00
Candleholders, single branch, pair			
☐ blue	75.00	80.00	76.00
Candleholders, double branch, pair			
☐ pink	20.00	24.00	21.50
☐ aquamarine	22.00	26.00	23.50
Candy Dish, with cover			
☐ pink	50.00	60.00	52.00
☐ aquamarine	70.00	75.00	72.00
Candy Dish, without lid, three-legged			
☐ pink	5.00	7.00	5.50
☐ aquamarine	8.00	9.00	8.25
Cereal Bowl, diameter 5¼″			
☐ pink	4.00	6.00	4.50
☐ aquamarine	6.50	8.50	7.00
☐ delphite	7.50	9.50	8.00
Coaster, diameter 3¼″			
☐ pink	5.00	6.00	5.25
☐ aquamarine	6.00	7.00	6.25
Creamer, footed			
☐ pink	6.00	7.00	6.25
☐ aquamarine	9.00	10.00	9.25
☐ delphite	7.00	8.00	7.25
Cup			
☐ pink	3.00	5.00	3.50
☐ aquamarine	6.00	8.00	6.00
☐ delphite	4.00	6.00	4.50
Dinner Plate, diameter 9¼″			
☐ pink	5.50	7.50	6.00

	Current Price Range		Prior Year Average
☐ aquamarine	10.00	12.00	10.50
☐ delphite	5.00	7.00	5.50
Pitcher, footed, 48 oz.			
☐ aquamarine	725.00	775.00	740.00
Plate, diameter 7¼"			
☐ pink	4.00	5.00	4.25
☐ aquamarine	7.00	8.00	7.25
Plate, diameter 10½"			
☐ delphite	9.00	11.00	9.50
Platter, oval, length 12"			
☐ delphite	18.00	22.00	19.00
Salad Bowl, diameter 9"			
☐ pink	8.50	10.50	9.00
☐ aquamarine	14.00	16.00	14.50
☐ delphite	15.00	17.00	15.50
Salad Plate, diameter 8"			
☐ pink	4.00	6.00	5.00
☐ aquamarine	8.00	10.00	9.00
☐ delphite	3.50	5.50	4.00
Salt and Pepper Shakers			
☐ aquamarine	25.00	30.00	27.00
Sandwich Plate, diameter 12½"			
☐ pink	7.00	8.00	7.25
☐ aquamarine	12.50	14.50	13.00
Saucer			
☐ pink	1.50	2.50	1.70
☐ aquamarine	2.00	3.00	2.25
☐ delphite	1.75	2.50	2.00
Sherbet Dish, footed			
☐ pink	4.50	6.50	5.00
☐ aquamarine	8.00	10.00	9.00
Sherbet Plate, height 6½"			
☐ pink	1.50	2.50	1.75
☐ aquamarine	3.00	4.00	3.50
☐ delphite	2.50	3.50	2.75
Soup Bowl, tab handles			
☐ pink	11.50	13.50	12.00
☐ aquamarine	13.00	13.50	15.50
Sugar Bowl, footed			
☐ pink	5.50	7.50	6.00
☐ aquamarine	9.00	10.00	9.25
☐ delphite	7.00	8.00	7.25
Tumbler, 9 oz., height 4"			
☐ pink	6.50	8.50	7.00
☐ aquamarine	10.50	12.50	11.00
Tumbler, 9 oz., height 4⅝"			
☐ pink	9.00	11.00	10.00

	Current Price Range		Prior Year Average
Tumbler, footed, 9 oz.			
☐ pink	11.50	13.50	12.00
☐ aquamarine	18.00	22.00	19.00
Tumbler, 12 oz., height 4¾″			
☐ pink	14.00	16.00	15.00
☐ aquamarine	33.00	38.00	34.00
Vase, footed, height 6½″			
☐ pink	10.50	12.50	11.00
☐ aquamarine	14.00	16.00	15.00
Vase, footed, height 8½″			
☐ aquamarine	16.50	18.50	17.00

TEA ROOM
Indiana

This pattern resembles a telescope pulled to its full length. Nesting ridges, high off the smooth surface, run horizontally in wide panels from the base to the ridge. The plates carry the same design, translated into octagonal bands, creating the look of a cobweb. The effect is simple, well designed and definitely Art Deco.

Candlesticks			
☐ pink	23.00	28.00	24.00
☐ green	28.00	33.00	29.00
Celery Bowl, length 8½″			
☐ pink	16.00	18.00	16.50
☐ green	20.00	25.00	21.50
Creamer, rectangular			
☐ pink	9.00	11.00	9.50
☐ green	11.50	13.50	12.00

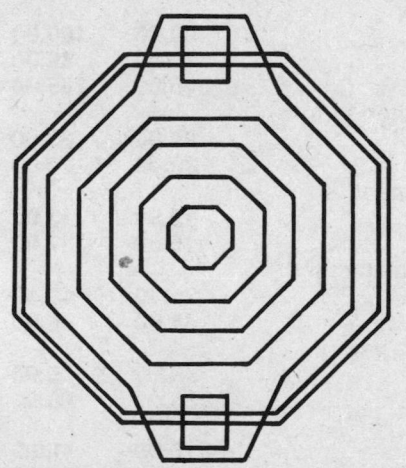

Tea Room

	Current Price Range		Prior Year Average

Creamer, round, diameter 4"
☐ pink	9.00	11.00	9.50
☐ green	11.50	13.50	12.00
☐ amber	38.00	43.00	39.00

Creamer and Sugar Bowl Set, with tray
☐ pink	48.00	53.00	49.00
☐ green	50.00	55.00	51.50

Cup
☐ pink	16.50	18.50	17.00
☐ green	20.00	25.00	22.00

Goblet, height 8"
☐ pink	40.00	45.00	42.00
☐ green	50.00	55.00	51.50

Ice Bucket
☐ pink	35.00	40.00	36.50
☐ green	30.00	35.00	32.00

Lamp, electric fittings
☐ pink	28.00	33.00	29.00
☐ green	30.00	35.00	32.00

Lunch Plate, diameter 8"
☐ pink	18.00	23.00	19.00
☐ green	18.00	23.00	19.00

Mustard Bowl, with lid
☐ pink	65.00	70.00	67.00
☐ green	75.00	80.00	77.00

Parfait Glass
☐ pink	30.00	35.00	32.00
☐ green	35.00	40.00	36.00

Pitcher, two quart capacity
☐ pink	90.00	100.00	92.50
☐ green	75.00	80.00	76.00
☐ amber	245.00	255.00	247.50

Plate, loop handled, diameter 11"
☐ pink	28.00	33.00	28.50
☐ green	30.00	35.00	32.00

Relish Dish, two compartment
☐ pink	12.00	13.00	12.25
☐ green	15.00	17.00	15.50

Salad Bowl, steep sided, diameter 9"
☐ pink	35.00	40.00	36.50
☐ green	45.00	50.00	47.50

Salt and Pepper Shakers, pair
☐ pink	35.00	40.00	36.50
☐ green	35.00	40.00	36.50

Saucer
☐ pink	10.00	12.00	10.50
☐ green	10.00	12.00	10.50

	Current Price Range		Prior Year Average
Sherbet Dish, footed			
☐ pink	12.50	14.50	13.00
☐ green	15.00	17.00	15.50
Sherbet Plate, diameter 6″			
☐ pink	11.00	13.00	11.50
☐ green	11.00	13.00	11.50
Sugar Bowl, diameter 4″			
☐ pink	9.00	11.00	9.50
☐ green	11.50	13.50	12.00
☐ amber	38.00	43.00	39.00
Sugar Bowl, rectangular			
☐ pink	9.00	11.00	9.50
☐ green	11.50	13.50	12.00
Sugar, with lid			
☐ pink	30.00	35.00	32.00
☐ green	35.00	40.00	36.50
Sundae Dish, pedestal foot, scalloped edge			
☐ pink	20.00	25.00	22.00
☐ green	25.00	30.00	27.00
Tumbler, collar base			
☐ pink	35.00	40.00	37.00
☐ green	45.00	50.00	47.00
Tumbler, pedestal foot, 6 oz.			
☐ pink	14.00	16.00	14.50
☐ green	16.50	18.50	17.00
Tumbler, pedestal foot, 9 oz.			
☐ pink	15.50	17.50	16.00
☐ green	18.00	22.00	19.00
☐ amber	43.00	48.00	44.00
Tumbler, pedestal foot, 11 oz.			
☐ pink	20.00	25.00	22.00
☐ green	25.00	30.00	26.50
Tumbler, pedestal foot, 12 oz.			
☐ pink	25.00	30.00	26.50
☐ green	28.00	33.00	29.50
Vase, height 9″			
☐ pink	35.00	40.00	36.50
☐ green	45.00	50.00	46.50
Vase, height 11″			
☐ pink	50.00	55.00	52.00
☐ green	60.00	65.00	62.00
Vegetable Bowl, oblong, length 10″			
☐ pink	33.00	38.00	34.00
☐ green	38.00	43.00	39.50

THISTLE
Macbeth-Evans

This lovely etched pattern consists of an overall feathery foliage design with bunches of fat thistles, nicely detailed and attractively arranged in sprays. The wide outer band that decorates the smooth edge is a wreath of these thistles, with stippled bodies and ridged puffs, connected with pairs of oak leaves. The bowls carry only this wreath with no center medallion.

	Current Price Range		Prior Year Average
Cake Plate, diameter 12"			
☐ pink	68.00	73.00	69.00
☐ green	83.00	88.00	84.00
Cereal Bowl, diameter 5½"			
☐ green	14.00	16.00	14.50
☐ pink	11.00	13.00	11.50
Cup			
☐ pink	13.00	15.00	13.50
☐ green	16.50	18.50	17.00
Fruit Bowl, diameter 10"			
☐ green	95.00	105.00	96.50
☐ pink	155.00	160.00	156.50
Grill Plate, diameter 11"			
☐ pink	11.50	13.50	12.00
☐ green	11.50	13.50	12.00

THREADING
Indiana

From a distance, these pieces have the appearance of a satin finish, showing off the lovely colors from the Indiana Glass Company. At close inspection, it can be seen that the matte surface is achieved by row after row of tiny ridges, rather like the grooves on a record album. The pieces are devoid of decoration other than this nice moldwork and the effect is a simple elegance.

Threading

	Current Price Range		Prior Year Average
Bowl, diameter 4″			
☐ pink	9.00	11.00	9.50
☐ amber	9.00	11.00	9.50
☐ green	9.00	11.00	9.50
Bowl, diameter 9½″			
☐ pink	20.00	24.00	21.00
☐ amber	20.00	24.00	21.00
☐ green	20.00	24.00	21.00
Candlesticks, height 4″			
☐ pink	20.00	24.00	21.00
☐ amber	20.00	24.00	21.00
☐ green	20.00	24.00	21.00
Candy Jar, with cover			
☐ pink	33.00	37.00	34.00
☐ amber	33.00	37.00	34.00
☐ green	33.00	37.00	34.00
Compote, diameter 7″			
☐ pink	11.00	14.00	11.50
☐ amber	11.00	14.00	11.50
☐ green	11.00	14.00	11.50
Compote Tray			
☐ pink	16.50	18.50	17.00
☐ amber	16.50	18.50	17.00
☐ green	16.50	18.50	17.00
Creamer			
☐ pink	11.00	12.00	11.25
☐ amber	11.00	12.00	11.25
☐ green	11.00	12.00	11.25
Fan Vase, height 5½″			
☐ pink	30.00	34.00	31.50
☐ amber	30.00	34.00	31.50
☐ green	30.00	34.00	31.50
Fruit Bowl, pedestal foot, height 6″			
☐ pink	20.00	25.00	22.00
☐ amber	20.00	25.00	22.00
☐ green	20.00	25.00	22.00
Fruit Bowl, diameter 9″			
☐ pink	18.50	20.50	19.00
☐ amber	18.50	20.50	19.00
☐ green	18.50	20.50	19.00
Goblet, height 6″			
☐ pink	16.50	18.50	17.00
☐ amber	16.50	18.50	17.00
☐ green	16.50	18.50	17.00
Pitcher, with lid			
☐ pink	78.00	83.00	79.50
☐ amber	78.00	83.00	79.50
☐ green	78.00	83.00	79.50

	Current Price Range		Prior Year Average
Sandwich Tray			
☐ pink	25.00	30.00	26.50
☐ amber	25.00	30.00	26.50
☐ green	25.00	30.00	26.50
Sherbet Dish			
☐ pink	13.50	15.50	14.00
☐ amber	13.50	15.50	14.00
☐ green	13.50	15.50	14.00
Sugar Bowl			
☐ pink	10.00	12.00	10.50
☐ amber	10.00	12.00	10.50
☐ green	10.00	12.00	10.50
Tumbler, pedestal foot, height 4½″			
☐ pink	11.50	13.50	12.00
☐ amber	11.50	13.50	12.00
☐ green	11.50	13.50	12.00
Tumbler, pedestal foot, height 5½″			
☐ pink	18.50	20.50	19.00
☐ amber	18.50	20.50	19.00
☐ green	18.50	20.50	19.00

WINDSOR DIAMOND
Jeannette

Similar in conception to "Waffle," the diamonds that cover these pieces in high relief are elongated and prismed. The star medallion is a continuation of these prisms, terminating in the center with a small circle. The light reflections are wonderful, and the clear colors show off the effect to the maximum degree. The shapes are straightforward, usually with smooth rims and flat bases, although a stubby footed bowl does exist.

Ashtray

☐ pink	28.00	33.00	29.00

Windsor Diamond

	Current Price Range		Prior Year Average
☐ crystal	10.50	12.50	11.00
☐ green	40.00	44.00	41.00

Berry Bowl, diameter 4¾"

☐ pink	4.00	6.00	4.50
☐ crystal	2.00	3.00	2.25
☐ green	5.00	7.00	5.50

Berry Bowl, diameter 8½"

☐ pink	9.00	11.00	9.50
☐ crystal	4.00	5.00	4.25
☐ green	10.00	12.00	10.50

Bowl, boat-shaped, 7¼" x 11¾"

☐ pink	17.00	19.00	17.50
☐ crystal	10.00	12.00	10.50
☐ green	17.50	22.50	18.00

Bowl, tri-legged, diameter 7⅛"

☐ pink	13.00	15.00	13.50
☐ crystal	3.50	4.50	3.75

Cake Plate, diameter 13"

☐ pink	10.50	12.50	11.00
☐ crystal	4.00	6.00	4.75
☐ green	11.50	13.50	12.00

Candlesticks, pair, 3"

☐ pink	48.00	53.00	49.50
☐ crystal	11.50	13.50	12.00

Candy Jar, with cover

☐ pink	18.00	22.00	19.00
☐ crystal	7.50	9.50	8.00

Bowl, diameter 5⅛"

☐ pink	9.00	11.00	9.50
☐ crystal	3.00	4.00	3.25
☐ green	11.00	12.00	11.25

Bowl, diameter 5⅝"

☐ pink	9.00	11.00	9.50
☐ crystal	3.00	4.00	3.25
☐ green	11.00	12.00	11.25

Bowl, diameter 12½"

☐ pink	48.00	53.00	49.00
☐ crystal	9.00	11.00	9.50

Bowl, diameter 5"

☐ pink	11.50	12.50	11.75
☐ crystal	4.00	5.00	4.25
☐ green	12.50	13.50	13.00

Bowl, sugar, lidded

☐ pink	3.50	4.50	3.75

Coaster

☐ pink	4.50	5.50	4.75
☐ crystal	2.00	3.00	2.25

	Current Price Range		Prior Year Average
Creamer			
☐ pink	2.50	3.50	2.75
☐ crystal	2.50	3.50	2.75
☐ green	7.00	8.00	7.25
Pitcher, 16 oz., height 4⅝"			
☐ pink	75.00	80.00	76.00
☐ crystal	16.50	18.50	17.00
Pitcher, 52 oz., height 6⅝"			
☐ pink	17.50	19.50	18.00
☐ crystal	10.00	12.00	10.50
☐ green	42.00	47.00	44.50
Plate, diameter 13½"			
☐ pink	14.00	15.00	14.25
☐ crystal	7.00	8.00	7.25
☐ green	14.00	16.00	14.75
Plate, dinner, diameter 9"			
☐ pink	9.00	10.00	9.25
☐ crystal	3.00	4.00	3.25
☐ green	9.00	10.00	9.25
Plate, oval, diameter 11⅜"			
☐ pink	9.00	10.00	9.25
☐ crystal	4.00	5.00	4.25
☐ green	9.00	11.00	9.50
Plate, salad, diameter 7"			
☐ pink	9.00	10.00	9.25
☐ crystal	2.50	3.50	2.75
☐ green	9.00	11.00	9.75
Plate, sandwich, with handle, diameter 10¼"			
☐ pink	8.00	10.00	8.50
☐ crystal	3.50	4.50	3.75
☐ green	9.00	11.00	9.50
Plate, serving, diameter 15½"			
☐ crystal	4.50	5.50	4.75
Plate, sherbet, diameter 6"			
☐ pink	2.00	3.00	2.25
☐ crystal	1.00	2.00	1.25
☐ green	3.00	4.00	3.25
Relish Platter, divided, length 11½"			
☐ crystal	5.00	6.00	5.25
Salt and Pepper, pair			
☐ pink	25.00	30.00	27.00
☐ crystal	11.50	13.50	12.00
☐ green	33.00	38.00	34.00
Tray, oval, 4¼" x 9"			
☐ pink	6.00	7.00	6.25
☐ crystal	2.50	3.50	2.75
☐ green	7.00	8.00	7.25

	Current Price Range		Prior Year Average
Tray, square, 4"			
☐ pink	4.00	5.00	4.25
☐ crystal	2.00	3.00	2.25
☐ green	6.00	7.00	6.25
Tumbler, 5 oz., height 3¼"			
☐ pink	9.00	10.00	9.25
☐ crystal	3.50	4.50	3.75
☐ green	9.00	11.00	9.50
Tumbler, 9 oz., height 4"			
☐ pink	8.00	9.00	8.25
☐ crystal	4.00	5.00	5.25
☐ green	9.50	10.50	9.75
Tumbler, 12 oz., height 5"			
☐ pink	14.00	16.00	14.50
☐ crystal	5.00	6.00	5.25
☐ green	18.00	22.00	19.50

ELEGANT PATTERNS

A.H. HEISEY—THE GLASS LIVES ON

Augustus Henry Heisey was born August 25, 1842 in Hanover, Germany. When he was still a very small child, his family left Germany and settled in Merrittown, Pennsylvania. Soon after their arrival, Heisey's father died. His mother returned to Germany, but he remained in Merrittown, cared for by an older sister until he had finished his schooling.

He then went to Pittsburgh and took a job at the King Glass Co. as a clerk. He enjoyed working in the glassware business but his stay there was interrupted by the civil war. In 1862 he entered the United States Army as a first sergeant and left three years later as a captain. The same qualities of discipline and perseverance that earned him his commission would also distinguish his career in business.

When he returned to Pittsburgh and private life, Heisey went to work for George Duncan at Ripley Glass Works. Five years later, in 1870, he married Duncan's daughter Susan. When Duncan set up his own glassware company, Heisey went to work for him there; an association that was to last until Duncan's death in 1877. Two years later, Heisey and one of Duncan's sons, James, became co-owners of George Duncan & Sons, which by then had become a successful company.

The thought of owning his own glass company outright had always attracted Heisey though, and he began laying plans for the project in 1893. Construction of the new plant began in 1895 and it was ready for business a year later. Heisey started small, but the company grew steadily until it employed over 700 people.

In addition to being the president of the company, Heisey wasn't afraid of designing glass himself. Back in his days with George Duncan, he designed the unusual umbrella vase. He was also responsible for designing one of A.H. Heisey & Co.'s most popular patterns: Shell and Tassel. Although most of the designing was done by professionals at the company, Heisey remained involved in design; as well as all other aspects of the company.

Heisey's sons, E. Wilson and T. Clarence (who would each in their turn head the company), also worked with their father, but he remained an energetic leader. Sadly, on February 13, 1922, at the age of 79, Augustus Heisey passed away.

The business continued to grow. The Heisey reputation spread throughout the United States and Europe and customer demand was high. But even good things must end and the company closed in 1957.

But the story doesn't end there. The reputation of this fine glass continued to grow and new collectors were drawn to the hobby every day. Clubs were formed, and people met to enjoy their glass, talk about a bargain, and enjoy each other's company.

One day in 1969, nine Heisey collectors from the Newark, Ohio area decided to form the Newark Heisey Collectors Club. They displayed their glass several times over the next two years and it was warmly received by the public. By the middle of 1971, their membership had grown to twenty collectors.

At just about the same time, a short-lived national club devoted to Heisey glass was disbanded, creating a void. Someone was needed to coordinate the clubs around the country and so the Newark group stepped in. They formed the Heisey Collectors of America (HCA); a non-profit corporation dedicated to the collection and preservation of the products of A.H. Heisey & Co. Membership was opened to collectors on January 1, 1972, and now includes 4,600 members.

The organization continued to grow. In July of 1973, the HCA was given the Samuel Dennis King house in Newark to use as a museum. After extensive renovation work, the museum opened in September of 1974 and has done very well ever since. The club also owns a building next to the museum and it's used as a library and administrative office.

But the last chapter of this story is the most exciting of all. When A.H. Heisey & Co. closed its doors in 1957, the molds they used to make the glass were bought by Imperial Glass Co. The molds were often used by Imperial until finally, in December of 1984, Imperial filed for bankruptcy and was acquired by Consolidated Colony. The HCA had thought about buying the molds for years, and now they had their chance. Through gifts and loans, they raised enough money to go ahead with the purchase. The cost was $229,150, an impressive sum for a small, private organization to raise. Included in the sale were 4,200 molds as well as several hundred etching plates (at least seventy-five of which are new). Thousands of mold drawings, some of which identify previously unknown molds were also in the sale.

A new warehouse facility was also acquired by the HCA. This made it possible to store the molds and many miscellaneous items from the museum in one place. Volunteers donated their time and money while companies such as the Ford Motor Corporation donated valuble equipment. Somehow the monumental task of sorting, preparing, packing, and moving the molds was completed.

So Heisey collectors can now breathe more easily. Their glass won't lose its value to reproductions. It was a bold venture and one worthy of praise. It showed that collectors who love their hobby can pull together for a common cause. Congratulations to the family and friends of the Heisey Collectors of America and thank you for preserving a piece of America for future generations.

AMERICAN
Fostoria

This classic cube style design has become a favorite glass of collectors. Prices should escalate as a result of Fostoria's announcement that its manufacturing process will no longer include handwork. American was mostly made in crystal, some green, amber, blue, and yellow was also made. Some pieces of American are still being produced.

	Current Price Range		Prior Year Average
Appetizer, individual, 3¼"			
☐ crystal	15.00	40.00	20.00
Ashtray, square, 5"			
☐ crystal	17.00	25.00	19.00
Baby Set, tumbler and bowl			
☐ crystal	40.00	50.00	42.00
Banana Split Bowl, 9"			
☐ crystal	28.00	42.00	32.00
Bell			
☐ crystal	17.00	27.00	19.00
Bon Bon Dish, 3 toes, 6"			
☐ crystal	8.00	13.00	9.50
Bowl, rolled edge, 11½"			
☐ crystal	30.00	45.00	33.00
Bread and Butter Plate, 6"			
☐ crystal	5.00	7.50	6.00
Bud Vase, footed, flared, 6"			
☐ crystal	13.00	17.00	14.00

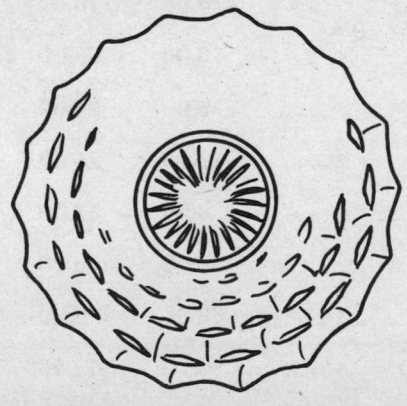

American

	Current Price Range		Prior Year Average
Bud Vase, footed, flared, 8½"			
☐ crystal	20.00	26.00	21.00
Butter Dish, with lid, round			
☐ crystal	95.00	108.00	98.00
Butter Dish, oblong, ¼ lb.			
☐ crystal	30.00	40.00	32.00
Cake Plate, footed, 12"			
☐ crystal	37.00	46.00	39.00
Candlesticks, pair, 3"			
☐ crystal	22.00	35.00	25.00
Candlesticks, pair, 6"			
☐ crystal	50.00	70.00	57.00
Centerpiece Bowl, 3 corners, 11"			
☐ crystal	30.00	45.00	34.00
Coaster, 3¾"			
☐ crystal	4.00	8.00	5.00
Cocktail Goblet, footed, 3 oz., 2⅞"			
☐ crystal	11.00	14.00	12.00
Cologne Bottle, 8 oz., 7½"			
☐ crystal	43.00	60.00	46.00
Comport, flat, 8½"			
☐ crystal	40.00	50.00	42.00
Comport, flat, 9½"			
☐ crystal	40.00	50.00	42.00
Condiment Tray, 4 sections			
☐ crystal	30.00	40.00	32.00
Cream Soup			
☐ crystal	20.00	30.00	22.50
Creamer, 9½ oz., 4¼"			
☐ crystal	9.00	14.00	11.00
Creamer, tea			
☐ crystal	6.00	9.00	7.00
Cup, footed, 7 oz.			
☐ crystal	6.00	10.00	7.00
Decanter, with stopper, 24 oz., 9¼"			
☐ crystal	68.00	85.00	72.00
Dinner Plate, 9½"			
☐ crystal	18.00	24.00	20.00
Finger Bowl, 4½"			
☐ crystal	17.00	24.00	18.00
Finger Bowl Plate, 6½"			
☐ crystal	8.00	12.00	9.00
Fruit Bowl, footed, 12"			
☐ crystal	85.00	110.00	90.00
Fruit Bowl, footed, 16"			
☐ crystal	60.00	90.00	68.00
Fruit Nappy, flared, 4¾"			
☐ crystal	8.00	12.00	9.00

	Current Price Range		Prior Year Average

Goblet, footed, 10 oz., 6⅞"
☐ crystal .... 14.00 | 19.00 | 15.00

Goblet, low, 9 oz., 5½"
☐ crystal .... 9.00 | 13.00 | 10.00

Handkerchief Box, with cover, 5½" x 4½" x 2"
☐ crystal .... 110.00 | 140.00 | 115.00

Hurricane Lamp, 12"
☐ crystal .... 70.00 | 80.00 | 72.00

Ice Bucket
☐ crystal .... 40.00 | 50.00 | 42.00

Iced Tea Tumbler, footed, flared, 12 oz., 5¾"
☐ crystal .... 13.00 | 17.00 | 14.00

Jam Pot, with cover, 4½"
☐ crystal .... 40.00 | 50.00 | 42.00

Jelly Comport, regular, 4¼"
☐ crystal .... 12.00 | 18.00 | 13.00

Juice Tumbler, footed, 5 oz., 4¾"
☐ crystal .... 10.00 | 14.00 | 11.00

Lemon Dish, with cover, 5½"
☐ crystal .... 26.00 | 34.00 | 28.00

Mayonnaise Dish, with liner
☐ crystal .... 24.00 | 32.00 | 25.00

Mayonnaise Ladle
☐ crystal .... 10.50 | 14.50 | 11.50

Muffin Tray, handled
☐ crystal .... 21.00 | 29.00 | 22.50

Mustard Dish, with cover and spoon, 3¾"
☐ crystal .... 28.00 | 35.00 | 30.00

Napkin Ring
☐ crystal .... 5.00 | 8.00 | 6.00

Nappy, flared, 7"
☐ crystal .... 30.00 | 40.00 | 32.00

Nappy, flared, 9"
☐ crystal .... 30.00 | 45.00 | 33.00

Nappy, shallow, 7"
☐ crystal .... 27.00 | 35.00 | 28.00

Nappy, 3 corners, handle, 5"
☐ crystal .... 8.00 | 12.00 | 9.00

Oil Cruet, 7 oz., 6¾"
☐ crystal .... 35.00 | 45.00 | 37.00

Old Fashioned Tumbler, flat, 6 oz., 3⅜"
☐ crystal .... 9.00 | 13.00 | 10.00

Oyster Cocktail, 4½ oz., 3½"
☐ crystal .... 11.00 | 14.00 | 12.00

	Current Price Range		Prior Year Average
Pickle Jar, with cover, 6″			
☐ crystal	135.00	165.00	142.00
Pitcher, with lip, 3 pints, 6½″			
☐ crystal	45.00	55.00	47.00
Pitcher, with lip, ½ gallon, 8¼″			
☐ crystal	70.00	80.00	72.00
Platter, oval, 12″			
☐ crystal	60.00	70.00	62.00
Preserve Bowl, with cover and handle, 5½″			
☐ crystal	30.00	45.00	33.00
Puff Box, with cover, 3″ x 3″ x 2⅞″			
☐ crystal	68.00	85.00	72.00
Punch Bowl, with base, 3¾ gallons, 18″			
☐ crystal	230.00	260.00	240.00
Punch Cup, flared, 6 oz.			
☐ crystal	6.00	9.00	7.00
Relish Tray, for olives, oval, 6″			
☐ crystal	8.00	12.00	9.00
Relish Tray, for pickles, oval, 8″			
☐ crystal	11.00	15.00	12.00
Relish Tray, oval, 3 sections, 11″			
☐ crystal	28.00	35.00	30.00
Rose Bowl, 3½″			
☐ crystal	13.00	22.00	15.00
Rose Bowl, 5″			
☐ crystal	18.00	25.00	19.00
Salad Plate, 8½″			
☐ crystal	13.00	17.00	14.00
Salt and Pepper, round bottom, 3½″			
☐ crystal	13.00	17.00	14.00
Salt Dish, individual			
☐ crystal	3.00	7.00	4.00
Sandwich Plate, 11½″			
☐ crystal	20.00	30.00	22.00
Saucer			
☐ crystal	2.50	4.50	3.00
Serving Bowl, with handle, 9″			
☐ crystal	20.00	30.00	22.00
Sherbet, low, flared, 5 oz., 3¼″			
☐ crystal	7.50	11.50	8.50
Sherbet, with handle, 4½ oz., 3½″			
☐ crystal	13.00	17.00	14.00
Sugar, tea			
☐ crystal	5.50	8.50	6.00
Sugar, with cover and handle, 5¼″			
☐ crystal	19.00	25.00	21.00
Sugar Shaker, 4¾″			
☐ crystal	110.00	140.00	120.00

	Current Price Range		Prior Year Average
Sundae, 6 oz., 3⅛″			
☐ crystal	8.00	11.50	9.00
Sweet Pea Vase, 4½″			
☐ crystal	88.00	105.00	92.00
Toothpick, 2¼″			
☐ crystal	16.00	23.00	17.00
Urn, square, 7½″			
☐ crystal	30.00	40.00	32.00
Utility Tray, handled, round, 9″			
☐ crystal	21.00	29.00	22.00
Vase, 8″			
☐ crystal	32.00	45.00	34.00
Vase, 10″			
☐ crystal	42.00	55.00	44.00
Vegetable Bowl, oval, 2 sections, 10″			
☐ crystal	27.00	37.00	30.00
Water Bottle, 44 oz., 9¼″			
☐ crystal	130.00	160.00	138.00
Water Tumbler, footed, 9 oz., 4⅜″			
☐ crystal	9.00	15.00	10.00
Wedding Bowl, pedestal, 6½″			
☐ crystal	28.00	37.00	30.00
Whiskey Tumbler, flat, 2 oz., 2½″			
☐ crystal	7.00	11.00	8.00
Wine Goblet, footed, 2½ oz., 4¾″			
☐ crystal	12.00	17.00	13.00

BAROQUE
Fostoria

Made in crystal, blue, and yellow, this elegant pattern features ornamental scrolls and designs on simple, delicately scalloped pieces.

Ashtray, oval			
☐ blue	13.00	17.00	14.00
☐ yellow	11.00	14.00	12.00
☐ crystal	7.00	10.00	8.00

Baroque

	Current Price Range		Prior Year Average
Bowl, flared, 12″			
☐ blue	26.00	34.00	28.00
☐ yellow	21.00	29.00	22.00
☐ crystal	15.00	20.00	16.00
Bowl, handles, 10½″			
☐ blue	31.00	39.00	32.00
☐ yellow	26.00	34.00	28.00
☐ crystal	17.00	23.00	18.00
Bowl, oval, 6½″			
☐ blue	13.00	20.00	14.00
☐ yellow	11.00	16.00	12.00
☐ crystal	8.00	12.00	9.00
Bread and Butter Plate, 6″			
☐ blue	5.00	7.00	5.50
☐ yellow	3.50	5.50	4.00
☐ crystal	2.00	4.00	2.50
Cake Plate, handles, 10″			
☐ blue	20.00	25.00	21.00
☐ yellow	15.00	20.00	16.00
☐ crystal	11.00	14.00	12.00
Candelabra, 3 lights, 9¼″			
☐ blue	68.00	82.00	71.00
☐ yellow	54.00	66.00	56.00
☐ crystal	40.00	50.00	42.00
Candlesticks, 4″			
☐ blue	22.00	29.00	23.00
☐ yellow	18.00	22.00	19.00
☐ crystal	13.00	17.00	14.00
Candlesticks, 5½″			
☐ blue	26.00	34.00	28.00
☐ yellow	22.00	28.00	23.00
☐ crystal	18.00	22.00	19.00
Celery Dish, oval, 11″			
☐ blue	22.00	29.00	23.00
☐ yellow	14.00	19.00	15.00
☐ crystal	11.00	14.00	12.00
Cereal Bowl, 6″			
☐ blue	26.00	34.00	28.00
☐ yellow	20.00	25.00	21.00
☐ crystal	14.00	20.00	15.00
Cocktail Tumbler, footed, 3¾ oz., 3″			
☐ blue	15.00	20.00	16.00
☐ yellow	12.00	16.00	13.00
☐ crystal	8.00	12.00	9.00
Compote, 6½″			
☐ blue	18.00	22.00	19.00
☐ yellow	14.00	18.00	15.00
☐ crystal	8.00	11.00	10.00

	Current Price Range		Prior Year Average
Cream Soup			
☐ blue	26.00	34.00	28.00
☐ yellow	20.00	25.00	21.00
☐ crystal	14.00	19.00	15.00
Creamer, footed, 3¾"			
☐ blue	14.00	18.00	15.00
☐ yellow	11.00	14.00	12.00
☐ crystal	6.00	10.00	7.00
Cruet, with stopper, 3½ oz., 5½"			
☐ blue	230.00	270.00	240.00
☐ yellow	230.00	270.00	240.00
☐ crystal	23.00	29.00	24.00
Dinner Plate, 9"			
☐ blue	26.00	34.00	28.00
☐ yellow	20.00	25.00	21.00
☐ crystal	13.00	17.00	14.00
Floating Garden Bowl, 10"			
☐ blue	35.00	45.00	37.00
☐ yellow	31.00	39.00	32.00
☐ crystal	21.00	29.00	22.00
Ice Bucket, metal handle			
☐ blue	78.00	97.00	82.00
☐ yellow	55.00	65.00	57.00
☐ crystal	31.00	39.00	32.00
Iced Tea Tumbler, 14 oz., 5¾"			
☐ blue	31.00	39.00	32.00
☐ yellow	25.00	30.00	26.00
☐ crystal	15.00	20.00	16.00
Juice Tumbler, 5 oz., 3¾"			
☐ blue	20.00	25.00	21.00
☐ yellow	18.00	22.00	19.00
☐ crystal	11.00	14.00	12.00
Luncheon Plate, 8"			
☐ blue	9.00	13.00	10.00
☐ yellow	7.00	11.00	8.00
☐ crystal	5.00	9.00	6.00
Mayonnaise, 5½"			
☐ blue	24.00	31.00	26.00
☐ yellow	20.00	24.00	21.00
☐ crystal	17.00	21.00	18.00
Nappy, 5"			
☐ blue	14.00	20.00	15.00
☐ yellow	11.00	15.00	12.00
☐ crystal	8.00	12.00	9.00
Old Fashioned Tumbler, 6¾ oz., 3½"			
☐ blue	21.00	29.00	22.00
☐ yellow	18.00	22.00	19.00
☐ crystal	11.00	14.00	12.00

	Current Price Range		Prior Year Average

Pickle Dish, 8¼"

☐ blue	14.00	19.00	15.50
☐ yellow	11.00	16.00	12.00
☐ crystal	7.50	11.50	8.50

Pitcher, 44 oz.

☐ blue	625.00	675.00	635.00
☐ yellow	525.00	575.00	535.00
☐ crystal	135.00	165.00	145.00

Punch Cup, 6 oz.

☐ blue	18.00	22.00	19.00
☐ crystal	6.00	9.00	7.00

Relish Tray, 3 sections, handled

☐ blue	24.00	31.00	26.00
☐ yellow	20.00	25.00	21.00
☐ crystal	11.00	14.00	12.00

Rose Bowl, 3¾"

☐ blue	26.00	34.00	28.00
☐ yellow	19.00	26.00	21.00
☐ crystal	13.00	17.00	14.00

Rose Bowl, 8¾"

☐ yellow	26.00	34.00	28.00

Salad Plate, 7"

☐ blue	7.00	11.00	8.00
☐ yellow	6.00	10.00	7.00
☐ crystal	4.00	7.00	5.00

Salt and Pepper Shakers

☐ blue	100.00	130.00	110.00
☐ yellow	87.00	103.00	90.00
☐ crystal	30.00	40.00	32.00

Saucer

☐ blue	4.50	6.50	5.00
☐ yellow	3.00	5.00	3.50
☐ crystal	1.00	3.00	1.50

Serving Plate, center handle, 11"

☐ crystal	14.00	19.00	15.00

Sherbet, 5 oz.

☐ blue	16.00	21.00	17.00
☐ yellow	12.00	16.00	13.00
☐ crystal	7.00	10.00	8.00

Sugar, footed, 3½"

☐ blue	12.00	15.00	13.00
☐ yellow	9.00	13.00	10.00
☐ crystal	6.00	9.00	6.50

Tray, oval, 11¼"

☐ blue	20.00	25.00	21.00
☐ yellow	15.00	20.00	16.00
☐ crystal	11.00	14.00	12.00

		Current Price Range		Prior Year Average
Vase, 8¼"				
☐ blue		26.00	34.00	28.00
☐ yellow		21.00	28.00	22.00
☐ crystal		16.00	20.00	17.00
Water Goblet, 9 oz.				
☐ blue		26.00	34.00	28.00
☐ yellow		18.00	22.00	19.00
☐ crystal		13.00	17.00	14.00
Water Tumbler, 9 oz.				
☐ blue		25.00	30.00	26.00
☐ yellow		20.00	25.00	21.00
☐ crystal		12.00	16.00	13.00

CANDLEWICK
Imperial

Introduced in 1936, Candlewick is still made today. A popular and simple pattern, it has mostly been made in crystal. Some colors have also been made.

Ashtray				
☐ crystal		4.00	6.50	5.00
Ashtray, heart shaped, 5½"				
☐ crystal		3.50	6.00	4.50
Ashtray, oblong, 4½"				
☐ crystal		3.50	6.00	4.50
Ashtray, round, 2¾"				
☐ crystal		2.50	4.50	3.25
Ashtray, square, 4½"				
☐ crystal		4.00	6.00	4.50
Baked Apple Bowl, rolled edge, 6"				
☐ crystal		11.00	14.00	12.00
Banana Bowl, 10"				
☐ crystal		16.00	20.00	17.50
Bell, 4"				
☐ crystal		14.00	18.00	15.00
Bon Bon Bowl, handled, 5"				
☐ crystal		14.00	18.00	15.00

Candlewick

	Current Price Range		Prior Year Average

Bouillon Bowl
□ crystal 11.50 14.50 12.50
Bowl, basket shape, handle, 11″
□ crystal 37.00 45.00 40.00
Bowl, bell shaped, 10″
□ crystal 14.00 17.00 15.00
Bowl, square, fancy edge, footed, 9″
□ crystal 14.00 18.00 15.50
Bread and Butter Plate, 6″
□ crystal 5.00 8.00 6.50
Butter Dish, with cover, round, 5½″
□ crystal 16.00 20.00 17.00
Butter Knife
□ crystal 18.00 23.00 19.00
Candy Box, with round lid, 6½″
□ crystal 16.00 19.00 17.00
Candleholder, 5½″
□ crystal 14.00 17.00 15.00
Candleholder, flat
□ crystal 9.50 12.00 10.50
Candleholder, flower shaped, 4″
□ crystal 7.00 10.00 8.00
Candleholder, mushroom shape
□ crystal 7.00 10.00 8.00
Candy Jar, footed with cover
□ crystal 18.00 23.00 19.00
Celery Bowl, oval, 11″
□ crystal 20.00 26.00 22.00
Claret Goblet, 5 oz.
□ crystal 16.00 19.00 17.00
Coaster, 4″
□ crystal 4.00 6.50 5.00
Cocktail Goblet, 4 oz.
□ crystal 16.00 19.00 17.00
Compote, 4½″
□ crystal 8.50 11.50 9.50
Compote, beaded stem, 8″
□ crystal 16.00 20.00 17.00
Condiment Tray, 5½″ x 9¼″
□ crystal 14.00 17.00 15.00
Cream Soup, 5″
□ crystal 11.00 14.00 12.00
Creamer, footed
□ crystal 5.00 7.50 6.00
Cruet, with stopper, etched "oil"
□ crystal 18.00 23.00 19.00
Cruet, with stopper, etched "vinegar"
□ crystal 18.00 23.00 19.00

	Current Price Range		Prior Year Average

Decanter, with stopper
☐ crystal 21.00 26.00 22.00
Dinner Plate, 10″
☐ crystal 11.00 14.00 12.00
Egg Cup
☐ crystal 11.00 14.00 12.00
Finger Bowl
☐ crystal 9.00 12.00 10.00
Floating Garden Bowl, 12″
☐ crystal 16.00 20.00 17.00
Fruit Bowl, beaded stem, 10″
☐ crystal 16.00 20.00 17.00
Fruit Bowl, handles, 4¾″
☐ crystal 10.50 13.00 11.50
Fruit Bowl, 6½″
☐ crystal 11.00 14.00 12.00
Goblet, 11 oz.
☐ crystal 11.00 15.00 12.00
Hurricane Lamp, flared and crimped, edge globe, 3 pieces
☐ crystal 48.00 62.00 53.00
Iced Tea Tumbler, beaded foot, 14 oz.
☐ crystal 13.00 16.00 14.00
Jam Bowl, 3 sections, 10½″
☐ crystal 20.00 25.00 22.00
Jelly Bowl, with lid, 5½″
☐ crystal 14.00 18.00 15.00
Juice Tumbler, beaded foot, 5 oz.
☐ crystal 14.00 18.00 15.00
Luncheon Plate, 9″
☐ crystal 7.00 10.00 8.00
Mayonnaise Dish, with liner, 7″
☐ crystal 16.00 20.00 17.00
Mayonnaise Ladle, 6¼″
☐ crystal 2.50 4.50 3.00
Mint Bowl, 6″
☐ crystal 8.50 11.50 9.50
Mustard Jar, with spoon
☐ crystal 25.00 30.00 26.00
Nappy, footed, 8½″
☐ crystal 12.50 15.00 13.50
Old Fashioned Tumbler, 7 oz.
☐ crystal 11.00 14.00 12.00
Parfait, 6 oz.
☐ crystal 14.00 18.00 15.00
Pickle Bowl, 7½″
☐ crystal 11.00 13.50 12.00

	Current Price Range		Prior Year Average

Pickle Bowl, 8½″
☐ crystal 11.00 14.00 12.00
Pitcher, beaded handle, lip, 40 oz.
☐ crystal 31.00 36.00 32.00
Pitcher, short, round, 14 oz.
☐ crystal 18.00 23.00 19.00
Pitcher, 20 oz.
☐ crystal 23.00 29.00 25.00
Pitcher, 64 oz.
☐ crystal 31.00 36.00 32.00
Plate, oval, 12″
☐ crystal 16.00 19.00 17.00
Punch Cup
☐ crystal 3.50 5.50 4.00
Punch Set, 8 cup, ladle, lid
☐ crystal 110.00 150.00 120.00
Relish Bowl, 7″
☐ crystal 14.00 17.00 15.00
Relish Bowl, footed, 3 sections, 10″
☐ crystal 18.00 23.00 19.50
Relish Bowl, oval, 12″
☐ crystal 18.00 23.00 20.00
Relish Tray, 13″
☐ crystal 25.00 35.00 27.00
Rose Bowl, footed, crimped edge, 7¼″
☐ crystal 15.00 19.00 16.00
Salad Bowl, 10½″
☐ crystal 18.00 23.00 20.00
Salad, Fork and Spoon
☐ crystal 11.00 14.00 12.00
Salad Plate, 8″
☐ crystal 6.00 9.00 7.00
Salad Plate, oval, 9″
☐ crystal 12.00 15.00 13.00
Salt and Pepper, beaded stem, chrome top
☐ crystal 5.00 8.00 6.00
Sugar, beaded handle, 6 oz.
☐ crystal 4.50 7.00 5.50
Tid Bit Server, 2 tier
☐ crystal 35.00 45.00 38.00
Tray, 5″
☐ crystal 11.00 15.00 12.00
Water Goblet, 9 oz.
☐ crystal 16.00 20.00 17.00
Wine Goblet, beaded foot, 5 oz.
☐ crystal 15.00 19.00 16.00
Wine Goblet, 4 oz.
☐ crystal 15.00 19.00 16.00

	Current Price Range		Prior Year Average

Tea Cup
☐ crystal 6.50 8.50 7.00
Vase, tab shaped, 6½"
☐ crystal 16.00 20.00 17.00
Vase, pitcher shape, handle
☐ crystal 18.00 24.00 20.00

CAPRICE
Cambridge

Caprice was first made in the 1940s. Colors are crystal, blue, amber, and amethyst. Pieces in blue are the most collectible and sought after.

Ashtray, triangle shape, 4½"
☐ blue 13.00 18.00 14.00
☐ crystal 9.00 12.00 10.00
Bon Bon Dish, square with handle, 6"
☐ blue 26.00 34.00 28.00
☐ crystal 16.00 20.00 17.00
Bread and Butter Plate, 6½"
☐ blue 17.00 21.00 18.00
☐ crystal 11.00 14.00 12.00
Cake Plate, footed, 13"
☐ blue 230.00 275.00 240.00
☐ crystal 95.00 110.00 98.00
Candy Box, footed, with lid, 6"
☐ blue 82.00 92.00 84.00
☐ crystal 47.00 55.00 50.00
Claret Goblet, 4½" oz.
☐ blue 40.00 50.00 42.00
☐ crystal 23.00 30.00 25.00
Coaster, 3½"
☐ blue 23.00 28.00 25.00
☐ crystal 13.00 18.00 15.00
Cocktail Goblet, 3½ oz.
☐ blue 37.00 45.00 39.00

Caprice

	Current Price Range		Prior Year Average
☐ crystal	22.00	29.00	24.00
Creamer, medium			
☐ blue	13.00	18.00	14.50
☐ crystal	6.00	9.00	7.00
Decanter, with stopper, 36 oz.			
☐ blue	130.00	170.00	140.00
☐ crystal	72.00	90.00	77.00
Dinner Plate, 9½″			
☐ blue	87.00	110.00	90.00
☐ crystal	35.00	45.00	37.00
Luncheon Plate, 8½″			
☐ blue	23.00	30.00	24.00
☐ crystal	13.00	19.00	14.00
Pitcher, ball shaped, 32 oz.			
☐ blue	170.00	185.00	175.00
☐ crystal	87.00	100.00	90.00
Rose Bowl, footed, 8″			
☐ blue	93.00	105.00	95.00
☐ crystal	56.00	68.00	60.00
Salad Bowl, footed, 8″			
☐ blue	40.00	50.00	42.00
☐ crystal	22.00	32.00	25.00
Salad Plate, 7½″			
☐ blue	18.00	24.00	20.00
☐ crystal	13.00	17.00	14.00
Sherbet, tall, 7 oz.			
☐ blue	23.00	30.00	25.00
☐ crystal	18.00	24.00	20.00
Sugar, medium size			
☐ blue	13.00	18.00	15.00
☐ crystal	6.50	9.00	7.50
Tumbler, footed, 3 oz.			
☐ blue	21.00	26.00	22.00
☐ crystal	15.00	20.00	16.00
Tumbler, footed, 5 oz.			
☐ blue	21.00	26.00	22.00
☐ crystal	15.00	20.00	16.00
Tumbler, footed, 10 oz.			
☐ blue	30.00	37.00	32.00
☐ crystal	18.00	24.00	20.00
Tumbler, footed, 12 oz.			
☐ blue	33.00	40.00	35.00
☐ crystal	21.00	27.00	22.00
Vase, 5½″			
☐ blue	57.00	65.00	59.00
☐ crystal	43.00	49.00	45.00

Cherokee Rose

CHEROKEE ROSE
Tiffin

This elegant glassware pattern was manufactured by the Tiffin Glass Company. The alternating design, around the rim of the plates and covering the other pieces, features a rose design and a cameo design. There is no decoration on the center of the plates. Handles on pieces look like beadwork.

	Current Price Range		Prior Year Average
Bud Vase, 6″			
☐ crystal	8.50	11.50	9.00
Bud Vase, 8″			
☐ crystal	11.00	14.00	12.00
Cake Plate, handle, 12½″			
☐ crystal	18.00	22.00	19.00
Candleholder, double branch			
☐ crystal	29.00	35.00	31.00
Cocktail, stemmed, 2 oz.			
☐ crystal	11.00	14.00	12.00
Creamer			
☐ crystal	8.50	11.50	9.00
Finger Bowl, 5″			
☐ crystal	6.50	9.50	7.00
Iced Tea Tumbler, footed, 10½ oz.			
☐ crystal	8.50	11.50	9.00
Luncheon Plate, 8″			
☐ crystal	6.00	9.00	7.00
Pitcher			
☐ crystal	83.00	93.00	85.00
Relish Tray, 3 compartments, 6½″			
☐ crystal	15.00	20.00	16.00
Salad Bowl, 7″			
☐ crystal	8.50	11.50	9.00
Salad Bowl, 10″			
☐ crystal	15.00	20.00	16.00
Sandwich Plate, 14″			
☐ crystal	12.50	15.50	13.00

	Current Price Range		Prior Year Average
Sherbet Plate, 6″			
☐ crystal	2.50	4.50	3.00
Sherbet, stemmed, 5½ oz.			
☐ crystal	10.00	13.00	11.00
Sugar			
☐ crystal	7.50	10.50	8.00
Vase, flared, 12″			
☐ crystal	22.00	29.00	23.00
Water Tumbler, footed, 8 oz.			
☐ crystal	8.00	11.00	9.00
Wine, stemmed, 3½ oz.			
☐ crystal	13.00	17.00	14.00

COLONY
Fostoria

Colony was made from the 1920's to the 1970's. This pattern was mostly made in crystal, though other colors include green, blue, and yellow.

Almond Bowl, footed			
☐ crystal	3.00	5.00	3.50
Bowl, low foot, 9″			
☐ crystal	13.00	17.00	14.00
Candlestick, 9¾″			
☐ crystal	11.00	14.00	12.00
Candy Dish, with lid, 6½″			
☐ crystal	18.00	22.00	19.00
Celery Bowl, 11½″			
☐ crystal	10.50	13.50	11.50
Cocktail Goblet, 3½ oz., 4″			
☐ crystal	7.50	10.50	8.50

Colony

	Current Price Range		Prior Year Average

Creamer
☐ crystal 6.50 9.50 7.50
Finger Bowl, 4¾"
☐ crystal 5.00 8.00 6.00
Goblet, 9 oz., 5¼"
☐ crystal 10.50 13.50 11.50
Oyster Cocktail, 4 oz., 3⅜"
☐ crystal 7.00 10.00 8.00
Pickle Bowl, 9½"
☐ crystal 8.50 11.50 9.50
Plate, 6"
☐ crystal 1.50 3.50 2.00
Plate, 7"
☐ crystal 2.00 4.00 2.50
Plate, 8"
☐ crystal 2.50 4.50 3.00
Plate, 9"
☐ crystal 3.50 5.50 4.00
Plate, 10"
☐ crystal 6.00 9.00 7.00
Sherbet, 5 oz., 3⅝"
☐ crystal 7.50 11.50 8.50
Sugar
☐ crystal 4.00 6.00 4.50
Tumbler, 5 oz.
☐ crystal 6.50 9.50 7.50
Tumbler, 9 oz.
☐ crystal 8.50 11.50 9.50
Tumbler, footed, 5 oz., 4½"
☐ crystal 8.00 11.00 9.00
Tumbler, footed, 12 oz., 5¾"
☐ crystal 10.00 13.00 11.00
Tumbler, 12 oz.
☐ crystal 10.50 13.50 11.50
Vase, 8"
☐ crystal 15.00 20.00 16.50
Wine Goblet, 3¼ oz., 4¼"
☐ crystal 8.50 11.50 9.50

CRYSTOLITE
A. H. Heisey

This pattern was produced on blank #1503 in crystal, blue, green, yellow, and amber.

Ashtray, square, 3½"
☐ crystal 2.00 4.00 2.50
Bon Bon Dish, shell shaped, 7"
☐ crystal 15.00 19.00 16.00

Crystolite

	Current Price Range		Prior Year Average
Candlestick, footed, 1 lite			
☐ crystal	10.50	13.50	11.50
Candy Dish, swan shape, 6½″			
☐ crystal	31.00	39.00	32.00
Cigarette Box, with cover, 4½″			
☐ crystal	15.00	19.00	16.00
Claret Goblet, wide blown, 3½ oz.			
☐ crystal	22.00	28.00	24.00
Cocktail Goblet, wide optic, blown, 3½ oz.			
☐ crystal	18.00	22.00	19.00
Cordial Goblet, wide optic, blown, 10 oz.			
☐ crystal	55.00	65.00	57.00
Creamer			
☐ crystal	8.50	11.50	9.50
Flower Urn, 7″			
☐ crystal	13.00	17.00	14.00
Iced Tea Tumbler, wide optic, blown, 10 oz.			
☐ crystal	18.00	22.00	19.00
Juice Tumbler, footed, wide optic, blown, 5 oz.			
☐ crystal	13.00	17.00	14.00
Mayonnaise Ladle			
☐ crystal	6.00	9.00	6.50
Mustard Dish, with lid			
☐ crystal	26.00	34.00	28.00

	Current Price Range		Prior Year Average
Nut Bowl, handle, 3″			
☐ crystal	13.00	17.00	14.00
Pitcher, swan shape, ice lip, 2 quart			
☐ crystal	625.00	675.00	635.00
Puff Box, with lid, 4¾″			
☐ crystal	42.00	49.00	43.50
Punch Bowl, 7½ quart			
☐ crystal	70.00	80.00	72.00
Punch Cup			
☐ crystal	8.50	11.50	9.50
Relish Tray, 3 sections, 12″			
☐ crystal	18.00	22.00	19.00
Salad Bowl, round, 10″			
☐ crystal	20.00	24.00	21.00
Salad Plate, 7″			
☐ crystal	5.50	8.50	6.50
Salad Plate, 8½″			
☐ crystal	13.00	17.00	14.00
Salt and Pepper			
☐ crystal	21.00	29.00	23.00
Sandwich Plate, 12″			
☐ crystal	18.00	22.00	19.00
Saucer			
☐ crystal	4.00	6.00	4.50
Sherbet, 6 oz.			
☐ crystal	8.50	11.50	9.50
Sugar			
☐ crystal	8.50	11.50	9.50
Syrup Bottle, drip and cut top			
☐ crystal	45.00	55.00	47.00
Vase, footed, 6″			
☐ crystal	13.00	17.00	14.00

Cupid

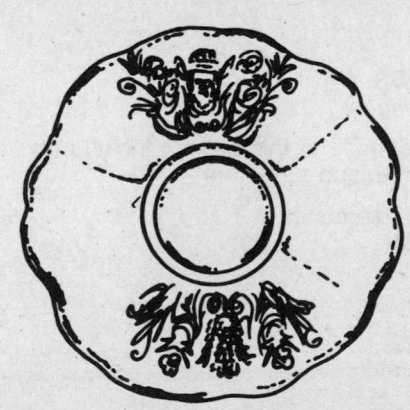

CUPID
Paden City

Manufactured by Paden City in the 1930's, Cupid was made in blue, green, and pink. Most pieces have delicately scalloped rims, and the repeating etched design features two cupids, in profile, facing an urn. They are surrounded by flowers and scrollwork.

	Current Price Range		Prior Year Average
Bowl, handled in center, 9¼″			
☐ blue	32.00	38.00	34.00
☐ green	32.00	38.00	34.00
☐ pink	32.00	38.00	34.00
Cake Plate, 11¾″			
☐ blue	32.00	38.00	34.00
☐ green	32.00	38.00	34.00
☐ pink	32.00	38.00	34.00
Candleholders, pair			
☐ blue	30.00	35.00	31.00
☐ green	30.00	35.00	31.00
☐ pink	30.00	35.00	31.00
Candy Holder, with lid			
☐ blue	42.00	52.00	45.00
☐ green	42.00	52.00	45.00
☐ pink	42.00	52.00	45.00
Creamer, footed, 5″			
☐ blue	30.00	35.00	31.00
☐ green	30.00	35.00	31.00
☐ pink	30.00	35.00	31.00
Dinner Plate, 10½″			
☐ blue	20.00	25.00	21.00
☐ green	20.00	25.00	21.00
☐ pink	20.00	25.00	21.00
Fruit Bowl, footed, 9¼″			
☐ blue	28.00	32.00	29.00
☐ green	28.00	32.00	29.00
☐ pink	28.00	32.00	29.00

EMPRESS
A.H. Heisey

Colors made in this pattern include crystal, green, yellow, pink, blue, alexandrite, and tangerine.

Ashtray, diamond			
☐ crystal	22.00	28.00	23.00
☐ pink	100.00	125.00	110.00
☐ yellow	75.00	90.00	82.00
☐ green	200.00	225.00	210.00
☐ cobalt	130.00	150.00	140.00
☐ alexandrite			

Empress

	Current Price Range		Prior Year Average
Candlestick, dolphin footed, 6″			
☐ crystal	26.00	34.00	28.00
☐ pink	90.00	110.00	100.00
☐ yellow	100.00	125.00	110.00
☐ green	150.00	175.00	160.00
☐ alexandrite	250.00	275.00	265.00
Celery Tray, 10″			
☐ crystal	15.00	18.00	16.00
☐ pink	20.00	25.00	22.00
☐ yellow	25.00	30.00	27.00
☐ green	30.00	35.00	32.00
Comport, footed, 6″, round			
☐ crystal	22.00	28.00	23.00
☐ pink	36.00	44.00	38.00
☐ yellow	50.00	60.00	53.00
☐ green	60.00	70.00	63.00
Comport, square, 6″			
☐ crystal	31.00	39.00	33.00
☐ pink	60.00	70.00	63.00
☐ yellow	63.00	77.00	67.00
☐ green	69.00	82.00	63.00
Cream Soup			
☐ crystal	10.00	12.00	9.00
☐ pink	15.00	20.00	16.00
☐ yellow	20.00	25.00	22.00
☐ green	25.00	30.00	27.00
☐ alexandrite	30.00	35.00	31.00
Creamer, dolphin footed			
☐ crystal	15.00	20.00	17.00
☐ pink	30.00	35.00	23.00
☐ yellow	35.00	40.00	33.00
☐ green	40.00	45.00	35.00
☐ alexandrite	200.00	230.00	190.00

	Current Price Range		Prior Year Average
Cup			
☐ crystal	12.00	15.00	7.50
☐ pink	22.00	28.00	23.00
☐ yellow	26.00	34.00	28.00
☐ green	31.00	39.00	33.00
☐ alexandrite	95.00	115.00	100.00
☐ tangerine	500.00	600.00	525.00
Floral Bowl, rolled edge, 9″			
☐ crystal	20.00	24.00	21.00
☐ pink	26.00	34.00	28.00
☐ yellow	31.00	39.00	33.00
☐ green	34.00	41.00	36.00
Ice Bucket, metal handles, D. F.			
☐ crystal	45.00	50.00	47.00
☐ pink	100.00	120.00	110.00
☐ yellow	115.00	130.00	120.00
☐ green	100.00	125.00	115.00
☐ alexandrite	400.00	450.00	420.00
Iced Tea, flat bottom, 12 oz.			
☐ crystal	13.00	17.00	14.00
☐ pink	18.00	22.00	19.00
☐ yellow	23.00	30.00	25.00
☐ green	26.00	34.00	28.00
Marmalade Dish, with lid, dolphin footed			
☐ crystal	45.00	50.00	47.00
☐ pink	65.00	70.00	67.00
☐ yellow	75.00	90.00	70.00
☐ green	100.00	115.00	110.00
☐ alexandrite	250.00	300.00	270.00
Mayonnaise Dish, footed, 5½″			
☐ crystal	20.00	25.00	22.00
☐ pink	30.00	35.00	32.00
☐ yellow	30.00	35.00	32.00
☐ green	45.00	55.00	50.00
☐ alexandrite	170.00	200.00	180.00
Mint Bowl, dolphin, footed, 6″			
☐ crystal	15.00	20.00	17.00
☐ pink	30.00	35.00	32.00
☐ yellow	30.00	35.00	32.00
☐ green	40.00	45.00	42.00
☐ alexandrite	130.00	150.00	140.00
Mustard Dish, with lid			
☐ crystal	25.00	30.00	27.00
☐ pink	45.00	55.00	50.00
☐ yellow	65.00	75.00	70.00
☐ green	75.00	85.00	80.00
Nappy, 4½″			
☐ crystal	5.00	8.00	6.00

	Current Price Range		Prior Year Average
☐ pink	10.00	12.00	10.50
☐ yellow	12.00	15.00	13.00
☐ green	15.00	20.00	17.00
Nappy, 8″			
☐ crystal	20.00	24.00	21.00
☐ pink	26.00	34.00	28.00
☐ yellow	31.00	39.00	33.00
☐ green	34.00	42.00	36.00
Oyster Cocktail			
☐ crystal	13.00	17.00	14.00
☐ pink	18.00	22.00	19.00
☐ yellow	22.00	28.00	23.00
☐ green	26.00	34.00	28.00
Pickle/Olive, 2 sections, 13″, relish			
☐ crystal	18.00	22.00	20.00
☐ pink	30.00	35.00	32.00
☐ yellow	40.00	50.00	44.00
☐ green	35.00	40.00	37.00
Plate, 4½″			
☐ crystal	4.00	5.00	4.50
☐ pink	8.00	10.00	9.00
☐ yellow	10.00	12.00	11.00
☐ green	12.00	15.00	13.00
Plate, round or square, 6″			
☐ crystal	6.00	8.00	7.00
☐ pink	9.00	12.00	10.00
☐ yellow	10.00	12.00	11.00
☐ green	12.00	15.00	13.00
☐ alexandrite	35.00	45.00	40.00
☐ tangerine	100.00	125.00	110.00
Plate, round or square, 7″			
☐ crystal	7.00	9.00	8.00
☐ pink	10.00	13.00	11.00
☐ yellow	13.00	17.00	14.00
☐ green	15.00	19.00	16.00
☐ alexandrite	40.00	50.00	42.00
☐ cobalt............................	35.00	40.00	37.00
Plate, 8″			
☐ crystal	9.00	12.00	10.00
☐ pink	18.00	22.00	19.00
☐ yellow	18.00	22.00	19.00
☐ green	22.00	26.00	23.00
☐ tangerine	150.00	175.00	160.00
☐ alexandrite	50.00	60.00	55.00
☐ cobalt	45.00	50.00	47.00
Plate, 9″, round			
☐ crystal	10.50	13.50	11.50
☐ pink	22.00	28.00	23.00

	Current Price Range		Prior Year Average
☐ yellow	32.00	38.00	33.00
☐ green	36.00	44.00	37.00
Plate, round or square, 10½"			
☐ crystal	25.00	30.00	27.00
☐ pink	50.00	60.00	55.00
☐ yellow	60.00	70.00	64.00
☐ green	70.00	80.00	74.00
Plate, round, 12"			
☐ crystal	22.00	27.00	23.00
☐ pink	60.00	70.00	64.00
☐ yellow	60.00	70.00	64.00
☐ green	70.00	80.00	74.00
Platter, oval, 14"			
☐ crystal	25.00	30.00	27.00
☐ pink	30.00	35.00	32.00
☐ yellow	35.00	40.00	37.00
☐ green	40.00	45.00	42.00
Punch Cup, 4 oz.			
☐ crystal	8.50	11.50	9.50
☐ pink	22.00	28.00	23.00
☐ yellow	25.00	31.00	26.00
☐ green	26.00	34.00	28.00
Relish Bowl, 3 sections, triplex, 7"			
☐ crystal	20.00	25.00	21.00
☐ pink	30.00	35.00	32.00
☐ yellow	40.00	45.00	42.00
☐ green	50.00	55.00	51.50
☐ alexandrite	175.00	225.00	190.00
Relish Tray, 3 sections, triplex, 10"			
☐ crystal	22.00	30.00	25.00
☐ pink	40.00	50.00	44.00
☐ yellow	50.00	60.00	54.00
☐ green	60.00	70.00	63.00
Salad Bowl, square, handles, 10"			
☐ crystal	30.00	40.00	32.00
☐ pink	40.00	50.00	42.00
☐ yellow	50.00	60.00	52.00
☐ green	60.00	70.00	62.00
☐ tangerine (one known)	1200.00	1500.00	
Salt and Pepper			
☐ crystal	36.00	44.00	38.00
☐ pink	60.00	70.00	63.00
☐ yellow	80.00	90.00	84.00
☐ green	90.00	100.00	94.00
Sandwich Tray, handle, 12"			
☐ crystal	26.00	34.00	28.00
☐ pink	45.00	55.00	50.00
☐ yellow	55.00	65.00	60.00

	Current Price Range		Prior Year Average
☐ green	75.00	85.00	77.00
☐ alexandrite	175.00	200.00	185.00
Saucer			
☐ crystal	7.00	10.00	8.00
☐ pink	10.00	15.00	12.00
☐ yellow	10.00	15.00	12.00
☐ green	10.00	15.00	12.00
☐ alexandrite	25.00	30.00	27.00
☐ tangerine	100.00	125.00	110.00
Sherbet, 4 oz.			
☐ crystal	13.00	17.00	14.00
☐ pink	18.00	22.00	19.00
☐ yellow	22.00	28.00	23.00
☐ green	26.00	34.00	27.00
Sugar, dolphin-footed			
☐ crystal	15.00	20.00	17.00
☐ pink	30.00	35.00	32.00
☐ yellow	35.00	40.00	37.00
☐ green	40.00	45.00	42.00
☐ alexandrite	200.00	225.00	210.00
Tumbler, dolphin, footed, 8 oz.			
☐ crystal	55.00	65.00	57.00
☐ pink	80.00	90.00	82.00
☐ yellow	115.00	133.00	115.00
☐ green	110.00	140.00	117.00
Tumbler, flat bottom, 8 oz.			
☐ crystal	15.00	20.00	17.00
☐ pink	30.00	35.00	32.00
☐ yellow	35.00	40.00	37.00
☐ green	40.00	45.00	42.00
Vase, flared, 3 handled, 8″			
☐ crystal	41.00	49.00	43.00
☐ pink	60.00	70.00	62.00
☐ yellow	69.00	82.00	63.00
☐ green	78.00	93.00	82.00
Vase, dolphin footed, 9″			
☐ crystal	45.00	55.00	47.00
☐ pink	110.00	125.00	83.00
☐ yellow	110.00	125.00	85.00
☐ green	110.00	145.00	117.00
☐ alexandrite	400.00	450.00	420.00
Vegetable Bowl, oval, 10″			
☐ crystal	25.00	30.00	26.00
☐ pink	31.00	39.00	33.00
☐ yellow	40.00	50.00	42.00
☐ green	50.00	60.00	52.00

Fairfax

FAIRFAX
Fostoria

This plain simple pattern was made from the 1920's to the 1940's. Other patterns were created using Fairfax and adding a design.

	Current Price Range		Prior Year Average
Ashtray			
☐ blue	18.00	22.00	19.00
☐ orchid	18.00	22.00	19.00
☐ pink	16.00	20.00	17.00
☐ green	16.00	20.00	17.00
☐ amber	11.00	15.00	12.00
Bon Bon Dish			
☐ blue	15.00	20.00	16.00
☐ orchid	15.00	20.00	16.00
☐ pink	13.00	17.00	14.00
☐ green	13.00	17.00	14.00
☐ amber	10.00	14.00	11.00
Bowl, footed, 11¾″			
☐ blue	21.00	25.00	22.00
☐ orchid	21.00	25.00	22.00
☐ pink	17.00	21.00	18.00
☐ green	17.00	21.00	18.00
☐ amber	13.00	17.00	14.00
Bowl, oval, 10½″			
☐ blue	25.00	30.00	26.00
☐ orchid	25.00	30.00	26.00
☐ pink	22.00	28.00	23.00
☐ green	22.00	28.00	23.00
☐ amber	15.00	20.00	16.00
Bread and Butter Plate, 6″			
☐ blue	3.50	5.50	4.00
☐ orchid	3.50	5.50	4.00
☐ pink	3.00	5.00	3.50
☐ green	3.00	5.00	3.50
☐ amber	2.00	4.00	2.50

	Current Price Range		Prior Year Average
Cake Plate, handles, 10″			
☐ blue	15.00	20.00	16.00
☐ orchid	15.00	20.00	16.00
☐ pink	13.00	17.00	14.00
☐ green	13.00	17.00	14.00
☐ amber	11.00	14.00	12.00
Candy Dish, with lid, 3 sections			
☐ blue	42.00	52.00	44.00
☐ orchid	42.00	52.00	44.00
☐ pink	33.00	41.00	34.00
☐ green	33.00	41.00	34.00
☐ amber	29.00	35.00	31.00
Cereal Bowl, 6″			
☐ blue	13.00	17.00	14.00
☐ orchid	13.00	17.00	14.00
☐ pink	11.00	14.00	12.00
☐ green	11.00	14.00	12.00
☐ amber	8.50	11.50	9.50
Cigarette Box			
☐ blue	31.00	39.00	33.00
☐ orchid	31.00	39.00	33.00
☐ pink	23.00	33.00	25.00
☐ green	23.00	33.00	25.00
☐ amber	20.00	25.00	21.00
Claret Goblet, 4 oz.			
☐ blue	23.00	28.00	24.00
☐ orchid	23.00	28.00	24.00
☐ pink	20.00	25.00	21.00
☐ green	20.00	25.00	21.00
☐ amber	17.00	21.00	18.00
Coaster, 3½″			
☐ blue	5.00	7.00	5.50
☐ orchid	5.00	7.00	5.50
☐ pink	3.00	5.00	3.50
☐ green	3.00	5.00	3.50
☐ amber	2.00	4.00	2.50
Cocktail Goblet, 3 oz.			
☐ blue	20.00	25.00	21.00
☐ orchid	20.00	25.00	21.00
☐ pink	18.00	22.00	19.00
☐ green	18.00	22.00	19.00
☐ amber	15.00	20.00	16.00
Compote, 7″			
☐ blue	20.00	25.00	21.00
☐ orchid	20.00	25.00	21.00
☐ pink	18.00	22.00	19.00
☐ green	18.00	22.00	19.00
☐ amber	14.00	18.00	15.00

	Current Price Range		Prior Year Average
Cordial Goblet, ¾ oz.			
☐ blue	26.00	34.00	28.00
☐ orchid	26.00	34.00	28.00
☐ pink	25.00	30.00	26.00
☐ green	25.00	30.00	26.00
☐ amber	21.00	26.00	23.00
Cream Soup			
☐ blue	12.00	15.00	13.00
☐ orchid	12.00	15.00	13.00
☐ pink	10.50	13.50	11.50
☐ green	10.50	13.50	11.50
☐ amber	8.50	11.50	9.50
Creamer, footed			
☐ blue	8.50	11.50	9.50
☐ orchid	8.50	11.50	9.50
☐ pink	6.50	9.50	7.50
☐ green	6.50	9.50	7.50
☐ amber	5.00	7.00	5.50
Cruet, footed, with handle			
☐ blue	112.00	140.00	117.00
☐ orchid	112.00	140.00	117.00
☐ pink	98.00	122.00	104.00
☐ green	98.00	122.00	104.00
☐ amber	82.00	98.00	85.00
Cup, footed			
☐ blue	7.00	10.00	8.00
☐ orchid	7.00	10.00	8.00
☐ pink	4.50	7.50	5.50
☐ green	4.50	7.50	5.50
☐ amber	4.00	6.00	4.50
Dinner Plate, 10¼"			
☐ blue	25.00	30.00	26.00
☐ orchid	25.00	30.00	26.00
☐ pink	22.00	28.00	23.00
☐ green	22.00	28.00	23.00
☐ amber	18.00	22.00	19.00
Finger Bowl, 4⅝" x 2"			
☐ blue	13.00	17.00	14.00
☐ orchid	13.00	17.00	14.00
☐ pink	11.00	15.00	12.00
☐ green	11.00	15.00	12.00
☐ amber	8.50	11.50	9.50
Fruit Bowl, 5"			
☐ blue	7.50	11.50	8.50
☐ orchid	7.50	11.50	8.50
☐ pink	5.00	8.00	6.00
☐ green	5.00	8.00	6.00
☐ amber	5.00	7.00	5.50

	Current Price Range		Prior Year Average

Grill Plate, 10¼″
☐ blue	15.00	20.00	16.00
☐ orchid	15.00	20.00	16.00
☐ pink	11.00	14.00	12.00
☐ green	11.00	14.00	12.00
☐ amber	8.50	11.50	9.50

Ice Bucket, with metal handle
☐ blue	36.00	44.00	38.00
☐ orchid	36.00	44.00	38.00
☐ pink	31.00	39.00	33.00
☐ green	31.00	39.00	33.00
☐ amber	25.00	30.00	26.00

Luncheon Plate, 9½″
☐ blue	7.50	10.50	8.50
☐ orchid	7.50	10.50	8.50
☐ pink	6.50	9.50	7.50
☐ green	6.50	9.50	7.50
☐ amber	6.00	8.00	6.50

Mayonnaise Dish
☐ blue	13.00	17.00	14.00
☐ orchid	13.00	17.00	14.00
☐ pink	9.50	12.50	10.50
☐ green	9.50	12.50	10.50
☐ amber	7.50	10.50	8.50

Mayonnaise Ladle
☐ blue	18.00	22.00	19.00
☐ orchid	18.00	22.00	19.00
☐ pink	13.00	17.00	14.00
☐ green	13.00	17.00	14.00
☐ amber	13.00	17.00	14.00

Oyster Cocktail, footed, 5½ oz.
☐ blue	14.50	18.50	15.50
☐ orchid	14.50	18.50	15.50
☐ pink	12.00	16.00	13.00
☐ green	12.00	16.00	13.00
☐ amber	8.50	11.50	9.50

Parfait, footed, 6½ oz.
☐ blue	15.00	20.00	16.00
☐ orchid	15.00	20.00	16.00
☐ pink	12.00	16.00	13.00
☐ green	12.00	16.00	13.00
☐ amber	11.00	14.00	12.00

Pitcher, footed, 48 oz.
☐ blue	175.00	220.00	180.00
☐ orchid	175.00	220.00	180.00
☐ pink	150.00	190.00	160.00
☐ green	150.00	190.00	160.00
☐ amber	120.00	150.00	127.00

	Current Price Range		Prior Year Average
Platter, oval, 15″			
☐ blue	42.00	52.00	45.00
☐ orchid	42.00	52.00	45.00
☐ pink	38.00	46.00	40.00
☐ green	38.00	46.00	40.00
☐ amber	32.00	39.00	33.00
Relish Tray, 2 sections, 8½″			
☐ blue	13.00	16.00	14.00
☐ orchid	13.00	16.00	14.00
☐ pink	11.00	14.00	12.00
☐ green	11.00	14.00	12.00
☐ amber	8.50	11.50	9.00
Relish Tray, 3 sections, 11½″			
☐ blue	20.00	25.00	21.00
☐ orchid	20.00	25.00	21.00
☐ pink	15.00	20.00	16.00
☐ green	15.00	20.00	16.00
☐ amber	11.00	14.00	12.00
Relish Tray, 3 sections, round			
☐ blue	15.00	20.00	16.00
☐ orchid	15.00	20.00	16.00
☐ pink	12.00	15.00	13.00
☐ green	12.00	15.00	13.00
☐ amber	8.50	11.50	9.50
Sauce Boat			
☐ blue	31.00	39.00	33.00
☐ orchid	31.00	39.00	33.00
☐ pink	26.00	34.00	28.00
☐ green	26.00	34.00	28.00
☐ amber	23.00	28.00	24.00
Saucer			
☐ blue	2.50	4.50	3.00
☐ orchid	2.50	4.50	3.00
☐ pink	1.50	3.50	2.00
☐ green	1.50	3.50	2.00
☐ amber	1.50	3.50	2.00
Sherbet, low, 6 oz.			
☐ blue	14.00	17.00	15.00
☐ orchid	14.00	17.00	15.00
☐ pink	12.00	15.00	13.00
☐ green	12.00	15.00	13.00
☐ amber	11.00	14.00	12.00
Sherbet, tall, 6 oz.			
☐ blue	15.00	20.00	16.00
☐ orchid	15.00	20.00	16.00
☐ pink	12.00	16.00	13.00
☐ green	12.00	16.00	13.00
☐ amber	12.00	16.00	13.00

		Current Price Range		Prior Year Average
Soup Bowl				
☐ blue		15.00	20.00	16.00
☐ orchid		15.00	20.00	16.00
☐ pink		13.00	17.00	14.00
☐ green		13.00	17.00	14.00
☐ amber		11.00	14.00	12.00
Sugar, footed				
☐ blue		7.50	10.50	8.50
☐ orchid		7.50	10.50	8.50
☐ pink		6.00	8.00	6.50
☐ green		6.00	8.00	6.50
☐ amber		4.00	6.00	4.50
Tray, handle, 11″				
☐ blue		25.00	30.00	26.00
☐ orchid		25.00	30.00	26.00
☐ pink		20.00	25.00	21.00
☐ green		20.00	25.00	21.00
☐ amber		15.00	20.00	16.00
Tumbler, footed, 12 oz.				
☐ blue		18.00	22.00	19.00
☐ orchid		18.00	22.00	19.00
☐ pink		16.00	20.00	17.00
☐ green		16.00	20.00	17.00
☐ amber		14.00	18.00	15.00
Tumbler, footed, 9 oz.				
☐ blue		15.00	20.00	16.00
☐ orchid		15.00	20.00	16.00
☐ pink		12.00	16.00	13.00
☐ green		12.00	16.00	13.00
☐ amber		10.50	13.50	12.50
Tumbler, footed, 5 oz.				
☐ blue		12.00	16.00	13.00
☐ orchid		12.00	16.00	13.00
☐ pink		9.50	12.50	10.50
☐ green		9.50	12.50	10.50
☐ amber		7.50	10.50	8.50
Tumbler, footed, 2½ oz.				
☐ blue		12.50	15.50	13.50
☐ orchid		12.50	15.50	13.50
☐ pink		9.50	12.50	10.50
☐ green		9.50	12.50	10.50
☐ amber		7.50	10.50	8.50
Water Goblet, 10 oz.				
☐ blue		20.00	25.00	21.00
☐ orchid		20.00	25.00	21.00
☐ pink		16.00	20.00	17.00
☐ green		16.00	20.00	17.00
☐ amber		15.00	18.00	16.00

	Current Price Range		Prior Year Average
Wine Goblet, 3 oz.			
☐ blue	25.00	30.00	26.00
☐ orchid	25.00	30.00	26.00
☐ pink	21.00	25.00	22.00
☐ green	21.00	25.00	22.00

GREEK KEY
A.H. Heisey

Greek Key was mostly made in crystal, though some pink was also made. Punch bowl, underplate, and punch cup were the only items made in pink.

Almond Bowl, footed, 5″			
☐ crystal	26.00	34.00	28.00
Banana Split Dish, flat, 9″			
☐ crystal	20.00	25.00	22.00
Bowl, low footed, shallow, 10″			
☐ crystal	45.00	50.00	46.00
Bowl, low footed, straight sides, 7″			
☐ crystal	35.00	40.00	37.00
Bowl, low footed, straight sides, 9″			
☐ crystal	55.00	60.00	57.00
Burgundy, 3½ oz.			
☐ crystal	100.00	125.00	110.00
Candy Jar, with lid, ½ lb.			
☐ crystal	100.00	125.00	105.00
Celery Tray, oval, 9″			
☐ crystal	30.00	35.00	32.00
Cheese and Cracker Set, 10″ (1 piece)			
☐ crystal	100.00	125.00	105.00
Claret, 4½ oz.			
☐ crystal	80.00	90.00	82.00

Greek Key

	Current Price Range		Prior Year Average
Cocktail, 3 oz.			
☐ crystal	40.00	50.00	44.00
Compote, 5″			
☐ crystal	45.00	55.00	47.00
Cordial, ¾ oz.			
☐ crystal	175.00	200.00	140.00
Creamer			
☐ crystal	22.00	28.00	23.00
Egg Cup, 5 oz.			
☐ crystal	41.00	49.00	43.00
Finger Bowl			
☐ crystal	25.00	30.00	27.00
Goblet, 7 oz.			
☐ crystal	125.00	150.00	130.00
Goblet, 9 oz.			
☐ crystal	150.00	175.00	160.00
Hair Receiver			
☐ crystal	80.00	90.00	85.00
Horseradish Jar, with lid, large			
☐ crystal	150.00	175.00	160.00
Ice Bucket, tab handles, large			
☐ crystal	125.00	150.00	140.00
Jelly Bowl, handle, 5″			
☐ crystal	40.00	45.00	42.00
Nappy, 4″			
☐ crystal	25.00	30.00	27.00
Nappy, scalloped, 8″			
☐ crystal	40.00	50.00	42.00
Nappy, shallow, 6″			
☐ crystal	30.00	35.00	32.00
Nappy, shallow, 11″			
☐ crystal	75.00	85.00	77.00
Pickle Jar, with lid			
☐ crystal	125.00	150.00	132.00
Pitcher, 1 pint			
☐ crystal	125.00	150.00	130.00
Pitcher, 3 pints			
☐ crystal	125.00	150.00	130.00
Plate, 4½″			
☐ crystal	12.00	15.00	14.00
Plate, 5½″			
☐ crystal	12.00	15.00	14.00
Plate, 6½″			
☐ crystal	15.00	20.00	17.00
Plate, 7″			
☐ crystal	20.00	25.00	22.00
Plate, 8″			
☐ crystal	25.00	30.00	27.00

	Current Price Range		Prior Year Average
Plate, 9″			
☐ crystal	40.00	50.00	44.00
Plate, 10″			
☐ crystal	75.00	85.00	80.00
Punch Bowl, footed, 12″			
☐ crystal	175.00	200.00	182.00
Punch Bowl, footed, 15″			
☐ crystal	200.00	250.00	210.00
☐ pink	650.00	750.00	700.00
Punch Cup, 4½ oz.			
☐ crystal	16.00	20.00	17.00
☐ pink	26.00	34.00	28.00
Salt and Pepper			
☐ crystal	45.00	55.00	47.00
Sherbet, footed, flared rim, 4½ oz.			
☐ crystal	12.50	15.00	13.00
Sherbet, footed, straight rim, 4½ oz.			
☐ crystal	12.50	15.00	13.00
Sherbet, low footed, 6 oz.			
☐ crystal	12.50	15.00	13.00
Sherry			
☐ crystal	100.00	130.00	110.00
Sugar			
☐ crystal	22.00	28.00	23.00
Tankard, 1 pint			
☐ crystal	110.00	125.00	115.00
Tumbler, flared or straight side, 5 oz.			
☐ crystal	30.00	35.00	32.00
Tumbler, flared or straight side, 7 oz.			
☐ crystal	35.00	40.00	37.00
Tumbler, flared or straight side, 10 oz.			
☐ crystal	35.00	40.00	37.00
Tumbler, flared or straight side, 12 oz.			
☐ crystal	35.00	40.00	37.00
Tumbler, flared or straight side, 13 oz.			
☐ crystal	35.00	40.00	37.00
Water Tumbler, 5½ oz.			
☐ crystal	30.00	35.00	32.00
Wine, 2 oz.			
☐ crystal	150.00	175.00	160.00

IPSWICH
A.H. Heisey

This distinctive pattern was produced on blank #1405 in crystal, green (Moongleam), pink (Flamingo), yellow (Sahara), cobalt, and alexandrite.

Ipswich

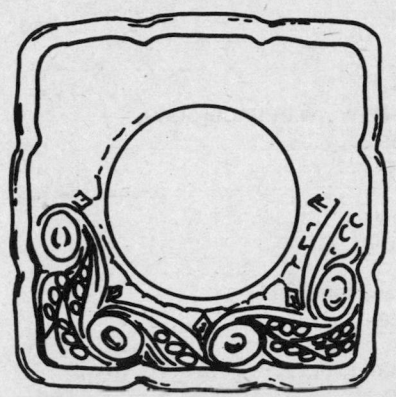

	Current Price Range		Prior Year Average
Bowl, footed, diameter 11″, floral			
☐ crystal	35.00	40.00	37.00
☐ cobalt...........................	350.00	400.00	370.00
☐ sahara	175.00	200.00	180.00
Candlestick, height 6″			
☐ crystal	150.00	175.00	160.00
☐ green	175.00	200.00	180.00
☐ pink	175.00	200.00	180.00
☐ yellow	175.00	200.00	180.00
Candy Jar, with lid			
☐ crystal	45.00	50.00	47.00
☐ green	240.00	260.00	245.00
☐ pink	240.00	260.00	245.00
☐ yellow	190.00	210.00	197.00
Champagne, 5 oz.			
☐ crystal	9.00	11.00	9.50
Cocktail, 4 oz.			
☐ crystal	9.00	11.00	9.50
Cocktail Shaker, with strainer and stopper			
☐ crystal	140.00	160.00	145.00
☐ green	440.00	460.00	445.00
☐ pink	240.00	260.00	245.00
☐ yellow	340.00	360.00	345.00
Creamer			
☐ crystal	15.00	20.00	17.00
☐ green	30.00	40.00	32.00
☐ pink	30.00	40.00	32.00
☐ yellow	30.00	40.00	32.00
Cruet, with stopper, footed, 2 oz.			
☐ crystal	60.00	65.00	62.00
☐ green	115.00	130.00	120.00

	Current Price Range		Prior Year Average
□ pink	115.00	130.00	120.00
□ yellow	115.00	130.00	120.00
Finger Bowl, with underplate			
□ crystal	14.00	18.00	15.00
□ green	40.00	45.00	42.00
□ pink	40.00	45.00	42.00
□ yellow	35.00	40.00	37.00
Goblet, 10 oz.			
□ crystal	14.00	16.00	14.50
Iced Tea, footed, 12 oz.			
□ crystal	24.00	26.00	24.50
Pitcher, 64 oz.			
□ crystal	90.00	110.00	100.00
□ green	400.00	450.00	420.00
□ pink	250.00	275.00	260.00
□ yellow	250.00	275.00	260.00
Plate, square, diameter 7"			
□ crystal	13.00	16.00	14.00
□ green	24.00	30.00	26.00
□ pink	24.00	28.00	26.00
□ yellow	20.00	28.00	27.00
Plate, square, diameter 8"			
□ crystal	15.00	20.00	17.50
□ green	30.00	35.00	32.00
□ pink	30.00	35.00	32.00
□ yellow	30.00	35.00	32.00
Sherbet, 4 oz.			
□ crystal	8.00	10.00	9.00
□ green	18.00	25.00	20.00
□ pink	18.00	25.00	20.00
□ yellow	18.00	25.00	20.00
Sugar Bowl			
□ crystal	15.00	20.00	17.00
□ green	30.00	40.00	34.00
□ pink	30.00	40.00	34.00
□ yellow	30.00	40.00	34.00
Tumbler, 10 oz. cupped			
□ crystal	10.00	16.00	12.00
□ green	30.00	40.00	34.00
□ pink	30.00	40.00	34.00
□ yellow	30.00	40.00	34.00
Tumbler, footed, 5 oz.			
□ crystal	8.00	10.00	9.00
□ green	24.00	30.00	26.00
□ pink	24.00	30.00	26.00
□ yellow	24.00	30.00	26.00

	Current Price Range		Prior Year Average
Tumbler, footed, 8 oz.			
☐ crystal	10.00	12.00	9.00
☐ green	20.00	26.00	22.00
☐ pink	20.00	26.00	22.00
☐ yellow	20.00	26.00	22.00
Tumbler, footed, 12 oz.			
☐ crystal	10.00	15.00	11.00
☐ green	40.00	45.00	42.00
☐ pink	40.00	45.00	42.00
☐ yellow	40.00	45.00	42.00

LARIAT
A.H. Heisey

This unique pattern was produced on blank #1540 and features pronounced circular loops around exterior rims. It was primarily made in crystal and very infrequently in black.

	Current Price Range		Prior Year Average
Ashtray, 4″			
☐ crystal	5.00	10.00	6.00
Basket, 7½″			
☐ crystal	58.00	65.00	60.00
Basket, footed, 8½″			
☐ crystal	95.00	120.00	100.00
Basket, footed, 10″			
☐ crystal	125.00	135.00	125.00
Bowl, 4″			
☐ crystal	13.00	20.00	14.00
Bowl, flat, 8″			
☐ crystal	12.00	16.00	12.50
Buffet Plate, 21″			
☐ crystal	33.00	43.00	34.00

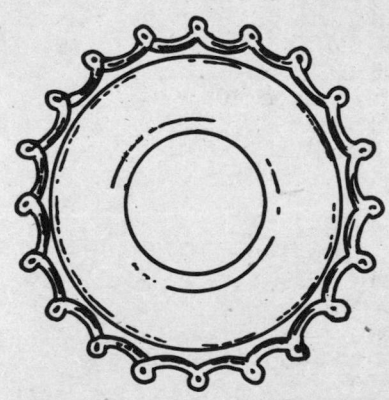

Lariat

	Current Price Range		Prior Year Average
Cake Plate, rolled edge, 12″			
☐ crystal	18.00	25.00	19.50
Camellia Bowl, 9½″			
☐ crystal	20.00	25.00	22.00
Candlestick, one candle			
☐ crystal	10.00	12.00	11.00
Candlestick, two candles			
☐ crystal	20.00	25.00	22.00
Candlestick, three candles			
☐ crystal	60.00	70.00	64.00
Candy Box, covered			
☐ crystal	28.00	35.00	29.00
Candy Dish, covered, 7″			
☐ crystal	28.00	40.00	30.00
Celery Bowl, handled, 10″			
☐ crystal	24.00	30.00	25.00
Celery Bowl, 13″			
☐ crystal	18.00	25.00	19.00
Champagne, blown, 5½ oz.			
☐ crystal	8.00	12.00	8.50
Cheese Dish, covered and footed, 5″			
☐ crystal	23.00	32.00	24.00
Cheese Dish, covered and footed, 8″			
☐ crystal	33.00	42.00	34.00
Cigarette Box			
☐ crystal	18.00	25.00	19.50
Claret, blown, 4 oz.			
☐ crystal	9.00	14.00	9.50
Coaster, 4″			
☐ crystal	6.00	10.00	6.00
Cocktail, blown, 3½ oz.			
☐ crystal	8.00	10.00	9.00
Cocktail, 3½ oz.			
☐ crystal	8.00	10.00	9.00
Compote, covered, 10″			
☐ crystal	45.00	60.00	48.00
Cookie Plate, 11″			
☐ crystal	20.00	25.00	21.00
Cordial, 1 oz.			
☐ crystal	125.00	135.00	128.00
Cordial, blown, 1 oz.			
☐ crystal	88.00	100.00	90.00
Creamer			
☐ crystal	12.00	15.00	11.00
Creamer and Sugar Set, with tray			
☐ crystal	40.00	45.00	42.00
Cruet, with handle and stopper, 4 oz.			
☐ crystal	70.00	80.00	72.00

	Current Price Range		Prior Year Average

Cup
☐ crystal 9.00 12.00 9.50
Deviled Egg Plate, 13″
☐ crystal 110.00 125.00 112.00
Flower Bowl, oval, 13″
☐ crystal 23.00 30.00 24.00
Fruit Bowl, 12″
☐ crystal 15.00 20.00 15.00
Gardenia Bowl, 13″
☐ crystal 18.00 25.00 19.00
Goblet, 9 oz.
☐ crystal 10.00 14.00 11.00
Goblet, blown, 10 oz.
☐ crystal 12.00 16.00 12.50
Ice Tub
☐ crystal 48.00 58.00 50.00
Iced Tea Tumbler, footed, 12 oz.
☐ crystal 11.00 18.00 12.00
Iced Tea Tumbler, footed, blown, 12 oz.
☐ crystal 12.00 19.00 13.00
Jar, with lid, 12″
☐ crystal 90.00 105.00 95.00
Juice Tumbler, footed, 5 oz.
☐ crystal 8.00 11.00 6.00
Juice Tumbler, footed, blown, 5 oz.
☐ crystal 8.00 11.00 6.50
Mayonnaise Bowl, with underplate
☐ crystal 28.00 38.00 30.00
Nappy, 7″
☐ crystal 12.00 16.00 12.50
Oyster Cocktail, 4¼ oz.
☐ crystal 8.00 10.00 6.50
Oyster Cocktail, blown, 4½ oz.
☐ crystal 8.00 10.00 6.50
Platter, oval, 15″
☐ crystal 25.00 35.00 25.00
Punch Bowl
☐ crystal 58.00 70.00 60.00
Punch Cup
☐ crystal 6.00 8.00 4.00
Relish Bowl, divided, 7″
☐ crystal 18.00 22.00 15.00
Relish Bowl, two handles, 11″
☐ crystal 15.00 23.00 16.00
Salad Bowl, 10½″
☐ crystal 25.00 30.00 25.00
Salad Bowl, two handles, 10½″
☐ crystal 23.00 33.00 25.00

	Current Price Range		Prior Year Average
Salad Plate, 7″			
☐ crystal	5.00	12.00	6.00
Salad Plate, 8″			
☐ crystal	8.00	12.00	9.00
☐ black (only 6 known of)	800.00	1000.00	900.00
Salt and Pepper Shakers, pair			
☐ crystal	140.00	160.00	145.00
Sandwich Plate, two handles, 14″			
☐ crystal	28.00	38.00	30.00
Saucer			
☐ crystal	5.00	6.00	4.00
Sherbet, low, 6 oz.			
☐ crystal	7.00	10.00	5.00
Sherbet/Champagne, 6 oz.			
☐ crystal	9.00	11.00	6.50
Sugar Bowl			
☐ crystal	12.00	15.00	10.00
Tray, for sugar and creamer			
☐ crystal	12.00	15.00	12.00
Wine, blown, 2½ oz.			
☐ crystal	15.00	23.00	16.00
Wine, 3½ oz.			
☐ crystal	10.00	13.00	6.50
Vase, fan shaped, footed, 7″			
☐ crystal	30.00	35.00	25.00

LODESTAR
A.H. Heisey

Produced from 1945 to 1956. It was made only in Dawn.

	Current Price Range		Prior Year Average
Ashtray			
☐ dawn	22.50	26.50	20.50
Bowl, crimped, 6″			
☐ dawn	30.00	36.00	29.00
Bowl, crimped, 7½″			
☐ dawn	32.00	38.00	30.00
Bowl, crimped, 11″			
☐ dawn	40.00	45.00	39.00
Bowl, cupped, 4″			
☐ dawn	15.00	21.00	14.00
Bowl, cupped, 8″			
☐ dawn	37.00	43.00	35.00
Bowl, deep, fruit design, 12″			
☐ dawn	80.00	87.50	78.00
Bowl, deep, floral design, 12″			
☐ dawn	80.00	87.50	78.00
Candlestick, 1 lite star			
☐ dawn	35.00	42.00	35.00

	Current Price Range		Prior Year Average

Candlestick, 1 lite centerpiece
☐ dawn 47.50 57.50 46.00

Candlestick, 2 lite
☐ dawn 100.00 115.00 95.00

Candy Box, covered, 5″
☐ dawn 27.00 32.00 26.00

Celery Tray, 10″
☐ dawn 30.00 35.00 28.00

Cigarette Urn
☐ dawn 15.00 19.00 14.00

Creamer or Sugar
☐ dawn 17.00 22.00 16.00

Jar, covered
☐ dawn 20.00 25.00 18.00

Juice, 6 oz.
☐ dawn 12.00 16.00 10.00

Mayonnaise, 5″
☐ dawn 22.00 27.50 20.00

Nappy, 5″
☐ dawn 22.00 27.00 22.00

Party Plate, 14″
☐ dawn 29.00 34.00 27.50

Pitcher, 1 quart
☐ dawn 30.00 34.00 28.00

Relish Tray, 3 compartment, 7½″
☐ dawn 22.00 26.00 20.00

Salt or Pepper
☐ dawn 6.00 9.00 6.00

Torte Plate, 8½″
☐ dawn 25.00 32.50 24.00

Tray, 4 compartment, 12″
☐ dawn 37.00 42.00 35.00

Vase, crimped, 8″
☐ dawn 28.00 33.00 26.00

PINEAPPLE AND FAN
A.H. Heisey

This pattern was produced from 1898 through 1907. It was manufactured in crystal, canary, emerald, ivorina verde, and vaseline.

Berry Bowl, round, 4½″
☐ crystal 6.50 9.00 6.00
☐ canary 7.50 10.00 7.00
☐ emerald 8.50 12.00 8.00
☐ ivorina verde 7.50 10.00 7.00
☐ vaseline 8.00 11.00 7.50

Berry Bowl, round, 9″
☐ crystal 10.00 13.00 9.00

	Current Price Range		Prior Year Average
☐ canary	11.00	14.50	11.00
☐ emerald	12.00	16.00	12.00
☐ ivorina verde	11.00	14.50	11.00
☐ vaseline	11.50	15.00	12.00
Berry Bowl, oval, straight, 12″			
☐ crystal	37.00	42.00	36.00
☐ canary	39.50	45.00	39.00
☐ emerald	43.00	48.00	42.00
☐ ivorina verde	39.50	45.00	39.00
☐ vaseline	41.50	46.50	41.00
Bonbon			
☐ crystal	16.00	19.50	15.50
☐ canary	17.00	20.50	16.00
☐ emerald	17.00	20.50	16.00
☐ ivorina verde	17.00	20.50	16.00
☐ vaseline	17.00	20.50	16.00
Bowl, footed, straight, 7″			
☐ crystal	27.50	31.50	27.00
☐ canary	28.50	32.50	28.00
☐ emerald	29.50	34.50	29.00
☐ ivorina verde	28.50	32.50	28.00
☐ vaseline	28.50	32.50	28.00
Bowl, footed, straight, 8″			
☐ crystal	29.00	34.50	28.50
☐ canary	30.50	35.50	29.50
☐ emerald	31.50	36.50	30.00
☐ ivorina verde	30.50	35.50	29.50
☐ vaseline	30.50	35.50	29.50
Bowl, footed, straight, 9″			
☐ crystal	33.00	37.00	32.00
☐ canary	34.50	39.00	33.00
☐ emerald	36.50	42.50	34.00
☐ ivorina verde	34.50	39.00	33.00
☐ vaseline	34.50	39.00	33.00
Bowl, footed, straight, 10″			
☐ crystal	36.00	41.50	35.00
☐ canary	38.50	43.00	37.00
☐ emerald	41.00	46.00	40.00
☐ ivorina verde	38.50	43.00	37.00
☐ vaseline	38.50	43.00	37.00
Bowl, footed, shallow, 7″			
☐ crystal	27.50	31.50	27.00
☐ canary	28.50	32.50	28.00
☐ emerald	30.00	35.00	29.00
☐ ivorina verde	28.50	32.50	28.00
☐ vaseline	29.00	33.50	28.50
Bowl, footed, shallow, 10″			
☐ crystal	37.00	42.00	36.00

	Current Price Range		Prior Year Average
☐ canary	39.50	45.00	39.00
☐ emerald	43.00	48.00	42.00
☐ ivorina verde	39.50	45.00	39.00
☐ vaseline	41.50	46.50	41.00
Butter, covered			
☐ crystal	42.00	46.00	40.00
☐ canary	44.00	49.00	43.00
☐ emerald	47.00	53.00	46.00
☐ ivorina verde	44.00	49.00	43.00
☐ vaseline	45.00	48.00	44.00
Celery, tall			
☐ crystal	30.00	33.00	28.00
☐ canary	32.00	36.00	30.00
☐ emerald	34.00	38.50	32.00
☐ ivorina verde	32.00	36.00	30.00
☐ vaseline	33.00	37.00	31.50
Celery Tray, 11″			
☐ crystal	11.00	15.00	10.00
☐ canary	12.50	17.00	11.00
☐ emerald	14.50	19.00	13.00
☐ ivorina verde	12.50	17.00	11.00
☐ vaseline	13.50	18.00	12.00
Cheese Plate, 7″			
☐ crystal	9.00	12.00	8.00
☐ canary	10.00	14.00	8.50
☐ emerald	12.00	16.50	10.00
☐ ivorina verde	10.00	14.00	8.50
☐ vaseline	11.00	15.00	9.00
Creamer, regular			
☐ crystal	27.00	30.00	26.00
☐ canary	29.00	31.00	28.00
☐ emerald	32.00	36.00	31.00
☐ ivorina verde	29.00	31.00	28.00
☐ vaseline	29.50	33.00	29.00
Creamer, half pint			
☐ crystal	30.00	33.00	29.00
☐ canary	32.00	35.00	30.00
☐ emerald	34.00	37.50	32.00
☐ ivorina verde	32.00	35.00	30.00
☐ vaseline	33.00	36.00	31.00
Custard, handled			
☐ crystal	15.00	18.00	14.50
☐ canary	17.00	19.00	15.50
☐ emerald	19.00	22.00	17.50
☐ ivorina verde	17.00	19.00	15.50
☐ vaseline	18.00	20.00	16.00
Jelly, footed, 5″			
☐ crystal	29.00	33.00	28.00

	Current Price Range		Prior Year Average
☐ canary	31.00	35.00	30.00
☐ emerald	32.00	37.00	32.00
☐ ivorina verde	31.00	35.00	30.00
☐ vaseline	31.50	36.00	31.00
Molasses can, 13 oz.			
☐ crystal	30.00	34.00	29.00
☐ canary	32.00	36.00	32.00
☐ emerald	34.50	39.00	33.00
☐ ivorina verde	32.00	36.00	32.00
☐ vaseline	33.00	37.50	32.50
Mug, handled, 7 oz.			
☐ crystal	24.00	27.00	23.00
☐ canary	26.00	29.00	25.00
☐ emerald	28.00	31.50	27.00
☐ ivorina verde	26.00	29.00	25.00
☐ vaseline	27.00	30.00	26.00
Nappy, straight, 4½"			
☐ crystal	5.50	8.50	6.00
☐ canary	7.00	10.00	7.00
☐ emerald	8.00	11.00	7.50
☐ ivorina verde	7.00	10.00	7.00
☐ vaseline	7.50	11.00	7.50
Nappy, straight, 8"			
☐ crystal	8.00	11.50	8.00
☐ canary	10.00	13.00	9.00
☐ emerald	12.00	14.50	11.00
☐ ivorina verde	10.00	13.00	9.00
☐ vaseline	11.00	13.50	10.00
Nappy, shallow, 6"			
☐ crystal	7.50	12.00	6.50
☐ canary	9.00	15.00	8.50
☐ emerald	10.50	16.50	9.50
☐ ivorina verde	9.00	15.00	8.50
☐ vaseline	10.00	16.00	9.00
Nappy, flared, 5"			
☐ crystal	8.00	10.50	7.00
☐ canary	9.00	11.50	8.00
☐ emerald	10.50	14.50	10.00
☐ ivorina verde	9.00	11.50	8.00
☐ vaseline	10.00	13.00	9.00
Nappy, nut, 4½"			
☐ crystal	8.00	10.50	7.00
☐ canary	9.00	11.50	8.00
☐ emerald	10.50	14.50	10.00
☐ ivorina verde	9.00	11.50	10.00
☐ vaseline	10.00	13.00	9.00
Nappy, orange, 4½"			
☐ crystal	10.00	13.00	9.00

	Current Price Range		Prior Year Average
☐ canary	11.00	15.00	10.00
☐ emerald	12.50	16.50	12.00
☐ ivorina verde	11.00	15.00	10.00
☐ vaseline	11.50	15.50	11.00
Oil, 6 oz.			
☐ crystal	38.00	42.00	37.00
☐ canary	41.00	45.00	40.00
☐ emerald	43.00	47.00	42.00
☐ ivorina verde	41.00	46.00	40.00
☐ vaseline	42.00	46.50	41.50
Olive, 5″			
☐ crystal	5.00	7.00	5.00
☐ canary	6.00	8.00	5.00
☐ emerald	8.00	9.50	7.00
☐ ivorina verde	6.00	8.00	5.00
☐ vaseline	7.00	8.50	6.50
Olive, 6″			
☐ crystal	6.00	8.00	5.50
☐ canary	7.50	9.50	6.00
☐ emerald	9.00	12.00	8.00
☐ ivorina verde	7.50	9.50	6.00
☐ vaseline	8.00	10.50	7.50
Pickle Jar, covered			
☐ crystal	24.00	28.00	23.50
☐ canary	26.00	29.00	26.00
☐ emerald	28.50	32.50	27.00
☐ ivorina verde	26.00	29.00	26.00
☐ vaseline	27.00	30.50	26.50
Pickle Tray, 6″			
☐ crystal	7.00	9.00	6.50
☐ canary	8.00	10.50	7.00
☐ emerald	9.50	12.00	8.50
☐ ivorina verde	8.00	10.50	7.00
☐ vaseline	9.00	11.00	8.00
Pitcher, ½ pint			
☐ crystal	18.00	24.00	17.00
☐ canary	20.00	26.00	20.00
☐ emerald	23.00	28.00	21.00
☐ ivorina verde	20.00	26.00	20.00
☐ vaseline	21.00	27.00	20.00
Pitcher, 1 pint			
☐ crystal	22.00	26.00	21.00
☐ canary	25.00	28.50	24.00
☐ emerald	27.00	33.00	25.00
☐ ivorina verde	25.00	28.50	24.00
☐ vaseline	26.00	31.00	24.50
Pitcher, 3 pint			
☐ crystal	40.00	45.00	40.00

	Current Price Range		Prior Year Average
☐ canary	42.00	46.00	40.00
☐ emerald	45.00	52.00	44.00
☐ ivorina verde	42.00	46.00	40.00
☐ vaseline	44.00	50.00	42.00
Pitcher, ½ gallon			
☐ crystal	44.00	50.00	42.00
☐ canary	46.50	49.00	44.00
☐ emerald	49.00	55.00	46.00
☐ ivorina verde	46.50	49.00	44.00
☐ vaseline	47.50	53.00	46.00
Salver, 10″			
☐ crystal	20.00	24.00	20.00
☐ canary	22.00	26.00	22.00
☐ emerald	24.00	28.00	23.00
☐ ivorina verde	22.00	26.00	22.00
☐ vaseline	23.00	25.00	22.50
Salver, footed, 11″			
☐ crystal	30.00	33.00	29.00
☐ canary	31.50	35.00	31.00
☐ emerald	34.00	37.50	33.00
☐ ivorina verde	31.50	35.00	31.00
☐ vaseline	32.50	36.00	32.00
Spooner			
☐ crystal	33.00	38.00	32.00
☐ canary	35.00	39.00	33.00
☐ emerald	37.50	42.00	35.00
☐ ivorina verde	35.00	39.00	33.00
☐ vaseline	36.00	40.00	35.00
Sugar, covered			
☐ crystal	27.00	32.00	26.00
☐ canary	29.00	34.00	26.50
☐ emerald	31.00	37.00	30.00
☐ ivorina verde	29.00	34.00	26.50
☐ vaseline	30.00	35.00	28.00
Tumbler, 8½ oz.			
☐ crystal	12.00	16.00	12.00
☐ canary	14.00	19.00	14.00
☐ emerald	16.00	22.00	16.00
☐ ivorina verde	14.00	19.00	14.00
☐ vaseline	15.00	20.50	15.00
Vase, 6″			
☐ crystal	20.00	24.00	20.00
☐ canary	23.00	27.00	22.00
☐ emerald	24.00	29.00	23.00
☐ ivorina verde	23.00	27.00	22.00
☐ vaseline	23.50	28.00	22.00
Vase, 8″			
☐ crystal	22.00	25.00	20.00

	Current Price Range		Prior Year Average
☐ canary	24.00	28.00	22.00
☐ emerald	26.00	30.50	25.00
☐ ivorina verde	24.00	28.00	22.00
☐ vaseline	25.00	29.00	23.00
Vase, 10″			
☐ crystal	24.00	28.00	23.00
☐ canary	27.00	30.00	26.00
☐ emerald	29.00	32.00	27.00
☐ ivorina verde	27.00	30.00	26.00
☐ vaseline	28.00	31.00	26.50
Vase, 12″			
☐ crystal	40.00	45.00	37.00
☐ canary	44.00	48.00	40.00
☐ emerald	48.00	55.00	45.00
☐ ivorina verde	44.00	49.00	40.00
☐ vaseline	46.00	53.00	43.00

PLANTATION
A.H. Heisey

One of the most graceful of all the elegant patterns, Plantation features the pineapple motif which has historically symbolized Southern hospitality. Produced on blank #1567 primarily in crystal, there are also rare pieces which have appeared in amber.

Ashtray, 3½″			
☐ crystal	14.00	23.00	15.50
Buffet Plate, 18″			
☐ crystal	35.00	40.00	37.00

Plantation

	Current Price Range		Prior Year Average
Butter Dish, covered, ¼ lb.			
☐ crystal	50.00	55.00	52.00
Butter Dish, covered, round			
☐ crystal	55.00	65.00	60.00
Cake Plate, footed, 13"			
☐ crystal	64.00	74.00	65.00
Candelabra, 3 lite			
☐ crystal	75.00	80.00	70.00
Candlestick, one candle			
☐ crystal	30.00	40.00	32.00
Candlestick, two candles			
☐ crystal	50.00	60.00	45.00
Candlestick, three candles			
☐ crystal	60.00	75.00	60.00
Candy Box, covered, 7"			
☐ crystal	74.00	83.00	75.50
Candy Jar, covered, footed, 5"			
☐ crystal	105.00	135.00	112.50
Celery Dish, two sections, 13"			
☐ crystal	30.00	35.00	33.00
Celery Dish, 13"			
☐ crystal	20.00	25.00	21.00
Champagne, blown, 6½ oz.			
☐ crystal	17.00	22.00	14.50
Cheese Dish, covered, footed, 5"			
☐ crystal	29.00	38.00	29.50
Claret, blown, 4½ oz.			
☐ crystal	20.00	26.00	18.50
Claret, pressed, 4½ oz.			
☐ crystal	20.00	24.00	16.50
Coaster, 4"			
☐ crystal	15.00	20.00	12.50
Cocktail, pressed, 3½ oz.			
☐ crystal	17.00	26.00	18.50
Compote, covered, 5"			
☐ crystal	39.00	48.00	40.50
Compote, 5"			
☐ crystal	17.00	26.00	18.50
Cordial, 1 oz.			
☐ crystal	75.00	95.00	82.00
Creamer, footed			
☐ crystal	18.00	23.00	14.50
Cruet, with stopper, 3 oz.			
☐ crystal	70.00	80.00	72.00
Cup and Saucer			
☐ crystal	15.00	20.00	16.00
Epergne, footed, with candleholder, 5"			
☐ crystal	60.00	75.00	64.00

	Current Price Range		Prior Year Average

Fruit Bowl, fluted edge, 9½"
☐ crystal .... 40.00 | 45.00 | | 42.00
Fruit Bowl, fluted edge, 12"
☐ crystal .... 55.00 | 60.00 | | 56.00
Fruit Cocktail Goblet, 4 oz.
☐ crystal .... 18.00 | 22.00 | | 14.50
Gardenia Bowl, 9½"
☐ crystal .... 24.00 | 28.00 | | 20.00
Gardenia Bowl, footed, 11½"
☐ crystal .... 25.00 | 35.00 | | 30.00
Gardenia Bowl, 13"
☐ crystal .... 27.00 | 36.00 | | 28.50
Honey Bowl, footed, 6½"
☐ crystal .... 21.00 | 30.00 | | 22.50
Hurricane Candleholder
☐ crystal .... 125.00 | 175.00 | | 145.00
Iced Tea Tumbler, footed, blown, 12 oz.
☐ crystal .... 26.00 | 35.00 | | 27.50
Iced Tea Tumbler, footed, pressed, 12 oz.
☐ crystal .... 24.00 | 33.00 | | 24.50
Jelly Bowl, flared rim, 6½"
☐ crystal .... 17.00 | 26.00 | | 18.50
Jelly Bowl, two handles, 6½"
☐ crystal .... 25.00 | 30.00 | | 26.00
Juice Tumbler, footed, blown, 5 oz.
☐ crystal .... 25.00 | 30.00 | | 27.00
Juice Tumbler, footed, pressed, 5 oz.
☐ crystal .... 19.00 | 28.00 | | 21.00
Marmalade Jar, covered
☐ crystal .... 70.00 | 80.00 | | 72.00
Mayonnaise Bowl, footed, 4½"
☐ crystal .... 25.00 | 35.00 | | 28.00
Mayonnaise Bowl, includes liner, 5¼"
☐ crystal .... 30.00 | 35.00 | | 32.00
Nappy, 5"
☐ crystal .... 15.00 | 20.00 | | 12.50
Nappy, 5½"
☐ crystal .... 15.00 | 21.00 | | 13.50
Oyster Cocktail Goblet, blown, 4½ oz.
☐ crystal .... 20.00 | 24.00 | | 17.50
Pitcher, ice lip, blown, 64 oz.
☐ crystal .... 125.00 | 150.00 | | 130.00
Plate, 10½"
☐ crystal .... 30.00 | 35.00 | | 18.50
Punch Bowl, 2½ gal.
☐ crystal .... 100.00 | 135.00 | | 95.00

	Current Price Range		Prior Year Average
Punch Bowl Underplate, 18″			
☐ crystal	50.00	60.00	52.00
Punch Cup			
☐ crystal	15.00	20.00	12.50
Relish Dish, divided, three sections, 11″			
☐ crystal	18.00	27.00	19.50
Relish Dish, oval, divided, five sections, 13″			
☐ crystal	40.00	45.00	42.00
Relish Dish, round, divided, four sections, 8″			
☐ crystal	30.00	35.00	32.00
Salad Bowl, 9″			
☐ crystal	25.00	30.00	22.50
Salad Plate, 7″			
☐ crystal	12.00	17.00	9.50
Salad Plate, 8″			
☐ crystal	15.00	20.00	11.50
Salt and Pepper Shakers, pair			
☐ crystal	45.00	55.00	50.00
Sandwich Plate, 14″			
☐ crystal	35.00	40.00	37.00
Serving Bowl, divided, two sections, 8½″			
☐ crystal	30.00	35.00	32.00
Sugar Bowl, footed			
☐ crystal	18.00	23.00	20.00
Tray, holds sugar bowl and creamer, 8½″			
☐ crystal	30.00	35.00	32.00
Water Goblet, blown, 10 oz.			
☐ crystal	18.00	24.00	15.50
Water Goblet, pressed, 10 oz.			
☐ crystal	16.00	23.00	15.50
Water Tumbler, 10 oz.			
☐ crystal	25.00	34.00	26.50
Wine Goblet, blown, 3 oz.			
☐ crystal	30.00	35.00	32.00
Vase, footed, 5″			
☐ crystal	35.00	40.00	37.00
Vase, footed, 9″			
☐ crystal	50.00	55.00	53.00

PLEAT AND PANEL
A.H. Heisey

Produced on blank #1170, this very simple pattern is found in crystal, pink (Flamingo), and green (Moongleam).

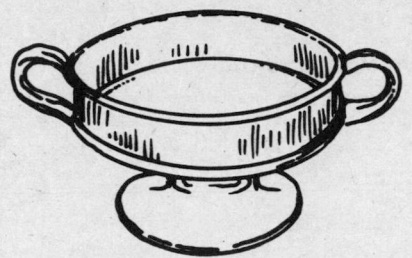

Pleat and Panel

	Current Price Range		Prior Year Average
Bouillon Bowl, two handles, with plate, 5″			
☐ crystal	10.00	15.00	10.00
☐ pink	20.00	30.00	24.00
☐ green	25.00	35.00	26.00
Bouillon Underplate, part of set, 6¾″			
☐ crystal	2.00	9.00	3.50
☐ pink	5.00	12.00	6.50
☐ green	7.00	14.00	8.50
Bowl, 4″			
☐ crystal	4.00	13.00	5.50
☐ pink	10.00	16.00	9.00
☐ green	10.00	18.00	9.00
Bread Plate, 7″			
☐ crystal	3.00	10.00	4.50
☐ pink	6.00	13.00	7.50
☐ green	8.00	15.00	9.50
Cereal Bowl, 6½″			
☐ crystal	8.00	13.00	7.50
☐ pink	15.00	20.00	14.00
☐ green	15.00	20.00	14.00
Champagne Goblet, 5 oz.			
☐ crystal	10.00	13.00	5.50
☐ pink	12.00	20.00	14.00
☐ green	25.00	35.00	24.00
Cheese and Cracker Set, 10½″			
☐ crystal	19.00	28.00	20.50
☐ pink	25.00	37.00	30.50
☐ green	34.00	40.00	35.50
Compote, covered, footed, 5″			
☐ crystal	24.00	33.00	25.50
☐ pink	50.00	65.00	50.00
☐ green	60.00	75.00	65.00
Creamer, hotel			
☐ crystal	10.00	15.00	12.00
☐ pink	15.00	20.00	17.00
☐ green	25.00	30.00	27.00

	Current Price Range		Prior Year Average
Cruet, with stopper, 3 oz.			
☐ crystal	16.00	25.00	17.50
☐ pink	45.00	55.00	50.00
☐ green	55.00	65.00	60.00
☐ amber	350.00	450.00	375.00
Cup			
☐ crystal	10.00	15.00	10.00
☐ pink	20.00	27.00	22.00
☐ green	20.00	30.00	24.00
Dinner Plate, 10¾″			
☐ crystal	15.00	20.00	15.00
☐ pink	19.00	28.00	20.50
☐ green	24.00	33.00	25.50
Goblet, 7½ oz.			
☐ crystal	8.00	17.00	9.50
☐ pink	14.00	23.00	15.50
☐ green	19.00	28.00	20.50
Goblet, 8 oz.			
☐ crystal	11.00	20.00	12.50
☐ pink	19.00	28.00	20.50
☐ green	24.00	33.00	25.50
Iced Tea Tumbler, 12 oz.			
☐ crystal	10.00	17.00	9.50
☐ pink	13.00	22.00	14.50
☐ green	16.00	25.00	17.50
Jelly Bowl, two handles, 5″			
☐ crystal	5.00	14.00	6.50
☐ pink	15.00	20.00	10.50
☐ green	15.00	20.00	12.50
Lemon Bowl, covered, 5″			
☐ crystal	15.00	18.00	10.50
☐ pink	25.00	30.00	14.50
☐ green	35.00	45.00	16.50
Luncheon Plate, 8″			
☐ crystal	4.00	13.00	5.50
☐ pink	9.00	18.00	10.50
☐ green	11.00	20.00	12.50
Marmalade Jar, 4¾″			
☐ crystal	6.00	15.00	7.50
☐ pink	11.00	20.00	12.50
☐ green	16.00	25.00	17.50
Nappy, 4½″			
☐ crystal	4.00	13.00	5.50
☐ pink	7.00	16.00	8.50
☐ green	8.00	17.00	9.50
Nappy, 8″			
☐ crystal	9.00	18.00	10.50
☐ pink	14.00	23.00	15.50

	Current Price Range		Prior Year Average
☐ green	16.00	25.00	17.50
Pitcher			
☐ crystal	30.00	40.00	32.00
☐ pink	50.00	60.00	52.00
☐ green	65.00	75.00	67.00
☐ sahara	120.00	135.00	130.00
Pitcher, ice lip			
☐ crystal	40.00	50.00	42.50
☐ pink	60.00	70.00	62.50
☐ green	75.00	85.00	72.50
Plate, 6″			
☐ crystal	2.00	9.00	3.50
☐ pink	5.00	12.00	6.50
☐ green	7.00	14.00	8.50
Platter, oval, 12″			
☐ crystal	16.00	25.00	17.50
☐ pink	29.00	38.00	30.50
☐ green	34.00	43.00	35.50
Sandwich Plate, 14″			
☐ crystal	14.00	23.00	15.50
☐ pink	24.00	33.00	25.50
☐ green	29.00	38.00	30.50
Saucer			
☐ crystal	2.00	9.00	3.50
☐ pink	4.00	11.00	5.50
☐ green	5.00	12.00	6.50
Sherbet, footed, 5 oz.			
☐ crystal	3.00	10.00	4.50
☐ green	7.00	14.00	8.50
Sugar Bowl, covered, institutional			
☐ crystal	6.00	15.00	7.50
☐ green	21.00	30.00	22.50
Tray, compartments, 10″			
☐ crystal	14.00	23.00	15.50
☐ green	29.00	38.00	30.50
Tumbler, 8 oz.			
☐ crystal	7.00	16.00	8.50
☐ green	14.00	23.00	15.50
Vase, 8″			
☐ crystal	24.00	33.00	25.50
☐ green	44.00	53.00	45.50
Vegetable Bowl, oval, 9″			
☐ crystal	10.00	19.00	11.50
☐ green	18.00	27.00	19.50

PRINCE OF WALES PLUMES
A.H. Heisey

This pattern was made between 1901 to 1912 in crystal and emerald.

	Current Price Range		Prior Year Average
Almond Tray			
☐ crystal	9.00	13.00	8.00
☐ emerald	11.00	16.00	10.00
Berry Bowl, 11″			
☐ crystal	28.00	32.00	27.00
☐ emerald	30.00	35.00	29.00
Bonbon			
☐ crystal	18.00	23.00	17.00
☐ emerald	22.00	27.50	20.00
Bowl, 8″			
☐ crystal	14.00	19.00	12.00
☐ emerald	18.00	24.00	17.00
Bowl, 9″			
☐ crystal	17.00	22.00	16.00
☐ emerald	19.50	24.50	18.50
Bowl, footed, 9″			
☐ crystal	17.50	21.00	16.50
☐ emerald	20.00	25.00	19.00
Bowl, footed, 10″			
☐ crystal	20.00	25.00	20.00
☐ emerald	23.00	27.00	22.00
Bowl, footed, flared, 10″			
☐ crystal	22.00	27.00	22.00
☐ emerald	25.00	30.00	24.00
Bowl, 10″			
☐ crystal	19.00	23.00	18.00
☐ emerald	21.00	24.00	19.50
Bowl, footed, shallow, 11″			
☐ crystal	20.00	23.00	19.00
☐ emerald	22.00	25.00	21.00
Butter, covered			
☐ crystal	75.00	85.00	77.00
☐ emerald	77.50	87.50	79.00
Celery Tray, 10″			
☐ crystal	18.00	22.00	17.00
☐ emerald	20.00	24.00	20.00
Celery Tray, 12″			
☐ crystal	20.00	23.00	20.00
☐ emerald	23.00	26.00	22.00
Creamer, hotel			
☐ crystal	27.00	32.00	27.00
☐ emerald	30.00	34.00	30.00
Creamer, regular			
☐ crystal	30.00	35.00	28.00
☐ emerald	33.00	38.00	32.00
Custard, handled			
☐ crystal	17.00	21.00	18.50
☐ emerald	19.00	23.00	20.00

	Current Price Range		Prior Year Average
Dish, 7½″			
☐ crystal	13.00	17.00	12.00
☐ emerald	16.00	20.00	16.00
Dish, 9″			
☐ crystal	15.00	19.00	14.00
☐ emerald	18.00	22.00	17.00
Dish, 10½″			
☐ crystal	17.00	21.00	16.00
☐ emerald	19.00	23.00	19.00
Dish, 12″			
☐ crystal	19.00	23.00	18.00
☐ emerald	21.00	25.00	21.00
Egg Cup			
☐ crystal	10.00	14.00	10.00
☐ emerald	13.00	16.00	13.00
Jelly, round, handled, 5″			
☐ crystal	9.00	12.00	8.00
☐ emerald	11.00	15.00	10.00
Jelly, footed, 5″			
☐ crystal	24.00	29.00	24.00
☐ emerald	26.00	32.00	26.00
Jelly, footed, 6″			
☐ crystal	17.00	21.00	16.50
☐ emerald	19.00	23.50	18.50
Molasses Can			
☐ crystal	52.50	57.50	50.00
☐ emerald	57.50	67.50	55.00
Nappy, 4″			
☐ crystal	5.00	7.00	5.00
☐ emerald	6.00	8.00	6.00
Nappy, 4½″			
☐ crystal	6.00	8.00	5.50
☐ emerald	7.50	9.50	6.50
Nappy, 7″			
☐ crystal	7.50	9.50	7.00
☐ emerald	9.50	11.00	9.00
Nappy, 8″			
☐ crystal	11.00	14.00	10.00
☐ emerald	13.00	15.00	12.00
Nappy, 9″			
☐ crystal	13.00	16.00	12.00
☐ emerald	14.00	17.00	12.50
Nappy, flared, 10″			
☐ crystal	38.00	42.00	37.00
☐ emerald	40.00	45.00	40.00
Orange Bowl, 10″			
☐ crystal	28.00	32.00	27.00
☐ emerald	32.00	36.00	31.00

	Current Price Range		Prior Year Average
Pickle Tray, 6″			
☐ crystal	12.00	16.00	13.00
☐ emerald	14.00	18.00	15.00
Pickle Tray, 9″			
☐ crystal	15.00	19.00	16.00
☐ emerald ....:...............	17.00	21.00	18.00
Pitcher, 64 oz.			
☐ crystal	80.00	90.00	82.00
☐ emerald	90.00	100.00	92.00
Punch Bowl, 10″			
☐ crystal	85.00	95.00	82.50
☐ emerald	90.00	100.00	92.50
Punch Bowl, 14″			
☐ crystal	130.00	140.00	127.50
☐ emerald	135.00	145.00	137.50
Rose Bowl, footed, 3″			
☐ crystal	28.00	33.00	27.00
☐ emerald	30.00	35.00	29.00
Salad Bowl, 10½″			
☐ crystal	26.00	28.00	25.00
☐ emerald	28.00	30.00	27.00
Salad Bowl, 12″			
☐ crystal	30.00	34.00	29.50
☐ emerald	32.00	37.00	32.00
Salver, cake.			
☐ crystal	72.00	76.00	71.00
☐ emerald	75.00	79.00	74.00
Sherbet, footed			
☐ crystal	8.00	11.00	8.50
☐ emerald	9.00	12.00	9.50
Spooner			
☐ crystal	30.00	34.00	29.00
☐ emerald	32.00	36.00	31.00
Sugar, covered			
☐ crystal	33.00	37.00	32.00
☐ emerald	36.00	41.00	35.00
Syrup Jug, 7 oz.			
☐ crystal	34.00	38.00	35.00
☐ emerald	37.00	42.00	36.00
Tankard, 64 oz.			
☐ crystal	90.00	95.00	93.00
☐ emerald	95.00	100.00	97.50
Tumbler, 8 oz.			
☐ crystal	27.50	32.50	27.00
☐ emerald	30.00	35.00	30.00

PRISCILLA
A.H. Heisey

This pattern was manufactured from 1905 through 1933 and was produced only in crystal.

	Current Price Range		Prior Year Average
Bar, 2 oz.			
☐ crystal	30.00	34.00	29.00
Celery Tray, 9″			
☐ crystal	10.00	14.00	9.00
Celery Tray, 13″			
☐ crystal	13.00	17.00	11.50
Claret, 4½ oz.			
☐ crystal	12.00	17.00	11.00
Cocktail, 2½ oz.			
☐ crystal	25.00	32.00	24.00
Cordial, 1 oz.			
☐ crystal	29.00	35.00	30.00
Custard, 5 oz.			
☐ crystal	17.00	23.00	17.00
Mayonnaise Dish			
☐ crystal	8.00	11.50	8.50
Mustard Dish, covered			
☐ crystal	17.00	23.00	17.00
Nappy, 4½″			
☐ crystal	5.00	7.00	5.00
Nappy, 6″			
☐ crystal	7.00	7.50	7.00
Nappy, 7″			
☐ crystal	8.00	10.00	8.00
Nappy, 8″			
☐ crystal	9.00	11.50	9.00
Nappy, 9″			
☐ crystal	11.00	15.00	10.00
Nappy, 10″			
☐ crystal	12.00	16.00	11.00
Oil, 4 oz.			
☐ crystal	20.00	24.00	21.00
Oil, 6 oz.			
☐ crystal	23.00	27.00	24.00
Pitcher, 64 oz.			
☐ crystal	75.00	80.00	72.00
Plate, 5″			
☐ crystal	6.50	9.00	6.00
Plate, 6″			
☐ crystal	7.50	10.00	7.00
Plate, 9″			
☐ crystal	8.50	11.50	7.50
Plate, 10″			
☐ crystal	10.00	12.00	9.00

	Current Price Range		Prior Year Average
Punch Bowl, footed, 14″			
☐ crystal	185.00	210.00	195.00
Sherbet, 3 oz.			
☐ crystal	4.00	6.00	5.00
Sherbet, 4 oz.			
☐ crystal	5.50	8.50	6.00
Sherbet, 5 oz.			
☐ crystal	7.00	9.00	7.50
Tumbler			
☐ crystal	7.00	9.50	7.50
Vase			
☐ crystal	17.50	25.00	20.00

PROVINCIAL
A.H. Heisey

Reminiscent of Early Thumbprint pattern glass, Provincial was produced on blank #1506 in crystal and limelight (blue-green).

	Current Price Range		Prior Year Average
Ashtray, square, 3″			
☐ crystal	15.00	20.00	12.50
Bonbon Dish, two handles, 7″			
☐ crystal	9.00	18.00	10.50
☐ limelight	29.00	38.00	30.50
Bread Plate, 7″			
☐ crystal	9.00	18.00	10.50
Buffet Plate, 18″			
☐ crystal	24.00	33.00	25.50
Butter Dish, covered			
☐ crystal	65.00	85.00	67.00
Candleholder, one candle			
☐ crystal	14.00	23.00	15.50
☐ limelight	125.00	150.00	130.00

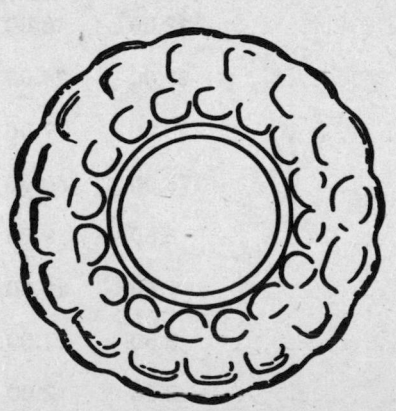

Provincial

	Current Price Range		Prior Year Average
Candleholder, three candles			
☐ crystal	34.00	43.00	35.50
Candy Box, covered, footed, 5½"			
☐ crystal	80.00	100.00	85.00
☐ green	250.00	300.00	270.00
Celery Tray, oval, 13"			
☐ crystal	19.00	28.00	20.50
Champagne Goblet, 5 oz.			
☐ crystal	6.00	15.00	7.50
Cigarette Lighter			
☐ crystal	24.00	33.00	25.50
Coaster, 4"			
☐ crystal	8.00	13.00	9.00
Creamer and Sugar Bowl Set, on tray, small individual			
☐ crystal	40.00	50.00	44.00
Creamer & Sugar, footed			
☐ crystal	14.00	23.00	15.50
☐ limelight	175.00	200.00	190.00
Cruet, with stopper, 4 oz.			
☐ crystal	35.00	40.00	37.00
Epergne, with three candles, 5"			
☐ crystal	44.00	53.00	45.50
Flower Bowl, 12"			
☐ crystal	29.00	38.00	30.50
Gardenia Bowl, 13"			
☐ crystal	29.00	38.00	30.50
Iced Tea Tumbler, footed, 12 oz.			
☐ crystal	14.00	23.00	15.50
☐ limelight	50.00	55.00	52.00
Iced Tea Tumbler, 13"			
☐ crystal	14.00	21.00	15.50
Jelly Bowl, two handles, 5"			
☐ crystal	15.00	20.00	12.50
Juice Tumbler, footed, 5 oz.			
☐ crystal	9.00	18.00	10.50
☐ limelight	45.00	55.00	48.00
Luncheon Plate, 8"			
☐ crystal	14.00	23.00	17.00
☐ limelight	45.00	50.00	47.00
Mayonnaise Set, includes bowl plate and ladle, 7"			
☐ crystal	25.00	34.00	30.00
☐ limelight	70.00	80.00	73.00
Nappy, 4½"			
☐ crystal	9.00	18.00	12.00
☐ limelight	30.00	35.00	31.00

	Current Price Range		Prior Year Average
Nappy, 5½"			
☐ crystal	12.00	20.00	14.00
☐ limelight	35.00	40.00	37.00
Nappy, round, with handle, 5½"			
☐ crystal	14.00	23.00	18.00
Nappy, triangular, with handle, 5½"			
☐ crystal	16.00	25.00	18.50
Nut Bowl, individual			
☐ crystal	20.00	28.00	23.00
Oyster Cocktail, 3½ oz.			
☐ crystal	9.00	15.00	12.00
Plate, footed, 5"			
☐ crystal	9.00	18.00	12.00
Plate, 14"			
☐ crystal	19.00	28.00	22.00
Plate, 18"			
☐ crystal	35.00	40.00	37.00
☐ limelight	100.00	125.00	110.00
Punch Bowl, 5 quart			
☐ crystal	60.00	80.00	70.00
Punch Cup			
☐ crystal	9.00	18.00	12.00
Relish Bowl, divided, four sections, 10"			
☐ crystal	29.00	38.00	34.00
☐ limelight	170.00	180.00	175.00
Salt and Pepper, pair			
☐ crystal	14.00	23.00	16.50
Snack Plate, two handles, 7"			
☐ crystal	11.00	20.00	12.50
Tumbler, 8 oz.			
☐ crystal	11.00	20.00	12.50
Tumbler, footed, 9 oz.			
☐ crystal	13.00	22.00	16.00
☐ limelight	50.00	55.00	52.00

CHILDREN'S DISHES

Many manufacturers of Depression Glass also produced children's dishes. Such makers often turned to these miniature items in an effort to stimulate a new interest in the glassware.

While many companies produced dishes for children, Akro Agate Co. is among the best known. Established in Akron, Ohio, Akro Agate Co. later moved to West Virginia. Along with small dish sets, the company also made games and marbles. Other makers of children's Depression Glass include Jeannette Glass Co., McKee Glass Co., Hazel Atlas Co., and Anchor Hocking.

CHERRY BLOSSOM
Jeannette

Made in pink and delphite, this pattern was called "Jeannette's Junior Dinner Set," in catalogues of the period.

	Current Price Range		Prior Year Average
Creamer, 2¾"			
☐ pink	26.00	28.00	26.50
☐ delphite	23.00	26.00	24.00
Cup, 1½"			
☐ pink	21.00	23.00	21.50
☐ delphite	21.00	23.00	21.50
Plate, 5⅞"			
☐ pink	8.00	10.00	8.50
☐ delphite	5.50	7.00	6.00
Saucer, 4½"			
☐ pink	4.50	6.00	5.00
☐ delphite	4.50	6.00	5.00
Sugar, 2⅝"			
☐ pink	23.00	26.00	24.00
☐ delphite	21.00	24.00	22.00

CHIQUITA
Akro Agate

Green opaque is the most common color found in this pattern made for J. Pressman.

	Current Price Range		Prior Year Average
Complete Set, 16 pieces, in box			
☐ green opaque	48.00	60.00	51.00
☐ cobalt	110.00	125.00	114.00
☐ crystal	150.00	180.00	160.00
☐ baked-on color	57.00	60.00	58.00
Complete Set, 22 pieces, in box			
☐ green opaque	63.00	75.00	65.00
Creamer, 1½"			
☐ green opaque	4.00	5.00	4.25
☐ cobalt	9.00	10.00	9.25
☐ crystal	13.00	15.00	13.50
☐ baked-on color	5.50	6.50	5.75
Cup, 1½"			
☐ green opaque	3.50	4.50	3.75
☐ cobalt	5.00	6.00	5.25
☐ crystal	10.00	12.00	10.50
☐ baked-on color	4.25	5.00	4.50
Plate, 3¾"			
☐ green opaque	2.00	2.50	2.15
☐ cobalt	5.25	6.00	5.50
☐ crystal	10.00	12.00	10.50
☐ baked-on color	1.75	2.25	1.85

	Current Price Range		Prior Year Average
Saucer, 3⅛″			
☐ green opaque	1.75	2.25	1.85
☐ cobalt	2.75	3.25	2.85
☐ crystal	4.75	5.75	5.00
☐ baked-on color	1.25	1.50	1.30
Sugar, 1½″			
☐ green opaque	3.75	4.25	3.85
☐ cobalt	7.00	8.00	7.25
☐ crystal	11.00	13.00	11.50
☐ baked-on color	4.25	4.75	4.35

CONCENTRIC RIB
Akro Agate

	Current Price Range		Prior Year Average
Complete Set, 7 pieces, in box			
☐ green and white	23.00	27.00	24.50
☐ other opaque colors	27.00	32.00	28.00
Creamer, 1¼″			
☐ green and white	3.75	4.75	4.00
☐ other opaque colors	4.50	6.00	5.00
Cup, 1¼″			
☐ green and white	2.25	2.75	2.35
☐ other opaque colors	2.75	3.75	3.00
Plate, 3¼″			
☐ green and white	1.75	2.50	2.00
☐ other opaque colors	2.75	3.50	3.00
Saucer, 2¾″			
☐ green and white	1.75	2.25	1.85
☐ other opaque colors	1.75	2.50	2.00
Sugar, 1¼″			
☐ green and white	4.00	5.00	4.25
☐ other opaque colors	4.50	6.00	5.00

CONCENTRIC RING
Akro Agate

Made in a large and small children's size, this pattern is similar to Concentric Rib. However, Concentric Ring is of better quality than Concentric Rib.

	Current Price Range		Prior Year Average
Complete Set, 21 pieces, large size, in box			
☐ cobalt	335.00	385.00	345.00
☐ blue marble	430.00	470.00	440.00
Complete Set, 16 pieces, small size, in box			
☐ cobalt	240.00	270.00	250.00
☐ blue marble	300.00	335.00	310.00
Cereal Bowl, 3⅜″			
☐ cobalt	24.00	26.00	24.50

	Current Price Range		Prior Year Average
☐ blue marble	29.00	33.00	30.00
☐ other opaque colors	16.00	19.00	17.00
Creamer, 1⅜″			
☐ cobalt	23.00	26.00	24.00
☐ blue marble	32.00	37.00	33.00
☐ other opaque colors	11.00	14.00	12.00
Creamer, 1¼″			
☐ cobalt	19.00	22.00	20.00
☐ blue marble	25.00	28.00	26.00
☐ other opaque colors	9.00	11.00	9.50
Cup, 1⅜″			
☐ cobalt	23.00	26.00	24.00
☐ blue marble	27.00	31.00	28.00
☐ other opaque colors	13.00	15.00	13.50
Cup, 1¼″			
☐ cobalt	25.00	28.00	26.00
☐ blue marble	28.00	31.00	29.00
☐ other opaque colors	9.00	11.00	9.50
Plate, 4¼″			
☐ cobalt	11.00	14.00	12.00
☐ blue marble	16.00	19.00	17.00
☐ other opaque colors	6.50	8.00	7.00
Plate, 3¼″			
☐ cobalt	11.00	13.00	11.50
☐ blue marble	12.00	14.00	12.50
☐ other opaque colors	4.50	6.00	5.00
Saucer, 3⅛″			
☐ cobalt	6.00	8.00	6.50
☐ blue marble	8.50	10.00	9.00
☐ other opaque colors	4.50	5.50	4.75
Saucer, 2¾″			
☐ cobalt	8.00	10.00	8.50
☐ blue marble	9.00	11.00	9.50
☐ other opaque colors	3.00	4.00	3.25
Sugar, 1⅞″			
☐ cobalt	31.00	34.00	32.00
☐ blue marble	37.00	42.00	39.00
☐ other opaque colors	17.00	20.00	18.00
Sugar, 1¼″			
☐ cobalt	19.00	22.00	20.00
☐ blue marble	25.00	27.00	25.50
☐ other opaque colors	9.00	11.00	9.50

DORIC AND PANSY
Jeannette

This pattern was made for only a short period of time. The colors were pink and ultramarine and catalogues called it "Pretty Polly Party Dishes."

	Current Price Range		Prior Year Average
Creamer, 2¾"			
☐ pink	26.00	29.00	27.00
☐ ultramarine	29.00	32.00	30.00
Cup, 1½"			
☐ pink	24.00	26.00	24.50
☐ ultramarine	24.00	26.00	24.50
Plate, 5⅞"			
☐ pink	6.50	8.00	7.00
☐ ultramarine	6.50	8.00	7.00
Saucer, 4½"			
☐ pink	4.00	5.50	4.50
☐ ultramarine	5.00	6.50	5.50
Sugar, 2½"			
☐ pink	21.00	24.00	22.00
☐ ultramarine	23.00	26.00	24.00

FIRE-KING
Anchor Hocking

Period catalogues called this pattern "Sunny Suzy Baking Set, No. 261."

	Current Price Range		Prior Year Average
Complete Set			
☐ 8 pieces, in box	38.00	44.00	40.00
☐ crystal	3.25	4.00	3.50
Custard Cup, 5 oz.			
☐ crystal	2.00	2.50	2.15
Pastry Board			
☐ crystal	2.75	3.75	3.00
Rolling Pin			
☐ crystal	2.25	3.25	2.50

HOMESPUN
Jeannette

	Current Price Range		Prior Year Average
Complete Set, 14 pieces, in box			
☐ pink	195.00	220.00	200.00
Complete Set, 12 pieces, in box			
☐ crystal	75.00	90.00	80.00
Cup, 1⅝"			
☐ pink	28.00	32.00	29.00
☐ crystal	13.00	15.00	13.50
Plate, 4½"			
☐ pink	5.50	7.00	6.00
☐ crystal	4.00	5.50	4.50

HOUZEX
Houze

This pattern, made only in opaque colors, is very similar to Miss America by Akro Agate Co.

	Current Price Range		Prior Year Average
Complete Set, 18 pieces, in box			
☐ green	210.00	240.00	215.00
☐ yellow	210.00	240.00	215.00
☐ blue	240.00	280.00	247.00
Creamer, 1¾"			
☐ green	19.00	21.00	19.50
☐ yellow	19.00	21.00	19.50
☐ blue	21.00	23.00	21.50
Cup, 1¼"			
☐ green	19.00	22.00	20.00
☐ yellow	19.00	22.00	20.00
☐ blue	21.00	23.00	21.50
Plate, 4"			
☐ green	8.50	10.50	9.25
☐ yellow	8.50	10.50	9.25
☐ blue	11.00	13.00	11.50
Saucer, 3¼"			
☐ green	6.50	8.50	7.00
☐ yellow	6.50	8.50	7.00
☐ blue	6.50	8.50	7.00
Sugar, with lid, 2⅞"			
☐ green	26.00	29.00	27.00
☐ yellow	26.00	29.00	27.00
☐ blue	28.00	31.00	29.00

INTERIOR PANEL
Akro Agate

This pattern was made in a large and a small children's size.

Complete Set, 21 pieces, in box, large size			
☐ green	130.00	145.00	135.00
☐ yellow	110.00	130.00	115.00
☐ blue and white	305.00	330.00	310.00
☐ red and white	330.00	360.00	335.00
☐ green and white	245.00	275.00	250.00
☐ lemonade and oxblood	320.00	350.00	330.00
Complete Set, 8 pieces, in box, small size			
☐ pink	38.00	50.00	40.00
☐ green	38.00	50.00	40.00
☐ blue	110.00	115.00	105.00
☐ yellow	110.00	115.00	105.00
☐ green	33.00	45.00	35.00
☐ topaz	33.00	45.00	35.00

	Current Price Range		Prior Year Average
☐ blue and white	105.00	120.00	110.00
☐ red and white	90.00	100.00	93.00
☐ green and white	60.00	70.00	63.00
Complete Set, 16 pieces, in box, small size			
☐ pink	110.00	125.00	115.00
☐ green	110.00	125.00	115.00
☐ blue	215.00	240.00	220.00
☐ yellow	215.00	240.00	220.00
☐ green	80.00	95.00	85.00
☐ topaz	80.00	95.00	85.00
☐ blue and white	215.00	230.00	220.00
☐ red and white	200.00	225.00	210.00
☐ green and white	120.00	140.00	125.00
Creamer, 1⅜"			
☐ blue and white	21.00	24.00	22.00
☐ red and white	23.00	26.00	24.00
☐ green and white	17.00	19.00	17.50
☐ lemonade and oxblood	23.00	27.00	24.00
☐ green	10.00	12.00	10.50
☐ topaz	9.00	11.00	9.50
Creamer, 1¼"			
☐ pink	21.00	23.00	21.50
☐ green	21.00	23.00	21.50
☐ blue	25.00	28.00	26.00
☐ yellow	25.00	28.00	26.00
☐ green	9.00	11.00	9.50
☐ topaz	9.00	11.00	9.50
☐ blue and white	21.00	24.00	22.00
☐ red and white	23.00	27.00	24.00
☐ green and white	14.00	17.00	15.00
Cup, 1⅜"			
☐ green	5.50	7.00	6.00
☐ topaz	4.50	6.00	5.00
☐ blue and white	19.00	21.00	19.50
☐ red and white	20.00	23.00	21.00
☐ green and white	14.00	17.00	15.00
☐ lemonade and oxblood	19.00	22.00	20.00
Cup, 1¼"			
☐ pink	7.00	9.00	7.50
☐ green	7.00	9.00	7.50
☐ blue	24.00	27.00	25.00
☐ yellow	24.00	27.00	25.00
☐ green	6.00	7.50	6.50
☐ topaz	6.00	7.50	6.50
☐ blue and white	19.00	22.00	20.00
☐ red and white	21.00	24.00	22.00
☐ green and white	14.00	17.00	15.00

	Current Price Range		Prior Year Average

Plate, 4¼"
☐ green	4.50	6.00	5.00
☐ topaz	3.50	6.00	4.00
☐ blue and white	9.00	11.00	9.50
☐ red and white	9.00	11.00	9.50
☐ green and white	7.50	10.00	8.00
☐ lemonade and oxblood	10.00	12.00	10.50

Plate, 3¾"
☐ pink	4.00	5.00	4.25
☐ green	4.00	5.00	4.25
☐ blue	4.50	6.50	5.00
☐ yellow	4.50	6.50	5.00
☐ green	3.00	4.00	3.25
☐ topaz	3.00	4.00	3.25
☐ blue and white	9.00	10.00	9.25
☐ red and white	6.50	8.00	7.00
☐ green and white	5.50	7.00	6.00

Saucer, 3⅛"
☐ green	3.00	4.00	3.25
☐ topaz	2.50	3.50	3.00
☐ blue and white	6.50	8.00	7.00
☐ red and white	7.50	9.00	8.00
☐ green and white	6.50	8.00	7.00
☐ lemonade and oxblood	6.50	8.00	7.00

Saucer, 2⅜"
☐ pink	3.00	4.00	3.25
☐ green	3.00	4.00	3.25
☐ blue	6.00	8.00	6.50
☐ yellow	6.00	8.00	6.50
☐ green	3.25	4.00	3.50
☐ topaz	3.25	4.00	3.50
☐ blue and white	6.50	8.00	7.00
☐ red and white	6.50	8.00	7.00
☐ green and white	3.25	4.00	3.50

Sugar, 1⅞"
☐ green	14.00	17.00	15.00
☐ topaz	14.00	17.00	15.00
☐ blue and white	29.00	32.00	30.00
☐ red and white	30.00	33.00	31.00
☐ green and white	22.00	25.00	23.00
☐ lemonade and oxblood	30.00	33.00	31.00

Sugar, 1¼"
☐ pink	21.00	24.00	22.00
☐ green	21.00	24.00	22.00
☐ blue	25.00	28.00	26.00
☐ yellow	25.00	28.00	26.00
☐ green	9.00	11.00	9.50
☐ topaz	9.00	11.00	9.50

	Current Price Range		Prior Year Average
☐ blue and white	21.00	24.00	22.00
☐ red and white	23.00	26.00	24.00
☐ green and white	15.00	18.00	16.00

J.P.
Akro Agate

This pattern was made for the J. Pressman Company.

Complete Set, 17 pieces, in box
☐ blue	163.00	187.00	167.00
☐ brown	225.00	265.00	235.00
☐ crystal	240.00	270.00	230.00
☐ green	163.00	187.00	167.00
☐ red	225.00	265.00	235.00
☐ baked-on colors	55.00	70.00	58.00

Complete Set, 21 pieces, in box
☐ baked-on colors	75.00	92.00	78.00

Cereal Bowl, 3¾"
☐ baked-on colors	5.50	7.00	6.00

Creamer, 1½"
☐ green	21.00	24.00	22.00
☐ blue	21.00	24.00	22.00
☐ crystal	26.00	30.00	27.00
☐ red	26.00	30.00	27.00
☐ brown	26.00	30.00	27.00
☐ baked-on colors	5.50	7.00	6.00

Cup, 1½"
☐ blue	12.00	15.00	13.00
☐ brown	16.00	19.00	17.00
☐ crystal	16.00	20.00	17.00
☐ green	12.00	15.00	13.00
☐ red	16.00	19.00	17.00
☐ baked-on colors	4.00	5.00	4.25

Plate, 4¼"
☐ blue	8.00	10.00	8.50
☐ brown	11.00	13.00	11.50
☐ crystal	11.00	14.00	12.00
☐ green	8.00	10.00	8.50
☐ red	11.00	14.00	12.00
☐ baked-on colors	2.00	3.50	2.50

Saucer, 3¼"
☐ blue	4.00	5.00	4.25
☐ brown	6.50	8.00	7.00
☐ crystal	6.00	9.00	7.00
☐ green	4.00	5.00	4.25
☐ red	6.50	8.00	7.00
☐ baked-on colors	1.50	2.00	1.65

Sugar, with lid, 1½"
☐ blue	23.00	26.00	24.00

	Current Price Range		Prior Year Average
☐ brown	31.00	33.00	31.50
☐ crystal	30.00	34.00	32.00
☐ green	23.00	26.00	24.00
☐ red	31.00	33.00	31.50
☐ baked-on colors	6.50	8.00	7.00

LAUREL
McKee

Creamer, 2⅝"
☐ ivory	22.00	24.00	22.50
☐ ivory with decorated trim	26.00	30.00	27.00
☐ jade	23.00	26.00	24.00
☐ scottie dog decal	34.00	38.00	35.00

Cup, 1½"
☐ ivory	22.00	26.00	23.00
☐ ivory with decorated trim	25.00	29.00	26.00
☐ jade	23.00	26.00	24.00
☐ scottie dog decal	30.00	34.00	31.00

Plate, 5⅞"
☐ ivory	8.00	10.00	8.50
☐ ivory with decal	10.00	13.00	11.00
☐ jade	8.00	10.00	8.50
☐ scottie dog decal	13.00	15.00	13.50

Saucer, 4⅜"
☐ ivory	5.00	6.50	5.50
☐ ivory with decorated trim	6.25	8.25	7.00
☐ jade	5.50	7.00	6.00
☐ scottie dog decal	5.50	7.00	6.00

Sugar, 2⅜"
☐ ivory	19.00	23.00	20.00
☐ ivory with decorated trim	24.00	29.00	25.00
☐ jade	21.00	24.00	22.00
☐ scottie dog decal	34.00	37.00	35.00

MISS AMERICA
Akro Agate

Complete Set, in box
☐ white	300.00	330.00	307.00
☐ white with decal	450.00	480.00	460.00
☐ orange and white	360.00	385.00	370.00
☐ green	360.00	385.00	370.00

Creamer
☐ white	26.00	29.00	27.00
☐ white with decal	38.00	44.00	40.00
☐ orange and white	33.00	38.00	35.00
☐ green	33.00	38.00	35.00

Cup
☐ white	26.00	29.00	27.00

	Current Price Range		Prior Year Average
☐ white with decal	38.00	44.00	40.00
☐ orange and white	30.00	34.00	31.00
☐ green	30.00	34.00	31.00
Plate			
☐ white	15.00	17.00	15.50
☐ white with decal	22.00	25.00	23.00
☐ orange and white	16.00	19.00	17.00
☐ green	16.00	19.00	17.00
Saucer			
☐ white	9.00	12.00	10.00
☐ white with decal	12.00	15.00	13.00
☐ orange and white	10.00	13.00	11.00
☐ green	10.00	13.00	11.00
Sugar			
☐ white	33.00	38.00	35.00
☐ white with decal	46.00	52.00	48.00
☐ orange and white	47.00	50.00	48.00
☐ green	47.00	50.00	48.00
Teapot, with lid			
☐ white	52.00	57.00	54.00
☐ white with decal	75.00	82.00	77.00
☐ orange and white	67.00	73.00	69.00
☐ green	67.00	73.00	69.00

MODERNTONE
Hazel Atlas

Catalogues called this pattern "Little Hostess Party Set." It sold in sets of pastel colors and dark colors. Colors included light green, light yellow, light blue, light pink, orange, gold, gray, turquoise, dark green, maroon, and chartreuse.

Complete Set, in box			
☐ pastel colors	35.00	42.00	37.00
☐ dark colors	58.00	64.00	60.00
Creamer, 1¾"			
☐ pastel colors	3.50	4.50	3.75
☐ dark colors	3.50	4.50	3.75
Cup, 1¾"			
☐ pastel colors	3.00	4.50	3.50
☐ dark colors	3.00	4.50	3.50
Plate, 5¼"			
☐ pastel colors	2.50	3.50	2.75
☐ dark colors	3.00	3.75	3.25
Saucer, 3⅞"			
☐ pastel colors	1.25	2.00	1.75
☐ dark colors	2.50	3.25	2.75
Sugar, 1¾"			
☐ pastel colors	3.50	4.50	3.75
☐ dark colors	3.50	4.75	4.00

OCTAGONAL
Akro Agate

This pattern was made in small and large children's sizes.

	Current Price Range		Prior Year Average
Complete Set, 21 pieces, in box, large size			
☐ green	46.00	52.00	48.00
☐ white	46.00	52.00	48.00
☐ dark blue	46.00	52.00	48.00
☐ lemonade and oxblood	280.00	310.00	290.00
☐ pink	75.00	90.00	80.00
☐ yellow	75.00	90.00	80.00
Complete Set, 16 pieces, in box, small size			
☐ green	85.00	110.00	92.00
☐ blue	85.00	110.00	92.00
☐ white	85.00	110.00	92.00
Cereal Bowl, 3⅜"			
☐ green	4.00	5.00	4.25
☐ white	4.00	5.00	4.25
☐ dark blue	4.00	5.00	4.25
☐ lemonade and oxblood	22.00	25.00	23.00
☐ pink	6.00	7.00	6.25
☐ yellow	6.00	7.00	6.25
Creamer, closed handle, 1½"			
☐ green	3.50	4.50	3.75
☐ white	3.50	4.50	3.75
☐ dark blue	3.50	4.50	3.75
☐ ivory	11.00	14.00	12.00
☐ orange	11.00	14.00	12.00
☐ light blue	11.00	14.00	12.00
☐ lemonade and oxblood	21.00	24.00	22.00
☐ pink	4.50	6.00	5.00
☐ yellow	4.50	6.00	5.00
Creamer, open handle, 1½"			
☐ green	4.50	5.50	4.75
☐ white	4.50	5.50	4.75
☐ dark blue	4.50	5.50	4.75
☐ ivory	13.00	15.00	13.50
☐ orange	13.00	15.00	13.50
☐ light blue	13.00	15.00	13.50
☐ lemonade and oxblood	25.00	29.00	26.00
☐ pink	5.00	7.00	5.50
☐ yellow	5.00	7.00	5.50
Creamer, 1¼"			
☐ green	11.00	14.00	12.00
☐ blue	11.00	14.00	12.00
☐ white	11.00	14.00	12.00
Cup, closed handle, 1½"			
☐ green	1.75	2.50	2.00

	Current Price Range		Prior Year Average
☐ white	1.75	2.50	2.00
☐ dark blue	1.75	2.50	2.00
☐ ivory	9.00	12.00	10.00
☐ orange	19.00	24.00	20.00
☐ light blue	9.00	12.00	10.00
☐ lemonade and oxblood	16.00	19.00	17.00
☐ pink	3.25	4.00	3.50
☐ yellow	3.25	4.00	3.50
Cup, open handle, 1½″			
☐ green	2.50	3.75	2.75
☐ white	2.50	3.75	2.75
☐ dark blue	2.50	3.75	2.75
☐ ivory	11.00	14.00	12.00
☐ orange	24.00	28.00	25.00
☐ light blue	11.00	14.00	12.00
☐ lemonade and oxblood	19.00	22.00	20.00
☐ pink	4.50	5.50	4.75
☐ yellow	4.50	5.50	4.75
Cup, closed handle, 1¼″			
☐ green	8.50	10.00	9.00
☐ blue	8.50	10.00	9.00
☐ white	8.50	10.00	9.00
☐ orange	15.00	18.00	16.00
☐ yellow	15.00	18.00	16.00
☐ light green	15.00	18.00	16.00
Cup, open handle, 1¼″			
☐ green	7.00	9.00	7.50
☐ blue	7.00	9.00	7.50
☐ white	7.00	9.00	7.50
☐ orange	12.00	14.00	12.50
☐ yellow	12.00	14.00	12.50
☐ light green	12.00	14.00	12.50
Plate, 4½″			
☐ green	2.00	2.75	2.25
☐ white	2.00	2.75	2.25
☐ dark blue	2.00	2.75	2.25
☐ ivory	6.00	8.00	6.50
☐ orange	6.00	8.00	6.50
☐ light blue	6.00	8.00	6.50
☐ lemonade and oxblood	9.00	11.00	9.50
☐ pink	2.75	3.50	3.00
☐ yellow	2.75	3.50	3.00
Plate, 3⅜″			
☐ green	4.00	4.75	4.25
☐ blue	4.00	4.75	4.25
☐ white	4.00	4.75	4.25
☐ orange	5.00	6.50	5.50
☐ yellow	5.00	6.50	5.50

	Current Price Range		Prior Year Average
☐ light green	5.00	6.50	5.50
Saucer, 3⅜"			
☐ green	1.25	1.75	1.35
☐ white	1.25	1.75	1.35
☐ dark blue	1.25	1.75	1.35
☐ lemonade and oxblood	5.50	7.00	6.00
☐ pink	1.75	2.50	2.00
☐ yellow	1.75	2.50	2.00
Saucer, 2¾"			
☐ green	2.50	3.50	2.75
☐ blue	2.50	3.50	2.75
☐ white	2.50	3.50	2.75
☐ orange	3.50	5.50	4.00
☐ yellow	3.50	5.50	4.00
☐ light green	3.50	5.50	4.00
Sugar, closed handle			
☐ green	5.00	6.00	5.25
☐ white	5.00	6.00	5.25
☐ dark blue	5.00	6.00	5.25
☐ ivory	15.00	18.00	16.00
☐ orange	15.00	18.00	16.00
☐ light blue	15.00	18.00	16.00
☐ lemonade and oxblood	27.00	30.00	28.00
☐ pink	6.50	8.00	7.00
☐ yellow	6.50	8.00	7.00
Sugar, open handle			
☐ green	7.00	9.00	7.50
☐ white	7.00	9.00	7.50
☐ dark blue	7.00	9.00	7.50
☐ ivory	19.00	22.00	20.00
☐ orange	19.00	22.00	20.00
☐ light blue	19.00	22.00	20.00
☐ lemonade and oxblood	31.00	35.00	32.00
☐ pink	8.00	11.00	9.00
☐ yellow	8.00	11.00	9.00
Sugar, 1¼"			
☐ green	11.00	14.00	12.00
☐ blue	11.00	14.00	12.00
☐ white	11.00	14.00	12.00
Tumbler, 2"			
☐ green	4.50	6.00	5.00
☐ blue	4.50	6.00	5.00
☐ white	4.50	6.00	5.00
☐ orange	13.00	16.00	14.00
☐ yellow	13.00	16.00	14.00
☐ light green	13.00	16.00	14.00

RAISED DAISY
Akro Agate

This pattern was made using only opaque colors.

	Current Price Range		Prior Year Average
Creamer, 1¾″			
☐ yellow	25.00	28.00	26.00
Cup, 1¾″			
☐ blue	25.00	28.00	26.00
☐ green	13.00	16.00	13.50
Plate, 3″			
☐ blue	10.00	12.00	10.50
Saucer, 2½″			
☐ yellow	7.00	9.00	7.50
☐ tan	7.00	9.00	7.50
Sugar			
☐ yellow	26.00	28.00	26.50
Tumbler, 2″			
☐ yellow	16.00	19.00	17.00
☐ blue	30.00	33.00	31.00
☐ tan	17.00	19.00	17.50

STACKED DISK
Akro Agate

This pattern is most commonly found in opaque green and white.

Complete Set, 21 pieces, in box			
☐ green	35.00	40.00	36.00
☐ white	35.00	40.00	36.00
Creamer, 1¼″			
☐ green	3.00	3.50	3.15
☐ white	3.00	3.50	3.15
☐ orange	10.00	12.00	10.50
Cup, 1¼″			
☐ green	1.75	2.25	1.90
☐ white	1.75	2.25	1.90
Plate, 3¼″			
☐ green	1.75	2.00	1.80
☐ white	1.75	2.00	1.80
Saucer, 2¾″			
☐ green	1.75	2.00	1.80
☐ white	1.75	2.00	1.80
Sugar, 1¼″			
☐ green	3.00	3.75	3.25
☐ white	3.00	3.75	3.25
☐ orange	10.00	13.00	11.00
Teapot, with lid, 3⅜″			
☐ green	7.00	8.50	7.25
☐ white	7.00	8.50	7.25
☐ orange	18.00	22.00	19.00

	Current Price Range		Prior Year Average

Tumbler, 2"

☐ green	3.25	4.50	3.50
☐ white	3.25	4.50	3.50
☐ orange	8.00	11.00	9.00

STACKED DISC AND INTERIOR PANEL
Akro Agate

This pattern was made in small and large children's sizes. There are many opaque colors as well as clear blue and green. Blue marble is the most rare.

Complete Set, 21 pieces, large, in box

☐ opaque colors	215.00	245.00	225.00
☐ blue marble	405.00	440.00	415.00
☐ clear green	250.00	280.00	257.00
☐ clear blue	310.00	340.00	320.00

Complete Set, 8 pieces, small, in box

☐ opaque colors	52.00	60.00	54.00
☐ blue marble	142.00	160.00	147.00
☐ clear green	130.00	145.00	132.00
☐ clear blue	180.00	210.00	185.00

Cereal Bowl, 3⅜"

☐ opaque colors	15.00	19.00	16.00
☐ blue marble	28.00	31.00	29.00
☐ clear green	16.00	19.00	17.00
☐ clear blue	19.00	22.00	20.00

Creamer, 1⅜"

☐ opaque colors	11.00	13.00	11.50
☐ blue marble	26.00	29.00	27.00
☐ clear green	15.00	18.00	16.00
☐ clear blue	23.00	26.00	24.00

Creamer, 1¼"

☐ opaque colors	5.50	7.00	6.00
☐ blue marble	26.00	29.00	27.00
☐ clear green	14.00	16.00	14.50
☐ clear blue	19.00	22.00	20.00

Cup, 1⅜"

☐ opaque colors	14.00	16.00	14.50
☐ blue marble	25.00	28.00	26.00
☐ clear green	14.00	17.00	15.00
☐ clear blue	17.00	19.00	17.50

Cup, 1¼"

☐ opaque colors	9.50	11.00	10.00
☐ blue marble	25.00	28.00	26.00
☐ clear green	10.00	11.00	10.25
☐ clear blue	14.50	17.00	15.50

Pitcher, 2¾"

☐ clear green	9.50	11.00	10.00
☐ clear blue	16.00	19.00	17.00

	Current Price Range		Prior Year Average
Plate, 4¾"			
☐ opaque colors	6.50	8.00	7.00
☐ blue marble	11.00	13.00	11.50
☐ clear green	9.00	11.00	9.50
☐ clear blue	9.50	11.00	10.00
Plate, 3¼"			
☐ opaque colors	4.00	5.00	4.25
☐ blue marble	11.00	13.00	11.50
☐ clear green	6.50	8.00	7.00
☐ clear blue	8.50	11.00	9.00
Saucer, 3⅛"			
☐ opaque colors	4.50	5.50	4.75
☐ blue marble	9.50	11.00	10.00
☐ clear green	6.50	8.00	7.00
☐ clear blue	7.50	9.00	8.00
Saucer, 2¾"			
☐ opaque colors	3.25	3.75	3.40
☐ blue marble	9.50	11.00	10.00
☐ clear green	4.50	5.50	4.75
☐ clear blue	5.50	7.00	6.00
Sugar, with lid, 1⅞"			
☐ opaque colors	17.00	19.00	17.50
☐ blue marble	38.00	41.00	39.00
☐ clear green	24.00	27.00	25.00
☐ clear blue	31.00	34.00	32.00
Sugar, 1¼"			
☐ opaque colors	5.50	7.00	6.00
☐ blue marble	26.00	29.00	27.00
☐ clear green	14.00	17.00	15.00
☐ clear blue	19.00	21.00	19.50
Tumbler, 2"			
☐ opaque colors	19.00	23.00	20.00
☐ clear green	7.50	9.00	8.00
☐ clear blue	9.50	11.00	10.00

STIPPLED BAND
Akro Agate

This pattern was made in small and large children's sizes.

Complete Set, 17 pieces, in box			
☐ clear amber	130.00	160.00	140.00
☐ clear green	75.00	90.00	78.00
☐ clear blue	220.00	260.00	225.00
Complete Set, 8 pieces, small, in box			
☐ clear amber	37.00	45.00	39.00
☐ clear green	32.00	37.00	34.00
Creamer, 1½"			
☐ clear amber	13.00	15.00	13.50
☐ clear green	5.50	7.00	6.00

	Current Price Range		Prior Year Average
☐ clear blue	21.00	23.00	21.50
Creamer, 1¼″			
☐ clear amber	5.50	7.00	6.00
☐ clear green	5.00	6.00	5.25
Cup, 1½″			
☐ clear amber	8.50	10.50	9.00
☐ clear green	4.50	5.50	4.75
☐ clear blue	16.00	19.00	17.00
Cup, 1¼″			
☐ clear amber	4.50	5.50	4.75
☐ clear green	4.25	4.75	4.40
Plate, 4¼″			
☐ clear amber	6.50	7.50	6.75
☐ clear green	4.00	5.00	4.25
☐ clear blue	9.00	11.00	9.50
Plate, 3¼″			
☐ clear amber	3.00	4.00	3.25
☐ clear green	2.75	3.75	3.00
Saucer, 3¼″			
☐ clear amber	4.25	5.50	4.50
☐ clear green	1.75	2.50	2.00
☐ clear blue	8.50	11.50	9.50
Saucer, 2¾″			
☐ clear amber	2.00	2.75	2.25
☐ clear green	1.75	2.50	2.00
Sugar, with lid, 1⅞″			
☐ clear amber	17.00	20.00	18.00
☐ clear green	9.00	11.00	9.50
☐ clear blue	26.00	30.00	27.00
Sugar, 1¼″			
☐ clear amber	5.50	7.00	6.00
☐ clear green	5.00	6.00	5.25
Tumbler, 1¾″			
☐ clear amber	5.50	7.00	6.00
☐ clear green	5.00	6.00	5.25

TWENTIETH CENTURY
Hazel Atlas

This pattern was made in mixed pastel colors.

Creamer			
☐ pastel colors	2.75	3.50	3.00
Cup			
☐ pastel colors	2.25	3.00	2.25
Plate			
☐ pastel colors	1.75	2.25	1.90
Saucer			
☐ pastel colors	1.25	1.75	1.35

	Current Price Range		Prior Year Average
Sugar			
☐ pastel colors	2.75	3.25	2.90

THE HEISEY ANIMALS

As all Heisey collectors know, outstanding workmanship and beauty were combined with great skill in all Heisey glass. Nowhere is this more apparent than in the dazzling array of Heisey animals.

Heisey began animal-related items as far back as the late 1920's, but only a few pieces were made. These included the lion's head bowl, the eagle plate and several of the dolphin items.

It wasn't until 1933 that Heisey's animal production started in earnest. It was in this year that the animal figurines were first made. Perhaps it was their great beauty, or their craftmanship, or their reasonable price, but whatever the reason, the Heisey animals were received warmly by adults and children alike.

New items were added yearly, popularity increased steadily, but the year 1943 proved to be a turning point. It was in that year that Horace King joined the company as a glassware designer and took an immediate interest in the animals. He introduced many popular items such as the lion covered trinket box and the sleeping fox ashtray. Also one of his creations was the hard to find elephant-handled children's mug.

Mr. King's greatest contribution, though, is probably the animal head stoppers. Heisey had already been manufacturing cocktail sets, but the addition of Mr. King's animal motif made them more in demand than they had ever been before. The best example is probably the goose cocktail set. In this set, not only was the stopper animal related, but the glasses were as well. The glasses were also made in cordial and sherry sizes.

In addition to the animal items, Heisey also made some human related items such as two Madonna figures and cherub candlesticks.

The animal items were manufactured until the company closed in 1957. When Imperial acquired the Heisey molds in the following year, they continued production of several of the Heisey animals such as the dolphin candlesticks. Even though many are clearly marked with the Imperial glass symbol, they are still popular with collectors. The secret of the Heisey animals' popularity lies in their versatility. They're all unusual, beautiful, well made, and many are useful as well. Children love them as playthings, and animal lovers appreciate them as skillful representations of nature.

It can truly be said without fear of contradiction that there is something for everyone in Heisey animals.

	Current Price Range		Prior Year Average
HEISEY ANIMALS			
Airedale, 5¾" high			
☐ crystal	115.00	135.00	120.00
Asiatic Pheasant, 10½" high			
☐ crystal	425.00	455.00	440.00

	Current Price Range		Prior Year Average
Bull, 4" high			
☐ crystal	290.00	335.00	297.50
Bunny, head up, 2⅜" high			
☐ crystal	85.00	95.00	90.00
Bunny, head down, 2⅜" high			
☐ crystal	75.00	100.00	85.00
Chick, 1" high, head up or head down			
☐ crystal	50.00	65.00	53.00
Clydesdale, 7¼" high			
☐ crystal	360.00	410.00	370.00
Cygnet, 2⅛" high			
☐ crystal	70.00	90.00	80.00
Doe Head Book End, 6¼" high, pair			
☐ crystal	350.00	425.00	370.00
Donkey, 6½" high			
☐ crystal	260.00	300.00	270.00
Duckling, floating, 2¼" high			
☐ crystal	75.00	100.00	82.00
Duckling, standing, 2⅝" high			
☐ crystal	75.00	100.00	82.00
Elephant, 4½" high			
☐ crystal	235.00	270.00	240.00
Elephant, 4" high (the body, minus the trunk, is actually bigger than the 4½" size)			
☐ crystal	230.00	270.00	240.00
Elephant, 5⅞" high			
☐ crystal	300.00	335.00	310.00
Fighting Rooster, 8" high			
☐ crystal	130.00	155.00	140.00

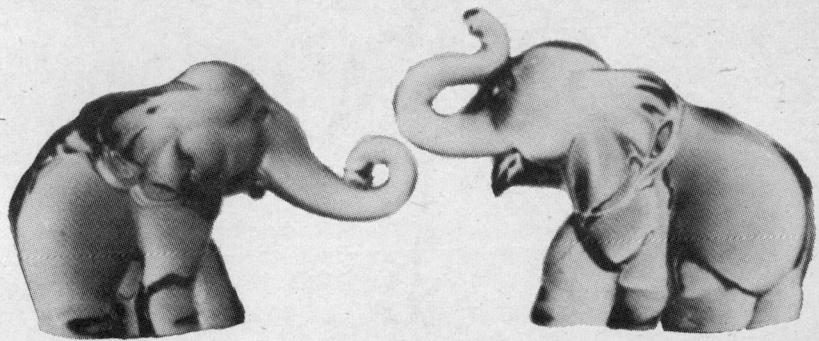

Heisey Elephants, *crystal,* $235.00–$335.00 *(Courtesy of Frank Hahn)*

	Current Price Range		Prior Year Average
Filly Horse, head forward, 8¼" high			
☐ crystal	375.00	430.00	385.00
Filly Horse, head backward, 8¼ high			
☐ crystal	375.00	430.00	385.00
Fish Book End, 6" high			
☐ crystal	175.00	205.00	190.00
Fish Bowl, 9" high			
☐ crystal	700.00	775.00	720.00
Fish Candlestick, 5" high			
☐ crystal	180.00	215.00	195.00
Fish Match Holder, 3" high			
☐ crystal	130.00	165.00	140.00
Flying Mare, 8⅞" high			
☐ crystal	775.00	875.00	800.00
☐ Sahara	1500.00	1850.00	1650.00
Gazelle, 11" high			
☐ crystal	1075.00	1180.00	1120.00
Giraffe, 11" high (Two models are available; one with its head turned to the side and the other with the head to the rear. They were made from the same mold; the head was turned to make the two models.)			
☐ crystal	135.00	165.00	142.00

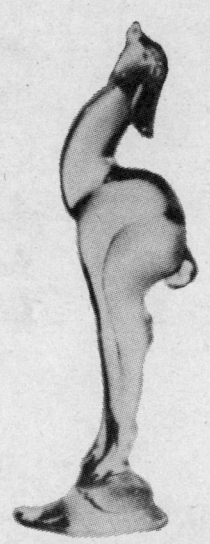

Heisey Gazelle, *crystal,* **$1075.00–$1120.00** *(Courtesy of Frank Hahn)*

Heisey Geese, *crystal,* $55.00-$65.00 *(Courtesy of Frank Hahn)*

	Current Price Range		Prior Year Average
Goose, wings up, 6½" high			
☐ crystal	55.00	80.00	65.00
Goose, wings halfway, 4½" high			
☐ crystal	55.00	80.00	65.00
Goose, wings down, 2¾" high			
☐ crystal	55.00	80.00	65.00
Hen, 4¼" high			
☐ crystal	360.00	395.00	365.00
Horse Head Book End, 6⅞" high, pair			
☐ crystal	135.00	180.00	167.00
Mallard, wings up, 6¾" high			
☐ crystal	155.00	175.00	160.00
Mallard, wings halfway, 5" high			
☐ crystal	135.00	155.00	135.00
Mallard, wings down, 4½" high			
☐ crystal	110.00	125.00	110.00
Me, You, and Us Cocktail Set, 1 shaker, 11½" high; 2 glasses, 5" high			
☐ crystal	290.00	335.00	310.00
Pig, 3⅛" high			
☐ crystal	100.00	125.00	110.00
Piglet, sitting, 1" high			
☐ crystal	50.00	65.00	55.00
Piglet, standing, ⅞" high			
☐ crystal	40.00	50.00	42.00
Plug Horse, 4" high			
☐ crystal	50.00	67.50	57.50
Pony, standing, 5" high			
☐ crystal	110.00	125.00	115.00

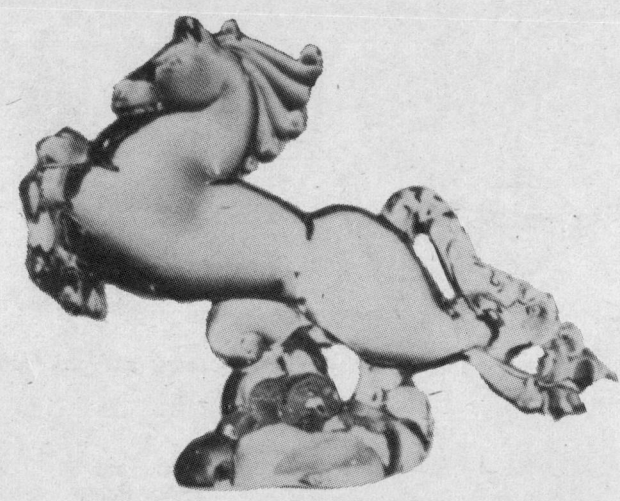

Heisey Flying Mare, *crystal,* **$775.00–$875.00** *(Courtesy of Frank Hahn)*

	Current Price Range		Prior Year Average
Pony, rearing, 3¾" high			
☐ crystal	100.00	120.00	110.00
Pony, kicking, 4⅛" high			
☐ crystal	110.00	125.00	115.00
Pouter Pigeon, 6¼" high			
☐ crystal	660.00	750.00	680.00
Rabbit, 4⅝" high			
☐ crystal	160.00	190.00	170.00
Rabbit, paperweight, 2¾" high			
☐ crystal	160.00	190.00	180.00
Rearing Horse Book End, 7⅞" high			
☐ crystal	225.00	360.00	240.00
Ringneck Pheasant, 4¾" high			
☐ crystal	125.00	160.00	145.00
Rooster, 5⅝" high			
☐ crystal	350.00	390.00	360.00
Rooster Cocktail Set, special issue, 1 shaker with 4 glasses			
☐ crystal	275.00	330.00	300.00
Rooster Cocktail Shaker, standard issue, 14" high			
☐ crystal	100.00	125.00	110.00
Rooster Cocktail Glass, 4¼" high			
☐ crystal	20.00	28.00	22.00

	Current Price Range		Prior Year Average
Rooster Vase, 6½" high			
☐ crystal	80.00	105.00	87.50
Scotty, 3½" high			
☐ crystal	95.00	120.00	100.00
Show Horse, 7⅜" high			
☐ crystal	250.00	400.00	325.00
Sparrow, 2¼" high			
☐ crystal	70.00	85.00	70.00
Swan, 7" high			
☐ crystal	300.00	350.00	340.00
Tropical Fish Piece, 12" high			
☐ crystal	950.00	1050.00	1000.00
Wood Duck, 4½" high			
☐ crystal	425.00	480.00	440.00

PRESSED PATTERN GLASS

INTRODUCTION

Glass historians are still undecided as to whether the Americans or the British first invented pressed glass. Small objects and feet for footed bowls were first hand pressed in England in the early 1800's, but this method was crude compared to the mechanical process which later evolved. Pressing glass with machinery to produce a wide range of glass objects appears to have originated in America.

No one really knows which American company produced the first pressed glass. Early patent records reveal the manufacture of pressed door knobs in the mid 1820's. Other companies are known to have been experimenting in glass pressing during that time. Deming Jarvis of Sandwich, Massachusetts obtained a patent in 1828 for pressed glass and another patent in 1830 for a device which pressed handled glass in one piece. Jarvis is no longer regarded by experts to be the originator of pressed glass, but his many contributions to the advancement of the process make him the dominant figure in the early stages of the field.

Pressing glass allowed for a wide variety of tableware sets to be mass produced at very low cost. The earliest patterns were very basic, followed by the simplistic Lacy glass. However, the molds for Lacy glass were expensive to produce and in 1836–1840, America suffered a depression which forced glass manufacturers to economize.

Shortly after 1840, Lacy glass declined and new simple geometric designs were produced in an effort to attract new buyers. This glass is what we refer to today as the early Pressed Pattern glass.

These new patterns became popular and one important factor in their success was the use of fire polishing, which was developed in England in 1834. Fire polishing is a process which removes mold and tool marks and polishes the glass by reheating it. Although fire polishing was used on Lacy glass, the very nature of the designs and motifs prevented any real change in appearance. In addition, Lacy glass did not withstand the process well at all. However, when fire polishing was done on the geometric designs the glassware took on the appearance of cut and fine blown glass.

Glass companies began producing pressed glass in matching tableware sets during the 1840's. Some of the names originally used for patterns are different than those used today. For example, thumbprint is a very common pattern which is found on more articles than any other motif. It was originally produced under the name of Argus, probably by the Bakewell, Pears and Company. They undoubtedly produced it for many years with many variations in pattern, shape, and type of object. It is impossible to attribute all thumbprint or Argus to Bakewell, Pears and Company because glass houses copied each other without hesitation.

Another extremely popular pattern was Bellflower. It features ribbing and vining. The vining is sometimes single and at other times appears with a single and double vine. Only a few pieces were produced with double vines only. Many manufacturers produced Ribbed Bellflower which accounts for the numbers available and for the numerous variations in detail. For this reason an entire table setting is fairly easy for the collector to accumulate. Other popular early patterns were Tulip, Frosted Roman Key, and Cable.

One interesting point in discussing Ribbed Bellflower is the amethyst tinge which is found in many pieces. This has probably resulted from an excess of manganese or from prolonged exposure to the sun. Colorless glass, when exposed to sunlight for many years, will turn colored, the shade depending on the intensity of the exposure and the substances used to make the glass. Even diffused light will affect colorless glass. Some colors will continue to deepen with exposure; whereas the color will stabilize in some articles regardless of continuing exposure. The only exception to this is some of the white flint glass.

This type of color change can be reversed by firing the article in a kiln. Such a process will restore the original color; however, if exposed to light afterward, the color will be altered once again.

In 1864, William Leighton of the Hobbs, Brockunier and Company developed a practical formula for less expensive glass using lime. The lime glass had a brilliancy similar to that of flint glass but was far cheaper to produce. Within a few years, most glass companies were using lime glass. The New England Glass Company and the Boston and Sandwich Glass Company continued to produce only flint glasswares, determined to maintain the quality of their pieces. But a decade or so later, the Boston and Sandwich Glass Company was forced to use lime in order to compete effectively.

The early patterns continued to garner popularity up through the 1860's and 1870's until they were gradually replaced with more intricate cut glass-type designs. Naturalistic motifs were also introduced, such as flowers, leaves, fruits and grapes along with the greater use of high relief. The most popular of these were Lion, Three Face, and Westward Ho. The basic form of the article also became more varied during this period. Most of these late patterns were produced in full-colored glass tableware sets as well as in the traditional clear glass. Also opaque white and variegated marble became very popular in the 1870's. Knowledgeable collectors feel that there are no complete colored table settings in the earlier patterns; in fact, they doubt that a very large variety of different colored pieces were made in the earlier periods.

HINTS ON CARE AND DISPLAY

1. Wash one piece at a time in lukewarm water using a very mild soap. Line the sink with toweling as an extra precaution.
2. Dry with a soft cloth.
3. Display pressed pattern glass away from sunlight.
4. Do not crowd pieces as chipping and breakage could result.

IDENTIFYING PRESSED PATTERN GLASS

Although pressed glass was originally made to imitate cut glass, you will have no problem differentiating one from the other. Despite the similarities in patterns, pressed glass lacks the deep faceted appearance of cut—the edges of the patterns look rounded, the earlier pieces contain many imperfections—bubbles, lumps, impurities, and sometimes cloudiness. The intricacy of Lacy glass attracted many buyers because the busy patterns disguised flaws. These pieces are rarely available to the average collector. Most of them have been acquired by museums and wealthy collectors.

Later pieces made between 1850 and 1890 are available to the average collector. This glass appears clearer and brighter than the earlier glass whether it is flint or nonflint glass. There also seems to be a preference for pieces that were produced in the East.

Although identification of pieces is mainly by pattern name, the novice collector will have some confusion in this area. This is due to the fact that most of the original names have been discarded by advanced collectors who have renamed the pattern in descriptive terms. For the most part these collectors have found it impossible to attribute most patterns to a particular maker. Manufacturers' marks are exceedingly rare and there are few catalogs available from the period before 1850. By studying the old catalogs that do exist, along with shards found at old factory sites, some sketchy information has been provided. But because patterns were so quickly copied by the competition, absolute verification of the manufacturer is impossible.

Reproductions can pose a definite problem to the beginning pressed pattern glass collector. Two very popular patterns, Bellflower, Daisy and Button, have been reproduced extensively. With careful, informed scrutiny, you will be able to detect the dullness and lack of sparkle characteristic of remakes. If the reproduction was made from a new mold (formed from an original object), the details will not possess the clarity and preciseness of the original article. By comparing known reproductions to their originals, you will develop the ability to differentiate between the two. By studying about pressed pattern glass and seeing as many of the best examples as possible, and by dealing only with reputable professionals who are knowledgeable in this specific area, you will avoid many of the pitfalls mentioned.

ABERDEEN

This is an elegant pattern, consisting of a wide band of curvy ridges in a keyhole motif. The connecting motifs are decorated with beadwork in high relief. The rest of the body is devoid of decoration.

	Current Price Range		Prior Year Average
☐ **Butter,** with cover	45.00	55.00	47.50
☐ **Compote,** high	30.00	40.00	35.00
☐ **Creamer**	40.00	50.00	42.50
☐ **Egg Cup**	30.00	40.00	35.00

	Current Price Range		Prior Year Average
☐ Goblet	30.00	40.00	35.00
☐ Sauce, flat	18.00	22.00	17.50
☐ Sauce, footed	25.00	35.00	27.50
☐ Sugar, with cover	40.00	50.00	45.50
☐ Water Pitcher	60.00	70.00	62.50

ACTRESS
La Belle Glass Company

Actors and actresses are immortalized on these pieces formed in portrait by light ridges. The pieces are always framed by stippled shell forms that rise off the side of the glass; the borders are often bands of light ridges.

☐ Bowl, flat	18.00	27.00	22.00
☐ Bowl, footed	32.00	38.00	34.00
☐ Bread Tray	50.00	60.00	53.00
☐ Butter, with cover	68.00	80.00	72.00
☐ Cake Stand	140.00	160.00	145.00
☐ Candlestick	85.00	115.00	87.50
☐ Celery	148.00	162.00	151.00
☐ Cheese Dish	180.00	200.00	185.00
☐ Compote, with cover	140.00	160.00	145.00
☐ Creamer	35.00	47.00	38.00
☐ Goblet	48.00	62.00	51.00
☐ Jam Jar, with lid	80.00	92.00	85.00
☐ Milk Pitcher	190.00	215.00	200.00
☐ Mustard, with lid	35.00	47.00	38.00
☐ Pickle Dish, says "Love's Request Is Pickles"	35.00	47.00	39.00
☐ Platter, oval	130.00	150.00	135.00
☐ Platter, round	150.00	170.00	155.00
☐ Salt	30.00	37.00	32.00
☐ Sauce Bowl, flat	20.00	30.00	23.00
☐ Sauce Bowl, footed	30.00	40.00	35.00
☐ Spooner	58.00	72.00	62.00
☐ Sugar	78.00	93.00	81.00
☐ Water Pitcher	190.00	215.00	200.00

APOLLO
Adams and Company

A simple pattern of an oval prism band rims the bottom or middle. The edges are slightly scalloped; the glass is smooth,

Bowl, diameter 7"

☐ frosted	25.00	30.00	22.50
☐ clear	20.00	25.00	22.50
☐ red flash	30.00	40.00	35.00

	Current Price Range		Prior Year Average
Bowl, diameter 8″			
☐ frosted	35.00	40.00	37.50
☐ clear	30.00	35.00	32.50
☐ red flash	40.00	45.00	42.50
Butter, with cover			
☐ frosted	50.00	60.00	52.50
☐ clear	45.00	55.00	47.50
☐ red flash	55.00	60.00	57.50
Cake Stand			
☐ frosted	40.00	50.00	45.00
☐ clear	35.00	40.00	37.50
☐ red flash	45.00	50.00	47.50
Celery			
☐ frosted	40.00	50.00	45.00
☐ clear	35.00	40.00	37.50
☐ red flash	45.00	50.00	47.50
Cheese Dish, with cover			
☐ frosted	50.00	60.00	52.50
☐ clear	40.00	50.00	42.50
☐ red flash	55.00	60.00	57.50
Compote, high, with cover			
☐ frosted	60.00	65.00	62.50
☐ clear	50.00	60.00	55.00
☐ red flash	65.00	70.00	67.50
Compote, low			
☐ frosted	40.00	45.00	42.50
☐ clear	35.00	40.00	37.50
☐ red flash	45.00	55.00	47.50
Creamer			
☐ frosted	40.00	50.00	42.50
☐ clear	35.00	45.00	37.50
☐ red flash	45.00	50.00	47.50
Egg Cup			
☐ frosted	25.00	30.00	27.50
☐ clear	20.00	25.00	22.50
☐ red flash	35.00	40.00	37.50
Goblet			
☐ frosted	45.00	55.00	50.00
☐ clear	40.00	50.00	45.00
☐ red flash	50.00	60.00	55.00
Pickle Dish, oval			
☐ frosted	28.00	37.00	32.00
☐ clear	22.00	28.00	24.00
☐ red flash	32.00	39.00	35.00
Sauce, flat			
☐ frosted	15.00	20.00	17.50
☐ clear	10.00	16.00	12.00
☐ red flash	20.00	30.00	25.00

	Current Price Range		Prior Year Average
Sauce, footed			
☐ frosted	20.00	30.00	25.00
☐ clear	15.00	20.00	17.50
☐ red flash	25.00	30.00	27.50
Spooner			
☐ frosted	35.00	45.00	37.50
☐ clear	25.00	35.00	27.50
☐ red flash	40.00	50.00	42.50
Sugar, with cover			
☐ frosted	50.00	60.00	52.50
☐ clear	45.00	50.00	47.50
☐ red flash	55.00	65.00	57.50
Sugar Shaker			
☐ frosted	50.00	60.00	52.50
☐ clear	45.00	55.00	47.50
☐ red flash	60.00	70.00	65.00
Syrup Pitcher			
☐ frosted	45.00	50.00	47.50
☐ clear	40.00	50.00	45.00
☐ red flash	50.00	60.00	55.00
Tumbler			
☐ frosted	35.00	45.00	37.50
☐ clear	30.00	40.00	32.50
☐ red flash	40.00	50.00	42.50
Water Pitcher			
☐ frosted	60.00	70.00	62.50
☐ clear	50.00	60.00	55.00
☐ red flash	70.00	80.00	72.50
Water Tray			
☐ frosted	36.00	43.00	38.00
☐ clear	32.00	42.00	35.00
☐ red flash	40.00	48.00	42.00
Wine Glass			
☐ frosted	35.00	40.00	37.50
☐ clear	25.00	35.00	27.50
☐ red flash	40.00	50.00	42.50

ARCHED LEAF

This is an intricate, interconnected pattern of banded scrolls untwisting from a medallion center to form a rim of broken arches. These rounded ridges frame heavily veined leaves which are separated with knobby buttons in high relief. The background is stippled and gives the pieces a frosty, opaque look.

☐ **Bowl,** diameter 6″	28.00	38.00	29.50
☐ **Goblet**	40.00	50.00	42.50
☐ **Pitcher**	65.00	85.00	67.50
☐ **Plate,** diameter 9″	30.00	40.00	35.50

Arched Leaf

	Current Price Range		Prior Year Average
☐ **Plate**, diameter 10″	40.00	50.00	42.50
☐ **Salt**	25.00	35.00	27.50

ATLAS

This is a simple pattern of smooth glass with a heavy band of thumb-prints along the base. The moldwork is deep and sharp, making this an interesting geometrical pattern.

☐ **Berry Bowl**	20.00	30.00	25.00
☐ **Butter**, with cover	40.00	50.00	42.50
☐ **Cake Stand**	30.00	40.00	32.50
☐ **Celery**	25.00	34.00	28.00
☐ **Compote**, high, with cover	70.00	80.00	73.00
☐ **Compote**, low	40.00	50.00	42.50
☐ **Compote**, low, with cover	40.00	50.00	42.50
☐ **Cordial Glass**	25.00	32.00	27.00
☐ **Creamer**	25.00	35.00	27.50
☐ **Goblet**	25.00	30.00	27.50
☐ **Jam Jar**	50.00	60.00	53.00
☐ **Relish Bowl**	35.00	40.00	37.50
☐ **Salt**	20.00	30.00	24.00
☐ **Sauce**, flat	10.00	15.00	12.50
☐ **Sauce**, footed	15.00	20.00	17.50
☐ **Spooner**	30.00	40.00	32.50
☐ **Sugar**, with cover	30.00	40.00	32.50
☐ **Toothpick**	18.00	22.00	19.50
☐ **Tumbler**	18.00	27.00	21.00
☐ **Water Pitcher**	40.00	50.00	42.50
☐ **Wine Glass**	25.00	30.00	27.00

BAKEWELL BLOCK
Bakewell Pears

There is a diamond design at the base with a row of thumbprints on top. Above the thumbprints is a plain band.

	Current Price Range		Prior Year Average
☐ Butter Dish, covered	185.00	195.00	180.00
☐ Celery	100.00	107.00	96.00
☐ Champagne	100.00	108.00	95.00
☐ Creamer	165.00	175.00	160.00
☐ Decanter	135.00	145.00	131.00
☐ Spooner	65.00	75.00	60.00
☐ Sugar Bowl, covered	85.00	95.00	80.00
☐ Tumbler, bar	85.00	95.00	81.00
☐ Tumbler, whiskey	85.00	95.00	80.00
☐ Whiskey Tumbler, handle	105.00	115.00	100.00
☐ Wine	70.00	80.00	64.00

BAMBOO

Cane-like pillars run around the body of these pieces in a wide vertical band. Each column is broken by thumbprint decorations. The upper band is gently scalloped.

☐ Butter	40.00	50.00	42.50
☐ Celery	25.00	35.00	25.00
☐ Compote, high, with cover	35.00	45.00	37.50
☐ Compote, low, diameter 7″	30.00	40.00	32.50
☐ Compote, low, diameter 8″	40.00	45.00	47.50
☐ Cordial Glass	35.00	45.00	37.50
☐ Creamer	40.00	50.00	45.00
☐ Relish Bowl, two compartments	15.00	20.00	17.50
☐ Salt	15.00	20.00	17.50
☐ Sauce, flat	9.00	12.00	9.50
☐ Sauce, footed	12.00	16.00	12.50
☐ Spooner	20.00	30.00	25.00
☐ Sugar, with cover	35.00	45.00	37.50
☐ Toothpick	20.00	30.00	22.50
☐ Tumbler	25.00	35.00	27.50
☐ Water Pitcher	60.00	80.00	62.50
☐ Wine Glass	30.00	40.00	35.00

BANDED BUCKLE

The long sawtoothed ovals are framed in ridged panels around the middle of the pieces. A thin sawtooth band decorates the rim, pleating resolves the base or center.

☐ Butter, with cover	55.00	65.00	57.50
☐ Compote, high, with cover	65.00	75.00	67.50
☐ Cordial Glass	25.00	35.00	27.50
☐ Creamer	75.00	87.00	78.00

	Current Price Range		Prior Year Average
☐ **Egg Cup**	25.00	35.00	27.50
☐ **Goblet**	30.00	40.00	35.00
☐ **Pickle Dish,** oval	18.00	22.00	18.50
☐ **Salt,** pedestal base	20.00	30.00	22.50
☐ **Sauce,** flat	15.00	20.00	17.50
☐ **Sauce,** footed	20.00	30.00	25.00
☐ **Spooner**	20.00	30.00	22.50
☐ **Sugar,** with cover	25.00	35.00	27.50
☐ **Syrup Pitcher**	40.00	50.00	42.50
☐ **Tumbler**	25.00	35.00	27.50
☐ **Water Pitcher**	70.00	80.00	75.50
☐ **Wine Glass**	25.00	35.00	27.50

BARBERRY

Berries and a leaf design are found on lower half of piece. There is a wide plain band across top.

Bowl, covered, diameter 8″			
☐ clear	35.00	45.00	30.00
☐ amber	52.00	59.00	45.00
☐ blue	55.00	65.00	50.00
Butter			
☐ clear	60.00	70.00	63.00
☐ amber	70.00	80.00	74.00
☐ blue	85.00	97.00	90.00
Cake Plate			
☐ clear	41.00	48.00	35.00

Barberry

		Current Price Range		Prior Year Average
☐ amber		61.00	68.00	55.00
☐ blue		70.00	78.00	65.00
Celery				
☐ clear		32.00	42.00	35.00
☐ amber		42.00	52.00	45.00
☐ blue		50.00	60.00	53.00
Compote, covered				
☐ clear		45.00	52.00	40.00
☐ amber		60.00	70.00	53.00
☐ blue		70.00	78.00	65.00
Compote, open				
☐ clear		33.00	38.00	28.00
☐ amber		45.00	50.00	40.00
☐ blue		52.00	58.00	45.00
Cordial				
☐ clear		35.00	40.00	30.00
☐ amber		48.00	55.00	43.00
☐ blue		55.00	60.00	50.00
Creamer				
☐ clear		35.00	45.00	38.00
☐ amber		45.00	55.00	50.00
☐ blue		60.00	72.00	65.00
Egg Cup				
☐ clear		20.00	28.00	15.00
☐ amber		35.00	40.00	30.00
☐ blue		38.00	45.00	33.00
Goblet				
☐ clear		22.00	28.00	25.00
☐ amber		30.00	37.00	32.00
☐ blue		37.00	45.00	39.00
Jug, pewter lid				
☐ clear		68.00	75.00	63.00
☐ amber		80.00	88.00	75.00
☐ blue		90.00	100.00	85.00
Pitcher, water, handled				
☐ clear		80.00	88.00	74.00
☐ amber		100.00	110.00	95.00
☐ blue		110.00	118.00	105.00
Plate, diameter 6″				
☐ clear		28.00	34.00	30.00
☐ amber		32.00	37.00	33.00
☐ blue		35.00	40.00	37.00
Relish				
☐ clear		18.00	25.00	15.00
☐ amber		30.00	35.00	25.00
☐ blue		33.00	38.00	28.00
Salt, footed				
☐ clear		18.00	24.00	14.00

	Current Price Range		Prior Year Average
☐ amber	23.00	27.00	18.00
☐ blue	27.00	31.00	24.00
Sauce, flat			
☐ clear	15.00	20.00	12.00
☐ amber	20.00	25.00	18.00
☐ blue	23.00	28.00	21.00
Sauce, footed			
☐ clear	10.00	15.00	8.00
☐ amber	15.00	20.00	13.00
☐ blue	17.00	22.00	15.00
Spoon Holder			
☐ clear	25.00	30.00	20.00
☐ amber	32.00	37.00	28.00
☐ blue	38.00	44.00	34.00
Sugar, covered			
☐ clear	60.00	66.00	55.00
☐ amber	75.00	80.00	70.00
☐ blue	88.00	95.00	81.00
Wine			
☐ clear	25.00	30.00	20.00
☐ amber	35.00	40.00	30.00
☐ blue	38.00	45.00	35.00

BARRED FORGET-ME-NOT
Canton Glass

Vining flower design overlaid with Greek key pattern. At base of design is short, diagonal ribbings. Top of motif has deep prism cut line. Wide plain band at top of piece.

Butter, covered			
☐ clear	37.00	42.00	34.00
☐ yellow	50.00	56.00	48.00
☐ amber	51.00	55.00	47.00
☐ blue	74.00	80.00	70.00
☐ green	82.00	90.00	76.00
Cake Plate, small, handled			
☐ clear	45.00	52.00	41.00
☐ yellow	55.00	63.00	50.00
☐ amber	56.00	61.00	49.00
☐ blue	73.00	82.00	69.00
☐ green	85.00	91.00	80.00
Cake Plate, large			
☐ clear	50.00	55.00	46.00
☐ yellow	66.00	72.00	61.00
☐ amber	65.00	71.00	60.00
☐ blue	73.00	79.00	69.00
☐ green	78.00	85.00	74.00
Celery			
☐ clear	35.00	42.00	31.00

	Current Price Range		Prior Year Average
☐ yellow	45.00	51.00	42.00
☐ amber	44.00	50.00	41.00
☐ blue	53.00	56.00	50.00
☐ green	58.00	63.00	54.00
Compote, covered			
☐ clear	37.00	43.00	33.00
☐ yellow	45.00	50.00	42.00
☐ amber	44.00	49.00	41.00
☐ blue	52.00	57.00	48.00
☐ green	60.00	65.00	56.00
Compote, open			
☐ clear	32.00	36.00	29.00
☐ yellow	42.00	46.00	38.00
☐ amber	40.00	45.00	37.00
☐ blue	50.00	55.00	46.00
☐ green	53.00	57.00	50.00
Cordial			
☐ clear	17.00	20.00	14.00
☐ yellow	23.00	26.00	20.00
☐ amber	22.00	25.00	19.00
☐ blue	27.00	31.00	25.00
☐ green	32.00	36.00	28.00
Goblet			
☐ clear	35.00	40.00	31.00
☐ yellow	42.00	47.00	38.00
☐ amber	40.00	45.00	36.00
☐ blue	50.00	55.00	46.00
☐ green	60.00	67.00	55.00
Pitcher			
☐ clear	42.00	48.00	38.00
☐ yellow	58.00	63.00	54.00
☐ amber	59.00	64.00	55.00
☐ blue	62.00	67.00	58.00
☐ green	71.00	75.00	67.00
Plate, diameter 9″			
☐ clear	31.00	35.00	28.00
☐ yellow	43.00	47.00	40.00
☐ amber	44.00	46.00	41.00
☐ blue	49.00	54.00	45.00
☐ green	59.00	65.00	56.00
Relish, handled			
☐ clear	15.00	19.00	12.00
☐ yellow	22.00	26.00	19.00
☐ amber	21.00	25.00	18.00
☐ blue	25.00	30.00	22.00
☐ green	27.00	32.00	24.00
Sauce, flat			
☐ clear	12.00	16.00	10.00

		Current Price Range		Prior Year Average
☐ yellow		17.00	20.00	14.00
☐ amber		16.00	19.00	13.00
☐ blue		20.00	24.00	17.00
☐ green		24.00	27.00	20.00

Spoon Holder

☐ clear	22.00	26.00	19.00
☐ yellow	32.00	36.00	28.00
☐ amber	31.00	35.00	27.00
☐ blue	38.00	44.00	32.00
☐ green	44.00	48.00	40.00

Sugar Bowl, covered

☐ clear	33.00	37.00	30.00
☐ yellow	46.00	50.00	41.00
☐ amber	45.00	49.00	40.00
☐ blue	49.00	53.00	45.00
☐ green	57.00	63.00	54.00

Wine

☐ clear	23.00	27.00	20.00
☐ yellow	33.00	38.00	30.00
☐ amber	32.00	37.00	29.00
☐ blue	39.00	45.00	36.00
☐ green	42.00	48.00	38.00

BARREL ASHBURTON

Oval- and circle-shaped fluting is placed horizontally on pieces. There are variations on this pattern.

☐ **Celery**	100.00	110.00	95.00
☐ **Cordials**	50.00	60.00	45.00
☐ **Creamer**	170.00	180.00	165.00
☐ **Decanter**	100.00	125.00	95.00
☐ **Egg Cup**	40.00	50.00	35.00
☐ **Goblet**	40.00	50.00	35.00
☐ **Honey Dish**	15.00	20.00	12.00
☐ **Sugar Bowl,** covered	95.00	105.00	90.00
☐ **Tumbler**	60.00	70.00	63.00
☐ **Water Pitcher**	350.00	360.00	345.00
☐ **Wine Glass**	50.00	60.00	45.00

BARREL EXCELSIOR

Loops and circles are placed horizontally. Difference between this pattern and the Barrel Ashburton is a smaller design.

☐ **Ale Glass**	35.00	45.00	30.00
☐ **Butter Dish,** covered	85.00	95.00	80.00
☐ **Candlesticks,** pair	200.00	250.00	195.00
☐ **Celery,** plain top	45.00	55.00	40.00

	Current Price Range		Prior Year Average
☐ **Celery,** scalloped top	75.00	85.00	70.00
☐ **Goblet**	75.00	85.00	70.00
☐ **Lamp**	130.00	140.00	125.00
☐ **Mug**	40.00	48.00	38.00
☐ **Spoon Holder**	45.00	55.00	40.00
☐ **Sugar Bowl,** covered	155.00	165.00	150.00
☐ **Tumbler**	35.00	45.00	33.00
☐ **Wine Bottle,** with tumble-up	135.00	145.00	130.00

BEADED GRAPE
U.S. Glass

This is a delicate pattern of branches, leaves and high relief grapes on a gently stippled background. Beadwork decorates the sides and upper rim, giving the design an elegant finish and separating each group of foliage into distinct panels. This is a popular pattern, made into many pieces.

Bowl, rectangular			
☐ clear	32.00	42.00	35.00
☐ green	50.00	62.00	53.00
Butter, covered			
☐ clear	62.00	75.00	65.00
☐ green	85.00	95.00	87.00
Cake Stand, height 9″			
☐ clear	57.00	65.00	52.00
☐ green	75.00	80.00	70.00
Cake Stand, height 10″			
☐ clear	67.00	75.00	62.00
☐ green	85.00	90.00	80.00

Beaded Grape

	Current Price Range		Prior Year Average
Celery, tall			
☐ clear	40.00	52.00	43.00
☐ green	60.00	75.00	64.00
Compote, covered			
☐ clear	50.00	55.00	45.00
☐ green	80.00	86.00	75.00
Compote, open, high			
☐ clear	39.00	45.00	35.00
☐ green	58.00	64.00	53.00
Compote, open, low			
☐ clear	44.00	49.00	40.00
☐ green	60.00	65.00	55.00
Cordial			
☐ clear	45.00	50.00	40.00
☐ green	63.00	68.00	58.00
Creamer			
☐ clear	47.00	55.00	41.00
☐ green	65.00	70.00	60.00
Cruet, stoppered			
☐ clear	63.00	76.00	67.00
☐ green	88.00	100.00	92.00
Dish, handled			
☐ clear	25.00	30.00	20.00
☐ green	40.00	45.00	35.00
Dish, oblong			
☐ clear	24.00	26.00	20.00
☐ green	42.00	48.00	38.00
Dish, square			
☐ clear	24.00	29.00	20.00
☐ green	38.00	44.00	34.00
Egg Cup			
☐ clear	20.00	25.00	15.00
☐ green	32.00	38.00	27.00
Goblet			
☐ clear	35.00	43.00	30.00
☐ green	54.00	58.00	50.00
Pitcher, round			
☐ clear	70.00	76.00	65.00
☐ green	100.00	110.00	90.00
Pitcher, square			
☐ clear	65.00	70.00	60.00
☐ green	90.00	100.00	85.00
Plate, square, diameter 8½"			
☐ clear	26.00	30.00	21.00
☐ green	42.00	48.00	38.00
Platter, oblong			
☐ clear	70.00	75.00	65.00
☐ green	100.00	110.00	92.00

	Current Price Range		Prior Year Average
Relish Dish			
☐ clear	19.00	24.00	14.00
☐ green	30.00	35.00	25.00
Salt and Pepper Shakers, pair			
☐ clear	52.00	65.00	58.00
☐ green	70.00	85.00	72.00
Sauce, handled			
☐ clear	10.00	18.00	13.00
☐ green	25.00	33.00	27.00
Spoon Holder			
☐ clear	30.00	36.00	25.00
☐ green	48.00	54.00	44.00
Sugar, covered			
☐ clear	50.00	62.00	53.00
☐ green	70.00	85.00	73.00
Sugar, open			
☐ clear	20.00	25.00	15.00
☐ green	40.00	45.00	35.00
Sugar Shaker			
☐ clear	40.00	45.00	35.00
☐ green	56.00	63.00	51.00
Toothpick Holder			
☐ clear	48.00	60.00	54.00
☐ green	70.00	83.00	72.00
Tray, bread, oblong			
☐ clear	42.00	48.00	38.00
☐ green	65.00	70.00	60.00
Tray, celery, flat, rectangular			
☐ clear	27.00	33.00	24.00
☐ green	45.00	50.00	40.00
Tumbler			
☐ clear	30.00	36.00	26.00
☐ green	50.00	55.00	45.00
Wine			
☐ clear	50.00	55.00	45.00
☐ green	70.00	75.00	65.00
Vase, height 6″			
☐ clear	25.00	30.00	20.00
☐ green	40.00	45.00	35.00

BELLFLOWER
Boston & Sandwich Co.

This is one of the most avidly collected patterns in patterned glass for good reason. Simple and well balanced, the design focuses mainly on the coarse ribbing that covers the pieces, providing a background for the sparse vines and pretty bellflowers that entwine around the piece. This pattern has been reproduced by other firms but the Sandwich is the oldest and most collectible.

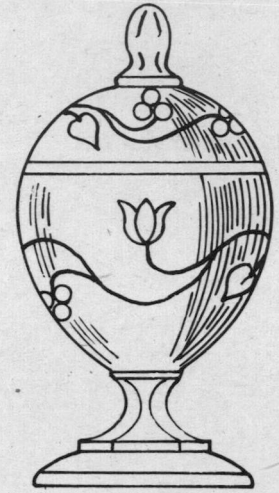

Bellflower

	Current Price Range		Prior Year Average
☐ **Butter,** covered	85.00	97.00	90.00
☐ **Celery Vase**	120.00	135.00	125.00
☐ **Champagne Glass**	70.00	82.00	73.00
☐ **Compote,** open, diameter 6½″	60.00	70.00	60.00
☐ **Compote,** diameter 7″	70.00	80.00	65.00
☐ **Cordial**	95.00	110.00	100.00
☐ **Creamer**	140.00	160.00	140.00
☐ **Egg Cup**	30.00	36.00	28.00
☐ **Hat,** made from tumbler mold, scarce	360.00	370.00	350.00
☐ **Honey Dish**	15.00	20.00	12.00
☐ **Lamp,** marble base	130.00	140.00	126.00
☐ **Mug,** handled, scarce	170.00	185.00	175.00
☐ **Pitcher,** syrup, handle	340.00	360.00	350.00
☐ **Pitcher,** water	195.00	215.00	200.00
☐ **Plate,** diameter 6″, scarce	90.00	100.00	85.00
☐ **Salt,** footed	30.00	40.00	28.00
☐ **Sauce,** flat	15.00	20.00	10.00
☐ **Spoon Holder**	28.00	40.00	33.00
☐ **Sugar Bowl,** open	30.00	42.00	35.00
☐ **Tumbler,** footed	200.00	220.00	180.00
☐ **Whiskey,** small, scarce	145.00	160.00	150.00
☐ **Wine**	60.00	72.00	65.00

BIGLER

Big, huge thumbprints are the main motifs on these pieces, creating a scalloped effect that is reminiscent of cut glass. Most articles have two rows of the circles, separated by long spears of ridged glass. The finish is smooth, glossy and refracts the light beautifully.

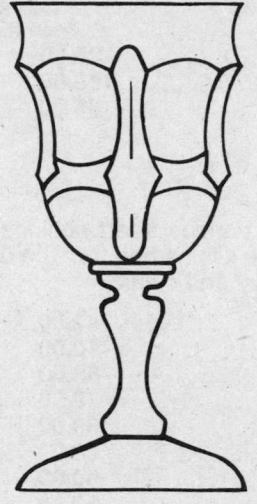

Bigler

	Current Price Range		Prior Year Average
☐ **Bowl**	75.00	85.00	70.00
☐ **Celery**	80.00	90.00	75.00
☐ **Champagne Glass**	90.00	100.00	85.00
☐ **Cordial**	85.00	95.00	80.00
☐ **Decanter**, quart	65.00	75.00	62.00
☐ **Egg Cup**, double	55.00	65.00	53.00
☐ **Goblet**	45.00	55.00	41.00
☐ **Mug**, handle	70.00	80.00	68.00
☐ **Tumbler**, water	55.00	65.00	50.00
☐ **Tumbler**, whiskey	60.00	70.00	58.00
☐ **Wine Glass**	50.00	60.00	47.00

BIRD AND STRAWBERRY
Beatty

The upper and lower bands are hexagons arranged in a fence filled in with stippling. Around the body, a scene with flying birds, berries, and foliage is molded in high relief. Some of the pieces are enameled over with color.

☐ **Bowl**, oval	25.00	35.00	27.50
☐ **Butter**, with lid	80.00	92.00	83.00
☐ **Cake Stand**, height 12″	65.00	75.00	67.00
☐ **Compote**, with cover	85.00	95.00	87.00
☐ **Creamer**	40.00	55.00	45.00
☐ **Goblet**	35.00	45.00	38.00
☐ **Relish**, three compartments	35.00	45.00	37.50
☐ **Spooner**	45.00	55.00	47.50

	Current Price Range		Prior Year Average
☐ Tumbler	35.00	45.00	37.00
☐ Water Pitcher	185.00	200.00	190.00
☐ Wine Glass	35.00	45.00	38.00

BLAZE
New England

The fire effect is created by various sized ribbings, flickering up and down these pieces like the blaze it is named for. The design is simple but balanced and the glass is heavy and clear.

☐ **Bowl,** diameter 8″	42.00	49.00	38.00
☐ **Celery**	70.00	78.00	66.00
☐ **Champagne**	63.00	69.00	59.00
☐ **Compote,** covered	70.00	80.00	66.00
☐ **Compote,** open	60.00	70.00	55.00
☐ **Cordial**	63.00	70.00	58.00
☐ **Creamer**	80.00	90.00	76.00
☐ **Egg Cup,** handled	52.00	58.00	48.00
☐ **Egg Cup,** regular	40.00	48.00	37.00
☐ **Goblet**	50.00	58.00	47.00
☐ **Plate,** with cheese cover	70.00	80.00	65.00
☐ **Plate,** diameter 6″	35.00	39.00	32.00
☐ **Plate,** diameter 7″	38.00	43.00	35.00
☐ **Salt,** rectangular	38.00	43.00	34.00
☐ **Sauce**	20.00	27.00	17.00
☐ **Spoon Holder**	45.00	53.00	42.00
☐ **Sugar,** covered	71.00	78.00	66.00
☐ **Tumbler,** footed	53.00	63.00	50.00

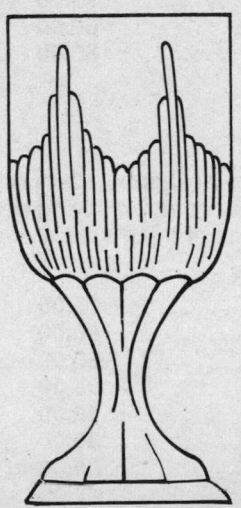

Blaze

	Current Price Range		Prior Year Average
☐ **Tumbler,** lemonade	45.00	53.00	40.00
☐ **Wine**	60.00	67.00	58.00

BLEEDING HEART

Flower and leaf design with wide plain band across top.

☐ **Bowl**	32.00	37.00	28.00
☐ **Butter,** covered	55.00	63.00	50.00
☐ **Cake Plate,** large	60.00	68.00	56.00
☐ **Compote,** covered	68.00	75.00	63.00
☐ **Compote,** open	30.00	36.00	25.00
☐ **Compote,** oval shaped	53.00	59.00	49.00
☐ **Cordial**	32.00	38.00	27.00
☐ **Creamer,** handled	53.00	60.00	48.00
☐ **Dish,** oval	30.00	36.00	26.00
☐ **Egg Cup,** barrel shape	38.00	45.00	35.00
☐ **Egg Cup,** straight sided	32.00	37.00	27.00
☐ **Goblet,** knob stem	37.00	44.00	33.00
☐ **Goblet,** plain stem	32.00	38.00	28.00
☐ **Jelly Glass**	28.00	34.00	24.00
☐ **Mug,** handled	35.00	42.00	30.00
☐ **Pickle Dish,** oval	28.00	35.00	24.00
☐ **Pitcher,** handled	160.00	180.00	165.00
☐ **Plate,** scarce	70.00	80.00	65.00
☐ **Platter,** oval	70.00	78.00	64.00
☐ **Salt,** footed	30.00	36.00	26.00
☐ **Sauce,** flat	15.00	19.00	12.00
☐ **Sauce,** flat, oval	28.00	32.00	25.00
☐ **Spoon Holder**	30.00	38.00	33.00
☐ **Tumbler,** footed	36.00	45.00	31.00
☐ **Wine**	68.00	75.00	65.00

BLOCK AND PALM

Palm leaves at base of pattern, band of stars at top of design. Large plain band at top of piece.

Bowl, diameter 8″			
☐ clear.............................	20.00	25.00	15.00
☐ milk white	22.00	27.00	18.00
Butter, covered			
☐ clear.............................	30.00	35.00	25.00
☐ milk white	34.00	39.00	29.00
Cake Stand			
☐ clear.............................	38.00	45.00	34.00
☐ milk white	42.00	48.00	38.00
Celery			
☐ clear.............................	20.00	25.00	15.00
☐ milk white	23.00	28.00	18.00

	Current Price Range		Prior Year Average
Creamer			
☐ clear	20.00	25.00	17.00
☐ milk white	22.00	27.00	19.00
Goblet			
☐ clear	25.00	30.00	20.00
☐ milk white	29.00	34.00	25.00
Pitcher			
☐ clear	40.00	45.00	35.00
☐ milk white	45.00	50.00	40.00
Salt and Pepper Shakers, pair			
☐ clear	30.00	40.00	34.00
☐ milk white	35.00	45.00	37.00
Sauce, flat			
☐ clear	18.00	22.00	15.00
☐ milk white	20.00	24.00	18.00
Sugar Shaker			
☐ clear	20.00	25.00	18.00
☐ milk white	23.00	28.00	19.00
Spoon Holder			
☐ clear	15.00	20.00	12.00
☐ milk white	17.00	22.00	15.00
Sugar, covered			
☐ clear	30.00	35.00	26.00
☐ milk white	34.00	38.00	30.00

BLOCK AND THUMBPRINT

Block design with thumbprint indented into each block.

☐ **Celery**	25.00	35.00	23.00
☐ **Compote,** covered	60.00	70.00	55.00
☐ **Compote,** open	30.00	40.00	28.00
☐ **Creamer**	40.00	50.00	37.00
☐ **Goblet**	45.00	53.00	40.00
☐ **Sugar Bowl,** covered	35.00	45.00	33.00
☐ **Tumbler,** footed	30.00	40.00	30.00

BROKEN COLUMN

This is an interesting "frozen motion" pattern. Vertical columns of heavy, rounded flutes are decorated with thumbprints, giving the impression of raindrops on a window pane.

☐ **Banana**	85.00	95.00	88.00
☐ **Basket**	120.00	140.00	128.00
☐ **Berry Bowl,** with cover	40.00	50.00	45.00
☐ **Bowl**	35.00	40.00	37.50
☐ **Butter,** with cover	50.00	60.00	55.00
☐ **Cake Stand**	65.00	75.00	68.00

	Current Price Range		Prior Year Average
☐ **Carafe**	60.00	70.00	65.00
☐ **Celery Bowl**	20.00	30.00	25.00
☐ **Celery Vase**	40.00	50.00	42.50
☐ **Champagne**	60.00	70.00	65.00
☐ **Compote**, high, with cover	60.00	70.00	65.00
☐ **Compote**, low	60.00	70.00	63.00
☐ **Cookie Jar**, with cover	70.00	80.00	75.00
☐ **Creamer**	35.00	45.00	37.50
☐ **Cruet**	50.00	60.00	54.00
☐ **Goblet**	50.00	60.00	54.00
☐ **Jam Jar**, with fitted cover	60.00	70.00	65.00
☐ **Mug**	45.00	55.00	47.50
☐ **Pickle Jar**	80.00	90.00	85.00
☐ **Punch Bowl**	100.00	130.00	110.00
☐ **Punch Cup**	25.00	35.00	27.50
☐ **Relish Bowl**	20.00	30.00	25.00
☐ **Salt**	15.00	20.00	17.50
☐ **Sauce**, flat	10.00	15.00	12.50
☐ **Sauce**, footed	15.00	20.00	17.50
☐ **Spooner**	28.00	36.00	30.00
☐ **Sugar**, with cover	45.00	55.00	47.50
☐ **Syrup Pitcher**	60.00	70.00	65.00
☐ **Toothpick**	25.00	35.00	27.50
☐ **Tumbler**	30.00	40.00	35.00
☐ **Water Pitcher**	60.00	70.00	65.00
☐ **Wine Glass**	50.00	60.00	52.50

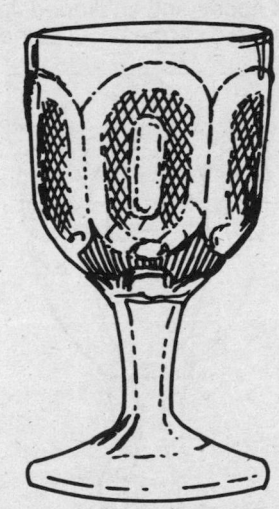

Buckle

BUCKLE

Long ovals of sawtooth filler, stippling, and a marquise of smooth, glossy glass are arranged in a wide band around most of the body of these pieces. It hovers over the pleating that resolves in the center of the plates and bowls, under the stem on footed pieces.

	Current Price Range		Prior Year Average
☐ **Bowl**	55.00	70.00	60.00
☐ **Butter,** with cover	55.00	70.00	60.00
☐ **Champagne**	90.00	110.00	95.00
☐ **Cordial Glass**	80.00	90.00	85.00
☐ **Creamer,** on pedestal	120.00	150.00	125.00
☐ **Egg Cup**	35.00	45.00	37.50
☐ **Goblet**	25.00	34.00	28.00
☐ **Pickle Dish,** oval	15.00	25.00	17.00
☐ **Salt,** flat	45.00	55.00	42.50
☐ **Salt,** footed	30.00	40.00	35.00
☐ **Sauce,** flat	10.00	15.00	12.00
☐ **Sauce,** footed	25.00	30.00	27.50
☐ **Spooner**	25.00	35.00	28.00
☐ **Sugar,** with cover	60.00	70.00	62.50
☐ **Tumbler**	27.00	37.00	30.00
☐ **Water Pitcher**	250.00	300.00	275.00

BULL'S EYE
New England

These bull's eyes look very much like the circular decorations on the end of a peacock's tail. The pattern repeats in panels around the piece, framed with arched ridges and scalloped fluting. The finish is smooth; the glass is heavy enough to appear cut rather than pressed.

Bull's Eye

	Current Price Range		Prior Year Average
☐ Bitter Bottle	80.00	90.00	75.00
☐ Celery Vase	70.00	80.00	68.00
☐ Cologne Bottle	75.00	87.00	78.00
☐ Creamer	130.00	140.00	131.00
☐ Decanter, bar lip, pint	100.00	115.00	105.00
☐ Decanter, bar lip, quart	130.00	140.00	125.00
☐ Decanter, usual type, pint	100.00	110.00	95.00
☐ Decanter, usual type, quart	115.00	125.00	110.00
☐ Egg Cup, covered, rare	170.00	180.00	165.00
☐ Egg Cup, open	60.00	72.00	64.00
☐ Goblet	72.00	85.00	70.00
☐ Lamp	85.00	95.00	80.00
☐ Mug, handled, small	50.00	60.00	45.00
☐ Mug, large	80.00	90.00	82.00
☐ Relish Dish, oval	45.00	55.00	40.00
☐ Salt, footed	35.00	45.00	30.00
☐ Salt, footed, oblong, covered, rare ...	105.00	115.00	100.00
☐ Spoon Holder	46.00	56.00	41.00
☐ Sugar Bowl, covered	115.00	125.00	113.00
☐ Tumbler	90.00	100.00	85.00
☐ Water Bottle, with tumble-up	105.00	115.00	100.00
☐ Wine Glass	50.00	60.00	45.00

BULL'S EYE AND BAR
Boston & Sandwich

Alternating pattern of bull's eye and ribbing. Wide plain band at top.

☐ Egg Cup	110.00	120.00	105.00
☐ Goblet	120.00	130.00	115.00

BULL'S EYE AND CUBE

The bull's eye band is directly under the smooth rim; the rest of the piece is covered with waffling.

☐ Goblet	60.00	80.00	65.00

BULL'S EYE AND SAWTOOTH

The bull's eyes are flattened in a band under the slightly flared rim. The rest of the piece is covered with deeply molded sawtooth.

☐ Goblet	75.00	100.00	77.50

BULL'S EYE WITH DIAMOND POINT

Bull's eye surrounded by diamond point cut and deep oval prism cuts, plain band around rim.

☐ Butter Dish, covered	210.00	220.00	205.00
☐ Celery	110.00	120.00	105.00

	Current Price Range		Prior Year Average
☐ Champagne Bottle	125.00	130.00	120.00
☐ Cologne Bottle	130.00	135.00	125.00
☐ Cordial	110.00	120.00	105.00
☐ Creamer	180.00	190.00	175.00
☐ Decanter, bar lip, quart	180.00	190.00	173.00
☐ Decanter, stopper, quart	205.00	215.00	205.00
☐ Egg Cup	90.00	100.00	93.00
☐ Goblet	110.00	115.00	96.00
☐ Honey Dish	40.00	45.00	42.00
☐ Pitcher	230.00	240.00	232.00
☐ Sauce Dish	15.00	20.00	14.00
☐ Sugar Bowl, covered	130.00	145.00	135.00
☐ Tumbler	65.00	75.00	60.00
☐ Wine Glass	60.00	70.00	62.00

BULL'S EYE WITH FLEUR-DE-LYS

Inverted button shape set into circle is the bull's eye; below the bull's eye are upside down tear drops. Entire design is surrounded by long oval prism cuts with a small plain band around the rim. Pieces are scarce.

☐ Ale Glass, rare	145.00	155.00	135.00
☐ Butter Dish, covered	180.00	205.00	175.00
☐ Compote, open	110.00	120.00	100.00
☐ Creamer, rare	250.00	260.00	243.00
☐ Decanter, pint	70.00	80.00	72.00
☐ Decanter, stopper, quart	90.00	100.00	93.00
☐ Goblet	85.00	95.00	80.00
☐ Lamp, marble base, brass stem	280.00	290.00	275.00
☐ Sugar Bowl, covered	140.00	160.00	130.00
☐ Water Pitcher, rare	280.00	300.00	283.00

CABBAGE ROSE

The roses are small and tightly petaled, set amidst leaves and thin vines. The flora and foliage is decorated with stippling in sharp contrast to the smooth, glossy finish of the rest of the body. On occasional pieces, there is an upper band of beadwork that lends an elegant touch to the pattern.

☐ Basket, handled	80.00	87.00	56.00
☐ Butter Dish, covered	48.00	55.00	45.00
☐ Cake Stand, small	50.00	60.00	62.00
☐ Cake Stand, large	67.00	74.00	63.00
☐ Celery	40.00	50.00	37.00
☐ Compote, covered	60.00	70.00	58.00
☐ Compote, open	40.00	47.00	37.00
☐ Cordial	38.00	45.00	36.00
☐ Creamer, handled	64.00	72.00	60.00
☐ Custard Cup, scarce	85.00	93.00	80.00

Cabbage Rose

	Current Price Range		Prior Year Average
☐ **Egg Cup**	27.00	35.00	29.00
☐ **Goblet**	38.00	45.00	40.00
☐ **Pitcher,** 3 pints, scarce	140.00	150.00	134.00
☐ **Pitcher,** water, quart	105.00	115.00	98.00
☐ **Relish Dish,** oval	30.00	36.00	27.00
☐ **Salt,** footed	30.00	37.00	25.00
☐ **Sauce,** flat, diameter 4″	15.00	20.00	13.00
☐ **Sauce,** flat, diameter 5″	20.00	24.00	17.00
☐ **Sauce,** flat, diameter 6″	25.00	30.00	22.00
☐ **Sauce,** flat, diameter 7″	30.00	34.00	28.00
☐ **Spoon Holder**	32.00	40.00	36.00
☐ **Sugar,** covered	63.00	70.00	60.00
☐ **Sugar Bowl,** open	30.00	38.00	27.00
☐ **Tumbler**	45.00	53.00	42.00
☐ **Wine**	45.00	55.00	41.00

CABLE

This popular pattern consists of vertical rows of rope-like cables in opposition to each other. The ridges are rounded and deeply molded, and the cables alternate in width.

☐ **Berry Bowl,** diameter 5″	20.00	30.00	22.50
☐ **Bowl,** diameter 6″	30.00	40.00	35.00
☐ **Butter,** with cover	70.00	80.00	72.00
☐ **Celery**	57.00	68.00	60.00
☐ **Champagne**	130.00	140.00	135.00
☐ **Compote,** high	50.00	60.00	52.50

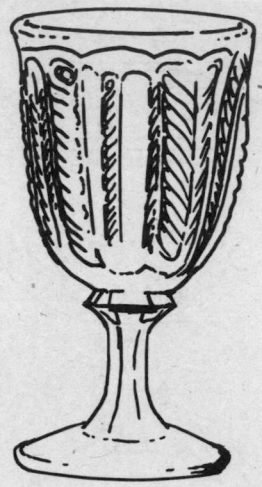

Cable

	Current Price Range		Prior Year Average
☐ **Creamer,** limited edition	400.00	500.00	425.00
☐ **Cruet,** one pint	150.00	160.00	155.00
☐ **Egg Cup**	300.00	400.00	325.00
☐ **Goblet**	70.00	80.00	75.00
☐ **Lamp,** marble base	90.00	100.00	95.00
☐ **Plate**	40.00	50.00	42.00
☐ **Salt**	20.00	30.00	22.50
☐ **Salt,** footed	50.00	60.00	52.50
☐ **Sauce,** flat	15.00	20.00	17.50
☐ **Spooner**	40.00	50.00	42.50
☐ **Sugar,** with cover	55.00	70.00	60.00
☐ **Syrup Pitcher**	150.00	200.00	175.00
☐ **Tumbler**	160.00	200.00	165.00
☐ **Wine Glass**	30.00	40.00	35.00

CANADIAN

The scenic panels that decorate the sides of pieces in this pattern are framed by a keyhole arch with straight sides. Mountains in the background with foliage in the front are molded in low relief.

☐ **Butter,** with cover	60.00	70.00	62.50
☐ **Celery**	45.00	55.00	47.50
☐ **Compote,** high, with cover	100.00	120.00	105.00
☐ **Compote,** low	45.00	65.00	55.00
☐ **Cordial**	40.00	50.00	42.50
☐ **Creamer**	40.00	50.00	42.50
☐ **Goblet**	55.00	65.00	57.50
☐ **Jam Jar**	50.00	60.00	55.00

Canadian

	Current Price Range		Prior Year Average
☐ **Milk Pitcher,** large	85.00	95.00	87.50
☐ **Milk Pitcher,** small	70.00	80.00	72.50
☐ **Plate,** diameter 6½″	45.00	55.00	47.50
☐ **Plate,** diameter 7½″	60.00	70.00	65.50
☐ **Sauce,** flat	16.00	18.00	16.50
☐ **Sauce,** footed	22.00	32.00	22.50
☐ **Spooner**	40.00	50.00	42.50
☐ **Sugar,** with cover	65.00	75.00	67.50
☐ **Water Pitcher,** large	90.00	100.00	95.00
☐ **Water Pitcher,** small	70.00	80.00	72.50
☐ **Wine**	50.00	60.00	52.50

CAPE COD

The upper half of these pieces is devoid of decoration—a wide expanse of smooth, clear glass. The design is carried around the bottom of the body, with twists of foliage around an oval sea scene.

☐ **Bowl,** tab handle, diameter 6″	30.00	40.00	32.50
☐ **Butter,** with lid	55.00	65.00	57.50
☐ **Celery**	35.00	47.50	45.00
☐ **Compote,** high, no cover	65.00	85.00	67.50
☐ **Compote,** high, with cover	70.00	80.00	75.00
☐ **Compote,** low, with cover	60.00	80.00	65.00
☐ **Cordial**	50.00	60.00	52.50
☐ **Creamer**	30.00	40.00	32.00
☐ **Cup**	25.00	30.00	27.50
☐ **Goblet**	50.00	60.00	52.50
☐ **Jam Jar**	50.00	60.00	55.50
☐ **Milk Pitcher**	40.00	50.00	42.50

	Current Price Range		Prior Year Average
☐ **Plate,** loop handle	30.00	40.00	35.50
☐ **Plate,** tab handle	45.00	65.00	47.50
☐ **Sauce,** flat	14.00	16.00	15.00
☐ **Sauce,** foot	18.00	22.00	19.00
☐ **Saucer**	20.00	30.00	22.50
☐ **Spooner**	35.00	40.00	37.50
☐ **Sugar,** with lid	60.00	70.00	62.50
☐ **Water Pitcher**	60.00	80.00	62.50
☐ **Wine**	40.00	50.00	42.50

CARDINAL BIRD

A cardinal perched on tree branch makes design. Horizontal ribbing top of pattern. Wide plain band across top of piece.

☐ **Butter,** covered, three birds labeled Redbird-Pewitt-Titmouse	80.00	90.00	73.00
☐ **Butter,** covered, regular	45.00	50.00	40.00
☐ **Cake Stand**	50.00	58.00	45.00
☐ **Creamer**	40.00	47.00	35.00
☐ **Goblet**	40.00	45.00	35.00
☐ **Pitcher**	115.00	122.00	110.00
☐ **Sauce,** flat	15.00	20.00	12.00
☐ **Sauce,** footed	20.00	25.00	15.00
☐ **Spoon Holder**	33.00	38.00	28.00
☐ **Sugar,** covered	58.00	65.00	53.00
☐ **Sugar,** open	25.00	30.00	20.00

CELTIC CROSS
Duncan, Miller Co.

Wide prism cuts alternating with plain panel.

☐ **Butter,** covered	42.00	52.00	38.00
☐ **Compote,** covered	33.00	38.00	28.00
☐ **Creamer**	30.00	40.00	25.00
☐ **Goblet**	25.00	35.00	20.00
☐ **Spoon Holder**	30.00	38.00	28.00
☐ **Sugar Bowl,** covered	40.00	50.00	36.00

CHAIN

This is an interesting pattern using many motifs in an interconnected band. The main design is an oval shape with diamond point filler. Behind the connections is a series of round rosettes. Each design repeats around the body; the rest of the glass is clear.

☐ **Butter,** with cover	45.00	55.00	47.50
☐ **Cake Stand**	30.00	40.00	32.50
☐ **Compote,** high	40.00	50.00	42.50
☐ **Cordial**	30.00	40.00	35.00

Chain

	Current Price Range		Prior Year Average
☐ **Creamer**	20.00	30.00	22.50
☐ **Goblet**	25.00	35.00	27.50
☐ **Sauce,** flat	12.00	16.00	12.50
☐ **Sauce,** footed diameter 4″	12.00	17.00	14.00
☐ **Sauce,** footed, diameter 5″	15.00	20.00	17.00
☐ **Spooner**	20.00	30.00	22.50
☐ **Sugar,** with cover	40.00	50.00	45.00
☐ **Tumbler**	30.00	40.00	35.00
☐ **Water Pitcher**	40.00	50.00	42.50

CHAIN WITH STAR

The chain is made up of a series of circles filled in with caning, framed by a scalloped band. The star, a finely petaled rosette with teardrops, is in the base.

	Current Price Range		Prior Year Average
☐ **Bread Plate,** tab handles	25.00	30.00	27.50
☐ **Butter,** with cover	40.00	50.00	45.00
☐ **Cake Stand,** diameter 10″	40.00	50.00	42.50
☐ **Compote,** high with cover	50.00	60.00	52.50
☐ **Compote,** low	30.00	40.00	32.50
☐ **Cordial Glass**	30.00	40.00	32.50
☐ **Creamer**	30.00	40.00	35.00
☐ **Goblet**	40.00	50.00	42.50
☐ **Pickle Dish**	20.00	30.00	22.50
☐ **Plate,** diameter 8″	25.00	35.00	27.50
☐ **Relish,** two compartments	25.00	35.00	27.50
☐ **Sauce,** flat	10.00	15.00	10.50

	Current Price Range		Prior Year Average
☐ **Sauce**, footed	15.00	20.00	16.50
☐ **Spooner**	30.00	40.00	35.00
☐ **Sugar**	40.00	45.00	42.50
☐ **Sugar**, with cover	45.00	50.00	47.50
☐ **Water Pitcher**	50.00	60.00	52.50
☐ **Wine Glass**	25.00	30.00	27.50

CHERRY
Bakewell, Pears & Co.

This is a prolific pattern, widely collected in its many pieces and variations. It is molded in high relief, with the triple cherry bunch rising high off the surface. The fruit is connected around the sides with stippled leaves and heavy vines. The finish is smooth, the glass is heavy.

Butter, covered

☐ clear	60.00	68.00	55.00
☐ milk white	120.00	130.00	110.00

Compote, covered

☐ clear	60.00	68.00	54.00
☐ milk white	118.00	128.00	114.00

Compote, open

☐ clear	40.00	50.00	33.00
☐ milk white	80.00	90.00	74.00

Creamer

☐ clear	45.00	50.00	40.00
☐ milk white	90.00	95.00	85.00

Goblet

☐ clear	33.00	38.00	28.00

Cherry

	Current Price Range		Prior Year Average
☐ milk white	60.00	66.00	55.00
Pitcher, handled			
☐ clear	50.00	60.00	45.00
☐ milk white	100.00	110.00	90.00
Sauce, flat			
☐ clear	20.00	25.00	15.00
☐ milk white	40.00	47.00	35.00
Spoon Holder			
☐ clear	25.00	30.00	20.00
☐ milk white	50.00	60.00	45.00
Sugar, covered			
☐ clear	50.00	55.00	45.00
☐ milk white	100.00	110.00	90.00
Wine			
☐ clear	20.00	25.00	15.00
☐ milk white	40.00	50.00	35.00

CLASSIC

This pattern alternates arched panels of English quilting with a Venus-like nude with draping. The arches are formed by heavy ridges in a doric pillar form. Some pieces contain portraits of historical figures instead of the nymph. This pattern is considered the height of molded art.

☐ **Bowl**	135.00	175.00	140.00
☐ **Butter,** with lid	200.00	225.00	215.00
☐ **Celery**	135.00	145.00	140.00
☐ **Compote,** collar base	140.00	160.00	145.00
☐ **Compote,** with lid	180.00	190.00	185.00
☐ **Creamer**	115.00	125.00	120.00

Classic

	Current Price Range		Prior Year Average
☐ Goblet	185.00	200.00	190.00
☐ Jam Jar	200.00	225.00	215.00
☐ Plate, with historical figures	175.00	200.00	180.00
☐ Sauce	40.00	50.00	42.50
☐ Spooner	95.00	115.00	100.00
☐ Sugar	100.00	115.00	105.00
☐ Sugar, with lid	170.00	200.00	175.00
☐ Water Pitcher	300.00	400.00	325.00

CLASSIC MEDALLION

The glass is clear and smooth with the exception of a beadwork oval frame which contains the profile of a lady. The general shape is angular, with ridged rims and spouts.

☐ Bowl, footed, diameter 6″	25.00	30.00	27.50
☐ Bowl, footed, diameter 8″	20.00	30.00	35.00
☐ Butter, with lid	45.00	55.00	47.50
☐ Celery	23.00	31.00	25.00
☐ Compote, with lid	55.00	60.00	57.50
☐ Creamer, flat	25.00	30.00	32.50
☐ Creamer, footed	45.00	55.00	47.50
☐ Goblet	40.00	52.00	42.00
☐ Spooner	23.00	31.00	25.00
☐ Sugar, with lid	45.00	55.00	47.50
☐ Water Pitcher	100.00	115.00	105.00

CLEMATIS

Vine pattern with flowers hanging down. Thin prism line cut above design. Wide plain band at top.

Classic Medallion

Clematis

	Current Price Range		Prior Year Average
☐ **Butter,** covered	40.00	46.00	38.00
☐ **Creamer**	42.00	47.00	40.00
☐ **Goblet**	37.00	43.00	40.00
☐ **Pitcher,** handled	48.00	56.00	45.00
☐ **Sauce,** flat	15.00	20.00	12.00
☐ **Sugar,** covered	48.00	55.00	45.00
☐ **Sugar,** open	30.00	37.00	27.00

Comet

COMET
Boston & Sandwich Co.

This is one of the most intricate geometric patterns in pressed glass. Swirls of ridging form whirlpools, then travel off again to surround rows of three large beads. The bottom rim is decorated with kite shaped panels which point to different designs above. The glass is smooth and clear; the mold work is excellent. Unfortunately, this pattern is rare and therefore costly.

	Current Price Range		Prior Year Average
☐ **Butter Dish,** covered	220.00	230.00	210.00
☐ **Goblet**	80.00	90.00	83.00
☐ **Mug**	140.00	150.00	135.00
☐ **Water Pitcher**	380.00	390.00	375.00
☐ **Water Tumbler**	135.00	145.00	130.00
☐ **Whiskey Tumbler**	135.00	150.00	130.00

CORD AND TASSEL

This is a simple, lightly molded pattern consisting of a cord band waving in deep scallops around the waist, decorated with beads and tassels within.

☐ **Butter**	50.00	60.00	52.50
☐ **Cake Stand,** diameter 8″	40.00	50.00	45.00
☐ **Cake Stand,** diameter 9″	50.00	60.00	55.00
☐ **Celery**	40.00	50.00	42.50
☐ **Compote,** low	40.00	50.00	42.50
☐ **Creamer**	40.00	50.00	45.00
☐ **Dish**	15.00	20.00	16.50
☐ **Egg Cup**	30.00	40.00	35.00
☐ **Goblet**	30.00	40.00	35.00
☐ **Lamp**	75.00	85.00	77.50
☐ **Sauce,** flat	7.00	10.00	8.00
☐ **Sauce,** footed	10.00	12.00	11.00
☐ **Spooner**	30.00	40.00	35.00
☐ **Sugar,** with cover	45.00	55.00	47.50
☐ **Syrup**	70.00	80.00	75.00
☐ **Tumbler**	60.00	70.00	65.00
☐ **Water Pitcher**	60.00	70.00	65.00
☐ **Whiskey**	70.00	80.00	75.00
☐ **Wine Glass**	40.00	50.00	42.50

COTTAGE

This is an elegant pattern consisting of a wide band of diamond point ovals connected with glossy glass flutes. The bottom or the center is a rounded petal rosette.

☐ **Butter,** with cover	40.00	50.00	42.50
☐ **Cake Stand**	40.00	50.00	45.00
☐ **Celery**	30.00	40.00	35.00
☐ **Compote,** high	30.00	40.00	35.00

	Current Price Range		Prior Year Average
☐ **Compote,** high, with cover	40.00	50.00	45.00
☐ **Creamer**	30.00	40.00	35.00
☐ **Cruet**	30.00	40.00	35.00
☐ **Fruit Bowl,** stemmed	40.00	50.00	45.00
☐ **Goblet**	25.00	35.00	27.00
☐ **Plate,** diameter 6″	20.00	25.00	22.00
☐ **Plate,** diameter 7″	22.00	28.00	24.00
☐ **Plate,** diameter 8″	24.00	30.00	26.00
☐ **Plate,** diameter 9″	26.00	32.00	28.00
☐ **Salt Shaker**	15.00	20.00	17.50
☐ **Spooner**	30.00	40.00	35.00
☐ **Sugar,** with cover	40.00	50.00	42.50

CRYSTAL
McKee Co.

Narrow fluting covering entire piece with scalloped edge at top.

	Current Price Range		Prior Year Average
☐ **Ale Glass**	40.00	45.00	37.00
☐ **Bowl,** covered, diameter 8″	55.00	65.00	51.00
☐ **Bowl,** diameter 10″	65.00	75.00	61.00
☐ **Butter Dish,** covered	70.00	80.00	66.00
☐ **Celery**	45.00	55.00	42.00
☐ **Champagne**	40.00	48.00	38.00
☐ **Compote,** covered, diameter 6″	55.00	65.00	52.00
☐ **Compote,** covered, diameter 8″	70.00	78.00	67.00
☐ **Compote,** open, diameter 10″	63.00	69.00	60.00
☐ **Creamer**	70.00	80.00	64.00
☐ **Decanter,** quart	70.00	78.00	66.00
☐ **Egg Cup,** handled	40.00	50.00	37.00

Crystal

	Current Price Range		Prior Year Average
☐ Goblet	35.00	45.00	31.00
☐ Pitcher	90.00	100.00	86.00
☐ Tumbler	30.00	36.00	28.00
☐ Wine	45.00	55.00	40.00

CUPID AND VENUS

A beadwork cameo frames a detailed Venus standing over a winged cupid. The rest of the ground is smooth with the exception of a connecting Ribbon of Rail fence decorating the middle.

☐ **Bowl,** diameter 10″	130.00	150.00	135.00
☐ **Bowl,** oval	40.00	45.00	42.50
☐ **Bowl,** with cover, diameter 8″	100.00	115.00	105.00
☐ **Bread Tray**	40.00	60.00	45.00
☐ **Butter,** with lid	80.00	95.00	83.00
☐ **Cake Plate**	60.00	80.00	65.00
☐ **Celery**	50.00	60.00	55.00
☐ **Champagne Glass**	50.00	60.00	52.50
☐ **Compote,** high	70.00	80.00	75.00
☐ **Compote,** low	50.00	60.00	55.00
☐ **Compote,** with lid, high	70.00	80.00	75.00
☐ **Compote,** with lid, low	60.00	75.00	62.50
☐ **Cordial**	50.00	60.00	52.50
☐ **Creamer**	40.00	50.00	42.50
☐ **Cruet,** with stopper	80.00	90.00	82.00
☐ **Goblet**	65.00	75.00	67.50
☐ **Jam Jar**	50.00	60.00	52.50
☐ **Milk Pitcher**	60.00	70.00	62.50

Cupid and Venus

	Current Price Range		Prior Year Average
☐ **Mug,** height 4½″	30.00	40.00	32.00
☐ **Plate,** diameter 9½″	40.00	60.00	42.50
☐ **Relish,** two compartments	25.00	35.00	27.50
☐ **Sauce,** flat	8.00	10.00	8.50
☐ **Sauce,** footed	12.00	14.00	16.50
☐ **Spooner**	40.00	50.00	42.50
☐ **Sugar,** with lid	60.00	80.00	62.50
☐ **Water Pitcher**	70.00	80.00	75.50

CURTAIN
Bryce Bros.

Deeply molded and well balanced, this pattern is an achievement in pressed glass. Sweeps of drapery flow across the middle body in parallel rows, tied together in panels of vertical bows. The central medallion or the bottom of the body is pleated.

☐ **Berry Bowl**	10.00	15.00	12.50
☐ **Bowl,** diameter 12″	20.00	30.00	25.00
☐ **Butter,** with cover	50.00	60.00	52.50
☐ **Cake Stand**	25.00	35.00	27.50
☐ **Celery Boat**	30.00	40.00	32.50
☐ **Celery Vase**	30.00	40.00	32.50
☐ **Compote,** high	25.00	35.00	27.50
☐ **Compote,** high, with cover	40.00	50.00	42.50
☐ **Creamer**	40.00	50.00	42.50
☐ **Goblet**	30.00	40.00	32.50
☐ **Plate,** round	18.00	22.00	19.50
☐ **Plate,** square	25.00	35.00	27.50
☐ **Relish Bowl,** two compartments	17.00	22.00	17.50
☐ **Salt Shaker**	18.00	22.00	15.50

Curtain

	Current Price Range		Prior Year Average
☐ **Sauce,** flat	8.00	12.00	9.50
☐ **Sauce,** footed	12.00	15.00	12.50
☐ **Spooner**	30.00	40.00	35.00
☐ **Sugar,** with cover	40.00	50.00	42.50
☐ **Tumbler**	25.00	35.00	27.50
☐ **Water Pitcher**	60.00	80.00	65.00
☐ **Water Tray**	50.00	60.00	55.00

DAHLIA

This elegant pattern is formed by a wide, stippled band containing the smooth decoration of a rosette-like flower with foliage. The wide band is edged on both sides with rounded ridgework and beading. The pieces are usually based or set on pedestals which are sharply scalloped and very heavy. It is a very popular pattern.

Bowl			
☐ clear	20.00	25.00	15.00
☐ blue	30.00	35.00	25.00
☐ green	30.00	35.00	25.00
☐ yellow	50.00	60.00	46.00
☐ amber	50.00	60.00	46.00
Butter, covered			
☐ clear	35.00	40.00	31.00
☐ blue	55.00	65.00	50.00
☐ green	55.00	65.00	50.00
☐ yellow	75.00	85.00	70.00
☐ amber	75.00	85.00	70.00

Dahlia

	Current Price Range		Prior Year Average

Cake Stand
☐ clear	33.00	38.00	28.00
☐ blue	53.00	63.00	48.00
☐ green	53.00	63.00	48.00
☐ yellow	68.00	75.00	63.00
☐ amber	68.00	75.00	63.00

Champagne
☐ clear	85.00	92.00	80.00
☐ blue	95.00	105.00	90.00
☐ green	95.00	105.00	90.00
☐ yellow	115.00	125.00	105.00
☐ amber	115.00	125.00	105.00

Compote, covered, large
☐ clear	58.00	63.00	54.00
☐ blue	75.00	83.00	70.00
☐ green	75.00	83.00	70.00
☐ yellow	105.00	115.00	100.00
☐ amber	105.00	115.00	100.00

Compote, open
☐ clear	35.00	40.00	30.00
☐ blue	53.00	58.00	49.00
☐ green	53.00	58.00	49.00
☐ yellow	62.00	68.00	58.00
☐ amber	62.00	68.00	58.00

Cordial
☐ clear	35.00	40.00	30.00
☐ blue	53.00	58.00	49.00
☐ green	53.00	58.00	49.00
☐ yellow	60.00	65.00	55.00
☐ amber	60.00	65.00	55.00

Creamer
☐ clear	25.00	30.00	20.00
☐ blue	32.00	38.00	28.00
☐ green	32.00	38.00	28.00
☐ yellow	38.00	44.00	34.00
☐ amber	38.00	44.00	34.00

Egg Cup, double, scarce
☐ clear	48.00	55.00	43.00
☐ blue	58.00	65.00	53.00
☐ green	58.00	65.00	53.00
☐ yellow	80.00	90.00	75.00
☐ amber	80.00	90.00	75.00

Egg Cup, single
☐ clear	20.00	26.00	15.00
☐ blue	26.00	32.00	23.00
☐ green	26.00	32.00	23.00
☐ yellow	35.00	40.00	30.00
☐ amber	35.00	40.00	30.00

	Current Price Range		Prior Year Average
Goblet, scarce			
☐ clear	43.00	48.00	39.00
☐ blue	55.00	63.00	50.00
☐ green	55.00	63.00	50.00
☐ yellow	66.00	74.00	61.00
☐ amber	66.00	74.00	61.00
Mug, handled, small			
☐ clear	35.00	40.00	30.00
☐ blue	48.00	53.00	44.00
☐ green	48.00	53.00	44.00
☐ yellow	58.00	63.00	53.00
☐ amber	58.00	63.00	53.00
Mug, handled, large			
☐ clear	40.00	45.00	35.00
☐ blue	58.00	65.00	53.00
☐ green	58.00	65.00	53.00
☐ yellow	70.00	75.00	65.00
☐ amber	70.00	75.00	65.00
Pickle			
☐ clear	23.00	26.00	20.00
☐ blue	34.00	38.00	30.00
☐ green	34.00	38.00	30.00
☐ yellow	40.00	45.00	35.00
☐ amber	40.00	45.00	35.00
Pitcher, milk, handled			
☐ clear	40.00	45.00	35.00
☐ blue	48.00	55.00	44.00
☐ green	48.00	55.00	44.00
☐ yellow	63.00	68.00	59.00
☐ amber	63.00	68.00	59.00
Pitcher, water, handled			
☐ clear	63.00	68.00	59.00
☐ blue	79.00	86.00	75.00
☐ green	79.00	86.00	75.00
☐ yellow	90.00	100.00	86.00
☐ amber	90.00	100.00	86.00
Plate, diameter 7″			
☐ clear	26.00	31.00	21.00
☐ blue	33.00	39.00	29.00
☐ green	33.00	39.00	29.00
☐ yellow	45.00	50.00	40.00
☐ amber	45.00	50.00	40.00
Platter, handled, oval			
☐ clear	32.00	38.00	28.00
☐ blue	43.00	49.00	37.00
☐ green	43.00	49.00	37.00
☐ yellow	55.00	60.00	50.00
☐ amber	55.00	60.00	50.00

	Current Price Range		Prior Year Average
Salt, footed			
☐ clear	10.00	15.00	8.00
☐ blue	15.00	20.00	10.00
☐ green	15.00	20.00	10.00
☐ yellow	20.00	25.00	15.00
☐ amber	20.00	25.00	15.00
Sauce, flat			
☐ clear	7.00	12.00	5.00
☐ blue	12.00	16.00	10.00
☐ green	12.00	16.00	10.00
☐ yellow	16.00	20.00	12.00
☐ amber	16.00	20.00	12.00
Sauce, footed			
☐ clear	15.00	20.00	12.00
☐ blue	21.00	26.00	16.00
☐ green	21.00	26.00	16.00
☐ yellow	32.00	37.00	28.00
☐ amber	32.00	37.00	28.00
Spoon Holder			
☐ clear	20.00	25.00	15.00
☐ blue	26.00	33.00	23.00
☐ green	26.00	33.00	23.00
☐ yellow	45.00	50.00	40.00
☐ amber	45.00	50.00	40.00
Sugar, covered			
☐ clear	43.00	49.00	38.00
☐ blue	56.00	63.00	51.00
☐ green	56.00	63.00	51.00
☐ yellow	70.00	75.00	65.00
☐ amber	70.00	75.00	65.00
Sugar, open			
☐ clear	25.00	30.00	20.00
☐ blue	35.00	40.00	30.00
☐ green	35.00	40.00	30.00
☐ yellow	40.00	45.00	35.00
☐ amber	40.00	45.00	35.00
Wine			
☐ clear	40.00	46.00	36.00
☐ blue	52.00	58.00	47.00
☐ green	52.00	58.00	47.00
☐ yellow	63.00	69.00	58.00
☐ amber	63.00	69.00	58.00

DAKOTA

A lovely floral band of lightly etched foliage rounds the outside, decorating pieces with this pattern. A thumbprint band of thick glass combines with the delicacy of the flowers creating a well-balanced, popular pattern.

	Current Price Range		Prior Year Average
Berry Bowl			
☐ etched	30.00	40.00	35.00
☐ plain	20.00	25.00	22.50
Bowl			
☐ etched	30.00	40.00	35.00
☐ plain	15.00	25.00	17.50
Bread Tray			
☐ etched	30.00	40.00	35.00
☐ plain	15.00	25.00	17.50
Butter, with cover			
☐ etched	40.00	50.00	45.00
☐ plain	20.00	25.00	22.50
Cake Stand			
☐ etched	60.00	80.00	65.00
☐ plain	30.00	50.00	32.50
Celery			
☐ etched	40.00	50.00	42.50
☐ plain	20.00	30.00	25.00
Compote, high			
☐ etched	45.00	55.00	47.50
☐ plain	25.00	35.00	27.50
Compote, low, with cover			
☐ etched	45.00	55.00	47.50
☐ plain	20.00	30.00	25.00
Cordial Glass			
☐ etched	30.00	40.00	32.50
☐ plain	15.00	20.00	17.50
Creamer			
☐ etched	60.00	70.00	65.00
☐ plain	30.00	40.00	35.00
Cruet			
☐ etched	50.00	60.00	52.00
☐ plain	20.00	30.00	25.00
Egg Cup			
☐ etched	20.00	30.00	25.00
☐ plain	10.00	15.00	12.50
Goblet			
☐ etched	35.00	45.00	37.50
☐ plain	20.00	30.00	25.00
Milk Pitcher			
☐ etched	40.00	50.00	45.00
☐ plain	20.00	40.00	22.50
Mug			
☐ etched	20.00	30.00	25.00
☐ plain	15.00	20.00	17.50
Sauce, flat			
☐ etched	10.00	12.00	11.00
☐ plain	8.00	10.00	9.00

	Current Price Range		Prior Year Average
Sauce, footed			
☐ etched	15.00	20.00	17.50
☐ plain	10.00	15.00	11.50
Spooner			
☐ etched	30.00	40.00	32.50
☐ plain	15.00	20.00	17.50
Sugar, with cover			
☐ etched	50.00	60.00	55.00
☐ plain	25.00	35.00	45.00
Tumbler			
☐ etched	40.00	50.00	42.50
☐ plain	25.00	30.00	27.50
Water Pitcher			
☐ etched	60.00	80.00	52.50
☐ plain	30.00	40.00	32.50
Wine Glass			
☐ etched	40.00	50.00	42.50
☐ plain	20.00	30.00	22.50

DEER AND PINE TREE

Panel of deer and pine trees alternating with panel of diamonds.

Bowl			
☐ clear	35.00	40.00	30.00
☐ yellow	52.00	63.00	55.00
☐ apple green	52.00	63.00	55.00
☐ blue	52.00	63.00	55.00
☐ amber	52.00	63.00	55.00
Butter, covered			
☐ clear	60.00	65.00	55.00
☐ yellow	90.00	100.00	92.00
☐ apple green	90.00	100.00	92.00
☐ blue	90.00	100.00	92.00
☐ amber	90.00	100.00	92.00
Cake Stand			
☐ clear	72.00	78.00	68.00
☐ yellow	100.00	115.00	105.00
☐ apple green	100.00	115.00	105.00
☐ blue	100.00	115.00	105.00
☐ amber	100.00	115.00	105.00
Celery			
☐ clear	50.00	55.00	45.00
☐ yellow	75.00	85.00	78.00
☐ apple green	75.00	85.00	78.00
☐ blue	75.00	85.00	78.00
☐ amber	75.00	85.00	78.00
Compote, covered			
☐ clear	60.00	65.00	55.00

	Current Price Range		Prior Year Average
☐ yellow	90.00	100.00	93.00
☐ apple green	90.00	100.00	93.00
☐ blue	90.00	100.00	93.00
☐ amber	90.00	100.00	93.00
Compote, open			
☐ clear	35.00	42.00	30.00
☐ yellow	50.00	60.00	52.00
☐ apple green	50.00	60.00	52.00
☐ blue	50.00	60.00	52.00
☐ amber	50.00	60.00	52.00
Creamer			
☐ clear	40.00	50.00	42.00
☐ yellow	60.00	70.00	63.00
☐ apple green	60.00	70.00	63.00
☐ blue	60.00	70.00	63.00
☐ amber	60.00	70.00	63.00
Goblet			
☐ clear	32.00	40.00	34.00
☐ yellow	60.00	70.00	62.00
☐ apple green	60.00	70.00	62.00
☐ blue	60.00	70.00	62.00
☐ amber	60.00	70.00	62.00
Jar, covered			
☐ clear	45.00	50.00	40.00
☐ yellow	65.00	77.00	68.00
☐ apple green	65.00	77.00	68.00
☐ blue	65.00	77.00	68.00
☐ amber	65.00	77.00	68.00
Pitcher			
☐ clear	90.00	102.00	94.00
☐ yellow	130.00	145.00	134.00
☐ apple green	130.00	145.00	134.00
☐ blue	130.00	145.00	134.00
☐ amber	130.00	145.00	134.00
Plate			
☐ clear	45.00	50.00	40.00
☐ yellow	60.00	65.00	55.00
☐ apple green	64.00	69.00	60.00
☐ blue	68.00	75.00	65.00
☐ amber	68.00	75.00	65.00
Platter			
☐ clear	53.00	58.00	48.00
☐ yellow	75.00	87.00	79.00
☐ apple green	75.00	87.00	79.00
☐ blue	75.00	87.00	79.00
☐ amber	75.00	87.00	79.00
Relish			
☐ clear	25.00	30.00	20.00

	Current Price Range		Prior Year Average
☐ yellow	32.00	38.00	28.00
☐ apple green	37.00	42.00	35.00
☐ blue	40.00	45.00	37.00
☐ amber	40.00	45.00	37.00
Sauce, flat			
☐ clear	15.00	20.00	10.00
☐ yellow	25.00	32.00	27.00
☐ apple green	25.00	32.00	27.00
☐ blue	25.00	32.00	27.00
☐ amber	25.00	32.00	27.00
Sauce, footed			
☐ clear	18.00	24.00	15.00
☐ yellow	30.00	40.00	32.00
☐ apple green	30.00	40.00	32.00
☐ blue	30.00	40.00	32.00
☐ amber	30.00	40.00	32.00

DEWDROP WITH STAR

Double bands of beadwork wind up and down around the body, capturing a row of high point stars in high relief. Underscoring each star is a herringbone panel ending at the base.

☐ **Bread Tray**	30.00	40.00	32.50
☐ **Bowl,** collared	20.00	25.00	22.50
☐ **Bowl,** footed	45.00	55.00	47.50
☐ **Butter,** with cover	60.00	80.00	62.50
☐ **Cake Stand**	60.00	80.00	62.50
☐ **Cheese Dish,** with cover	80.00	100.00	85.00
☐ **Compote,** high	80.00	100.00	85.00
☐ **Compote,** high, with cover	80.00	100.00	85.00
☐ **Compote,** low, with cover	75.00	85.00	77.50
☐ **Creamer**	40.00	50.00	42.50
☐ **Honey Jar,** with cover	80.00	100.00	85.00
☐ **Lamp**	150.00	200.00	165.00
☐ **Plate,** large	35.00	45.00	37.50
☐ **Plate,** small	25.00	35.00	27.50
☐ **Saucer**	20.00	30.00	22.50
☐ **Spooner**	25.00	35.00	27.50
☐ **Sugar,** with cover	40.00	50.00	42.50
☐ **Water Pitcher**	90.00	100.00	95.00

DIAMOND POINT
Boston & Sandwich

Diamond design with plain band at top.

☐ **Ale Glass**	35.00	45.00	32.00
☐ **Cake Stand**	195.00	205.00	190.00

Diamond Point

	Current Price Range		Prior Year Average
☐ **Candlesticks,** pair	160.00	170.00	155.00
☐ **Celery Vase**	70.00	80.00	67.00
☐ **Compote,** open, diameter 6″	45.00	53.00	43.00
☐ **Compote,** open, diameter 7″	50.00	60.00	47.00
☐ **Compote,** open, diameter 8″	65.00	75.00	60.00
☐ **Decanter,** stoppered, pint	80.00	90.00	76.00
☐ **Decanter,** stoppered, quart	110.00	120.00	105.00
☐ **Egg Cup**	35.00	45.00	30.00
☐ **Goblet,** small	65.00	75.00	60.00
☐ **Goblet,** large	55.00	65.00	50.00
☐ **Honey Dish**	25.00	35.00	20.00
☐ **Jelly Glass**	30.00	40.00	28.00
☐ **Pitcher,** handle, half pint	50.00	60.00	47.00
☐ **Pitcher,** handle, pint	60.00	70.00	58.00
☐ **Pitcher,** handle, quart	135.00	145.00	130.00
☐ **Plate,** diameter 6″	40.00	50.00	40.00
☐ **Plate,** diameter 8″	55.00	65.00	50.00
☐ **Salt,** footed	55.00	65.00	51.00
☐ **Sauce,** flat	12.00	17.00	12.00
☐ **Spoon Holder**	55.00	65.00	50.00
☐ **Wine**	45.00	53.00	43.00

DIAMOND POINT WITH PANELS
Boston & Sandwich

☐ **Butter,** covered	80.00	90.00	75.00
☐ **Celery**	100.00	110.00	95.00
☐ **Champagne**	65.00	75.00	60.00
☐ **Creamer**	70.00	80.00	68.00
☐ **Goblet**	50.00	60.00	45.00
☐ **Salt,** footed	40.00	50.00	35.00

	Current Price Range		Prior Year Average
☐ **Spoon Holder**	45.00	55.00	40.00
☐ **Sugar,** covered	75.00	85.00	70.00
☐ **Whiskey,** handled, footed	55.00	65.00	51.00
☐ **Wine**	50.00	60.00	45.00

DIAMOND QUILTED

This is one of the most popular patterns in pressed glass for good reason. The honey comb texture covers the piece in its entirety, creating a play of light that is unequaled in non-flint glass.

Bowl, oval
☐ yellow	35.00	45.00	37.50
☐ amber	30.00	40.00	32.50
☐ blue	40.00	50.00	45.00
☐ periwinkle	50.00	60.00	55.00
☐ amethyst	60.00	70.00	65.00
☐ clear.............................	15.00	25.00	17.50

Bowl, round
☐ yellow	35.00	45.00	37.50
☐ amber	30.00	40.00	32.50
☐ blue	40.00	50.00	45.00
☐ periwinkle	50.00	60.00	55.00
☐ amethyst	60.00	70.00	65.00
☐ clear.............................	15.00	20.00	15.50

Butter, with cover
☐ yellow	130.00	150.00	135.00
☐ amber	125.00	135.00	127.00
☐ blue	125.00	135.00	127.50
☐ periwinkle	150.00	175.00	155.00
☐ amethyst	160.00	180.00	165.00
☐ clear.............................	45.00	55.00	47.50

Celery
☐ yellow	80.00	90.00	85.00
☐ amber	75.00	85.00	77.50
☐ blue	80.00	90.00	85.00
☐ periwinkle	90.00	100.00	95.00
☐ amethyst	100.00	110.00	105.00
☐ clear.............................	30.00	40.00	37.50

DIAMOND THUMBPRINT

Deep prism diamonds with large thumbprint in the center of each diamond, plain band around top.

☐ **Butter Dish,** covered	147.00	157.00	145.00
☐ **Cake Stand**	220.00	250.00	222.00
☐ **Celery**	130.00	152.00	143.00
☐ **Champagne Glass,** rare	230.00	250.00	220.00

	Current Price Range		Prior Year Average
☐ Creamer	125.00	140.00	120.00
☐ Compote, footed, scalloped edge ...	40.00	50.00	42.00
☐ Decanter, no stopper, pint size	75.00	80.00	75.00
☐ Decanter, original stopper, quart size	100.00	120.00	105.00
☐ Goblet, rare	350.00	365.00	345.00
☐ Honey Dish	15.00	20.00	15.00
☐ Sauce Dish	10.00	15.00	11.00
☐ Spooner	80.00	90.00	75.00
☐ Sugar Bowl, covered	130.00	145.00	135.00
☐ Tumbler	100.00	110.00	95.00
☐ Waste Bowl	85.00	95.00	80.00
☐ Water Pitcher, rare	350.00	370.00	352.00
☐ Whiskey Tumbler, handled	275.00	300.00	280.00
☐ Wine Glass, rare	220.00	240.00	205.00
☐ Wine Jug, places for holding glasses	750.00	950.00	600.00

DIVIDED HEARTS
Boston & Sandwich

Wide oval fluting with loops inside of the fluting. Wide plain band across top.

☐ Butter Dish, covered	130.00	140.00	125.00
☐ Compote, covered	115.00	125.00	110.00
☐ Compote, open	110.00	120.00	105.00
☐ Creamer	105.00	115.00	100.00
☐ Egg Cup	65.00	75.00	63.00
☐ Lamp, marble base	115.00	125.00	110.00
☐ Salt, footed	35.00	45.00	31.00
☐ Spoon Holder	50.00	60.00	47.00
☐ Sugar Bowl, covered	125.00	137.00	120.00
☐ Sugar Bowl, open	60.00	70.00	55.00

DOUBLE SPEAR

This is a well balanced design consisting of a wide band of ovals with cane filler framed on either side with wide scallops.

☐ Butter, with cover	40.00	50.00	42.50
☐ Celery	30.00	40.00	35.00
☐ Compote, high, with cover	50.00	60.00	52.50
☐ Creamer	35.00	45.00	37.50
☐ Egg Cup	20.00	30.00	22.50
☐ Goblet	30.00	40.00	32.50
☐ Pickle Plate	15.00	25.00	17.50
☐ Sauce, flat	16.00	22.00	17.50
☐ Sauce, footed	20.00	25.00	22.50
☐ Spooner	30.00	40.00	35.50
☐ Sugar, with cover	40.00	50.00	42.50
☐ Toothpick	25.00	35.00	27.50

	Current Price Range		Prior Year Average
☐ **Tumbler**	30.00	40.00	32.50
☐ **Water Pitcher**	60.00	80.00	65.00

DRUM

The geometric pattern is the motif of a toy drum, with light ridges running vertically into long triangles around the flat base.

☐ **Butter,** with lid	125.00	145.00	130.00
☐ **Creamer**	110.00	125.00	115.00
☐ **Mustard Jar,** with cover	110.00	125.00	115.00
☐ **Spooner**	75.00	100.00	80.00
☐ **Sugar,** with cover	110.00	125.00	115.00

ELONGATED THUMBPRINT

The thumbprints are pulled out into pointed egg shapes and arranged in a wide band. Around the bottom of the base is a series of rounded thumbprints, resolving under the stem and base.

☐ **Goblet**	150.00	200.00	175.00

EUGENIE
McKee and Bros.

Three rows of thumbprints. Middle row also has long ovals between thumbprints. Scalloped line at top.

☐ **Butter Dish,** covered	80.00	90.00	77.00
☐ **Castor Bottle**	30.00	38.00	26.00
☐ **Celery**	80.00	90.00	74.00
☐ **Champagne**	60.00	70.00	56.00

Eugenie

	Current Price Range		Prior Year Average
☐ **Compote,** covered	105.00	115.00	100.00
☐ **Cordial**	50.00	58.00	46.00
☐ **Egg Cup**	50.00	60.00	47.00
☐ **Goblet**	55.00	65.00	51.00
☐ **Sauce,** flat	20.00	28.00	18.00
☐ **Sugar Bowl,** covered, dolphin finial, scarce	75.00	90.00	80.00
☐ **Tumbler**	45.00	55.00	39.00
☐ **Wine**	50.00	60.00	45.00

EUREKA

Large loops with several parallel lines running full length inside of loop. Wide plain band at top.

☐ **Bowl,** diameter 8″	35.00	45.00	30.00
☐ **Butter Dish,** covered	70.00	80.00	66.00
☐ **Compote,** covered	90.00	100.00	86.00
☐ **Compote,** open	50.00	60.00	46.00
☐ **Creamer**	55.00	63.00	57.00
☐ **Egg Cup**	30.00	38.00	32.00
☐ **Plate**	45.00	55.00	41.00
☐ **Salt,** footed	25.00	35.00	20.00
☐ **Sauce,** flat	14.00	18.00	12.00
☐ **Spooner**	35.00	45.00	30.00
☐ **Sugar,** covered	60.00	70.00	55.00
☐ **Sugar,** open	35.00	45.00	30.00
☐ **Wine Glass**	27.00	35.00	29.00

Eureka

Excelsior

EXCELSIOR

Circles and loops combine to make this design, space between the figures, wide plain band at top.

	Current Price Range		Prior Year Average
☐ **Ale Glass**	55.00	65.00	50.00
☐ **Bowl**	130.00	135.00	128.00
☐ **Bitters Bottle**	30.00	40.00	25.00
☐ **Butter Dish,** covered	105.00	115.00	100.00
☐ **Candlesticks,** pair	240.00	250.00	230.00
☐ **Compote,** covered, low foot	125.00	135.00	120.00
☐ **Compote,** open, high foot	90.00	98.00	88.00
☐ **Creamer**	75.00	85.00	70.00
☐ **Decanter,** one pint	55.00	65.00	50.00
☐ **Decanter,** quart	65.00	75.00	60.00
☐ **Egg Cup,** double	40.00	50.00	35.00
☐ **Egg Cup,** single	45.00	55.00	40.00
☐ **Goblet,** Maltese cross	60.00	68.00	57.00
☐ **Goblet,** plain	45.00	55.00	42.00
☐ **Lamp,** Maltese cross	145.00	155.00	140.00
☐ **Pitcher,** milk, rare	220.00	240.00	200.00
☐ **Pitcher,** syrup	115.00	125.00	110.00
☐ **Pitcher,** water, rare	175.00	200.00	160.00
☐ **Spoon Holder**	80.00	90.00	78.00
☐ **Sugar Bowl,** covered	90.00	100.00	88.00
☐ **Whiskey Glass,** Maltese cross	75.00	85.00	70.00
☐ **Wine Glass**	50.00	60.00	45.00

FAN BAND

This is a simple pattern consisting of a row of flashed fans connected with feathering. The rest of the piece is smooth and glossy, devoid of decoration.

	Current Price Range		Prior Year Average
☐ Bowl	15.00	20.00	17.50
☐ Butter, with cover	35.00	45.00	37.50
☐ Celery	25.00	35.00	27.50
☐ Creamer	18.00	22.00	19.00
☐ Compote, low	20.00	30.00	22.50
☐ Compote, high, with cover	35.00	45.00	37.50
☐ Sauce, footed	12.00	15.00	13.50
☐ Spooner	10.00	14.00	11.50
☐ Sugar	8.00	10.00	8.50
☐ Sugar, with cover	8.00	10.00	8.50
☐ Water Pitcher	25.00	35.00	27.50
☐ Water Tray	20.00	30.00	25.50

FEATHER

This pattern is reminiscent of cut glass designs with alternating swirling panels of rosette point and beaded flutes. The motif is overall, the mold work deep.

	Current Price Range		Prior Year Average
☐ Banana	65.00	75.00	67.50
☐ Berry Bowl	15.00	20.00	17.50
☐ Berry Bowl, square	20.00	30.00	25.00
☐ Bowl, oval	15.00	20.00	17.50
☐ Butter, with cover	40.00	50.00	55.00
☐ Cake Stand, large	30.00	40.00	35.00
☐ Cake Stand, small	35.00	45.00	37.50
☐ Compote, high, with cover	50.00	60.00	52.50
☐ Compote, low	25.00	30.00	27.50
☐ Compote, low	30.00	40.00	35.00
☐ Cordial Glass	70.00	80.00	75.00
☐ Creamer	25.00	35.00	27.50
☐ Cruet	40.00	50.00	45.00
☐ Goblet	50.00	60.00	55.00
☐ Jam Jar	80.00	90.00	85.00
☐ Milk Pitcher	50.00	60.00	55.00
☐ Plate, diameter 7"	20.00	25.00	22.50
☐ Plate, diameter 8"	22.00	26.00	23.50
☐ Platter	28.00	32.00	30.00
☐ Relish Bowl	20.00	30.00	25.00
☐ Sauce, flat	10.00	15.00	12.00
☐ Sauce, footed	15.00	20.00	17.50
☐ Spooner	30.00	40.00	35.00
☐ Sugar, with cover	30.00	40.00	35.00
☐ Toothpick	40.00	50.00	42.50
☐ Tumbler	32.00	40.00	33.50
☐ Water Pitcher	60.00	80.00	65.00
☐ Wine Glass	40.00	50.00	42.50

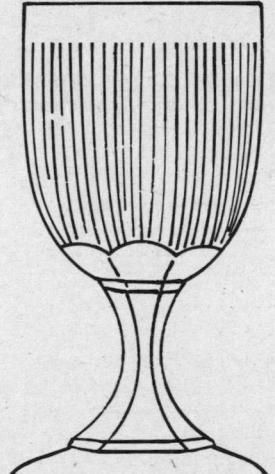

Fine Rib

FINE RIB
New England

This is a simple pattern of ribbing which covers the pieces with length-wise panels. Most based pieces have scalloped bottom panels and some bowls and compotes have waved rims. The glass is clear and heavy; the moldwork is excellent.

	Current Price Range		Prior Year Average
☐ **Bottle,** bitters	55.00	65.00	58.00
☐ **Bowl,** covered, diameter 7″	93.00	103.00	87.00
☐ **Butter,** covered	110.00	120.00	105.00
☐ **Castor Bottle**	33.00	38.00	30.00
☐ **Castor Set**	30.00	38.00	28.00
☐ **Celery**	55.00	65.00	51.00
☐ **Champagne**	55.00	63.00	57.00
☐ **Compote,** covered	110.00	120.00	95.00
☐ **Compote,** open	70.00	80.00	66.00
☐ **Creamer,** handled	95.00	107.00	98.00
☐ **Decanter,** stoppered, pint	105.00	115.00	100.00
☐ **Decanter,** stoppered, quart	140.00	150.00	135.00
☐ **Egg Cup**	35.00	45.00	30.00
☐ **Goblet**	50.00	60.00	53.00
☐ **Lamp,** handled	158.00	168.00	153.00
☐ **Mug,** handled	63.00	73.00	60.00
☐ **Pitcher,** water	190.00	200.00	185.00
☐ **Plate,** diameter 6″	55.00	65.00	50.00
☐ **Plate,** diameter 7″	55.00	65.00	50.00
☐ **Salt,** footed, covered	95.00	105.00	90.00
☐ **Water Bottle,** with tumbler	110.00	120.00	105.00
☐ **Wine**	40.00	48.00	37.00

FLEUR-DE-LYS
Adams and Company

A well-balanced design, this pattern alternates upright fleur-de-lys with upside down tassles. Both motifs are molded in high relief with voluptuous feathering.

	Current Price Range		Prior Year Average
Butter, with cover			
☐ opal	60.00	70.00	65.00
☐ green	60.00	70.00	65.00
☐ clear	40.00	50.00	42.50
Cake Stand			
☐ opal	50.00	60.00	55.00
☐ green	50.00	60.00	55.00
☐ clear	30.00	40.00	32.50
Celery			
☐ opal	30.00	40.00	32.50
☐ green	30.00	40.00	32.50
☐ clear	20.00	30.00	22.50
Compote, high			
☐ opal	60.00	70.00	62.50
☐ green	60.00	70.00	62.50
☐ clear	40.00	50.00	42.50
Creamer			
☐ opal	40.00	50.00	42.50
☐ green	40.00	50.00	42.50
☐ clear	35.00	45.00	37.50
Milk Pitcher			
☐ opal	100.00	110.00	105.00
☐ green	100.00	110.00	105.00
☐ clear	65.00	75.00	67.50
Spooner			
☐ opal	20.00	30.00	22.50
☐ green	20.00	30.00	22.50
☐ clear	15.00	20.00	17.50
Sugar, with cover			
☐ opal	30.00	40.00	35.00
☐ green	30.00	40.00	35.00
☐ clear	20.00	30.00	28.00
Tumbler			
☐ opal	40.00	50.00	42.50
☐ green	40.00	50.00	42.50
☐ clear	20.00	30.00	25.00
Water Pitcher			
☐ opal	60.00	70.00	62.50
☐ green	60.00	70.00	62.50
☐ clear	40.00	50.00	42.50
Wine Glass			
☐ opal	30.00	40.00	35.00
☐ green	30.00	40.00	35.00
☐ clear	15.00	20.00	17.50

FLOWER POT

Horizontal ribbing overlaid with flower pot and flowers.

	Current Price Range		Prior Year Average
☐ **Butter,** covered	60.00	70.00	55.00
☐ **Cake Stand**	52.00	59.00	46.00
☐ **Compote,** covered	45.00	53.00	40.00
☐ **Creamer**	37.00	43.00	33.00
☐ **Goblet**	30.00	36.00	28.00
☐ **Pitcher,** milk	38.00	45.00	34.00
☐ **Pitcher,** water	56.00	63.00	50.00
☐ **Salt Shaker**	26.00	31.00	22.00
☐ **Sauce,** footed	15.00	20.00	12.00
☐ **Sauce,** square, handled	20.00	25.00	15.00
☐ **Spoon Holder**	30.00	36.00	26.00
☐ **Sugar,** covered	45.00	52.00	40.00
☐ **Sugar,** open	30.00	37.00	26.00
☐ **Tray**	43.00	49.00	38.00
☐ **Tumbler**	20.00	26.00	17.00

FLUTE

Fluting design with plain band across top. There were more than 14 different flute patterns produced between 1850 and 1880. Some of the pattern names include New England Flute, Bessimer Flute, Brooklyn Flute, and Sandwich Flute. Since all of the flute designs have similar prices, the list is basic prices and not specific to any pattern.

☐ **Ale Glass**	30.00	40.00	28.00
☐ **Bottle,** bitters	30.00	37.00	28.00
☐ **Bowl,** scalloped edge	30.00	38.00	27.00
☐ **Candlesticks,** pair.................	40.00	50.00	37.00

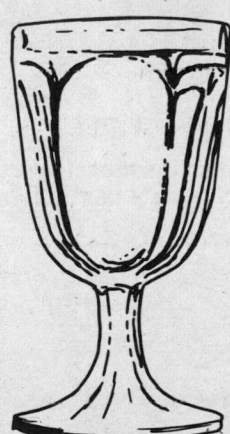

Flute

	Current Price Range		Prior Year Average
☐ **Champagne**	30.00	35.00	27.00
☐ **Compote,** open, diameter 8″	32.00	38.00	30.00
☐ **Decanter,** quart	50.00	56.00	47.00
☐ **Egg Cup,** single	15.00	19.00	13.00
☐ **Egg Cup,** double	30.00	35.00	28.00
☐ **Goblet**	30.00	40.00	25.00
☐ **Honey Dish**	15.00	19.00	13.00
☐ **Lamp**	70.00	77.00	67.00
☐ **Mug**	50.00	60.00	48.00
☐ **Pitcher,** water	60.00	70.00	55.00
☐ **Salt,** footed	20.00	25.00	17.00
☐ **Sauce,** flat	14.00	18.00	12.00
☐ **Sugar Bowl,** open	27.00	35.00	25.00
☐ **Tumbler**	13.00	19.00	14.00
☐ **Whiskey,** handled	25.00	33.00	23.00
☐ **Wine**	15.00	20.00	16.00

FLUTE WITH BULL'S EYE

Widely spaced bull's eyes hover above long arched fluting from the bottom of the body to the waist.

☐ **Goblet**	50.00	70.00	55.00
☐ **Wine Glass**	40.00	60.00	45.00

FOUR PETAL

Two rows of diamonds with indented thumbprint in center of each.

☐ **Bowl**	40.00	48.00	35.00
☐ **Compote,** open, diameter 6″	60.00	68.00	57.00
☐ **Creamer,** handle	75.00	85.00	73.00
☐ **Jar**	40.00	50.00	35.00
☐ **Sugar Bowl,** domed lid	55.00	65.00	50.00
☐ **Sugar Bowl,** regular lid	40.00	48.00	41.00

FORGET-ME-NOT-IN-SCROLL

Wide band of Roman rosettes, leaves, and scrolls alternating with plain bands. At bottom of base a band of leaves.

☐ **Butter Dish,** covered	30.00	37.00	27.00
☐ **Creamer**	26.00	35.00	21.00
☐ **Goblet**	25.00	32.00	20.00
☐ **Pitcher,** handled	36.00	43.00	31.00
☐ **Sauce,** flat	15.00	20.00	12.00
☐ **Spoon Holder**	20.00	28.00	17.00
☐ **Sugar Bowl,** covered	30.00	38.00	26.00
☐ **Sugar,** open	20.00	26.00	17.00

FRAMED OVALS

The heavy architectural base ends in a wide collar at the bottom of the body. Then, in lighter glass, long squared flutes contain ovals of plain polished glass.

	Current Price Range		Prior Year Average
☐ Goblet	150.00	200.00	165.00
☐ Vase	75.00	85.00	77.50

FROSTED ARTICHOKE

The finely ridged artichoke with foliage has alternate petals frosted, the rest a clear glossy glass. The fruit is in low relief.

☐ Berry Bowl, diameter 6″	28.00	32.00	29.50
☐ Berry Bowl, diameter 8″	28.00	32.00	29.50
☐ Bowl, diameter 7″	15.00	25.00	15.50
☐ Bowl, diameter 8″	40.00	50.00	42.50
☐ Butter	70.00	80.00	75.00
☐ Cake Stand	55.00	65.00	57.50
☐ Candlestick	35.00	45.00	37.50
☐ Celery	40.00	60.00	42.50
☐ Compote, with lid	55.00	65.00	57.50
☐ Creamer	70.00	80.00	75.00
☐ Cruet, honeycomb stopper	40.00	60.00	42.50
☐ Finger Bowl	45.00	55.00	47.50
☐ Hurricane Lamp	75.00	85.00	77.50
☐ Lamp	40.00	60.00	42.50
☐ Sauce, flat	10.00	15.00	11.50
☐ Sauce, footed	12.00	16.00	12.50
☐ Saucer	10.00	15.00	11.50
☐ Spooner	25.00	35.00	27.50
☐ Sugar	70.00	80.00	75.00
☐ Tumbler	35.00	45.00	37.50
☐ Water Pitcher, bulbous	65.00	75.00	67.50
☐ Water Pitcher, tankard style	60.00	80.00	62.50
☐ Vase	15.00	25.00	15.50

FROSTED FRUITS

Design composed of various fruits with leaves and vines. Pattern usually covers entire piece.

Bowl, berry			
☐ clear	15.00	20.00	10.00
☐ frosted	30.00	37.00	25.00
Butter			
☐ clear	55.00	65.00	50.00
☐ frosted	70.00	80.00	60.00
Celery			
☐ clear	25.00	30.00	20.00
☐ frosted	40.00	45.00	35.00

	Current Price Range		Prior Year Average
Creamer			
☐ clear	35.00	40.00	30.00
☐ frosted	45.00	55.00	40.00
Goblet			
☐ clear	30.00	35.00	25.00
☐ frosted	40.00	45.00	35.00
Pitcher			
☐ clear	75.00	80.00	70.00
☐ frosted	90.00	100.00	85.00
Sauce			
☐ clear	20.00	25.00	15.00
☐ frosted	25.00	30.00	20.00
Sugar			
☐ clear	50.00	55.00	45.00
☐ frosted	60.00	70.00	50.00
Tumbler			
☐ clear	35.00	40.00	30.00
☐ frosted	45.00	55.00	40.00

FROSTED LEAF

The bottom band on these pieces is fluted with wide panels, which creates an anchor for the meandering vine that winds around the rim. The full, spade-shaped leaves are frosted and opaque. The contrast is excellent; the design is well-balanced.

☐ **Butter Dish,** covered	155.00	160.00	151.00
☐ **Celery**	130.00	138.00	126.00
☐ **Compote,** covered	255.00	265.00	238.00
☐ **Creamer**	125.00	128.00	125.00

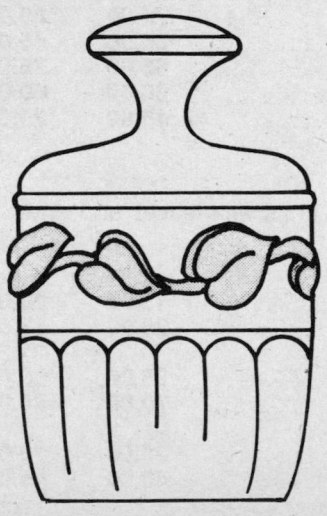

Frosted Leaf

	Current Price Range		Prior Year Average
☐ **Decanter,** no stopper	110.00	118.00	105.00
☐ **Decanter,** stoppered, quart	250.00	255.00	250.00
☐ **Egg Cup**	100.00	105.00	96.00
☐ **Goblet**	80.00	86.00	78.00
☐ **Pitcher,** scarce	360.00	370.00	350.00
☐ **Salt**	55.00	65.00	51.00
☐ **Sauce Dish**	30.00	35.00	21.00
☐ **Spoon Holder**	80.00	90.00	74.00
☐ **Sugar Bowl,** covered	130.00	140.00	126.00
☐ **Sugar Bowl,** open	70.00	80.00	64.00
☐ **Tumbler**	145.00	150.00	145.00
☐ **Tumbler,** footed	100.00	108.00	98.00
☐ **Wine**	25.00	35.00	21.00

FROSTED MEDALLION

This is an interesting pattern of sunbursts of geometrical ridges in smooth glass over a finely stippled body. The rosettes are decorated with beading and the same little knobs form a band around the top and bottom.

☐ **Bowl,** oval	20.00	30.00	22.50
☐ **Bowl,** round	25.00	35.00	27.50
☐ **Butter,** with cover	35.00	45.00	37.50
☐ **Creamer**	30.00	40.00	32.50
☐ **Compote**	30.00	40.00	37.50
☐ **Compote,** with cover	45.00	55.00	47.50
☐ **Goblet**	18.00	20.00	19.00
☐ **Relish,** two compartments	15.00	20.00	25.00
☐ **Sauce,** flat	20.00	25.00	22.50
☐ **Sauce,** footed	25.00	35.00	22.50
☐ **Spooner**	25.00	35.00	27.50
☐ **Syrup Pitcher**	35.00	45.00	37.50
☐ **Tray**	35.00	45.00	37.50
☐ **Tumbler**	25.00	35.00	27.50
☐ **Water Pitcher**	50.00	60.00	52.50

FROSTED STORK
Crystal Glass

A playful stork in cameo, the design on these pieces is well-molded in low relief. The frames are rounded ridges, filled in at the connection with rounded fans.

☐ **Bowl,** round	40.00	50.00	45.00
☐ **Butter,** with lid	60.00	80.00	65.00
☐ **Creamer**	45.00	55.00	47.00
☐ **Dish,** oval	40.00	50.00	45.00
☐ **Goblet**	50.00	80.00	55.00
☐ **Jam Jar**	60.00	80.00	65.00

Frosted Stork

	Current Price Range		Prior Year Average
☐ **Pickle Jar**	60.00	80.00	65.00
☐ **Plate,** tab handles	50.00	60.00	55.50
☐ **Platter**	60.00	80.00	65.00
☐ **Sauce,** flat	15.00	20.00	17.50
☐ **Sauce,** footed	20.00	25.00	22.50
☐ **Spooner**	35.00	45.00	38.00
☐ **Sugar**	30.00	40.00	35.00
☐ **Water Pitcher**	95.00	110.00	100.00

Garfield Drape

GARFIELD DRAPE
Adams

This elegant pattern was made to commemorate President Garfield after his assassination. Subsequently beadwork draping in this style has shown up on other patterns and the motif has taken the name Garfield Drape.

	Current Price Range		Prior Year Average
☐ **Berry Bowl**	30.00	40.00	35.00
☐ **Bread Plate**, oval	45.00	55.00	47.50
☐ **Butter**, with cover	70.00	90.00	75.00
☐ **Cake Stand**	60.00	80.00	65.00
☐ **Celery**	37.00	48.00	40.00
☐ **Compote**, high, with cover	80.00	100.00	85.00
☐ **Compote**, low	40.00	50.00	45.00
☐ **Creamer**	60.00	80.00	65.00
☐ **Goblet**	32.00	41.00	34.00
☐ **Milk Pitcher**	70.00	80.00	72.50
☐ **Plate**, says "It's Gods Way"	60.00	80.00	65.00
☐ **Plate**, says "We mourn our loss"	65.00	85.00	67.50
☐ **Plate**, star center	40.00	50.00	42.50
☐ **Relish Dish**, two compartments	20.00	30.00	22.50
☐ **Sauce**, flat	10.00	15.00	11.50
☐ **Sauce**, footed	14.00	16.00	14.50
☐ **Spooner**	30.00	40.00	32.50
☐ **Sugar**	20.00	30.00	22.50
☐ **Sugar**, with cover	50.00	60.00	62.00
☐ **Tumbler**	30.00	40.00	32.50
☐ **Water Pitcher**	60.00	72.00	63.00

GIANT BULL'S EYE

A band of large bull's eyes with indented centers takes up most of the waist on these massive pieces. The stem and base are fluted.

☐ **Creamer**	65.00	75.00	67.50
☐ **Goblet**	110.00	140.00	115.00

GOTHIC
McKee and Bros.

Pattern resembles stained glass window design. Thumbprint in center enclosed by large loop. Diagonal lines run from thumbprint to edge of loop. Deep prism line around bottom half of pattern.

☐ **Bowl**, diameter 8″	55.00	65.00	52.00
☐ **Butter Dish**	55.00	70.00	60.00
☐ **Cake Stand**	55.00	65.00	50.00
☐ **Castor Bottle**	20.00	30.00	21.00
☐ **Champagne**	60.00	70.00	62.00
☐ **Compote**, covered, diameter 8″	115.00	130.00	120.00
☐ **Compote**, open, footed, diameter 7″	60.00	70.00	62.00

	Current Price Range		Prior Year Average
☐ **Egg Cup**	30.00	40.00	32.00
☐ **Goblet**	55.00	67.00	58.00
☐ **Pitcher**	75.00	85.00	67.00
☐ **Plate**	45.00	55.00	40.00
☐ **Salt,** footed	45.00	55.00	40.00
☐ **Sauce,** flat	23.00	33.00	20.00
☐ **Spoon Holder**	40.00	50.00	42.00
☐ **Sugar Bowl,** covered	85.00	95.00	80.00

GRAPE BAND

Here is another pattern with contrast as the central motif. The glass background is clear and smooth while the grape vine and leaves that crisscross around the middle are lightly stippled and are in high relief. Beadwork bands frame the vine on the bottom above the scalloped pedestal. The rims on many bowls and vases are pulled out and scalloped.

	Current Price Range		Prior Year Average
☐ **Butter,** covered	42.00	57.00	48.00
☐ **Compote,** covered, high	40.00	45.00	35.00
☐ **Compote,** covered, low	25.00	30.00	20.00
☐ **Compote,** open	30.00	35.00	25.00
☐ **Creamer**	30.00	35.00	25.00
☐ **Egg Cup**	20.00	25.00	15.00
☐ **Goblet**	20.00	26.00	16.00
☐ **Honey**	10.00	15.00	8.00
☐ **Pitcher**	55.00	63.00	50.00
☐ **Relish**	15.00	20.00	12.00
☐ **Salt,** footed	15.00	20.00	12.00
☐ **Sauce,** flat	10.00	15.00	8.00

Grape Band

	Current Price Range		Prior Year Average
☐ **Spoon Holder**	25.00	30.00	20.00
☐ **Wine**	20.00	25.00	15.00

HAIRPIN
Boston & Sandwich

Extremely long oval design, plain band at top.

☐ **Celery**	35.00	45.00	37.00
☐ **Champagne**	55.00	65.00	50.00
☐ **Compote**, covered	80.00	90.00	76.00
☐ **Compote**, open	30.00	40.00	26.00
☐ **Creamer**	75.00	85.00	71.00
☐ **Decanter**	42.00	52.00	37.00
☐ **Egg Cup**	30.00	38.00	27.00
☐ **Goblet**	40.00	50.00	36.00
☐ **Pitcher**, handled	130.00	140.00	125.00
☐ **Salt**, footed	23.00	30.00	20.00
☐ **Sauce**, flat	14.00	18.00	12.00
☐ **Sugar Bowl**, covered	60.00	70.00	55.00
☐ **Sugar Bowl**, open	40.00	50.00	36.00
☐ **Spooner**	35.00	45.00	30.00

HARP
Bryce Bros.

Each fluted panel contains an ornate lyre harp in high relief. The shape of most of the pieces is very classical and geometric, following the antiquity theme presented by the harp. The finish is clear, the glass is heavy.

☐ **Butter Dish**, covered, low foot	130.00	140.00	125.00
☐ **Compote**, covered	180.00	190.00	175.00

Hairpin

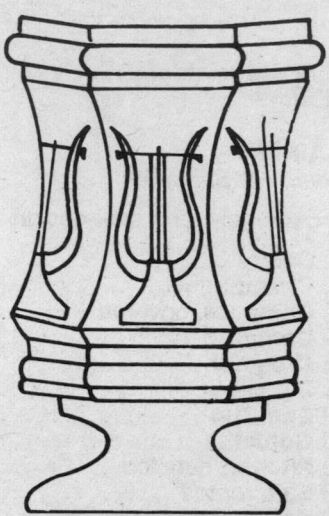

Harp

	Current Price Range		Prior Year Average
☐ **Goblet,** flared sides, rare	360.00	370.00	363.00
☐ **Goblet,** straight sides, rare	260.00	270.00	250.00
☐ **Lamp,** handled, small, double wick ..	160.00	170.00	155.00
☐ **Lamp,** large	130.00	140.00	133.00
☐ **Spill Holder**	50.00	60.00	48.00
☐ **Spoon Holder**	60.00	70.00	55.00

Horn of Plenty

HORN OF PLENTY

Alternating diagonal panels of squares and inverted thumbprints. Plain band around top.

	Current Price Range		Prior Year Average
☐ **Butter Dish,** covered, diameter 6" ...	115.00	120.00	110.00
☐ **Butter Dish,** shape of acorn	135.00	145.00	130.00
☐ **Butter Dish,** Washington's head, rare, round	450.00	475.00	440.00
☐ **Cake Stand,** rare	370.00	400.00	360.00
☐ **Celery**	170.00	180.00	172.00
☐ **Champagne**	155.00	165.00	150.00
☐ **Compote,** open	70.00	75.00	72.00
☐ **Compote,** oval, scalloped edge	150.00	180.00	155.00
☐ **Creamer,** large, handled	150.00	160.00	145.00
☐ **Creamer,** regular	210.00	220.00	205.00
☐ **Egg Cup**	55.00	65.00	53.00
☐ **Flat Bowl,** diameter 8½"	105.00	115.00	98.00
☐ **Goblet**	75.00	85.00	70.00
☐ **Honey Dish,** covered, rectangular ...	550.00	575.00	525.00
☐ **Lamp,** all glass, large	175.00	183.00	170.00
☐ **Lamp,** marble base	105.00	115.00	100.00
☐ **Mug,** small, handled	165.00	175.00	160.00
☐ **Plate,** diameter 6"	48.00	58.00	45.00
☐ **Round Bowl**	80.00	90.00	75.00
☐ **Sauce Dish,** diameter 3½"	10.00	15.00	8.00
☐ **Sauce Dish,** diameter 4¼"	20.00	25.00	18.00
☐ **Sauce Dish,** diameter 5"	50.00	55.00	48.00
☐ **Sauce Bottle**	185.00	195.00	180.00
☐ **Water Pitcher**	310.00	320.00	305.00
☐ **Whiskey Glass**	58.00	68.00	55.00
☐ **Wine**	120.00	130.00	122.00

HORSESHOE

This pattern consists of an upper band of interconnected horseshoes with beaded feet. The band just below the rim is a series of small knobs corresponding with the top of the arches on the horseshoes. The body has a diagonally placed rectangle made up of foliage and beadwork. Ivy sprigs run around the pieces.

☐ **Bowl,** oval	40.00	60.00	45.00
☐ **Bowl,** with cover, oval	130.00	140.00	135.00
☐ **Bread Tray,** horseshoe handles	40.00	50.00	42.50
☐ **Butter,** with cover	70.00	90.00	72.50
☐ **Cake Stand,** diameter 7½"	40.00	50.00	42.50
☐ **Cake Stand,** diameter 8½"	45.00	55.00	42.50
☐ **Cake Stand,** diameter 9½"	50.00	60.00	55.00
☐ **Celery**	50.00	60.00	55.00
☐ **Cheese Dish,** with cover	250.00	290.00	260.00
☐ **Compote,** high	40.00	60.00	42.50

	Current Price Range		Prior Year Average
☐ **Compote,** high, with cover	60.00	80.00	62.50
☐ **Creamer**	50.00	60.00	55.00
☐ **Finger Bowl**	25.00	35.00	27.50
☐ **Goblet,** knob stem	40.00	50.00	42.50
☐ **Goblet,** straight stem	30.00	40.00	35.00
☐ **Jam Jar**	20.00	30.00	22.50
☐ **Jam Jar,** with cover	30.00	40.00	35.00
☐ **Plate,** diameter 7″	37.50	45.00	40.00
☐ **Plate,** diameter 8″	45.00	50.00	47.50
☐ **Plate,** diameter 10″	50.00	60.00	52.50
☐ **Relish Dish,** three compartments ...	15.00	20.00	16.00
☐ **Salt Shaker,** horseshoe shape	60.00	80.00	62.50
☐ **Sauce,** flat	30.00	40.00	32.50
☐ **Sauce,** footed	18.00	25.00	19.50
☐ **Spooner**	30.00	40.00	32.50
☐ **Sugar**	25.00	30.00	27.50
☐ **Sugar,** with cover	55.00	65.00	57.50
☐ **Waste Bowl**	45.00	65.00	47.50
☐ **Water Pitcher**	80.00	95.00	85.00
☐ **Wine Goblet**	160.00	180.00	165.00

HUBER

This is a ribbed pattern with the wide, long panels reaching all the way to the straight rims. The design is voluptuous and deeply molded. The emphasis here is on the texture rather than on decoration and the effect is simple but elegant.

☐ **Bowl,** covered, diameter 6″	25.00	30.00	23.00
☐ **Bowl,** covered, diameter 7″	35.00	43.00	31.00

Huber

	Current Price Range		Prior Year Average
☐ **Celery**	35.00	43.00	33.00
☐ **Compote**, covered, diameter 8"	70.00	78.00	66.00
☐ **Compote**, covered, diameter 10"	65.00	70.00	62.00
☐ **Decanter**, stoppered, pint	55.00	65.00	50.00
☐ **Decanter**, stoppered, quart	65.00	73.00	62.00
☐ **Egg Cup**, handled	40.00	46.00	38.00
☐ **Egg Cup**, regular	25.00	32.00	24.00
☐ **Goblet**, small	32.00	38.00	30.00
☐ **Goblet**, large	40.00	50.00	38.00
☐ **Jelly Glass**	20.00	30.00	17.00
☐ **Jug**, three pints	28.00	34.00	25.00
☐ **Jug**, quart	32.00	38.00	30.00
☐ **Mug**	30.00	40.00	26.00
☐ **Pitcher**	55.00	65.00	52.00
☐ **Salt**, footed	25.00	35.00	20.00
☐ **Salt**, small	20.00	30.00	17.00
☐ **Sauce**, flat	15.00	20.00	10.00
☐ **Spoon Holder**	25.00	35.00	23.00
☐ **Sugar Bowl**, covered	50.00	58.00	48.00
☐ **Sugar Bowl**, open	30.00	40.00	27.00
☐ **Tumbler**, water	20.00	28.00	18.00
☐ **Wine**	25.00	35.00	22.00

HUMMINGBIRD

Bird is center of design with flowers and leaves surrounding it. Deep prism cuts at base of bowl.

Bowl

☐ clear	22.00	28.00	17.00

Hummingbird

	Current Price Range		Prior Year Average
☐ canary	31.00	36.00	27.00
☐ amber	38.00	43.00	33.00
☐ blue	38.00	43.00	33.00
Butter, covered			
☐ clear	47.00	54.00	43.00
☐ canary	56.00	63.00	52.00
☐ amber	78.00	84.00	72.00
☐ blue	78.00	84.00	72.00
Celery			
☐ clear	45.00	50.00	40.00
☐ canary	52.00	57.00	48.00
☐ amber	63.00	68.00	58.00
☐ blue	63.00	68.00	58.00
Compote			
☐ clear	50.00	57.00	45.00
☐ canary	70.00	75.00	65.00
☐ amber	78.00	85.00	72.00
☐ blue	78.00	85.00	72.00
Creamer, footed			
☐ clear	30.00	35.00	25.00
☐ canary	42.00	47.00	36.00
☐ amber	55.00	60.00	50.00
☐ blue	55.00	60.00	50.00
Goblet			
☐ clear	33.00	38.00	28.00
☐ canary	45.00	50.00	40.00
☐ amber	52.00	58.00	46.00
☐ blue	52.00	58.00	46.00
Pitcher, water, height 8″			
☐ clear	45.00	50.00	40.00
☐ canary	52.00	60.00	46.00
☐ amber	57.00	65.00	53.00
☐ blue	57.00	65.00	53.00
Sauce, flat			
☐ clear	13.00	18.00	10.00
☐ canary	20.00	25.00	15.00
☐ amber	24.00	29.00	20.00
☐ blue	24.00	29.00	20.00
Sauce, footed			
☐ clear	17.00	24.00	13.00
☐ canary	26.00	35.00	21.00
☐ amber	30.00	36.00	25.00
☐ blue	30.00	36.00	25.00
Spoon Holder			
☐ clear	32.00	38.00	27.00
☐ canary	46.00	52.00	41.00
☐ amber	55.00	60.00	50.00
☐ blue	55.00	60.00	50.00

	Current Price Range		Prior Year Average
Sugar, covered			
☐ clear	50.00	55.00	45.00
☐ canary	64.00	68.00	60.00
☐ amber	70.00	75.00	65.00
☐ blue	70.00	75.00	65.00
Tray			
☐ clear	55.00	60.00	50.00
☐ canary	75.00	80.00	70.00
☐ amber	84.00	88.00	80.00
☐ blue	84.00	88.00	80.00
Tumbler			
☐ clear	30.00	35.00	25.00
☐ canary	45.00	50.00	40.00
☐ amber	52.00	58.00	48.00
☐ blue	52.00	58.00	48.00
Wine			
☐ clear	32.00	38.00	27.00
☐ canary	45.00	50.00	40.00
☐ amber	53.00	58.00	48.00
☐ blue	53.00	58.00	48.00

HUNDRED LEAVED ROSE

Single rose with stem surrounded by leaves. Next to rose pattern is fishbone design which runs from base to top of piece.

☐ **Bowl**	20.00	18.00	17.00
☐ **Butter,** covered	35.00	45.00	30.00
☐ **Creamer**	35.00	42.00	31.00
☐ **Pitcher**	50.00	56.00	46.00

Hundred Leaved Rose

	Current Price Range		Prior Year Average
☐ **Sauce,** flat	20.00	23.00	18.00
☐ **Spoon Holder**	25.00	30.00	23.00
☐ **Sugar Bowl,** covered	52.00	62.00	48.00
☐ **Sugar Bowl,** open	40.00	50.00	35.00

ICICLE

Icicle design beginning at base of the body.

☐ **Bowl,** oval	25.00	32.00	21.00
☐ **Butter,** covered, footed	63.00	70.00	58.00
☐ **Butter Dish,** flat	50.00	58.00	46.00
☐ **Compote,** open, diameter 8″	40.00	·48.00	36.00
☐ **Creamer**	42.00	50.00	38.00
☐ **Goblet**	40.00	50.00	35.00
☐ **Lamp**	58.00	68.00	52.00
☐ **Pitcher,** water	60.00	70.00	55.00
☐ **Relish Dish,** oval	25.00	30.00	20.00
☐ **Salt,** footed	28.00	35.00	24.00
☐ **Sauce,** flat	15.00	18.00	13.00
☐ **Spoon Holder**	40.00	50.00	36.00
☐ **Sugar Bowl,** covered	53.00	60.00	48.00
☐ **Sugar Bowl,** open	22.00	28.00	18.00

INVERTED FERN

Alternating fern and inverted fern design with ribbing. Small plain band at top.

☐ **Compote,** open	60.00	68.00	57.00
☐ **Creamer,** handled	90.00	100.00	92.00

Icicle

Inverted Fern

	Current Price Range		Prior Year Average
☐ **Egg Cup**	25.00	35.00	28.00
☐ **Pitcher**	210.00	220.00	200.00
☐ **Salt,** footed	28.00	32.00	28.00
☐ **Sauce,** flat	10.00	15.00	10.00
☐ **Spoon Holder**	28.00	34.00	25.00
☐ **Sugar Bowl,** covered	55.00	65.00	51.00
☐ **Sugar Bowl,** open	30.00	38.00	27.00
☐ **Wine**	25.00	35.00	28.00

Ivy-in-Snow

IVY-IN-SNOW
Cooperative Flint

Frosted band overlaid with ivy leaves covering most of the piece. Wide plain band across top.

	Current Price Range		Prior Year Average
☐ **Bowl,** diameter 8″	30.00	35.00	25.00
☐ **Butter,** covered	60.00	65.00	55.00
☐ **Cake Stand,** large	55.00	60.00	50.00
☐ **Cake Stand,** small	40.00	47.00	35.00
☐ **Celery**	55.00	60.00	50.00
☐ **Compote,** covered, small	35.00	40.00	30.00
☐ **Compote,** covered, medium	55.00	60.00	50.00
☐ **Compote,** covered, large	70.00	80.00	65.00
☐ **Creamer**	25.00	30.00	20.00
☐ **Goblet**	30.00	37.00	25.00
☐ **Jar,** covered	30.00	35.00	25.00
☐ **Pitcher**	62.00	68.00	55.00
☐ **Plate,** diameter 6″	25.00	30.00	20.00
☐ **Plate,** diameter 8″	30.00	40.00	25.00
☐ **Plate,** diameter 10″	35.00	45.00	30.00
☐ **Relish**	15.00	20.00	12.00
☐ **Sauce,** flat	12.00	15.00	10.00
☐ **Sauce,** diameter 6″	15.00	21.00	13.00
☐ **Spoon Holder**	30.00	35.00	25.00
☐ **Sugar,** covered	45.00	52.00	40.00
☐ **Sugar,** open	30.00	35.00	25.00
☐ **Tumbler**	40.00	45.00	35.00
☐ **Wine**	30.00	35.00	25.00

JACOB'S LADDER
Bryce Brothers

Reminiscent of cut glass, this pattern is sharply molded in high relief. Diamond point panels alternate with horizontal flutes under a scalloped rim. This pattern is very popular and desirable to collectors.

Bowl			
☐ yellow	65.00	75.00	67.50
☐ amber	65.00	75.00	67.50
☐ clear	30.00	40.00	35.00
Bowl, footed			
☐ yellow	75.00	85.00	80.00
☐ amber	75.00	85.00	80.00
☐ clear	35.00	45.00	37.50
Butter			
☐ yellow	150.00	200.00	175.00
☐ amber	150.00	200.00	175.00
☐ clear	80.00	90.00	85.00
Cake Stand			
☐ yellow	70.00	80.00	75.00

	Current Price Range		Prior Year Average
☐ amber	70.00	80.00	75.00
☐ clear	35.00	45.00	37.50
Celery			
☐ yellow	70.00	80.00	75.00
☐ amber	70.00	80.00	75.00
☐ clear	35.00	45.00	37.50
Compote, high			
☐ yellow	90.00	110.00	100.00
☐ amber	90.00	110.00	100.00
☐ clear	45.00	55.00	47.50
Compote, low			
☐ yellow	40.00	50.00	45.00
☐ amber	40.00	50.00	45.00
☐ clear	25.00	35.00	27.50
Creamer			
☐ yellow	80.00	90.00	85.00
☐ amber	80.00	90.00	85.00
☐ clear	40.00	50.00	45.50
Goblet			
☐ yellow	70.00	80.00	75.00
☐ amber	70.00	80.00	75.00
☐ clear	35.00	45.00	37.50
Honey Jar, with cover			
☐ yellow	120.00	130.00	125.00
☐ amber	120.00	130.00	125.00
☐ clear	60.00	70.00	65.00
Jam Jar			
☐ yellow	140.00	180.00	145.00
☐ amber	140.00	180.00	145.00
☐ clear	70.00	80.00	75.00
Pickle Dish			
☐ yellow	50.00	60.00	52.50
☐ amber	50.00	60.00	52.50
☐ clear	25.00	35.00	27.50
Plate			
☐ yellow	60.00	80.00	62.50
☐ amber	60.00	80.00	62.50
☐ clear	30.00	40.00	32.50
Platter			
☐ yellow	40.00	60.00	42.50
☐ amber	40.00	60.00	42.50
☐ clear	20.00	30.00	22.50
Platter, round			
☐ yellow	60.00	80.00	62.50
☐ amber	60.00	80.00	62.50
☐ clear	30.00	40.00	35.00
Relish Bowl			
☐ yellow	60.00	80.00	62.50

	Current Price Range		Prior Year Average
☐ amber	60.00	80.00	62.50
☐ clear	30.00	40.00	35.00
Sauce, flat			
☐ yellow	20.00	30.00	25.00
☐ amber	20.00	30.00	25.00
☐ clear	10.00	15.00	12.00
Sauce, footed			
☐ yellow	45.00	55.00	47.50
☐ amber	45.00	55.00	47.50
☐ clear	20.00	25.00	22.50
Spooner			
☐ yellow	60.00	70.00	65.00
☐ amber	60.00	70.00	65.00
☐ clear	30.00	40.00	35.00
Sugar, with cover			
☐ yellow	70.00	80.00	75.00
☐ amber	70.00	80.00	75.00
☐ clear	35.00	45.00	37.50
Syrup Pitcher			
☐ yellow	180.00	200.00	190.00
☐ amber	180.00	200.00	190.00
☐ clear	90.00	110.00	95.00
Tumbler			
☐ yellow	120.00	140.00	130.00
☐ amber	120.00	140.00	130.00
☐ clear	60.00	70.00	62.50
Water Pitcher			
☐ yellow	250.00	300.00	275.00
☐ amber	250.00	300.00	275.00
☐ clear	125.00	135.00	127.50
Wine Glass			
☐ yellow	70.00	90.00	75.00
☐ amber	70.00	90.00	75.00
☐ clear	35.00	45.00	37.50

JOB'S TEARS

An overall pattern of elongated ovals, this design has the look of emeralds in line. The texture is voluptuous.

☐ **Berry Bowl,** footed	15.00	20.00	17.50
☐ **Bowl,** diameter 6″	20.00	30.00	22.50
☐ **Bowl,** diameter 8″	30.00	40.00	32.50
☐ **Bread Tray**	30.00	40.00	32.50
☐ **Butter**	30.00	40.00	32.50
☐ **Butter,** with cover	40.00	50.00	42.50
☐ **Cake Stand**	35.00	45.00	37.50
☐ **Celery**	20.00	30.00	22.50
☐ **Compote,** low	20.00	30.00	22.50
☐ **Cordial Glass**	20.00	30.00	22.50

	Current Price Range		Prior Year Average
☐ Creamer	30.00	40.00	32.50
☐ Dish	15.00	20.00	17.50
☐ Egg Cup	20.00	30.00	22.50
☐ Goblet	15.00	20.00	17.50
☐ Milk Pitcher	20.00	30.00	22.50
☐ Mug	20.00	30.00	22.50
☐ Plate	15.00	20.00	17.50
☐ Platter	25.00	35.00	27.50
☐ Relish Bowl	20.00	30.00	25.50
☐ Salt	25.00	35.00	27.50
☐ Sauce, flat	10.00	15.00	10.50
☐ Sauce, footed	12.00	15.00	12.50
☐ Spooner	20.00	30.00	25.00
☐ Toothpick	22.50	30.00	27.50
☐ Tumbler	30.00	40.00	32.50
☐ Water Pitcher	60.00	80.00	65.00
☐ Wine Glass	25.00	35.00	27.50

KNOB STEM SAWTOOTH

Sawtooth design with high knob on stem.

☐ Cake Stand, large	80.00	90.00	75.00
☐ Celery	45.00	53.00	43.00
☐ Creamer	45.00	53.00	42.00
☐ Egg Cup	35.00	40.00	30.00
☐ Goblet	45.00	55.00	40.00
☐ Jar, covered	40.00	50.00	35.00
☐ Pitcher	90.00	110.00	85.00
☐ Salt, covered	55.00	63.00	52.00
☐ Salt, open	20.00	30.00	17.00
☐ Sauce, flat	15.00	20.00	12.00
☐ Spoon Holder	25.00	35.00	20.00
☐ Sugar Bowl, covered	45.00	55.00	40.00
☐ Wine	35.00	45.00	30.00

LAMINATED PETALS

Layered petal-shaped design, clear band across top.

☐ Creamer	85.00	95.00	75.00
☐ Goblet	70.00	80.00	65.00
☐ Sugar Bowl, covered	90.00	110.00	80.00
☐ Wine Glass	75.00	90.00	65.00

LEAF AND FLOWER

Wandering stem with flowers and leaves. Edge of design is scalloped. Design usually found on lower half of piece. Upper half is plain.

Leaf and Flower

	Current Price Range		Prior Year Average
Bowl			
☐ clear	20.00	26.00	16.00
☐ frosted	25.00	30.00	20.00
☐ amber	33.00	39.00	29.00
☐ green	36.00	42.00	32.00
☐ red	43.00	48.00	38.00
Butter, covered			
☐ clear	35.00	42.00	30.00
☐ frosted	45.00	50.00	40.00
☐ amber	56.00	62.00	51.00
☐ green	58.00	64.00	53.00
☐ red	80.00	86.00	75.00
Castor Set			
☐ clear	45.00	50.00	40.00
☐ frosted	53.00	58.00	48.00
☐ amber	69.00	75.00	65.00
☐ green	73.00	78.00	68.00
☐ red	88.00	95.00	84.00
Creamer			
☐ clear	26.00	31.00	21.00
☐ frosted	32.00	37.00	28.00
☐ amber	43.00	48.00	38.00
☐ green	45.00	50.00	41.00
☐ red	65.00	73.00	61.00
Pitcher			
☐ clear	45.00	53.00	40.00
☐ frosted	55.00	60.00	50.00
☐ amber	59.00	65.00	53.00
☐ green	68.00	73.00	64.00
☐ red	88.00	94.00	83.00

	Current Price Range		Prior Year Average
Salt and Pepper Shakers, pair			
☐ clear	30.00	36.00	25.00
☐ frosted	36.00	43.00	31.00
☐ amber	48.00	55.00	44.00
☐ green	51.00	57.00	47.00
☐ red	60.00	65.00	55.00
Sauce, flat			
☐ clear	17.00	24.00	14.00
☐ frosted	23.00	28.00	20.00
☐ amber	30.00	36.00	25.00
☐ green	33.00	38.00	30.00
☐ red	36.00	40.00	31.00
Sugar, covered			
☐ clear	33.00	38.00	29.00
☐ frosted	37.00	43.00	34.00
☐ amber	52.00	56.00	48.00
☐ green	55.00	60.00	50.00
☐ red	65.00	70.00	60.00
Tray, long, flat			
☐ clear	24.00	29.00	20.00
☐ frosted	30.00	35.00	25.00
☐ amber	40.00	44.00	36.00
☐ green	43.00	48.00	39.00
☐ red	50.00	55.00	45.00
Tumbler			
☐ clear	15.00	20.00	12.00
☐ frosted	22.00	27.00	18.00
☐ amber	24.00	30.00	20.00
☐ green	27.00	32.00	23.00
☐ red	30.00	35.00	25.00

LEE

Teardrop shaped pattern, thumbprints band around top.

☐ **Celery Dish**	110.00	120.00	105.00
☐ **Champagne Glass**	140.00	148.00	135.00
☐ **Creamer**	130.00	140.00	125.00
☐ **Decanter**	75.00	90.00	75.00
☐ **Goblet**	135.00	145.00	130.00
☐ **Sugar Bowl,** covered	130.00	140.00	125.00
☐ **Tumbler**	100.00	110.00	96.00

LIBERTY BELL

The cracked Liberty Bell is the main motif on these pieces, with "1776–1876, Declaration of Independence" in block letters. The bell is well detailed with a series of fine ridges to represent the metal.

Liberty Bell

	Current Price Range		Prior Year Average
☐ **Butter,** with cover	130.00	145.00	133.00
☐ **Candy Dish,** bell cover	125.00	135.00	130.00
☐ **Compote**	60.00	80.00	65.00
☐ **Creamer**	110.00	115.00	112.50
☐ **Goblet**	55.00	65.00	57.50
☐ **Miniatures**	500.00	600.00	550.00
☐ **Nappy,** tab handle	30.00	40.00	35.00
☐ **Platter,** milk glass	300.00	330.00	310.00
☐ **Platter,** oval	125.00	140.00	130.00
☐ **Platter,** round	130.00	140.00	135.00
☐ **Relish,** three compartments	50.00	60.00	55.00
☐ **Salt**	25.00	35.00	27.50
☐ **Salt Shaker,** bell shape	110.00	125.00	115.00
☐ **Spooner**	115.00	125.00	117.50
☐ **Sauce,** flat	25.00	35.00	27.50
☐ **Sauce,** footed	30.00	40.00	35.00
☐ **Sugar**	60.00	80.00	65.00
☐ **Sugar,** with cover	110.00	125.00	115.00
☐ **Water Pitcher**	750.00	850.00	775.00

LIGHTNING

This is an interesting geometrical pattern comprised of fluting, heavy cuttings, and bands. The mold is deep, the glass is heavy.

☐ **Berry Bowl**	15.00	20.00	17.50
☐ **Bowl,** oval	20.00	30.00	25.00
☐ **Bowl,** round	22.00	30.00	26.00
☐ **Butter**	40.00	50.00	42.50

	Current Price Range		Prior Year Average
☐ Celery	30.00	40.00	32.50
☐ Compote, high, with cover	45.00	55.00	47.50
☐ Compote, low	20.00	30.00	22.50
☐ Cordial Glass	15.00	20.00	17.50
☐ Creamer	42.00	44.00	43.50
☐ Goblet	30.00	40.00	35.00
☐ Spooner	35.00	45.00	37.50
☐ Water Pitcher	60.00	80.00	62.50

LILY-OF-THE-VALLEY

Large flower design with wide plain band at top.

	Current Price Range		Prior Year Average
☐ Butter, footed, three-legged	58.00	64.00	54.00
☐ Cake Stand	59.00	66.00	55.00
☐ Celery	30.00	37.00	26.00
☐ Compote, covered	80.00	90.00	75.00
☐ Compote, open	40.00	45.00	35.00
☐ Creamer, handled	63.00	70.00	58.00
☐ Creamer, handled, three legged	65.00	70.00	60.00
☐ Cruet, stoppered	57.00	64.00	53.00
☐ Dish, oval	26.00	35.00	21.00
☐ Egg Cup	43.00	48.00	40.00
☐ Goblet	42.00	48.00	38.00
☐ Pitcher, milk, scarce	98.00	105.00	92.00
☐ Pitcher, water	92.00	98.00	88.00
☐ Relish, oval	87.00	94.00	83.00
☐ Salt, covered, three-legged	190.00	205.00	181.00
☐ Sauce, flat	20.00	26.00	15.00
☐ Spoon Holder	35.00	40.00	30.00
☐ Sugar, covered, three-legged	70.00	78.00	65.00

Lily-of-the-Valley

	Current Price Range		Prior Year Average
☐ **Sugar,** covered, no legs	50.00	56.00	45.00
☐ **Sugar,** open	40.00	46.00	36.00
☐ **Vegetable,** oval	28.00	35.00	25.00
☐ **Wine,** scarce	53.00	60.00	48.00

LINCOLN DRAPE
Boston & Sandwich

This ornate design is reminiscent of the heavy folds on a velvet curtain, pulled back and held with jewelled medallions. This decoration loops around the rims on these pieces, with fine pleating below to the base. The central medallion is a series of nested six point stars. The glass is clear and heavily molded.

☐ **Butter Dish**	105.00	115.00	100.00
☐ **Celery**	85.00	95.00	83.00
☐ **Compote,** covered	155.00	165.00	150.00
☐ **Compote,** open	70.00	80.00	73.00
☐ **Decanter**	80.00	90.00	83.00
☐ **Egg Cup**	50.00	60.00	45.00
☐ **Lamp,** marble base	130.00	140.00	126.00
☐ **Lamp,** miniature	50.00	60.00	48.00
☐ **Salt,** footed	40.00	50.00	38.00
☐ **Spoon Holder**	60.00	70.00	55.00

Lincoln Drape

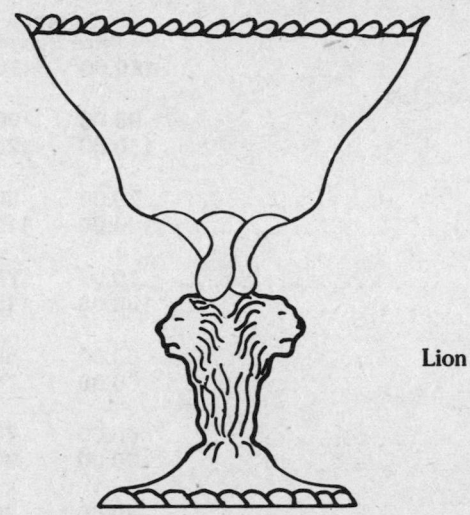

Lion

LION

This pattern is a favorite with collectors because of its great design and its availability in a wide variety of pieces. The wildly maned lion perches either on the finial of covered pieces or on the middle band in high relief. The decorative band is heavily stippled giving an opaque look which contrasts with the smoothness of the rest of the piece. The lion is pictured crouching or sitting and occasionally on smaller pieces, the head alone appears.

	Current Price Range		Prior Year Average
Bread Plate			
☐ clear	35.00	40.00	30.00
☐ frosted	60.00	65.00	53.00
Butter, covered			
☐ clear	100.00	110.00	90.00
☐ frosted	140.00	150.00	130.00
Celery			
☐ clear	80.00	90.00	70.00
☐ frosted	110.00	120.00	100.00
Champagne			
☐ clear	105.00	115.00	100.00
☐ frosted	140.00	150.00	130.00
Cheese, covered, scarce			
☐ clear	300.00	320.00	290.00
☐ frosted	390.00	410.00	380.00
Cologne Bottle, scarce			
☐ clear	300.00	400.00	250.00
☐ frosted	400.00	480.00	350.00
Compote, covered, high			
☐ clear	130.00	140.00	120.00

	Current Price Range		Prior Year Average
☐ frosted	160.00	170.00	150.00
Compote, covered, low			
☐ clear	90.00	100.00	80.00
☐ frosted	110.00	125.00	100.00
Compote, open			
☐ clear	70.00	80.00	60.00
☐ frosted	100.00	110.00	90.00
Creamer			
☐ clear	70.00	78.00	65.00
☐ frosted	100.00	110.00	90.00
Egg Cup			
☐ clear	50.00	60.00	40.00
☐ frosted	60.00	70.00	50.00
Goblet			
☐ clear	60.00	70.00	50.00
☐ frosted	70.00	80.00	60.00
Jar, covered			
☐ clear	80.00	90.00	72.00
☐ frosted	105.00	110.00	95.00
Lamp, scarce			
☐ clear	500.00	600.00	400.00
☐ frosted	750.00	850.00	650.00
Paperweight, lions reclining			
☐ clear	160.00	170.00	150.00
☐ frosted	200.00	215.00	190.00
Pitcher, milk, scarce			
☐ clear	420.00	550.00	400.00
☐ frosted	600.00	700.00	500.00
Pitcher, syrup, metal top			
☐ clear	200.00	250.00	150.00
☐ frosted	275.00	340.00	220.00
Pitcher, water			
☐ clear	180.00	210.00	170.00
☐ frosted	250.00	300.00	230.00
Relish, oval			
☐ clear	60.00	70.00	50.00
☐ frosted	85.00	95.00	75.00
Salt, footed			
☐ clear	155.00	160.00	150.00
☐ frosted	200.00	235.00	185.00
Sauce, footed, diameter 4"			
☐ clear	20.00	30.00	15.00
☐ frosted	40.00	50.00	30.00
Sauce, footed, diameter 5"			
☐ clear	25.00	35.00	20.00
☐ frosted	45.00	55.00	40.00
Spoon Holder			
☐ clear	55.00	65.00	48.00

	Current Price Range		Prior Year Average
☐ frosted	70.00	80.00	62.00
Sugar, covered			
☐ clear	90.00	100.00	80.00
☐ frosted	120.00	130.00	110.00
Sugar, open			
☐ clear	40.00	50.00	35.00
☐ frosted	55.00	65.00	50.00
Wine			
☐ clear	120.00	130.00	110.00
☐ frosted	160.00	168.00	155.00

LOBULAR BULL'S EYE

The petal-shaped bull's eyes are arranged in rows opposing each other. This deep molded design gives the heavy glass an interesting surface texture.

☐ **Goblet**	110.00	125.00	115.00

MAPLE LEAF
Gillinder & Sons

Large maple leaf design with scalloped edge across top of pieces.

	Current Price Range		Prior Year Average
Bowl			
☐ clear	26.00	31.00	22.00
☐ canary	35.00	40.00	30.00
☐ amber	40.00	45.00	35.00
☐ blue	40.00	45.00	35.00
Butter, covered			
☐ clear	70.00	75.00	65.00
☐ canary	90.00	100.00	85.00
☐ amber	95.00	105.00	90.00
☐ blue	95.00	105.00	90.00
Cake Stand			
☐ clear	45.00	50.00	40.00
☐ canary	55.00	60.00	50.00
☐ amber	60.00	65.00	55.00
☐ blue	60.00	65.00	55.00
Celery			
☐ clear	33.00	38.00	28.00
☐ canary	45.00	50.00	40.00
☐ amber	48.00	54.00	44.00
☐ blue	48.00	54.00	44.00
Compote, covered			
☐ clear	80.00	85.00	75.00
☐ canary	100.00	108.00	95.00
☐ amber	105.00	110.00	100.00
☐ blue	105.00	110.00	100.00

	Current Price Range		Prior Year Average
Compote, open, footed			
☐ clear	40.00	45.00	35.00
☐ canary	53.00	58.00	48.00
☐ amber	58.00	63.00	52.00
☐ blue	58.00	63.00	52.00
Creamer			
☐ clear	40.00	45.00	36.00
☐ canary	53.00	57.00	48.00
☐ amber	58.00	63.00	53.00
☐ blue	58.00	63.00	53.00
Goblet			
☐ clear	40.00	45.00	36.00
☐ canary	56.00	60.00	51.00
☐ amber	60.00	65.00	55.00
☐ blue	60.00	65.00	55.00
Pitcher, large			
☐ clear	55.00	63.00	50.00
☐ canary	73.00	78.00	68.00
☐ amber	77.00	81.00	71.00
☐ blue	77.00	81.00	71.00
Pitcher, small			
☐ clear	40.00	46.00	36.00
☐ canary	50.00	56.00	46.00
☐ amber	58.00	64.00	52.00
☐ blue	58.00	64.00	52.00
Platter, diameter 10½″			
☐ clear	35.00	40.00	30.00
☐ canary	48.00	55.00	43.00
☐ amber	53.00	58.00	48.00
☐ blue	53.00	58.00	48.00
Relish			
☐ clear	15.00	20.00	12.00
☐ canary	18.00	24.00	15.00
☐ amber	23.00	28.00	20.00
☐ blue	23.00	28.00	20.00
Sauce, footed			
☐ clear	13.00	17.00	10.00
☐ canary	18.00	24.00	14.00
☐ amber	20.00	26.00	18.00
☐ blue	20.00	26.00	18.00
Spoon Holder			
☐ clear	22.00	27.00	18.00
☐ canary	30.00	36.00	25.00
☐ amber	35.00	40.00	30.00
☐ blue	35.00	40.00	30.00
Sugar, covered			
☐ clear	35.00	40.00	30.00
☐ canary	45.00	50.00	40.00

	Current Price Range		Prior Year Average
☐ amber	52.00	58.00	48.00
☐ blue	52.00	58.00	48.00
Tumbler			
☐ clear	22.00	28.00	18.00
☐ canary	30.00	35.00	25.00
☐ amber	38.00	44.00	33.00
☐ blue	38.00	44.00	33.00

MARSH PINK

Panel of flowers alternating with narrow plain panel. Design runs from base of bowl to top.

☐ **Bowl,** covered	40.00	45.00	35.00
☐ **Bowl,** open	30.00	35.00	25.00
☐ **Butter,** covered	40.00	50.00	42.00
☐ **Cake Stand,** small	18.00	28.00	20.00
☐ **Compote,** covered	43.00	48.00	38.00
☐ **Jam Jar,** covered	35.00	43.00	30.00
☐ **Pitcher**	45.00	50.00	40.00
☐ **Plate,** square	32.00	38.00	28.00
☐ **Salt and Pepper Shakers,** pair	33.00	39.00	28.00
☐ **Sauce,** flat	18.00	24.00	15.00
☐ **Spoon Holder**	16.00	25.00	18.00
☐ **Sugar,** covered	36.00	43.00	32.00
☐ **Sugar,** open	26.00	32.00	20.00

MASCOTTE

The pattern is large diamond point bands running on either side—one wide, one thin. The effect is almost that of cut glass with the deep mold-work.

☐ **Butter**	60.00	70.00	65.00
☐ **Celery**	20.00	30.00	24.00
☐ **Compote,** high	50.00	60.00	55.00
☐ **Compote,** low	30.00	40.00	35.00
☐ **Dish**	20.00	30.00	25.00
☐ **Goblet**	40.00	50.00	42.50
☐ **Milk Pitcher**	50.00	60.00	55.00
☐ **Platter**	40.00	50.00	45.00
☐ **Sauce,** flat	10.00	15.00	12.50
☐ **Sauce,** footed	15.00	20.00	17.50
☐ **Spooner**	18.00	22.00	19.00
☐ **Water Pitcher**	60.00	80.00	65.00
☐ **Wine Glass**	20.00	30.00	25.00

Medallion

MEDALLION

An intricate, well-balanced pattern, Medallion was made in many pieces and colors. The central motif is a flowery medallion with scroll decoration and sawtooth filler. The center is a ridged star. The rest of the piece has oval bands of parallel ridges, creating a frame for the medallion.

	Current Price Range		Prior Year Average
Butter, with cover			
☐ green	55.00	70.00	57.50
☐ yellow	40.00	50.00	45.00
☐ amber	42.00	52.00	46.00
☐ blue	55.00	65.00	57.00
☐ vaseline	45.00	47.00	47.00
☐ clear	30.00	35.00	32.00
Castor Bottle			
☐ green	32.00	40.00	35.00
☐ yellow	17.00	22.00	19.00
☐ amber	17.00	22.00	19.00
☐ blue	32.00	36.00	34.00
☐ vaseline	22.00	30.00	24.00
☐ clear	12.00	17.00	15.00
Celery			
☐ green	45.00	55.00	47.00
☐ yellow	30.00	35.00	32.00
☐ amber	30.00	35.00	32.00
☐ blue	45.00	50.00	47.00
☐ vaseline	35.00	40.00	37.00
☐ clear	20.00	30.00	25.00
Compote, high, with cover			
☐ green	70.00	90.00	75.00
☐ yellow	47.00	52.00	50.00

	Current Price Range		Prior Year Average
☐ amber	47.00	52.00	50.00
☐ blue	70.00	90.00	75.00
☐ vaseline	52.00	65.00	56.00
☐ clear	42.00	45.00	46.00
Creamer			
☐ green	47.00	50.00	48.00
☐ yellow	35.00	40.00	37.00
☐ amber	35.00	40.00	37.00
☐ blue	47.00	52.00	50.00
☐ vaseline	35.00	40.00	37.00
☐ clear	27.00	35.00	30.00
Egg Cup			
☐ green	40.00	50.00	42.00
☐ yellow	30.00	40.00	35.00
☐ amber	30.00	40.00	35.00
☐ blue	40.00	50.00	42.00
☐ vaseline	35.00	40.00	37.00
☐ clear	20.00	25.00	22.00
Goblet			
☐ green	47.00	52.00	50.00
☐ yellow	30.00	40.00	32.00
☐ amber	30.00	40.00	32.00
☐ blue	47.00	52.00	50.00
☐ vaseline	35.00	45.00	37.00
☐ clear	20.00	30.00	25.00
Pickle			
☐ green	35.00	40.00	37.00
☐ yellow	25.00	30.00	27.00
☐ amber	25.00	30.00	27.00
☐ blue	35.00	40.00	37.00
☐ vaseline	30.00	40.00	32.00
☐ clear	20.00	25.00	22.00
Sauce, flat			
☐ green	25.00	30.00	27.00
☐ yellow	20.00	25.00	22.00
☐ amber	20.00	25.00	22.00
☐ blue	25.00	30.00	27.00
☐ vaseline	22.00	35.00	25.00
☐ clear	15.00	20.00	17.00
Sauce, footed			
☐ green	30.00	35.00	32.50
☐ yellow	25.00	30.00	27.00
☐ amber	25.00	30.00	26.00
☐ blue	30.00	35.00	31.00
☐ vaseline	30.00	35.00	31.00
☐ clear	15.00	20.00	17.00
Spooner			
☐ green	30.00	35.00	34.00

	Current Price Range		Prior Year Average
☐ yellow	25.00	30.00	27.00
☐ amber	25.00	30.00	27.00
☐ blue	30.00	35.00	32.00
☐ vaseline	27.00	32.00	30.00
☐ clear	15.00	20.00	17.00
Sugar, with cover			
☐ green	40.00	60.00	45.00
☐ yellow	25.00	45.00	27.00
☐ amber	25.00	45.00	27.00
☐ blue	40.00	50.00	45.00
☐ vaseline	30.00	40.00	35.00
☐ clear	20.00	30.00	25.00
Tumbler			
☐ green	40.00	50.00	45.00
☐ yellow	25.00	40.00	27.00
☐ amber	25.00	40.00	27.00
☐ blue	40.00	50.00	45.00
☐ vaseline	30.00	40.00	35.00
☐ clear	20.00	30.00	25.00
Water Pitcher			
☐ green	70.00	100.00	75.00
☐ amber	65.00	85.00	67.00
☐ blue	70.00	80.00	75.00
☐ vaseline	65.00	75.00	70.00
☐ clear	60.00	65.00	62.00
☐ yellow	65.00	70.00	67.00
Wine Glass			
☐ green	35.00	40.00	37.00
☐ amber	30.00	35.00	32.00
☐ blue	35.00	40.00	37.00
☐ vaseline	45.00	55.00	47.00
☐ clear	25.00	30.00	27.00
☐ yellow	35.00	40.00	37.00

MINERVA

The central figure of a nymph in a flowing gown is surrounded in cameo by shiny beadwork. The borders are also beaded with scalloped bands.

☐ **Butter,** with cover	58.00	70.00	62.00
☐ **Cake Plate,** diameter 12″	115.00	125.00	117.50
☐ **Compote,** high	85.00	110.00	95.00
☐ **Compote,** low	75.00	100.00	78.00
☐ **Compote,** with lid	70.00	75.00	72.50
☐ **Creamer**	45.00	57.00	48.00
☐ **Goblet,** small	75.00	85.00	75.50
☐ **Goblet,** large	90.00	100.00	95.00
☐ **Jam Jar,** with cover	85.00	95.00	87.50
☐ **Plate,** tab handled	65.00	75.00	67.50

Minerva

	Current Price Range		Prior Year Average
☐ **Platter,** oval	50.00	60.00	52.50
☐ **Pickle Dish,** oval, says "Love's Request is Pickles"	40.00	50.00	42.50
☐ **Relish Dish,** three compartment	35.00	45.00	37.50
☐ **Sauce,** flat	25.00	35.00	27.50
☐ **Sauce,** footed	30.00	35.00	32.50
☐ **Spooner**	40.00	50.00	42.50
☐ **Sugar**	75.00	85.00	77.50
☐ **Sugar,** with cover	80.00	90.00	82.00
☐ **Water Pitcher**	145.00	160.00	152.00

NAILHEAD

A wide band of heavy diamonds rims the waist, formed by heavy ridge-work. Each diamond has bead and teardrop decoration and they hover over a stippled background.

☐ **Butter**	55.00	65.00	47.50
☐ **Cake Stand**	40.00	50.00	42.50
☐ **Compote,** high	40.00	50.00	42.50
☐ **Compote,** low	30.00	40.00	32.50
☐ **Cordial Glass**	30.00	40.00	35.00
☐ **Creamer**	20.00	32.00	22.00
☐ **Goblet**	35.00	45.00	37.50
☐ **Plate**	20.00	30.00	22.00
☐ **Relish Bowl**	40.00	50.00	45.00
☐ **Salt**	40.00	50.00	42.50
☐ **Sauce,** flat	10.00	12.00	11.50
☐ **Sauce,** footed	15.00	20.00	17.50
☐ **Spooner**	30.00	40.00	35.00
☐ **Sugar,** with cover	35.00	45.00	37.50

	Current Price Range		Prior Year Average
☐ Tumbler	25.00	30.00	27.50
☐ Water Pitcher	60.00	80.00	65.00
☐ Wine Glass	20.00	30.00	25.50

NEW ENGLAND PINEAPPLE
Boston & Sandwich

This is an ornate pattern, with decoration covering most of the piece. The central focus is a stylized pineapple, elongated into a pointed oval with a teardropped shape medallion resolving the top. The pineapple motif is surrounded with swirled ridging that forms a tulip blossom. The moldwork is deep and sharp; the glass is heavy.

☐ **Castor Bottle**	30.00	40.00	25.00
☐ **Castor Set,** 4 bottles	320.00	350.00	310.00
☐ **Champagne Bottle**	110.00	120.00	105.00
☐ **Compote,** covered	120.00	130.00	115.00
☐ **Compote,** open	65.00	75.00	63.00
☐ **Decanter,** no stopper, pint	80.00	90.00	80.00
☐ **Decanter,** stopper, quart	110.00	120.00	105.00
☐ **Egg Cup**	40.00	50.00	36.00
☐ **Goblet**	45.00	55.00	40.00
☐ **Honey Dish**	20.00	30.00	22.00
☐ **Jug,** stopper	160.00	170.00	163.00
☐ **Mug,** handled	105.00	115.00	100.00
☐ **Plate,** diameter 6"	95.00	105.00	90.00
☐ **Salt,** footed	45.00	53.00	43.00
☐ **Sugar Bowl,** covered	90.00	100.00	85.00
☐ **Sugar Bowl,** open	45.00	55.00	40.00

New England Pineapple

	Current Price Range		Prior Year Average
☐ Spoon Holder	45.00	55.00	40.00
☐ Tumbler	80.00	90.00	75.00
☐ Whiskey Tumbler, handled	110.00	120.00	108.00
☐ Wine Glass	80.00	90.00	75.00

OAKEN BUCKET

The illusion of bark is created by rippling ridges covering the pieces. Heavy bands of clear glass simulate the brass bands on a bucket, completing the decoration on these novelties. Full size and miniature pieces were made in many colors.

Butter
☐ yellow	45.00	55.00	47.50
☐ amber	40.00	50.00	42.50
☐ blue	45.00	55.00	47.50
☐ amethyst	35.00	45.00	37.50
☐ clear	25.00	35.00	27.50

Creamer
☐ yellow	25.00	35.00	27.50
☐ amber	30.00	40.00	35.50
☐ blue	25.00	35.00	27.50
☐ amethyst	35.00	45.00	47.50
☐ clear	25.00	35.00	27.50

Toothpick
☐ yellow	10.00	15.00	12.50
☐ amber	15.00	20.00	17.50
☐ blue	10.00	15.00	12.50
☐ amethyst	17.00	22.00	18.00
☐ clear	8.00	12.00	9.00

OPEN ROSE

This elegant pattern is a floral delight. The pieces are sparsely covered with roses in full bloom perched on branches and leaves. The background is clear; the design is stippled except for the rose which rises in high relief.

☐ **Butter,** covered	60.00	68.00	56.00
☐ **Compote,** covered	68.00	75.00	65.00
☐ **Compote,** open	35.00	44.00	31.00
☐ **Creamer**	43.00	50.00	40.00
☐ **Egg Cup**	23.00	27.00	20.00
☐ **Goblet**	28.00	33.00	25.00
☐ **Pitcher,** handled	105.00	115.00	100.00
☐ **Relish,** oval	19.00	25.00	16.00
☐ **Saucer,** flat, diameter 4″	12.00	16.00	10.00
☐ **Sugar,** covered	50.00	58.00	47.00
☐ **Sugar,** open	20.00	26.00	18.00
☐ **Tumbler**	33.00	38.00	30.00
☐ **Vegetable Dish,** oval	24.00	30.00	20.00

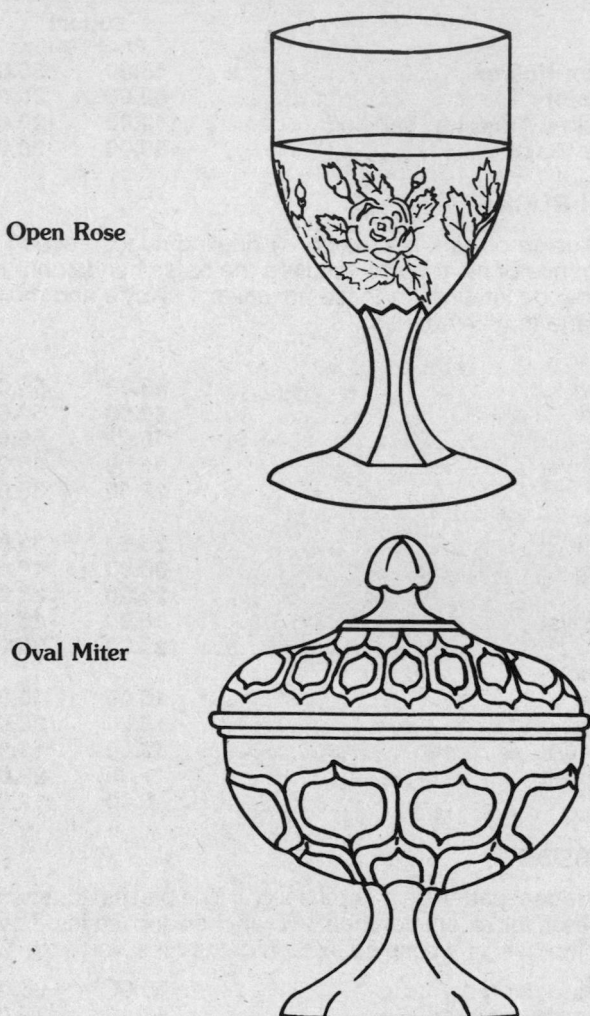

Open Rose

Oval Miter

OVAL MITER

This geometric pattern is a series of lemon shaped thumbprints, rising off the surface by deep moldwork. These bands repeat around the body of the piece until they resolve under the base. The effect is of cut glass with the deep mitre between each oval. The glass is heavy; the texture is excellent.

	Current Price Range		Prior Year Average
☐ **Bowl**	40.00	50.00	37.00
☐ **Butter Dish,** covered	80.00	90.00	77.00

	Current Price Range		Prior Year Average
☐ Compote, covered	60.00	70.00	57.00
☐ Compote, open, diameter 8″	40.00	50.00	38.00
☐ Goblet	45.00	53.00	47.00
☐ Saucer, flat	15.00	20.00	12.00
☐ Spooner	35.00	45.00	30.00
☐ Sugar Bowl, covered	60.00	70.00	55.00
☐ Sugar Bowl, open	55.00	65.00	50.00

PALMETTE

This overall pattern consists of a series of leaf shapes interconnected to form a wide band. The fillers alternate between geometrical sawtoothing and veinlike ridgework. The background is stippled.

☐ Butter, with cover	65.00	75.00	67.50
☐ Cake Stand	40.00	52.00	43.00
☐ Celery	35.00	45.00	37.50
☐ Compote, high	37.00	42.00	40.00
☐ Compote, low, with cover	55.00	65.00	57.50
☐ Creamer	60.00	70.00	65.00
☐ Goblet	30.00	40.00	35.00
☐ Salt	25.00	35.00	27.50
☐ Saucer, flat	15.00	20.00	17.50
☐ Saucer, footed	20.00	30.00	25.00
☐ Spooner	30.00	40.00	35.00
☐ Sugar, with cover	35.00	45.00	37.50

Palmette

Paneled Daisy

PANELED DAISY
Bryce Bros.

This is an elegant overall pattern consisting of long bands of trellised daisies, meandering up the side with foliage and vines. The panels are framed with scalloped rows divided by straight, smooth bands. The decoration is stippled which contrasts nicely with the smooth background.

	Current Price Range		Prior Year Average
☐ **Bowl,** oval	15.00	20.00	12.00
☐ **Bowl,** open, diameter 10½"	16.00	22.00	13.00
☐ **Bowl,** square	24.00	29.00	20.00
☐ **Butter,** covered, footed	43.00	48.00	38.00
☐ **Cake Stand,** height 8"	43.00	48.00	37.00
☐ **Cake Stand,** large	50.00	58.00	45.00
☐ **Celery**	42.00	50.00	34.00
☐ **Compote,** covered, short	41.00	48.00	36.00
☐ **Compote,** covered, high	58.00	68.00	52.00
☐ **Compote,** open, high	50.00	57.00	45.00
☐ **Creamer,** scarce	45.00	50.00	40.00
☐ **Goblet**	32.00	37.00	27.00
☐ **Mug,** large	33.00	39.00	30.00
☐ **Pickle,** flat	21.00	26.00	17.00
☐ **Pitcher,** syrup	55.00	60.00	50.00
☐ **Pitcher,** water	64.00	70.00	58.00
☐ **Plate,** diameter 7"	26.00	32.00	22.00
☐ **Plate,** square, diameter 9"	32.00	38.00	27.00
☐ **Relish Dish**	19.00	25.00	14.00
☐ **Salt and Pepper Shakers,** pair	41.00	48.00	36.00
☐ **Saucer,** flat	15.00	20.00	10.00
☐ **Saucer,** footed	20.00	26.00	15.00

	Current Price Range		Prior Year Average
☐ Spoon Holder	30.00	35.00	26.00
☐ Sugar Bowl, covered	45.00	52.00	38.00
☐ Sugar Shaker	40.00	47.00	35.00
☐ Syrup	26.00	32.00	22.00
☐ Tray	50.00	56.00	45.00
☐ Tumbler	28.00	33.00	24.00
☐ Waste Bowl	24.00	30.00	20.00

PANELED FORGET-ME-NOT
Bryce Bros.

Panel of flowers and leaves alternate with plain panels and diamond panels. Serrated ribbing separates the panels.

☐ Bowl, covered	18.00	26.00	15.00
☐ Butter, covered	40.00	46.00	38.00
☐ Cake Plate	25.00	32.00	22.00
☐ Celery	50.00	56.00	46.00
☐ Compote, covered	56.00	64.00	53.00
☐ Compote, open	35.00	43.00	32.00
☐ Cordial	30.00	38.00	28.00
☐ Creamer	28.00	36.00	25.00
☐ Goblet	38.00	45.00	35.00
☐ Jar, covered	35.00	43.00	32.00
☐ Pitcher	43.00	50.00	40.00
☐ Platter	30.00	37.00	27.00
☐ Relish Dish, oval	15.00	22.00	12.00
☐ Sauce, flat	15.00	20.00	12.00
☐ Sauce, footed	20.00	26.00	16.00
☐ Sugar Bowl, covered	40.00	47.00	36.00

Paneled Forget-Me-Not

	Current Price Range		Prior Year Average
☐ **Spoon Holder**	30.00	36.00	26.00
☐ **Wine**	37.00	45.00	35.00

PANELED OVALS

A row of large ovals with diamond band across top of ovals. A wide plain band above the diamond strip.

☐ **Butter Dish,** covered	65.00	75.00	60.00
☐ **Compote,** covered	50.00	60.00	45.00
☐ **Compote,** open	25.00	35.00	20.00
☐ **Creamer**	45.00	55.00	40.00
☐ **Egg Cup**	30.00	40.00	28.00
☐ **Goblet**	40.00	50.00	38.00
☐ **Pitcher,** handled	50.00	60.00	45.00
☐ **Spooner**	45.00	55.00	42.00

PANELED THISTLE
J.B. Higbee Co.

Panels of flowers with deep prism cuts separating the panels. Top of design is scalloped. Some pieces have small outline of bee in the base. These pieces are worth 20% more.

☐ **Banana Stand**	60.00	68.00	55.00
☐ **Basket**	40.00	46.00	36.00
☐ **Berry Bowl,** footed	43.00	48.00	38.00
☐ **Butter,** covered	43.00	47.00	38.00
☐ **Cake Stand,** large	30.00	36.00	25.00
☐ **Cake Stand,** small	25.00	30.00	22.00

Paneled Thistle

	Current Price Range		Prior Year Average
☐ **Celery,** height 11"	27.00	33.00	24.00
☐ **Compote,** open	20.00	25.00	16.00
☐ **Cordial**	28.00	34.00	24.00
☐ **Cups,** sherbert	23.00	28.00	20.00
☐ **Creamer,** knob feet	30.00	37.00	26.00
☐ **Cruet,** stoppered	40.00	45.00	35.00
☐ **Egg Cup**	23.00	28.00	19.00
☐ **Goblet**	39.00	45.00	35.00
☐ **Honey,** covered	50.00	55.00	45.00
☐ **Honey,** oval	45.00	50.00	40.00
☐ **Honey,** round	46.00	50.00	42.00
☐ **Pitcher,** milk	43.00	48.00	38.00
☐ **Pitcher,** water	55.00	63.00	50.00
☐ **Plate,** diameter 7"	30.00	35.00	25.00
☐ **Plate,** diameter 8"	33.00	38.00	28.00
☐ **Plate,** diameter 9"	30.00	34.00	26.00
☐ **Plate,** diameter 10"	33.00	37.00	29.00
☐ **Punch Cup**	25.00	30.00	21.00
☐ **Relish Dish,** flat	26.00	31.00	21.00
☐ **Rose Bowl,** large	50.00	58.00	46.00
☐ **Salt**	15.00	19.00	12.00
☐ **Salt and Pepper Shakers,** pair	45.00	53.00	40.00
☐ **Sauce,** flat	13.00	18.00	10.00
☐ **Sauce,** footed	15.00	20.00	12.00
☐ **Spoon Holder**	22.00	26.00	18.00
☐ **Sugar,** covered, handled	37.00	45.00	35.00
☐ **Sugar,** open	20.00	25.00	16.00
☐ **Tray,** celery	22.00	27.00	18.00
☐ **Tumbler**	30.00	35.00	26.00
☐ **Vase,** height 5"	18.00	24.00	15.00
☐ **Vase,** height 9"	20.00	25.00	15.00
☐ **Wine**	28.00	34.00	25.00

PATHFINDER

The wide paneled flutes flare from the knobbed stem with beadwork trim.

☐ **Goblet**	100.00	125.00	105.00

PETAL AND LOOP
Boston & Sandwich Co.

One row of large loop and petal designs.

☐ **Butter Dish,** covered	90.00	100.00	85.00
☐ **Compote,** covered	120.00	130.00	116.00
☐ **Creamer**	115.00	125.00	110.00
☐ **Sugar Bowl,** covered	115.00	125.00	110.00

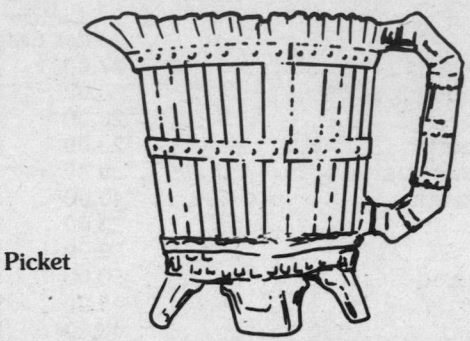

Picket

PICKET

This pattern is reminiscent of Oaken Bucket, with a vertical band of panels arranged to resemble a pointed fence. The horizontal bands that connect the pickets are wide and stippled, with beadwork decoration.

	Current Price Range		Prior Year Average
☐ Butter, with cover	55.00	65.00	57.00
☐ Celery	45.00	55.00	47.50
☐ Compote, high, with cover	60.00	70.00	65.00
☐ Compote, low	40.00	50.00	42.00
☐ Creamer	40.00	50.00	42.00
☐ Goblet	55.00	50.00	42.00
☐ Jam Jar	44.00	50.00	46.00
☐ Pickle Dish, with cover	45.00	55.00	47.50
☐ Salt	20.00	30.00	25.00
☐ Spooner	25.00	35.00	27.50
☐ Sugar, with cover	52.00	55.00	53.00
☐ Toothpick	35.00	40.00	37.50
☐ Tumbler	40.00	50.00	42.50
☐ Water Pitcher	65.00	75.00	67.50
☐ Wine Glass	30.00	40.00	32.50

PILLAR
Bakewell, Pears & Co.

Several rows of thumbprints with a vertical prism line running between. Plain band across top.

☐ Ale Glass	45.00	55.00	40.00
☐ Cordial	65.00	75.00	65.00
☐ Creamer	65.00	75.00	60.00
☐ Decanter, no stopper	50.00	60.00	45.00
☐ Goblet	50.00	60.00	45.00
☐ Sauce, flat	20.00	28.00	18.00
☐ Sugar Bowl, covered	65.00	75.00	60.00

PILLAR AND BULL'S EYE

Row of bull's eye at base, fluting above the bull's eye.

	Current Price Range		Prior Year Average
☐ Goblet	60.00	70.00	57.00
☐ Pitcher, water	140.00	150.00	130.00
☐ Tumbler	75.00	85.00	70.00
☐ Wine	55.00	65.00	50.00

PILLARED LOOP

The body is fully covered with long, arched fluting, the upper rim is a band of stretched triangles. The collar at the bottom of the body is outwardly flared, the stem and base are squatty.

☐ Goblet	75.00	85.00	77.50
☐ Spooner	100.00	125.00	110.00

PINEAPPLE STEM

The pattern is characterized by a round pineapple textured ball on the pedestal—the only decoration on smooth glass. Some pieces are etched with a delicate floral motif.

☐ Berry Bowl	20.00	30.00	25.00
☐ Bowl	15.00	20.00	22.50
☐ Bread Tray	30.00	40.00	32.50
☐ Butter	50.00	60.00	52.00
☐ Cake Stand	60.00	70.00	62.50
☐ Celery	40.00	50.00	45.00
☐ Compote, high	25.00	35.00	27.50
☐ Compote, low	20.00	30.00	25.00
☐ Cordial Glass	20.00	30.00	25.00
☐ Creamer	25.00	35.00	27.50
☐ Dish	15.00	20.00	17.50
☐ Egg Cup	20.00	30.00	22.50
☐ Goblet	20.00	30.00	22.50
☐ Milk Pitcher	30.00	40.00	35.00
☐ Mug	20.00	30.00	22.50
☐ Plate	10.00	15.00	12.50
☐ Platter, oval	20.00	30.00	25.00
☐ Platter, round	25.00	35.00	27.50
☐ Relish Bowl, two compartments	20.00	30.00	25.00
☐ Salt	15.00	20.00	17.50
☐ Sauce, footed	15.00	20.00	17.50
☐ Spooner	20.00	30.00	25.00
☐ Toothpick	12.00	16.00	12.50
☐ Tumbler	20.00	30.00	22.50
☐ Water Pitcher	50.00	60.00	52.50
☐ Wine Glass	20.00	30.00	25.00

PITT HONEYCOMB

Honeycomb design with small plain band across top.

	Current Price Range		Prior Year Average
☐ **Celery**	43.00	50.00	40.00
☐ **Creamer**	45.00	55.00	41.00
☐ **Egg Cup**	20.00	27.00	18.00
☐ **Pitcher,** water	75.00	85.00	70.00
☐ **Sugar Bowl,** covered	43.00	52.00	40.00
☐ **Tumbler**	28.00	35.00	25.00
☐ **Whiskey,** handled	30.00	40.00	25.00

PLUME

The wide feather band is formed by heavy teardrop shapes. The plumes are opposed vertically, the feather runs horizontally around the waist.

	Current Price Range		Prior Year Average
☐ **Berry Bowl**	20.00	30.00	22.50
☐ **Butter,** with cover	20.00	28.00	22.00
☐ **Cake Stand**	45.00	55.00	47.50
☐ **Celery**	30.00	40.00	32.00
☐ **Compote,** high, with cover	40.00	50.00	42.50
☐ **Compote,** low	30.00	40.00	35.00
☐ **Cordial Glass**	15.00	20.00	17.50
☐ **Creamer**	30.00	40.00	35.00
☐ **Goblet**	20.00	30.00	25.00
☐ **Pickle Plate**	25.00	35.00	27.50
☐ **Platter,** oval	40.00	50.00	42.50
☐ **Relish Bowl,** two compartments	30.00	40.00	35.00
☐ **Sauce,** flat	10.00	15.00	12.50
☐ **Sauce,** footed	20.00	30.00	25.00
☐ **Spooner**	20.00	30.00	25.00

Polar Bear

POLAR BEAR
Crystal Glass Co.

Polar bear on panel. Wide plain band at top of piece.

	Current Price Range		Prior Year Average
Bowl, ice			
☐ clear	83.00	90.00	76.00
☐ frosted	86.00	93.00	78.00
Butter			
☐ clear	105.00	110.00	100.00
☐ frosted	110.00	115.00	105.00
Creamer			
☐ clear	70.00	78.00	65.00
☐ frosted	75.00	83.00	68.00
Goblet			
☐ clear	90.00	100.00	85.00
☐ frosted	105.00	110.00	100.00
Pitcher, water			
☐ clear	170.00	180.00	160.00
☐ frosted	190.00	205.00	180.00
Platter, handled			
☐ clear	90.00	100.00	85.00
☐ frosted	100.00	110.00	95.00
Relish			
☐ clear	30.00	35.00	25.00
☐ frosted	33.00	38.00	27.00
Sauce			
☐ clear	30.00	36.00	25.00
☐ frosted	34.00	39.00	28.00
Spoon Holder			
☐ clear	60.00	65.00	55.00
☐ frosted	65.00	70.00	60.00
Tray, round			
☐ clear	140.00	150.00	130.00
☐ frosted	155.00	165.00	145.00
Tray, oval			
☐ clear	150.00	160.00	140.00
☐ frosted	165.00	175.00	155.00

PORTLAND TREE OF LIFE

A wonderful pattern, Tree of Life in this version is an overall bark motif made up of veining that covers the piece. With the exception of the upper rim, which is smooth, the entire piece is completely covered with texture. It is a very popular pattern.

Bowl			
☐ amber	40.00	60.00	45.00
☐ blue	35.00	45.00	37.50
☐ yellow	35.00	45.00	37.50
☐ amethyst	40.00	60.00	45.00

	Current Price Range		Prior Year Average
☐ clear	25.00	35.00	27.50
Butter, with cover			
☐ amber	80.00	90.00	85.00
☐ blue	75.00	80.00	77.50
☐ yellow	80.00	90.00	85.00
☐ amethyst	80.00	90.00	85.00
☐ clear	60.00	70.00	65.00
Cake Stand			
☐ amber	80.00	90.00	85.00
☐ blue	70.00	80.00	75.00
☐ yellow	80.00	90.00	85.00
☐ amethyst	80.00	90.00	85.00
☐ clear	60.00	70.00	65.00
Celery			
☐ amber	80.00	90.00	85.00
☐ blue	70.00	80.00	85.00
☐ yellow	80.00	90.00	85.00
☐ amethyst	80.00	90.00	85.00
☐ clear	50.00	60.00	55.00
Champagne			
☐ amber	60.00	70.00	62.50
☐ blue	55.00	65.00	57.00
☐ yellow	60.00	70.00	62.50
☐ amethyst	60.00	70.00	62.50
☐ clear	40.00	50.00	42.50
Compote, high			
☐ amber	100.00	110.00	105.00
☐ blue	95.00	100.00	97.00
☐ yellow	100.00	110.00	105.00
☐ amethyst	100.00	110.00	105.00
☐ clear	80.00	90.00	85.00
Compote, low, with cover			
☐ amber	110.00	125.00	115.00
☐ blue	100.00	110.00	105.00
☐ yellow	110.00	125.00	115.00
☐ amethyst	110.00	125.00	115.00
☐ clear	90.00	100.00	95.00
Creamer			
☐ amber	90.00	100.00	95.00
☐ blue	85.00	95.00	87.50
☐ yellow	90.00	100.00	95.00
☐ amethyst	90.00	100.00	95.00
☐ clear	70.00	80.00	75.00
Goblet			
☐ amber	80.00	90.00	85.00
☐ blue	75.00	85.00	77.50
☐ yellow	80.00	90.00	85.00
☐ amethyst	80.00	90.00	85.00

	Current Price Range		Prior Year Average
☐ clear	60.00	70.00	62.50
Plate			
☐ amber	40.00	50.00	42.50
☐ blue	35.00	40.00	37.00
☐ yellow	40.00	50.00	42.50
☐ amethyst	40.00	50.00	42.50
☐ clear	20.00	30.00	27.00
Relish Bowl, two compartments			
☐ amber	40.00	50.00	45.00
☐ blue	45.00	55.00	47.50
☐ yellow	45.00	55.00	47.50
☐ amethyst	45.00	55.00	47.50
☐ clear	25.00	35.00	27.00
Sauce, flat			
☐ amber	20.00	30.00	25.00
☐ blue	15.00	20.00	17.50
☐ yellow	20.00	30.00	25.00
☐ amethyst	20.00	30.00	25.00
☐ clear	12.00	15.00	13.00
Sauce, footed			
☐ amber	20.00	30.00	25.00
☐ blue	30.00	40.00	35.00
☐ yellow	30.00	40.00	35.00
☐ amethyst	30.00	40.00	35.00
☐ clear	15.00	20.00	17.50
Spooner			
☐ amber	35.00	45.00	37.00
☐ blue	30.00	40.00	35.00
☐ amethyst	35.00	45.00	37.00
☐ yellow	35.00	45.00	37.00
☐ clear	25.00	30.00	27.00
Sugar, with cover			
☐ amber	100.00	125.00	115.00
☐ blue	100.00	120.00	115.00
☐ yellow	100.00	125.00	115.00
☐ amethyst	100.00	125.00	115.00
☐ clear	60.00	80.00	65.00
Tumbler			
☐ amber	60.00	80.00	65.00
☐ blue	55.00	60.00	57.00
☐ yellow	60.00	80.00	65.00
☐ amethyst	60.00	80.00	65.00
☐ clear	40.00	50.00	42.50
Water Pitcher			
☐ amber	125.00	150.00	135.00
☐ blue	120.00	140.00	125.00
☐ yellow	125.00	150.00	135.00
☐ amethyst	125.00	150.00	135.00

	Current Price Range		Prior Year Average
☐ clear	80.00	100.00	95.00
Wine Glass			
☐ amber	80.00	90.00	85.00
☐ blue	70.00	75.00	72.00
☐ yellow	80.00	90.00	85.00
☐ amethyst	80.00	90.00	85.00
☐ clear	50.00	60.00	55.00

POWDER AND SHOT
Boston & Sandwich

This is an interesting pattern consisting of clear glass with a stippled bottom band decorated with a beadwork powder horn and buck shot. The different textures work well together, creating glittering refractions of the light.

☐ **Berry Bowl,** footed	50.00	60.00	55.00
☐ **Butter,** with cover	90.00	100.00	95.00
☐ **Castor Bottle**	40.00	50.00	45.00
☐ **Celery**	60.00	80.00	65.00
☐ **Compote,** high, with cover	100.00	150.00	110.00
☐ **Compote,** low	60.00	80.00	62.50
☐ **Creamer**	75.00	95.00	77.50
☐ **Egg Cup**	70.00	90.00	75.00
☐ **Goblet**	50.00	60.00	55.00
☐ **Salt Dip**	30.00	50.00	32.50

Powder and Shot

Pressed Leaf

PRESSED LEAF

Contrast is the key to the interest in this pattern. The background and the majority of the piece is smooth and clear, but the tall, bold oak leaves that run lengthwise for more than half of the body are heavily stippled and almost opaque.

	Current Price Range		Prior Year Average
☐ Bowl, open	25.00	30.00	20.00
☐ Butter, covered	45.00	50.00	40.00
☐ Cake Stand	65.00	70.00	60.00
☐ Champagne	45.00	53.00	40.00
☐ Compote, covered, high	55.00	65.00	50.00
☐ Compote, covered, low	48.00	55.00	43.00
☐ Cordial	40.00	47.00	35.00
☐ Creamer, handled	50.00	55.00	45.00
☐ Egg Cup	23.00	28.00	19.00
☐ Goblet	22.00	28.00	18.00
☐ Lamp, handled	45.00	55.00	40.00
☐ Pitcher, handled	80.00	90.00	75.00
☐ Salt, footed	25.00	30.00	20.00
☐ Sauce, flat	12.00	17.00	10.00
☐ Spoon Holder	23.00	28.00	18.00
☐ Sugar, covered	40.00	46.00	35.00
☐ Wine	40.00	45.00	35.00

PRIMITIVE

A heavy plain design accents the architectural stem and thick, squared base.

☐ Goblet	75.00	100.00	77.50

Primrose

PRIMROSE
Canton Glass

Fine horizontal ribbing overlaid with rose and leaves. Prism cuts on base of piece.

	Current Price Range		Prior Year Average
☐ **Bowl**	23.00	28.00	20.00
☐ **Butter Dish,** covered	45.00	52.00	42.00
☐ **Cake Plate,** handled	30.00	35.00	27.00
☐ **Compote,** covered	30.00	36.00	27.00
☐ **Goblet,** knob stem	28.00	34.00	25.00
☐ **Goblet,** plain stemmed	25.00	30.00	23.00
☐ **Pitcher,** milk	36.00	43.00	33.00
☐ **Pitcher,** water	30.00	35.00	28.00
☐ **Plate,** diameter 4½"	15.00	20.00	12.00
☐ **Plate,** diameter 6"	18.00	23.00	15.00
☐ **Plate,** diameter 7"	20.00	26.00	18.00
☐ **Sauce,** flat	8.00	12.00	5.00
☐ **Sauce,** footed	18.00	22.00	15.00
☐ **Spoon Holder**	25.00	30.00	20.00
☐ **Sugar,** covered	30.00	37.00	27.00
☐ **Tray**	35.00	43.00	30.00
☐ **Toothpick Holder**	20.00	26.00	18.00

PRISM

This simple, well-balanced design consists of long spears, sharply molded and arranged in a long vertical band which covers the majority of the body. The light refracts beautifully due to the jagged texture and the deep moldwork. The glass is clear and heavy.

☐ **Champagne**	35.00	45.00	30.00
☐ **Compote,** open	45.00	50.00	40.00
☐ **Decanter**	45.00	55.00	40.00
☐ **Egg Cup**	32.00	39.00	30.00
☐ **Goblet**	45.00	55.00	40.00
☐ **Pitcher,** water	75.00	85.00	70.00

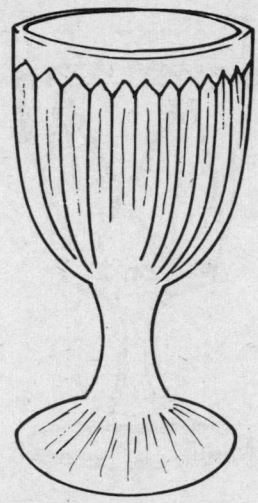

Prism

	Current Price Range		Prior Year Average
☐ **Salt**, footed	30.00	38.00	28.00
☐ **Wine**	45.00	55.00	40.00

PRISM WITH DIAMOND POINTS
Boston & Sandwich

Prism cut design with band of diamond motif at bottom and top of piece.

☐ **Bowl**	35.00	43.00	30.00
☐ **Butter Dish**, covered	80.00	88.00	74.00
☐ **Celery**	40.00	48.00	38.00
☐ **Compote**, covered, diameter 6"	95.00	105.00	90.00
☐ **Compote**, open	60.00	70.00	55.00
☐ **Creamer**	65.00	75.00	60.00
☐ **Egg Cup**, single	36.00	43.00	33.00
☐ **Egg Cup**, double	45.00	53.00	41.00
☐ **Goblet**	50.00	60.00	46.00
☐ **Jelly Dish**, covered	48.00	55.00	45.00
☐ **Pitcher**, water	110.00	120.00	100.00
☐ **Salt**, footed	30.00	38.00	27.00
☐ **Spoon Holder**	35.00	45.00	30.00
☐ **Sugar Bowl**, covered	55.00	65.00	51.00
☐ **Tumbler**	40.00	50.00	37.00
☐ **Wine**	45.00	55.00	40.00

Reticulated Cord

RETICULATED CORD

Diamond shapes made up of thin cables crisscross over the bodies of these pieces, framed on the bottom and top by a horizontal band of the cording. The pattern is simple but well balanced and popular with collectors.

	Current Price Range		Prior Year Average
☐ **Butter**, with cover	25.00	35.00	27.50
☐ **Cake Stand**	30.00	40.00	35.00
☐ **Celery**	20.00	30.00	22.50
☐ **Compote**, high	25.00	30.00	27.50
☐ **Creamer**	20.00	30.00	22.50
☐ **Goblet**	15.00	20.00	17.50
☐ **Plate**	20.00	30.00	25.00
☐ **Relish Bowl**	15.00	30.00	16.50
☐ **Sauce**, flat	6.00	8.00	6.50
☐ **Spooner**	15.00	20.00	17.50
☐ **Sugar**	18.00	22.00	19.00
☐ **Sugar**, with cover	30.00	40.00	35.00
☐ **Tumbler**	15.00	20.00	17.50
☐ **Wine Glass**	20.00	25.00	22.50

RIBBED FORGET-ME-NOT

Vining flowers in middle of piece with vertical ribbing on top and bottom of piece.

☐ **Butter**, covered	25.00	33.00	23.00
☐ **Cup**	15.00	22.00	12.00
☐ **Creamer**	26.00	35.00	24.00
☐ **Jam**, covered	25.00	35.00	21.00

	Current Price Range		Prior Year Average
☐ **Pitcher**	40.00	48.00	36.00
☐ **Spoon Holder**	25.00	32.00	22.00
☐ **Sugar Bowl,** covered	33.00	38.00	29.00

RIBBED GRAPE

The ribbed pieces are particulary interesting because of the voluptuousness that is achieved by the rounded ridges. Ribbed Grape adds interest to this background with grape bunches and vines interrupting the flow of the ribbing in high relief. The upper rim on some pieces is often a jagged sawtooth.

☐ **Butter,** covered	90.00	100.00	85.00
☐ **Compote,** open, low	70.00	80.00	66.00
☐ **Cordial**	55.00	65.00	50.00
☐ **Creamer,** handled	130.00	140.00	126.00
☐ **Goblet**	45.00	55.00	41.00
☐ **Jelly Compote,** scarce	130.00	140.00	125.00
☐ **Pitcher,** handled	130.00	140.00	126.00
☐ **Plate,** diameter 6"	60.00	70.00	55.00
☐ **Sauce,** flat	28.00	34.00	25.00
☐ **Spoon Holder**	55.00	65.00	51.00
☐ **Sugar Bowl,** covered	90.00	100.00	85.00
☐ **Sugar Bowl,** open	50.00	60.00	45.00
☐ **Wine**	100.00	110.00	98.00

RIBBED IVY

Ivy design with vertical ribbing.

Ribbed Grape

	Current Price Range		Prior Year Average
☐ **Butter,** covered	90.00	100.00	85.00
☐ **Castor Bottle**	40.00	48.00	37.00
☐ **Champagne**	105.00	115.00	100.00
☐ **Celery,** scarce	310.00	320.00	300.00
☐ **Compote,** large, scalloped edge	65.00	75.00	60.00
☐ **Compote,** low, scalloped edge	60.00	70.00	56.00
☐ **Compote,** jelly, covered, scarce	130.00	138.00	126.00
☐ **Compote,** tall	50.00	60.00	48.00
☐ **Decanter,** with stopper, half pint	80.00	90.00	75.00
☐ **Decanter,** without stopper, one quart	110.00	119.00	106.00
☐ **Egg Cup**	30.00	37.00	27.00
☐ **Goblet**	45.00	55.00	41.00
☐ **Hat,** scarce	360.00	370.00	350.00
☐ **Honey Dish**	18.00	23.00	15.00
☐ **Salt,** covered	135.00	145.00	131.00
☐ **Salt,** scalloped edge, open	45.00	55.00	41.00
☐ **Sauce,** flat	15.00	20.00	13.00
☐ **Spoon Holder**	30.00	40.00	25.00
☐ **Tumbler**	70.00	80.00	66.00
☐ **Tumbler,** whiskey, handled	70.00	80.00	66.00
☐ **Wine**	100.00	110.00	95.00

RIBBED LOOP

The long, stylized flutes contain an elongated flute. The stem is knobbed above the base and hexagonal shaped.

☐ **Goblet**	55.00	75.00	58.50

RIBBED OPAL
A. J. Beatty

Vertical ribbing is heavily molded, creating high squared peaks and deep valleys. The panels cover the piece, the rest of the glass is smooth and glossy.

Ribbed Opal

	Current Price Range		Prior Year Average
☐ **Bowl,** diameter 8″	20.00	25.00	22.50
☐ **Cookie Jar**	55.00	65.00	57.50
☐ **Creamer**	25.00	35.00	27.50
☐ **Mug**	45.00	55.00	47.50
☐ **Powder Box,** with lid	40.00	50.00	42.50
☐ **Relish,** two compartments	50.00	60.00	55.00
☐ **Salt**	25.00	35.00	27.50
☐ **Sauce Dish**	25.00	35.00	27.50
☐ **Sugar**	35.00	45.00	37.50
☐ **Toothpick**	25.00	35.00	27.50
☐ **Tumbler**	45.00	60.00	50.00
☐ **Water Pitcher**	55.00	65.00	57.50

RIBBED PALM
McKee and Bros.

Palm tree in center surrounded by ribbing. Wide plain band across top.

☐ **Bowl,** diameter 8″	45.00	55.00	40.00
☐ **Butter Dish,** covered	90.00	100.00	85.00
☐ **Celery**	75.00	85.00	76.00
☐ **Champagne**	70.00	80.00	68.00
☐ **Compote,** jelly, covered	110.00	120.00	105.00
☐ **Compote,** open, diameter 8″	65.00	75.00	60.00
☐ **Compote,** open, diameter 10″	85.00	95.00	80.00
☐ **Egg Cup**	20.00	28.00	22.00
☐ **Lamp,** all glass	90.00	100.00	85.00
☐ **Lamp,** marble base	90.00	100.00	85.00
☐ **Pitcher,** handled	130.00	140.00	125.00
☐ **Plate,** diameter 6″	56.00	66.00	52.00

Ribbed Palm

	Current Price Range		Prior Year Average
☐ Salt, footed	35.00	45.00	31.00
☐ Sauce, flat, diameter 4″	20.00	28.00	18.00
☐ Sugar Bowl, covered	65.00	75.00	60.00
☐ Tumbler	76.00	86.00	74.00
☐ Wine	55.00	65.00	53.00

RIBBED SAWTOOTH

This pattern is an overall design of stepped panels, arranged vertically and broken by a beaded chain at the waist. All of the available space is ribbed; the effect is busy and textured.

☐ Berry Bowl	10.00	20.00	12.50
☐ Butter, with cover	20.00	30.00	25.00
☐ Cake Stand	30.00	40.00	35.00
☐ Celery	25.00	35.00	27.50
☐ Compote, high	25.00	35.00	27.50
☐ Cordial Glass	15.00	20.00	17.50
☐ Creamer	25.00	35.00	27.50
☐ Egg Cup	20.00	30.00	25.00
☐ Goblet	15.00	25.00	17.50
☐ Milk Pitcher	35.00	45.00	37.50
☐ Mug	15.00	20.00	17.50
☐ Platter	20.00	30.00	25.00
☐ Relish Bowl	20.00	30.00	25.00
☐ Salt	25.00	35.00	27.50
☐ Sauce, flat	10.00	15.00	25.00
☐ Sauce, footed	15.00	20.00	25.00
☐ Spooner	20.00	30.00	25.00
☐ Sugar, with cover	30.00	40.00	35.00
☐ Toothpick	15.00	20.00	17.50
☐ Tumbler	20.00	30.00	25.00
☐ Water Pitcher	20.00	30.00	25.00
☐ Wine Glass	15.00	20.00	17.50

RIPPLE

This simple pattern is one wide band of fine horizontal ridges, waving slightly around the piece. The mold is light, the rest of the glass devoid of decoration.

☐ Bowl	25.00	35.00	27.50
☐ Butter, with cover	30.00	40.00	35.00
☐ Compote, high	30.00	40.00	35.00
☐ Compote, low, with cover	40.00	50.00	45.00
☐ Creamer	30.00	40.00	32.50
☐ Goblet	25.00	30.00	27.50
☐ Lamp	42.00	50.00	45.00
☐ Salt, pedestal foot	20.00	30.00	25.00
☐ Spooner	25.00	30.00	35.00

Roman Key

ROMAN KEY

This popular motif has been used since antiquity on art of all kinds. Here, in pressed glass, we see the key band framed on both sides with heavy ridges, deeply molded and set off with a stippled background. The shape of most pieces is significantly classical in keeping with the ancient aura these pieces project.

	Current Price Range		Prior Year Average
☐ **Bowl**, diameter 8″	40.00	46.00	38.00
☐ **Butter**, covered	40.00	50.00	36.00
☐ **Cake Stand**, diameter 12″	58.00	66.00	55.00
☐ **Castor Set**, three pieces	100.00	110.00	95.00
☐ **Celery**	47.00	53.00	45.00
☐ **Compote**, covered	60.00	70.00	55.00
☐ **Compote**, open, diameter 7″	53.00	59.00	50.00
☐ **Creamer**, handled	70.00	80.00	66.00
☐ **Decanter**, stoppered	100.00	110.00	95.00
☐ **Egg Cup**	37.00	42.00	35.00
☐ **Goblet**	50.00	60.00	47.00
☐ **Pitcher**	210.00	218.00	205.00
☐ **Plate**	55.00	63.00	53.00
☐ **Relish Dish**	40.00	47.00	37.00
☐ **Salt**, footed	42.00	48.00	40.00
☐ **Spoon Holder**	50.00	60.00	45.00
☐ **Sugar Bowl**, covered	60.00	70.00	57.00
☐ **Tumbler**	53.00	63.00	50.00

Roman Rosette

ROMAN ROSETTE

Rounded, voluptuous rosettes are arranged in a middle row in high relief. The background is lightly stippled giving the body a frosty look. The bottom of the goblets or the center of plates and dishes carry the rosette also.

	Current Price Range		Prior Year Average
☐ **Bowl,** diameter 5½″	30.00	40.00	32.50
☐ **Bowl,** diameter 6½″	35.00	45.00	37.50
☐ **Bowl,** diameter 7½″	40.00	45.00	42.50
☐ **Bowl,** diameter 8½″	45.00	55.00	47.50
☐ **Butter Dish,** with cover	55.00	65.00	57.50
☐ **Cake Plate,** stemmed	75.00	85.00	77.50
☐ **Casters,** set of eight	75.00	85.00	77.50
☐ **Celery**	45.00	55.00	47.50
☐ **Compote,** high, with cover, diameter 6″	50.00	60.00	52.50
☐ **Compote,** high, with cover, diameter 7½″	60.00	70.00	62.50
☐ **Compote,** low, with cover, diameter 6″	55.00	65.00	57.50
☐ **Compote,** low, with cover, diameter 8½″	65.00	75.00	67.50
☐ **Creamer**	45.00	50.00	47.50
☐ **Goblet**	45.00	55.00	47.50
☐ **Mug**	15.00	20.00	16.00
☐ **Pickle Dish**	35.00	45.00	37.50
☐ **Salt Shaker,** sterling fittings	65.00	75.00	67.50
☐ **Sauce,** flat	15.00	20.00	17.50
☐ **Spooner**	55.00	70.00	60.00
☐ **Sugar,** with cover	55.00	65.00	57.50
☐ **Syrup Pitcher**	60.00	70.00	62.50
☐ **Tumbler**	45.00	65.00	47.50
☐ **Wine Glass**	35.00	43.00	37.00

Rose in Snow

ROSE IN SNOW
Bryce Bros.

Rose and stem design over frosted glass. Scalloped edge at top of pattern. Plain band at top. Pieces are either round or square form. Prices listed are for either form.

	Current Price Range		Prior Year Average
Bowl, diameter 4"			
☐ clear	48.00	55.00	45.00
☐ amber	55.00	60.00	51.00
☐ canary	55.00	60.00	51.00
☐ blue	70.00	75.00	65.00
Butter, covered			
☐ clear	48.00	55.00	45.00
☐ amber	55.00	60.00	50.00
☐ canary	55.00	60.00	50.00
☐ blue	70.00	75.00	64.00
Cake Stand, diameter 9"			
☐ clear	85.00	93.00	82.00
☐ amber	95.00	100.00	90.00
☐ canary	95.00	100.00	90.00
☐ blue	110.00	115.00	105.00
Compote, covered			
☐ clear	70.00	75.00	66.00
☐ amber	84.00	88.00	80.00
☐ canary	84.00	88.00	80.00
☐ blue	95.00	100.00	90.00

	Current Price Range		Prior Year Average
Compote, open			
☐ clear	35.00	43.00	32.00
☐ amber	42.00	48.00	38.00
☐ canary	42.00	48.00	38.00
☐ blue	48.00	55.00	44.00
Creamer, round or square			
☐ clear	32.00	40.00	28.00
☐ amber	40.00	45.00	35.00
☐ canary	40.00	45.00	35.00
☐ blue	50.00	55.00	45.00
Goblet			
☐ clear	35.00	43.00	32.00
☐ amber	40.00	45.00	36.00
☐ canary	40.00	45.00	36.00
☐ blue	50.00	55.00	45.00
Jar, covered, scarce			
☐ clear	60.00	70.00	55.00
☐ amber	73.00	78.00	68.00
☐ canary	73.00	78.00	68.00
☐ blue	85.00	90.00	80.00
Jelly, covered			
☐ clear	45.00	55.00	40.00
☐ amber	54.00	60.00	50.00
☐ canary	54.00	60.00	50.00
☐ blue	65.00	70.00	60.00
Mug, "In Fond Remembrance"			
☐ clear	40.00	48.00	36.00
☐ amber	48.00	55.00	43.00
☐ canary	48.00	55.00	43.00
☐ blue	60.00	65.00	55.00
Pickle, double, scarce			
☐ clear	90.00	100.00	86.00
☐ amber	108.00	115.00	103.00
☐ canary	108.00	115.00	103.00
☐ blue	120.00	130.00	110.00
Pitcher, water, handled			
☐ clear	100.00	110.00	95.00
☐ amber	108.00	115.00	103.00
☐ canary	108.00	115.00	103.00
☐ blue	122.00	128.00	115.00
Plate, diameter 6"			
☐ clear	25.00	30.00	22.00
☐ amber	31.00	36.00	25.00
☐ canary	31.00	36.00	25.00
☐ blue	37.00	43.00	33.00
Plate, diameter 7"			
☐ clear	23.00	28.00	20.00
☐ amber	30.00	35.00	25.00

	Current Price Range		Prior Year Average
☐ canary	30.00	35.00	25.00
☐ blue	34.00	40.00	30.00
Plate, diameter 10″, handled			
☐ clear	40.00	48.00	36.00
☐ amber	48.00	55.00	44.00
☐ canary	48.00	55.00	44.00
☐ blue	60.00	65.00	55.00
Platter, oval, scarce			
☐ clear	80.00	90.00	75.00
☐ amber	95.00	100.00	90.00
☐ canary	95.00	100.00	90.00
☐ blue	105.00	110.00	100.00
Relish Dish, oval			
☐ clear	23.00	27.00	20.00
☐ amber	30.00	35.00	25.00
☐ canary	30.00	35.00	25.00
☐ blue	40.00	45.00	35.00
Sauce, flat			
☐ clear	13.00	18.00	10.00
☐ amber	15.00	20.00	12.00
☐ canary	15.00	20.00	12.00
☐ blue	22.00	28.00	18.00
Sauce, footed			
☐ clear	10.00	15.00	8.00
☐ amber	12.00	17.00	10.00
☐ canary	12.00	17.00	10.00
☐ blue	15.00	20.00	12.00
Spoon Holder			
☐ clear	30.00	35.00	25.00
☐ amber	38.00	44.00	34.00
☐ canary	38.00	44.00	34.00
☐ blue	45.00	50.00	40.00
Sugar, covered			
☐ clear	45.00	50.00	40.00
☐ amber	54.00	58.00	50.00
☐ canary	54.00	58.00	50.00
☐ blue	63.00	68.00	58.00
Tumbler, handled			
☐ clear	43.00	48.00	38.00
☐ amber	52.00	57.00	48.00
☐ canary	52.00	57.00	48.00
☐ blue	65.00	70.00	60.00
Vegetable Dish			
☐ clear	70.00	80.00	66.00
☐ amber	84.00	88.00	80.00
☐ canary	84.00	88.00	80.00
☐ blue	95.00	105.00	90.00

	Current Price Range		Prior Year Average

Wine

☐ clear	35.00	42.00	32.00
☐ amber	48.00	55.00	44.00
☐ canary	48.00	55.00	44.00
☐ blue	52.00	58.00	48.00

ROSE SPRIG
Campbell, Jones

Single rose surrounded by leaves. This panel alternates with panel of vertical ribbing. Plain band across top.

☐ **Butter Dish**	30.00	36.00	28.00
☐ **Cake Stand**	30.00	37.00	27.00
☐ **Celery**	35.00	42.00	32.00
☐ **Compote,** covered	40.00	47.00	37.00
☐ **Creamer**	31.00	36.00	28.00
☐ **Dish**	20.00	27.00	17.00
☐ **Goblet**	32.00	37.00	30.00
☐ **Nappy,** handled	20.00	26.00	17.00
☐ **Pickle,** oval	22.00	28.00	20.00
☐ **Pitcher**	50.00	55.00	46.00
☐ **Plate,** diameter 8"	28.00	32.00	25.00
☐ **Plate,** diameter 10"	31.00	35.00	28.00
☐ **Relish,** boat shaped	29.00	35.00	25.00
☐ **Salt,** sleigh	28.00	35.00	25.00
☐ **Sauce,** footed	15.00	20.00	12.00
☐ **Spoon Holder**	25.00	31.00	22.00
☐ **Sugar,** covered	42.00	48.00	39.00
☐ **Sugar,** open	30.00	35.00	28.00

Rose Sprig

	Current Price Range		Prior Year Average
☐ **Tray**	45.00	55.00	42.00
☐ **Tumbler**	28.00	35.00	25.00
☐ **Tumbler,** handled	32.00	40.00	28.00

ROSETTE

Rounded petal flowers are the main focus on these pieces, scattered across the body in neat order. The upper and lower bands are a series of horizontal ridges with rimmed bull's eyes interrupting the flow every half-inch or so.

☐ **Butter Dish,** with cover	35.00	47.00	37.00
☐ **Cake Plate,** stemmed, diameter 10½"	25.00	35.00	27.00
☐ **Celery**	40.00	50.00	42.50
☐ **Compote,** high with cover, diameter 7"	50.00	60.00	52.50
☐ **Compote,** high, with cover, diameter 8½"	55.00	65.00	57.50
☐ **Compote,** stemmed, diameter 8"	50.00	60.00	52.50
☐ **Creamer**	20.00	30.00	22.00
☐ **Goblet**	25.00	35.00	27.00
☐ **Mug**	45.00	55.00	47.50
☐ **Plate,** diameter 7"	30.00	40.00	32.50
☐ **Plate,** tab handles	45.00	55.00	47.50
☐ **Relish,** three compartments	15.00	25.00	17.00
☐ **Sauce,** flat	7.00	11.00	7.50
☐ **Spooner**	25.00	35.00	27.00

Rosette

Sandwich Star

SANDWICH STAR
Boston & Sandwich

The texture on these pieces is the main focus of this pattern. With geometric rosettes interconnecting like a kaleidoscopic scene, the surface rises and falls with deeply molded prisms that make up the stars. The glass is heavy and clear; the light refracts wonderfully on the surface.

	Current Price Range		Prior Year Average
☐ **Compote,** large, covered	300.00	330.00	305.00
☐ **Compote,** open	300.00	320.00	275.00
☐ **Compote,** tall, covered, rare	1000.00	1200.00	1000.00
☐ **Compote,** open, supported by three dolphins	800.00	1000.00	775.00
☐ **Cordial**	250.00	280.00	225.00
☐ **Decanter,** no stopper, pint	100.00	120.00	90.00
☐ **Decanter,** no stopper, quart	120.00	135.00	115.00
☐ **Goblet,** rare	400.00	430.00	400.00
☐ **Relish Dish,** flat	70.00	85.00	75.00
☐ **Spooner**	50.00	60.00	45.00
☐ **Water Dish,** rare	375.00	400.00	350.00
☐ **Wine Glass**	130.00	140.00	125.00

SAWTOOTH AND STAR

The interesting aspect of this pattern is the sawtooth band—it rims the mid-waist of the piece, rising off the surface like a tossed ring on a stake. The facets are decorated with a row of small stars.

☐ **Banana Plate**	30.00	40.00	35.00
☐ **Butter,** with cover	35.00	45.00	37.50
☐ **Compote,** high	45.00	50.00	42.50
☐ **Creamer**	25.00	35.00	27.50
☐ **Cruet**	25.00	35.00	27.50
☐ **Cup**	15.00	20.00	17.50

Sawtooth and Star

	Current Price Range		Prior Year Average
☐ Goblet	24.00	28.00	25.50
☐ Lamp	35.00	45.00	37.50
☐ Pickle	20.00	25.00	22.50
☐ Plate	18.00	22.00	19.00
☐ Sauce, flat	10.00	15.00	12.50
☐ Sauce, footed	15.00	20.00	17.50
☐ Salt Shaker	15.00	20.00	16.50
☐ Sugar, with cover	30.00	40.00	32.50
☐ Tumbler	35.00	40.00	37.50
☐ Wine Glass	25.00	35.00	27.50

SAXON
Adams

Narrow fluting beginning at base of body and extending halfway up pieces. A band of blocking in the middle of fluting.

☐ Bowl, oval	31.00	37.00	28.00
☐ Butter Dish, covered	50.00	58.00	46.00
☐ Cake Stand	45.00	53.00	40.00
☐ Compote, covered	35.00	40.00	33.00
☐ Compote, open	20.00	26.00	18.00
☐ Creamer	30.00	36.00	27.00
☐ Egg Cup	30.00	38.00	26.00
☐ Goblet	26.00	32.00	22.00
☐ Jar, covered	45.00	53.00	41.00
☐ Mug, handled	33.00	40.00	29.00
☐ Plate, diameter 6″	30.00	36.00	27.00
☐ Platter, oval	35.00	43.00	30.00

Saxon

	Current Price Range		Prior Year Average
☐ Relish Dish	17.00	22.00	15.00
☐ Salt	15.00	20.00	12.00
☐ Sauce, flat	15.00	21.00	12.00
☐ Spoon Holder	26.00	32.00	21.00
☐ Sugar Bowl, covered	42.00	48.00	38.00
☐ Sugar Bowl, open	25.00	30.00	21.00
☐ Toothpick Holder	27.00	34.00	23.00
☐ Tray	45.00	54.00	40.00
☐ Tumbler	23.00	28.00	20.00
☐ Wine	23.00	28.00	20.00

SCALLOPED DIAMOND POINT

The bottom of the body is covered with diamond point, ending just under the flared, scalloped rim. The glass is heavy and well-molded, the pattern refracts the light well.

☐ Bowl	25.00	35.00	27.50
☐ Butter, with cover	35.00	45.00	37.50
☐ Cake Stand	40.00	50.00	45.50
☐ Celery	25.00	35.00	27.50
☐ Creamer	30.00	40.00	35.00
☐ Dish, with cover	40.00	50.00	42.50
☐ Sauce, flat	12.00	16.00	14.00
☐ Sauce, footed	15.00	20.00	17.50
☐ Spooner	25.00	35.00	27.50
☐ Sugar, with cover	35.00	45.00	37.50
☐ Tumbler	25.00	35.00	27.50
☐ Water Pitcher	60.00	70.00	67.50
☐ Wine Glass	30.00	40.00	35.00

SCROLL

The motif is a wide band of stippled background with elegant scrolls of glossy glass. The bottoms are pleated, the upper two-thirds is smooth and devoid of decoration.

	Current Price Range		Prior Year Average
☐ **Butter**	35.00	45.00	37.00
☐ **Celery**	30.00	40.00	35.00
☐ **Compote,** high	25.00	30.00	32.50
☐ **Compote,** low	20.00	30.00	22.50
☐ **Creamer**	25.00	30.00	27.50
☐ **Egg Cup**	15.00	22.00	16.00
☐ **Goblet**	15.00	20.00	17.50
☐ **Relish Bowl**	20.00	30.00	22.50
☐ **Salt**	15.00	20.00	17.50
☐ **Sauce,** flat	10.00	12.00	11.00
☐ **Sauce,** footed	20.00	30.00	25.00
☐ **Spooner**	22.00	30.00	24.00
☐ **Sugar,** with cover	30.00	40.00	32.50
☐ **Water Pitcher**	40.00	60.00	45.00
☐ **Wine Glass**	20.00	30.00	22.50

SCROLL WITH FLOWERS
Central Glass Co.

Star design in middle of pattern surrounded by double scrolling. Small bands of horseshoe shaped ribbing top of design.

Butter, covered

☐ clear	40.00	45.00	36.00
☐ amber	52.00	57.00	48.00
☐ blue	60.00	68.00	55.00

Scroll with Flowers

	Current Price Range		Prior Year Average
☐ green	61.00	67.00	56.00
Cake Plate, handled			
☐ clear	21.00	26.00	17.00
☐ amber	30.00	35.00	27.00
☐ blue	32.00	38.00	29.00
☐ green	31.00	37.00	28.00
Compote, covered			
☐ clear	35.00	41.00	30.00
☐ amber	46.00	51.00	41.00
☐ blue	55.00	60.00	50.00
☐ green	54.00	59.00	51.00
Celery			
☐ clear	28.00	32.00	25.00
☐ amber	35.00	42.00	31.00
☐ blue	45.00	50.00	41.00
☐ green	44.00	49.00	40.00
Cordial			
☐ clear	33.00	38.00	30.00
☐ amber	45.00	50.00	41.00
☐ blue	56.00	62.00	51.00
☐ green	57.00	63.00	52.00
Creamer			
☐ clear	26.00	31.00	21.00
☐ amber	34.00	39.00	30.00
☐ blue	43.00	48.00	39.00
☐ green	44.00	49.00	40.00
Egg Cup, double, handled			
☐ clear	27.00	33.00	23.00
☐ amber	36.00	42.00	31.00
☐ blue	41.00	48.00	36.00
☐ green	42.00	49.00	37.00
Egg Cup, single			
☐ clear	15.00	19.00	12.00
☐ amber	20.00	25.00	15.00
☐ blue	26.00	31.00	21.00
☐ green	25.00	30.00	20.00
Goblet			
☐ clear	30.00	36.00	26.00
☐ amber	38.00	45.00	32.00
☐ blue	49.00	56.00	44.00
☐ green	50.00	57.00	45.00
Jar, covered, small			
☐ clear	36.00	42.00	31.00
☐ amber	45.00	50.00	40.00
☐ blue	55.00	62.00	51.00
☐ green	56.00	63.00	52.00
Pickle, handled, oval			
☐ clear	21.00	26.00	17.00

	Current Price Range		Prior Year Average
☐ amber	25.00	30.00	20.00
☐ blue	32.00	38.00	28.00
☐ green	31.00	37.00	27.00
Pitcher			
☐ clear	75.00	83.00	70.00
☐ amber	110.00	120.00	102.00
☐ blue	125.00	135.00	120.00
☐ green	126.00	136.00	121.00
Salt, footed			
☐ clear	20.00	26.00	16.00
☐ amber	25.00	30.00	20.00
☐ blue	31.00	37.00	27.00
☐ green	30.00	36.00	26.00
Salt and Pepper Shakers, pair			
☐ clear	32.00	37.00	28.00
☐ amber	44.00	49.00	40.00
☐ blue	53.00	60.00	48.00
☐ green	52.00	59.00	49.00
Sauce, handled			
☐ clear	15.00	20.00	12.00
☐ amber	19.00	25.00	16.00
☑ blue	25.00	30.00	20.00
☐ green	26.00	31.00	21.00
Spoon Holder			
☐ clear	24.00	30.00	20.00
☐ amber	28.00	36.00	24.00
☐ blue	32.00	40.00	28.00
☐ green	33.00	41.00	29.00
Sugar, covered			
☐ clear	40.00	47.00	36.00
☐ amber	52.00	58.00	48.00
☐ blue	68.00	75.00	62.00
☐ green	66.00	73.00	60.00
Sugar, open			
☐ clear	18.00	23.00	15.00
☐ amber	25.00	30.00	20.00
☐ blue	33.00	39.00	29.00
☐ green	32.00	38.00	28.00
Wine			
☐ clear	26.00	32.00	21.00
☐ amber	35.00	40.00	30.00
☐ blue	43.00	50.00	38.00
☐ green	42.00	49.00	37.00

SCROLL WITH STAR

Overlapping loops with top of loop design scalloped. Star appears in center of flat pieces, such as the plate, with loop design around it.

	Current Price Range		Prior Year Average
☐ **Bowl**	10.00	15.00	8.00
☐ **Butter Dish,** covered	30.00	40.00	25.00
☐ **Cup**	15.00	25.00	12.00
☐ **Cup and Saucer Set**	25.00	35.00	20.00
☐ **Creamer**	20.00	28.00	18.00
☐ **Goblet**	20.00	25.00	17.00
☐ **Plate,** diameter 6″	18.00	25.00	15.00
☐ **Plate,** diameter 10″	25.00	30.00	22.00
☐ **Sauce**	18.00	23.00	15.00
☐ **Spoon Holder**	25.00	30.00	21.00
☐ **Sugar Bowl,** covered	25.00	35.00	21.00

SENECA LOOP

One row of large loops with smaller loops inside of the large. Plain band at top.

☐ **Bowl,** diameter 9″	55.00	65.00	50.00
☐ **Butter,** covered	50.00	55.00	46.00
☐ **Cake Stand**	70.00	77.00	68.00
☐ **Celery**	40.00	50.00	36.00
☐ **Champagne**	30.00	35.00	27.00
☐ **Compote,** covered	65.00	70.00	61.00
☐ **Compote,** open	40.00	48.00	38.00
☐ **Compote,** scalloped edge	50.00	60.00	48.00
☐ **Creamer**	50.00	60.00	45.00
☐ **Egg Cup**	30.00	36.00	27.00
☐ **Goblet**	30.00	35.00	28.00
☐ **Pitcher,** handled	80.00	90.00	76.00
☐ **Salt,** footed	25.00	32.00	22.00
☐ **Spoon Holder**	30.00	36.00	28.00
☐ **Sugar Bowl,** covered	60.00	68.00	57.00
☐ **Sugar Bowl,** open	40.00	50.00	38.00

SPIREA BAND

This is a simple pattern consisting of two opposed rows of diamond point, rimming the top and bottom or middle of the pieces. The rest of the piece is devoid of decoration, showing off the clear colors.

Butter

☐ blue	60.00	70.00	65.00
☐ yellow	60.00	70.00	65.00
☐ amber	60.00	70.00	65.00
☐ clear	40.00	50.00	42.50

Cake Stand

☐ blue	60.00	70.00	65.00
☐ yellow	60.00	70.00	65.00
☐ amber	60.00	70.00	65.00
☐ clear	40.00	50.00	42.50

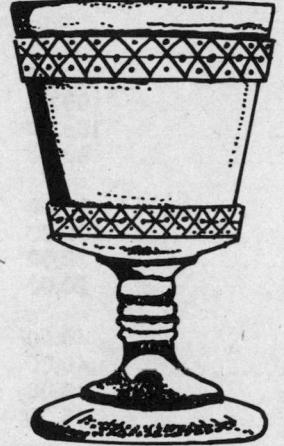

Spirea Band

	Current Price Range		Prior Year Average
Celery			
☐ blue	40.00	50.00	45.00
☐ yellow	40.00	50.00	45.00
☐ amber	40.00	50.00	45.00
☐ clear	35.00	45.00	37.50
Compote, high, with cover			
☐ blue	60.00	70.00	65.00
☐ amber	60.00	70.00	65.00
☐ yellow	60.00	70.00	65.00
☐ clear	45.00	55.00	47.50
Creamer			
☐ blue	45.00	55.00	47.50
☐ amber	45.00	55.00	47.50
☐ yellow	45.00	55.00	47.50
☐ clear	30.00	40.00	35.00
Dish			
☐ blue	25.00	35.00	27.50
☐ yellow	25.00	35.00	27.50
☐ amber	25.00	35.00	27.50
☐ clear	15.00	20.00	17.50
Egg Cup			
☐ blue	45.00	55.00	47.50
☐ yellow	45.00	55.00	47.50
☐ amber	45.00	55.00	47.50
☐ clear	25.00	35.00	27.50
Goblet			
☐ blue	60.00	70.00	65.00
☐ amber	60.00	70.00	65.00
☐ yellow	60.00	70.00	65.00
☐ clear	40.00	50.00	45.00

	Current Price Range		Prior Year Average
Platter			
☐ blue	100.00	110.00	105.00
☐ yellow	100.00	110.00	105.00
☐ amber	100.00	110.00	105.00
☐ clear	80.00	90.00	85.00
Salt			
☐ blue	30.00	40.00	35.00
☐ amber	30.00	40.00	35.00
☐ yellow	30.00	40.00	35.00
☐ clear	20.00	30.00	25.00
Spooner			
☐ blue	40.00	50.00	45.00
☐ amber	40.00	50.00	45.00
☐ yellow	40.00	50.00	45.00
☐ clear	35.00	45.00	37.50
Sugar, with cover			
☐ blue	45.00	55.00	47.00
☐ yellow	45.00	55.00	47.00
☐ amber	45.00	55.00	47.00
☐ clear	37.00	43.00	40.00
Tumbler			
☐ blue	20.00	30.00	25.00
☐ yellow	20.00	30.00	25.00
☐ amber	20.00	30.00	25.00
☐ clear	15.00	20.00	17.50
Water Pitcher			
☐ blue	75.00	85.00	80.00
☐ yellow	75.00	85.00	80.00
☐ amber	75.00	85.00	80.00
☐ clear	60.00	80.00	65.00
Wine Glass			
☐ blue	45.00	55.00	47.00
☐ yellow	45.00	55.00	47.00
☐ amber	45.00	55.00	47.00
☐ clear	30.00	40.00	35.00

SPRIG
Bryce Higbee & Co.

Long, fluted panels make up the main decoration on these pieces. Every other one contains a sparse branch, lightly etched with leaves and little flowers. It is a simple but elegant pattern that refracts the light beautifully.

☐ **Berry Bowl**	28.00	33.00	24.00
☐ **Bowl,** footed, diameter 10"	43.00	48.00	38.00
☐ **Butter,** covered	43.00	50.00	38.00
☐ **Cake Stand,** small	31.00	36.00	26.00

Sprig

	Current Price Range		Prior Year Average
☐ **Celery**	33.00	38.00	28.00
☐ **Compote**, covered	45.00	50.00	41.00
☐ **Compote**, open	30.00	38.00	26.00
☐ **Creamer**	25.00	30.00	21.00
☐ **Goblet**	32.00	38.00	28.00
☐ **Pitcher**	50.00	58.00	46.00
☐ **Platter**, oval	40.00	45.00	35.00
☐ **Relish**, oval	20.00	26.00	16.00
☐ **Sauce**, flat	10.00	15.00	7.00
☐ **Sauce**, footed	15.00	20.00	10.00
☐ **Spoon Holder**	30.00	35.00	25.00
☐ **Sugar**, covered, handled	40.00	45.00	35.00
☐ **Sugar**, open	25.00	32.00	20.00
☐ **Tumbler**	22.00	26.00	18.00
☐ **Wine**	45.00	50.00	40.00

ST. BERNARD

The big dog lies in the center surrounded by a smooth and beaded band. The edges are gently scalloped.

☐ **Berry Bowl**	15.00	20.00	17.50
☐ **Bowl**, diameter 8″	20.00	30.00	25.00
☐ **Bread Tray**, oval	25.00	35.00	27.50
☐ **Butter**	20.00	30.00	25.00
☐ **Butter**, with cover	25.00	35.00	37.50
☐ **Cake Stand**	20.00	30.00	22.50
☐ **Celery**	30.00	40.00	35.00
☐ **Compote**, high	30.00	40.00	35.00

	Current Price Range		Prior Year Average
☐ **Compote,** low	20.00	30.00	25.00
☐ **Cordial Glass**	15.00	25.00	17.50
☐ **Creamer**	20.00	30.00	22.50
☐ **Dish**	20.00	30.00	22.50
☐ **Egg Cup**	15.00	20.00	17.50
☐ **Goblet**	20.00	30.00	22.50
☐ **Milk Pitcher**	30.00	40.00	35.00
☐ **Mug**	15.00	20.00	17.50
☐ **Plate**	15.00	20.00	17.50
☐ **Platter**	20.00	30.00	22.50
☐ **Relish Bowl**	25.00	35.00	22.50
☐ **Salt**	15.00	25.00	17.50
☐ **Sauce,** flat	8.00	12.00	10.00
☐ **Sauce,** footed	15.00	20.00	17.50
☐ **Spooner**	20.00	30.00	25.00
☐ **Sugar,** with cover	25.00	35.00	27.00
☐ **Toothpick**	20.00	30.00	25.00
☐ **Tumbler**	20.00	30.00	25.00
☐ **Water Pitcher**	40.00	60.00	45.00
☐ **Wine Glass**	25.00	35.00	27.50

STAR ROSETTED

This overall pattern is row after row of tiny five pointed stars, giving these pieces an interesting texture.

☐ **Butter,** with cover	45.00	55.00	47.50
☐ **Compote**	30.00	40.00	35.00
☐ **Compote,** with cover	50.00	60.00	52.50
☐ **Creamer**	30.00	40.00	32.50

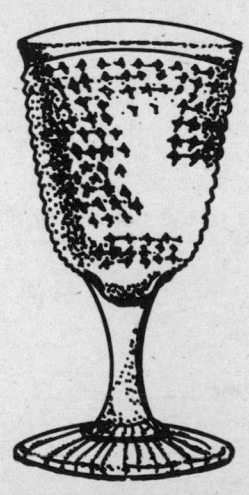

Star Rosetted

	Current Price Range		Prior Year Average
☐ Goblet	25.00	35.00	27.00
☐ Pickle Dish	15.00	20.00	17.50
☐ Plate, diameter 7"	18.00	22.00	19.50
☐ Plate, says "A Good Mother Makes a Happy Home"	50.00	60.00	55.00
☐ Relish, three compartments	15.00	22.00	16.00
☐ Sauce, flat	7.00	10.00	7.50
☐ Sauce, footed	15.00	20.00	17.50
☐ Sugar	20.00	25.00	22.50
☐ Sugar, with cover	40.00	50.00	42.50
☐ Water Pitcher	50.00	60.00	55.00

STEDMAN

Pleating design beginning at base extending either halfway or full length depending on piece.

☐ Champagne	36.00	42.00	32.00
☐ Compote, covered	80.00	85.00	76.00
☐ Compote, open	55.00	63.00	52.00
☐ Creamer	80.00	87.00	76.00
☐ Decanter, no stopper	80.00	90.00	75.00
☐ Egg Cup	40.00	48.00	36.00
☐ Plate, diameter 6"	35.00	43.00	31.00
☐ Salt, footed	17.00	24.00	15.00
☐ Spoon Holder	36.00	42.00	32.00
☐ Tumbler	42.00	48.00	40.00
☐ Wine	55.00	63.00	51.00

STIPPLED FORGET-ME-NOT
Bryce Bros.

Vining flowers in center of design with band of ribbed beading around bottom and top. Plain band at top of piece.

☐ Butter Dish, covered	55.00	63.00	50.00
☐ Cake Plate, small	40.00	46.00	37.00
☐ Cake Plate, large	60.00	65.00	56.00
☐ Celery	37.00	43.00	39.00
☐ Cup and Saucer Set	30.00	36.00	25.00
☐ Compote, covered, diameter 6"	48.00	55.00	44.00
☐ Compote, covered, diameter 8"	64.00	69.00	60.00
☐ Goblet	30.00	40.00	32.00
☐ Mug	22.00	29.00	18.00
☐ Pitcher, water	54.00	59.00	50.00
☐ Plate, kitten center	44.00	48.00	40.00
☐ Plate, star center	35.00	39.00	31.00
☐ Sauce, flat	12.00	17.00	10.00
☐ Sauce, footed	18.00	22.00	14.00

	Current Price Range		Prior Year Average
☐ Spoon Holder	27.00	35.00	29.00
☐ Sugar Bowl, covered	48.00	55.00	44.00
☐ Toothpick, hat shaped	80.00	86.00	75.00
☐ Tray, bread	40.00	46.00	36.00
☐ Tray, water scene with aquatic birds and life	50.00	56.00	46.00
☐ Tumbler	25.00	35.00	27.00
☐ Wine	34.00	38.00	30.00

STIPPLED PEPPERS

The upper band is a double band of beadwork, framing the molded flowers and foliage below. The blooms are textured with stippling, the background is smooth.

☐ Creamer	40.00	50.00	42.50
☐ Egg Cup	25.00	35.00	27.50
☐ Goblet	25.00	35.00	27.50
☐ Pitcher	40.00	50.00	42.00
☐ Salt, footed	18.50	20.00	19.00
☐ Sauce	10.00	15.00	11.50
☐ Sugar, with lid	40.00	50.00	42.50
☐ Tumbler, footed	25.00	35.00	27.50

Stippled Peppers

STIPPLED STAR
Gillander and Sons

This is a popular pattern because of the use of texture. The body is covered with light stippling giving the piece an icy look. Five pointed stars, arranged in horizontal rows, rise off this background, refracting the light with smooth glass.

	Current Price Range		Prior Year Average
☐ **Butter,** with cover	40.00	60.00	42.50
☐ **Celery**	35.00	45.00	37.50
☐ **Compote,** high	40.00	50.00	42.50
☐ **Compote,** with cover, high	70.00	80.00	75.00
☐ **Creamer**	55.00	60.00	57.50
☐ **Egg Cup**	30.00	40.00	35.50
☐ **Goblet**	30.00	40.00	35.50
☐ **Pickle Dish,** oval	35.00	40.00	37.50
☐ **Sauce,** flat	15.00	20.00	17.50
☐ **Sauce,** footed	20.00	30.00	22.50
☐ **Spooner**	30.00	40.00	35.50
☐ **Sugar,** with cover	50.00	60.00	52.50
☐ **Tumbler**	25.00	32.00	27.00
☐ **Water Pitcher**	80.00	100.00	82.50
☐ **Wine Goblet**	30.00	40.00	32.50

SUNFLOWER

Square panels with sunflowers and leaves cover entire piece except for narrow plain band across top.

	Current Price Range		Prior Year Average
Butter, covered			
☐ clear	50.00	55.00	45.00
☐ amber	75.00	80.00	70.00
☐ milk white	100.00	108.00	94.00
Creamer			
☐ clear	35.00	40.00	30.00
☐ amber	50.00	60.00	42.00
☐ milk white	70.00	80.00	65.00
Goblet			
☐ clear	20.00	25.00	17.00
☐ amber	30.00	35.00	25.00
☐ milk white	40.00	45.00	35.00
Pitcher			
☐ clear	55.00	60.00	50.00
☐ amber	75.00	80.00	70.00
☐ milk white	105.00	115.00	100.00
Spoon Holder			
☐ clear	25.00	30.00	20.00
☐ amber	33.00	40.00	28.00
☐ milk white	48.00	53.00	44.00
Sugar, covered			
☐ clear	45.00	50.00	40.00

	Current Price Range		Prior Year Average
☐ amber	50.00	58.00	45.00
☐ milk white	70.00	75.00	65.00
Sugar, open			
☐ clear	30.00	35.00	28.00
☐ amber	45.00	50.00	40.00
☐ milk white	60.00	65.00	55.00

TALL ARGUS

Varies slightly from Argus pattern in position of knob on stem and number of thumbprints in design. Tall Argus has large oval thumbprints with a roll of small thumbprints in center. Knob placed high on stem. Plain band across top.

☐ **Goblet**	75.00	85.00	70.00
☐ **Pitcher**	150.00	160.00	145.00

TEARDROP

This is a simple pattern of two opposed rows of heavy teardrops taking up the bottom two-thirds of the pieces. The mold is deep giving the body a wonderful texture.

☐ **Berry Bowl**	20.00	30.00	25.00
☐ **Bowl**	30.00	40.00	32.50
☐ **Bread Tray**	25.00	35.00	27.50
☐ **Butter**	20.00	30.00	25.00
☐ **Butter,** with cover	30.00	40.00	35.00
☐ **Cake Stand**	25.00	35.00	27.50
☐ **Celery**	25.00	35.00	27.50
☐ **Compote,** high	25.00	35.00	27.50
☐ **Compote,** low	25.00	30.00	27.50
☐ **Cordial Glass**	30.00	40.00	35.00
☐ **Creamer**	35.00	45.00	37.50
☐ **Dish**	25.00	35.00	27.50
☐ **Egg Cup**	20.00	30.00	25.00
☐ **Goblet**	15.00	20.00	17.50
☐ **Milk Pitcher**	20.00	30.00	25.50
☐ **Mug**	20.00	30.00	22.50
☐ **Plate**	25.00	35.00	27.50
☐ **Platter**	20.00	30.00	22.50
☐ **Relish Bowl**	15.00	20.00	17.50
☐ **Salt**	15.00	20.00	17.50
☐ **Sauce,** flat	15.00	20.00	17.50
☐ **Sauce,** footed	20.00	30.00	22.50
☐ **Spooner**	20.00	30.00	22.50
☐ **Sugar,** with cover	25.00	35.00	27.50
☐ **Toothpick**	15.00	20.00	17.50
☐ **Tumbler**	12.00	18.00	12.50

	Current Price Range		Prior Year Average
☐ **Water Pitcher**	40.00	60.00	45.00
☐ **Wine Glass**	15.00	20.00	17.50

TEARDROP AND TASSEL

This is an elegant, deeply molded glass in high relief. Sweeping over the body is a jeweled band of beadwork, with oval gems dangling from it. Beadwork decorates each motif creating a sparkling effect. This pattern is in great demand in all colors.

Berry Bowl

☐ blue	60.00	80.00	65.00
☐ green	58.00	62.00	59.00
☐ amber	65.00	75.00	67.50
☐ yellow	65.00	75.00	67.50
☐ milk glass	50.00	60.00	55.00
☐ clear	50.00	60.00	55.00

Butter, with cover

☐ blue	85.00	95.00	87.50
☐ green	85.00	95.00	87.50
☐ amber	90.00	100.00	95.00
☐ yellow	100.00	110.00	105.00
☐ milk glass	60.00	80.00	65.00
☐ clear	60.00	80.00	65.00

Creamer

☐ blue	90.00	100.00	95.00
☐ green	90.00	100.00	95.00
☐ amber	95.00	105.00	100.00
☐ yellow	100.00	110.00	105.00
☐ milk glass	60.00	80.00	65.00
☐ clear	60.00	80.00	65.00

Teardrop and Tassel

	Current Price Range		Prior Year Average
Goblet			
☐ blue	90.00	100.00	95.00
☐ green	80.00	95.00	82.50
☐ amber	60.00	80.00	62.50
☐ yellow	80.00	90.00	85.00
☐ milk glass	60.00	80.00	65.00
☐ clear	60.00	80.00	65.00
Milk Pitcher			
☐ blue	160.00	210.00	175.00
☐ green	200.00	250.00	225.00
☐ amber	300.00	400.00	225.00
☐ yellow	150.00	160.00	155.00
☐ milk glass	80.00	100.00	85.00
☐ clear	80.00	100.00	85.00
Platter			
☐ blue	90.00	110.00	95.00
☐ green	90.00	110.00	95.00
☐ amber	100.00	125.00	105.00
☐ yellow	125.00	150.00	130.00
☐ milk glass	80.00	90.00	85.00
☐ clear	80.00	90.00	85.00
Relish Bowl			
☐ blue	90.00	110.00	95.00
☐ green	90.00	110.00	95.00
☐ amber	100.00	120.00	110.00
☐ yellow	120.00	125.00	122.50
☐ milk glass	60.00	80.00	65.00
☐ clear	60.00	80.00	65.00
Spooner			
☐ blue	50.00	60.00	55.00
☐ green	50.00	60.00	55.00
☐ amber	60.00	80.00	62.50
☐ yellow	70.00	75.00	72.50
☐ milk glass	40.00	50.00	45.00
☐ clear	40.00	50.00	45.00
Sugar, with cover			
☐ blue	90.00	100.00	95.00
☐ green	90.00	100.00	95.00
☐ amber	100.00	110.00	105.00
☐ yellow	110.00	120.00	115.00
☐ milk glass	80.00	90.00	85.00
☐ clear	80.00	90.00	85.00
Water Pitcher			
☐ blue	130.00	150.00	135.00
☐ green	130.00	150.00	135.00
☐ amber	140.00	150.00	145.00
☐ yellow	150.00	160.00	155.00
☐ milk glass	80.00	90.00	85.00

	Current Price Range		Prior Year Average
☐ clear	80.00	90.00	85.00
Wine Glass			
☐ blue	60.00	80.00	65.00
☐ green	60.00	80.00	65.00
☐ amber	70.00	80.00	75.00
☐ yellow	80.00	90.00	85.00
☐ milk glass	50.00	60.00	55.00
☐ clear	50.00	60.00	55.00

TERRACED BULL'S EYE

The squared flute base ends at the bottom of the body with tiny pleats tucked into a hexagonal collar. Inside the frames above are heavy double bull's eyes.

Goblet	200.00	300.00	225.00

THREE FACE
Duncan Miller Glass

The cameo motif is treated here with rope framing in large interconnecting circles. Three such panels take up most of the body on these pieces.

☐ **Butter,** with cover	135.00	165.00	145.00
☐ **Cake Stand,** height 14″	200.00	250.00	275.00
☐ **Cake Stand,** height 8″	150.00	200.00	175.00
☐ **Celery**	100.00	120.00	105.00
☐ **Claret Glass**	78.00	92.00	82.00
☐ **Champagne**	350.00	400.00	375.00
☐ **Compote,** with cover	225.00	250.00	230.00
☐ **Cracker Jar**	600.00	700.00	625.00

Three Face

	Current Price Range		Prior Year Average
☐ Goblet	75.00	100.00	77.50
☐ Hurricane Lamp	125.00	150.00	130.00
☐ Milk Pitcher	300.00	400.00	325.00
☐ Salt Dip	35.00	45.00	37.50
☐ Salt Shaker	50.00	60.00	55.00
☐ Sauce, footed, diameter 6″	20.00	30.00	25.00
☐ Sauce, footed, diameter 8″	30.00	40.00	35.00
☐ Spooner	75.00	100.00	77.50
☐ Sugar, with cover	100.00	125.00	115.00
☐ Water Pitcher	250.00	300.00	260.00
☐ Wine Glass	200.00	300.00	225.00

TIDY

This is a lightly molded floral pattern with bud flowers and foliage. The design is sparse with lots of clear glass in the background. On covered pieces the filial is shaped like a tree trunk.

☐ Berry Bowl, diameter 5″	15.00	20.00	17.50
☐ Berry Bowl, diameter 6″	20.00	30.00	25.00
☐ Bowl	20.00	30.00	25.00
☐ Bread Tray	30.00	40.00	35.00
☐ Butter	25.00	35.00	27.50
☐ Butter, with cover	30.00	40.00	35.00
☐ Cake Stand	25.00	35.00	27.50
☐ Creamer	30.00	40.00	32.50
☐ Celery	30.00	40.00	35.00
☐ Compote, high	25.00	35.00	27.50
☐ Compote, low	20.00	30.00	27.50
☐ Cordial Glass	20.00	30.00	27.50
☐ Creamer	25.00	35.00	27.50
☐ Dish	30.00	42.00	35.00
☐ Egg Cup	25.00	35.00	27.50
☐ Goblet	27.00	32.00	27.50
☐ Milk Pitcher	30.00	40.00	35.00
☐ Mug	30.00	40.00	35.00
☐ Plate	20.00	30.00	25.00
☐ Platter	30.00	40.00	35.00
☐ Relish Bowl	20.00	30.00	25.00
☐ Salt	20.00	30.00	25.00
☐ Sauce, flat	10.00	15.00	12.50
☐ Sauce, footed	15.00	20.00	27.00
☐ Spooner	20.00	30.00	25.00
☐ Sugar, with cover	30.00	40.00	35.00
☐ Toothpick	20.00	30.00	25.00
☐ Tumbler	15.00	20.00	17.50
☐ Water Pitcher	40.00	60.00	45.00
☐ Wine Glass	20.00	30.00	25.00

Tulip with Sawtooth

TULIP WITH SAWTOOTH

Tulip design with small triangle of sawtooth pattern at base. Wide plain band across top.

	Current Price Range		Prior Year Average
☐ **Champagne**	80.00	88.00	76.00
☐ **Compote,** covered, diameter 6″	105.00	115.00	100.00
☐ **Compote,** open, diameter 7″	45.00	55.00	41.00
☐ **Compote,** open, diameter 9″	55.00	65.00	50.00
☐ **Creamer**	105.00	115.00	101.00
☐ **Decanter,** handled, stoppered, quart	110.00	120.00	105.00
☐ **Egg Cup**	45.00	53.00	40.00
☐ **Egg Cup,** covered	130.00	140.00	127.00
☐ **Goblet,** height 7″	55.00	70.00	60.00
☐ **Jug,** quart	115.00	125.00	110.00
☐ **Mug**	85.00	93.00	81.00
☐ **Pitcher**	155.00	165.00	150.00
☐ **Plate,** diameter 6″	65.00	75.00	60.00
☐ **Salt,** footed	40.00	50.00	35.00
☐ **Salt,** footed, scalloped edge	50.00	58.00	48.00
☐ **Spoon Holder**	35.00	45.00	31.00
☐ **Sugar Bowl,** covered	105.00	115.00	100.00
☐ **Sugar Bowl,** open	55.00	63.00	50.00
☐ **Tumbler,** footed	60.00	70.00	55.00

U.S. COIN-DIME

This highly collectible pattern is rare because the U.S. mint took a dim view of using currency for resale and profit. They shut down the manufacturing shortly after it began—causing the piece to become instantly collectible. The glass is heavy, the bottom band consists of dimes implanted in squared flutes.

	Current Price Range		Prior Year Average
☐ Berry Bowl, diameter 5½"	400.00	500.00	425.00
☐ Bowl, diameter 8"	600.00	700.00	625.00
☐ Bread Tray	200.00	300.00	225.00
☐ Cake Stand, diameter 9"	400.00	500.00	425.00
☐ Celery Tray	225.00	300.00	250.00
☐ Celery Vase	350.00	400.00	375.00
☐ Champagne	325.00	400.00	350.00
☐ Claret	325.00	400.00	350.00
☐ Compote, high, large	230.00	300.00	275.00
☐ Compote, high, with cover	425.00	475.00	430.00
☐ Creamer	400.00	500.00	425.00
☐ Cruet, with stopper	600.00	700.00	625.00
☐ Epergne	600.00	700.00	625.00
☐ Finger Bowl	300.00	400.00	325.00
☐ Goblet	200.00	300.00	225.00
☐ Goblet, flare rim	400.00	500.00	425.00
☐ Lamp, round	375.00	425.00	390.00
☐ Lamp, square	400.00	450.00	415.00
☐ Mug	400.00	500.00	425.00
☐ Pickle Dish	175.00	225.00	190.00
☐ Salt Shaker, sterling top	135.00	175.00	150.00
☐ Sauce, flat	130.00	150.00	135.00
☐ Sauce, footed	175.00	225.00	185.00
☐ Sugar	150.00	300.00	175.00
☐ Sugar, with cover	400.00	500.00	425.00
☐ Spooner	250.00	350.00	260.00
☐ Syrup Pitcher	500.00	600.00	525.00
☐ Toothpick	70.00	90.00	72.50
☐ Waste Bowl	260.00	300.00	275.00
☐ Water Pitcher	500.00	600.00	525.00
☐ Water Tray, rectangular	350.00	400.00	375.00
☐ Wine Glass	300.00	400.00	325.00

U.S. COIN-HALF DOLLAR

This pattern is equally as collectable as the dime version for the same reasons. Production was stopped a few short months after it began and although it was made in the widest variety of pieces, few ever make it to the marketplace. Besides the difference in the coin, the most notable variation from the dime pattern is the round, ridge decorated frames that contain the half dollars.

☐ Berry Bowl, diameter 5½"	400.00	500.00	425.00
☐ Bowl, diameter 8"	600.00	700.00	625.00
☐ Bread Tray	200.00	300.00	225.00
☐ Cake Stand, diameter 9"	400.00	500.00	425.00
☐ Celery Tray	225.00	300.00	250.00
☐ Celery Vase	350.00	400.00	375.00
☐ Champagne	325.00	400.00	350.00
☐ Claret	325.00	400.00	350.00

		Current Price Range		Prior Year Average
☐ **Compote,** high, large		230.00	300.00	275.00
☐ **Compote,** high, with cover		425.00	475.00	430.00
☐ **Creamer**		400.00	500.00	425.00
☐ **Cruet,** with stopper		600.00	700.00	625.00
☐ **Epergne**		600.00	700.00	625.00
☐ **Finger Bowl**		300.00	400.00	325.00
☐ **Goblet**		200.00	300.00	225.00
☐ **Goblet,** flare rim		400.00	500.00	425.00
☐ **Lamp,** round		375.00	425.00	390.00
☐ **Lamp,** square		400.00	450.00	415.00
☐ **Mug**		400.00	500.00	425.00
☐ **Pickle Dish**		175.00	225.00	190.00
☐ **Salt Shaker,** sterling top		135.00	175.00	150.00
☐ **Sauce,** flat		130.00	150.00	135.00
☐ **Sauce,** footed		175.00	225.00	185.00
☐ **Spooner**		250.00	350.00	260.00
☐ **Sugar**		150.00	300.00	175.00
☐ **Sugar,** with cover		400.00	500.00	425.00
☐ **Syrup Pitcher**		500.00	600.00	525.00
☐ **Toothpick**		70.00	90.00	72.50
☐ **Waste Bowl**		260.00	300.00	275.00
☐ **Water Pitcher**		500.00	600.00	525.00
☐ **Water Tray,** rectangular		350.00	400.00	375.00
☐ **Wine Glass**		300.00	400.00	325.00

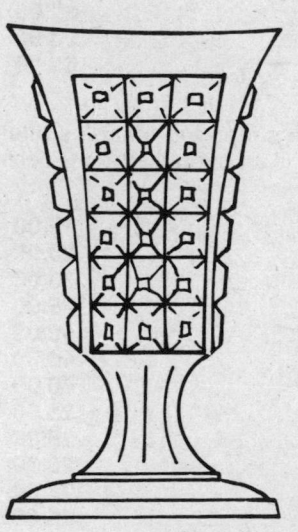

Waffle

WAFFLE
Boston and Sandwich

Waffling has been used on every type of glassware for a good reason. The deeply molded prism square shows off the light refractions that make collecting glassware so popular. In pressed glass, Waffle is an overall design, texturing the surface with wide panels. The glass has to be heavy to allow for the deep molding.

	Current Price Range		Prior Year Average
☐ Butter, covered	130.00	140.00	126.00
☐ Compote, covered	135.00	145.00	130.00
☐ Compote, open	70.00	80.00	65.00
☐ Creamer	115.00	125.00	110.00
☐ Decanter, no stopper	60.00	70.00	55.00
☐ Decanter, stoppered	105.00	115.00	100.00
☐ Egg Cup	30.00	40.00	28.00
☐ Goblet	55.00	65.00	50.00
☐ Lamp, all glass	180.00	190.00	173.00
☐ Lamp, marble base	130.00	140.00	122.00
☐ Pitcher, water	110.00	120.00	105.00
☐ Plate, diameter 6"	30.00	40.00	25.00
☐ Salt, covered	110.00	120.00	105.00
☐ Salt, footed	40.00	50.00	35.00
☐ Sauce, flat	20.00	25.00	18.00
☐ Spoon Holder	60.00	70.00	55.00
☐ Tumbler, water, footed	80.00	90.00	75.00
☐ Whiskey, handled	90.00	100.00	85.00
☐ Wine Glass	65.00	75.00	63.00

WASHBOARD

The stepped panels are shaped in triangles alternating with opposed spears of vertical flutes. It is an overall pattern, occupying all of the available space.

☐ Berry Bowl	15.00	25.00	15.50
☐ Bowl	20.00	30.00	25.00
☐ Bread Tray	30.00	40.00	35.00
☐ Butter	25.00	30.00	25.00
☐ Butter, with cover	40.00	50.00	45.00
☐ Cake Stand	40.00	50.00	45.00
☐ Creamer	40.00	50.00	45.00
☐ Celery	25.00	35.00	27.50
☐ Compote, high	25.00	35.00	27.50
☐ Compote, low	20.00	30.00	22.50
☐ Cordial Glass	25.00	35.00	27.50
☐ Creamer	25.00	35.00	27.50
☐ Dish	30.00	40.00	35.00
☐ Egg Cup	25.00	35.00	27.50
☐ Goblet	20.00	30.00	25.50
☐ Milk Pitcher	30.00	40.00	35.00

	Current Price Range		Prior Year Average
☐ **Mug**	20.00	30.00	22.50
☐ **Plate**	20.00	30.00	25.00
☐ **Platter**	30.00	40.00	35.00
☐ **Relish Bowl**	25.00	35.00	27.50
☐ **Salt**	30.00	40.00	35.00
☐ **Sauce,** flat	10.00	12.00	10.50
☐ **Sauce,** footed	15.00	20.00	17.50
☐ **Spooner**	20.00	30.00	25.00
☐ **Sugar,** with cover	30.00	40.00	35.00
☐ **Toothpick**	35.00	45.00	37.50
☐ **Tumbler**	20.00	30.00	25.00
☐ **Water Pitcher**	60.00	80.00	65.00
☐ **Wine Glass**	20.00	30.00	25.00

WASHINGTON
New England Glass

Thumbprint rows, arranged vertically, alternate with elongated ovals made up of smooth glass. The two motifs are separated by draped ridging which stretches out to sharp prism. The finish is smooth, the design well-balanced.

☐ **Bitters Bottle**	80.00	90.00	75.00
☐ **Bowl,** low, covered	70.00	80.00	73.00
☐ **Bowl,** tall, covered	100.00	110.00	95.00
☐ **Butter Dish,** covered, on pedestal	180.00	190.00	175.00
☐ **Celery**	105.00	115.00	100.00
☐ **Champagne Glass**	105.00	115.00	103.00

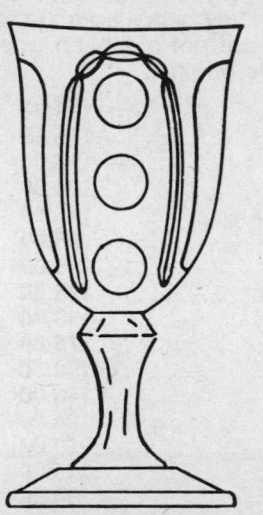

Washington

	Current Price Range		Prior Year Average
☐ **Cordial**	158.00	168.00	155.00
☐ **Creamer**	205.00	215.00	200.00
☐ **Decanter**, no stopper	90.00	100.00	85.00
☐ **Decanter**, with stopper	155.00	165.00	150.00
☐ **Egg Cup**	75.00	85.00	70.00
☐ **Goblet**	80.00	90.00	74.00
☐ **Pitcher**, syrup	125.00	135.00	120.00
☐ **Salt**, footed	60.00	70.00	55.00
☐ **Sauce Dish**, diameter 4½″	25.00	35.00	20.00
☐ **Spooner**	70.00	80.00	68.00
☐ **Sugar**, covered	110.00	120.00	105.00
☐ **Sugar**, open	50.00	60.00	45.00
☐ **Water Pitcher**	260.00	270.00	255.00
☐ **Wine Glass**	70.00	80.00	68.00

WEDDING RING

One row of overlapping rings with plain band at top.

☐ **Champagne**	35.00	45.00	30.00
☐ **Creamer**	38.00	46.00	35.00
☐ **Decanter**	50.00	60.00	45.00
☐ **Goblet**	35.00	45.00	31.00
☐ **Pitcher**	50.00	58.00	47.00
☐ **Tumbler**	35.00	45.00	32.00
☐ **Wine**	30.00	35.00	27.00

WESTWARD HO

A low panel of deer, foliage, and mountains covers the bottom half of these pieces. A double row of tiny beads from the scene on the top and bottom along the base. This pattern has been extensively reproduced, although less sharply than the original.

☐ **Bread Platter**, oval	110.00	125.00	115.00
☐ **Butter**, with lid	175.00	200.00	185.00
☐ **Celery**	125.00	150.00	130.00
☐ **Champagne**	300.00	400.00	325.00
☐ **Compote**, high, with cover	145.00	155.00	150.00
☐ **Compote**, large	95.00	110.00	100.00
☐ **Compote**, low, with cover	135.00	145.00	140.00
☐ **Compote**, small, with cover	175.00	200.00	185.00
☐ **Cordial Glass**	160.00	180.00	165.00
☐ **Creamer**	175.00	200.00	180.00
☐ **Jam Jar**, with lid	190.00	210.00	195.00
☐ **Pickle Jar**, oval	145.00	155.00	147.00
☐ **Sauce**, flat	24.00	26.00	24.50
☐ **Sauce**, footed	28.00	32.00	30.00
☐ **Sugar**, with lid	155.00	165.00	160.00
☐ **Spooner**	90.00	110.00	95.00

	Current Price Range		Prior Year Average
☐ **Water Pitcher**	225.00	250.00	230.00
☐ **Wine Goblet**	140.00	160.00	145.00

WHEAT AND BARLEY
Bryce Bros.

Wheat and barley hanging down on piece. Design is also fluted.

Bowl, covered, diameter 8″			
☐ clear.............................	26.00	30.00	22.00
☐ canary	38.00	43.00	32.00
☐ amber	38.00	43.00	32.00
☐ blue	42.00	46.00	38.00
Butter, covered			
☐ clear.............................	40.00	45.00	35.00
☐ canary	55.00	63.00	50.00
☐ amber	55.00	63.00	50.00
☐ blue	64.00	68.00	60.00
Cake Stand, height 8″			
☐ clear.............................	22.00	27.00	17.00
☐ canary	33.00	37.00	28.00
☐ amber	33.00	37.00	28.00
☐ blue	36.00	40.00	31.00
Cake Stand, height 9″			
☐ clear.............................	26.00	31.00	21.00
☐ canary	39.00	44.00	35.00
☐ amber	39.00	44.00	35.00
☐ blue	43.00	48.00	40.00
Cake Stand, height 10″			
☐ clear.............................	30.00	35.00	25.00
☐ canary	45.00	50.00	40.00
☐ amber	45.00	50.00	40.00
☐ blue	48.00	53.00	44.00
Compote, covered			
☐ clear.............................	40.00	45.00	35.00
☐ canary	55.00	60.00	50.00
☐ amber	55.00	60.00	50.00
☐ blue	57.00	63.00	53.00
Creamer, plain, footed			
☐ clear.............................	25.00	30.00	21.00
☐ canary	37.00	43.00	32.00
☐ amber	37.00	43.00	32.00
☐ blue	40.00	45.00	35.00
Goblet			
☐ clear.............................	20.00	25.00	16.00
☐ canary	30.00	35.00	25.00
☐ amber	30.00	35.00	25.00
☐ blue	35.00	40.00	30.00
Mug			
☐ clear.............................	23.00	28.00	20.00

	Current Price Range		Prior Year Average
☐ canary	34.00	38.00	30.00
☐ amber	34.00	38.00	30.00
☐ blue	37.00	41.00	32.00
Nappy, handled			
☐ clear	15.00	20.00	12.00
☐ canary	24.00	30.00	20.00
☐ amber	24.00	30.00	20.00
☐ blue	27.00	33.00	22.00
Pitcher, water			
☐ clear	32.00	40.00	27.00
☐ canary	47.00	53.00	44.00
☐ amber	47.00	53.00	44.00
☐ blue	50.00	56.00	45.00
Plate, diameter 7"			
☐ clear	20.00	25.00	16.00
☐ canary	30.00	35.00	25.00
☐ amber	30.00	35.00	25.00
☐ blue	33.00	40.00	28.00
Plate, handled, diameter 9"			
☐ clear	25.00	30.00	20.00
☐ canary	35.00	40.00	30.00
☐ amber	35.00	40.00	30.00
☐ blue	38.00	43.00	34.00
Relish			
☐ clear	15.00	20.00	12.00
☐ canary	22.00	28.00	18.00
☐ amber	22.00	28.00	18.00
☐ blue	25.00	30.00	20.00
Sauce, flat			
☐ clear	15.00	20.00	12.00
☐ canary	24.00	29.00	20.00
☐ amber	24.00	29.00	20.00
☐ blue	26.00	30.00	22.00
Sauce, footed			
☐ clear	17.00	22.00	15.00
☐ canary	25.00	30.00	20.00
☐ amber	25.00	30.00	20.00
☐ blue	28.00	33.00	24.00
Salt and Pepper Shakers, pair			
☐ clear	32.00	36.00	28.00
☐ canary	42.00	48.00	37.00
☐ amber	42.00	48.00	37.00
☐ blue	45.00	52.00	40.00
Spoon Holder			
☐ clear	23.00	28.00	20.00
☐ canary	32.00	37.00	28.00
☐ amber	32.00	37.00	28.00
☐ blue	35.00	40.00	30.00

	Current Price Range		Prior Year Average
Sugar, covered			
☐ clear	33.00	39.00	27.00
☐ canary	45.00	50.00	40.00
☐ amber	45.00	50.00	40.00
☐ blue	48.00	55.00	44.00
Tumbler			
☐ clear	21.00	26.00	17.00
☐ canary	30.00	35.00	25.00
☐ amber	30.00	35.00	25.00
☐ blue	34.00	39.00	30.00
Toothpick Holder			
☐ clear	14.00	18.00	11.00
☐ canary	20.00	25.00	15.00
☐ amber	20.00	25.00	15.00
☐ blue	24.00	29.00	20.00

WILDFLOWER
Adams

This is one of the most popular patterns in pressed glass because of its intricate but well-balanced design. The upper bands are wide waffle ridges of varying sizes. The bottom bands are fat ribbings. The rest of the glass is smooth except for lightly stippled vines and flowers which twist around the mid-body. The shape of the pieces is ornate in keeping with the elegant design.

Bowl, round			
☐ clear	15.00	19.00	12.00

Wildflower

	Current Price Range		Prior Year Average
☐ light amber	20.00	24.00	16.00
☐ yellow	32.00	38.00	28.00
☐ deep amber	32.00	38.00	28.00
☐ blue	32.00	38.00	28.00
☐ green	32.00	38.00	28.00
Bowl, square			
☐ clear	23.00	28.00	19.00
☐ light amber	26.00	33.00	21.00
☐ yellow	48.00	56.00	43.00
☐ deep amber	48.00	56.00	43.00
☐ blue	48.00	56.00	43.00
☐ green	48.00	56.00	43.00
Butter, covered, footed			
☐ clear	42.00	49.00	37.00
☐ light amber	52.00	58.00	46.00
☐ yellow	64.00	70.00	60.00
☐ deep amber	64.00	70.00	60.00
☐ blue	64.00	70.00	60.00
☐ green	64.00	70.00	60.00
Butter, flat, covered			
☐ clear	36.00	41.00	31.00
☐ light amber	45.00	50.00	40.00
☐ yellow	58.00	65.00	54.00
☐ deep amber	58.00	65.00	54.00
☐ blue	58.00	65.00	54.00
☐ green	58.00	65.00	54.00
Cake Stand, large, metal handle			
☐ clear	50.00	58.00	45.00
☐ light amber	60.00	65.00	55.00
☐ yellow	80.00	90.00	75.00
☐ deep amber	80.00	90.00	75.00
☐ blue	80.00	90.00	75.00
☐ green	80.00	90.00	75.00
Cake Stand, small			
☐ clear	45.00	50.00	40.00
☐ light amber	54.00	59.00	50.00
☐ yellow	73.00	80.00	68.00
☐ deep amber	73.00	80.00	68.00
☐ blue	73.00	80.00	68.00
☐ green	73.00	80.00	68.00
Celery			
☐ clear	30.00	36.00	26.00
☐ light amber	39.00	45.00	33.00
☐ yellow	55.00	63.00	50.00
☐ dark amber	55.00	63.00	50.00
☐ blue	55.00	63.00	50.00
☐ green	55.00	63.00	50.00

	Current Price Range		Prior Year Average
Champagne			
☐ clear	35.00	40.00	30.00
☐ light amber	44.00	51.00	40.00
☐ yellow	70.00	76.00	65.00
☐ dark amber	70.00	76.00	65.00
☐ blue	70.00	76.00	65.00
☐ green	70.00	76.00	65.00
Compote, covered			
☐ clear	40.00	48.00	36.00
☐ light amber	50.00	56.00	45.00
☐ yellow	75.00	82.00	70.00
☐ dark amber	75.00	82.00	70.00
☐ blue	75.00	82.00	70.00
☐ green	75.00	82.00	70.00
Compote, open			
☐ clear	35.00	40.00	30.00
☐ light amber	48.00	55.00	43.00
☐ yellow	60.00	68.00	55.00
☐ dark amber	60.00	68.00	55.00
☐ blue	60.00	68.00	55.00
☐ green	60.00	68.00	55.00
Cordial			
☐ clear	30.00	36.00	26.00
☐ light amber	38.00	43.00	33.00
☐ yellow	55.00	65.00	50.00
☐ dark amber	55.00	65.00	50.00
☐ blue	55.00	65.00	50.00
☐ green	55.00	65.00	50.00
Creamer			
☐ clear	25.00	30.00	21.00
☐ light amber	33.00	39.00	28.00
☐ yellow	49.00	56.00	44.00
☐ dark amber	49.00	56.00	44.00
☐ blue	49.00	56.00	44.00
☐ green	49.00	56.00	44.00
Goblet			
☐ clear	27.00	32.00	24.00
☐ light amber	35.00	43.00	31.00
☐ yellow	48.00	55.00	44.00
☐ dark amber	48.00	55.00	44.00
☐ blue	48.00	55.00	44.00
☐ green	48.00	55.00	44.00
Pitcher			
☐ clear	50.00	55.00	45.00
☐ light amber	58.00	65.00	54.00
☐ yellow	75.00	85.00	70.00
☐ dark amber	75.00	85.00	70.00
☐ blue	75.00	85.00	70.00

	Current Price Range		Prior Year Average
☐ green	75.00	85.00	70.00
Plate, round			
☐ clear	20.00	25.00	16.00
☐ light amber	26.00	31.00	21.00
☐ yellow	35.00	40.00	30.00
☐ dark amber	35.00	40.00	30.00
☐ blue	35.00	40.00	30.00
☐ green	35.00	40.00	30.00
Plate, square			
☐ clear	30.00	36.00	26.00
☐ light amber	38.00	43.00	33.00
☐ yellow	53.00	60.00	48.00
☐ dark amber	53.00	60.00	48.00
☐ blue	53.00	60.00	48.00
☐ green	53.00	60.00	48.00
Platter, oblong, diameter 10″			
☐ clear	35.00	40.00	30.00
☐ light amber	43.00	49.00	38.00
☐ yellow	62.00	69.00	57.00
☐ dark amber	62.00	69.00	57.00
☐ blue	62.00	69.00	57.00
☐ green	62.00	69.00	57.00
Relish			
☐ clear	22.00	26.00	18.00
☐ light amber	30.00	35.00	25.00
☐ yellow	44.00	49.00	40.00
☐ dark amber	44.00	49.00	40.00
☐ blue	44.00	49.00	40.00
☐ green	44.00	49.00	40.00
Salt and Pepper Shakers, pair			
☐ clear	43.00	49.00	39.00
☐ light amber	48.00	55.00	43.00
☐ yellow	68.00	76.00	63.00
☐ dark amber	68.00	76.00	63.00
☐ blue	68.00	76.00	63.00
☐ green	68.00	76.00	63.00
Salt, turtle			
☐ clear	40.00	46.00	36.00
☐ light amber	53.00	59.00	48.00
☐ yellow	66.00	72.00	61.00
☐ dark amber	66.00	72.00	61.00
☐ blue	66.00	72.00	61.00
☐ green	66.00	72.00	61.00
Sauce, flat			
☐ clear	12.00	17.00	10.00
☐ light amber	20.00	25.00	15.00
☐ yellow	26.00	30.00	21.00
☐ dark amber	26.00	30.00	21.00

	Current Price Range		Prior Year Average
☐ blue	26.00	30.00	21.00
☐ green	26.00	30.00	21.00
Sauce, footed			
☐ clear	15.00	19.00	12.00
☐ light amber	23.00	28.00	20.00
☐ yellow	30.00	36.00	25.00
☐ dark amber	30.00	36.00	25.00
☐ blue	30.00	36.00	25.00
☐ green	30.00	36.00	25.00
Sauce, round			
☐ clear	11.00	16.00	9.00
☐ light amber	19.00	24.00	14.00
☐ yellow	25.00	29.00	20.00
☐ dark amber	25.00	29.00	20.00
☐ blue	25.00	29.00	20.00
☐ green	25.00	29.00	20.00
Sauce, square			
☐ clear	13.00	16.00	12.00
☐ light amber	21.00	26.00	16.00
☐ yellow	27.00	31.00	22.00
☐ dark amber	27.00	31.00	22.00
☐ blue	27.00	31.00	22.00
☐ green	27.00	31.00	22.00
Spoon Holder			
☐ clear	20.00	25.00	15.00
☐ light amber	31.00	36.00	28.00
☐ yellow	41.00	48.00	37.00
☐ dark amber	41.00	48.00	37.00
☐ blue	41.00	48.00	37.00
☐ green	41.00	48.00	37.00
Sugar, covered			
☐ clear	35.00	43.00	30.00
☐ light amber	48.00	55.00	44.00
☐ yellow	63.00	72.00	58.00
☐ dark amber	63.00	72.00	58.00
☐ blue	63.00	72.00	58.00
☐ green	63.00	72.00	58.00
Syrup			
☐ clear	45.00	50.00	40.00
☐ light amber	53.00	58.00	49.00
☐ yellow	65.00	75.00	60.00
☐ dark amber	65.00	75.00	60.00
☐ blue	65.00	75.00	60.00
☐ green	65.00	75.00	60.00
Tray			
☐ clear	45.00	53.00	40.00
☐ light amber	56.00	64.00	51.00
☐ yellow	75.00	83.00	69.00

	Current Price Range		Prior Year Average
☐ dark amber	75.00	83.00	69.00
☐ blue	75.00	83.00	69.00
☐ green	75.00	83.00	69.00
Tumbler			
☐ clear	23.00	27.00	19.00
☐ light amber	28.00	35.00	24.00
☐ yellow	40.00	46.00	35.00
☐ dark amber	40.00	46.00	35.00
☐ blue	40.00	46.00	35.00
☐ green	40.00	46.00	35.00
Wine			
☐ clear	31.00	38.00	26.00
☐ light amber	39.00	45.00	35.00
☐ yellow	57.00	65.00	54.00
☐ dark amber	57.00	65.00	54.00
☐ blue	57.00	65.00	54.00
☐ green	57.00	65.00	54.00

WILLOW OAK
Bryce Bros.

A panel of flower and leaves alternates with a slender panel of two flowers. Band of scroll design on top and bottom of panel. Narrow beaded strip on top of entire pattern while vertical ribbon at bottom of piece. Plain band at top of piece.

Bowl, berry			
☐ clear	28.00	35.00	24.00
☐ amber	45.00	50.00	40.00
☐ blue	55.00	60.00	50.00
Bowl, covered			
☐ clear	38.00	44.00	34.00

BIBLIOGRAPHY

Often glass collectors are attracted to more than one type of glass. For this reason, the following bibliography lists a variety of books pertaining to glass.

Addis, Wily P., *What's Behind Old Carnival: A Study of Patterns Seldom Seen,* Lakewood, OH, privately printed, 1971.

Arwas, Victor, *Glass: Art Nouveau to Art Deco,* New York, Rizzoli International, 1977.

Avila, George C., *The Pairpont Glass Story,* Reynolds-DeWalt Printing, 1968.

Barret, Richard Carter, *A Collector's Handbook of Blown and Pressed American Glass,* Manchester, VT, Forward's Color Productions, 1967.

Barret, Richard Carter, *A Collector's Handbook of American Art Glass,* Manchester, VT, Forward's Color Productions, 1971.

Belknap, E.M., *Milk Glass,* New York, Crown Publishers.

Boggess, Bill and Louise, *American Brilliant Cut Glass,* Crown Publishers, New York, 1977.

Bones, Frances, *The Book of Duncan Glass,* Des Moines, Wallace-Homestead, 1973.

Bount, Henry, and Blount, Berniece, *French Cameo Glass,* Des Moines, Wallace-Homestead, 1968.

Brahmer, Bonnie J., *Custard Glass,* Springfield, MO, privately published, 1966.

Bridgeman, Harriet, and Elizabeth Drury, *The Encyclopedia of Victoriana,* Macmillan, 1975.

Brown, Clark W., *A Supplement To Salt Dishes,* Des Moines, Wallace-Homestead, 1970.

Butler, Joseph T., *American Antiques 1800–1900,* Odyssey Press, 1965.

Carved and Decorated European Glass, Rutland, VT, Charles E. Tuttle Co., Inc., 1970.

Cole, Ann Kilborn, *Golden Guide to American Antiques,* New York, Golden Press, 1967.

Contemporary Art Glass, New York, Crown Publishers, 1975.

Cooke, Lawrence S., ed., *Lighting in America. From Colonial Rushlights to VictorianChandeliers,* Antiques Magazine Library, New York, Main Street/Universe Books, 1977.

Cosentino, Geraldine, and Regina Stewart, *Carnival Glass, A Guide for the Beginning Collector,* New York, Golden Press, 1976.

Daniel, Dorothy, *Cut and Engraved Glass 1771–1905,* New York, M. Barrows & Company, 1950.

Darr, Patrick, *A Guide to Art and Pattern Glass,* Pilgrim House Publishing Co., 1960.

Davidson, Marshall B., ed., *The American Heritage History of Colonial Antiques,* New York, American Heritage, 1967.

Davis, Derek C. and Keith Middlemas, *Colored Glass,* New York, Clarkson N. Potter, Inc.

Davis, Frank, *Antique Glass and Glass Collecting,* London, Hamlyn, 1973.

Davis, Frank, *The Country Life Book of Glass,* Glasgow, The University Press, 1966.

DiBartolomeo, Robert E., ed., *American Glass From the Pages of Antiques,* Vol. II, Pressed and Cut, Princeton, The Pyne Press, 1974.

Drepperd, Carl W., *ABC's of Old Glass,* New York, Doubleday & Company, 1968.

Drepperd, Carl W., *A Dictionary of American Antiques,* New York, Doubleday & Company, 1968.

Edwards, Bill, *Millersburg, The Queen of Carnival Glass,* Collector Books, 1976.

Elville, E.M., *English and Irish Cut Glass,* Country Life Limited, 1953.

Ericson, Eric E., *A Guide To Colored Steuben Glass (1903-1933),* two vols., Colorado, The Lithographic Press, 1963–65.

Florence, Gene, *Elegant Glassware of the Depression Era,* Paducah, Collector Books, 1983.

Florence, Gene, *Kitchen Glassware of the Depression Years,* Paducah, Collector Books, 1981.

Florence, Gene, *Pocket Guide to Depression Glass,* revised 3rd ed., Paducah, Collector Books, 1983.

Florence, Gene, *The Collector's Encyclopedia of Akro Agate Glassware,* Paducah, Collector Books, 1982.

Florence, Gene, *The Collector's Encyclopedia of Depression Glass,* 6th ed., Paducah, KY, Collector Books, 1984.

Frazer, Margaret, *Colored Glass, Discovering Antiques,* Vol. 8, New York, Greystone Press, 1973, pp. 904–907.

Gardner, Paul V., *The Glass of Frederick Carder,* New York, Crown Publishers, 1971.

Greguire, Helen, *Carnival in Lights,* 103 Trimmer Road, Hilton, NY 14468, privately published, 1975.

Grover, Ray and Grover, Lee, *Art Glass Nouveau,* Rutland, VT, Charles E. Tuttle Co., 1967.

Grover, Ray and Grover, Lee, *Carved & Decorated European Art Glass,* Rutland, VT, Charles E. Tuttle Co., 1967.

Hammond, Dorothy, *Confusing Collectibles,* IA, Mid-American Book Company, 1969.

Hammond, Dorothy, *More Confusing Collectibles,* KS, C.B.P. Publishing Company, 1972.

Hand, Sherman, *Colors in Carnival Glass,* Books 1–4, Des Moines, Wallace-Homestead Book Co., 1967–1974.

Hartley, Julia M., and Cobb, Mary M., *The States Series, Early American Pattern Glass,* privately published, 1976.

Hartung, Marion T., *Carnival Glass,* Books 1–10, 718 Constitution Street, Emporia, KS 66801, privately published, 1967–1973.

Hartung, Marion T., *Northwood Pattern Glass In Color,* privately published, 1969.

Haslam, Malcolm, *Marks and Monograms of the Modern Movement, 1875–1930,* New York, Charles Scribner's Sons, 1977.

Heacock, William, *Encyclopedia of Victorian Colored Pattern Glass, Book III,* Antique Publications, 1976.

Hinds, Maxine, *Smashed Glass Reclaimed and Restored,* Route 2, P.O. Box 540, Galt, CA 95632, privately printed, 1972.

Hollister, Paul, Jr., *The Encyclopedia of Glass Paperweights,* New York, Clarkson N. Potter, 1969.

Hotchkiss, John F., *Art Glass Handbook,* New York, Hawthorn Books, 1972.

Hunter, Frederick William, *Stiegel Glass,* NY, Dover Publications, 1950.

Innes, Lowell, *Pittsburgh Glass 1797–1891: A History and Guide for Collectors,* Houghton Mifflin Company, 1976.

Jenkins, Dorothy H., *A Fortune In The Junk Pile,* New York, Crown Publishing, 1963.

Kamm, Minnie Watson, *Two Hundred Pattern Glass Pitchers,* six volumes., Grosse Pointe Farms, MI, privately published.

Kamm, Minnie Watson, *A Second Two Hundred Pattern Glass Pitchers,* Kamm Publications, 1940.

Kamm, Minnie Watson, *A Fourth Pitcher Book,* Kamm Publications, 1950.

Kamm, Minnie W., and Wood, Serry (editors), *Encyclopedia of Antique Pattern Glass I,* Kamm Publications, 1961.

Kamm, Minnie W., and Wood, Serry (editors), *Encyclopedia of Antique Pattern Glass II,* Kamm Publications, 1961.

Klamkin, Marion, *The Collector's Guide to Carnival Glass,* Hawthorn Books, Inc., 1976.

Klein, William Karl, *Repairing and Restoring China and Glass,* New York, Harper & Row, 1962.

Koch, Robert, *Louis C. Tiffany, Rebel in Glass,* New York, Crown Publishers, 1964.

Koch, Robert, *Louis C. Tiffany's Glass—Bronzes—Lamps,* New York, Crown Publishers.

Lagerberg, Theodore and Viola, *Collectible Glass,* vols. 1, 2, and 4, New Port Richey, FL, privately published, 1963–1968.

Lee, Ruth Webb, *Early American Pressed Glass,* Wellesley Hills, MA, Lee Publications, 105 Suffolk Road, Wellesley Hills, MA 02181, 1933.

Lee, Ruth Webb, *Nineteenth Century Art Glass,* New York, M. Barrows and Company, 1952.

Lee, Ruth Webb, *Sandwich Glass,* Wellesley Hills, MA, Lee Publications, 1966.

Lee, Ruth Webb, *Victorian Glass Handbook,* Wellesley Hills, MA, Lee Publications, 1946.

Lee, Ruth Webb, and Rose, James H., *American Glass Cup Plates,* Wellesley Hills, MA, Lee Publications, 1948.

Libbey Glass, A Tradition of 150 Years, Toledo Museum of Art, 1968.

Lindsey, Bessie M., *American Historical Glass,* Rutland, VT, Charles E. Tuttle, 1967.

Malone, Laurence Adams, *How to Mend Your Treasures: Porcelain—(China)—Pottery—Glass,* New York, Phaedra Publishers, 1972.

McClinton, Katharine M., *Collecting American Victorian Antiques,* Charles Scribner's Sons, 1966.

McKean, Hugh F., *The "Lost" Treasures of Louis Comfort Tiffany,* Garden City, NY, Doubleday, 1980.

McKearin, George and Helen, *American Glass,* New York, Crown Publishers, 1966.

Mebane, John, *Collecting Brides' Baskets and Other Glass Fancies,* Des Moines, Wallace-Homestead Book Co., 1976.

Metz, Alice Hulett, *Early American Pattern Glass,* Chicago, privately published.

Metz, Alice Hulett, *More Early American Pattern Glass*, Vol. II, Chicago, privately published, 1965.

Moore, Donald E., *The Shape of Things in Carnival Glass*, 2101 Shoreline Drive, Alameda, CA 94501, privately published, 1975.

New England Glass Co. 1818–1888, Toledo Museum of Art, 1963.

Newman, Harold, *An Illustrated Dictionary of Glass*, London, Thames and Hudson, 1977.

Oliver, Elizabeth, *American Antique Glass*, New York, Golden Press, 1977.

Owens, Richard E., *Carnival Glass Tumblers*, 2611 Brass Lantern Drive, La Habra, CA 90361, privately published, 1975.

Papert, Emma, *The Illustrated Guide to American Glass*, Hawthorn Books, Inc., 1972.

Pearson, J. Michael, *Encyclopedia of American Cut and Engraved Glass (1880–1917), Vol. I: Geometric Conceptions*, 402844 Ocean View Station, Miami Beach, FL 33140, privately printed, 1975.

Pearson, J. Michael, *Encyclopedia of American Cut and Engraved Glass (1880–1917), Vol. II: Realistic Patterns*, 402844 Ocean View Station, Miami Beach, FL 33140, privately printed, 1977.

Pearson, J. Michael and Dorothy T., *American Cut Glass for the Discriminating Collector*, Miami, The Franklin Press, 1965.

Pennsylvania Glassware, 1870–1904, American Historical Catalog Collection, Princeton, The Pyne Press, 1972.

Peterson, Arthur G., *400 Trademarks on Glass*, Takoma Park, MD, Washington College Press, 1968.

Peterson, Arthur G., *Glass Salt Shakers: 1,000 Patterns*, Des Moines, Wallace-Homestead Book Company.

Peterson, Arthur G., *Salt and Salt Shakers*, Washington, D.C. Washington College Press.

Peterson, Arthur G., *333 Glass Salt Shakers*, Washington, D.C. Washington College Press.

Polak, Ada, *Glass, Its Tradition and Its Makers*, G.P. Putnam's Sons, 1975.

Presznick, Rose M., *Carnival Glass*, Books 1–6, 7810 Avon Lake Road, Lodi, OH 44254, privately published, 1966.

Presznick, Rose M., *Encyclopedia of New Carnival Glass and Iridescent Glass*, 7810 Avon Lake Road, Lodi, OH 44254, privately published, 1974.

Rainwater, Dorothy T. and H. Ivan, *American Silverplate*, Nashville, Thomas Nelson, Inc., and Hanover, PA, Everybody's Press.

Rainwater, Dorothy T., and H. Ivan, *Sterling Silver Holloware*, Princeton, Pyne Press.

Revi, Albert Christian, *American Art Nouveau Glass*, Nashville, Thomas Nelson, 1968.

Revi, Albert C., *American Cut and Engraved Glass*, Nashville, Thomas Nelson, Inc., 1970.

Revi, Albert C., *American Pressed Glass and Figure Bottles*, Nashville, Thomas Nelson, 1964.

Revi, Albert Christian, *Nineteenth Century Glass*, New York, Galahad Books, 1967.

Revi, Albert Christian, (ed.), *The Spinning Wheel's Complete Book of Antiques*, New York, Grosset & Dunlap, 1972.

Rose, James H., *The Story of American Pressed Glass of the Lacy Period, 1825–1850*, The Corning Museum of Glass, 1954.

Schrijver, Elka, *Glass and Crystal,* Universe Books, Inc., 1964.

Schwartz, Marvin D., *American Glass: Blown and Moulded,* New Jersey, The Pyne Press, 1974.

Schwartz, Marvin D., *Collector's Guide to Antique American Glass,* Doubleday & Company, Inc., 1969.

Shull, Thelma, *Victorian Antiques,* Rutland, VT, Charles E. Tuttle.

Springer, L. Elsinore, *The Collector's Book of Bells,* New York, Crown Publishers.

Stout, Sandra McPhee, *Depression Glass in Color,* Ephrata, WA, privately published.

Stout, Sandra M., *Depression Glass III,* Wallace-Homestead Book Co., 1976.

Swan, Frank H., *Portland Glass,* Des Moines, Wallace-Homestead Book Co.

Traub, Jules S., *The Glass of Desire Christian,* Chicago, The Art Glass Exchange, 1978.

Warren, Phelps, *Irish Glass,* Charles Scribner's Sons, 1970.

Watkins, Laura W., *Cambridge Glass, 1818–1888,* Bramhill House, 1930.

Weatherman, Hazel Marie, *Colored Glassware of the Depression Era,* revised and expanded edition, Springfield, MO, privately published.

Weatherman, Hazel Marie, *Colored Glassware of the Depression Era 2,* privately printed, 1970.

Webb, Jack Lawton, *A Guide to New Carnival Glass,* Joplin, Imperial Publishing Company.

Webber, Norman W., *Collecting Glass,* New York, Arco, 1972.

Weiss, Gustav, *Books of Glass,* Praeger Publishers, Inc., 1971.

Whitlow, Harry H., *Art, Colored and Cameo Glass,* Riverview, MI, privately published, 1967.

Whitmyer, Margaret and Kenn, *Children's Dishes,* Paducah, Collector Books, 1984.

Wiener, Herbert, and Freda Lipkowitz, *Rarities in American Cut Glass,* The Collectors House of Books Publishing Co., 1975.

Wilson, Kenneth M., *New England Glass and Glassmaking,* Old Sturbridge, Inc., 1972.

Ziegfeld, Edwin, Faulkner, Ray, and Hill, Gerald, *Art Today,* New York, Holt, Rinehart and Winston, 1965.

INDEX

The HOUSE OF COLLECTIBLES Series

☐ Please send me the following price guides—
☐ I would like the most current edition of the books listed below.

THE OFFICIAL PRICE GUIDES TO:

☐ 199-3	American Silver & Silver Plate 5th Ed.	$11.95
☐ 513-1	Antique Clocks 3rd Ed.	10.95
☐ 283-3	Antique & Modern Dolls 3rd Ed.	10.95
☐ 287-6	Antique & Modern Firearms 6th Ed.	11.95
☐ 738-X	Antiques & Collectibles 8th Ed.	10.95
☐ 289-2	Antique Jewelry 5th Ed.	11.95
☐ 539-5	Beer Cans & Collectibles 4th Ed.	7.95
☐ 521-2	Bottles Old & New 10th Ed.	10.95
☐ 532-8	Carnival Glass 2nd Ed.	10.95
☐ 295-7	Collectible Cameras 2nd Ed.	10.95
☐ 548-4	Collectibles of the '50s & '60s 1st Ed.	9.95
☐ 740-1	Collectible Toys 4th Ed.	10.95
☐ 531-X	Collector Cars 7th Ed.	12.95
☐ 538-7	Collector Handguns 4th Ed.	14.95
☐ 748-7	Collector Knives 9th Ed.	12.95
☐ 361-9	Collector Plates 5th Ed.	11.95
☐ 296-5	Collector Prints 7th Ed.	12.95
☐ 001-6	Depression Glass 2nd Ed.	9.95
☐ 589-1	Fine Art 1st Ed.	19.95
☐ 311-2	Glassware 3rd Ed.	10.95
☐ 243-4	Hummel Figurines & Plates 6th Ed.	10.95
☐ 523-9	Kitchen Collectibles 2nd Ed.	10.95
☐ 291-4	Military Collectibles 5th Ed.	11.95
☐ 525-5	Music Collectibles 6th Ed.	11.95
☐ 313-9	Old Books & Autographs 7th Ed.	11.95
☐ 298-1	Oriental Collectibles 3rd Ed.	11.95
☐ 746-0	Overstreet Comic Book 17th Ed.	11.95
☐ 522-0	Paperbacks & Magazines 1st Ed.	10.95
☐ 297-3	Paper Collectibles 5th Ed.	10.95
☐ 744-4	Political Memorabilia 1st Ed.	10.95
☐ 529-8	Pottery & Porcelain 6th Ed.	11.95
☐ 524-7	Radio, TV & Movie Memorabilia 3rd Ed.	11.95
☐ 288-4	Records 7th Ed.	10.95
☐ 247-7	Royal Doulton 5th Ed.	11.95
☐ 280-9	Science Fiction & Fantasy Collectibles 2nd Ed.	10.95
☐ 747-9	Sewing Collectibles 1st Ed.	8.95
☐ 358-9	Star Trek/Star Wars Collectibles 2nd Ed.	8.95
☐ 086-5	Watches 8th Ed.	12.95
☐ 248-5	Wicker 3rd Ed.	10.95

THE OFFICIAL:

☐ 445-3	Collector's Journal 1st Ed.	4.95
☐ 549-2	Directory to U.S. Flea Markets 1st Ed.	4.95
☐ 365-1	Encyclopedia of Antiques 1st Ed.	9.95
☐ 369-4	Guide to Buying and Selling Antiques 1st Ed.	9.95
☐ 414-3	Identification Guide to Early American Furniture 1st Ed.	9.95
☐ 413-5	Identification Guide to Glassware 1st Ed.	9.95
☐ 448-8	Identification Guide to Gunmarks 2nd Ed.	9.95
☐ 412-7	Identification Guide to Pottery & Porcelain 1st Ed.	$9.95
☐ 415-1	Identification Guide to Victorian Furniture 1st Ed.	9.95

THE OFFICIAL (SMALL SIZE) PRICE GUIDES TO:

☐ 309-0	Antiques & Flea Markets 4th Ed.	4.95
☐ 269-8	Antique Jewelry 3rd Ed.	4.95
☐ 085-7	Baseball Cards 8th Ed.	4.95
☐ 647-2	Bottles 3rd Ed.	4.95
☐ 544-1	Cars & Trucks 3rd Ed.	5.95
☐ 519-0	Collectible Americana 2nd Ed.	4.95
☐ 294-9	Collectible Records 3rd Ed.	4.95
☐ 306-6	Dolls 4th Ed.	4.95
☐ 359-7	Football Cards 7th Ed.	4.95
☐ 540-9	Glassware 3rd Ed.	4.95
☐ 526-3	Hummels 4th Ed.	4.95
☐ 279-5	Military Collectibles 3rd Ed.	4.95
☐ 745-2	Overstreet Comic Book Companion 1st Ed.	4.95
☐ 278-7	Pocket Knives 3rd Ed.	4.95
☐ 527-1	Scouting Collectibles 4th Ed.	4.95
☐ 494-1	Star Trek/Star Wars Collectibles 3rd Ed.	3.95
☐ 307-4	Toys 4th Ed.	4.95

THE OFFICIAL BLACKBOOK PRICE GUIDES OF:

☐ 743-6	U.S. Coins 26th Ed.	3.95
☐ 742-8	U.S. Paper Money 20th Ed.	3.95
☐ 741-X	U.S. Postage Stamps 10th Ed.	3.95

THE OFFICIAL INVESTORS GUIDE TO BUYING & SELLING:

☐ 534-4	Gold, Silver & Diamonds 2nd Ed.	12.95
☐ 535-2	Gold Coins 2nd Ed.	12.95
☐ 536-0	Silver Coins 2nd Ed.	12.95
☐ 537-9	Silver Dollars 2nd Ed.	12.95

THE OFFICIAL NUMISMATIC GUIDE SERIES:

☐ 254-X	The Official Guide to Detecting Counterfeit Money 2nd Ed.	7.95
☐ 257-4	The Official Guide to Mint Errors 4th Ed.	7.95

SPECIAL INTEREST SERIES:

☐ 506-9	From Hearth to Cookstove 3rd Ed.	17.95
☐ 530-1	Lucky Number Lottery Guide 1st Ed.	4.95
☐ 504-2	On Method Acting 8th Printing	6.95

TOTAL

SEE REVERSE SIDE FOR ORDERING INSTRUCTIONS

▬ FOR IMMEDIATE DELIVERY ▬

VISA & MASTER CARD CUSTOMERS
ORDER TOLL FREE!
1-800-638-6460

This number is for orders only; it is not tied into the customer service or business office. Customers not using charge cards must use mail for ordering since payment is required with the order—sorry, no C.O.D.'s.

OR SEND ORDERS TO

THE HOUSE OF COLLECTIBLES
201 East 50th Street
New York, New York 10022

—————— POSTAGE & HANDLING RATES ——————

First Book $1.00
Each Additional Copy or Title $0.50

Total from columns on order form. Quantity_____ $_____

☐ Check or money order enclosed $_____ (include postage and handling)

☐ Please charge $_____ to my: ☐ MASTERCARD ☐ VISA

Charge Card Customers Not Using Our Toll Free Number Please Fill Out The Information Below

Account No. _____ Expiration Date_____
(All Digit:
Signature_____

NAME (please print)_____ PHONE_____

ADDRESS_____ APT. #_____

CITY_____ STATE_____ ZIP_____

"Sir," said he, "I cannot express all the admiration that I feel on regarding the wonders with which you are surrounded. The hand of God has been with you, and here you live happily, far away from the strife of the world, among the works of creation, alone with your family. I came from England to seek repose: where can I find it better than here? and I shall esteem myself the happiest of men if you will allow me to establish myself in a corner of your domains."

This proposition of Mr. Wolson filled me with joy, and I immediately assured him that I would willingly share with him the half of my patriarchal empire.

Mr. Wolson hastened to communicate to his wife the success of his application, and the morning was devoted to the joy and pleasure that this news caused. But considerations of a painful nature occupied my mind: the ship which now presented itself was the second only we had seen in ten years, and probably as long a period might elapse before another appeared, should we let Captain Littleton and his ship leave us without any addition to his crew. These questions affected the dearest interests of my family. My wife did not wish to return to Europe; I was myself too much attached to my new life to leave it, and we were both at an age when hazards and dangers have no attraction, and ambition has resolved itself into a desire for repose. But our children were young, their life was but just commencing, and I did not think it right to deprive them of the advantages which civilization and a contact with the world presented; and then again, Emily, since she had heard that her father was in England, did not conceal her desire to return; and although we regretted losing this amiable girl, yet it was impossible to detain her. So at last I decided to call my children together, and ascertain their sentiments. I spoke to them of civilized Europe, of the resources of every kind which society offered to its members, and I asked them if they would depart with Captain Littleton, or be content to pass the remainder of their lives upon this coast.

Jack and Ernest declared that they would rather remain. Ernest, the philosopher, had no need of the world to interrupt his studies; and Jack, the hunter, found the domain of Falcon's Nest large enough for his excursions. Fritz was silent, but I saw by his countenance that he had decided to go. I encouraged him to speak; he confessed that he had a great desire to return to Europe, and his younger brother, Francis, declared that he would willingly accompany him.

Mr. Wolston also dismembered his family: he kept but one of his daughters; the other went on to New Holland.

These family arrangements were very painful, and when they were finished I hastened to inform the captain of the *Unicorn*. He readily consented to take our three passengers.

"I resign three persons," said he, "Mr. and Mrs. Wolston and one of their daughters; I take three more, and my complement will not be affected."

The *Unicorn* remained eight days at anchor, and we employed them in preparing the cargo which was to be the fortune of our voyagers on arriving in Europe. All the riches that we had amassed—pearls, ivory, spices, furs, and all our rare productions, were carefully packed and put on board the ship, which we also furnished with meat and fruits.

On the eve of their departure, after having exhausted myself in a last conversation, in which I advised my sons always to carry out the principles in which they had been instructed, and so to live in this world that we might, through the merits of our Saviour, be united in the next, I gave Fritz this narration of our shipwreck and establishment on the desert coast, enjoining him expressly to have it published as soon after his arrival as he possibly could; and this desire on my part, exempt from all vanity of authorship, had for its only object and hope that it might be useful to others as a lesson of morality, patience, courage, perseverance, and of Christian submission to the will of God. Perhaps some day a father may take courage from the manner in which we supported our tribulations; perhaps some young person will see, in the course of this narrative, the value of a varied education and the importance of becoming acquainted with first principles.

I have not written this as a learned man would have done, and all my results may not have been arrived at according to the correct theory; but we were in an extraordinary position, and were obliged to depend on our own resources. We placed our entire trust in the mercy of God; and He ever watched over and protected us.

We none of us slept much during the last night. At the dawn of day the cannon of the ship announced the order to go on board. We conducted our children to the shore; there they received our last embraces and benedictions.

The anchor has been weighed, the sails unfurled, the flag run up to the mast-head, and a rapid wind promises speedily to separate us from our children.

I will not attempt to paint the grief of my dear Elizabeth—it is the grief of a mother, silent and profound. Jack and Ernest are weeping bitterly, and my own grief and heartfelt sorrow is, I must confess, but badly concealed.

I finish these few lines whilst the ship's boat is waiting.

My sons will thus receive my last blessing. May God ever be with you. Adieu, Europe! adieu, dear Switzerland! Never shall I see you again! May your inhabitants be always happy, pious, and free!

AN ALADDIN READING GROUP GUIDE TO

THE SWISS FAMILY
ROBINSON

ABOUT THIS BOOK

A storm at sea leads to a terrible shipwreck. The only survivors are a Swiss couple and their four young sons. Can they survive on the Pacific island on which they find themselves? Will they ever see their homeland again?

DISCUSSION QUESTIONS

◆ When *The Swiss Family Robinson* begins, the ship on which they are sailing has been ravaged by storms for six days. How does the family manage to leave the ship? Why don't the sailors come with them? How and why do they return to the ship?

◆ Describe the personalities of each person in the family. What role does each individual play in the family? In the story?

◆ What are some of the first household items the family makes? What are some of the first sources of food and drink they find on the island?

◆ When the family fears for their lives in the storm, they pray together; when they land safely on their island, they offer up a prayer of thanks. What role do you think prayer had in their lives before the shipwreck? What roles do religion and prayer play on the island?

◆ The mother's life is very different from that of the other members of the family. Describe some of her tasks, her accomplishments, and her "magic bag." Why do you think her contributions differ from those of her husband and sons?

◆ The first home that the family constructs is their beloved tree house, which they call the Falcon's Nest. Why don't they live in the Falcon's Nest all the time? What other homes and shelters do they build and why?

◆ The family encounters many animals on the island: monkeys, tortoises, wild asses and pigs, a kangaroo, and a whale, among others. Which of these are useful? Which are dangerous? What do they do when they come upon an animal new to them?

◆ Is the life the family creates for themselves a European mainland one or a Pacific island one? Why did you choose the answer you did?

ACTIVITIES

◆ The family finds many different animals and plants, and uses them in many different ways: for transportation, clothing, and food. Learn more about the specific plants and animals that would likely thrive on an island like the one in the story. Learn more about the various ways that people have cultivated, domesticated, and used plants and animals over human history. Try raising a new plant or animal at home or at school; record your observations.

◆ The family kills many of the animals they encounter. Why? What else might they have done, especially if this book was written today? Have a debate with your friends or family about how humans should treat animals.

◆ Pretend that you are going on a long ocean journey. You need to develop some practical skills that would help you survive in case of shipwreck. Take a course or get some books from the library on living in the wilderness.

Try to predict which of your new abilities will be most helpful on an island like the one in the book.

◆ The family builds different homes and lives in them at different times of year. Learn about houses built around the world. Try to figure out why societies create different kinds of houses in which to live.

◆ *The Swiss Family Robinson* is one of several famous tales of shipwreck survival. Try reading some others! The earliest-written and best-known is *Robinson Crusoe*. The Robinson family is probably named for that novel, which was already famous when *The Swiss Family Robinson* was written in the early nineteenth century. Or try other island adventure stories, like *Treasure Island* by Robert Louis Stevenson, or *Island of the Blue Dolphins* by Scott O'Dell. You might also watch the movie *Cast Away*, starring Tom Hanks as a man who is marooned on an island by a plane crash. Which of these do you like best and why?

◆ *The Swiss Family Robinson* has been made into a movie, directed by Ken Annakin, that's available on DVD. It was also made into a television series, *The Adventures of Swiss Family Robinson*, starring television's Richard Thomas, which had thirty episodes, also available on

DVD. Watch one or more of these and compare them to the book. Which adaptation is most like the book? Which do you like best and why?